THE LAND OF THE LIVING

THE LAND OF THE LIVING

THE DANISH FOLK HIGH SCHOOLS AND DENMARK'S NON-VIOLENT PATH TO MODERNIZATION

STEVEN M. BORISH

BLUE DOLPHIN

Copyright © 1991 Steven M. Borish
All rights reserved.

Published by Blue Dolphin Publishing, Inc.
P.O. Box 1908, Nevada City, California 95959

ISBN: 0-931892-62-7

Library of Congress Cataloging in Publication Data

Borish, Steven M., 1943–
    The land of the living : the Danish folk high schools and Denmark's
non-violent path to modernization / Steven M. Borish.
        512 p.   cm.
        Includes bibliographical references and index.
        ISBN 0-931892-62-7
        1. Folk high schools—Denmark—History.   2. Denmark—History.
    3. Borish, Steven M., 1943–   . I. Title.
    LC5256.D4B66 1991
    948.9—dc20   91-12365
                                                                      CIP

See List of Maps, Tables, and Photographs (xii ff.) for credits and permissions.

Printed in the United States of America
Blue Dolphin Press, Inc., Grass Valley, California

9   8   7   6   5   4   3   2   1

I want to dedicate this book
to my grandmother,
Helen Borish
and to my mother,
Annette Peck Borish

to the blessed memory
of my father,
Bernard Borish
and my grandparents,
Barney Borish
David Peck
Ida Steinberg Peck

Without their love and support
not a word of it
could have been written

This book is also
dedicated to the memory of
Roar Skovmand: scholar, teacher, friend

Table of Contents

List of Maps, Tables and Photographs

Foreword

DENMARK IS MORE THAN Hans Christian Andersen and Tivoli, more than Søren Kierkegaard and the little mermaid. It is a society with 5 million inhabitants who try to manage their present lives in the light of both yesterday and tomorrow's experience. It is a modern society, perhaps a happy one, but at any rate it is a society in a state of rapid change.

It is a pleasure for me to write the foreword to Dr. Steven Borish's excellent and timely analysis of the Danish society. Dr. Borish first came to Professor Roar Skovmand and myself at the Royal Danish School of Educational Studies in the winter of 1983. He was conducting a participant-observation study of three Danish folk high schools at the time. It was our pleasure to make available to him some of the relevant documents and literature that could provide additional background for his study.

Since then, we have watched with interest and satisfaction as his initial field study turned into a historical investigation of some of the roots of our modern Danish culture. I think it is important that Dr. Borish began his study with a real understanding of the Danish folk high schools. He himself has lived at three of these schools, is fluent in Danish, and through talks with pupils and teachers has been able to draw precise, well-formed conclusions about the theory and practice behind these schools.

Dr. Borish's experience in the folk high schools led him to a confrontation with Danish history, and to a most unusual and interesting interpretation of its long-run historical trends. His interpretation of Danish history and culture is one that needs to be discussed, and will be discussed, both within and outside of Danish borders. Making the necessary connections between his ethnographic fieldwork and the documentary evidence from several key periods in the Danish history of the last two hundred years, he has presented a detailed, intimate view of Denmark that at the same time has the advantage of professional and cultural distance. He shows why it is a good society for most people, yet he does not forget its problems and its failings. He studies professionally as an anthropologist, but his analysis gains depth by his fascination for and deep emotional involvement with the object of his study. And, I should add, he is a master of the charming art of writing.

We note with great sorrow the death of Roar Skovmand in November, 1987. As the recognized Danish authority on the folk high schools, Professor Skovmand would doubtless have had great pleasure from the finished volume. *The Land of the Living* is a marvelous study, one that will be useful for foreigners as well as for Danes. It demonstrates convincingly how fertile and productive anthropological analysis can be.

Vagn Skovgaard-Petersen
Director, Institute for Danish Educational History
The Royal Danish School of Educational Studies, Copenhagen

Preface and Acknowledgments

THIS BOOK, THE CULMINATION of ten years' research, could not have been written without the help of many people. During my first year in Denmark (1982), I was fortunate enough to come into contact with Roar Skovmand and Vagn Skovgaard-Petersen, respectively the former and present director of the Institute for Danish Educational History at the Royal Danish School of Educational Studies in Copenhagen. Both Dr. Skovmand and Dr. Skovgaard-Petersen enthusiastically shared their extensive knowledge of Danish history and education with me in subsequent years, and I wish here to gratefully acknowledge both their stimulating questions and their continued kind support to a foreign colleague. I will never forget the wonderful atmosphere and enlightening discussion over coffee round a conference table in the Institute. These discussions informed me, guided my research efforts, and deepened my knowledge both of the folk high schools and Danish educational history.

Both men read early drafts of the manuscript, and after Professor Skovmand's death in the fall of 1987, Professor Skovgaard-Petersen was kind enough to read the manuscript in its entirety. Needless to say, I have benefited enormously from his searching and knowledgeable critique. The encouragement given me by both men since our initial meeting is one of the most important factors in my having the courage to undertake the writing of this book. The support given me during the final two years by Professor Skovgaard-Petersen and his wife, Inge Skovgaard-Petersen, has been a major factor in its successful completion.

I would like to express my deepest thanks to Hon. Bertel Haarder, the Danish Minister of Education, and to Ebbe Lundgaard and Arne Andresen of the Association for Danish High Schools for their critical support in the final stages of this research project. Their aid and support made possible its timely completion.

I owe an enormous debt of gratitude to Niels Højlund for his practical support, his Grundtvig scholarship, and his intimate knowledge of the folk high school movement. I want to thank Klaus Rifbjerg and Per Hedeman of Gyldendal Publishing for their generous permission to use illustrated materials. The United States Educational Foundation in Denmark and the Institute of International Education supported the initial field research in three Danish folk high schools with a Fulbright-Hayes Grant (1982–83). A Swarthmore College Faculty Research Grant enabled me to do follow-up fieldwork in Denmark during the summer of 1988. I am grateful for both of these sources of support.

Many in Denmark were instrumental in aiding this project at various stages of its development. Mogens Pedersen answered my letter of inquiry about the folk high schools, written from the United States in the spring of 1981, with a wise suggestion that when in Denmark I try to contact Roar Skovmand. It was my good fortune to receive this fine advice. Kjeld Erik Brødsgaard was kind enough to speak Danish with me at a time when my vocabulary did not exceed twenty words. Steve Sampson made available to me on his own initiative numerous sources that turned out later to be critical to my research. Jonathan Matthew Schwartz introduced me in a knowledge-able way to the study of the folk high school. Kjeld, Steve, and Jonathan were not only extremely generous in their personal support but made available their professional expertise in areas relevant to my study. Margarethe Balle-Petersen was the first who made me see that Grundtvig's influence was something that went far beyond the single institution of the folk high school.

I owe a debt of gratitude to many of those at the three folk high schools. At Kolding, Benny Christensen, Suzanne Petersen, and Axel Nielsen did much to make my initial period of learning a productive one. At Silkeborg, Terkel Berg-Sørensen, Vibeke Bøelt, Hans Førgård, Hanne Lauridsen, Erik and Inger Lindebjerg, Bent Martinsen, Leif Rasmussen, and Anders Sørensen assisted me in the intermediate stages of language learning and the learning of Danish culture. At Askov, I received further guidance and insight from Hans Møller Christensen, Hans Henningsen, Karen Holst, Mogens Melbye, and Finn Thrane. From Carl, Marie, and Birgitte Andersen I received a taste of Danish farm life. Finn and Eila Lauridsen were a valuable source of enlightenment about the Danish welfare system. Britt Hansen and Hans-Ole Haarder shared with me their many sharp critical insights about Danish education and national character. Else Lund, Bodil Lund, Anne-Lise Malter, Mogens Thorsen, Niels Torsleff, and Elin Torsleff gave rich descriptions of their experience of Denmark in the 1940s and 1950s. Michael and Susan Whyte and Jonathan Friedman supported me while I was a Visiting

Guest Lecturer at the Institute of Ethnology and Anthropology at the
University of Copenhagen in the autumn of 1984.

I must express my appreciation to those of my American colleagues
who read one or more chapters and gave me the invaluable benefit of their
insight and expertise. Ward Watt, an evolutionary biologist at Stanford
University, read some of my initial drafts: his sharp and incisive critique
helped the resulting manuscript a great deal. Harumi Befu, an anthropologist at Stanford University; Steve Piker, an anthropologist at Swarthmore
College; Bob Bannister, an historian at Swarthmore; Richard Estes, a
specialist in international development at the University of Pennsylvania;
and Mike Scherer, a former Swarthmore economist now at the John F.
Kennedy School of Government at Harvard, each read one or more chapters.
I am extremely grateful to them for taking the time to review portions of
the manuscript and for their helpful and stimulating comments. I continue
to be amazed at the depth of George and Louise Spindler's cross-cultural
perspective on education: I have learned much from our conversations and
dialogues. I have also been grateful to Gil Herdt for his sharp insight into
questions of psychology and culture, and his willingness to challenge
accepted dogma.

I have benefited greatly from the support of my colleagues at
Swarthmore while this manuscript was in process. I wish to thank, in the
Department of Sociology and Anthropology, Joy Charlton, Miguel Diez-
Barriga, Sam Kaplan, Jennie Keith, Asmarom Legesse, Braulio Muñoz,
Steve Piker, and Robin Wagner-Pacifici. In the Department of Biology, I
would like to thank, for their exemplary collegiality to a visiting anthropol-
ogist, Scott Gilbert, Mark Jacobs, John Jenkins, Bob Savage, and Jake
Weiner. I thank my students at Swarthmore College, especially those in the
Cultural Transmission course, for giving me a fresh perspective on education
and culture. I want also to thank Jim England, Provost at Swarthmore, for
his generous aid and support while this manuscript was being written. The
following people at Swarthmore have provided invaluable technical aid:
Debbie Brown, Pauline Federman, Maria Musika, Marie Ominsky, Anne
Rawson, and Etta Zweig. I owe a special thanks to George Flickinger for his
high-quality photographic reproduction of maps, charts, and photographs.
And to Wendy Piccard and Genoa Carver for their moral support.

Without the course in Danish made possible by the Program in Special
Linguistics at Stanford University, I am not sure I would have had the
courage to go about learning the Danish language on my own. Clara Bush
gave me an outstanding course in phonetics at Stanford. Claus Lund
provided a skilled and competent introduction to Danish within the Special

Linguistics Program at Stanford; later I was fortunate enough to have additional instruction from Søren Sølberg of Bornholm.

Early drafts of this manuscript were written while in residence at a rural retreat center in southern Norway, Forbundssenteret Haugtun. I want to gratefully acknowledge the aid and friendship given to me while I was in Norway by Trygve and Greta Natvig, Leif and Gro Lyngstad, Dag Magne Staurheim, Knut Ola, Åse, and Britte of the Center. I thank also Ragnhild Garthus, Harry and Kristel Trainer, Nora, Anna, Elisabeth, and Nils-Petter Grøndal. The final work on the manuscript was done while a Visiting Fulbright Scholar at the Norwegian Centre for Child Research at the University of Trondheim. I wish to thank Karin Ekberg, Marianne Gullestad, Anne Trine Kjørholt, Tora Korsvald, Svein Lorentzen, Turid Midjo, Per Egil Mjaavatn, Barbro Nilsson, Gunvor Risa, Alfred Oftedal Telhaug, Per Olav Tiller, Rolf Tønnessen, and Eli Åm for our many stimulating discussions of Scandinavian education and culture.

Finally, I want to express my thanks to Paul Clemens and to his talented group of co-workers at Blue Dolphin Publishing, Nevada City, California, in particular Christine Barnes, Jeff Case, Linda Maxwell, and John Mello, for their dedicated work in transforming an author's manuscript into the finished book that you hold in your hands. They are enormously skilled professionals, and it has been a great pleasure to work with them. I am especially indebted to Jeff Case for his photographic work, including the book cover, and to Paul Clemens who is not only a very capable editor and publisher but a wise counselor and friend.

A note on Danish phonetics for the English reader: the letters å, æ, and ø are the orthographic representation of three common unpronounceable Danish vowels.

In several places, such as Hans Christian Andersen's poetic description of Denmark cited at the beginning of *Excursus Four,* I have taken the liberty of making slight changes in the original text in order to preserve the flow of the narrative. This has only been done with passages used for their poetic content, not with passages cited to develop a political, cultural, or historical argument; in each case I have nonetheless been at pains not to change the meaning of the original passage or to leave out any significant material. The Notes providing documentation begin at the conclusion of the text in Chapter Twelve and are followed by a selected English and Danish bibliography. For reasons of space the bibliography does not list all works mentioned in the text (it does, however, contain all the major sources on which I have relied, together with some suggestions for further reading). All photos and translations from the Danish are by the author except where otherwise indicated.

In addition to many published works, I have benefited greatly from two unpublished dissertations: the late Judith Friedman Hansen's "Danish Social Interaction" (Department of Anthropology, University of California Berkeley, 1970); and Ole Christensen, Poul Christensen, and Peter Warrer, *Højskolebevægelse og Almendannelse* (The high school movement and general education), Institut for Statskundskab, Århus University, 1981.

A brief note about the book as a whole: Chapters Four and Five, which provide a historical analysis of the Danish Land Reforms and the origin of the folk high schools, are probably the most important chapters in the book. The arguments presented in the other chapters all follow, in one way or another, from the material presented in these two chapters. I have included a brief note on ethnographic method in the first chapter (Section IV). I encourage the reader who is not interested in such things to go directly from the initial discussion of Grundtvig to the map section (The History of Denmark Through Maps).

Many people have helped in the completion of this project, and I am grateful to all of them for their time and effort on my behalf. Nevertheless, I alone bear responsibility for whatever errors of fact and interpretation have persisted in spite of their generous efforts. For reasons of space I am not able to list more than a few of the many fellow students at the three folk high schools I attended, nor have I been able to list many others, both in the United States and in Scandinavia, who have contributed both professionally and personally to the completion of this project. I beg their indulgence for not being able to list them all here. The debt I owe to the many people who have been part of the writing of this book is and remains an enormous one.

Steven M. Borish
Norwegian Centre for Child Research
University of Trondheim
Dragvoll, Norway
May, 1991

PART I

INTRODUCTION

—He knew what money was, Mr. Deasy said. He made money. A poet but an Englishman too. Do you know what is the pride of the English? Do you know what is the proudest word you will ever hear from an Englishman's mouth?

The seas' ruler. His seacold eyes looked on the empty bay: history is to blame: on me and on my words, unhating.

—That on his empire, Stephen said, the sun never sets.

—from James Joyce, Ulysses (1922)

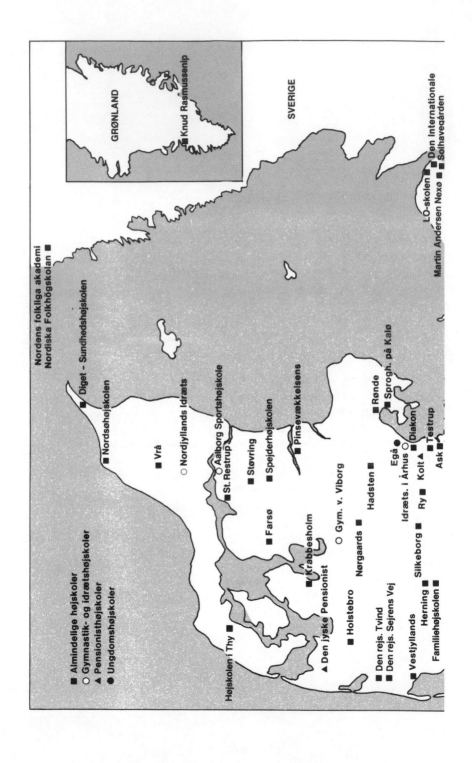

GRØNLAND
Knud Rasmussenip
SVERIGE

Nordens folkliga akademi ■
Nordiska Folkhögskolan ■

Diget – Sundhedshøjskolen ■
Nordsøhøjskolen ■

■ Almindelige højskoler
○ Gymnastik- og idrætshøjskoler
▲ Pensionisthøjskoler
● Ungdomshøjskoler

Vrå ■
○ Nordjyllands Idræts
○ Aalborg Sportshøjskole
○ St. Restrup ■
Støvring ■
Spejderhøjskolen ■
Pinsevækkelsens ■

Farsø ■

Krabbesholm ■
○ Gym. v. Viborg

▲ Den jyske Pensionist

Nørgaards ■
Hadsten ■

Rønde ■
Sprogh. på Kalø
Egå ●
Idræts. i Århus ▲
Ry ■ Kolt ▲
Ask ■
Diakon ■
Testrup ■

■ Højskolen i Thy

Holstebro ■

Den rejs. Tvind ■
Den rejs. Sejrens Vej ■
Vestjyllands ■
Herning ■ Silkeborg ■
Familiehøjskolen ■

LO-skolen ■
Martin Andersen Nexø ■
Den Internationale ■
Solhavegården ■

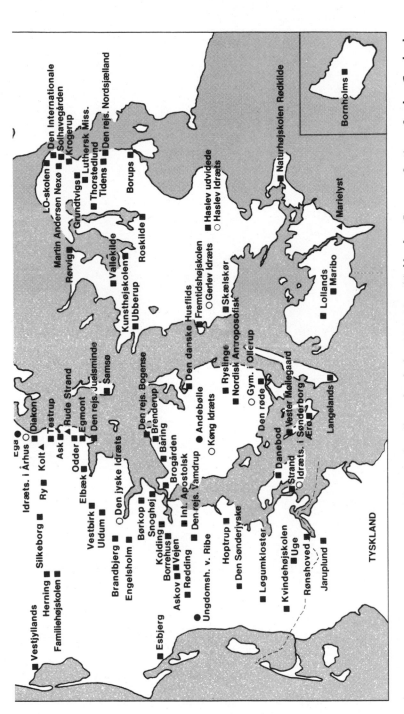

Map of Denmark showing the location of the Danish Folk High Schools, 1988. Note: Tyskland = Germany; Sverige = Sweden; Grønland = Greenland. (Courtesy of the Folkehøjskole Sekretariat, Farvegade 27, 1463 Copenhagen K)

CHAPTER ONE

Nature and Purpose
of the Inquiry

I. ON THE RELATIVE DECLINE OF AMERICAN POWER

IN RECENT YEARS there has been a focus by journalists, financial experts, and scholars in a number of disciplines on what is widely perceived as the decline of American power in the world.[1] This literature of relative decline has addressed a wide range of problems. At its best it has contributed elegant analyses of long-term historical trends relating to the rise and fall of empires, such as Paul Kennedy's conclusion that "a new, multipolar economic world" is emerging to replace the bipolar world that dominated global events during the past five decades.[2] The works belonging to this genre have encouraged a useful questioning of national purpose, priorities, and values. The difficult themes they treat suggest that some hard questions need to be asked about fundamental American institutions. It is true that the United States has reemerged from the Gulf crisis as the world's dominant military power, but the deteriorating state of our non-military infra-structure—of our schools, cities, hospitals, prisons, farms, business and financial institutions and much of the natural environment—does not provide convincing evidence for a long term reversal of the pattern of decline.

One question that must be asked is this: what can we in the United States learn from the decline of past empires—of seventeenth-century Spain, of France under Napoleon, of Great Britain in the late nineteenth and early twentieth centuries? Another and related question: what helpful lessons can we learn from contemporary powers? One obvious strategy here is to try to learn from present competitors, especially those that seem in many ways already to have overtaken us. Ezra Vogel provides a compelling examination of the Japanese model: ". . . given its limited resources, Japan has dealt more successfully with more of the basic problems of postindustrial society than any other country. It is in this sense, I have come to believe, that the Japanese are number one."[3]

The present book is aimed at making a contribution to this rapidly expanding area of discussion and debate. Its conclusion, based on a decade of research, will be a surprising one to many. That conclusion is this: the citizens of both large postindustrial superpowers (such as the United States) and of developing third world nations could learn some valuable lessons from studying the history and culture of Denmark.

It is anticipated that the results of this inquiry will be of interest to those in a number of fields and situations: (a) to those concerned with problems of welfare and development in the contemporary world, regardless of their discipline; (b) to Europeanists as another case study of a modern European society; (c) to students of cross-cultural education interested in learning about a successful alternative school form that has endured for nearly 150 years; (d) to historians of American society in search of challenging comparative material to use in the teaching of American history; (e) to citizens of the newly liberated Eastern European countries and the three Baltic Republics; (f) to Americans, Chinese, Russians, and in fact to citizens of any larger nation who might be willing to derive insight and example from the historical experience of a smaller nation; and (g) to Scandinavians and especially to Danes themselves, who, it is hoped, will be tolerant of these interpretations offered by a foreigner of their own history and culture.

II. DEVELOPMENT WITH A HUMAN FACE: THE DANISH PATH TO MODERNIZATION

The Central Importance of Education

What are the unique features of the Danish path to modernization? How can one best approach this topic in order to make explicit whatever lessons it has to teach? One critical feature of any society undergoing modernization is the kind of education it provides to its citizens. The ensuing discussion of modernization will focus initially on Danish educational history. Consider the following questions. If it is possible to show that a particular society has a special and unusual educational institution, one that plays a social role unique to that society, what can an analysis of this reveal about its history and culture? This question suggests in turn two others: (a) what more general features can be learned about the society *from a study of the historical circumstances under which this particular school form emerged?* and (b) what can be learned about the society from a study of the school's *present-day functioning,* from an investigation of how it has changed in order to adapt to changes in the surrounding society?

The Danish Folk High Schools

These questions are relevant because precisely such a school does exist in Denmark. Viewed from a comparative and cross-cultural perspective on education, it must be regarded as quite an unusual school.[4] Both its nineteenth-century origins and its present-day functioning provide excellent illustrations of the Danish concern for "development with a human face."[5] The school is popularly referred to as a folk high school (the Danish term is *folkehøjskole,* or more simply *højskole).* Although such schools or closely related ones are found in the neighboring countries of Norway, Sweden, Finland, and Iceland,[6] the first folk high school was created in Denmark in the mid-nineteenth century (1844). The schools are thus a particularly Danish innovation, an original and authentic contribution made by Denmark to the field of education. Interestingly enough, their present function in Danish society differs strikingly from the function they performed from the time of their origin until shortly after the Second World War, that is, for over a century. Once set up to serve almost exclusively the children of farmers, the schools have been subjected to far-reaching change in the past four decades. In its wake they have found themselves serving the needs of a different clientele, challenged by the demands of a new cultural context, and coping with the implications of an altered social role. This forced redefinition of their original social function has been neither an easy nor a comfortable process. Yet these schools continue to be a vital and important part of Danish society, as even a brief look at their present number and pattern of distribution suggests.

The folk high schools in the 1980s are distributed throughout the Danish countryside, all the way from the predominantly rural west coast of Jutland, the large peninsula that shares a land border with West Germany, to the urban milieu of Copenhagen and the far-off island of Bornholm in the North Baltic. The 1988 catalogue of the folk high school secretariat in Copenhagen lists 106 such schools. Close to fifty thousand students (in a nation of just over 5 million people) will pass through them this year. Many Danes choose to spend at least a part of their summer vacation taking a folk high school course. Some return year after year to the same school. Prospective students in 1987, for example, can choose among the 809 different short courses of one, two, or three weeks' duration,[7] or one of the long courses (which typically take from three to ten months).

What type of person is one likely to encounter at a folk high school today? A middle-aged Danish farmer, spending a month with easel and canvas, finally surrenders to his lifelong desire to paint. A woman with a six-year-old son comes to shape clay on a potter's wheel. While she molds clay on long afternoons, the boy plays soccer, tries his hand with waterpainting, finds other children with whom to explore a friendly rural environment. Here is a man of thirty who has been unemployed for the past two years; there is a young woman taking a year off from her veterinary studies at the university. There are some who have just finished *gymnasium,*[8] and others who never finished the eighth grade. Some come in hopes of finding a girlfriend or a boyfriend. Some are trying to kick a drug habit or control a problem with alcohol. Some come only because a social worker has urged them to do so and perhaps conveniently arranged their stay. Some want to see a different part of the country than the one they have always known or have come to escape the devastation of a recent and traumatic divorce. Some don't know what they want or why they have come here. Some will meet a future wife or husband. Some charm everybody and leave without paying all their bills. In truth, all kinds of people come to a Danish folk high school, and they come for all kinds of reasons.

What in the world is this thing called a folk high school? The concept behind it is not easy to explain. Furthermore, an easy, word-to-word translation only confuses the issue. A Danish *folkehøjskole* is not really what the literal English equivalent suggests: a "folk high school." The translation is not entirely incorrect because these schools are for the "folk," for the people. Yet it is also misleading. The term "high school" means a secondary school for most Americans. It is commonly understood to refer to the school that handles the tasks of learning and socialization after primary and middle (or junior high) school and before university education. As such, it is (a) geared to those in a limited and specific age-group; (b) avowedly competence-giving, in the sense of intending to prepare students for vocational or professional employment; (c) competitive, with examinations and grading; and (d) an integral part of universalistic mainstream education; that is, it is felt that all citizens should complete their high school education.

A Danish *folkehøjskole,* in contrast to an American secondary school, is (a) open to all those above eighteen years of age; (b) avowedly and by law *not* competence-giving; (c) *not* academically competitive, with no grades or marks at all given; and (d) outside of the mainstream Danish educational system. Two further features will astonish outside observers. First, in spite of their officially marginal status, these schools presently receive approximately 85% of their expenses from the state. Second, in spite of this high degree of state support, the point of view and philosophical framework adopted by an individual school are entirely free from state control. It is true that a certain amount of mumbling is heard from time to time, usually by local officials unhappy with something they believe to be taking place at one of the more radical and experimental schools.[9] But even such officials do not publicly challenge the right of the school to exist. Their maneuvering is usually limited to attempting to deny local subsidies to students who wish to attend such schools. And it should be added that this type of conflict is quite rare, almost certainly the exception rather than the rule.

The diversity of the Danish folk high schools in the 1980s and early 1990's is quite extraordinary. There are perhaps half a dozen schools with a radical communist or feminist orientation. There are, on the other hand, at least the same number of schools that teach some particular brand of ultraconservative Christian theology. Side by side with these can be found folk high schools that specialize in ecology and biodynamic agriculture, folk high schools for athletic instruction, folk high schools for instruction in music, and folk high schools for various kinds of travel abroad. There are folk high schools for the study of foreign languages, folk high schools for retired people, and at least one folk high school for teenagers under the age of eighteen. There are several "folk high schools for consciousness develop- ment," one of which teaches the Maharishi's transcendental meditation techniques and philosophy. In addition to these, there are many schools that call themselves by the perplexing (to the outsider) label of general "Grundtvigian" folk high schools. Use of this label entails a claim that a school is following in the footsteps of the tradition set by N. F. S. Grundtvig (1783–1872), who first proposed establishing such a school form in 1830.

Grundtvig's original vision of the folk high school was couched in both clear and compelling terms; yet his specific mandate concerning how this vision was to be realized has left many of the particulars open to debate and interpretation. And ever since the first folk high school came into existence in 1844, precisely what these schools should be doing and how they should go about doing it have been matters for continual debate, interpretation, and reinterpretation. It is not a static tradition. The very least one can say is this: a broader range of diversity than presently exists could scarcely be imagined, and all of this diversity is essentially state supported.

The Problem of Contextualization

The goal of the analysis is twofold. In tracing the folk high schools of today to their origins in the folk high schools of the previous century, we will learn something about the process of change in a single institution. This is the narrow focus of the study. From this treatment of a single Danish institution over time, both the achievements and some of the dilemmas faced by Danish society in today's postmodern world will be brought into sharper perspective. This is the broader focus of the study.

Reform Acts took some of the power and traditional prerogatives out of the hands of a landed feudal aristocracy. In the process at least one group within the stratified peasant-farmer class (the *gaardmænd*) was liberated from its previous serflike status. Members of this social group only a few decades later were sending their children to be the original students at the Danish folk high schools (the first such school was founded at *Rødding* in south Jutland in 1844).

Less than half a century after the passage of the Land Reforms, a second major transformation in Danish society took place: the transition from absolutist monarchy to parliamentary democracy. Although demands for greater political representation had been heard even before the time of the French Revolution (1789), these cries began to intensify in the third decade of the nineteenth century. The already liberated farmers *(gaardmænd)*, who constituted one group among the internally stratified agricultural community, formed a temporary alliance with an emerging urban bourgeoisie (they were later to find themselves betrayed by this former ally). After two decades of political struggle, the revolutionary events of 1848 and 1849 laid the foundation for a new form of government. The adoption of the Danish Constitution on 25 May 1849 (by a vote of 119 to 4) brought to a close almost two hundred years of rule under an absolutist monarchy.

Primary and Secondary Agents of Transformation

How is one to make sense of the relationship between these and subsequent developments? It is useful to distinguish in this context between the primary and the secondary agents of transformation. The Land Reform Acts, together with the acquisition of constitutional government, constitute what I would call the *primary agents of transformation.* The justification for calling them "the primary agents" is that they appear to have been a historical prerequisite, a change in baseline conditions of the society, making possible the additional forms of democratization that were to follow. Two conclusions must be emphasized. First, these actions were truly major reforms with fundamental consequences for power relationships in Danish society; they were not mere cosmetic face-lifts. Second, although it is unquestionably true that similar political and social developments took place in other European countries during this period, a closer look will show some unique and fascinating aspects to the Danish case.

In introducing this second theme, it should be underscored that these developments toward democratization took place during difficult times. It is well known that crisis does not necessarily lead to democratization; in fact, a score of examples from the historical record (including the tragic events of 1989 in Tiananmen Square) could be cited to support the opposite contention. And the nineteenth century was a period of cataclysmic events in Danish history, one containing great risks as well as opportunities. The risks were so severe that there is every reason to believe those who argued that the territorial integrity and perhaps even the independent national identity of Denmark might cease to exist. Given the chaotic speed and direction of change, it would have been reasonable to predict a decline in democratic trends accompanied by a rise in centralized police authority. Yet this was precisely the opposite of what in fact occurred. In order to successfully negotiate these dangerous waters and to cope with their potentially devastating challenges, the formulation of wise and innovative strategies was required. In this case, the challenge posed by history was met by a successful Danish response.

The nineteenth century in Denmark was a period characterized, on the whole, by progressive and far-reaching social movements that attempted to cope with the multiple facets of change. There were forces working against as well as for social democratization.[13] Yet seen here in retrospect through the abstract and simplifying eye of the historian, this was a remarkable period in Danish history. It positively smolders, both with progressive new ideas and with willingness to try them out. Its course is rarely smooth and linear; indeed, there were interruptions and even periods of regression. It is rather more like "a broad flowing river" that, while it meanders through a series of divergent streams, is nonetheless always ultimately rejoined by them.[14] And it is the pattern created by these streams and the larger river to which they return that constitutes the unique Danish path to modernization, "the pattern that connects," in the apt words of the anthropologist Gregory Bateson.

During these trying times a complex of social movements already underway gained strength and gradually accomplished a major democratic restructuring of many Danish institutions. These social movements, the "secondary agents of transformation," are of great interest in making clear the reasons why development took the path it did in Denmark. Among the "secondary agents of transformation" are the well-known cooperative movement in Danish agriculture (*andelsbevægelse*), the less well known cottars' or tenant farmers' movement (*husmændsbevægelse*), the role of the village meetinghouses (*forsamlingshuse*) and independent congregations (*valgmenigheder*), the growth of the agricultural training centers (*landbrugshøjskoler*), and the beginnings of social health insurance (the *sygekasse* and *sygeforsikring*). A profoundly revitalized politics, economy, and society emerged in the wake of these "people's movements" (*folkelig bevægelser*).

To give just one example: the Danish farmers responded creatively and effectively to the loss of the international grain market in the 1880s. A farming community that had been prepared by the existence of folk high schools and agricultural training centers was able to plan a new strategy. The farmers organized into cooperatives, and in the course of just two decades changed their production from grains to meat and dairy. In every detail of technical production and marketing the new cooperatives were extraordinarily successful. Soon Danish eggs, butter, and bacon became known as the highest-quality items available in the European market. Writing in 1936, the American journalist Frederick Howe described a breakfast in a London hotel that eventually resulted in the writing of two books about Denmark:

> I discovered Denmark quite by accident some fifteen years ago while writing a series of magazine articles on the post-war changes which were taking place in Europe. . . . In a London hotel I had noticed strange markings on the shells of eggs served me at breakfast. As to why the shell of a hen's egg should have any mark upon it, I could not imagine. I sent for the head waiter and asked him about it. He said, "All of our eggs come from Denmark. Also all of our bacon. Danish eggs are strictly fresh. They are marked in that way to certify their freshness. Danish bacon is the best in the world."[15]

By the end of the nineteenth century, Danish agricultural products had succeeded in winning an uncontested place in the markets of England and Germany. Without benefit of bloody revolution or political reign of terror, through an essentially peaceful process of social revolution, the country gradually achieved both new prosperity and a series of further extensions of democracy.

Another of the movements of that time, the Danish Heath Society (*Det danske Hedeselskab*), has provided a slogan that serves as an apt symbol for the achievements of the entire period. Founded by the thirty-eight-year-old engineer Enrico Dalgas in 1866, the goal of this movement was to reclaim the barren heath country in Jutland for Danish agriculture. The words of its remarkable slogan were: "Outward loss, inward gain" (*Hvad udad tabes, det skal indad vindes*).[16] The wisdom and magnanimity of this slogan illustrate some quintessential features of the Danish response to forced modernization. The slogan joins an explicit acceptance of the loss of external territory with an inward refusal to be devastated by this loss. Its message is that inward progressive change must provide positive compensation for what has been lost externally. The term "inward" is apparently used in a dual sense, meaning both internal to the country (within Danish borders) and internal to the heart and mind of the individual Dane. Note that there is nothing here about mourning the lost territories, no bitter muttering about a Danish equivalent of "the treaty of Versailles."[17] There is no residual sense of being betrayed by history, nor are there any grandiose schemes to recover the lost territories.

I submit that these are remarkable attitudes for the late nineteenth century, a period known for its outbreak of incendiary and expansionist nationalisms.[18] Indeed, when one considers the behavior of most nation states throughout history, they would seem remarkable attitudes in any period. The slogan's terse eloquence, as I have indicated, encapsulates a major theme behind the constructive Danish response to the external loss of power and territory. It also facilitates a first insight into Danish national character (the central topic of Part IV: Chapters Six through Ten). Numerous facets of this long-term cultural response to crisis would richly repay further exploration. *The focus in this book will be limited to two of its many themes. The first of these is the origin and subsequent development of the Danish folk high schools.*

Two historical periods figure importantly in this discussion:

1. The period of emergence: the time of about a century that passed between the Land Reforms of the 1780s and the Educational Reform Act of 1892, which marked the final stage of acceptance of these schools as a normal part of the Danish educational scene. By 1892 a type of school had emerged that in its essential outlines was to remain fairly consistent for the next five decades. A discussion of the changes taking place between 1892 and the end of World War II would be relevant for any complete treatment of the history of these schools; nevertheless, the events of this period, including the important events of industrial and urban modernization, must be considered beyond the scope of this analysis.[19]

2. The period of contemporary change: the post–World War II decades, with particular focus on the 1980s.

The second focus to be taken up here is the question of Danish national character, a fundamental part of the cultural matrix for the developments discussed.

N. F. S. Grundtvig (1783–1872) and Danish Non-Violence

Although the folk high school movement originated among the peasant farmers, it is in large part traceable to the teachings of a single remarkable man whose life spanned much of the period during which these critical events occurred. Nikolaj Frederik Severin Grundtvig was a man of many talents—poet, educator, historian, theologian, translator, mythologist and mythmaker, composer of popular hymns, prophet, protestor, and social critic. Even this extensive list does not do full justice to his concerns and

N. F. S. Grundtvig (1783–1872), Danish minister, educator, theologian, poet, philosopher, historian, hymnwriter, and social critic, from a contemporary drawing by P. C. Skovgaard, 1847 (from Kaj Thaning, N. F. S. Grundtvig, 1972, Det Danske Selskab, reprinted with permission of Gyldendal).

commitments, his passions and his accomplishments. The man was in truth a living whirlwind. One can only say of him (with little fear of contradiction) that both his own time and the future of Denmark would not have been the same had he not been there to bequeath to them the unique stamp of his thoughts, actions, and feelings.

In those sections of Grundtvig's voluminous writings that deal with education, he bitterly protests the neglect of Danish language and culture found in the classical Latin schools of his time. Through their undue emphasis on Latin, Greek, and medieval classicism, these schools, he charges, "have been at work for hundreds of years widening the gulf between life and learning." It was his deeply held conviction that "life and learning are to go together in such a way that life is to be first and learning is to follow." Viewed from the present, Grundtvig emerges as a major prophetic figure whose views laid the foundation for a profound cultural synthesis that spoke eloquently to the question of nationalism and national identity. It is one that has played a vital role in Danish history from Grundtvig's time down to our own and has significantly influenced the unique path of Danish modernization.

Education was one of Grundtvig's major concerns. He wrote advocating the creation of a unique school that would serve the Danish people at all levels in society, proposing originally to call it the *"folkelig højskole"* (meaning loosely a school that would be "of and for the people"). His special passion was that these schools would give dignity to the life of the farmer. They would awaken in rural men and women not only a pride in the national culture but a love of learning that would continue long after a student had finished the formal course of study. Grundtvig's positive feelings for the working farmer were equaled only by his contempt for those he referred to scathingly as "the learned." One of his most well known poems, "Enlightenment," begins with these lines, which I have freely translated:

> Is the light of the spirit only something for the
> learned to spell with? No! Heaven has bequeathed
> more good things, and the light is the gift of heaven.
> The sun rises with the farmer, and not with those
> who possess learning. It illuminates, from top til toe,
> the one who is really on the go.

Grundtvig's original vision was a school not only for the children of farmers but for the Danish people at large in all their different walks of life. In 1830 the idea of the *folkelig højskole* is set forth for the first time in his writings (the first actual school was established fourteen years later). At the

opening of a school bearing his own name in 1856, he made these remarks
to those present, including the eight enrolled pupils:

> I saw life, real human life, as it is lived in this world, and saw at once
> that to be enlightened, to live a useful and enjoyable human life, most people
> did not need books at all, but only a genuinely kind heart, sound common
> sense, a kind good ear, a kind good mouth, and then liveliness to talk with
> really enlightened people, who would be able to arouse their interest and
> show them how human life appears when the light shines upon it.[20]

Grundtvig lived to be a very old man. He survived long enough to see
the schools whose existence he had envisioned begin to grow and take root.
It was an idea that reached fulfillment in his own lifetime. One reason for
this was that many of the "really enlightened people" of Grundtvig's day
and age came to devote their lives to the burgeoning folk high school
movement, attempting to show young farmers "how human life appears
when the sun shines upon it." Only a decade after the founding of the first
such school in 1844, others began springing up all across the countryside.
In the space of a single two-year period (1865–67), twenty-five new high
schools were formed. By 1870 there were already more than fifty schools;
by 1890, seventy-five.[21]

The folk high schools are of particular importance in understanding
the role played by farmers and the farming community in the Danish path
to modernization. Yet their importance goes beyond this, and it is no
exaggeration to say that these schools and the movement to which they
belong influenced the path modernization as a whole took in Denmark. This
entire fabric of historical events has had its unusual, even remarkable
features. Perhaps the most extraordinary of all (viewed from the outside as
a non-Dane) is the almost complete absence of armed conflict, systematic
political repression, and violent social revolution. Even during an extended
period of change, when the conditions of social, political, and economic life
were being fundamentally altered, there were few acts of serious mass
violence. Where violence occurred, it was in most cases little more than
stone throwing and shouting, followed by a shot or two fired into the air,
after which all sides gallantly withdrew from battle. The total body count
approaches zero. Violence as it is commonly known in the less fortunate
countries (accompanied by such doubtful features as inquisitorial tribunals,
mob persecutions, police states, death camps, and paramilitary assassination
squads) is to my knowledge conspicuous by its absence during this whole
period of Danish history.

How did the Danes do it? It can't all be attributed to the good taste
of their beer, their friendly smiles, or their open-faced sandwiches. We are

faced with an unresolved mystery, a jigsaw puzzle that has not yet been put together. Why did the same or parallel culture change processes that have resulted in violent repression, both in the past (for example, the French[22] and Russian[23] Revolutions) and in the present, occur without widespread social violence in Denmark? What is it about Denmark and the Danes that is responsible for this feature of their response to modernization and cultural change? Is there something of value here that has been missed? Is there anything that deserves closer examination? In a world marked by social violence these facts suggest a historical enigma that has gone for the most part both unnoticed and unexplored.

Let us remember that the contemporary literature of development and modernization is replete with examples of miscalculation and sheer human tragedy.[24] In spite of the Western tendency to regard change as progress, culture change is frequently a harsh, almost inhuman process. In his classic critique of the economics of modernization (1973), the British economist E. F. Schumacher wrote eloquently of the need to develop what he called "technology with a human face."[25] Schumacher's haunting image suggests several questions for this study of Denmark. Can we usefully abstract from the special features of the Danish case a potential alternative model of modernization "with a human face"? Are there any lessons from the Danish experience that should be part of the common knowledge of politicians, administrators, educators, and development theorists? Could any of these lessons, if they in fact exist, be usefully applied outside the Danish context?

The focus offered here is based on a perspective developed in the course of extended ethnographic fieldwork. While in Denmark carrying out this research, I had an insight that gave rise to the perspective set forth here. The folk high school is not merely an interesting school with a particular kind of curriculum. It is much more than that. An observation made by Thomas Rordam, a former folk high school principal, hints at these connections. Rordam wrote that "the Danish national character is reflected in the Folk High Schools, because the core of the Danish nation—earlier the country people but in this century also the townsfolk—took part in their formation."[26] The folk high schools, then, express a unique facet of both the social history and the national character of the Danish people.

The need to make these wider connections is acute in this case because so little is known in the world at large about either the history of Denmark or the Danish folk high schools. It is precisely because so little is known about Denmark—its heroes, history, and traditions—that fundamental questions must be asked. Who are the Danes? Which geopolitical realities have constrained their national and cultural development? What critical turning points can one identify in their history? How has their unique national character been shaped and molded over time? It is only when questions such as these have been addressed that the particular institution of the folk high school can be seen in the proper context and its own special lessons understood.

IV. On Ethnographic Method

Sources and Major Research Sites

From the tone of much of the preceding section, the reader may have begun to entertain images of dry historical research carried out in the stacks and shelves of isolated library collections. In actual fact I spent the largest proportion of my time neither peering through old books nor imprisoned in dusty libraries. On the contrary, I spent most of my time with diverse groups of Danes drawn from every conceivable age, social class background, geographic location, worldview, and personality type. I sat in classrooms, worked on windmills, and spread compost in gardens. I cleaned stalls, went to parties in dormitory rooms, and wandered in the streets of three small towns in Jutland. Much later I came to live for a time in the capital city of Copenhagen.

My understanding of Denmark came initially not through books or articles but most appropriately through the agency of "the living word" itself. My central thesis did not begin with library research. I went to the library only at a later stage, after experience itself had given rise to the series of insights around which this book is organized. At this later stage of the study I did use letters, documents, books, and historical records, the usual sources of the historian. By that time I felt that I had learned not only to read and translate the Danish words but to understand something of what they meant.

The use of traditional historical materials has been supplemented at every stage of the inquiry by the ethnographer's concern with "the forms of social discourse": the living communications of real people in everyday life situations. The methods used in gathering this material stem from the anthropological tradition of fieldwork, which requires the immersion of the investigator into the group some part of whose lifeways he or she proposes to investigate. Anthropologists traditionally collect their data by observing a range of situational behaviors, conducting interviews with informants, and using other, related techniques of participant observation (or "observant participation," as it has been called by psychologist Thomas Cottle). These concerns have been widened in the present study to include relevant material taken from a variety of written sources and from Danish media, including TV, newspapers, and magazines. These too are important textual elements in the ongoing social discourse of a literate population.

From September 1982 through July 1983 I attended the long courses at three Danish folk high schools. These schools served as my primary research sites. For my initial two courses I chose younger schools, then just into their second decade of existence. The first, Kolding Højskole, represents a rebellion within the folk high school movement against older and more traditional models of what a folk high school should be. In many details of its functioning it departs significantly from the conservative tradition. Some of these crucial areas of difference include the politics and preparation of food, details of course organization, and types of themes found in course offerings (the focus in this school was and is on feminist issues, world peace, ecological land use, and alternative energy forms).

The second, Silkeborg Højskole, was chosen because, in contrast to Kolding, it is strongly connected to the liberal religious tradition in Danish society. It is furthermore what may be called a "general" folk high school, one that attracts a wide and typical cross section of Danish youth to its programs. In many ways it provided a quite different kind of experience than what one would find at Kolding Højskole. Yet regardless of their different approaches, there are many similarities between these two institutions. One is that both are comparatively young schools founded only in the last two decades.

For my third long course I chose to attend Askov, the oldest and perhaps most celebrated of all Danish folk high schools. Its importance for the movement is emphasized by this comment found in a recent scholarly review of the folk high school tradition: "Well into the 20th century Askov Højskole remained the flagship of the high school movement."[27] This school, founded in 1844, has been at its present site in southern Jutland since 1865. No study of the Danish folk high schools would be complete without some time spent in attendance at Askov. Finally, it is of great interest that Kolding Højskole, the initial fieldwork site, was founded in the early 1970s by a breakaway group of teachers from Askov. The fact that the founders of Kolding were rebels from within the folk high school movement against its own traditions (perhaps best symbolized by Askov itself) is an additional factor underscoring the relevance of this particular choice of schools.

Following my year in three Danish folk high schools, I migrated (as did many of my fellow students) to Copenhagen, where I was to stay for nearly two more years. A succession of experiences, which included a semester of teaching at the Institute of Ethnology and Anthropology at the University of Copenhagen, broadened and deepened the process of understanding that had begun at the folk high schools. I did not return to the United States until June 1985, nearly two years after my originally scheduled date of return. I revisited the country for seven weeks during the summer of 1987 and again in the summer of 1988 in order to carry out follow-up studies.

   This study is one based on long-term fieldwork, a type of research that requires a stay of many months (or even years) in the culture to be investigated. Long-term fieldwork is full of psychological hazards for the unwary (some of these are described in Chapter Eleven) and is not to be recommended for everyone. The advantages of long-term fieldwork center on the fact that one almost cannot help learning to speak the language well. As a result, one gains not only a better understanding of the culture but deeper and more meaningful attachments with a large cross section of people in the group one has been "studying." The use of quotation marks in the previous sentence is deliberate. As a practitioner of long-term fieldwork in Denmark, I must admit that I never really mastered their aspirated plosives in accented position (the consonants *t, d, k*), their rich and complicated array of vowels (of which *y, æ,* and *å* are only the tip of the iceberg, phonetically speaking), or the final subtleties of irony in their humor and social relations. Yet in the end it was obvious to me (and to many of my Danish friends) that my fieldwork had been a success. The culture had brainwashed me. I came in many ways to see, feel, and think like a Dane. In short, what I learned while carrying out this research in Danish folk high schools was not so much how the Danes are, but how to be a Dane. At the same time I struggled to use what vestiges of professional distance and training remained to view Danish culture with the presumably cold, clear eye of an outsider.

   I do not mean to imply that the fieldwork lacked rigor. Not only was I required to develop a taste for Tüborg or Carlsberg (that was easy), but I had to learn how to drink half as many of them as fellow folk high school students out for a night on the town without falling under the table. For a determined nondrinker like myself, situations like these provided both pleasure and pain on occasion. And then, after I felt I had come to know the culture well, came the most difficult part of the experience, the time when I had to leave both people and places for whom I had come to feel the warmest of affection. I can report that for practitioners of long-term fieldwork the boundary-threatening processes begin, paradoxically, not when in the middle of the fieldwork, but when one must leave and go back to one's native culture. The irony is that one returns no longer seeing quite as a native, but at least in part through the eyes of the stranger that one has now become.

Ethnographic Reporting: Fieldwork and the Language of Description

> Any opposition between subjective and objective, internal and external, intrinsic and extrinsic, is as a rule overridden in practice; one is never either individual or impersonal but always both at the same time.
> —Perry Meisel, 1989

In a recent, much-discussed volume George Marcus and Michael Fischer, two American anthropologists, describe what they have called a "crisis of representation in the human sciences." They have called for a more "interpretive" anthropology, many of whose practices and procedures conflict with the more positivistic orientation of older traditions in ethnographic reporting. In arguing that ethnography has become an experimental genre, Marcus and Fischer have made an extraordinary suggestion: that the writing of each new ethnography is nothing less than an experiment in cultural communication. In their own words:

> Ethnographies of experience are now trying to make full use of the knowledge that the anthropologist achieves from fieldwork, which is much richer and more diverse than what he [or she] has been able to distill into conventional analytic monographs. The task of this trend of experimentation is thus to expand the existing boundaries of the ethnographic genre in order to write fuller and more richly evoked accounts of other cultural experience.[28]

The crisis of representation in the human sciences evoked by Marcus and Fischer is very real, and it is not limited to the discipline of anthropology. In the West German historiography of the last decade, for instance, there has been a strong tendency "to turn away from the great themes of state policy, national and economic development, and theories of fascism and modernization, to a new emphasis upon everyday life and the experiences of ordinary people in their family, occupational and regional settings."[29] Among American historians there has been an intense debate following Hayden White's assertion that the past should not be studied "for its own sake" but rather, in White's words, "to force . . . an awareness of how the past could be used to effect an ethically responsible transition from present to future."[30] A related set of concerns has been expressed in the deconstructionist approach characterizing much of contemporary literary criticism.[31] Indeed, there is an interesting and potentially productive convergence between much of this newest work in literary theory and the recent ethnographic concern with the subjective experience of the ethnographer.

The intellectual history of this crisis is older than Fischer and Marcus' recent and useful reformulation. At least one of its ancestral branches can be traced back to Husserl's (1938) views on "the crisis of European sciences," motivated in part by a dissatisfaction with what the English philosopher Roger Poole has called "the political-scientific-objective impersonality" that dominates much of the work in the human sciences.[32] These are some of the questions asked by Poole: What would full and adequate objectivity be like? What would it be like to re-encounter the world as a totality? After objectivity has been called before the bar of human responsibility and subjected to the ethical critique of deep subjectivity, what parts of it would be left?

What should be the relationship between subjectivity (the private and personal experience of doing fieldwork) and objectivity (the public and socially relevant presentation of what has been learned through fieldwork) in ethnographic writing? Older generations of anthropologists followed a paradigm in which properly "objective" ethnographies left out most or all of the "subjective" experience of fieldwork on which their writing was based. A new generation of anthropologists is more open to creative and alternative strategies of ethnographic reporting. It is perhaps appropriate for an ethnography of Denmark to suggest that a potential resolution to some of these questions can be found in the work of Danish physicist and philosopher Niels Bohr.

Among Bohr's many contributions was the notion of complementarity, which speaks precisely to this division between the subjective and objective. As Bohr wrote in a famous concluding passage: "Consequently, evidence obtained under different experimental conditions cannot be comprehended within a single picture, but must be regarded as *complementary* in the sense that only the totality of the phenomena exhausts the possible information about the objects."[33] Bohr did not see his notion of complementarity as a mere restatement of Heisenberg's uncertainty principle. Indeed, he hoped that it would bear fruit outside of the narrow areas within physics and the natural sciences to which he had originally applied it. He envisioned it as part of an all-embracing and unified framework that could be applied not only to the paradoxes of physics but to the paradoxes of culture and human history. Many interpretations have been made of Bohr's complementarity principle, and a voluminous literature exists on the subject.[34] The interpretation I shall offer is this: apparently irreconcilable contradictions at a lower level of meaning can form part of a harmonious whole at a higher level if the tension between them is not ignored or downplayed but sustained and allowed to run its course. In order for the insights of complementarity to emerge, a dialogue between oppositions must be allowed to take place.

This ethnography belongs in part to the newer experimental tradition described by Marcus and Fischer. Its particular experiment is to introduce

Bohr's theory of complementarity into the human sciences by constructing an ethnographic report based on three levels of complementarity. The first level is a "subject-object" complementarity. On this level it is suggested that the terms "subjective" and "objective," often seen as implying incompatible and contradictory languages of description, form (to use another of Gregory Bateson's memorable phrases) "a necessary unity." Included among them must be such competing languages of description as the poetic and the scientific, the personal and the impersonal, the subjective and the objective. Viewed through Bohr's lenses, such polarities of description are not really in opposition; rather, the apparent tension between them must be utilized to seek potential higher unities in our understanding of complex social issues.

This study alternates deliberately between different languages of description. It includes a movement between the details of "objective" social history and the "subjective" awareness and experience of those located within the described structures. The author himself is shown both in the process of fieldwork and in the period of problem formulation that preceded fieldwork. Analysis does not preclude poetry; logic may invite tears. The style is not an entirely unprecedented one in the social sciences, embedded as it is in the work of such perennial craftsmen as Colin Turnbull, as well as in some of the more recent interpretivist ethnographies discussed by Marcus and Fischer.[35]

A second type of complementarity is based on the alternation between present and past time perspectives. The ethnographic present of Denmark and its folk high schools can be seen as the leaves and foliage of an ancient tree. Many of its roots are buried in the subterranean intersections of the past. To study the present or the past in isolation does not usefully reflect qualities of what the American sociologist C. Wright Mills once referred to as "the sociological imagination." Mills' conclusion is worth citing: "No social study that does not come back to the problems of biography, of history and of their intersections within a society has completed its intellectual journey."[36] To make this journey successfully requires a complementarity in time perspectives. Such strategies have long been the recognized property of the creative writer (beautifully exemplified by the treatment of Dublin in Joyce's *Ulysses*). They ought to prove an equally valuable tool for the creative ethnographer.

A third type of complementarity emerges from the relationship between the limited set of protocols for ethnographic research that I brought with me to Denmark and what my fieldwork there taught me about a more intangible reality. For lack of a better term call it "the spirit of the Danish folk high school." As I confessed earlier, my fieldwork was a success in that

I not only studied the culture but came to feel a part of it. Having made this admission, I can hardly pretend to be the utterly detached observer demanded by the traditional ideal of objectivity, that mythical figure who weighs and measures all observations with impartial clarity to arrive at what are thought to be unbiased and "value-free" conclusions. Yet upon reflection it occurs to me that something may have been gained as well as lost by this failure to maintain the stance of traditional objectivity. What might have been gained is a greater freedom to enter sympathetically into the spirit of the folk high school and thus to communicate something of its deeper wisdom.

Let me give an example of what I mean. Can the Western scientific ideal of objectivity, with its emphasis on detached, rational calculation, speak not only to the practical but to the moral and spiritual problems of human existence? Many of those who have been educated in Western institutions of higher learning would answer in the affirmative. Yet there is a long line of thought in the Danish folk high school tradition that pointedly challenges this assumption. During one period of fieldwork, I could not help noticing that Bent Martinsen, the principal of Silkeborg Højskole, was a particularly effective spokesman for this critical point of view. He remarked to me once during an interview, "It's always that which can't be calculated, measured or weighed that means the most in our lives. Love, faith . . . I've never met a person yet who denies it." The point of view he was so succinctly expressing is one with deep roots in the Danish philosophical tradition; its underlying Christian existentialism can be traced back to the nineteenth-century writings of both Grundtvig and Kierkegaard. I had heard him express these views many times before that interview, both in classes and on other public occasions.

Such remarks can all too easily lead to furious debate. For that reason I must say that I do not cite them here either to take a position or to defend a point of view in this perennial controversy. My purpose is more narrowly conceived: I cite them because they make it possible for me to express lucidly and concisely the necessary tension that points to the third form of complementarity. That tension is the kind that exists between what one *studies* as a scientific observer (data that can in principle be "calculated, measured, or weighed") and what one *learns* as a subjective human participant (insights and transformations that often cannot be expressed no matter how hard one tries). During my fieldwork I tried stubbornly to do both at the same time. As part of my scientific self-image, I worked to keep these two processes separate and safely compartmentalized. But for all of my calculations, measures, and maneuvers, I found that I was never able to separate the two roles completely from each other. When I returned home to the United

States, my perception of American institutions was very different from the one I had before I left. This post-ethnographic change in cultural perspectives, where the strange becomes familiar and the familiar suddenly strange, ought not to be censored out in the interests of a truncated and biased "objectivity."

What do familiar American institutions and philosophies look like to an ethnographer after fieldwork? The issues potentially raised by this question can and ought not to be ignored. The ethnography therefore contains a third level of complementarity: an ongoing dialogue between "the culture of the observer" and "the observed culture." The dialogue is between the culture of the United States and the culture of Denmark, as experienced by an American anthropologist who has done long-term fieldwork in Denmark. The underlying intent is to provide the depth of cultural critique uniquely facilitated by a cross-cultural perspective. In this sense the dialogue falls squarely within the experimental area marked out by Marcus and Fischer (indeed the title of their volume is *Anthropology as Cultural Critique*). These, then, are the three forms of complementarity included in the present study. Their goal is to provide contrast and illumination for a set of observations made in today's postmodern world, a world of unprecedented geographic and spiritual mobility that is littered with the wreckage of disappearing traditions.

The History of Denmark Through Maps

A Series of Maps Illustrating the Theme of Long-Term Territorial Loss[37]

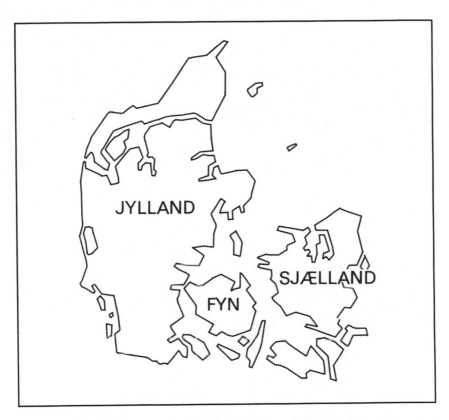

1. *An Overview of Denmark's Main Regions: Jylland (Jutland), Fyn and Sjælland (Reprinted with permission of Kort-og Matrikelstyrelsen, Danmarks Bolig-ministerium A390-90). South of Sjælland and Fyn, moving from east to west, the islands of Møn, Falster, Lolland, Langeland, Ærø, and Als are shown in outline. The island of Bornholm is not shown, nor is the land connection between Germany and peninsular Jylland. The circled regions in each of the three panels on the following page depict the above area; the area is shown here in greater detail.*

2. Denmark from the time of Knuth the Great (1030) to the Kalmar Union (1397–1523) (Adapted with permission from Gyldendals Historiske Atlas, *1973).*

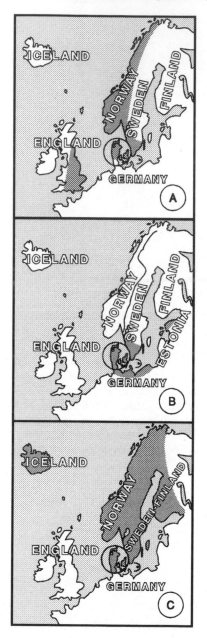

a) Under Knuth ("Canute") the Great in 1030 Denmark controlled most of England, Norway and parts of southern Sweden (as indicated by the dark shading). In order to emphasize the difference in size between historical Denmark and Denmark today, present Danish borders are circled in panels a), b), and c).

b) By the reign of Valdemar the Victorious two centuries later (1202–1241) Denmark had lost control over England and Norway, but gained possession of large areas in Northern Germany and Estonia, while retaining power in southern Sweden.

c) In the Kalmar Union (1397–1523) Queen Margarethe I brought Denmark, Sweden and Norway under one crown in a union which lasted 126 years. For the first and only time in its history all of Scandinavia was gathered together under the authority of a single monarch. A major factor facilitating her remarkable set of achievements was the growing anxiety in all three countries about an increasing German presence in Scandinavia, symbolized by the crowning of a German prince as king of Sweden in 1363. Margarethe I used her influence to have her son Oluf crowned king of Denmark at the age of 5 in 1375. When her husband Håkon VI (king of Norway) died in 1380, she had the boy crowned King of Norway as well. The resulting successful fusion of the Danish and Norwegian ruling families would characterize the new kingdom of Denmark-Norway. It was a kingdom which, dominated by Denmark, would endure until 1814 (more than 400 years).

3. The relationship between the kingdom of Denmark-Norway and Sweden, late medieval and early modern period (Adapted with permission from Gyldendals Historiske Atlas, 1973).*The provinces of Skåne, Halland, and Blekinge in what is today southern Sweden (indicated with light shading) were part of Denmark until 1658. Their loss to the Swedish king Karl Gustav X in the third of four major wars fought with Sweden during the seventeenth century dealt a crushing blow to Danish imperial ambitions. Denmark, fearful of a Swedish attack and doubtless encouraged by the fact that Russia and Austria had already broken the peace with Sweden, declared war in 1657. When the ice unexpectedly froze over on both the Great and the Little Belt in the winter of 1658, the Swedish king (on his way back from Poland) was able to cross over from Jylland and strike quickly at Copenhagen with his 9000 man army. Caught by surprise, Denmark suffered a military debacle. In the disastrous Treaty of Roskilde (1658), the concessions made by Danish king Frederic III included the surrender of all claims to Skåne, Halland and Blekinge, as well as the island of Bornholm. Of these, only Bornholm would return to Denmark after the death of Karl Gustav in 1660; the three "old provinces" were permanently lost. (The present Danish land border with Germany is indicated by the dotted line in the southern part of Jylland.)*

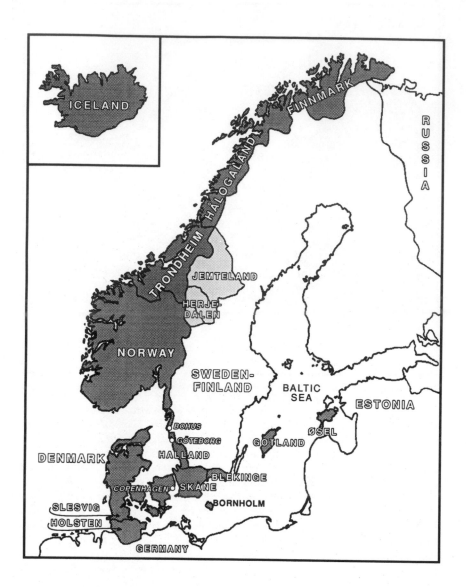

4. The territorial holdings of the kingdom of Denmark-Norway (*Adapted with permission from* Gyldendals Historiske Atlas, *1973*). *See explanation on following page.*

The kingdom of Denmark-Norway had extensive territorial holdings in late medieval and early modern times (roughly from the late fourteenth to the mid-seventeenth century). These holdings (indicated by the shaded area) included (1) the provinces of Skåne, Halland and Blekinge in what is today southern Sweden (see previous map); (2) the islands of Gotland (off the west coast of Sweden), Bornholm (directly south of Sweden), and Øsel (just east of Estland, or Estonia); (3) parts of Slesvig and Holsten in north Germany (see maps 6 and 7); (4) Iceland, the Faroe Islands and various coastal areas of Greenland, all acquired in 1380 along with Norway; (5) and Norway in its entirety. From 1380 Denmark made claims not only to south and mid-Norway, but to all of northern Norway, including Hålogaland and Finnmark.

It was in the second of four major wars with Sweden in the seventeenth century (the Torstensson War, 1643–45), that the pattern of Swedish military superiority was first clearly established in Scandinavia. At the Treaty of Brömsebro in 1645 which ended this war, the Danish king Christian IV was forced to surrender the islands of Gotland and Øsel as well as the areas of Herjedalen and Jemteland in mid-Norway

As a result of the next war with Sweden (King Gustav's War, 1657–60), the kingdom of Denmark-Norway had to give up not only its three provinces in southern Sweden but areas of Norway as well. The Norwegian concessions included the fief of Bohus (a small area on the west coast of Sweden north of Göteborg) and the province of Trondheim (a large and significant coastal area in mid-Norway).

The loss of Trondheim (together with the previous loss of Herjedalen and Jemteland) effectively split Norway in two. In 1660 (after the death of Karl Gustav) Trondheim as well as Bornholm reverted back to Denmark-Norway, but the areas of Herjedalen and Jemteland stayed under Swedish control and eventually became part of Sweden. The frozen expanses of north Norway remained in principal Norwegian (and thus part of Denmark-Norway), but the precise boundaries with Sweden and Russia in this area would be contested and thus insecure for a long time to come. Although successfully challenged by Sweden for the right to many of its possessions, the kingdom of Denmark-Norway did manage to preserve its union of the two countries until 1814.

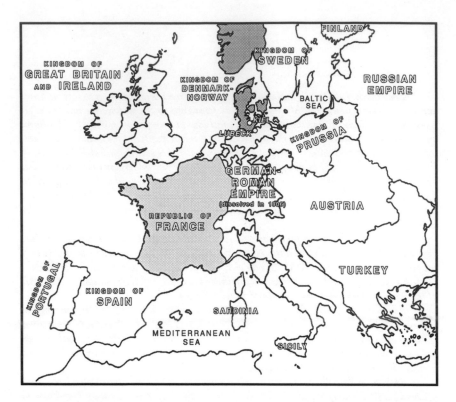

5. Europe in 1803, showing the consequences of the French Revolution and French territorial expansion under Napoleon (Adapted with permission from Gyldendals Historiske Atlas, 1973). *The extent of French territorial expansion is indicated by light shading. Denmark, which had stayed neutral to this point, remains in control of Norway (the kingdom of Denmark-Norway is shown with dark shading). Note that its southern border now extends south of Kiel all the way down to Lübeck in Germany.*

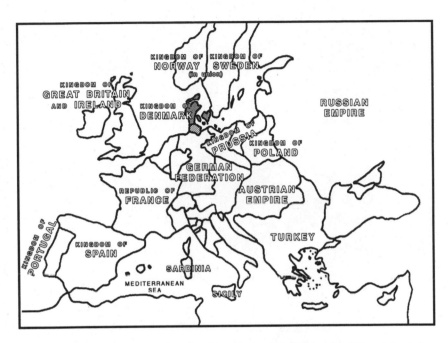

6. Europe in 1815 (Adapted with permission from Gyldendals Historiske Atlas, *1973). After being drawn into the general European war on the side of Napoleon, Denmark was forced to cede Norway to Sweden in 1814 following Napoleon's defeat (note that the map now shows separate kingdoms of Denmark and Norway). Norway remained under Swedish control until gaining its independence in 1905. In 1864 a tragic confrontation with Bismarck's Prussia meant that Denmark would be still further reduced in size by the loss of the hatched area.*

7. *Slesvig-Holsten* (*Adapted with permission from Roar Skovmand*, Danmarks
Historie, *Vol. 11, Politikens Forlag, 1978*). *"Denmark to the Eider River"* (Danmark
til Eideren) *was the hopeful but ill-fated slogan of the National Liberal party in the 1840s.
Its policies led to a series of tragic military confrontations with Bismarck's Germany,
culminating in the loss of Slesvig and Holsten in 1864. Denmark's southern border from
1864 to 1920 is indicated by the line just north of Ribe in the above map. The present border,
not far from the town of Tønder, is shown with dotted lines. In a referendum held in 1920
after World War I, a majority in north Slesvig (the area between the line above Ribe and the
present border) voted for reunification with Denmark. A majority in south Slesvig (the area
between the present Danish border and the northern boundary of Holsten) voted to remain
part of Germany. With this map, we enter the historical period of the Danish folk high schools.*

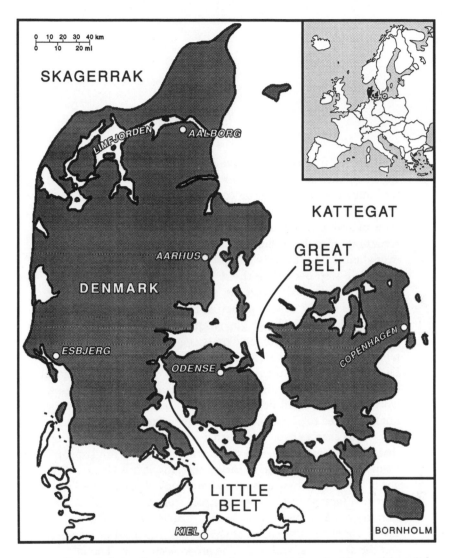

8. *Denmark in the late twentieth century* (*Adapted with permission of the Danish Tourist Board of New York*). *The box to the upper right shows Denmark in its contemporary European context: Norway is directly to the north, Sweden to the northeast, Germany and continental Europe to the south. Note the circled island of Bornholm to the east, south of Sweden (shown in greater detail in the inset, lower right). To round out the picture, Iceland gained its independence in 1944. Though still nominally part of Denmark, the Faroe Islands and Greenland have achieved independent "home rule" in most areas (each has two representatives in the Danish parliament, or* folketing). *This map and the previous seven have traced the theme of long-term territorial loss in Danish history.*

EXCURSUS ONE

Tivoli Gardens

In the first chapter I have introduced in outline some of the main themes and problems of this investigation. I have as well subjected the reader to concentrated discussion, alleging the existence of sweeping historical interconnections, troubling areas of ambiguity, and vast domains of paradox. Not only the reader but even the author may at times stand in danger of being overwhelmed by all this complexity. The reader is therefore invited to step back from the dry outlines of theoretical argument to make a small excursion. The point of this and following excursions will be to visit an actual region, a town, a time, or a place in Denmark. The single exception to this will be in the following chapter, where the Excursus is a consideration of some relevant themes in the cultural history of the United States. Discussion of these themes will introduce some key areas of contrast between Danish and American history. Each section labeled Excursus will provide concrete illustrations and living images related to points made in the chapter to which it belongs.

This chapter concludes with a visit to a Danish institution that came in many ways to represent for me the fundamental theme of limits discussed in earlier sections of this chapter. It is one of Denmark's best-known and most-loved places, the Tivoli Gardens, located just across the street from the central railway station in downtown Copenhagen. Come with me, then, to Tivoli, for the last weekend of the season. It is mid-September, and the sky is clear and cold. The mood is autumn. Though the leaves are still green on the trees, one can already feel the tremors of winter with its frosted mornings and dark afternoons, its bleak, leafless landscapes. Its smell and taste are already to be sensed in the crisp air of this flawless, late-summer day.

The Tivoli Gardens bears a superficial resemblance to an amusement park in the United States. Yet a closer inspection reveals important differences. To my eyes everything at Tivoli seems small and on a human scale. The ferris wheel and roller coaster are tame compared to those I have seen in some American amusement parks, where part of the fun is apparently tied up with the need to be terrified by the sense of being placed in almost real physical danger. A kind of evanescent pseudo-ordeal is created, perhaps supplying a testimonial proof of young macho competence. Could it be, I reflect to myself, that the relatively small size here reflects not so much the inability to construct large and dangerous-looking rides, but more a simple lack of the American obsession with speed and size?

Tivoli is not just an amusement park, but a series of worlds within worlds. It is like a set of Chinese boxes: gardens are mixed in with restaurants, restaurants hide alongside amusement concessions, amusement concessions are surrounded by snack bars. Taken together, the assortment of restaurants and snack bars scattered through the park can provide sources of satisfaction for every conceivable mood, taste, and budget. What Judith Friedman Hansen has called the "principle of inclusion"[38] is an essential principle of Tivoli's design. There is something for all age groups here, something for members of every social class. It is not, like so many amusement parks in the United States, noticeably dominated by the presence of the eighteen- to twenty-five-year-old crowd.

Some restaurants are modern and glow with fashionable chic. Others have been built to look like pubs or alehouses from Denmark or other lands, perhaps England or the Tyrolean Alps. Full-course international gourmet dinners, ice cream, pastry, Coke, hot dogs, and beer: all are served virtually side by side. Benches are set down through the entire park, some along the main thoroughfares, others in more private places, beside the duck ponds, or half-hidden under neighborly trees still pendant with late-summer foliage. Many of the benches face colorful gardens or fountains. They are often filled with older people who can secure seasonal passes guaranteeing them free admission. This is one of the advantages possessed by the city's senior residents, who can pass their time during these pleasant summer days and evenings in a vibrant setting surrounded by the moving flow of humanity.

I can't help noticing that I see almost no policemen, yet the evening moves along peaceably. The fences are small, but no one steps over them. A small playground is freely available to children during the daylight hours, and at night the theater and concerts attract the older visitors. One can choose from classical, traditional, popular, folk, and rock music, each of which is available and finds its own age- and taste-group. Theaters and performing pavilions are everywhere. The pantomime of Pierrot, Harlequin, and Columbine charms audiences just as it has since Tivoli was first opened in the summer of 1843. The members of the Tivoli Guard, all under the age of seventeen, are dressed in the style of the Queen's Guard; they march with their own band on the weekends. The brilliance of the Chinese Pagoda, the magnificent Peacock Theatre, the Illuminated Bubble Fountain, the rides, the restaurants, the sounds, the smells—it is all too much for the confused tourists, who peer at their maps and guidebooks, trying to find out where they are. At this late date in the summer the Danes outnumber the tourists, and it is easy to tell them apart. The Danes walk quickly and don't need to look at the maps to get where they are going. Or else they stroll along slowly—children, parents, lovers hand in hand. And there are always the loud and enthusiastic gangs of teenagers, having a robust good time.

A guard gestures to the middle-aged tourist couple waiting at the acrobats' performance. They are trying to make out the sign. "It's free," he says in English. When they look around suspiciously, he smiles and repeats, "Yes, it's free." They look at each other in disbelief, fearful that they are being tricked. But there are no tickets and no line, just rows of long green benches in front of the stage where soon the Czechoslovakian acrobats will perform again. It is in this square that the crowds gather on Wednesdays and Saturdays at midnight to watch the magnificent fireworks display that comes as a fitting climax to the evening's entertainment. Children stare openmouthed, dropping their ice cream cones as the night sky suddenly explodes in bright colors. One of everyone's favorites is the "chrysanthemum bomb," which momentarily transforms the midnight darkness into a cascade of shapes and colors resembling this lovely flower. The professional fireworks crew that is responsible for the evening's stirring conclusion also does "special effects" for rock groups, the Royal Ballet, or visiting orchestras. Sometimes the smoke and glow from these events light up the night sky.

The small ponds and fountains that dot the landscape give it in sudden places the almost rustic nature of a park in a provincial Danish town. Private corners can easily be found whether for the lonely or for lovers, for those immersed in solitary reflection, or for those who want to hold serious, deep personal conversations. All the while the throng of humanity continues to flow along the main avenues. There is an assortment of couples both with and without children. Sometimes one can see three generations of a family moving along in a stately and unhurried procession. The dress code is self-chosen; it varies all the way from blue jeans to spotless summer whites.

On leaving one of the park's more private and secluded places it is sometimes difficult to remember that you are in the center of downtown Copenhagen. Yet lingering for a while in all these places you find yourself swept back into the slow and stately movement of the crowds, to become again a part of their typical, twentieth-century minuet. From this description of Tivoli made by Edmund Gosse, an Englishman who visited Denmark in 1874, it is evident that it has not changed much in its essence:

> When you entered Tivoli, you found a huge crowd, of all ranks of society, engaged in sauntering along paths which diverged in various directions between stiff avenues of trees. A large piece of water lay at the end of the principal vista, on which fantastic boats slowly conducted happy groups of citizens. Fountains, *parterres,* terraces and statues, a large bazaar, a concert-room, a theatre, booths for jugglers, for games of skill, for mountebanks and athletes, made up the attractions of the place, which, as the night came on and a thousand lamps were lighted, was clothed in an atmosphere of charming gaiety. . . . The Danes are a quiet people, but their fondness for clinging to company is extravagant. They cannot go away. My own companions were

insatiable; not a swing, not a pavilion, not a gondola, was to be missed . . . not until the last illuminated tableaux had flared upon the night, and the last lamp-lit party had groped across the darkling lake, was I permitted to march home.

If anyone—a native of the city, a tourist, a world-weary traveler—were looking for a moment of peace in a world gone mad, that person could do much worse than to wind up in Tivoli in September, on the last weekend of this year's season. I stand by the railing of a pond, watching the intricate electric dragon-flies with their brightly oscillating wings. How is it done? Suddenly there is the chiming of a clock somewhere off in the distance. Ducks in the sleepy pond swim under bent willows in the shadows of early evening. A little girl and an old woman lean over a black railing, throwing bread crumbs to the ducks. The children ride the roller coaster one last time, saying goodbye to summer.

PART II

CLOUDED IMAGES, HOPEFUL REALITIES

The injustice which Denmark has, in general, sustained from the ignorance and prejudice of foreign travelers, originally suggested the expedience of this Publication.

The Author's endeavour has been to give a description of the Country and the People, in a manner which, he trusts, will prove satisfactory. His great object is to obey a call, at once just and generous, lately made in one of the eminent literary Journals of Britain, "requiring every man to contribute his mite to make nations better acquainted with each other, in the hope of repairing the breach which the fourth part of a century, spent in war and devastation, has made in mutual courtesy."

Edinburgh, 7th July, 1821
from the frontispiece to
A. Andersen Feldborg
DENMARK
DELINEATED
or
Sketches of the present State
of that Country
(1824)
Rosenkilde and Bagger
International Booksellers and Publishers

CHAPTER TWO

The Foreign Image
of Denmark

These Danes began to be knowne to the world, about the yeere of
Christ 570, for their piracies called Wiccings.

—Samuel Purchas, 1625

I. The Provisional Research Hypothesis

T
HOSE ANTHROPOLOGISTS WHO REPORT on some faraway group like the
Yanomamö or Kaingáng of Brazil can take it for granted that Western
readers will know very little about them. An individual who has done
this type of fieldwork may be surprised if the people back home know
anything about the people he or she has studied. When I first became
interested in Denmark and its folk high schools, I was surprised to find the
existence of a parallel: for all most Americans really knew about Denmark,
it might as well have been part of the Amazonian rain forest. It is unquestionably the case that with slightly more than 5 million inhabitants,
occupying a land area of 43,074 square kilometers, Denmark must be
reckoned as one of the smaller nations of the world. From an American
perspective, however, it is not only a small country but one that is almost
unknown.

The unfortunate lack of knowledge concerning Denmark was forcibly
brought home to me during the time that I was making preparations to
leave California in the summer of 1982 to begin my fieldwork. "Denmark?"
many asked in surprise when told where I was going upon finishing my
Ph.D. in anthropology. More than one well-meaning person even committed
the ultimate blunder of wishing me "a good time in Stockholm" or something of that sort.[1] When they heard what I planned to do there, the blank
look in their eyes gave clear testimony as to their puzzlement. Anyone could
understand going to Copenhagen for a tourist trip. But why would a sensible

person go there and waste valuable time *studying and learning about* Danish culture? This thought or something like it was clearly on most people's minds, even if they were too polite to say it aloud in my presence. It soon became clear to me that what little knowledge of Denmark exists in the American awareness is bound up with stereotypes about pornography and the welfare state, perhaps a memory of a fairy tale by Hans Christian Andersen read as a child, coupled with vague images of Viking ships sailing the open seas. Throw in a picture of blond Scandinavians in ski sweaters, Victor Borge at the piano, and perhaps a hunk of Danish blue cheese, and the American knowledge of Denmark is pretty much complete.

Given the existence of these stereotypes, and the appalling general lack of knowledge concerning not only Denmark but the other small countries of the world, perhaps the best way to introduce Danish culture is to sketch in something of the process by which I came to study it. In the beginning I had none of the more sophisticated formulations set forth in the previous chapter (e.g., an alternation between the "broad" and the "narrow" focus), for I hadn't yet even heard of the folk high school. I had only a glimmering, a kind of preliminary intuition that can best be called a "provisional research hypothesis." The provisional research hypothesis that guided this study in its early stages was a simple one and of greater generality than particular questions I later came to ask about the Danish folk high schools. It can be summed up in a sentence: there is something of real importance to be learned from a study of Danish culture and history.

This hypothesis had a corollary. If it is true that Denmark has something of value to teach the world, then not merely the lesson itself *but even the fact that such a lesson exists* have been well-kept secrets. These insights had begun to crystallize for me in the summer of 1979 shortly after returning from Israel, where I had carried out a two-year study of an Israeli kibbutz. The fact that few others shared my conviction failed to dampen the enthusiasm it aroused. On the contrary, the lack of consensual validation kindled something stubborn in my nature, and my conviction grew gradually into a small obsession. I began to study Danish at Stanford University just a month after returning from Israel, even though the completion of my doctoral thesis was at least two years away and I hadn't the faintest idea either of how I was going to get to Denmark or what I was going to study once I got there.

In spite of the lack of external reinforcement, my curiosity persisted during the difficult years of thesis writing. In part because of what was fast becoming a solitary and almost private endeavor, I thought at one point to ask if anyone before me outside of Denmark had asked the same questions I was now asking. This curiosity resulted in frequent side trips in the

Stanford University libraries to explore the dusty archives of the Danish collection. My review of the library files showed that a few writers, mostly Americans and Englishmen, had found pieces of what I was looking for. Some had even written valuable firsthand accounts of their visits to Denmark.

In 1911 Edmund Gosse published his *Two Visits to Denmark,* an account of travels made forty years earlier (1872 and 1874) to what he called "one of the smallest, but one of the most cultivated countries of Europe." Gosse, an Englishman, had timed his visits remarkably well. He was present at one of N. F. S. Grundtvig's final sermons and has left us a memorable account of the feelings Grundtvig evoked in his admirers (see p. 175). Hans Christian Andersen received him personally on several occasions. Although the great Danish author was not known for his talent in public relations, he nonetheless succeeded in making an exceptional impression on Gosse:

> Suddenly, however, as we were seated in the living-room, there appeared in the doorway a very tall, elderly gentleman, dressed in a complete suit of brown, and in a curly wig of the same shade of snuff-color. I was almost painfully struck, at the first moment, by the grotesque ugliness of his face and hands, and by his enormously long and swinging arms, but this impression passed away as soon as he began to speak. His eyes, although they were small, had great sweetness and vivacity of expression, while gentleness and ingenuousness breathed from everything he said. He had been prepared to expect a young English visitor, and he immediately took my hand in his two big ones, patting and pressing it. Though my hands have no delicacy to speak of, they seemed like pebbles in a running brook in his large ones. . . . The face of Hans Andersen was a peasant's face, and a long lifetime of sensibility and culture had not removed from it the stamp of the soil. But it was astonishing how quickly this first impression subsided, while a sense of his great inward distinction took its place. He had but to speak, almost but to smile, and the man of genius stood revealed.[2]

Gosse and a number of other writers—among them H. Rider Haggard, Frederick Howe, Josephine Goldmark, and A. H. Hollman—pointed with obvious enthusiasm and respect to some of the things they had seen with their own eyes in Denmark. Yet most of their accounts, however convincing, dated from the early years of this century, and their small volumes were now busy gathering dust in obscure corners of the library. Much had to have taken place in the half century and more since the writing of these books. If the Danes themselves knew what it was these men had been trying to say to the world, and what its contemporary sequel was, they had evidently persisted in speaking and writing about it in their own mother tongue. Word would never get out that way, and the mystery of Danish

culture would remain unavailable and inaccessible, a secret except perhaps
to a narrow handful of academic specialists.[3] Something had to be done, and
I had appointed myself the one to do it. As the saying goes, a fool rushes in
where angels fear to tread. But I am getting ahead of my story.

There were a number of other factors, in addition to this body of
literature, behind my interest in Denmark. A second thread that led to the
provisional research hypothesis was what I had come to know about the
relationship among the Scandinavian nations. I knew, for instance, that
Denmark exists as a cultural and national unit within the broader regional
setting of Scandinavia. And even as a nonspecialist in the history of that area,
I learned that these nations (Norway, Sweden, Denmark, and Finland),
which once regularly made war on each other and their neighbors, had long
since beaten their swords into ploughshares. Although continuing to maintain strong concerns for national defense in an admittedly unstable world,
what interested me most was an important detail that I thought I could
discern in their international policy statements. For in these countries the
public rhetoric of imperialism—of expansion and obsessive empire building—seemed notable in its absence. While the spirit of aggressive militarism unquestionably had not disappeared from all individuals at all times
in these countries, it apparently was no longer celebrated in the high
counsels of their governments. However maddening to American officials
such things as Sweden's complicated neutrality policies and dissenting
Danish footnotes to NATO decisions might be, the Scandinavian nations
seemed to me to represent both a positive "peace zone" and a much-needed
brake on the constant threat of spreading international conflict. These have
included both the superpowers' dangerous drift toward confrontation risk-
ing nuclear devastation, and the intractable web of regional wars such as
those seen in the Horn of Africa during the past three decades.

This fact in itself seemed to me a distinctive achievement. In a world
of increasing individual and social violence, where new militarism and
expansionary third world imperialisms conjoin those already existing in the
technologically postmodern Eastern and Western bloc states, the Scandinavian countries appeared to represent isolated yet potentially significant
models for the possibility of peaceful coexistence among nations. After all,
these were not small and isolated hunting-gathering cultures, but modern
European nations with a long and bloody history that at some particular
point in their development had ceased to believe in the usefulness of war
and political conquest. Denmark, in fact, had become part of the Scandinavian "peace zone," whose philosophy is perhaps nowhere better summed up
than in this brief statement by Olof Palme (1927–86), the former Prime
Minister of Sweden: "We have come to realize that peace is certainly more

than the absence of military violence. It is also stability in relations between states, based on observance of legal principles."

If a soldier in one of the Scandinavian countries experiences active duty today, it is likely to be with a United Nations peacekeeping force. "Soldiers can enforce peace as well as make war," argues Norway's Prime Minister Gro Harlem Brundtland, and United Nations officials state that the Scandinavian countries are among the most consistent and generous contributors, per capita, to internationally supported peacekeeping efforts.[4] More than thirty-two thousand Norwegian soldiers have served with the United Nations peacekeeping forces since 1947, their tour of duty underscoring the importance that the Scandinavian nations (together with many other small countries) place on volunteering for these difficult campaigns. Such a tour of duty is not without risk, and losses are inevitable. On 12 December 1988, a unique memorial service was held in the Oslo Cathedral for the 733 UN soldiers who have died while trying to keep the peace (twenty-five of them were Norwegians). "So far as we know, no one has ever held a memorial service like this before," remarked the Norwegian chaplain who conducted the service. Such actions plainly point to one of the guiding values that has characterized the modern Scandinavian nations in the field of international relations and diplomacy: a strong and consistent emphasis on the peaceful settlement of disputes.

Questions like these had to be asked: What did it mean to say that Denmark was a part of Scandinavia? What about Denmark was similar to the other Scandinavian nations, and which features were unique to its own history? At what point in their development, and for what reasons, did the Scandinavian countries "bury the hatchet" with each other? Is it meaningful to speak of a "postimperialist" state of national development, perhaps best exemplified by Denmark and the other Scandinavian countries? Although this book can only peripherally touch on these questions, I cite them in any case as relevant to the formation of the provisional research hypothesis.

The other factor that whetted my interest in Denmark was a tantalizing set of observations made during two years of residence on several Israeli kibbutzim. While carrying out the fieldwork for this research, I lived in the housing provided for foreign volunteers. Although my main attention at the time was on the myriad details of kibbutz social organization, I could not help noticing something very puzzling about our own volunteer existence. In short, I observed that whenever there was a Danish volunteer present, something remarkable seemed to happen to our social life. It was difficult to put your finger on it, but candles and flowers would suddenly appear on the wasted orange crates that we used for tables. The smiles seemed easier and the mood lighter. We laughed a lot more, and our parties were more relaxed. Because of my work I stayed far longer than any other resident of the volunteer quarter and so could watch this pattern come to life and then more or less flicker out when the last Dane had left. Both my personal and professional curiosity were aroused. Why did this mood seem to depend on there being a Dane present? Was this an accident of individual personalities, or was there something more to it? Just what was going on here? At the time it was a complete puzzle.

I left Israel in the spring of 1979 and returned to the United States to begin the more mundane task of writing and completing a Ph.D. thesis. Yet my mind was full of questions that pointed beyond my kibbutz research. Who were these people that not so many years ago had steadfastly refused to give up their Jewish neighbors to the cattle cars and gas chambers? Who were those smiling, friendly co-workers on the kibbutz, the fellow volunteers whose laughter and easy sociability had so often lit up our small cabins in the evenings when work was done? Who, in fact, were these people of the cold and far North, the Scandinavians, once among the world's most warlike nations, but long since having made a real and lasting peace with each other? I am not sure that I knew it then, but I can see now that I had already made a decision. When my doctoral thesis was finished, I would try to get to Denmark and to live there long enough to find some of the answers to these questions.

II. TWO COMMON NEGATIVE STEREOTYPES

As I pursued the provisional research hypothesis, I discovered that it is impossible to do the ethnography of a people without becoming sensitive to the images of them held in the world at large. Viewed overall, Denmark does not suffer in this regard; the current international image of Denmark is generally quite a favorable one. One finds inevitable exceptions, such as the rude Soviet author mentioned by Samuel Rachlin who dismissed it as "the country that has more pigs than people."[5] Yet given the predominantly positive nature of the evaluations, the negative images that do exist should be scrutinized with particular interest for what they might reveal. Such stereotypes might provide direct revelations by making available insights into Danish character. On the other hand, they may facilitate indirect revelations through their systematic misreadings of that character. In the latter case the stereotypes in question should be looked at even more closely with an eye toward clarifying their origin and functions.

The two images discussed in this section have been compiled from the informal oral traditions of several Western, non-Scandinavian nations and can in a sense be regarded as part of their folklore. They are, respectively, the welfare state as a destroyer of personal initiative and the melancholy Dane. The discussion of the welfare state stereotype serves to introduce Excursus Two, with its critical and comparative reading of Danish and American history. Its central theme is that in the Danish and the American case a different perception of limits on national action has profoundly influenced the nation's historical experience and its people's national character.

Stereotype One: A Boring Welfare State

The best dance is the dance of the Eastern clans,
the best people ourselves, of this I have always been sure.
—Dance song, Somalis of the Northern Horn of Africa[6]

A common stereotype about Denmark is reflected in frequent judgments made (especially in the United States) about the concept of welfare and the welfare state. Welfare destroys individual initiative, welfare keeps people in poverty, welfare leads to laziness and moral lassitude: this familiar litany of conservative Western social thought scarcely needs repeating. As a modern "welfare state," Denmark is presumably guilty of all of the above. Explicit judgments couched in these terms are often aimed at the Scandinavian countries in particular and constitute one aspect of the negative stereotype concerning welfare.

A second part of the stereotype exists at the implicit level, meaning that I have never heard it uttered in so many words. It can be summed up in the more or less unconscious attitude that Denmark is somehow a boring country, one altogether lacking in interest. Connected partly to size ("Isn't it tiny?") and partly to geography ("Isn't it flat as a pancake?"), this image draws much of its energy from attributions made on the basis of stereotyped political evaluations ("Isn't it one of those welfare states where the individual gets everything from the state?"). The Scandinavian countries, it is felt, are boring. Interestingly enough, this type of negative evaluation is not made of other European countries such as England, France, and Spain.

The ethnocentrism and naive cultural self-centeredness implied in such comments are nothing new to an anthropologist. I once lived and worked among the Somalis of the Northern Horn, a people whose magnificent oral tradition is not to be outdone when it comes to expressing the vainglorious themes of group self-love. The lines of the Somali poem cited above reflect a familiar mood, of which the previously noted American stereotypes are surely an indirect and minor instance. Nevertheless, such areas of deep-rooted cultural prejudice suggest a need for the most careful scrutiny. Let us pursue the matter a little further.

It must be asked at this point: what does a discussion of American ethnocentrism have to do with the present work? The connection is this: from my contact with Americans, I can only conclude that many will dismiss with unconscious condescension a subject like the history of Denmark on the assumption that it is a topic simply not worth pursuing. This particular manifestation of the American national character is in the first instance wrong and in the second instance a pity, but I would go even further. It is one that suggests to me the need for some cultural psychoanalysis. The image of Denmark as somehow a "boring" country should be seen clearly as the kind of unconscious defense mechanism that it is.

It is a virtual truism of modern anthropological research that culturally constituted defense mechanisms often function to keep from consciousness a set of potentially disturbing and unpleasant facts.[7] These mechanisms function as mental detergents, laundering and bleaching reality in order to bolster the comfortable and prejudiced state of mind that sociologist Peter Berger has labeled the "world-taken-for-granted." If the mirror is turned around in order to examine some of its own properties, we may find that the American image of Denmark as a boring culture can reveal at least as much about the observing American as it does about the observed Dane. It could also tell us what in particular about Denmark and the Danish experience might be most useful for Americans (and others) to consider at this precise juncture in their history. We are invited, at this moment, to peer through the anthropologist's window of cross-cultural exploration.

The Continually Expanding Frontier and the Absence of Limits: Two Root Themes in the Cultural Mythology of the U.S.A.

> The land was ours before we were the land's.
> She was our land more than a hundred years
> Before we were her people.
> —Robert Frost, "The Gift Outright"

I was still in high school when these lines from Robert Frost's poem were read aloud by John Fitzgerald Kennedy at his presidential inauguration in 1960. It is probably not surprising that Kennedy, a New England president, had chosen on that occasion to read from Frost, a New England poet. What may be more surprising, however, is that themes of the Western frontier echo through the words of a New England poet writing in the mid-twentieth century. "We did not know this land," the poet seems to be saying, and at the same time leaving us to draw the even more shocking yet unstated implication, "We did not know ourselves." The slogan for the Kennedy administration would be "The New Frontier."

The venerable frontier hypothesis, first put forth in 1893 by the American historian Frederick Jackson Turner, has been debated at length by subsequent generations of historians.[8] (This development would not have surprised Turner, who once wrote that "each age writes the history of the past anew with reference to the conditions uppermost in its own time.") Turner's thesis was twofold: first, that the frontier—defined as an ever-receding border "between savagery and civilization"—had been the most important factor shaping the American character; and second,

that as of 1890 the frontier was closed, and "with its going has
closed the first period of American history."[9]

Turner's frontier hypothesis has been chipped away at and
debunked in the ensuing decades. Charles Beard pointed out that
it could not explain slavery, industrialization, urbanization, and
the growth of organized labor, all of which existed before the
supposed closing of the frontier in 1890. Benjamin Wright
argued that the movement of democratic institutions had been
from east to west, and not from west to east in the wake of frontier
democracy as Turner maintained. Other parts of Turner's thesis
have been questioned, such as the degree to which the frontier
identity, if it in fact ever existed, did represent as clean a break
with the European past as Turner seems to have thought it was.
Beneath these more factual aspects of Turner's thesis, however,
lies an aspect that has touched a root theme in our cultural
mythology. And it is this aspect, deeply enshrined in the American awareness, that both gives the thesis its valid core of insight
and explains why Turner's thesis is still being debated a hundred
years after his first paper on the loss of the frontier was presented.

In my judgment this useful core can be stated in four
simple propositions. First, American identity and national character have been decisively shaped by the relationship of an
expanding nation to an apparently endless frontier. Second, even
after the frontier ceased to exist physically, it became a fundamental part of the mythology and character structure of the
American people and remains so today. Third, the myth of the
frontier is connected with a particularly American myth of
freedom without responsibility and without the acknowledgment of limits on personal or collective action. Fourth, in our
time, when declarations of interdependence must be joined to
those of independence, this myth becomes a dangerous one, and
a people thus imprisoned in its cultural mythology will ultimately reap a tragic harvest.

If Frost's lines cited above point to our ignorance of
ourselves as a people, it is probably not unfair to say that the
American knowledge of Europe as a whole is vanishingly small.
The lack of awareness and interest in Denmark must therefore
be seen as part of a broader "knowledge gap." Leaving the

discussion of stereotypes momentarily aside, it is typically only the educated American who has even *heard of* Denmark. Let us begin with an anecdote. A Danish acquaintance of mine, working as a busboy in a restaurant in the United States, happened to remark to one of his co-workers that he had been born in Europe. "Europe—hey, that's some nice country!" was the friendly and good-faith reply that he received.

As one who has taught in an inner city school and experienced a good deal of the class and ethnic diversity found on both coasts, I can claim with some degree of confidence that the above level of knowledge is not a rare exception. It is instead something closer to the American norm. Although its narrow vision of what exists outside American borders may suffice for understanding the world of the street corners, it does little to lighten up the street corners of the world. By this I mean not only to critique the isolated and insular quality of the typical American world-view (if one is permitted to speak of such an abstraction) but to point to just one of its many unfortunate consequences. I speak here of the dangerous asymmetry of knowledge that more and more has come to influence relationships between Americans and most of the rest of the world. The results of this asymmetry are as evident in the manifold details of American foreign policy as they are in the comments of the presumably "uneducated" individual cited above. To take one example, many educated Americans—among them highly placed policy and decision makers—share a happy misperception that English has become the world's dominant language. Yet as historian Paul Kennedy has observed, "In a world in which some of its businessmen, scientists and diplomats know only one language—English—and others know both it *and* a second language, who is the better equipped to deal with global complexities and cross-cultural misunderstandings?"[10]

What are some of the reasons for the American insularity? The imbalance and asymmetry of relative knowledge may be in part a historical consequence of the isolation imposed by geography. It locates us "under the celestial protection of two oceans," one off each coast. These large oceans provide enormously extended boundaries to both east and west; while to the north and

south are found peaceful neighbors, Canada and Mexico. Eliza-
beth Hardwick argues that the oceans are deeply rooted in the
American unconscious, and points out that they have fostered
an illusion of protection and separation from world events so
intensely held that "only a savage amount of nudging, shouting
and alarming can make the often exhorted American people feel
threatened."[11] The American historian C.Vann Woodward has
posed a thoughtful question: did the unique security provided
by this geography allow Americans to indulge in "the doubtful
luxury of a full-scale civil war of four years without incurring
the evils of foreign intervention and occupation?"[12] In the same
essay Woodward asks whether this free and easy security is
related to two other significant features of American national
character, the all-pervasive American optimism and the myth of
national innocence—the sense of being, in Woodward's words,
"an innocent nation in a wicked world."

But these accidents of geography, however suggestive and
important, are only part of the story and must be supplemented
by some basic facts of cultural history. Consider first the unique
way in which the United States came to be settled. The majority
of those who fled to the United States from other lands used it
as a physical and psychological refuge from traditions they
desperately wanted to escape. Once an individual arrived, the
idea was to lose the immigrant identity and become "an American." The fact of geographic isolation was compounded by the
existence of vast amounts of apparently open space in which
immigrants (a category including everyone except the Native
American Indians, who were there from the beginning) could
build a new American identity. A slogan from the Zionist
Movement has an odd relevance: "To build the land and be
rebuilt by it." The words of the slogan imply the need to basically
redefine the self, a need beautifully summed up in the phrase
"becoming a real American." Older cultural identities were to
be abandoned, if not in the first, then in the second or third
generations. Whatever connections to the past existed were to
be surrendered and (at least publicly) placed in the dustbin of
history where, it was felt, they belonged. Immigrant languages,

dialects, and traditions were to be given up; the future was here and now, in America.

Perhaps this is one reason for the odd ahistoricity of American culture, with its eyes so firmly fixed on the future and averted from the past. "History is bunk," said one famous American who made motor cars. When an American president scornfully remarks, "That's History," the American press and public meekly allow him to avoid discussing the matter at issue, even if the events in question took place only last week or last year. If it is history, the post-Reagan understanding is that it can no longer be relevant. Noam Chomsky has shown how this convenient "change of course" doctrine allows American politicians to sanitize, deny, and reinterpret past policies merely by making the simple counterclaim: "Oh, we're not doing that anymore." As Chomsky has written:

> One useful consequence of the doctrine of "change of course" is that all analytic work devoted to the study of American society and history is entirely irrelevant, no matter what it reveals. Since we have now changed course, we may dismiss the lessons of history and begin afresh, unburdened by any understanding of the nature of American society or the documentary and historical record. All studies of these topics may be shelved, as now irrelevant, apart from their antiquarian interest. Furthermore, analysis of current developments may also be dismissed when the conclusions are unacceptable, since we can, after all, always change course once again and set forth anew. . . .[13]

But a seemingly endless trajectory of economic growth, powered by the enormous web of natural resources the land originally possessed, was just one of the developments that seemed to confirm beyond all expectations the hopes and predictions of the immigrants. Given what many were fleeing from, it is understandable that they ignored the past, clung to the present, and took the future for granted. The American dream was somewhere out there waiting for them, and those who were clever, ambitious, and hardworking enough could expect to own a few shares in it even if they were Jewish, Irish, or their last name was Grabowski (though discriminatory subclauses of that dream built fences around the hopes of those whose ancestry was Mexican, Indian, or African).

If one wanted to symbolize and personify the American development experience, one could hardly choose a better event than the Oklahoma land rush that took place roughly a century ago. At noon on 22 April 1889, more than 40,000 settlers, on horseback and in wagons, raced in from the borders of the 2-million-acre "Unassigned Lands" (now central Oklahoma) to claim their 160-acre tracts. These so-called Unassigned Lands belonged to Indian tribes—to the Cheyenne, the Arapaho, and the Cherokees—but President Benjamin Harrison had now generously opened them to white settlement. Those who managed to enter the territories before the appointed time were called "Sooners"; it is from them that the state of Oklahoma gets its nickname. An explosive growth in population followed: the population of the Oklahoma territory was about 60,000 at the end of 1889; in 1892 it was 130,000, and by 1900 it had reached 389,000.[14] The frontier concept of progress that lay behind these events is still celebrated in American cultural mythology. In 1989, on the occasion of the centennial celebration of the original land rush, 150 participants raced a half mile across an open pasture with their cowboy hats flying in the wind. The winners were awarded wooden stakes similar to those their ancestors might have used to claim land in 1889. To their astonishment, members of surviving Indian groups were invited to participate in the event.

This single incident, so symbolic of "how the West was won," suggests a paradox that is equally a part both of the original American frontier heritage and the postfrontier American pattern of land settlement. The paradox is this: despite the continuous and successive waves of immigration from without, a state of dangerous psychological and cultural isolation has resulted in the United States. When the English poet William Blake wrote, may "God us keep / From single vision and Newton's sleep," he probably had the factories of England in mind. Yet Blake's lines speak with the acuity of prophetic insight to the clouded vision and cultural slumber of much of American society in the 1980s. In spite of the superficial appearance of cultural pluralism, a single distorted vision still clouds most American eyes.

The mood is of course not a new one. Even back in the nineteenth century when the frontier existed and Walt Whitman heard America singing, the tune played was frequently Yankee Doodle Dandy and the message one of Manifest Destiny.[15] "The deed of gift was many deeds of war," Frost had written in the poem read by Kennedy at his Inaugural. When in the wake of two world wars the United States emerged not merely as a world empire but as unquestioned *numero uno,* the temptation to take jingoistic preachings for divine revelation became an overpowering one. The arrogance of empire was transformed into an article of faith, and belief in the greatness of America a dogmatic artifact of American allegiance. It was as if a mindless hand-over-the-heart pledge had become a socially accepted substitute for reality testing.

Like a tower of Babel, the rhetoric grew and grew, especially in the 1980s. It would last forever, this inspired movement toward the stars, this unique and noble democracy. We could do no wrong, almost by definition. Fueled in the loyal shadow of the stars and stripes, sustained by a positive belief in American goodness and the limitless possibilities of American action, the rhetoric supported and nourished a perennial American illusion. It is one that persisted and persists. Even today it is rare that one hears publicly questioned the idea that American drive, enterprise, imagination, and technology might not be able to solve in the future all of the problems that American drive, enterprise, imagination, and technology are so busy creating today. In much of our recent history the hypnotic rhetoric of purchased TV commercials has been taken for reality. The omnipresent code of Americanism blinds us both to who we are and what we are becoming.[16]

The American frontier, once real and seemingly without limits, was initially an unfinished obstacle course to be traversed by successive trains of covered wagons traveling through dangerous Indian country over the plains and mountains that seemed to stretch out so endlessly before them. The English-American poet T. S. Eliot used the image of a river:

I think that the river is a strong brown god—
sullen, untamed and intractable,
Patient to some degree, at first recognized as a frontier;
Useful, untrustworthy, as a conveyor of commerce;
Then only a problem confronting the builder of bridges.

Whether it had physically vanished by 1890, as Turner
believed, or was eroded away by the twin forces of time and
history in the intervening hundred years, this once real frontier
continues to exist as an experienced territory of the American
mind. In his highly touted volume of short stories, *In a Father's
Place* (1990), American writer Christopher Tilghman portrays
characters whose inner lives often reflect metaphors of the frontier. In "Loose Reins, " the main character's mother, who gave
up a debutante's life for the hardships of Montana, says she
understands "what the pioneer wives felt as they waited in the
wagons, dreaming of the green hills of Ohio, while husbands
made homes out of sod and buffalo skin." And Grant, the hero
of "Hole in The Day," drives west across Montana in pursuit of
his wife, thinking of his great grandfather, "who traced a similar
route westward to the Pacific, and all the others who once left
their homes in search of an elusive frontier."[17] In his short story
"The Lion at Morning," the American novelist Thomas Wolfe,
writing in the 1930s, has left us an evocative portrait of an old
man's nostalgia for his lost youth and the vanished frontier:

> Had not he who was James Wyman fifty years ago—
> young and brave and an American who had the faith, and felt
> the strength and heard the singing, who had seen the plains, the
> rivers, and the mountains, the quiet blueness in a farmhand's
> eyes, and had heard the voices in the darkness talking, known
> how the land went, and the shapes of things, and known, too,
> that the dream was something more than dream, the great hope
> something more than hope. . . . Where had it gone to, then—all
> of the passion and the fire of youth, and the proud singing; all
> of the faith, the hope, the clean belief of fifty years ago? Where
> had it gone to, then—the strength, the faith, the wisdom, the
> sound health and substance of his lost America?[18]

The fate of the American Indians, treated as fond projections in American advertising and folklore, symbolizes in a tragic way the vanished frontier. Their present struggles are not with wagon trains, but with alcoholism and fetal alcohol syndrome on the reservations and in big city slums, or with lung cancer and cystic fibrosis after years of working in the uranium mines of the American Southwest.[19] The cultural imperialism of the dominant society struggles to take from them the shreds of traditional identity they have been able to save from their old and once proud cultures. They are asked to participate in such events as the centennial reenactment of the Oklahoma land rush, a request described by one Indian activist as "asking us to dance on the graves of our people." The apparently limitless frontier inhabited by the Indians and the immigrant cowboys endures now only in the archetypal regions of the (mostly white, mostly male) American mythical consciousness and its attendant self-image. Celebrated mainly in beer commercials and presidential rhetoric, it is a pretentious piece of self-deception that is only supported and kept alive in our time by what social historian Garry Wills has aptly described as "a vast communal exercise in make-believe."[20]

What is the conclusion of this Excursus into American mythology and its parade of reflected images? It is *that one of the critical problems confronting contemporary American society is its refusal to accept or even to seriously debate the idea of limits and what they imply, even while it is increasingly and inexorably faced with them on all fronts.* Some readers will ask how such a thesis can be seriously offered when bankers, journalists, and politicians can be heard preaching every day about American limits. The answer is that protagonists in the mainstream, in due deference to the recent "greening" of the American political climate, will in many cases give passionate lip service to the idea of limits. But their action (or in many cases, their inaction) speaks louder than their words. Take just one area of crisis that suggests the necessity of acknowledging limits: the environment. Here, as in other areas of crisis, it is important not to be taken in by the superficial appearance of serious commitment that is being so assiduously fostered by corporations and politicians eager to capitalize on the current wave of environmental anxiety.

When the Bush administration was asked to contribute the modest sum of $20 million to a new international fund to help poorer countries phase out chemicals that are destroying the earth's ozone layer, it initially refused. The justification given was that it did not want to set a precedent for expensive new foreign aid programs on the environment. Only after personal appeals from Margaret Thatcher, from the executive director of the United Nations Environmental Program, from environmental organizations, and even from the industries that make and use chlorofluorocarbons, did the Bush administration reluctantly agree to contribute.[21] Far from leading the way in developing realistic strategies to cope with the global ozone crisis, the United States has had to be dragged kicking and screaming to even a minimal confrontation with the nonmilitary challenges that a global leader must confront in the 1990s. Numerous parallel examples from the environmental policies of American corporations could be cited.[22]

Based on his visits to the American continent in the 1830s, the French aristocrat Alexis de Tocqueville made a series of perceptive observations about the United States of America. He admired some of the things he saw, such as the "manly independence" of Americans as they explored the wilderness of the new continent. Viewing a nation of twenty-four states and 13 million people, he called us "the most unmilitary people in the world," a comment that suggests that the present obsessive concern with annihilation by a foreign power had not yet become a part of the American experience. But de Tocqueville's observations also contained a darker side, and he made some disturbing prophecies about the future of American society. In his classic, *Democracy in America,* de Tocqueville wrote in particular of the danger that a subtle "tyranny of the majority" would one day come to subvert democratic structures in America. He foresaw that it was precisely the democratic and egalitarian strengths of the new country that would one day, through the ironies of history, be transformed into demolishing weaknesses. An unpleasant question must be asked: has the day foreseen by de Tocqueville already come?

Particularly in America, we must think again about this unpleasant theme of limits. Take the area of international power politics: the myth of American military invincibility painfully and agonizingly shattered in Vietnam, a tragic misadventure whose unrecognized contradictions and unadmitted human cost remain unresolved problem areas in the mainstream American awareness. In spite of the euphoria over the easy military victory in Iraq, its bitter heritage has not been vanquished and continues to cast a dark shadow over American life. The confident assertion that we can now forget about "the Vietnam syndrome" provides a perfect example of Chomsky's change of course doctrine, discussed earlier. In the words of a Marine Corps veteran: "Not once—not once in all of these years—have I ever heard a single high-level policy-maker of the Vietnam war apologize for what he did, ever admit that he made a mistake, ever show the slightest sign of remorse for all the havoc and misery, the shattered lives and shattered families and shattered nations left gasping in the wake of his decisions."[23] Take any of the increasingly competitive domains in which the American way, once the world's unquestioned best, has seen foreigners gain ascendancy: computer electronics, machine tools, semiconductors, space rocketry, steel manufacturing, public education, automobile assembly and performance.[24] Take the self-indulgent development of the throwaway economy: first, glass bottles replaced by no-return, non-deposit plastic containers, next disposable razors, cameras, and diapers (16 billion a year of the last-mentioned item).[25] Assault weapons proliferate; old growth rain forests vanish. Although the landfills rise in silent testimony to the contrary, and the ozone holes at both poles become larger each year, most Americans still seem to believe in a world without limits on American action.

Remember that the sun has set on many world empires in the course of history. Every world empire has seen its time of dominance and exclusive hegemony fade into memory. Can a study of history and anthropology provide any insight into our situation? One thing we must remember is that when faced with

deep crisis both cultures and individuals often tend to an un-
healthy conservatism, clinging to past values with a death grip.
Herbert Muller concluded in his classic study, *The Uses of the Past,*
that the writings of Arnold Toynbee "have shown that when
religious belief was strongest it bred the worldly pride from
which it is supposed to deliver us, and was most deeply involved
in the moral failure of both Eastern and Western Christen-
dom."[26] The desperate attempt of the morally bankrupt Communist party to retain power in the Soviet Union provides
another example of this process. In the postmodern United
States, our quasi-religious belief in the necessity of progress has
bred the same sort of worldly pride, and the consequences of its
moral failure are all around for those who have eyes to see it. As
Muller wrote of his own insightful work, "Our theme, in short,
is high Tragedy."

It will be easy enough for many Americans to dismiss these
arguments. Aren't they contradicted by the fact that the American economy had seven straight years of expansion going into
1990? Isn't the current failure of world communism—marked
by a desperate turn toward capitalism not only of Eastern Europe
but of the Soviet Union itself—clear evidence that the American
Way of Life is triumphant throughout the world? Doesn't the
military victory in Iraq in early 1991 by an American-led
international coalition prove that America is still Number One?
The Nicaraguan poet Rubén Darío wrote in 1905: ". . . the
United States is grand and powerful. Whenever it trembles, a
profound shudder runs down the enormous backbone of the
Andes."[27] Aren't these lines as true today as the day they were
written?

Many will want to answer yes to all of these questions. Yet
a sober and critical approach to history is never more sorely
needed than in such moments of apparent liberation from the
past. For, as David Brion Davis suggests, it is in such moments
of *kairos,* of abrupt discontinuity, that an inability to see the logic
of the past will have the most tragic consequences. It is at such
times we are most likely to be trapped in our illusions of triumph
(think, for instance, of the reception given the Treaty of Versailles by the Allied victors in World War I, the illusion that a

better future would immediately follow that predominated in the newly independent African nations in the early 1960s, and the short-sighted rejoicing of many Israelis at the conclusion of the Six Days War).

The present moment is just such a time of *kairos*. Let me suggest that the military victories we have won on the battle-fields of the Middle East may buy us time, but they will provide no long-run solutions for the non-military problems that currently threaten American enterprise and prosperity. We have not been able to deal with them because we Americans are a people who have not yet learned to live within the limitations being forced on us by our history.

I do not stand alone in writing of "the decline of empire." A spate of recent works have offered similar arguments.[28] If this analysis is correct, what kind of alternative social policies might better serve the citizens of the dominant world empire in an era of increasing interdependence and diminishing resources? From the experience of *which* other nations can something useful be learned? I propose here a surprising parallel: *a valuable perspective on the nature of the dilemma facing American society can be gained through contrast and comparison with the history of Denmark, one of the world's smaller nations.* For it is not merely that the Danes are a people who have learned to live with the idea of limits. It is that in doing so they have created a culture and a way of life that even in American terms has many positive features. In fact, Americans (and much of the rest of the world) might do well to take a closer look at just what it is the Danes have done in learning to live with the idea of limits.

POINTS OF CONTRAST: A REVIEW OF THE ESTES STUDY

There are obvious similarities between Denmark and the United States. Both are economically advanced, industrialized, Western nations possessing an outwardly democratic political structure. Both profess fierce allegiance to democracy and democratic values. Each is a member of NATO and the Western alliance. Yet there are striking contrasts between them as well. These contrasts include such nontrivial matters as the nature of their respective political party systems, dominant beliefs about the military and its proper role in the society, relative level of violent crime, extent and functioning of welfare institutions, policies in the field of education, and metaphors of national self-image.

It will come as a surprise to many Americans that Denmark has become a multicultural society in the last thirty years (see the section on "Cultural Collisions" in Chapter Ten). Nevertheless, the enormous differences in size, degree of ethnic heterogeneity, and international power between Denmark and the United States are obvious relevant factors in any comparison of these two countries. I suggest that for the purpose of this inquiry these factors are of only minor interest and should be regarded chiefly as background material. For its purposes the most interesting historical parallel is the one suggested by a comparative consideration of the theme of limits. For unlike the United States, Denmark is a country that in the course of its long history has been forced to accept and acknowledge many times the idea of limits. Let us remember that during the course of the nineteenth century alone a land area equal to more than four times the size of modern Denmark was permanently lost from its sovereignty. Viewed from the framework of international power politics, loss and contraction have been continually recurring themes in the last two centuries of Danish history. The Danes have been forced to acknowledge the theme of limits with what appears to be some finality on the part of history.

Yet it is not the mere external facts of contraction and loss that are critical. Denmark is certainly not the only nation even in its own European sphere to suffer such a fate (how many people today knew anything of Lithuania prior to the events of spring 1990 or can recall what happened to the Armenian nation?) What is of real interest, and should call for systematic investigation on the part of historians and other social scientists, has been the Danish response. As a nation the Danes gave up long ago their old dream of conquest and expansion, and with it all hope of reacquiring their former territories. They responded to the unfortunate facts of loss by making their peace with the regrettable unpleasantries of history. They abandoned the belief that the voluntary, systematic, and aggressive use of national force would in the long run help them to achieve major geopolitical ends. Finally, they gave up the illusory hope that Denmark would once again be a world power, and in a sense that many Americans might find it difficult to understand, they do not wish to make the world over in their own image.

To make these claims is not to argue that they are necessarily delighted with how it all worked out. The Danish perspective on these events is frequently cloaked in irony, with an elegant touch of gallows humor:

> But, forgetting all this, Denmark approaches the ideal. The Dane himself often admits it, and gladly, as false modesty is not usually among his faults. The nation today is, in reality, the result of a long process of selection. Through a wise and consistent foreign policy throughout the ages, the inferior parts of a once great nation have been carefully and methodically dropped—to begin with, Normandy and England, then Sweden, Estonia, Norway, Tranquebar, Iceland, the West Indies, until only the best is left.[29]

More to the point, in spite of their loss of innocence, the Danes have done well in the world. The point is a central one—the abandoning of even third-rank claims to world empire does not seem to have caused them to fare poorly in the end. This "soft" assertion is a proposition that can be supported with considerable "hard" statistical evidence. And it is a conclusion that holds regardless of which other nations of the world one wants to use as a standard of comparison. Those who question this claim ought to consider the results of two recent studies (*The Social Progress of Nations*, 1984 and *Trends in World Social Development*, 1988) conducted by Richard Estes of the University of Pennsylvania School of Social Work. A longitudinal study spanning the decade of the 1970s, Estes' 1984 research attempted to systematically assess the quality of life in 107 nations around the world. Based on statistics obtained from the UN, World Bank, and the Organization of Economic Cooperation and Development, these nations were evaluated according to forty-four separate indices.

Estes' indices included literacy, health and welfare programs, political participation, women's rights, infant mortality, male and female life expectancy at age one, the percentage of the GNP devoted to education, the percentage of arable land for food production, and the influence of the military (a negative). Political riots and natural disasters were scored, as were the number of deaths due to domestic violence. In order to observe changes and to gauge their progress, Estes assessed countries both at the beginning (1969–70) and at the end (1979–80) of the decade. Only four of his forty-four indices were strictly economic factors. "The major difference between my index and others is that the others emphasize economic development as an indication of social progress. That's why the United States generally comes out on top," Estes remarked in an interview. "America generally produces wealth in spectacular dimensions. But social conditions in the U.S. leave much to be desired."[30]

The goals behind this highly innovative approach to problems of international development included the following: (1) to develop a baseline data source for making longitudinal assessments of social progress among nations; (2) to suggest a good-sized number of discrete indicators of social progress for which reliable data could be collected over time; (3) to aid nations at different places on the scale to assess their own situation in a global and comparative perspective; (4) to help nations, regardless of their place on the scale, to plan possibilities of beneficial national and international social action; and (5) to assist in assigning strategic intervention priorities for nations with a range of social welfare problems.

The main purpose of the Estes study was to construct and validate an operational model of world social welfare development. In order to accomplish this goal, an Index of Social Progress (ISP) was constructed with rankings of social welfare that "could serve as valid indicators of the differential levels of human deprivation and suffering experienced by people living anywhere in the world." The forty-four indices were placed in one of eleven subindices: Education, Health, Women, Defense, Economic, Demographic, Geographic, Political Stability, Political Participation, Cultural Diversity, and Welfare. A critical point is that all assessments were made independently of the type of political or economic system characteristic of a country. In making the assessments Estes and his team simply chose their forty-four indices, gathered the data for two points with a ten-year interval (1969–79) between them, and calculated the relative rank order of each nation.

For analytic purposes, the ISP scores that resulted from the collection of longitudinal data within the forty-four indices used were collapsed and divided into eight regions referred to as Zones of Social Vulnerability. Each nation was not only given a relative individual ranking but was placed in a common "Zone of Social Vulnerability" together with those other nations that had similar scores. Those nations placed in a common Zone of Social Vulnerability on the basis of their ISP scores are presumed to have comparable social development criteria. Nations, in other words, are grouped together by their achievement in the area of social welfare, by their ability to provide their citizens with "social provisioning" in times of difficulty, rather than by the more traditional economic development classifications or by geopolitical region and alliances.

Where is the United States ranked in the Estes study? A look at Estes' matrices shows that the United States in 1969–70 was ranked 58th in the

TABLE 5–4. Index of Social Progress (ISP) Scores for World Social Leaders and Least Socially Developed Nations, 1970 and 1980.

World Social Leaders		Least Socially Developed Nations	
1969–70 (ISP)	1979–80 (ISP)	1969–70 (ISP)	1979–80 (ISP)
Denmark (198)	Denmark (201)	Nigeria (3)	Ethiopia* (-12)
Sweden (198)	Norway (193)	Vietnam (8)	Chad* (14)
Netherlands (187)	Austria (192)	Chad* (25)	Uganda* (21)
Austria (186)	Netherlands (190)	Indonesia (28)	Pakistan (31)
Norway (186)	Sweden (189)	Niger* (34)	Nigeria (33)
Ireland (185)	New Zealand (186)	Ethiopia* (36)	Zimbabwe (33)
New Zealand (178)	Australia (184)	Upper Volta* (37)	Upper Volta* (34)
Belgium (175)	Ireland (183)	PDR Yemen* (39)	Niger* (34)
FDR Germany (174)	Belgium (178)	Pakistan (40)	Tanzania* (29)
Australia (173)	Finland (174)	Togo (41)	Burundi* (24)
	FDR Germany (174)		

*Indicates nations officially designated by the United Nations as "Least Developing Countries" (United Nations 1971, 1975).

Index of Social Progress scores, from Richard Estes, The Social Progress of Nations, 1984, Table 5-4, p. 111 (reprinted by permission of Greenwood Publishing Group, Inc., Westport, CT, copyright Praeger Publishing Co.).

world. Its score (91) placed it in Zone 5, along with such countries as Algeria, Nicaragua, Turkey, and Bolivia. By 1979–80 the United States had moved up to Zone 4 status, which it shares with El Salvador, Tunisia, Mexico, and South Korea. With a score of 116, the United States was ranked 42nd in 1979–80, a long way behind such nations as Norway (193), Austria (192), the Netherlands (190), Sweden (189), New Zealand (186), Australia (184), Ireland (183), and Belgium (178).

Where is Denmark ranked in the Estes study? In 1969–70 Denmark's ISP score of 198 placed it in a tie with Sweden for the highest rank among all the nations studied (see Table 5-4). In 1979–80, it had the highest ISP score (201) among all 107 nations assessed in Estes' study. It was joined by such countries as Norway, Sweden, Austria, Belgium, the Netherlands, and New Zealand in Zone 1 of National Social Vulnerability in both 1969–70 and 1979–80.[31] The Soviet Union fell from 31st (Zone 3) at the beginning of the decade to 43rd (Zone 4) at its end.[32]

It may well be that many Americans do not want to accept either the assumptions or the results of Estes' study. They would not be alone in this regard: the study is, for instance, more than a little controversial among the many Swedes who question how Denmark could possibly have a higher rating than Sweden. But regardless of whether Americans (or for that matter the Russians, French, and Chinese) can accept the results of Estes' study, they ought at the very least to be intrigued by his findings. For these findings, supported by an elegant research design and enormous amounts of statistical documentation, should succeed in bringing into question some of our complacent assumptions.

Is it necessarily true that, as citizens of the world's largest and most modernized superpower, Americans enjoy the highest quality of life? The Estes study brings this conclusion into question. It implies other questions as well: Does "more" and "bigger" necessarily mean better? Can aggregate statistics of the private, individual "material standard of living" provide meaningful measures of the socially experienced "quality of life"? What social policies will be most effective in creating a better quality of life? (And of course, what do we mean by the elusive term "quality of life" in the first place?) Another mystery from the American point of view: how is it that Denmark, one of those "boring" welfare states with a presumably fixed and unenterprising social order, ranks first in Estes' painstaking, longitudinal study? And the same data show other welfare states, such as Norway, Sweden, and the Netherlands, not far behind, all of them scoring well in advance of the United States.

When reflecting on the results of the Estes study, we should recall briefly the events of nineteenth-century Danish history. "Outward loss,

inward gain" seems to have been neither a rationalization for public resignation nor a pathway to cultural passivity. On the contrary, the slogan aptly
symbolizes a viable collective strategy that enabled the Danes to cut their
losses and to begin dealing from a new deck. The results of their experiment
were already visible to foreign visitors in the early years of this century, long
before Richard Estes began to carry out his comparative study of international social welfare. I spoke of Edmund Gosse earlier in this chapter.
Another Englishman, the novelist H. Rider Haggard, published in 1913 a
volume entitled *Rural Denmark and Its Lessons.* In this volume Haggard
extols the virtues of three Danish institutions: the cooperative dairy, the folk
high school, and the agricultural school. Indeed, the book is dedicated "to
the Farmers of Denmark, in token of the admiration of a foreign agriculturalist, for the wisdom and brotherly understanding that have enabled them
to triumph over the difficulties of soil, climate, and low prices, and by the
practice of general co-operation, to achieve individual and national success."

Some of the lessons Haggard drew from his Danish visit are worth
quoting for the major themes they foreshadow. The lessons Haggard drew
were, first, "that in a free-trade country of limited area and lacking virgin
soil, co-operation is necessary to a full measure of agricultural success";
second, "that only free-holders, or farmers owning their own land (or having
some form of perpetual lease) will co-operate to any wide extent"; and third,
"that the accumulation of large estates with hired tenancy is not conducive
to the multiplication of free-holders, nor therefore to the establishment of
general co-operation." The implications of these observations for third world
economic development are, I believe, quite clear. Haggard's book certainly
suggests that at least in the area of agriculture the Danish path to modernization (based on the complex of social movements reviewed in the preceding
chapter) had borne fruit by the first decade of the twentieth century.
Denmark had even then "arisen from the ashes" of its threatened nineteenth-
century decline.

From a contemporary development perspective, the lessons are simply
that these positive responses to social crisis depended on the existence of a
free-holding class of farmers who had achieved a high level of mutual
cooperation. Haggard's conclusion (p. 188) is that "whatever else may be
doubtful or open to argument in connection with Danish agriculture, one
thing remains clear, namely, that it owes the greater part of such prosperity
as it possesses to the working of the co-operative movement. Or perhaps it
would be more accurate to say that this prosperity is due to the character of
its people, which renders co-operation popular among them. . . ." One
doubts very much whether this flexible and adaptive response to crisis would
have been possible among an agricultural class subjected to the "accumula-

tion of large estates with hired tenancy," that is, to the abuses and exploitation that accompany the systems of landless tenant farming still so common
in today's world.

The insights that resulted from Haggard's visit to Denmark constitute
in themselves an interesting minor reversal of history. For it was almost
exactly eighty years earlier that N. F. S. Grundtvig, who first proposed the
idea of the folk high school, had made three visits to England (1829–31).
It is generally acknowledged by those who have studied Grundtvig's development that these English experiences served as a critical catalyst for his
thinking. What grew out of them was an ideal that was to become the basis
for an enduring and influential model of both education and society in
Denmark. Based partly on Grundtvig's encounter with English institutions
(such as the tutorial system at Trinity College, Cambridge), the resulting
synthesis ("Grundtvigianism," as it was later called) was to be instrumental
from that time on in Danish cultural, economic, and political life. Detailed
discussion of Grundtvig's life and accomplishments is postponed to Chapter
Five. Here it is sufficient to note that by the time of Haggard's visit in 1911,
the successes of Danish cultural revitalization were already apparent in such
institutions as the cooperative dairies, the agricultural schools, and the folk
high schools. The tables have now been turned. An Englishman is coming
to Denmark to write about how *Danish* institutions and customs ought to
be used by *his own* countrymen for *their* benefit. Haggard's admiring
comments on Danish agriculture provide a useful and timely evaluation of
the Danish society that had by then emerged from the ashes of the nineteenth
century. Its success was in large measure due to the relatively high percentage
of its citizens who were effectively enfranchised and encouraged to improve
their lives through independent, small-scale local cooperation. By all indi-
cations it was a society that had moved significantly in the direction of that
earlier version of the American dream that went under the name of "Jeffersonian democracy."[33]

Haggard was not alone in his observations. In 1936 the National
Home Library Foundation published a two-part book entitled *Democracy in
Denmark*. The first section, "Democracy in Action," was by Josephine
Goldmark. The second section, "The Folk High School," was an English
translation of a work by A. H. Hollman, a German historian who had visited
Askov Højskole in 1908. Sherman F. Mittell, who edited the volume, wrote
in his preface some lines that echo the theme expressed by Haggard and
others:

> This book can be read with profit by all citizens. It tells the remarkable
> story of an enlightened people. For today Denmark as a nation spells

enlightened government, enlightened education, enlightened living. In these pages you will find no account of national barbarism, lust for subjection, program of conquest or aggrandizement.

Danish achievements have not come easily. They have been won not by war nor through abundance of natural resources. As Miss Goldmark so clearly records, democracy in Denmark has been accomplished rather through an abiding faith in her human resources and the capacity of her people to use the national intelligence for the improvement of her entire citizenry.

To my surprise and pleasure, one of the most interesting early commentators was the American reporter and social reformer Frederick C. Howe. Of all of those I read, Howe was the one who had a perspective closest to what I had hoped to find. He had written in 1921 a book entitled *Denmark: A Cooperative Commonwealth* (and in 1936 a revised and extended work, *Denmark: The Cooperative Way*). In the preface to his 1921 work Howe had even stated clearly his own version of my provisional research hypothesis:

> Denmark seems to me to be quite the most valuable political exhibit in the modern world. It should be studied by statesmen. It should be visited by commissions, especially by commissions from the agricultural states of the American West. Denmark is one of the few countries in the world that is using its political agencies in an intelligent, conscious way for the promotion of the economic well-being, the comfort and the cultural life of its people.

In that same preface, written in 1921, Howe wrote some prophetic lines: "At a time when a great part of Europe is fast drifting toward economic collapse, Denmark offers a demonstration of how a nation can come back to life, of how agriculture can be made both profitable and attractive, and how the hopelessness and poverty of the world can be corrected by orderly political action."

What does this discussion of the frontier thesis, the Estes study, and the Danish path to modernization suggest? Perhaps it suggests that this final, false stereotype about Denmark (that the Danish society and its history are topics possessing neither interest nor relevance for Americans) can no longer be maintained, or at least defended (stereotypes can be maintained, of course, regardless of the evidence). It may lead at least a few people to question the unconscious denial behind the idea that a society that has learned to live with limits and with loss, one of the smaller nations of the world, could have anything at all, in its history and its institutions, to teach the citizens of a much larger and more powerful nation. All of the preceding arguments have led to this conclusion.

Returning momentarily to Estes' study, I learned about it some time after completing my research in Denmark. His conclusions did not surprise me because by then I knew something about the quality of life in Denmark. I knew, for instance, that its standard of living was among the highest in the world and that the distribution of wealth through its population was among the world's most equitable. I also knew that in spite of this it was no Shangri La, especially in the eyes of the Danes themselves. Nothing illustrates this better than the Danish response to Estes' study. Those Danes who know of it tend to shrug off his results with stoic calmness, maintaining only that it shows more about the sad state of the rest of the world than anything admirable in their own society. This response is marvelously in consonance with what I have come to know of the Danish national character. Indeed, it is just about what I would expect a Dane to say on learning of such findings.

I cite Estes' study as a piece of evidence to try to counter the pervasive stereotype that a "welfare state" must be all wrong and that Denmark (as an example of such a state) is a boring and uninteresting society. Often held so deeply that it is never verbally expressed, this stereotype is one that came to bother me a great deal. In the years that I lived and worked in Denmark, I had very few moments of boredom. The deeper I dug, the more rewarding were the surprises and the discoveries that came my way. It was a little like the archeological technique called *decapagé*, in which the soil at a site is peeled back gradually layer by layer, leaving the artifacts in place (a technique that is especially effective in reconstructing the spatial organization of a prehistoric site). Yet as a cultural anthropologist I had the advantage that my archeology was done mostly among the living. My artifacts could both speak and be spoken for.

Stereotype Two: The Melancholy Dane

A second common negative stereotype about Denmark is that the Danes suffer from a kind of Scandinavian melancholy, popularly thought to predispose them to sadness and depression. After all, isn't it true that the Scandinavian nations (of which Denmark is one) have the world's highest suicide rates? Doesn't the northern climate with its dreary rain, bitter cold, and long periods of winter darkness make life difficult to endure? The short and unreliable summers—aren't they reminiscent of Mark Twain's aphorism that the worst winter he had ever experienced was a San Francisco summer? And leaving aside features of the physical climate, look at their intellectual life: isn't the essential message of their most famous philosopher, Kierkegaard, little more than a sustained and unremitting exercise in the possibilities of grief, melancholy, and *angst?* (Indeed—to stretch a point—doesn't the philosopher's very name, translated, mean a "churchyard," or cemetery?)

To set the record straight, studies of Scandinavian suicide (including Hendin's classic study made in the 1960s) show complex patterns whose meaning is still being debated by specialists in the field.[34] One puzzle is that although present-day Denmark and Sweden do have comparatively high suicide rates, the rate of their common neighbor Norway has been until recently quite low.[35] These facts are difficult to interpret because Norway superficially resembles both Denmark and Sweden in so many ways, among them religion, form of government, language, possession of a welfare state. In terms of climate the Norwegian winter is, if anything, considerably more extreme than that of Denmark, with greater cold and longer periods of winter darkness. While an analysis of differences in population density and town settlement patterns, combined with a further breakdown of regional variations within each country, might provide additional clues, a second puzzle is provided by changes in the relative mean suicide rates over time.[36] The Danish suicide rate has been high since the beginning of industrialization in the mid-nineteenth century. In contrast the Swedish rate, lower under preindustrial conditions, has climbed with the growth of industrialization to its present high rate. But these facts, while of interest, do not speak to the issue of the high suicide rates in Denmark.

It is not inconceivable that one reason for the relatively high suicide count could be the greater reliability of the Danish and Swedish statistics. After all, suicide is not exactly a neutral event, one that under all circumstances can be easily identified and reported. Where it causes not only grief but the possibility of social sanctions to fall upon the family or social network, there is good reason to expect that other explanations may be given for the cause of death. Thus in some Latin American countries with Catholicism as the dominant religion, an official suicide is often not declared unless an actual suicide note is found, no matter how incriminating the other evidence may be.[37] In the United States, given the primarily outer-directed expression of individual violence, the possibility exists that some unknown proportion of the high rate of homicides and traffic fatalities are in effect unacknowledged suicides. If one takes into account these possible discrepancies in identification and reporting, the real differences between Denmark and many other countries may not be as large as the reported statistics imply.

Yet suicide is not the only dimension of the depressing theme of melancholy. It is not necessary to commit suicide in order to be melancholic; one cannot therefore call into question the image of the melancholy Dane merely by posing an *a priori* challenge to the accuracy of the comparative suicide statistics. The issue here is not a simple one but considerably more complicated. For there *is* some truth to the image of melancholy in the Danish national character. One cannot help asking the question: was it just a historical accident, an unthinking acceptance of the stereotype, or could it have been some acute insight into the Danish character that led Shakespeare to fashion his primal portrait of Hamlet, Crown Prince of Denmark? In either case the image of the melancholy Dane, a long-held figure of foreign folklore, contains an important partial truth.

An obvious direction in which to look for the origin of Danish melancholy is the dark and cold northern climate. And there are in fact wry admissions in Danish song and story that the country's climate has its questionable features. The largest summer rock festival, held annually at Roskilde, is famous not only for high-quality popular music but for drowning in rain year after year. The same is true for the mid-June summer equinox celebration on the Evening of Saint Hans; it is said to rain on that day nine years out of ten, sometimes so fiercely that the fire in which the cloth witch is to be burned can only be lit with great difficulty. A much-loved song found in the Folk High School Songbook confesses in the very first line: "You Danish summer, I love you, even though you have so often betrayed me" *(Du danske sommer, jeg elsker dig, skønt du so ofte har sveget mig)*.[38] The dry, patient understatement that characterizes much of Danish humor can be seen in the dignified resignation expressed by this line of another song: "Showers, that come and go, that is the Danish summer" *(Byger, der går og kommer, det er den danske sommer)*.[39] The writer's sigh is nearly audible, for these showers come a lot more than they go. Such mournful themes are not at all uncommon in Danish songs that deal with summer.

Similar sentiments can sometimes be found in the newspapers. During the spring and summer of 1987 rain fell with a frequency unprecedented even by strict Danish standards. Then on a Sunday afternoon the miraculous took place: the clouds parted and the rain held up. This hopeful pause was actually followed by several consecutive hours of warm afternoon sun. Perhaps reflecting the feelings of a populace whose patience had been sorely tried, the front page headline in a Copenhagen paper that could be purchased during the next day's downpour was breathtaking in its eloquence: "Summer Fell on a Sunday." To live in Denmark is indeed to become a realist about the weather.

But when these and other images of climate are teased back into context and examined, it becomes evident that the Danes are in general fond of their climate, with its change not only of seasons, but of seasons within seasons. "There is nothing in the world as quiet as snow, with the cleanliness of snow, that can soften like snow" goes an encapsulated version of the first lines of one song in the Folk High School Songbook. And to speak on behalf of the defense, Danish weather is rarely dull. With 120 to 200 days of precipitation a year the air is kept clean and fresh. Even the fierce gales that can come with the westerly winds are widely thought to build character. These storms, which come most often in the western part of Jutland, leave a deep imprint on the minds of those who have seen and lived through them. A vivid testimony is contained in a childhood reminiscence by Danish writer and novelist Martin A. Hansen:

> When I was almost twelve years old, I was awakened one winter night. It was storm weather outside. My mother said, "Father wants you to go along with him down to the beach tonight, but stay close to him and be very careful." It already had been blowing for a couple of days. In the evening, when we lay down to go to sleep, the storm was like a heavy weight leaning on the house, so that wherever there was, here or there, a crack in the old windows, a horizontal string of air was blown into the room. A large branch was torn from a tree in the garden, it broke at the shoulder joint, sounding like a shot, but far away. My parents had talked it over, whether we all should stay up. We usually did when bad weather came. Something could all too easily happen with an old, straw-thatched house.
>
> Such night watches during storms, each of us sitting with a bunch of clothes ready in his or her lap, are later remembered as holy hours. The women and children sat inside, waited, listened, perhaps sang. Mother talked about sailors and poor people, while father was outside—as was the men's custom in bad weather—to keep an eye on the land, to look out for fires, and to be ready if the alarm rang. Now and then he would come in and report on the Lord's doings, saying that it had to let up soon. We knew well that this was said for our benefit, and that the storm could last a long time. But now it had occurred to father that the storm had slackened, and that we had gone to bed. We got up suddenly, the little girls almost nothing more than big eyes. I could hardly figure out how to get into my pants and shirt, I was so excited by the thought of going down to the ocean with father. He stood in the doorway, thickly clad and wearing his rubber boots.[40]

The picture that emerges from Hansen's description is true to the experiences I had in a wide range of travels within the country during all of its seasons. Though I did not live through the storms of which he writes, I saw the uprooted trees on the coast of West Jutland only a year after one of them had come in from the North Sea. The huge, twisted trunks that were still lying by the side of the road with their gnarled roots exposed gave clear and impressive evidence of its fury. I wore my rubber boots often while trudging through the rain and mud, and I felt the bitter cold winds and the darkness of winter on my back. I stayed for two Danish winters, and from what I saw on the basis of privileged glances into homes, fields, churches, and schools, as well as long walks along its coasts, I could not find much corroboration for the idea that the Danish climate is the source of a melancholy disposition. On the contrary, the experience of living through nature at its most intense seems to have a positive, even a spiritual quality to it. The need to face common dangers can bring people and families into a profound sense of community (as the passage taken from Hansen well illustrates). Although there are stretches of gray, sad, and cloudy days that leave their imprint as a challenge, the Danes are by and large more fond of their weather than they let on. It is my strong impression that most of them would not willingly exchange the intensities of their passing seasons even for the fabled sunshine of other, more southerly lands.

If climate is not the cause of the melancholy in the Danish temperament, then what is? I am not at all sure of its causes, but whether it is cause or consequence, I did notice a particular cultural patterning that is of interest: a surprising directness to Danish communication, combined with a willingness to acknowledge unpleasant realities. I think, for instance, of a group of ministers and Danish citizens who had gone to Central America for a fact-finding mission and were being interviewed on television upon their return. "Do you think that your mission contributed in any way to greater prospects for peace in Central America?" one of them was asked. "No, I don't think our mission contributed at all to greater prospects for peace in Central America" was the flat and direct answer of one of the ministers. It was a kind of unqualified, if honest, reply that I don't think would often be heard from an American asked such a question in these circumstances.

The same quick, flat directness is frequently seen in Danish humor. A good example is the joke cited by Judith Friedman Hansen:

— 240 miles per hour! Now someone's driven a car 240 miles per hour!
— Why'd he do that?

Another example is the joke told by a *folkehøjskole* teacher:

—Danish immigrant to America back to Denmark for a visit:
You should see the size of my farm over there! Why, I can get in my car in the morning and it takes three hours just to drive the length of my fields!
—Old Danish farmer:
Yeah, I used to have a car like that too.

A similar flat and direct quality can often be seen in the awareness of death and its meaning. A possible consequence of the overwhelmingly rural heritage that lies not far beneath the facade of modern urban Denmark, it is a theme expressed in the laconic, taken-for-granted acknowledgment of a basic human truth: that death awaits everyone and gives no exemptions. There is a much greater tendency than in the United States for the ever-present reality of the common human fate to be acknowledged by an open and direct introduction into songs, stories, and everyday conversations. It can even be seen in a characteristic style of humor in which Danes make wry little jokes about death. Danes not only refer to death with more openness and frequency than is found in the United States, but they make reference to it in a matter-of-fact way that would, I believe, seem just a little strange to American ears.[41]

One source in which this attitude toward death is frequently found is the tales of Hans Christian Andersen. The author and critic Johannes Møllehave has rightly observed that it is impossible for Danes to read Andersen "without discovering why we think and feel as we do."[42] Consider, for instance, the little-known story *Noget* (Something), in which five brothers compete with each other to become someone of importance in this world. In order to accomplish this goal one plans to become an architect and to design and construct a building a level higher than anyone else can manage to build. But (as in so many of Andersen's stories) the unfortunate hero meets an untimely demise:

> Then came the genius, the fourth brother, who wanted to invent something new, something different and one level higher, but it didn't work for him. He fell down and broke his neck—but he received a wonderful funeral with flags, emblems and music, with flowers in the newspaper, on the street and over the pavement. There were held three burial speeches in his honor, the one much longer than the other, and it would have pleased him, because he liked to be talked about. A monument was built on his grave. It was only one level high, but that's still something.

The superficial good humor of Andersen's story uses death and funerals to make a serious point about human folly. It is almost impossible not to laugh at the details of the funeral, yet at the same time the writer's scathing irony, barely hidden from view, emerges like a dagger in the last line.

A more contemporary example of this Danish mood can be seen in a comic interchange on an old film strip on Danish television. A patient is talking to his doctor:

> Patient to Doctor: Doctor, sometimes I feel so bad [he peers hopefully and nearsightedly at the doctor, as if anticipating that he will receive some nurturant advice] that I think I'm going to die.

Doctor: [slaps him good-naturedly on the shoulder and replies merrily without a second's hesitation] Hey, we're all going to die. Did you think that you could be let off? (*Det skal vi sgu alle. Troede du, at du kunne slippe?*)

The effect of the sudden shift was (forgive me) hilarious to watch. The unfortunate patient, anticipating a show of professional sympathy, receives instead a swift kick in the shins. Reaching out his hand in the hope of finding a measure of pity, commiseration, and compassion from his doctor, he becomes instead the unhappy recipient of a two-sentence lecture on death and existentialism. It was precisely the wounded look on the patient's face, the shock and utter surprise that the actor so convincingly managed to demonstrate, that made this comic sequence truly funny. For reasons I never could fully understand, I found that I was able to resonate well with the Danish mood of melancholy whether it was being expressed directly or more indirectly (as in the above examples through a sometimes quite harsh humor).

I have on occasion speculated that this mood has something to do with the age of Danish culture, which has grown and endured on the same land for well over a thousand years. It is worth recalling that long before the American Revolution of 1776, Denmark was already an old nation with centuries of history behind it. The University of Copenhagen, at which I taught for a semester, was founded in 1479, thirteen years before Columbus set sail. My theory, then, is that some of the cultural roots of this underlying mood of sadness that sometimes surfaces are to be found in the comparatively great age of the culture, combined with the historical patterns of loss and constraint that have defined it in recent centuries. Yet it must be remembered that these same Danes are by cultural training among the world's most intensely social peoples, and this is part of the paradox. They even possess a special behavioral code (*hygge:* see Chapter Eight) as part of the tradition that influences their informal socializing. Perhaps it is the capacity for sadness and melancholy that makes the Danish celebrations of life more meaningful in the end. I don't claim to be able to provide a simple answer. I only know that the better I got to know them, the more I came to respect their earthy qualities: their directness, their dry humor, and their uncanny ability to fill in the spaces of daily life with small, joyful celebrations.

CHAPTER THREE

A First Look at Modern Denmark

I. GEOLOGY, CLIMATE, AND PREHISTORY

> . . . the sea is full of things
> the great fish in their wanderings
> and the spread galleys of the old kings.
> —Hilaire Belloc, *Return to The Baltic* (1938)

T HE PRECEDING CHAPTER was concerned with stereotypes. We now ask about some of the pertinent realities in Denmark, what they are and what they have been. A more formal inquiry must begin with simple questions like these: Where in Europe is Denmark located? What are its borders, its coasts, its internal topography? What type of climate and resources does the land possess? The answers to these sorts of questions will provide the background material with which to address some of the more complex issues: What are the major geopolitical constraints faced by Denmark, and how have they influenced over time its history and the character of its people? Faced with this particular set of possibilities and constraints, what kind of society has evolved there? What were the most significant steps in its development? And ultimately, where is this society now in terms of its own history?

The broad framework required for this discussion requires a complementarity based on the telescoping of several different time scales. The first of these time scales is the geological, with its flowing and eternally unfolding millennia written with equal signature on eroding hillsides and in deep sea cores, in a language of rocks and crystals, a language that the human species has only recently begun to decipher and to understand. The second time scale is a historical one related to the process of modernization, that complex series of transitions that can come about in a society from the action of such forces as industrialization, mechanization, and urbanization.[1] It is measured in a pattern of historical events recorded in the last two, perhaps three centuries. The third time scale, a matter of a few recent decades, is that of our postmodern era. Together these three time perspectives enable one to look at the present so that, at least in outline, the nature of its debt to the past can be clarified and understood.

Present-day Denmark, consisting of a peninsula and some 406 islands, occupies a small area of northern Europe between the North Sea and the Baltic; it is, as Samuel Rachlin has remarked, a little like an appendix sitting on top of Europe (see Map 8 on p. 37). As the above lines cited by Hilaire Belloc suggest, Denmark is a nation with its history and geography closely tied to the sea, or more correctly, to the seas that surround it on three sides.[2] Its west coast meets the North Sea. Coming up from the North Sea on the western part of Jutland, the *Skagerrak* is the body of water that separates Denmark from Norway. To the north the *Kattegat* and to the south the Sound (*Øresund*) lie between it and neighboring Sweden. In addition to this area of "Denmark proper," the kingdom of Denmark includes the island of Bornholm just to the southwest of the southern tip of Sweden, the Faroe Islands[3] in the North Atlantic (about 300 km northwest of Scotland, 430 km from Iceland, and 600 km from Norway) and the ice-covered, subpolar expanses of Greenland. Greenland and the Faroe Islands exercise the right to home rule while remaining under the Danish crown (the Faroe Islands were granted Home Rule in 1948, Greenland in 1979).

As the first lines of the National Song (which I have freely translated) suggest, small and lovely hills can surprise the hiker or traveler:

> There is a lovely land.
> It stands with mighty beech trees
> Near the salty shores of the Baltic
> It bends in hills and valleys,
> Its name is Old Denmark.

Inspiring as these lines are, the sad truth is that the Danish landscape is in most places about as flat as the proverbial pancake. With its highest point in East Jutland only 568 feet above sea level, Denmark is the bicyclist's dream come true. Kilometers of nearly level roads stretch in every direction, most of them with clearly marked bicycle paths. In spite of its lack of severely mountainous topography, the Danish countryside is almost uniformly one of great beauty. To take an extended bike trip in the spring or summer through its characteristic scenery of farmhouses and open fields, small stretches of forest and attractive provincial towns, is an experience that I can heartily recommend to anyone.

Geologically, Denmark is an archipelago with its many islands sitting on a submerged shelf in a shallow inland sea. The city of Copenhagen is located on the largest island, Zealand *(Sjælland)* (7,014 sq km). The two next largest islands are Funen *(Fyn)* (2,984 sq km) and Lolland (1,283 sq km); after them comes the island of Bornholm, located in the Baltic about 150 km to the east of Denmark and 40 km off the south coast of Sweden. The waters of the Great Belt *(Storebælt)* lie between Zealand and Funen, while the Little Belt *(Lillebælt)* separates Funen from Jutland.

Jutland *(Jylland)*, the peninsular part of Denmark, projects out from the mainland of Europe just north of the flat plains of the Federal Republic of Germany. The two countries share a 68-kilometer land border that has changed several times in the course of their history. In 1975, for example, continental Denmark had an area of 43,074 sq km; yet in 1901 its area was just 38,473 sq km.[4] The difference between these two figures comes from the reunification with Denmark in 1920 of land areas in North Slesvig that had been lost to Germany in 1864. To give an idea of relative sizes, the peninsula of Jutland alone provides nearly 70% of the land area of Denmark.

The Danish coastline has some remarkable features. It is one of the most jagged and dissected in the world. If laid out in a straight line, its total distance would amount to more than 7,400 km (4,600 miles), which is almost one-sixth of the way around the globe. It possesses in addition some 613 sq km of inland water area. One consequence of this peninsula and island geography is that in Denmark one is never more than 52 km away from the sea. It does not take great acuity of insight to see that both the sailing ability of the early Vikings and the subsequent Danish skill in a variety of occupations associated with the sea are natural outcomes of this geography. And as a kind of historical footnote it ought to be mentioned that Denmark's periods of expansion and empire—from the ninth-century Viking era to medieval expansion in the Baltic and the mercantile adventures of the sixteenth century—were made possible by her naval power. At one time Denmark held colonies in India, on the Guinea Coast in Africa, and in the West Indies. In the seventeenth century, during a period of flourishing overseas trade, Danish ships even made adventurous voyages to China. The nearness of the sea, then, is an inescapable fact in Denmark and provides at least one clue to the shaping of its history.

A second clue to the shaping of Danish history is its appendix-like location on the continent of Europe. Placed at a significant junction of the northern seas, it lies at a crossroads between north and south, east and west. This location in a region of intense maritime transit has drawn it at various times in its history into a struggle for three seas: the North Sea (with its outlets to Britain and western Europe); the *Skaggerak* (with its proximity to the Norwegian and Swedish coasts); and the Baltic (with its inevitable sea routes to and from Germany, Sweden, Poland, and Russia). Denmark was thus forced to become both a Baltic and an Atlantic power, and in successive combinations it once clashed with English and German princes, as well as with Norwegian and Swedish kings. Its role in the area was not limited to maritime events. For many centuries it has also served as a land bridge between the countries of northern Europe and those of central and western Europe. The ideas of Christianity, the Reformation, and the Enlightenment first entered Scandinavia by moving to the north through Denmark. Invading armies and mercantile patterns (as well as new ideas) have followed this well-worn, centuries-old path.[5]

A third clue is given by its climate and the material features of the landscape. Located on the western fringe of the Eurasian continental block, Denmark faces an ocean traversed by the Gulf Stream, which is a series of water masses that come from more southern latitudes. In combination with prevailing westerly winds, the Gulf Stream tempers the Danish winters. At the same time, the waters of the Baltic provide a separation from the continental land masses, ensuring most of the time an independence from the cold airstreams of eastern Europe. It is the location in a temperature zone at the meeting point of extremely diverse air masses that is responsible for Denmark's extraordinarily changeable weather. Weather fronts come and go during the entire year, frequently releasing their precipitation as they swing over the country. Although there is rainfall year around, the precise amount varies from year to year and even from season to season. The annual mean precipitation is 60 cm, highest in southwest Jutland (80 cm). Snow is frequently, although not always, seen in the winter. Unlike Norway to the north, the Danish earth is only rarely covered with snow for the entire winter.

In the present era snow and ice come mainly to Denmark as well-behaved seasonal visitors. Such laudable restraint was not always seen. During much of the last 3 million years the Northern Hemisphere lay covered by huge fields of moving glacial ice. In contrast to the simple fourfold division of glacials and interglacials that was once accepted, geologists today distinguish some thirty cold spells punctuated by brief warmer times.[6] The last 2 million years constitutes the Pleistocene, which, taken together with the most recent ten thousand years—the Holocene—comprises the period known as the Quaternary. During the Quaternary period Denmark lay within the northern European area of glaciation, and it was the movement of the glaciers, their slow retreat followed by their inevitable return, that has given the Danish landscape its character: undulating plains alternating with gently rolling hills, a topography marked as well by an abundance of lakes and other inland bodies of water. Coastal plains created by the flat sand

and gravel of marine deposits make up one-tenth of a total land area, which is subject to constant change through marine deposit, erosion, and (more recently) human reclamation. Denmark's marine boundaries include vast areas of relatively shallow water. It has thus provided a favorable habitat for the countless sea birds, both year-round and migrant, that can be seen along its coasts, marshes and inland waterways.

At the end of the Pleistocene, about ten thousand years ago, a global warming occurred, and the retreating ice left many shallow depressions and new sediments that eventually became lakes and streams. Tundra species such as dwarf birches, lichens, reindeer, and horses played the role of initial colonizers. They were quickly followed by groups of late Paleolithic human hunters. Through normal processes of ecological succession the tundra was gradually replaced by light forests of birch and pine. The presence of wild cattle, moose, wild pigs, red and roe deer made the area an ideal one for the early human hunter-gatherers, as evidenced by the profusion of their artifacts. The first abundant traces of Mesolithic culture, with its even more sophisticated tool assemblages, are not found until after 7000 B.C.

The life-style of these sedentary foragers was apparently made possible by the warming trend of this postglacial period, a trend that profoundly changed some of the properties of the physical setting in southern Scandinavia.[7] The continental ice sheets melted, causing the seas to rise, but the land also rose, freed of the weight of the ice blanket it long had borne. The sea eventually won its slow race with the land, and by about 5000 B.C. many of the low-lying areas near today's coast had been flooded over. Southern Scandinavia was smaller than it is today, and the estuaries, inlets, and islands formed by this flooding became the focus for human settlement. The ongoing excavation of such coastal sites as Vedbæk shows that the coastal cultures of the late Mesolithic (5000 to 3200 B.C.) flourished in a favorable environment for human habitation. It was at about this time (the beginning of the third millennium B.C.) that the cultivation of barley and wheat first began.[8]

What were the conditions for agriculture encountered in Denmark, and what kinds of constraints did they place on its subsequent development? The Danish climate is in some ways an advantageous one. Denmark is a green land and, like England, it is rarely if ever burnt off and yellowed by a harsh summer sun. The climate is generally temperate with limited long-term fluctuations in precipitation and temperature. The Danish soils originated chiefly on a substratum of moraine and meltwater sand, which arose in the late glacial age by leaching of the moraine masses. Mixing with subterranean limestones, the moraine became calcareous. This fortunate accident of geology may explain the present ability of the Danish channels and lakes—at least up to the most recent report—to resist the devastating effects of the acid precipitation carried northward by atmospheric forces from England and Germany.

In some other respects the combined heritage of geology and climate is not so favorable. The seasonal precipitation patterns, for instance, are not ideally suited to agriculture. Lower levels of rain are usually found during the winter. The spring months also tend to be relatively dry. The latter fact is especially unfortunate, for at that time the crops are growing fast due to high temperatures. A dry May or June can restrict crop biomass growth and thus considerably reduce the harvest. The largest monthly volumes of rain typically fall in August and October, yet in the grain-ripening season in August large volumes of water are unnecessary. During the harvest period a major rainfall can be not only detrimental but disastrous.

In a final unfortunate accident of nature, the raw materials needed for industry are almost entirely lacking. In this regard the Danes have not shared in the good fortune of their Scandinavian neighbors, Sweden and Norway. The land possesses no metals, no minerals, no coal, no oil, or water power of any importance. About the only raw materials in good supply are chalk, clay, limestone, and wind (the latter increasingly used to power windmills that generate electricity). Having little in the way of natural resources, Denmark has had to import the essential raw materials for its industry and to rely on a skilled population to compensate for this primary disadvantage.

Although the climate is not optimal for agriculture, it is probably not surprising to learn that for most of their history the Danes have been principally dependent on it (and on what they could gather from the sea). And up to very recent times it was always the agricultural sector of the economy that employed the largest proportion of the population. In spite of the limitations, the Danish soil has been radically improved through many centuries of cultivation. Tillage, regulation of the water table, an increase in the amount of fertilization, improvement in plant strains, and reclamation of once barren land are only a few of the diverse practices that have created an agricultural land area now comprising nearly three-quarters of the land surface.[9]

At about the same time that agriculture was initially practiced, the first dolmens and, later, passage graves begin to appear. Early examples of monumental architecture, these impressive structures are made of heaps of enormous stones piled over and around a spacious common tomb. They are one of the distinguishing archeological features of the Danish landscape. Shaped from boulders carried down and then left by the glacial ice, they show a surprising amount of variation in form. Some of this variation may reflect the evolution of different religious beliefs among the early agricul-

Slåensø, a lake near Silkeborg.

Harvesting the roses, Sjælland.

turalists. In any case, the huge and impressive blocks of stone are the stuff of which legends are easily made. The medieval historian Saxo Grammaticus saw in them clear evidence that a race of giants had once inhabited Denmark. They were and still are popularly called by such names as "Giants Tombs" (*jættestuer*). Nearly five thousand such ancient structures have been mapped and described in Denmark, of which barely seven hundred are still standing. Many are protected by law, and Danish farmers simply plough around them in their fields. Johannes V. Jensen wrote of them: "And still the graves of the ancients stand, witness to the generations that pass through Denmark's land."

For visitor and native alike, these stone monuments speak to a special feature of Danish society. If one looks (and one does not have to look hard), one finds everywhere the sense of being connected to an ancient past. I was once shown, on a well-managed and prosperous Danish farm, a large drawerful of stone implements that had been gathered from their fields over the course of the last hundred years. As an anthropologist I know something about such tools, and I could see at once that these were not the chipped fragments or pebble cores that sometimes litter the old tool-making sites in great profusion. They were, on the contrary, finished products—a collection of well-worked scrapers, spear points, and axe blades that evoke in many of us now, more than a hundred centuries later, the same feeling of awe that they must have engendered in those who first learned to fashion them. Although small, it was a collection that any archeological museum might well regard with envy.

The twentieth-century Danish farmer who showed me these tools is a hardworking, practical man.[10] Even though he was then close to seventy, he rose at five and worked long days. I have only one snapshot of him, taken as he was striding out of one of his many greenhouses. It is a blurred study of a man in motion. Nearly half a dozen modern tractors are parked in his tractor garage, adjacent to the one barn with its large freezing unit and the spacious, well-organized garden outlet with its commercial bushes, trees, and flowers for retail sale to businesses and private families. There is always something to be done: roses to be budded, stalls to be cleaned, customers to serve. The small pickup truck is for business; when he goes to the nearest town for social occasions, the car he drives is a late model BMW sedan.

It is worth mentioning that he and his wife had met when both were students at Askov, the oldest of the Danish folk high schools. They met more than forty-five years ago during the years of the Second World War. Several times his wife told me that the experience at Askov had been one of the high points of their lives. The time I was shown these tools was not my first visit to their home; I had been there many times. Not a great deal was said about

A prosperous Danish farm, Jutland.

Land under cultivation, Jutland.

them. They were treasures to be held briefly and then returned to a sanctuary for safekeeping. I do not know this to be the case, but their feeling for these artifacts might have originated at a lecture heard at Askov as students back in the 1940s. Or it could have been something learned from their parents, from such a lecture given a generation earlier (attendance at a folk high school was and still is a proud tradition in many Danish farm families).

For the purposes of this inquiry, it is not critical to know where they gained their knowledge and appreciation of these implements. What is critical is that they, as a rural farm family working their land, did have this reverence for the past that is one mark of the truly educated person. They must have known, as did I, that the tools had lain on that land for many centuries and were already ancient when the Vikings set sail for North America and succeeded in building the first village at *L'Anse aux Meadows* on the coast of Newfoundland some five hundred years before the voyages of Columbus. They could feel, as did I, that the mute stone forms in front of us, a collection gathered from their own fields and backyards, linked them in a direct way to a vanished prehistoric past. Once profane objects for everyday use in the hands of earlier and other humans, these pieces of worked stone were now plainly sacred symbols, resonating and attesting to the continuity of human generations on a Danish landscape. The existence of so many different kinds of stone monuments, of spear points and passage graves, mirrors a stubborn continuity between the people and the land. We are reminded of this continuity by the simple fact that agriculture has existed in Denmark for some five thousand years.

Though I was able to appreciate the beauty of such ancestral testaments as twelfth-century village churches and the sense of a departed history they bring, I cannot claim to be a specialist in Danish history, feudal or modern. Nor am I a specialist in Danish prehistory, which long predates both the first conversion of a Danish king to Christianity in the tenth century A.D. and the earlier Norse legends, extending back at least some thirteen thousand years to the time when the land was first freed from the great glacial ice sheets that covered it during most of the last European ice age. But though I cannot dwell on it at length, I must report that there is a special quality about this theme of continuity in Denmark. The Danish author Karen Blixen (Isak Dinesen), best known for her stories of Africa, wrote of it in the eloquent opening lines of her short story "Sorrow-Acre":

> The low, undulating Danish landscape was silent and serene, mysteriously wide-awake in the hour before sunrise. There was not a cloud in the pale sky, not a shadow along the dim, pearly fields, hills and woods. The mist was lifting from the valleys and hollows, the air was cool, the grass and foliage dripping wet with morning dew. Unwatched by the eyes of man, and

A twentieth-century Danish farmer.

undisturbed by his activity, the country breathed a timeless life, to which language was inadequate. All the same, a human race had lived on this land for a thousand years, had been formed by its soil and weather, and had marked it with its thoughts, so that now no one could tell where the existence of the one ceased and the other began.[11]

In any investigation of Danish natural character, the existence of this long historical continuity must be stressed. One of its unique manifestations is that since the ninth century A.D., the kings and queens of Denmark have been descendants of a single royal family. Unlike many other royal families, the Danish kings were wise enough to voluntarily surrender their authority when asked to do so by the majority of the people. Perhaps because of this, the members of the ruling family continued to play a special role in Danish history long after the surrender of their absolute power.

Two examples from this century are worth citing. North Slesvig, lost to Bismarck's Germany in 1864, was reunited with Denmark in 1920 after a plebiscite held under the Treaty of Versailles. For fifty-six years the ruling Germans had attempted to forbid all expressions of Danish culture in North Slesvig. Danes had been conscripted into the German army at the same time that they were denied the right to use their native language. When the results of a plebiscite showed that North Slesvig would rejoin Denmark,

King Christian X rode into Slesvig on horseback to reclaim it for the Danish Crown. Crowds surrounded him as he rode, and his path was strewn with flowers for miles. There was universal celebration and rejoicing that day among the Danes of this part of Sønderjylland, who could again talk and sing and express themselves openly in their own language. Then a little girl fell into his path. The king stopped, bent down, took the child in his arms, and carried her for the rest of his ride. Francis Hackett, who was an eyewitness to this magnificent scene, wrote of the king:

> He was so absorbed in himself that this Reunion swept over him from time to time like a blessed miracle, and tears rolled down his cheeks. Emotions chased through him like sun and shower. He watered the new border with tears of joy and lit it with his smile.[12]

There was a time not so many decades ago when it was the custom for King Christian X to ride his horse through the streets of Copenhagen. Even after Copenhagen and Denmark were occupied by a foreign power, the king continued his daily ride through the city. The representatives of the foreign power were astonished that he would ride alone through the streets of an occupied city. What they did not know was that in Danish eyes the king was not alone. The Danes were very clear about that. It was said: "The king never rides alone when he rides, all of the people ride with him."

EXCURSUS THREE

The Rescue of The Danish Jews

> One is tempted to recommend the story as required reading in political science for all students who wish to learn something about the enormous power potential inherent in non-violent action and in resistance to an opponent possessing vastly superior means of violence.
> —Hannah Arendt, *Eichmann in Jerusalem*

When the Second World War broke out in 1939, the Scandinavian countries issued their declarations of neutrality as they had done in 1914. Only this time it was to be in vain. On 9 April 1940 Germany invaded both Denmark and Norway. After a brief and hopeless struggle the government yielded under protest. In the German-controlled "protectorate" that was established, the Danes were initially allowed a small degree of internal self-government. But when the war entered its later stages, the Germans encountered serious reverses on all fronts. By August 1943 the German offensive in Russia had failed, the Afrika Korps had surrendered in Tunisia, and the Allies had invaded Italy. The Danes were forced to pay a much higher price, and it was in these times that an effective Resistance Movement grew up against the Nazi Occupation. As the situation worsened, the facade of the model protectorate began to fall apart. A wave of sabotage swept the country. Riots broke out in Danish shipyards as dock workers went out on strike and refused to repair German ships. On 29 August 1943 the Germans declared martial law. The Danish army and navy were ordered to turn in all their weapons to make these resources available for the German war effort. In defiance, the Danish fleet was scuttled.

The conflict between the Nazi authorities and their model Danish "protectorate" began to focus on "the Jewish question." Hitler and the top Nazi leadership could neither tolerate nor understand the freedoms the Jews had in Danish society. Jews in Denmark had long been allowed to run their own businesses, attend synagogues, and move about with the freedom of all other Danish citizens. Full public rights had been given them as far back as 1814. When the Germans began the Occupation, they took the usual first steps toward isolation and stigmatization of the Jewish population. The difference between what happened in Denmark and what happened in many other European countries is that the Danes never cooperated. As Hannah Arendt remarks, "It is the only case we know of in which the Nazis met with *open* native resistance."

The consequences of this open resistance were immeasurable. Unlike the Jews in other European countries, the Danish Jews never saw their businesses taken. Nor did they ever come to wear the humiliating yellow badges shaped in the Star of David. The German authorities during the Occupation could never even succeed in getting the Danes to distinguish between native Danes of Jewish origin (of whom there were then about sixty-four hundred) and Jewish refugees from other lands (although some fourteen hundred stateless German Jewish refugees had been granted prewar asylum in Denmark, they were given neither work rights nor citizenship). The Germans were apparently caught flatfooted by the Danish refusal to discriminate against the latter category of Jew, it appearing utterly "illogical" to them for a government to protect people to whom it had denied naturalization and work rights. The most important consequence of the Danish refusal to cooperate is clearly noted by Hannah Arendt: "Thus, none of the preparatory moves, so important for the bureaucracy of murder, could be carried out, and operations were postponed until the fall of 1943."13

In the fateful autumn of that year, stung by the dock strike and infuriated by the losses on the international front, Himmler and the Nazi leadership in Berlin decided that this was the time to tackle the troublesome question of the Danish Jews. It is of great interest that opposition to the decisions being made in Berlin came not only from the Danes, but from some of the Germans who had been living in Denmark managing the German Occupation. General von Hannecken, the military commander, actually refused at one point to put troops at the disposal of Dr. Werner Best, the Nazi high commander. And Best himself was apparently an unreliable agent of Berlin policy. When the planned Danish version of the Final Solution was imminent (the night of October 1 had been set for seizure and immediate departure), the special police units that had arrived from Germany were told by Best that they were not permitted to break into apartments for fear that the Danish police might interfere. They could therefore only seize those Jews who voluntarily opened their doors (a fate that befell 477 of the 7,800 Jews then in Denmark).

Moreover, it was a German official, the embassy secretary (Georg F. Duckwitz: 1904–73) who provided the Danes with

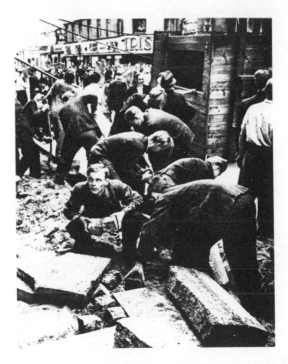

Strike against the Nazi Occupation, 1944. The stones of the street are being broken up for use in the barricades (from T. B. Jensen, ed., Danmark og Danskerne, *1979, reprinted with permission of Gyldendal).*

detailed advance notice of what was to happen. All Jews were to be rounded up and shipped off to die in concentration camps to the south. But this was never allowed to happen. Danish government officials quickly informed Jewish leaders, who openly communicated the news in the synagogues during the New Year services. In the autumn of 1943 a speedy emergency evacuation of Denmark's more than seven thousand Jews to nearby Sweden took place. The entire rescue operation was planned and carried out in two to three weeks' time. It was an almost complete success, for not more than a handful of Danish Jews were captured.

This action of the Danes was a just cause for admiration by the civilized peoples of the world. But something almost as remarkable as the rescue action was the later Danish response to it. As Israeli historian Leni Yahil astutely observes, "Perhaps the most astonishing phenomenon, and the very element in which greatness lay, was the fact that the Danes regarded their deeds as not in the least extraordinary or worthy of praise and admiration. In their opinion they merely did the natural and the necessary."[14]

Most of the cost of boat transportation for the indigent was paid for by wealthy Danish citizens. This assistance was given at a time when rich Jews elsewhere felt themselves lucky if they could pay thousands of dollars for exit permits. Poor Jews in other countries rarely escaped. Many years later a former veteran of fifteen crossings on the fishing boats that made the one-and-a-half-hour journey from Denmark to Sweden reminisced: "I would sit with the children, they were absolutely fantastic. You never heard anybody complain. I brought food to the children, I read to them, I turned on the light at night when they went to sleep. I told them, 'Yes, you will see mommy and daddy again. You will be reunited. There's nothing to worry about.' I never thought of it as dangerous at the time, but I could have ended up against the wall."[15]

Cases were recorded of complete strangers going up to Jews in the street and offering them the keys to their houses. The Torah, or sacred Hebrew scrolls, were hidden in the cellars of Copenhagen's Protestant churches. When the Danish Jews returned after the war, many found that records of their possessions had been kept and that their businesses and homes were intact. In some cases their lawns had even been mowed! In reviewing the course of these events, it is difficult to refrain from eulogizing and myth making. Yet as paleontologist Stephen Jay Gould has remarked in another context, God dwells in the details.

It is of course true that acts of heroism were recorded in other European countries. The Danes were not the only ones even in Scandinavia to engage in active resistance. Helped by the Norwegian resistance, 930 Norwegian Jews escaped to Sweden in 1941 and 1942 (although at the end of 1942 more than 800 men, women, and children were seized by the Nazi Occupation in Norway and deported to Auschwitz).[16] Successful rescue operations were also carried out, for instance, in Finland, Italy, and Bulgaria. Nevertheless, there are some questions that have to be asked about the Danish case. First, why did so many Danes risk ending up "against the wall" to save the Danish Jews? Second, how was it that the voices and actions of resistance came not only from ordinary individuals, but from those in high places of government?[17] Third, why was the anti-Semitism that flourished elsewhere so conspicuously lacking in the Danish nation as a whole, so much so that even members of the German Occupation did not remain untouched by Danish ways of thinking? The official Danish religion is the Lutheran Church, a sect of Christianity tracing its origins to the German theologian Martin Luther. It was this same Luther who condemned the Jews as a nation of traitors, calling for their homes to be demolished, their synagogues burned, and religious writings destroyed.[18]

The longer one ponders these things, the more remarkable they seem. Even now, when I think I have a much better understanding of some of the reasons behind the Danish response to Hitler, it seems to me no less of a marvel. But at that time, before I got to know the Danes better, I just plain and simply wanted to know why they had acted this way. Partly for reasons of personal history it was something that had always been important to me. The part about personal history is easily explained. I remember as a five-year-old child my grandfather speaking of his childhood in Czarist Russia. He spoke in a soft voice of what it was like to hide in a kind neighbor's cellar while screaming mobs ran through the Jewish ghetto chanting the timeless, eternal slogan: "Kill the Jews." Recited in a quiet tone of voice that lacked all outward signs of anguish or bitterness, communicated to inform and not to frighten, the stories served nonetheless in their own way as incendiary fairy tales. With their authentic lived content, amplified by images of screaming monsters I myself had never seen, they rang truer to me than any Arthurian legend ever could.

When he spoke, his tone was not harsh. It was more as if he were amazed that these things had actually happened. Perhaps this was because he had left Russia many years ago at the age of seventeen and was now sitting in his own living room speaking of events that were far distant in space and time. One day not long after that particular round of *pogroms* (persecutions), he left Mother Russia illegally, never to return. He used his employed older brother's passport to cross the border, sending it back in the mail when he had safely arrived. The next year his brother, traveling on the reclaimed passport, would join him in the United States after making a similar journey. The two of them started a small cigar store in a large Eastern city. They would work there the rest of their lives, rolling handmade cigars for a living. I can still remember the sight of his hands and the smell of cigar smoke.

We are now far from that period in history, and equally far from the time of the Nazi Occupation, and of those who preceded it. "Who, after all, speaks today of the annihilation of the Armenians?" was the rhetorical question put by Hitler to his military commanders on 22 August 1939 shortly before the invasion of Poland.[19] The arrest and murder of 200 Armenian leaders in Turkey in 1915 were the first acts in a systematic persecution that lasted eight years, during which an estimated 1.5 million Armenians were killed and 500,000 exiled from Turkey.[20] Other and more recent political mass murders have done much to take the peculiar horror of the Nazi period out of sharp focus. Consider a small random sample: Cambodia (Pol Pot era, 1975–80, 500,000+ deaths);[21] Indonesia (Chinese population, 1965–66, 800,000+ deaths);[22] Indonesia (invasion of East Timor, 1980–85, 200,000+ deaths);[23] Guatemala (1966–

85, 100,000+ deaths);[24] Mozambique (1980–87, 100,000+ deaths).[25] Other names come easily to mind: Uganda under Idi Amin and Milton Obote, Argentina, Chile, El Salvador. Still others might be included: South Africa, Angola, the United States in Indo-China (1955–75), the Chinese in Tibet, the refugee camps at Sabra and Shatila. And even this would be no complete rendering but a very partial and limited list of names. One looks in vain through this literature for a parallel to the rescue of the Danish Jews.

There are some wounds that even time can never heal, just as some nightmares cannot be forgotten even by those who never directly lived through them. One of those with her memories of the Nazi era is an elderly Danish woman I met while traveling on a train in north Germany. As we talked she remembered a small, lost detail of that time. Our conversation had turned to the war years, and as the countryside flashed by, she recalled something for me. Living then as a member of a Danish minority in the North German town of Flensburg, she recalled what was written on the wall in a room in the government office where she was required to go to obtain her foreigner's ration card. I asked her to write it down for me. She did so, prefacing it with the year (1933):

> *Trittst du in diesen*
> *Raum hinein*
> *So soll Dein Grüss*
> *"Heil Hitler" sein.*

"When you step into this room with me, then your greeting 'Heil Hitler' must be." Those entering the room had to pass a public test of loyalty. They were required to stretch out their arms and offer a public affirmation. It had to be performed with the appropriate enthusiasm. Refusal could mean more than just the loss of a ration card. It could result in being branded as an enemy of the state. A momentary poor mood on the part of the dispensing official, an unlucky first impression, even a single indiscreet gesture could bring tragic consequences. A small thing, perhaps, but it enables one nevertheless to recall momentarily something of that period of European history. And as our train continued through the north German town of Lübeck, I looked out the train window and saw that a large black swastika had been drawn on the underside of a bridge. The train was going by so quickly that I was unable to make out the writing that accompanied it.

Hannah Arendt wrote that "the story of the Danish Jews is *sui generis*, and the behavior of the Danish people and their government was unique among all the countries of Europe."[26] Leni Yahil concluded of the Danish rescue operation that it "indicates which elements enable a small nation to remain true to itself even under the most trying conditions. It restores to their special honor the humane values, so often distorted and underestimated under the impact of the worldwide struggle for power and predominance."[27] It remains, even after the passage of half a century, one of the more extraordinary series of events in the history of our time.

II. AN INTRODUCTION TO DANISH POLITICAL ECONOMY

We move now beyond the period covered in the preceding excursus to the ethnographic present. Political economy, an older term for the study of economics, goes back to a time when economics was not a kingdom unto itself but was studied as part of history, politics, and social thought. In their influential 1986 volume Marcus and Fisher note the resurgence of this term in recent times in the work of economists and political scientists. I follow a similar strategy here, assuming that economic factors can and ought not to be considered in isolation from their social, political, psychological, and cultural counterparts; all are interwoven, hence the use of the term "political economy." This short introduction to modern Denmark focuses on the period after 1945.

The Relationship Between Agriculture and Industry

Viewed from a macrohistorical, long-range point of view, Danish agriculture has been able to transcend nonoptimal features of land and climate to become one of the most sophisticated and successful in the world.[28] The spectacular success of the cooperative movement through most of the present century can be cited in support of this conclusion. It is supported as well by a first look at the performance of Danish agriculture in the modern world market, using the gross statistics of international export. Denmark was in 1981 the world's largest exporter of pigmeat, second largest exporter of butter, and third largest exporter of cheese. Export sales of pigmeat, for instance, were expected to yield 17 billion kroner in 1984 (more than $1.5 billion).

"The Danish pig is not what it has been," announces an article in the Danish newspaper *Information*. "It is first and foremost no longer Danish."[29] It is explained that the modern Danish pig is the result of careful artificial breeding, combining the virtues of its traditional Danish forebear with those of the English Yorkshire and the North American Hampshire and Duroc. The Black-and-White Danish cow, which combines a high milk yield with rapid growth and fine meat quality, has been exported to nearly thirty countries. Mink farming has become a specialty, and the 5 million mink a year raised on Danish farms account for nearly 20% of the world market. Selective plant cultivation based on control of seed and strain appropriate to the soil is only one of the innovations (along with effective fertilizer application, weed, disease, and pest controls) that have led to a 30% increase in overall crop yields over the last twenty-five years.

Given these encouraging facts, what then is the present relationship in the Danish economy between agriculture and industry? The answer is that in spite of the success in agriculture symbolized by this impeccable but no longer quite Danish pig, the Danish economy as a whole is one that has increasingly come to be dominated by industry. This observation is true, even though as the result of modernization both the agricultural and the industrial technologies have become rationalized, intensive, and advanced. There is often a human cost to the increased levels of productivity. In 1985 the Danish agricultural sector produced 40% more than it had in 1973 even though there were now forty-five thousand fewer farmers.[30]

Danish industry has recorded its successes even in the face of the added constraints posed by the lack of raw materials. It has compensated through use of the following strategies: (1) relying mainly on labor-intensive production strategies; (2) having many small companies in a large number of fields; (3) retaining the ability to adjust and adapt production lines quickly and at short notice; and (4) emphasizing innovation and the finding of special niches in which a strong competitive position can be quickly secured. Many Danish firms have become subcontractors for large foreign industrial concerns. Most are remarkably small: 53.4% of all employees work in firms of less than two hundred people, and only ninety-one Danish companies employ more than five hundred workers. Danish factories produce a wide variety of goods for export: from glass fiber-reinforced polyester sailboats to diesel motors, from nail varnish to concrete paints, from pharmaceuticals to automatic monitoring equipment for hospital patients. Their products are often highly specialized equipment such as automatic controls for refrigeration plants, controls for heating units, and sophisticated electronic components. In some recently emerging specialized fields of technology, such as the use of recombinant DNA technology for the production of insulin, Denmark is an acknowledged world leader.

In spite of its increased productivity, Danish agriculture in the 1960s found itself in an unenviable position. Though efficiency was continuing to improve, farmers were unable to find additional markets for their products. This situation resulted in a decline in numbers of those employed in agriculture. The Danish agricultural labor force in 1950 comprised more than 500,000 full-time employees; by 1960 it numbered just under 400,000 and by 1970 just over 250,000, or 10% of the total national work force. Even by the close of the 1950s the value of industrial exports was approaching that of agricultural exports. By 1979 agriculture accounted for just 27% of Danish exports, industry 73%. It is clear from these developments that the center of gravity of the Danish economy was slowly moving from agriculture to industry.

These developments continued, intensifying a trend toward urbanization that began in the second half of the nineteenth century. In 1801, 21% of the Danish population (which by 1811 consisted of 1 million inhabitants) resided in urban areas; 79% in rural areas. Thus four out of every five Danes were living in rural areas at that time, most of them employed in agriculture or related occupations. In 1950 the percentage of the population employed in agriculture (including fishing) had declined to 26%. In 1975 it had taken a further drop to 9%, and by 1988 it was down to 6%. The long-term processes of mechanization, urbanization, and industrialization have in the course of the last century utterly transformed the Danish social and occupational landscape.[31]

The demographic transition that has accompanied the path to modernization in Denmark has involved a typical three-phase process. An initial high rate of both mortality and fertility (stage one: "premodern") is followed by a fall in mortality rates (stage two: "modernizing") and then, after a comprehensive economic and social restructuring, a decline in rate of fertility as well (stage three: "postmodern"). To take some examples of mortality statistics alone, a newborn boy in 1840 could expect to live to forty-two, a girl to forty-seven. At the beginning of this century the figures were fifty-two and fifty-six; today they are seventy-two and seventy-seven.[32] The high life expectancy figures, reflecting the achievements of a modernized society, are viewed as desirable. The declining fertility rates, on the other hand, are viewed with alarm. "If present trends continue there will be fewer people in Denmark by the end of the century, and by the end of the next century the population will be halved."[33] In worst case scenarios, Denmark will become a society of old people surrounded by single parents and single children, the consequences of a putative decline in traditional marriage, child-bearing patterns, and the nuclear family.

Along with the growth in total population from an estimated 1 million (1811) to just over 5 million (about 5.1 million in 1989), the demographic transition has affected population density. This figure increased from about 20 persons per square kilometer in 1801 to 64 in 1901 and 117 in 1975. Of course these numbers are only averages for the whole. The citing of total average figures conceals the local variation in population density and thus can give a superficial or even misleading picture of the data. A more sensitive measure is the range, which extends from 11,616 persons per square kilometer in Frederiksberg in central Copenhagen, to 54 persons per square kilometer in Viborg Amt in central Jutland. In addition to rural-urban differentials, population density increases from west to east (it is three times greater in Zealand than in Jutland).

The demographic transition has brought about a series of long-term changes in the population structure. Its consequences include the following: (1) a radical change in the age distribution of the population (more older adults and proportionally fewer infants and children); (2) a long-term pattern of internal rural-urban migration (though after 1960 the greatest growth has been in the suburbs around the largest cities); (3) a marked slowing down of the rate of population growth for the population as a whole; and (4) the changes in occupational distribution patterns already noted (particularly the movement out of agriculture into the fields of manufacturing, construction, government, community, and business services).

Let us turn from these demographic developments to major trends that can be seen subsequent to the Second World War. The rise of industry for export was one significant postwar economic trend. Greater investment in building and housing was another, especially in the owner-occupied sector. By 1970 nearly half the population lived in homes they had purchased themselves. But the fastest-growing area of the Danish economy in the 1960s was beyond question the public sector. The share of the total national product consumed by the public sector more or less doubled during the 1960s, corresponding to the growth of the welfare state. This growth made possible more construction of schools, colleges, and hospitals, as well as an increase of time spent at school and in higher education. It provided expanded health service and extended the care available for preschool children and the elderly. An added policy of major importance implemented in this decade was the provision of a universal old-age pension, regardless of income. Unemployment benefits were also raised to a level making them among the most generous in the world.[34]

The Crisis of the 1980s

When I arrived in Denmark in September 1982, I made it a point for all the fall months to walk through the streets as much as possible. Besides providing exercise, it seemed a good thing for a curious ethnographer to do. I could not help noticing that even in September the days were beginning to shorten and there was a definite coldness in the air. But whether I was walking in Copenhagen or through provincial towns in Jutland, I saw the signs of what looked to me like a prosperous and vital society. The streets were clean, and everywhere there were healthy-looking children. There were many beautiful parks, some with inspiring sculptures. The shops were full of every imaginable ware including the irresistible Danish pastry (which in Denmark they modestly refer to as *Wienerbrød*, [lit.: "Vienna bread"]). There were coffee shops and outdoor cafes, department stores and supermarkets, the latter on a slightly smaller scale than found in the United States but containing just as many appetizing items. Those were my first impressions. The proverb that says "A happy face is the sign of a glad heart" still makes me think of the Danes more than any other people among whom I have lived. What I saw were the outward signs of a successful, modernized, and socially advanced society.

A variety of other indices add to and confirm this initial picture. Compulsory education exists for everyone between the ages of seven and sixteen. School standards are generally quite high compared to American norms. Illiteracy is virtually unknown. Public transportation is excellent and ubiquitous. Special caretaking institutions exist for infants, children, teenagers, and adults with every conceivable kind of problem or handicap. There are numerous public libraries, museums, and concerts. There are innumerable rock festivals, bars, and nightclubs. The various forms of social-security legislation are far more comprehensive than their parallels in the United States and include as a matter of course are such things as medical, hospital, and old-age care. Equal pay for men and women doing the same work was introduced in 1973; the law even specifies that it is forbidden for job advertisements to stipulate a particular gender for the job. These are some of the reasons why it looked like a very advanced and progressive society to me.

But I soon learned that what I saw was not what many Danes themselves saw as they gazed at the same sights. William Shakespeare, who wrote the immortal lines about the rottenness in the state of Denmark, once again showed his prescience; he succeeded in capturing (most likely well in advance of its actual appearance) a fundamental theme of the Danish psyche in the postmodern age. "There *is* something rotten about Denmark," many Danes will tell you. And in spite of the aforementioned indices of prosperity, this theme is one that should not be taken lightly. It can be seen in part as a tendency toward enlightened self-criticism that works against the expression of the worst sort of pride and bombastic foolishness (or at least makes it difficult to voice them in public). Yet over and above this, the mood of crisis expressed in this prosperous society reflects a very real set of concerns. One does not have to look very hard to see that the instability of the postmodern world has reached deeply into all sectors of Danish life. Its clammy and not-at-all invisible hand is felt on the backs of those employed in agriculture and in industry. It is felt by government employees and by teachers, even those within the previously untouchable ranks of tenured university professors. Every day the headlines from a variety of newspapers repeat their Cassandra chorus of alarming news. The following sample provides a thumbnail sketch of some of the issues that concern and perplex Danes today:

(1) "In Western Europe Some Countries Owe Big Sums to Foreigners; Unlike many poor nations, their borrowing is laid to huge social programs" (*The Wall Street Journal*, 14 Dec. 1982). Denmark has become a debtor nation, the article announces, and will have to accept a lower standard of living tomorrow. (2) "139 Died Of Narcotics In 1983; Shocking, says police chief" (*Politiken*, 29 March 1984). The article claims that there may be as many as ten to fifteen thousand narcotic addicts in Denmark. (3) "Prices Climbed 8 Percent; inflation not under control" (*Politiken*, 19 April 1984). (4) "100 Silent Witnesses To Terror on Train: No one interfered, when five Danes forced a young Pakistani to throw away his clothes" (*Extra Bladet*, 16 April 1984). (5) "The Young Are Turning To Weapons; more gross criminality" (*Politiken*, 29 Sept. 1984). (6) "Passive witnesses to ugly sex-violence, unjustifiable say police" (*Politiken*, 5 Oct. 1984). (7) "Bloody gang-confrontation close to ending with a slaying, two wounded in Vanløse, one critically" (*Politiken*, Jan. 1984). (8) "Denmark is for the Danes, immigrants, gays and left-oriented must be crushed. There is need for a Danish branch of the Ku Klux Klan, say young supporters of white power on Østerbro's dark side" (*Off Side, Information magasin*, 31 May 1985). (9) "The vacuum of the poor, 30,000 people live as outcasts" (*Politiken*, 30 July 1987). (10) "Poverty is made invisible" (*Nørrebro Avis*, 29 Jan. 1985).

These headlines, which are not unusual, conjure up a series of problematic images tied to a perception of social crisis. The sense of social crisis is confirmed by the unceasing parade of symptomatic images. "What is happening to our Denmark?" is a question on many people's minds. One hears it asked by members of the older generation who must cope with the startling news of drug addiction, unemployment, racism, and street violence. One hears it asked also among those in the younger generations whose life experience is being critically shaped by the bitter contradictions of this brave new world. There is a darker side to paradise, one that you will not read about in the tourist brochures. Although it is still true that you are much safer on the streets of Denmark than you would be in a comparable American city, you are not as safe as you once had been, and that only a short time ago.

Reminiscences can sometimes say more than a handful of statistics. A woman in her late sixties in a Copenhagen suburb, raised in a small town in West Jutland, remembers that when her mother was young there was perhaps one homicide a year. The entire country would discuss it for weeks. Now it is a rare day when the newspapers do not bring news of shocking violence. I spoke to some who recalled that in the postwar years of the late

1940s it was possible to leave your bicycle unlocked and come back to find it there at the end of the day. This was said to be true of Copenhagen as well as the small provincial towns. It is no longer true, and a bike left unlocked anywhere these days runs the risk of disappearing.

Two additional images should suffice. A headline (*Politiken*, 17 May 1984) announces, "Fishermen refuse to destroy 10,000 tons of fish." A group of Danish fishermen have been ordered by the European Economic Community (EEC) to drench highly edible fish with dye to turn them into fish oil and animal food. Though these are the highest-quality fish, they are ineligible in this case to receive even EEC's lowest prices for human consumption. "Why can't they be taken to third world countries where people are starving?" the fishermen ask, aggrieved at their loss of income and upset at the waste of highly edible foodstuff in a world where many are starving.

What this illustrates in the case of fishing can be matched in the area of agriculture. Niels and Steen were two young men with extensive agricultural experience who shared my stay at Silkeborg Højskole. More than once I heard them complain about similar events. One year the EEC would tell the farmers to build more stalls for their cattle. Then two years later it would pay them to have the cattle slaughtered or even to go out of business. As Steen once told me, the disgust evident in his voice, "In Denmark we have a lot of cows, as you know, and we *shot* a lot of these cows especially here in East Jutland, where we are living. There were a lot of cows two, three years ago. Now there are none. On my farm there were fifty-five cows, today there are none, only corn, and all because of the EEC."

I mention these unpleasant realities neither to create an unduly sensationalized picture nor to drown in a mood of social pessimism. It is true that there is a dark underside of culture change symbolized in these unpleasant images of economic instability, of irrational international constraints on production, of violent acts and helpless victims. Yet this negative picture is only one of Denmark's many moods. I have spoken of it here in order to introduce a notion fundamental to this study: the concept of social crisis. The existence of this crisis was something that I learned ultimately neither from newspaper accounts nor interviews. I learned it from lived experiences in the three folk high schools that I attended, and afterward, when I lived for half a year in a small apartment in one of Copenhagen's less desirable neighborhoods, an unemployed anthropologist struggling to keep dreams alive in a time of contracting opportunities.

In the course of my fieldwork, I came to appreciate that there are many in Denmark who are at least outwardly not at all touched by the atmosphere of crisis that I have briefly sketched. I came to know many of them well, and to see Denmark also from their point of view. Niels, my farmer friend from Silkeborg, was one who viewed his own society from this vantage point. The son of a hard-working and well-to-do farmer, he was trying one day to explain all of this to me. "You see," he said, "we have this crisis in the country. Or what we *call* a crisis. It's an economic crisis—we owe a lot of money to other countries."

From his point of view Niels was probably correct in talking about the so-called crisis. Trained by his father, a successful farmer before him, he was already a skilled and capable young agriculturalist at the age of twenty-one. Niels had a clear path before him. Yes, he did worry a little about how bound to the land he would be once he bought his own farm, and he wasn't sure how much longer he should put it off. He worried about finding a wife to share the joys and the drudgery of the farm that he was going to buy. He had just returned to Denmark from a year in Alberta working for a Canadian farm family, and he had made such a good impression that the family offered to pay his transportation back and a salary as well if he wanted to return. He had traveled through much of the continental United States and acquired the most extensive collection of American T-shirts that I have ever seen: Disneyland, Cape Canaveral, Golden Gate Bridge, Yellowstone National Park. There was hardly a place in the United States that he hadn't visited at least long enough to collect a T-shirt.

But although Niels wasn't sure of all the details, the larger picture still looked bright for him. Not all of those I met at the folk high schools, or afterward in Copenhagen, could look into their future with the same degree of optimism. When I talked with Niels I had been in the country for six months and was in the initial stage of conducting interviews at Silkeborg, the second of the two folk high schools I attended. At the time I accepted the judgment of Niels and people like him as authoritative. I remember how I dutifully wrote down the words in my field notebook: "the so-called crisis." It was a judgment I came to revise only later on the basis of personal experience. By then I had looked at Danish society from both sides of the tracks.

III. SUMMARY AND CONCLUSION

To speak of the social crisis in contemporary Denmark is not to say anything original. The Danes themselves speak and write continually about the crisis *(krisen)*; they certainly do not need a foreign anthropologist to point out its existence to them. What I would like to do here, however, is something broader; it is to use the concept of the social crisis to take a more general look at Denmark. The ultimate goal will be to see where Danish society is in terms of its own history. To briefly summarize: in spite of the many dire predictions and unfortunate events of the last century, Denmark had by the early years of this century succeeded in making an extraordinary series of internal renewals (recall, for instance, the admiring comments of the visiting English agriculturalist H. Rider Haggard in 1913 and those of the American reformer Frederick Howe just a few years later). It was not a smooth path, and the direction was not always forward and positive. Nevertheless, if one looks at the larger picture, the Danes were able to come back from a series of national defeats and disasters to construct a society that perhaps more than any other in recent history resembles the ideal of Jeffersonian democracy. A recent validation of these claims is suggested by the results of the Estes study.

Some of the evidence to be considered in following chapters suggests that much of this success was due to the development of cooperative, "people-intensive" strategies. These strategies (one of which is represented in the growth of the folk high schools) enabled the Danes to make up for their lack of natural resources by an intense series of investments in the human quality of their population. If this analysis is correct, Denmark stands at a crossroads today. The Danes are faced with a new set of challenges. These challenges center at first glance on their balance of payments deficit and the resulting pressures both from within and from without to formulate strategies to bring it back into balance. I say "at first glance," because I believe that there is another aspect to the dilemma that is at least as important as the issues connected with international debt. This aspect has to do with the means chosen to attain that end and the model of society that will be used to justify the use of those means.

Denmark is a small country. The Danes are well aware—I am almost tempted to say "painfully aware"—of its relative smallness. The expression "we are such a little country" falls frequently from their lips and in many different contexts. Most of them take for granted the achievements in the field of social welfare reflected in the results of the Estes study. Yet the model of society behind these achievements in the field of social welfare was based on a particularly Danish vision, formulated in the last two centuries by Grundtvig and numerous others. It was made possible by an emphasis on specific Danish values such as Grundtvig's *folkelighed* and associated strategies of mutual cooperation. The policies based on this model provided the Danish population with a broadened base of social, economic, and political participation. In many ways, this unique Danish vision was successful in achieving its overall goals of modernization "with a human face." Yet powerful forces are at work in present-day Denmark to undo this achievement, and to replace the vision that lay behind it with a quite different set of assumptions.

If I were asked to sum this up in a sentence, I would say that the social crisis has created an atmosphere of confusion in which the older assumptions about the necessity of small-scale cooperation and investments in human quality have been replaced by another vision. I would sum up that vision in these words: the Germanization/Thatcherization/Americanization of Denmark. However awkward it may sound to the human ear, this monstrous hybrid construct provides us with the necessary composite image. It effectively encapsulates both the varied sources and possible consequences of the privatized vision that many Danes now feel must guide "the new Denmark." This dilemma and the need to choose between competing visions of society is, I would argue, the deeper meaning of the social crisis in Denmark today.

In the first two chapters, the primary focus was on Danish achievements. This chapter reviewed further Danish achievements, but it included as well a first look at some of the bewildering complications of the present. In the next two chapters we will examine in depth the historical roots of the Danish "people-oriented" strategy of cultural modernization.

PART THREE

THE ORIGIN OF THE FOLK HIGH SCHOOLS

CHAPTER FOUR

Revolution Without Violence: The Danish Land Reforms of the Late Eighteenth Century

I. WINDOW OF PROSPERITY: THE AGE OF THE BERNSTORFFS (1751–97)

THE UNIQUE PATH taken by modernization in Denmark begins with a series of developments that affected the rural landscape in the second half of the eighteenth century. It is a period of history characterized by some truly extraordinary events. The central theme posed by this inquiry is the question of how the Danes were able to go through the radical social changes that accompanied the modernization process without the use of organized violence in their society. The response of Danish elites during times of deep social crisis is a very significant factor: when we examine several key episodes of "crisis-oriented" social change in Denmark, we will find that those in the highest stations of society acted in a most unusual way.[1] An entrenched aristocratic nobility and two Danish kings were faced with situations in which arguably the best solution (both for their own interests and the interests of Denmark as a whole) was for them to give up some of their power. Amazingly enough, this is exactly what they did. Moreover, not only did they assent non-violently to this type of change, but they could in some cases be seen in the very vanguard of the forces demanding its enactment. The pattern of events to be treated here represents a most unusual and neglected chapter of European Enlightenment history. Let us turn to the period in question and take a closer look at the process that gave birth to the Danish Land Reforms.

The course of Danish history in the eighteenth century is guided by a series of paradoxes. During an age of great wars, Danish commerce and possessions increased both in Europe and overseas. Yet these gains were made for the most part not by participation in these wars but by wise avoidance of involvement in them. Moreover, the astute and effective policies respon-

sible for securing these advantages were formulated not by the absolutist
Danish kings who then ruled but by a fortunate succession of clever advisers.
The success of these kings, for as long as it lasted, seems to have been due
chiefly to their ability to follow ministerial advice. As a British historian
has written in ironic yet admiring summary:

> The partial detachment of Denmark from the main current of European
> affairs, however, by no means robs her history of interest. In an age of absolute
> monarchies, she presents the spectacle of one entirely wielded by feeble
> Kings. Power soon fell to a series of remarkable Ministers, and Moltke,
> Bernstorff, Struensee, Guldberg, and the younger Bernstorff, furnish a dem-
> onstration, unique in its amplitude, of the range and possibilities of benev-
> olent despotism.[2]

Two of these ministers, both the younger and the elder Bernstorff, were
to play key roles in the historical process that led to the Land Reforms of
the 1780s. Baron Johann Hartwig Ernst von Bernstorff (the elder) was by
any standards a major statesman of the period. During a six-year stay at the
Court of Louis XV, he achieved for Denmark the profitable Treaty of Alliance
of April 1746. Beginning in 1751 he resided in Copenhagen for nearly
twenty years while serving as chief diplomatic consultant to the state.
Guided by the senior Bernstorff's astute maneuvering (1751–70), Denmark
was one of the few states in northern Europe to remain out of the Seven Years
War, thus avoiding armed conflict with more powerful European neighbors:
France, England, Sweden, and Russia. His wise and skillful policies are
mirrored in a reputed epigram of Frederic the Great: "Denmark has her fleet
and her Bernstorff."

Andreas Peter Bernstorff (the younger) held office as minister for
foreign affairs from 1784 to his death in 1797. Carrying on the diplomatic
tradition of his uncle, he succeeded in protecting Danish prosperity in the
late 1780s through a series of successful negotiations with Russia and Prussia
to ensure Danish neutrality. In the general European war against France that
began in 1792, A. P. Bernstorff continued the same prudent statesmanship
(Denmark's failure to continue these policies after his death was to have
disastrous consequences in the next two decades). Protected by its neutrality,
Danish trade flourished during these decades in both the Mediterranean and
the East and West Indies.

The administration of the younger Bernstorff was characterized by its
enlightened policies, among them abolishing the African slave trade within
Danish colonies (1792). To put Bernstorff's action in sharper historical
perspective, a relevant comparison may be cited. Within the same time
frame, the American Continental Congress had neatly excised all reference

to slavery and the slave trade, thus both weakening the Declaration of Independence and leaving the American revolutionaries "in the ambiguous position of asserting human rights without unequivocally branding the enslavement of blacks as a violation of those rights." No less a human rights advocate than Thomas Jefferson was caught in this dilemma, as is made clear by his statement in 1820: "We have the wolf by the ears; and we can neither hold him, nor safely let him go. Justice is on one scale, and self-preservation on the other."[3] (Part of Jefferson's agony and moral confusion may have been due to the fact that he was one of the nation's largest slaveholders.)

In addition to ending slavery in Danish colonies, A. P. Bernstorff dispensed with censorship of the press. He was also one of the prime movers behind a series of major land reforms that, beginning in the 1780s, completely transformed existing social relationships in the Danish countryside. The Danish Land Reforms, the most important of the primary agents of transformation, took place during a period of prosperity and rising economic expectations made possible at least in part by the wise statesmanship of the Bernstorffs.

II. LIFE ON THE FEUDAL ESTATES: THE PEASANT FARMER COMMUNITY BEFORE THE REFORM ERA

The year 1988 was by all accounts a golden year for Danish flag manufacturers.[4] This sudden windfall, made possible by the two hundredth-year celebration of a major Danish land reform (*stavnsbaandetsløsning,* 1788), took place in the midst of intense public commentary and debate. Recreated by an extraordinary exhibit at the Museum at Brede outside of Copenhagen, the enactment of the Land Reforms is something that most Danes would agree is an essential feature of their history.

In order to understand the significance of the Danish Land Reforms, one must begin by looking at the situation of the Danish farmer in the mid-eighteenth century in the decades immediately prior to their enactment. At this time three-fourths of all Danish land belonged to the nearly eight hundred existing estates.[5] The figure should not be interpreted to mean that this number of large landowners actually existed; it was not uncommon for a single landowner to have several estates. Some, in fact, owned many: the actual number of large landowners has been estimated at between five hundred and six hundred. This situation had developed over time. If one looks back to the period immediately after the Reformation (1536), the estates owned by the Crown constituted nearly 40% of the country's land, due to its seizure of church property. In the intervening period, however, many of these estates had been sold to members of the feudal aristocracy to provide revenues. As a result, the feudal estates *(gods)* that then dominated the Danish landscape were frequently owned by an individual, either one who was by birth a titled member of the landed aristocracy or someone, such as a former army officer, who had purchased the title.[6] The owner of an estate *(godsejer),* also called the estate proprietor, was the most powerful figure in the system of social relations found in the Danish countryside. As a Danish historian comments, "It has been pointed out correctly that Danish society in the eighteenth century was still feudally organized, with the large estate *(godset)* as the economic and administrative unit."[7]

From the last part of the fourteenth century a form of serfdom *(vornedskab)* had existed in Denmark that not only bound peasant farmers tightly to the feudal estate of their birth, but forced them to work the particular farm and holdings *(gaard)* to which they had been assigned. One function of this system was to ensure that the necessary labor force would be provided for agricultural production on the estate. Another function, the raising of armies, was facilitated by the estate owner's power to conscript those bound to the estate into army service. It was a system that for all practical purposes made the tenant farmers into a form of disposable property.

Long before the enactment of the Land Reforms, an attempt to loosen the obligations of the system had not only failed but led to a subsequent tightening of feudal control. In 1701 Frederic IV, the reigning Danish king, feared a Swedish invasion. In order to supplement a standing army composed chiefly of foreigners, he passed an ordinance creating the so-called land militia. Compulsory army duty facilitated by a conscription register now faced all rural young men.[8] In the belief that the old system *(vornedskab)* was no longer needed, it was abolished in 1702. Almost immediately two things happened. Many of the young farmers *(bonderkarle)* who were not written down for military service used their new freedom to leave the estates on which they had been born. And when Danish agriculture soon afterward faced an economic crisis, the estate proprietors feared that they would not have sufficient numbers of people to work the tenancies on their estates. Thus it was that in 1733 a new law was passed *(stavnsbaandet)* reinstating the requirement that young farmers remain on the estate where they were born. In the beginning the requirement was limited to those between fourteen and thirty-six years of age, but through a series of adjustments it was gradually extended until, by 1764, it included all males between the ages of four and forty.

What did this feudal system look like by the middle of the eighteenth century to a Danish farmer *(bonde)* and his family? The picture of their lives is grim and stark. Aided by the law that forbade men to leave the estate during their productive work years, a member of the nobility could compel a farmer to accept a position on his estate that he wanted filled *(fæstegaard)*. When positions became vacant, either through the death of the former tenant or his incapacity—for whatever reason—to work the land, it was in the estate owner's interest to have that position filled as quickly as possible. To add insult to injury, when a prospective farmer took over (or was forced to take over) such a position, he was officially required to pay the owner a lump sum of money *(indfæstning* or *stedsmaal)*. In practice, the onerous requirement of an initial payment was sometimes not enforced, particularly in cases when a new tenant would agree to clean up the farm he was about to live on and prepare it for operation (it was not uncommon for the farm to have been left in a wretched condition by the previous occupant).

In earlier times the estate owner's primary source of income from his tenants was a yearly payment in natural produce *(landgilden)*. This payment in goods, which typically amounted to between 20 and 25% of the harvest, had gradually been supplemented by a work requirement *(hoveri)* on the estate owner's fields. Much of the surviving literature of the time suggests that the latter obligation weighed hardest of all on the tenant farmers of an estate.[9] It was not uncommon for them to be required to work on the estate owner's fields as much as several hundred workdays a year. These workdays fell typically during the critical spring planting and autumn harvest times. As a result the farmer's own work had to be neglected in precisely those periods that were most crucial for his own economic success.

In addition to the payment in produce and the oppressive system of donated workdays (whose number could be increased by the estate owner at any time), the farmer was subjected to other systematic humiliations. If a man objected to the number of workdays required, it was well within the power of the estate owner to have him disciplined and punished. Punishment was usually carried out by the hated figure of the *ridefoged* (the bailiff, or overseer of the estate). The means employed were often severe, going beyond the bailiff's whip and cane to the devices of actual torture, to a ride on the Wooden Horse *(træhest)* or a stay in the Dog's Hole *(hundhullet)*. But indirect sanctions could be equally effective. Remember that a young farmer who contemplated resisting the estate owner knew that the latter could have him conscripted at any time into military service. Reluctant to leave the only home he had ever known, and perhaps wanting to avoid the discomfort and dangers of military service as well, a sensible tenant farmer would think twice before complaining about the details of estate life, however unfair he might feel they were.

If a tenant farmer needed spiritual counseling, he could always speak with the priest, who had been appointed by the estate owner. And if matters did get out of hand, most estates possessed their own local system of jurisdiction: it consisted of a court with a judge also appointed by the estate owner. This "judge" *(birkedommer)*, responsible for upholding Danish law, was rarely, if ever, a trained jurist. He usually turned out to be someone who had once worked for and served the estate owner in some capacity. Thus the "judge" stood in a clear dependency relation to the estate proprietor, who both appointed him and paid him his salary. Not surprisingly, the tenant farmers rarely received an independent hearing in this court.

Tenant farmers possessed no independent inheritance rights. If a farmer died at a young age, his widow was obligated to bring in a new tenant through marriage.[10] Whenever a tenant farmer died, the estate owner's overseer evaluated the condition of the property. It was nearly always decided that the farm had deteriorated during the tenant's occupancy, and in such cases the costs of repair were to be borne by the estate of the surviving family members. Given his responsibilities and his vested interests, it is understandable that an overseer tended to gloss over whatever improvements had accrued to the property as a result of a tenant's years of work. These practices frequently meant that a deceased tenant farmer's wife and heirs were deprived of any inheritance whatsoever. As one Danish historian of the period concludes: "After a life of work, toil and humiliation, the tenant farmers of Denmark went in poverty to their graves, stripped of the little they could gather together to support themselves." [11]

Yet the situation was probably even worse, a conclusion suggested by the fact that less than half of all tenant farmers managed to remain on the farm they had worked until the time of their death.[12] In theory they were to remain on the farm for life (the very term for the relationship, *livsfæste*, means literally "a fastening for life"). But fulfillment of one precondition of this tenantship, the requirement that all expenses were paid when due, could become difficult if not impossible in times of crisis. In spite of the fact that a tenant's contract was officially entered into for life, such events as disease (both of humans and animals), physical weakness, and old age forced nearly one-third to leave prematurely. A tenant farmer could also be forced to give up the farm because of what was perceived as insufficient will or ability to fulfill the expectation of the contract *(fæstekontrakt)*; about one-third of all tenants on Sjælland (which seems an amazingly high figure) suffered this fate in the years between 1770–90.[13] To resist too strenuously the continually required donations of rent, produce, and labor could lead to a final loss of the estate owner's patience. Those who lost their tenancy (*gaardforsidder*) suffered a personal tragedy: they were reduced to the lowest status in the peasant community, the position of landless day-worker. In their old age these individuals would often become beggars, dependent on other people's charity for their survival.

The distinction between the tenant farmer occupying his land (*bonde*) and the one who had seen it taken from him (*gaardforsidder*) is a critical one. It highlights a dimension of the social stratification in the Danish peasant community that was of equal importance both before and after the Land Reforms of the 1780s. For even with all of the above-cited difficulties, the tenant farmer was (from the limited and circumscribed point of view of the peasant community itself) a person with a higher status. As someone who had the use of land, as a *bonde* (plural: *bønder*), he and his family belonged to a higher class, the *bondeklass,* also known as *gaardmænd.* The landless, ex-tenant farmer, on the other hand, had now become a member of the agricultural underclass, known collectively as *husmænd.*[14] The conditions of this class varied. Some *husmænd* possessed a small house on the estate but little or no land to farm for themselves. They depended for their survival on seasonal and part-time agricultural employment by the estate owner. Others, the more fortunate ones, had steady positions as laborers and servants to the tenant farmers (often their wives served as well). Their compensation might include a plot of earth taken from the landed farmer with the understanding that they could keep whatever they grew on it. In order to understand what the folk high school would later come to mean to the Danish agricultural community, it is essential to grasp this distinction between the landed (*bønder*) and landless farmers (*husmænd*).

What was the underlying ethos behind the social relations of this system of feudal estates? It was at least outwardly dominated by the magisterial manor houses within which a life of lofty and cultivated elegance could be carefully fashioned. French, German, Latin, and Greek were the languages of European high culture; accordingly, it was a common practice for those in the estate owner's household to journey abroad to such cultural centers as Paris, London, and Vienna. For many it was a familiar custom to spend part of the winter in Copenhagen, where one could keep an eye on royal politics as well as stay abreast of the latest developments in literature, the arts, science, and philosophy. Members of this class frequently possessed dwellings in or near the capital that were of the same palatial quality as their manors back on the estates, replete with such helpful features as a well-stocked library and a special sitting room (*kabinettet*) in which the lady of the house could pursue her cultivated hobbies. Although the estate owners' wives were excluded from official power, they were not without a measure of indirect authority:

> They had great influence on what was seen as good taste, good art, good literature. It was to a large extent they who made order in the homes. They chose the artists who would paint portraits of them and their families, the books that should be read by both children and adults, and the theater pieces that in a good dilettante fashion, and with great enthusiasm, would be performed in the home with family and a circle of friends as both actors and audience.[15]

Wherever one happened to be at the time—in Paris, Copenhagen, or the manor of the estate—it was not unusual for an owner to leave many of the details of the estate's daily operation to the bailiff and other hired administrators. That this luxurious existence for the few was made possible by the labor of the many, by the labor of a bound community of landed and landless subsistence tenant farmers, was not a fact that often sprang to anyone's mind. What Michael Taussig has called "the veil of naturalness" effectively obscured the historical contingency of the system, its dependence on a particular set of social arrangements that could be first questioned and then changed. But during much of the time that it prevailed, the system functioned as a "world-taken-for-granted," in Peter Berger's apt phrase. Thus Jens Vibæk could write, "Something shared by everyone in the countryside, high as well as low, was the conception that this was the way it had to be. This is the way it had been from time immemorial, and here no changes could take place."[16]

What was the ethos, the kinds of feeling and sentiment expressed in everyday life by the peasants who were a part of this system? Were they both outwardly and inwardly accepting of its hierarchical rules, or did preconditions of resistance and dissent exist among them? Fridlev Skrubbeltrang, an expert on Danish rural history, has written this of the Danish peasant community: "The attitude of the common people to the gentry was outwardly respectful but not humble."[17] There is some evidence in the literature of the Danish peasant village that goes even further. It indicates that in certain kinds of contacts, particularly with agents such as the bailiff or overseer, even the show of outward respect was not necessarily given. Much conflict seems to have centered on the work requirements (*hoveri*) on the estate owner's fields. One author's description underlines the harshness of the authority relations that accompanied the mandatory work donations: "Probably the most resented aspect, although it had less economic importance, was the corporal punishment which was allowed in connection with *hove.* Peasants doing *hove* at the manor were treated as if they came under the Servants Law *(Tyende Lov)* which forbade servants to resist corporal punishment; this law was not repealed until 1862."[18]

Some oral eyewitness material collected by the nineteenth-century Danish folklorist Evald Tang Kristensen shows how the system might well have functioned informally, that is, in the face-to-face everyday encounters typically sustained by its members (as opposed to the ideal rules governing such encounters). Many of the narratives in Kristensen's massive collection provide unparalleled insight into (1) how the system weighed on the tenant farmers; (2) the spectrum of responses found among the farmers; and thus (3) grounds for reflecting upon the nature of Danish national character as it is seen in their behavior. Consider the following citation:

> Old Palle in *Voldum* was at *hove* one day, and they were carting in corn. It was chancy weather, and the peasants wanted to get their own corn in, but they had to take in the manor's corn first. They waited in a line, 12 or 13 wagons in a row, wanting to unload, but they had to go through the main gate first. The lord had trouble finding a bailiff who was good at beating the people, but he had got this fellow over from Sjælland, who was so clever at hitting people with a long dog-whip, and he stood at the gate and stuck his hand into the loads, to see if the corn was dry enough. But there was a good chance of a wet sheaf here and there, unsteady as the weather was. As he pulled out another handful of wet straw, he struck his whip right in the eyes of the first man in line and yelled, "If I find more of you with a load like this, I'll—so and so—beat them." Old Palle was right behind, and when he came up to him, he stood up on the load and said, "You rotten kid, if you touch me with that whip I'll put this fork into you up to the shaft." So the overseer had to back down, he was afraid of old Palle, who was a powerful fellow.[19]

Although they were virtually powerless in terms of formal rules, it is of interest that the Danish tenant farmers were permitted at the informal level areas of discretion that allowed the expression of autonomous resistance to the status quo. It was apparently expected that those strong enough to do so would resist on such occasions as the above. But even the weakest of the workers could strike back on occasion, and if they had the support of their fellow villagers, they might get away with it:

> There was a little girl who struck an overseer on *Krastrup* manor. He was bad to go, during harvest, and feel whether the sheaves were bound fast enough, and if he didn't think they were, he cut the string. But this made her angry, so she collected a whole handful of rye-blades, all the same length and with that lock she hit the overseer in the face the next time he cut one of her sheaves, so that he started over backwards. When he got on his feet he

was about to hit her, but the mowers all crowded around him and said they'd cut his head off with their scythes if he didn't let her alone. Then the owner is supposed to have come and calmed them down, so nothing more came of it, but that was a brave little girl.[20]

If these stories are to be believed, a bailiff seen as overstepping the legitimate exercise of his authority was not beyond powerful sanctions by the community. As the above citation indicates, even the owner of an estate could in effect sanction this autonomy by not pressing his legal powers too far. Several other stories tell how overseers were waylaid and beaten, often with the addition that "they smashed his right hand between two stones."[21] What emerges here is at least a limited trend toward the significant form of authority-related communication that the social psychiatrist Eric Berne has called "permissions."[22] The permission in this case allows the expression of independent, self-affirming behavior on the part of a structural inferior to a structural superior (given, of course, that the entire encounter takes place in a negative context created by the demands of the system itself).

In terms of Danish national character, several later themes concerning the handling of authority relations are foreshadowed here. These themes are: (1) a strong possibility that someone with power in the immediate environment will sympathize sufficiently with the underdog in a conflict situation to allow (2) a tendency to sanction "bending the rules," the granting of a *de facto* permission (in most cases to a victim or potential victim) to violate the strict letter of formal, legal rules, all of which has the effect that (3) a state of affairs less out of balance than would otherwise have been the case comes to exist. Thus two core values relevant to an understanding of Danish national character, egalitarianism (Chapter Six) and balance (Chapter Seven), are prefigured in the above social transactions.

It is important neither to exaggerate the scope of such defensive activity nor to romanticize its consequences. The following description of both poor working conditions and a failed attempt to improve them was probably much more typical:

> When I was at Lerkenfeldt to do *hove* at harvest, I was put in the threshing barn to cast out. We were all in stocking feet. When I had to turn in my work, the boards pinched my feet as they moved. The bailiff came in to oversee the work, and I turned to him and said, "Could we possibly be allowed another board to stand on, Mr. Overseer?" But what answer did I get? "Ah, they have damn well supported heavier fellows than you," he snarled, and went on his way. And only the day before, an old woman had fallen down from that same place and hurt herself so badly that she never got over it, as long as she lived.[23]

The images that have been presented to this point emphasize the dimensions of conflict and exploitation that were unquestionably present in the system. There is another side to it that is worth pointing out. Laziness and drunkenness were apparently common vices among the tenant farmers, and individuals frequently took liberties with their work obligations, confident that the estate owner would take care of them if they got into difficulty.[24] In many cases, this did happen. For one thing, many of the estate owners regarded their own tenant farmers with patriarchal feelings of responsibility. As long as the system itself wasn't challenged, certain kinds of misbehavior were perhaps best paternalistically tolerated in the name of a common humanity. For another, it made sense even from a strictly business point of view to give aid to an ordinarily competent tenant who had fallen on momentary need or committed some indiscretion. The alternative could be even more bothersome, especially if this was one of the frequent times when there was a scarcity of potential new tenants. Besides (to take a hypothetical case), everyone knew that old Jens had a fine and loyal wife, had once been a good worker, and if aided today might prove a useful source of information in the future.

A final point needs to be made about this system. Seen in modern terms, it was grossly inefficient in maximizing output and productivity. One set of factors responsible for its inefficiency was the pattern of human social relationships on which it was based. Bound without their consent to the land, taxed to the hilt without any form of representation, and forced to donate an inordinate number of days in the most critical parts of the planting and harvest season to labor without direct compensation on the estate owner's fields, the Danish peasant farmers have been bluntly described as "ignorant and poor."[25] Was this any wonder? Required to surrender most of what they produced, fundamentally insecure in their tenancy and way of life, unable either to provide for themselves in their old age or to dispose of what they had produced to their heirs, they were at the mercy of the overseer or the estate owner's kangaroo court if they stood up for themselves. When one considers what life must have been like under these arrangements, it is not in the least surprising that such breaches of virtue as intemperance and a lack of "individual initiative" were so widespread among the members of this feudal agricultural community.

Although not unrelated to the social relations of the estate system, a second set of factors rooted in the techniques of agricultural production shared responsibility for the relatively low output and productivity. First, the peasant villages (*dyrkningsfælleskaber*) of this period still cultivated all their lands in common. This meant that each owner worked numerous strips of land scattered in irregular and sometimes fantastically complex patterns. There were often great distances in between the strips of land assigned to an individual. The purpose of this distribution was to ensure some equality in the assignment of good and marginal lands, but the degree of its inefficiency is seen in the fact that a single tenant farmer could come to be responsible for as many as a hundred separate parcels. It took a considerable amount of time just to travel between the farmhouse and all of these separate fields.[26] Second, the system of cultivation used was medieval, requiring that four to six horses be yoked to heavy, clumsy wheeled ploughs. The lighter and more efficient swing-plough had not yet been invented.[27] And third, the cultivated land that lay outside of the peasant village was in most cases organized around a three-field system of tillage devoted monotonously to grains and to fallow land; it has been described as both primitive[28] and wasteful.[29]

It is easy to see why a modern economist would describe this system as relatively unproductive, for all of these conditions hindered the introduction of more modern methods of operation. What is perhaps even more remarkable is that many of the people of that period were beginning to reach the same conclusion. Among them are some names we have already encountered, such as the elder and the younger Bernstorff. Added to this list must be other names: Christian Ditlev Reventlow, Christian Colbjørnsen, Vilhelm August Hansen, Ernst Schimmelmann, and the young crown prince, Frederic VI. It is significant that this group included not only some of the most powerful and influential landowners in Denmark, but a sixteen-year-old regent prince who upon his *de facto* accession to power in 1784 would reign in Denmark for fifty-five years, until the time of his death in 1839.

III. THE MAJOR LAND REFORMS (1765–1799)

The Danish Land Reforms did not take place overnight. They were the work not of years, not even of decades, but of more than a century. The year cited above (1765) marked the beginning of a significant effort at private and voluntary reform. On J. H. E. Bernstorff's Sjælland estate, forty-two tenant farmers were simultaneously given: (1) hereditary rights to the land *(overgang til arvefæste)*, (2) a single parcel of land to replace the dozens of separate holdings that had previously been worked *(udskiftning)*, and (3) a lightening of the required work donated to the estate *(hoveri)*. Yet this action of Bernstorff was neither the earliest private reform effort, nor did it mark the beginning of public debate on the subject.[30] The later date of 1799 represents the passage of legislation significantly limiting the arbitrary power of the estate owner to set the conditions for the donated work requirement. Yet it was only in 1850 that the final legal abolition of this donated work took place. Perhaps even more significantly, the passage of legislation ending the last remnants of the tenant system did not occur until 1919. Thus the dates given above are not intended to be written into a stone tablet but merely to provide a convenient framework for discussion. There is an understandably large Danish literature dealing with the land reforms, and the deeper one gets into it, the more complicated and subtle the historical process behind them begins to appear. In the analysis that follows, the goal is not to give a complete rendering, but the more limited one of summarizing some of the significant highlights of the process. Once this has been accomplished, it will become clear how the land reforms functioned as a primary agent of transformation in the cultural and economic development of Denmark.

It was suggested in Chapter One that the process of land reform in Denmark had its unusual, even remarkable features. Perhaps most noteworthy is the fact that major transfers of power were accomplished gradually, over time, with little or no recourse to organized social violence. Angry voices were raised, unhappy petitions were circulated, and furious letters were written, but no heads rolled on the ground. Another of its remarkable features was that much of the impetus behind the Land Reforms came from a group of men that included some of the wealthiest, most highly placed, and most influential figures in Danish society. It was members of this group (among them the elder Bernstorff) who established the Royal Danish Agricultural Society *(Det Kgl. danske Landhusholdningsselskab)* in 1769. The establishment of this society (which held its founding meeting on the king's birthday) reflected reform trends already set in motion. Many of its members were to make further substantial contributions toward their fulfillment and realization.

Let us take a closer look at this process. For the sake of convenience, the major areas of land reform can be broken down into a fourfold classification (the dates given represent the passage of significant legislation): (1) the provision of secure rights to tenant farmers *(retssikerhed* and *fæstelovgivningen:* 1787), (2) the liberation of the tenant farmer from forced residence on the estate of birth *(stavnsbaandetsløsning:* 1788), (3) the formalization and control of the forced work requirement *(hoveriets bestemmelse:* 1769, 1791, 1799), and (4) the fundamental reorganization of agricultural land use and residence patterns *(udskiftningslovgivningen:* 1758, 1776, 1781). These were the major land reforms, and even merely to list them suggests the wide area of their sweep and scope. How, one asks, did all this happen?

Christian Ditlev Reventlow and
the Major Agricultural Commission (1786)

Although developments leading toward its establishment can be traced back to the 1750s, a large share of credit for the passage of the major reforms must be attributed to the work of a single committee, the Major Commission on Agriculture and Rural Land Use *(Den Store Landbokommission)*. Hereafter referred to as the Major Agricultural Commission, this body was established by royal decree on 25 August 1786. Its leader was Christian Ditlev Reventlow (1748–1827), a remarkably unconventional estate owner who remained throughout his life a clever, committed, and farsighted champion of the interests of the Danish tenant farmers. His life experience had prepared him well for this task. As an estate owner, he was well acquainted with the practical details of tenancy and its effects on the tenant farmers. As a member of the social class of estate owners, he was also familiar with both the opposition to reform that would most likely be expressed and the political strategies that would be most effective in circumventing them.

The background to the establishment of the Major Agricultural Commission is not without interest. In 1784, the same shift that brought A. P. Bernstorff back to power soon resulted in the appointment of Christian Reventlow to the position of first deputy (later president) of the *Rentekammer*, a governmental body controlling many of the affairs of agriculture. At thirty-six Reventlow was already a committed believer in agricultural reform. Yet there is little reason to believe that he had a fixed plan to guide him in accomplishing this objective. Furthermore, as later events were to show, he was as much a cautious reformer as a bold revolutionary. Indeed, he could be very much the patient and pragmatic diplomat when he thought that this strategy would best advance his cause.

Upon accepting the appointment as first deputy in 1784, Reventlow steeled himself to a long, slow course of development. A single, much-heralded conversation was soon to change his view of things. It was occasioned, surprisingly enough, by the action of a chief bailiff from Jutland, one Jens Biering, who had asked the Rentekammer in 1783 to provide an independent adjustor to estimate the worth of a deceased farmer's estate. As we have seen, the estimates given by the proprietor's agents were frequently unfair, amounting to little more than statements of debt against the deceased farmer's heirs. Biering's complaint drew attention to this sensitive and embarrassing situation. Although a number of reform actions had already been taken, the issue raised here was potential political dynamite. Its astounding implications were that the chamber would now begin to tamper with what had long been an unquestioned and taken-for-granted right of

Reventlow's main residence was Christianssæde on the island of Lolland, but he preferred his second and more modest estate, Pederstrup, shown here. Pederstrup is the site of the Reventlow Museum today (photographed from an aquarelle by Fr. Richardt, 1845, Reventlow Museum, reprinted by permission of Ole Koch Jensen).

estate proprietors. Reventlow's initial strategy was guarded and conservative. He asked for judicial opinions on the part of two leading lawyers, Oluf L. Bang and Christian Colbjørnsen. In January and March 1785, respectively, these advocates took positions strongly supporting the right of the tenant farmer to protection from this kind of misuse.

It was early in the summer of 1786 when Reventlow first announced these results in a meeting with the eighteen-year-old crown prince, later King Frederic VI. He spoke also of the more general situation, of the difficulties and obstacles faced by the tenant farmers, and of the need to make changes to ensure the general welfare. Unsure of what sort of response to expect, he could not have been more astonished by what was forthcoming. After listening with undivided attention and concentration, the crown prince reacted more strongly than Reventlow in his wildest dreams would have expected.[31] "It seems to me," replied the crown prince, "that in such an important matter, on which the welfare of the country depends, one shouldn't let a single day be lost. Can't we just as well take hold of it tomorrow as the day after tomorrow?"

Wildly elated by this conversation, Reventlow lost no time in bringing the good news to his friend and colleague A. P. Bernstorff (1735–97),

Christian Ditlev Reventlow together with his wife, eight children, and the children's
nursemaid (photographed from a sketch to a painting by Nicolaus Wolff, 1790, Reventlow
Museum, reprinted by permission of Ole Koch Jensen).

who for twenty years had been an open proponent of reform. "I see here a
wink from the Providence that watches over Denmark, " Bernstorff is
reputed to have said. "I would perhaps have been in doubt over whether it
would be best to wait a few years, but when the prince himself is so decided,
then we have permission to hope for the best." In early July 1786 the
conception of a new royal commission was emerging, one that would
reconsider in its entirety the relationship between tenant farmers and estate
proprietors.

Reventlow was so moved in the meantime that he fired off an extraordinary letter on July 14 to his married sister Louise Stolberg, with whom
he shared an enthusiasm for the cause of liberation and reform.[32] This letter
is a revealing one. It is a marvelous statement of his innermost thoughts and
feelings, constituting in effect a private forum in which he allowed himself
to mix fantasy with aspiration, dream with purpose, and anger with vision.
With only the barest minimum of poetic license, one can hear in it faint
echoes of contemporary figures from a faraway landscape, of the sentiments
that were even then being expressed by such men as Thomas Jefferson, Tom

Paine, James Madison, and later Abraham Lincoln. Without any exaggeration, it stands as one of the most moving documents of the period:

> Joyous and grateful to God, I am writing you these lines quickly. No, my Wife has not delivered, hasn't given birth to a Son, it's not that. She will probably give birth in about 14 days, but now a thousand Sons are born to me, a thousand Daughters, all with large and beautiful homes. Boldly they look over to that Land where once their ancestors were persecuted, with joy they drive the well-fed Horses before the light Plow to Work, and sing a little verse on the golden Warrior [i.e., Reventlow himself], who came out of his hole like a monster to battle against the dwarfs who held them bound. But for those who are made happy by Peace's message, by Freedom's message, a messenger of God's Blessing has come. There lies the old rubbish: the Chains, the Yoke, the Dog's Hole, the long Whip, the Wooden Horse, the Spanish Cape, away are they. Hurra, Hurra, Hurra, shout, scream it aloud toward me, so that our voices can blend together. . . . Hurra, there lies that rubbish, under His Feet it lies.[33] I have torn it apart with my hands, my feet and my teeth, I will burn it and cast the ash into the sea, to sink down to the earth's innards. The newspapers, the pamphlets, all who meet you on the streets, can tell you what has happened, what kind of man Christian the Smith has become. . . . For me neither body nor soul shall rest before all the work is completed, before the temple of bondage has been broken down and the temple of freedom built up.[34]

The use of the term "Christian the Smith" refers to Reventlow's free-time occupation as a metal-worker on his estate. When I first read these marvelous words in the 1988 exhibit commemorating the two hundredth anniversary of the Land Reforms, I assumed that they had been written after the smoke had cleared on the field of battle. I was surprised to learn later that they were written only as Reventlow was preparing to make his own entrance onto that field. What seems to have happened is that an initially careful and diplomatic movement in the direction of reform was transformed into a passionate calling once he had reason to believe that the crown prince would fully support his actions. The fact that even a proud and fiercely independent man like Reventlow could be so heavily influenced by a few spoken words on the part of the crown prince of Denmark underscores the enormous power of the absolute monarchy at that time (an authority that would itself be called into question and then peacefully surrendered some fifty years later).

Still, even if Reventlow had been guilty of celebrating his victory in advance, the unfolding pattern of events soon began to confirm his hopes and predictions. Immediately after his conversation with the crown prince, even before writing his letter to Louise Stolberg, he had submitted for royal consideration a detailed outline of the important points that he felt should be taken up by a new agricultural commission. Just six weeks later, on the 25th of August, the commission was established. Given the title of *Den Store Landbokommission* (the Major Commission on Agriculture and Rural Land Use), it was destined to play a major role in the enactment of the land reforms that were even then waiting in the wings. One thing clearly in its favor was a stacked deck. Reventlow, who had been instrumental in appointing the committee members, saw to it that the majority of the sixteen members initially appointed were sympathetic in various degrees to the prospect of agricultural reform. But such sentiments were not unanimous, and at least three of the initial members were strong and outspoken opponents of reform.

The names of two of its members, Oluf Bang and Christian Colbjørnsen, are already familiar to us. Let us recall that Reventlow had asked for their opinions in the case, initiated by Jens Biering, that dealt with the right of the tenant farmer to an independent evaluation of the farm's value upon his death. Their opinions in this case, whose disposition was instrumental in leading to the Commission's formation, give particular insight into the frame of mind of reform advocates at that time. The narrow question here was how to provide an independent evaluation of the worth of the deceased tenant farmer's estate. It can be seen to turn on the conflict of interest between, on the one side, the prospective new tenant and the estate proprietor (whose interests would be served by a *low* evaluation of the estate's worth) and, on the other, the heirs of the deceased tenant farmer (whose interests would be served by a *high* evaluation). What is most impressive about Bang's evaluation is his insistence on going beyond the formal question of providing on paper a legal remedy that sounds good but is actually unenforceable. In focusing attention on what has been called "the informal level of operation" of the system, Bang shows himself to be an excellent sociologist as well as a good lawyer. Witness his shrewd insight into the problem of choosing an assessor to evaluate the condition of the deceased farmer's estate:

> That the deceased's estate chooses one property assessor, and the proprietor a second, seems to me to be much better, and would be the best way, *when there is no cause to fear that this choice will degenerate and fall back into the proprietor's hands* [italics added]. There is now such cause, [because] a poor man has no friends at all, and a poor tenant farmer's widow and heirs even less, they are dispirited. When the proprietor's agent suggests to the widow and heirs a property assessor, they will not dare to refuse to hire him. If they choose one themselves, he will not dare go against the finding of the proprietor's agent and *his* assessor. Let the widow and heirs go so far as to find a firm man, when he disagrees with the proprietor's assessor, what will the

result be? Even if both parties each choose their own man, the result will be the same.[35]

Not content to limit his discussion to the particular topic at hand, Bang concludes with an eloquent critique that takes into account the characterological implications of the system under which the Danish tenant farmer was forced to live. In modern terms, he speaks to the critical issue of motivation and psychological incentive:

> Where this exists, the Farmer *(Bonden)* is utterly oppressed, [and] an oppressed man can neither desire nor act well; the concern that all Created Beings have for their deeds, which is their own welfare, is lacking in him. He may do as he will, he sees nothing other than Poverty and Oppression; he may finally stop wanting his own Best [interests]; because he sees that he can't attain it. This despair is the first thought that each upcoming generation drinks in. It sets roots, propagates itself, and becomes a source of corruption to entire generations. . . . I find this mode of treatment both completely destructive and completely unjust.[36]

Bang's colleague, the highly regarded Norwegian-born jurist Christian Colbjørnsen (1749–1814), is one of the most interesting figures of the time. Colbjørnsen was a gifted and brilliant advocate whose views on land reform placed him at least three degrees to the left even of Reventlow. The relationship between Colbjørnsen and Reventlow is complex. They were not always in agreement, with Reventlow on many occasions taking an intermediate position on pragmatic and political grounds. Colbjørnsen held extreme views on virtually all the questions touched by the Commission and often defended them with a rhetoric in which moderation and conciliation were conspicuous by their absence. He asked for no quarter and gave none. Nevertheless, it was impossible not to respect his intelligence and ability, and it is probably in recognition of this that Reventlow appointed him as secretary of the Commission. Throughout Colbjørnsen's written opinions, one finds a consistently expressed point of view based on his belief that the interests of the weak must be protected against those of the strong. The following statement—concerning tenant farmer's inheritance rights—quite clearly shows the thrust of his thought:

> The existence of the tenant farmers is all too insecure. . . . Even though they may be fortunate enough to have the best masters, they must yet always live in uncertainty about their own and their children's future fate when the estate comes into the hands of another owner. The tenant farmer's rights should therefore be decided by a law. This law, which shall protect a poorer class against a mightier, must therefore be given such strength and constancy,

that neither the might of the one nor the weakness of the other will be able to shake it, or hinder its serious enforcement.[37]

Although the Major Agricultural Commission *(Den Store Landbokommission)* had a majority that favored reform, a diverse spectrum of views existed among them about just what form its enactment should take. Not all of them were as passionate as Colbjørnsen, willing to act as quickly or go as far. The Commission included Reventlow's brother Ludwig, as well as a long-time friend and fellow reformer, the Sjælland estate owner Vilhelm August Hansen. The latter was known for a motto unusual in that day and age, namely that he did not want his tenant farmers to be treated differently than he himself would have wanted to be treated if he were a tenant farmer.[38] The Commission's membership also included at least two or three determined opponents of reform, such as the baron Poul A. Lehn and advocate Morten Qvistgaard. In order to gain insight into what the coming passage of the land reforms meant, it is important to sample the kinds of views found on both sides.

What kinds of arguments did those who were opposed to land reform typically offer? Given their general views and philosophy, it is not surprising that they refused in some cases even to consider its possibility. Thus in one case (admittedly some twenty years before the establishment of the Major Agricultural Commission), four estate owners in West Jutland had responded in these terms to a request for information sent out by regional authorities: "It is not possible, that *Hoveriet* [mandatory work donated to the estate] can be *in any way* [italics added] abolished, narrowed, regulated or set on another footing than it now is, without our becoming very aggrieved."[39]

As was the case with the proponents of reform, however, diverse opinions could be found together with a variety of arguments offered to support them. Writing in 1768, the estate owner H. Rosenkrantz admitted at least implicitly that reforms were possible. He then argued against them on the following grounds:

> Whether the tenant farmers *(Bonde-Standen)* are being aided or helped, when they are offered freedom in their young years to go from one estate to another against parents' and friends' advice and will, and whether that will not be the cause of animosity between neighbors, misunderstanding between parents and children, and a loss for the tenant farmer. . . . I cannot do otherwise than fear that such freedom will be misused.[40]

The paternalism expressed here by Rosenkrantz reflects a belief found among many estate owners at the time, namely that tenant farmers, like little children, could not be trusted to handle the freedom that might result from a change in their condition.[41] Another estate owner, writing anonymously in 1769, took a different tack, citing international developments. After admitting that the life of the tenant farmers was a difficult one ("his work is hard and continuous, his expenses almost always greater than his income"), he went on to argue that reform would nonetheless be harmful and a disservice to the national interest:

> There is good reason to fear that when the tenant farmer's children are no longer bound to the estate, that most of them—to the great loss and disadvantage of the country—will leave behind the field of agriculture. They will choose an easier but less useful occupation, or allow themselves to be talked into traveling to England and Holland, where serving folk and especially seamen's salaries are much higher than in Denmark. Holland is sending each year thousands of foreigners to the East Indies, collected from Germany, Norway, Holsten, Jutland and other places in the hope of making a large profit, and of these not one of a hundred returns to Europe or to the land of his fathers.[42]

These developments must be put into a larger European perspective. Beginning about 1750, there was a general rise in prices within the Western world economy. The industrialization and rapid population growth that accompanied it were seen, perhaps most spectacularly, in neighboring England. Once a major exporter of grains, England was transformed into a large grain importer whose voracious appetite provided an important new market for Danish grain products. Back on the Danish countryside, the belief in a quickly expanding export market for agricultural products led to a rise in the speculative purchase of estates and, not surprisingly, to pressures for increased agricultural production, especially on those estates just purchased.

The existence of this new market and its opportunities for increased profit did not benefit the tenant farmers. Indeed, the only immediate consequence for them was a greater instability, reflected primarily in the increased mandatory work donations to the fields of the estate (*hoveri*). The estate owners who could sell their best grain to England at a higher price were also able to continue sending the lower-quality crop to Norway (which was obliged through the terms of an agreement signed in 1735 to purchase all of its foreign grain from Denmark). Driven by the new possibilities of expanding markets and higher profits, the estate owners weren't going to let the complaints made by a bunch of lazy tenant farmers stand in their way. What resulted was the seemingly paradoxical situation that has been neatly summarized by Vibæk: "The closer one comes in time to the land reforms—but of course one didn't know it in advance—the heavier the burdens of the tenant farmer weighed."[43]

The destructive nature of these trends, clearly reflected in the literature of the time, suggests that the long dominant system of feudal relations had already entered a downward spiral of crisis-driven, potentially revolutionary social change. A high-ranking regional official *(amtmand)* writing in 1768 makes the comment that *"Hoveriet* in Denmark has finally become so exorbitant, that in some places it can be regarded as the yoke of slavery, since soon nothing on the estate can be done without the tenant farmer's help, even the smallest matters which do not directly concern him, such as bringing fuel and water to the kitchen, washing and slaughtering, transport to the mill, handling the bullocks and clipping the sheep."[44] The constantly increasing demands for donated work had become so burdensome that one group of farmers took the unprecedented step of taking a collective written complaint to the king:

> We must not alone thresh the grain that he grows on his own fields, but also all the other tithe-grain it pleases him to buy. If we don't want to do the threshing ourselves, then we must at great cost to ourselves send another out to do it. He takes from us the best servants, young men and young women, and if we ask him whether we can hold them in our service, he sets us up to ride the Wooden Horse or lets us be whipped or beaten as long as he wants. We must dig his gardens, cut his firewood, guard his sheep and pigs, clean his cowbarn, take care of his geese, and prepare his rubbish. If we dare to complain about his hard and evil treatment, that we can't get our own grain harvested, that it lies on the field and goes bad, then he answers only, "I don't care whether you get your grain into your houses or not, as long as you take care of the head corn [i.e., his own, the estate's]. . . ." When he understood that we will travel to Copenhagen to seek a remedy for his evil treatment of us, then he said, "When you Satan's peasants *(bønder)* get it into your minds to seek the King, then it is going to be a great catastrophe for us proprietors."[45]

Upon viewing the petition, this estate owner's response is to contemptuously dismiss it. He addresses none of the specific issues raised by the farmers, preferring instead to attribute all of their problems to their own "bad character" (this type of pathological communication, with its use of the defense mechanisms of discounting and denial, is all too familiar to therapists treating disturbed families).[46] What, one must ask, would it have been like to live as a tenant on this estate?

> These peasants are not good at being satisfied. They are unable to judge whether their situation is good or not. It's just enough for them, that they

mustn't be master of themselves, and can do and act as they please and as they have long been accustomed to, and as their nature dictates. That, which they will endeavour to do to the point of their own ruin, is games, drink, foolishness and feasts, which last from the beginning of the year until its end. And all this we have to tolerate, if we will be secure in life.[47]

The Land Reform Process

Having sampled some contributions to the debate that took place prior to the establishment of the Major Agricultural Commission *(Den Store Landbokommission)* in the summer of 1786, we are now ready to examine its operation and some of its accomplishments.[48] Once Reventlow and Bernstorff became aware that they could count on a high degree of royal support, matters proceeded with amazing speed. Their first task was to prepare significant legislation that would protect the security of the landed peasant farmer through legal clarification of his rights and duties. Its writing took less than a year, and the resulting document *(Forordningen om bondens rettigheder og pligter)* was completed in late May 1787. It was signed into law by King Christian VII on 7 June 1787. Its first two provisions, cited below in their entirety, provided direct and workable solutions to the thorny problem of inheritance. Old injustices were to be abolished and new freedoms put in their place:

> 1. Every estate owner, who leases out a farm, shall be required to supply written notification about the condition of its buildings, livestock and farm implements, through a lawful and orderly agent. Upon the loss of the tenancy through death or departure this agent shall investigate the condition of the property received by him, so that any rise or fall of its value can be determined.
> 2. If an estate owner fails to present a new tenant with this information in written form at the outset of his tenancy, he will be denied the right to demand compensation for any loss of value from the tenant farmer or from his heirs. Nor will he be allowed to force the farmer to leave the farm on the grounds that the buildings and livestock have not been properly cared for.[49]

This piece of landmark legislation went on to provide additional protections for the tenant farmer. If an estate owner felt he had grounds to remove a tenant from the land, it could no longer be done in the old arbitrary manner. The new legislation specified the forms of due process that were now legally binding on all parties (but primarily affected estate owners). First, the agent responsible for the initial evaluation could no longer be the proprietor's own bailiff; it had to be "an independent and experienced man, from a different estate." Second, to ensure that this took place, a high-ranking regional official *(amtmand)* was required to arrange free and independent legal assistance for the tenant farmer during the course of the entire proceedings. Third, if an estate owner acted on his own, ignoring due process, "he shall therefore be recognized and punished." If, for instance, an owner wanted to eject a tenant before the judgment had finally been reached, "it shall be his duty to pay the tenant's rent either on the estate or at some other place, until the matter has been rightly judged." Fourth, judges presiding over the disposition of these cases were specifically instructed "to see that the deceased tenant farmer's widow and children are not cheated [lit. "offended"], in spite of the fact that they themselves, through ignorance, might have neglected to take advantage of their rights." No longer could estate owners conveniently cut corners in the exercise of their authority.

The final paragraph of the legislation appears at first to be a masterful attempt at reconciliation. It begins with a call for balance: "Just as We on the one hand will protect the tenant farmers in their rights, those which are suited to their circumstances, so will We on the other side maintain estate owners in that authority which suits their condition." Yet its very last sentence grants the tenant farmers still another critical area of freedom: "The way of proceeding known from the old times, and still used by estate owners or their agents—that on their own authority they let the tenant farmers be punished by use of the Wooden Horse, the iron collar, the so-called prison in the hole, and the like—shall be completely forbidden."

The dreamlike prophecy about the abolition of these ancient instruments of torture that Reventlow had made only a year before in the jubilant letter to his sister was now to be realized. It would soon become enshrined in both the letter and spirit of the law. Yet this 1787 Ordinance of Rights and Duties (much of which is generally thought to be the work of Colbjørnsen) was in Reventlow's mind only the beginning.[50] He now began looking at *stavnsbaandet,* probably the central institution of the feudal system because it kept the tenant farmers physically and symbolically bound to the estate.

Reventlow's first success had only increased his determination and his sense of urgency. Tenant farmers, in his view, were still second-class citizens and would remain so as long as they were bound by law to the estate for the most productive years of their lives. After the initial meetings of the Commission, it was clear that reforms were going to be made. But Reventlow knew that when this issue was brought up for consideration, he would be met with fierce and determined opposition. The custom of binding peasants to the estate was at the heart of the existing system of property relations, and it was connected as well to the potentially incendiary issue of military service. Far-reaching as the 1787 Ordinance of Rights and Duties had been, even greater passions were aroused by the debate that was soon to take place over the abolition of *stavnsbaandet.*

In recognition of this problem, Reventlow made a preliminary proposal on 24 October 1786. His plan was to enlarge the selection districts and give the young farmers free movement within each district. Soldiers would be chosen not on the basis of crop size but of population, "since experience shows, that the number of men in relation to the crop size on the estates is quite unequal."[51] This would have led to the interesting but inequitable result that on some estates many work-competent but surplus unmarried young workers would have escaped army service, while on others it would become necessary to send everyone available, including married landless tenants *(husmænd)* and the only sons of older landed tenants *(bønder),* workers one would prefer to keep home.

Reventlow's proposal was quickly ridiculed by his political opponents. Baron P. A. Lehn, a Commission member who was one of the principal opponents of land reform, remarked scornfully, "There could hardly be imagined a better way of murdering all personal industry and decreasing the numbers of the general population than this one of tearing my own people out of my hands . . . the population can be increased, but not by taking my best people from me, in order to reward those that should be punished, and to punish those that should be rewarded."[52] Another member of the Commission, estate owner Morten Qvistgaard from West Jutland, even went as far as to directly address Christian Colbjørnsen in his written reply:

> But yet another question, and one of great significance: when everyone, after Hr. Colbjørnsen's suggestion, has permission to leave the estate or the place of their birth if they so desire, is that same proprietor obligated to keep on his estate all of the crippled, the old, the poor and the weak, who were born or have lived there? . . . I believe, after all natural right and economy, that the estate owner must have the power to say that "I will not have" those who are not fit to work, or earn their food, or pay their rent and taxes, or where now is all this wretchedness leading us?[53]

Colbjørnsen's characteristically acerbic response was not long in coming: "The class of tenant farmers has received its verdict as written by the hand of Herr Justice Counselor Qvistgaard. The Danish farmer shall remain bound to the estate *(stavnsbunden)* until the day of his death. After that time the learned Justice Counselor will make no further demands on him; he has, as a consequence, the freedom to allow himself to be buried outside of the estate, as long as he can prove that he is really dead."[54] In a report made public on 6 January 1787, Colbjørnsen expressed strong support for

Reventlow's ideas, and in at least one of his suggestions for the coming legislation he spoke directly and more seriously to Qvistgaard's arguments: "Those who really are found to be crippled or disabled, must, while still in their young years, be given certificates of release from military service attesting to this. They should receive as well training in craft-skills in the provincial towns, so that they can live without being a burden to the general public."[55]

Several additional political obstacles had to be overcome before the debate could be concluded. J. O. Schack-Rathlou, one of the government's most influential men, issued early in 1788 an angry pronouncement predicting that the proposed legislation would lead to financial ruin. Then a furious exchange took place between Colbjørnsen and another set of adversaries, in this case the military authorities. A brief selection from Colbjørnsen's reply is sufficient to convey its spirit: "At first glance, I was taken aback, when I saw the Fatherland described as being on the brink of a precipice. Mistrust of my own reasoning power and high regard for the Royal Council of Generals *{det Kgl. Generalitets-Collegium}* (whose collective wisdom, certainly in the area of agriculture, cannot be doubted, because the half part of its members are reputedly estate proprietors) made me sure in the first moment that my thesis about tenant farmers' freedom held nothing other than mistakes. But on more sober consideration, some thoughts occurred to me. . . . The other members of the commission, who are all known for their Knowledge, Experience and Love of country, can it be possible that all of them have allowed themselves to be influenced to make so remarkable a mistake in a matter that is this well known to them, and that directly touches the majority of them as owners of estates?"[56]

When the dust settled, Crown Prince Frederic together with A. P. Bernstorff had engineered the approval of King Christian VII for an "Ordinance for the Loosening of *Stavnsbaandet*" (*Forordning om Stavnsbaandets-løsning*). The document was prepared and signed into law on 20 June 1788. Its opening sentence stated that

> *Stavnsbaandet* to the estates shall be completely abolished from the first of January, in the year 1800, so that all of the tenant farmers (*Bondestanden*) in Denmark . . . shall from the aforesaid time have freedom to live in the Land Militia's prescribed districts [where they have been registered] until they have received from the board either a rejection or a free pass. After this, they are allowed to settle and seek sustenance anywhere in the Kingdom.[57]

The loosening of *stavnsbaandet* is probably the best known and the most celebrated of the Danish land reforms. In retrospect, however, the ordinance seems in many ways a quite moderate piece of legislation. What it proposed was a gradual loosening, first for those under fourteen years of age, next for those over thirty-six, and then for those who had served as soldiers. All others would be bound still another twelve years until the year 1800. This procedure allowed people to stay with the old system for at least a little while longer. In addition, it gave everyone on both sides some chance to work out strategic accommodations to the new situation as it evolved. Moreover, when one examines the original legislation, one is struck by the extent to which it emphasizes that the loosening of the feudal bond must be ordered so as to protect the vested interests of the military. After the initial programmatic statement quoted above, each of its first thirty-two clauses specifies how military conscription is to be conducted in the new situation.

It is true that some passages do contain what appears to be a remarkable new flexibility toward tenant farmers. One of them, for instance, states that "when a young member of the tenant farmer condition can prove with a trustworthy statement of witness from public teachers that he has made progress in his studies and provided evidence of his ability and industry, he should not be conscripted to soldier status." Yet the weight of military service is quite clearly to fall on certain shoulders and not on others. Even the language of the ordinance quoted above, which speaks of the landed tenant farmers *(Bondestanden)* and not of their landless counterparts *(Husmænd)*, makes it clear that the existing social stratification in the peasant community is not to be tampered with. Skrubbeltrang has remarked that the resulting liberation was "an encouragement to prospective agricultural investors in the provincial towns, to industrious lessees and tenant farmers together with the sons of prosperous farmers."[58]

It was not an encouragement to the entire agricultural community. The heritage of social stratification that remains is considerable. The children of the nobility, of public officials, and of all large landowners (even if they do not belong to the nobility) were exempted from military service. In these as in its other provisions a serious attempt was being made to protect the traditional privileges of estate owners and to reconcile them with the newly legislated freedoms of their tenant farmers. But as one might have predicted, the passage of this ordinance loosening the feudal bond was not received by the dissident estate owners in any generous spirit of compromise. Schack-Rathlou and one other member went so far as to resign from the Commission in protest after it had been passed.

Yet in spite of the very real limitations of this document there is another and equally valid sense in which the legislation it introduced must be seen as nothing less than a breathtaking accomplishment. Its superficial moderation masks truly radical consequences. Keep in mind what is happening here: a four-hundred-year-old system is being peacefully legislated out of existence. No longer will a tenant farmer and his family belong to the estate to be counted among the estate owner's property as a disposable item of inventory. No longer will an estate owner be able to coerce a farmer into tenancy by threatening him with conscription into military service. In the long run, its consequences went even further than any of these partial effects: it was instrumental in giving rise to a whole new class in Danish society, the self-owning farmers. (We shall meet them in the next chapter's description of the founding of the folk high schools.)

After passing this crucial piece of legislation, the Commission did something very Danish indeed. Instead of rushing blindly ahead, it took a two-year "tea pause" to take a look at what had happened. Between June 1788 and the beginning of 1790, it began to look at the question of donated work on the estates, the next question to be taken up. In the meantime, there was a major protest in the summer of 1790 against the previous land reform enactments, and a petition signed by 103 landowners from Jutland was presented to the crown prince. The petition made reference to fears of "general suppression, an attack on our rights, which are grounded in law, and the violation of our freedom, which with time will make us breadless, lead to a general disturbance, bring the country near to its demise, and make our descendants unhappy."[59] The series of incidents connected with the presentation of this petition must be recorded, both because this was the last significant act of protest by the nobility against the passage of the land reform acts and because the events themselves provide a certain measure of comic relief.

Due to an inexplicable and unfortunate sense of timing, the petition, most unconvincingly camouflaged as "an Expression of Confidence," was presented to Crown Prince Frederic in the high summer of 1790 just after the happy occasion of his marriage to Princess Marie of Hessen. Thinking it best to present the document in person, the plotters decided to send a deputation to Slesvig where the crown prince was honeymooning with his new bride. (For insurance they simultaneously presented a written letter of complaint, in German, to the crown prince's stepfather, Karl of Hessen.) Understandably less than delighted to receive this unusual wedding card, the crown prince took the expedient step of immediately handing the petition over to the Commission. The Commission passed it on in turn to Colbjørnsen. In the ensuing battle, Colbjørnsen proved to be more than a match for the petition's authors. It helped that he was able to obtain the crown prince's permission to publish the petition together with his own comments, which he did in a pamphlet available to the general public. A brief sample follows:

Is it Nero, Caligula or Tiberius, or merely the government of Christian VII we find described here? . . . It can hardly have been said with more precision, that the King has behaved in a tyrannical fashion, and that the men who have counseled and advised the legislators have been the hand-maidens of injustice and suppression. . . . Does one dare to say about Denmark's Fatherly Regent, that he mounts violence and suppression against the laws of the land, and through this the demise of the country and the unhappiness of our descendants?[60]

The significance of the last sentence is that it shows Colbjørnsen as one who was not above making veiled threats. To a knowledgeable contemporary the implications would have been obvious: the nobles' statement was not only misguided but bordered on actual insult to the royal authority. It could thus (admittedly by stretching a point) even be construed as treason. By the standards of the time, this was really playing hardball.

Upon publication of the petition a succession of additional events transpired, all of which worked to Colbjørnsen's advantage. One of the signatories claimed never to have signed the petition or, for that matter, even to have seen it; the incorrectly represented estate owner provided Colbjørnsen with a letter testifying to this state of affairs. Further investigation revealed that thirty-three of the signatories fell (or allegedly fell) into this category. The entire affair soon devolved into a sustained and ferocious legal feud between Colbjørnsen and the main author of the petition, Tønne Lüttichau. Lüttichau was a former army officer who through marriage and the purchase of a title had attained estate-owner status. He was by no means uneducated. He had studied at Göttingen, and, as if that were not enough, he also held a doctorate in jurisprudence from Oxford. Nevertheless, he came out second best in this encounter. Under the conditions of the royal decision on the matter that was finally announced in the summer of 1791, he was obliged to return both his title and the symbolic key that went along with it. In the accompanying private injury case against Colbjørnsen, he was also adjudged the loser and had to pay a fine of 1,000 *rigsdaler* to the Church of Our Savior in Copenhagen. The rear-guard action of a group of landowners against the passage of land reforms had failed abysmally, and it was clear that the reform process would continue.

The Commission now began to move forward on the troublesome issue of the donated work requirements (*hoveri*). An attempt at earlier reform, made in 1769, had not been able to settle the question to anyone's satisfaction. The need to take action on this question became even more acute in 1790, a year of marked unrest and a sharp rise in tenant farmer complaints. Some of them engaged in work slowdowns; others even went on strike. Settling this issue was not to be an easy task. An "Ordinance on Good Order in *Hoveri*" was passed on 25 March 1791, and a "Public Notice on Voluntary *Hoveri* Associations" on 24 June in the same year. These were followed by a "Government's Reluctant Finding" in August 1793 and the formation in 1795 of local commissions to deal with the problem. It was not until 6 December 1799 that a more or less conclusive "Ordinance on the Definition of *Hoveri*" could be set forth.

As the listing of these piecemeal and partial actions suggests, the question of donated labor proved to be more difficult and intractable than any of the other issues dealt with by the Major Agricultural Commission. Members of the Commission and other governmental representatives traveled up and down the land in these years, attempting to negotiate both with the tenant farmers and with estate owners. The estate owners were not the sole cause of the Commission's obstacles. Even as loyal a friend as Reventlow was heard to complain on occasion that the farmers were stubborn and intractable. As de Tocqueville was later to write: "Patiently endured so long as it seemed beyond redress, a grievance comes to appear intolerable once the possibility of removing it crosses men's minds."[61] Further movement and conflict would continue over the course of the next fifty years. Nevertheless, by the year 1800 even this troublesome issue had, for all practical purposes, received *some* degree of resolution. What once had been arbitrarily enforced by the estate owner was now formalized into the giving of specific and clear amounts of donated work or to the payment of specific amounts of money in its stead.[62]

The discussion to this point has focused on three critical areas of land reform: (1) the provision of secure rights to the tenant farmers (1787), (2) the loosening and eventual abolition of the law that bound them to the estates (1788), and (3) the establishment of limits and formal controls over the amount of work they were required to perform in the estate owner's sphere of interest (1799). We have seen how these three critical kinds of land reform were carried through between 1784 and 1799 by the Major Agricultural Commission, guided by Christian Ditlev Reventlow as its executive head. Another vital area of land reform had already been enacted in 1781, three years before the system shift that brought A. P. Bernstorff back to power and five years before the formation of the Major Agricultural Commission. It entailed the conversion of the multiple, separate, and often far distant strips of land for which each tenant farmer was responsible into a single collected parcel for each farm on the estate *(udskiftning)*. Once these collected parcels had been allotted, it was in many cases more convenient for a farmer to move out of the peasant village and build a new house on his own piece of land *(udflyttning)*. The following, taken from an actual case history for the town of Fjellerup in Jutland, illustrates the degree of social cooperation that was required for such a far-reaching transition to take place peacefully:

> The biggest change in the daily life of the tenant farmers was without a doubt the reorganization of holdings *(udskiftningen)* that took place in 1794, when the centuries-old peasant village community was broken up. From this time on Fjellerup's *bønder* and some of its *husmænd* held their land in individual parcels, which they could in reality cultivate as they wished without regard to their neighbors. *In 1794 all the land still belonged to the estate-owner at Østergaard, Ivar Ammitzboll, and it was also on his initiative that the reorganization was begun* [italics added].
>
> On the morning of August 22, 1794 a meeting was held on the estate. Present were the leading officials of the regional agricultural commission, all tenant farmers *(bønder)*, the priest, the parish clerk and of course the estate owner. All of them together studied the map which land inspector Krag had surveyed, and on which he had drawn up a plan for reorganization of their holdings. It was a very complicated matter. All wanted to remain in the village close to the church, and above all, no one wanted to live up in the sandy and storm-blown hills.
>
> The agricultural commission understood this well, and suggested a solution, in which seven farms together with the rectory could remain in the village and have their fields connected to their farm houses. The cost was, however, that they received parcels that were a good hundred meters broad and almost two kilometers in length. These "lucky" farmers, who escaped having to move out, would in the coming years have to do an enormous amount of work building fences and digging ditches along these long parcels.
>
> Five farms had to move up into the hills. In order to compensate them for the poorer quality soil they received extra big parcels, which still required a large effort in order to produce a reasonable yield. Every farm received as well a plot of meadow on the coast and a piece of heath land. . . . When none of those present protested, the plan was officially approved by the regional agricultural commission.[63]

This new arrangement had many implications for change. For one thing, it was now much easier for a knowledgeable farmer to introduce new techniques on his own fields. He no longer had to consult first with and then to convince the others in the peasant village. The ancient custom was that the landed farmers of the village met in a council *(bystæv)* that discussed common affairs and reached decisions (the landless farmers, or *husmænd*, were excluded from its meetings). The members of the council would decide, for instance, when to begin planting. Such collaboration was necessary because their fields lay intermingled in such a way that an individual farmer could hardly begin without some cooperation from his neighbors. Now, for better or for worse, the farmer was on his own. New systems of cultivation with different and more productive methods of shifting among fields were introduced. New crops, such as potatoes and clover, became a familiar part of the landscape. Further experiments could be carried out with gardens and fruit trees, with new kinds of tools, and with irrigation.

There was, however, a dark side to this new freedom. When a farmer moved out of the peasant village onto his own plot of land, both he and his family were more alone than ever before. Now the nearest neighbor could be many kilometers away. No longer could his wife expect to pursue a sociable chat with friends by the mere act of stepping outside her own front door. Peter Michelsen has written that "the fellowship that surrounded the old village council faded away, to be gradually replaced in the course of the nineteenth century by new forms of fellowship in communal work and later in the cooperative movement."[64] But the old and secure fellowship of the traditional peasant village was lost to them and would never be seen again. Its place was being taken by a new era of individualism and modernization.

IV. CONCLUDING REFLECTIONS

Any discussion of these land reforms must go beyond the particular areas of Danish life they affected. Their enactment both set in motion and was itself affected by a series of related developments. A new and more efficient swing-plough greatly aided productivity, increasing efficiency while reducing labor costs (although its first use in Denmark was in 1821, experiments with new kinds of ploughs had begun as early as 1770).[65] The formation of a state-operated credit institution (Kreditkassen) in 1786 offered cheap loans that were instrumental in helping newly liberated tenant farmers to purchase their land (this policy facilitated the rise of a new class of self-owning farmers). A new law for assistance to the poor (1803) required that each district support those living within it who needed assistance. A forestry ordinance (fredskovforordningen, 1805) began to give protection to the badly depleted Danish forests. Another development of great significance was a new school law (1814) that made education compulsory for those between seven and fourteen years of age.[66] These are some of the remarkable developments that accompanied the major land reforms or came soon after them. Taken together, they suggest the extent of the cultural revitalization that was taking place during this time.

How, one asks, did all of this happen? It was unquestionably facilitated by the continued existence of favorable economic conditions over a long period. A new era of European commerce ushered in a general prosperity beginning roughly in the 1750s: in the period 1788–1805 alone, increased demand raised the prices of grain 50%, those of butter and meat 35–40%.[67] These circumstances created a new situation in which the removal of inefficient feudal constraints on the tenant farmers and their agricultural production could benefit not only the farmers but the Danish economy as a whole (including, of course, the estate-owner class).

It is not enough, however, to show that these new possibilities existed; to explain the land reforms on this basis would be to reduce complex issues of history, culture, and personality to a simplistic techno-environmental determinism. Even presupposing the "objective" existence of these possibilities, the "subjectivity" of the Danish ruling aristocracy could equally well have led its members to attempt to preserve all of their privileges, regardless of the violence and conflict that this suppression might have caused. Indeed, this behavior is far more usual on the part of dominant groups who see their ascendancy and privileges being called into question. One has also to explain how a sufficient number of estate owners and members of the Danish aristocratic elite came first to have eyes to see that these new possibilities existed and second to have the determination to ensure that they would be realized. How is it possible to explain the existence of a Reventlow, a Colbjørnsen, and a Bernstorff?

We must remember that Denmark did not exist in isolation and that Europe in the last half of the eighteenth century was influenced by a range of new ideas. Jean Jacques Rousseau's romantic conception of nature made many of the European elite turn with naive, enthusiastic admiration to the life of the peasants around them. Rationalistic philosophies of the Enlightenment suggested that the proper use of logic and reason could lead to unlimited possibilities of human perfectibility and improvement. Adam Smith's *The Wealth of Nations* was influencing many with its new views on the social and economic importance of free enterprise. The estate-owning class in Denmark was very much a part of these and other trends of the time. As one Danish commentator has expressed it:

> The European literature of the Enlightenment, with its mixture of philosophy, careful social debate and practical instructions about agricultural techniques could be read by the educated upper class, as well as a priest here and there. It was decisive that enlightened and reform-minded men came to power at a point in time where a comparatively large number of the powerful and landholding class could gradually come to see that there were advantages in introducing certain changes. It has often been maintained, that these changes happened here in Denmark in a peaceful way, just before they were the cause of bloody revolution in other places.[68]

These observations do tell us something, but in my judgment much has been left unexplained. *Yes,* it is true that the Danish upper class was influenced by all of the European trends connected with the Enlightenment. *Yes,* it is also true that the changes happened without bloody revolution in Denmark. But to make these points in no way provides an explanation of *why* these changes were able to occur without bloodshed in Denmark. After all, the European elite in other countries were reading much of the same literature and debating the same issues. Why, then, did the resolution of these matters take the non-violent and cooperative course they did in Denmark? Instead of submitting a silly petition with 103 names, why didn't Lüttichau, a former military man, try to organize a palace revolt? Why didn't any other members of the about-to-be-slightly-disenfranchised nobility resort to violent measures during this period? And, to view the matter from the other side, why was it that Lüttichau's little rebellion was penalized, not by the loss of his head but by the loss of his title (and the symbolic key that accompanied it)?

I would like to suggest that even though we have considered some of the myriad details of the Danish Land Reforms and described the process of cultural revitalization with which they are connected, we are still faced with the same abominable mystery, the same unsolved historical dilemma, that was stated in the first chapter. The inquiry, far from being settled, must be continued (I will argue in coming chapters that a resolution of these issues turns on an understanding of Danish national character).

Let us conclude this chapter by reflecting momentarily on Crown Prince Frederic VI and on Christian Ditlev Reventlow. Reventlow's role in the land reform process has been discussed in some detail. But he was in addition intimately connected with two of the above-cited developments: the establishment of state-operated credit institutions (beginning with the *Kreditkassen* in 1786), which offered advantageous loans to tenant farmers, and the passage of the forest protection ordinance of 1805. It is worth mentioning that at that time Danish forests were among the poorest and least cared for in Europe. Reventlow's legislation provided for the fencing, care, and gradual increase of the state-owned forests. Under its provisions new owners had to wait ten years before cutting commercial timber from their land, and a variety of measures ensured that the existing forest areas would be maintained and protected.[69] His written dissertation on forest management, which was not published until 1879, establishes him as one of the major figures in Danish forestry.[70] It is a further tribute to him that his early forestry legislation (*fredskovforordningen*, 1805) required no revision until 1935 and that even the newer legislation continued to rely on many of his original principles.[71]

In 1804, after the successful passage of all of the major land reforms, Reventlow could write with satisfaction the following wonderful words: "God has blessed everything on my estate, the schools, the farmers, the forests, the poor-law authorities and my income."[72] As for the crown prince, later to be king of Denmark, the Danish historian Claus Bjørn has written that "when in 1839 farmers from Sjælland bore the coffin of King Frederic VI to the grave, it was a sincere expression of the gratitude that was deeply felt among the farming community toward that monarch who, when young, 'had loosened the farmer's chains.'"[73] Only five years later a new heritage of the Land Reforms would appear: the first Danish folk high school opened its doors to the children of the farmers.

EXCURSUS FOUR

In the Aftermath of Catastrophe

RURAL DENMARK IN 1830

The course of history is rarely smooth and linear. It would be pleasant to report that immediately after the passage of the Land Reforms the rural landscape was set free and the goals of the Major Agricultural Commission accomplished. Unfortunately, this was not what happened. International developments soon halted all internal progressive change. There was even regression on several fronts for the first three decades of the new century. Let us briefly visit the scene.

An educated foreigner traveling through the Danish countryside in the year 1830 would have been struck by a number of things. First, he would most likely have been surprised to find that he was not the only one of his class making such a journey, for in these years the life of the Danish farmer was being observed, investigated, and recorded by significant numbers of home-grown experts, among them priests, schoolteachers, and a variety of rural officials. Second, if his journey had taken him through the rural areas of Sjælland, Fyn, and Jutland, he probably would have been surprised at the extent of regional and local variation in style and quality of life. On Sjælland, for instance, the land reforms had changed only the face of rural life. When many farmers moved out on their own single parcel of land, it had effectively ended the community of the old peasant villages. Yet in other ways things seemed hardly to have changed at all. Even though the farmer no longer lived in the old peasant village, it was perhaps symbolic that the new house built on his own land resembled the old one both in exterior design and interior decoration. Moreover, four out of every five Sjælland farmers still cultivated the ground in the traditional medieval

way, using the clumsy and outmoded wheel-plough so heavy
that five or six horses were needed to pull it along.

The middle island of Fyn appeared to be quite different.
With its order, cleanliness, and prosperity, Fyn impressed many
travelers as a large and beautiful garden. "The villages and
farmhouses," wrote author H. C. Andersen in 1836, "appear
more prosperous than in Sjælland, where a house seen from the
road often resembles a heap of fertilizer raised up on four posts.
From a country road on the island of Fyn, you see only clean
houses."[1] Andersen, of course, was a resident of Fyn and might
have been showing a little hometown favoritism. Yet when one
looks at his description of Jutland, one has to admit that he could
transcend his provincial sentiments at least long enough to
recognize the unique features of the other regions of Denmark:

> The peninsula of Jutland possesses not only the same
> beauties of nature that Sjælland and Fyn offer—wonderful beech
> forests and fragrant fields of clover close to the salt sea—but it
> has also a wild and desolate nature in the heather-covered moor
> and wide expanses of marshland. There are no fences here to show
> the boundaries of property. . . . The land's west coast stands
> without trees and without bushes, only with white sand dunes
> by the storming sea that whips the dead, sorrowful coast with
> flying sand and sharp winds.[2]

These features rendered much of the windswept peninsula
of Jutland bleak and almost uninhabitable. Although some of
the farmland in East Jutland was of excellent quality, the heath
country found in much of West Jutland made the practice of
agriculture difficult and onerous in those places. Author and
priest Steen Steensen Blicher wrote in 1839 of Viborg in mid-
Jutland, "It is sorrowful to see the farmers here scrape the
surrounding sand banks to press out of the earth a few years of
starvation-level subsistence, and at the same time let these
magnificent bogs remain as playgrounds for the gray hens and
ravens."[3] Moving south, one would find that the territory belonging to Denmark extended far into present-day Germany, all
the way down to the cities of Lübeck and Hamburg in southern

Holsten. The provinces of Slesvig and Holsten were included within the Danish monarchy, the Slesvig city of Flensborg second in size only to Copenhagen among Danish seaports.

If our hypothetical foreign observer knew much about agriculture, he would not have been very impressed with the degree of modernization achieved by Danish farmers. In Jutland, the new land allotments had been made in such a way that they were nearly as confusing as the old ones with their dozens of separate holdings. Most farmers refrained from planting potatoes in the mistaken belief that cultivating them would harm the soil. It was a common sight to see sheep and pigs wandering on planted land. The harvested grains were not cleaned or dried properly. The stalls of the domestic animals were often in terrible condition, without air or light. And a closer look would show that the apparent prosperity of the farmers on Fyn, testified to by no less an authority than H. C. Andersen, was deceptive. Most estates still demanded burdensome donations of work and the self-owned farms remained in the minority. Furthermore, it was a common complaint among the authors of the time that the prevailing looseness of morals was greatest of all on the island of Fyn. As evidence the critics could point to the fact that an estimated one out of every seven births was illegitimate; this was the highest count in all of Denmark.[4]

The situation on Sjælland was equally depressing. Although the Land Reforms had created a new framework, the dreams of progress envisioned by the reformers thirty years earlier had not been realized. On this question all of those who looked at the Danish farmer during the 1820s were in agreement. The worst of it was that the farmer was not willing to read and study, lacked respect for science, and was not receptive to new ideas. He could in no sense be regarded as an educated person. The following words must be taken with a grain of salt because they come from a critic of the farming class. Yet this judgment of district bailiff Niels Blume, made shortly after 1830, is little more than a crude restatement of what many observers of the time saw: "The farmers' present position on the path of knowledge is so low, his thinking ability so restricted, his circle of vision so narrow and mixed with prejudice, his morality and religion so weak, that it will be necessary for a whole generation to go before he can appear among cultivated people with the authentic stamp of enlightenment."[5]

What had happened to the proud promise of the Land Reforms? The transition to self-ownership that was its spearhead had proceeded quickly during the two decades after the passage of legislation gradually dissolving the feudal bond *(stavnsbaandetsløsning,* 1788). It had gone so quickly that by the year 1807 the astounding figure of 60% of Danish *bønder* now lived on self-owned farms.[6] By the same year 75% percent of the farms on Fyn and Sjælland had been moved out of the old peasant villages *(udskiftning);* the figure for Jutland was 50%.[7] This rapid transformation was suddenly brought to a screeching halt.

It was Denmark's misguided entrance into the Napoleonic wars that had put a quick stop to these progressive developments. No longer guided by the diplomatic vision of the Bernstorffs, the monarchy, unable to avoid being caught up in the deadly enmity between England and France, allowed itself to be drawn into the general European war. It was a policy that soon had disastrous consequences. In August 1807 an English fleet with thirty thousand men bombarded Copenhagen for three days until the military authorities were finally forced to surrender. When the English forces sailed home a few weeks later, they took the Danish fleet with them. The events that followed this defeat were to mark an end to Denmark's time as a power of any real significance in Europe. The Congress of Vienna, which was held shortly after the Napoleonic wars came to an end, reached its unpleasant decisions about Denmark in the spring of 1815.

When these rulings were announced, it was a final staggering blow to Danish pride. In actual fact the real damage had already been done when the peace was made at Kiel on 14 January 1814. King Frederic VI had been forced to surrender Norway to the Swedish king and Helgoland to England (and the few small concessions that he received were no consolation for the loss of Norway). But the final terms to be given to Denmark were not yet clear. To make matters even worse, the Danish delegation to the Vienna Congress was kept waiting with evasions and half-promises for nearly six months while the decisions were being reached. An expansionist Sweden was not satisfied with what it had been given and wanted more.[8] The Danish diplomats believed that Russian and English strategic interests would be better served by the maintenance of a stable balance in northern Europe than by the creation of a Swedish superpower. Yet throughout this long waiting period (during which King Frederic VI tried unsuccessfully to win the czar to the Danish cause), they could not be certain that the Russians and the English would see it the same way. In the end the great powers, especially England, did support Denmark's existence on pragmatic grounds; it would be in their interests to preserve the existence of an independent state at the entrance to the Baltic Sea. Nevertheless, the mood of humiliation and despair that accompanied these events was so great that, as Vagn Skovgaard-Petersen writes, there was "a widespread doubt about whether the great powers would allow the continued existence of the Danish monarchy at all."[9]

This international debacle would have both immediate and long-term effects on the Danish nation. The series of domestic financial catastrophes that accompanied these events created a severe and long-lasting crisis in the economy. An unparalleled inflation rate appeared, causing prices to rise so sharply from 1807 to 1813 that the unit of currency declined to less than 10% of its original worth. This unpleasant development was followed by the specter of a state bankruptcy in 1813. As a result of this general crisis, the progressive developments being implemented in the wake of the land reforms were not only halted but for several decades went in reverse. These events make it clear why a foreign observer journeying through rural Denmark in 1830 would have seen conditions so discordant with the fulfillment of Reventlow's hopes.

Yet the movement begun under Reventlow and the other members of the Major Agricultural Commission had not come to an end. It was to begin again in earnest in the years after 1830. The statistics of increasing self-ownership, which can be taken as a critical measure of rural modernization, reflect these later developments. By 1850, self-ownership accounted for 67% of the land in agricultural use. In the year 1860 the percentage of self-owned land would rise to 76%; in 1873 it would reach 83%. By 1905, fully 94% of all land in agricultural production was self-owned.[10] It was only six years later that H. Rider Haggard would visit Denmark and make his observations on the success of the cooperative movement and the folk high schools.

THE PREDICAMENT OF THE RURAL UNDERCLASS

After 1830, a long and stable period of expansion and consolidation lay ahead for most members of the agricultural community. Having made this generalization, it is necessary to limit it in two ways. First, the expansion and consolidation that would be experienced by *some* farmers was not to be experienced by *all* of them. In order to understand the quality of rural life at that time, we must recall the critical distinction between the landed farmers (*bønder,* or members of the landed *gaardmænd* class) and those who were landless (the *husmænd,* singular: *husmand*).[11] Some landed farmers still held their land by contract from an estate, but many owned it themselves by this time (*selveje,* an increasingly common arrangement after the land reforms).[12] Palle Ove Christensen has written that "the reform laws were advantageous for the *gaardmænd* class, but for the *husmænd* group they were the beginning of the later, so utterly hopeless conditions."[13] How did this situation come about?

Whether members of the landless rural underclass lived in a house belonging to an estate owner or to a landed farmer, the tendency was for them to be even more exploited *after* the Land Reforms. The estate owners were limited by law in their power to press the landed farmers into donated labor on their fields. In order to recover what they had lost, they increased the burden that fell on the *husmænd.* They demanded higher payments of taxes, rent, and labor (this was even true for those members of the rural underclass who had signed leases for life). Moreover, it became a common practice to break up a large holding formerly given to a landed farmer into smaller parcels for a different class of *husmænd.* Many of this new class of *husmænd* did not obtain lifelong rights to the newly created parcel; they were treated as

mere renters, who could be evicted with no more than a three-
to six-month term of notice. In addition, they were forced to pay
for their small, rented holdings with greatly increased amounts
of donated work on the estate fields. At the same time, the
independent landed farmers, with their altered patterns of residence, ownership, and cultivation, developed a need for extra
labor in short and intensive periods during the agricultural
season. The *husmænd* came thus to function as an agricultural
underclass, as a deprived rural proletariat who existed under
conditions now increasingly set by the estate owners *and* the
landed farmers.

Thus the unfortunate side effect of the Land Reforms was
that they further weakened the position of the *husmænd*. One fact
in itself underlines the partial and incomplete nature of the
reforms: the 1787 legislation forbidding the use of torture
applied only to the landed farmers, to the *fæstebonde* and his wife.
The *husmand* and members of his family could still be subjected
to physical punishment and even to torture well into the second
half of the nineteenth century.[14] Even though it could be forbidden by the estate owner, it was a common practice for both
landed farmers and *husmænd* to rent out rooms. An even more
marginal group within the latter category consisted of the
servants or day laborers likely to rent such a room. This group
(*tyendehusmænd*) constituted a third grouping within the agricultural underclass. Beginning about 1850, it became increasingly common for estate owners to build separate houses for
married and steadily employed servants; often as many as eight
families would live together in a single house.[15] Thus the
husmænd group itself could be divided into three classes: those
with a lifelong contract (*fæstehusmænd*), the new class of renters
(*lejehusmænd*), and those who were servants (*tyendehusmænd*).

The dynamics of the situation are clearly shown by demographic developments. In 1700 there were nearly three times as
many landed tenants as those without land. When the major
Land Reforms were beginning to take effect a century later in
1800, there were about 60,000 *husmænd* and 55,000 *gaardmænd*
in Denmark, as well as 15,000 day laborers and servants. This
pattern of unequal growth rates was to continue, the numbers

of the landless underclass growing much faster than any other group in rural Denmark in the course of the nineteenth century. In the hundred-year period between 1785 and 1885, the number of *husmænd* actually tripled. If one takes the period of time from the Land Reforms until 1905, the landed tenants increased their numbers from 60,000 to 75,000, the *husmænd* from 60,000 to 213,000.[16] Thus the proportion of the population represented by the landless underclass grew enormously during the nineteenth century.

The significance of this deep status split within the agricultural community can only be appreciated when one remembers that the makeup of the Danish population throughout the nineteenth century was overwhelmingly rural. In the year 1800, 80% of the Danish population was part of this rural landscape, but even a half century later, in 1850, the rural sector constituted 80% of the total population. As late as 1870, the rural population accounted for 75% of the total, and even by 1901 the figure had only dropped to 61%.[17]

Who were these *husmænd?* They were the poor and forgotten members of the rural community. They were the ones who could be seen working their own small plots of land on Sundays. They were the ones whose children worked long hours. Both they and their children could be subjected to brutality in the service of the estate. Men and women in their class would often end their days in the poorhouse, separated even though they had been married for a lifetime. Powerful and charismatic reformers were to speak for them in the years to come, but the movement that would most effectively argue their cause was not to become really active until the first years of the present century.

THE CHALLENGE TO THE MONARCHY

The existence of a significant agricultural underclass provides one exception to the generalization that expansion and prosperity lay ahead for the Danish farmer in 1830. A second set of obstacles was connected to a fast-approaching pattern of historical events that would soon utterly transform a two-centu-

ries-old political system. Recall the somber mood that characterized the observations from about 1830. "A lazy, sluggish and
disconnected people" was the evaluation of Denmark given by
an advocate from Slesvig-Holsten as late as 1848.[18] A visitor
from Sweden remarked in 1825 that "the character of the Danish
people was weak; its body full of marrow but without bone, its
soul without strength or spirit." The Swedish visitor believed
that the most important reason for this condition was the
shocking lack of political freedom he had witnessed. Fridlev
Skrubbeltrang comments that "the absolute monarchy was in
ethical terms a depressing social phenomenon. It created the
conception of an infallible authority on Protestant religious
grounds."[19] Roar Skovmand speaks also to this point:

> In spite of the attractive air of integrity that characterized
> Frederic VI's conduct and way of thinking through and through,
> he lived in his later years in a delusion that bordered on a living
> lie. The truth, which he himself never was to recognize, was this:
> that the absolute monarchy, which in crown prince Frederic's
> younger days had been "enlightened," was now exhausted and
> impoverished. In the 1780s crown prince Frederic had his share
> of the honor for the fact that Denmark was in the vanguard of
> progress in Europe. As an old king he had to share responsibility
> for the fact that Denmark had become a backward land.[20]

In 1830, remembering the role that King Frederic VI had
played in their liberation some four decades ago, the landed
farmers were still positive about the authority of the absolute
monarchy. Yet coming events would soon shake their confidence
in this institution. Change was in the air, and storm clouds
brewing. The mood of the times is captured in these lines from
a letter written by a young university student to his brother in
the Christmas of 1840:

> We live in the most important time that Denmark has
> experienced since the Reformation. There has not been this
> much movement for three centuries. People against the King,
> Slesvigholsteners, Holstenlaueners, Scandinavians, Friends of
> the Monarchy, French-minded, Nordic-minded, liberals, royal-

ists, church conservatives and advocates of freedom, all standing against each other. No other land of Denmark's size would be likely to show so many sharp antagonisms.[21]

One of those in Denmark who was making his own judgment about these years was N. F. S. Grundtvig, who held in 1838 a series of lectures entitled *Mands Minde* (Man's Memory). In these lectures Grundtvig spoke of the period after 1814 as the trough of a wave, where "Denmark bowed under and sank down into a ten years time so deep in destitution and despondency, so deep in powerlessness and indifference, that I cannot think myself back to the years between 1820 and 1830 without feeling a certain horror."[22] It is to the part Grundtvig himself was to play in these events that we now turn.

CHAPTER FIVE

The Rise of the Danish Folk High Schools

I. THE LIFE AND WORK OF N. F. S. GRUNDTVIG (1782–1873)

A Biographical Sketch

URING THE YEAR 1983, the two hundredth anniversary of Grundtvig's birth was celebrated in Denmark. There was a veritable outpouring of books, articles, lectures, seminars, and public meetings, as well as numerous radio and television discussion programs. A week of consecutive articles dealing with Grundtvig appeared in the prestigious "Chronicle" section of a major newspaper (including one by Grundtvig himself never previously published). The title of the series, accompanied by a memorable picture of the white-bearded patriarch, was "Two Hundred Years Young." Other pictures of Grundtvig at all stages of his life could be seen in each and every corner of the land: in bookshops, schools, and public places. Connections were explored between Grundtvig and Marx, between Grundtvig and Christianity, between Grundtvig and the world crisis.[1] Speaking in practical terms, it was quite impossible for anyone not to know that this was the two hundredth-year celebration of Grundtvig's birth.

What accounts for the way in which this man is remembered? As Paul Hammerich points out, he never became an export-ware as did his younger contemporaries H. C. Andersen and Søren Kierkegaard.[2] Nor is it true that the words he wrote come quickly to the minds of all Danish citizens. One young commentator straightforwardly confesses, "Like all others I sing Grundtvig's hymns when it is Christmas, have *heard* about his work, and have a suspicion of its importance. But at the same time I have no real knowledge of it."[3] Another of a slightly older vintage writes, "Even I, of course, learned Grundtvig's hymns by heart in school in the 1950s, but they didn't say anything at all, either to me or to my urban middle class and cement worker class school comrades in Gl. Lindholm north of Aalborg."[4] Yet it is often said by these same Danes of Grundtvig, "You meet him at the border."[5] Who was this man, and why is his life so important for an understanding of Danish history?

Nikolaj Frederik Severin Grundtvig was the youngest son of the local minister in the small town of Udby in south Sjælland. He was born in 1783 into a family with a long history of religious involvement at a time when the philosophy of the Enlightenment permeated both the church and secular society. His mother tutored him at home, just as she had done with his four siblings. He was a slow starter, but came soon to read voraciously in the thick volumes of church history and the history of Denmark that would be found in a priest's home or in the nearby parish house. He learned from the adults around him, from the heated discussions of contemporary events that took place among the parish's guests, and from the songs, stories, and legends recounted by an old crippled woman, Malene Jensdatter, who after the custom of the time had found refuge in the parish house. The deep impression she gave him of the songs and myths of Sjælland may have had something to do with Grundtvig's later extraordinary sensitivity both to the beauty of the Danish language and to the spiritual quality that he saw lying latent in the common people.[6]

Grundtvig was accepted to the Aarhus Latin School in 1798, and after passing his student examinations he began to study theology at the University of Copenhagen in 1800. He passed his major university examination in 1803 but did not appear to have been engaged or truly excited by his studies. Hal Koch, one of his biographers, characterized him at this time: "If one reads Grundtvig's notes from the student years, one gets the impression of an awkward and clumsy student from the rural hinterlands, who to a high degree felt that he was burdened by his circumstances. Flight over existence and air under the wings, there isn't much of that."[7] There was still little evidence of the outstanding contributions that were to come.

In 1805 he traveled to the island of Langeland to live at the estate Egelykke and serve as tutor to the family's son. The twenty-two-year-old Grundtvig received at this point one of the shocks that life can give suddenly and without warning. He fell deeply in love with his employer's wife and pupil's mother, Constance Leth. As he wrote in his diary, "I came here. I read in this fair woman's eyes, and what were all the world's books against that?"[8] In the pain and confusion that followed, one thing became clear to him: his own view of human existence had been a narrow and impoverished one. Without knowing it Grundtvig had been a good and unquestioning eighteenth-century rationalist, a believer that reason was sufficient in all things. Now the unendurable tension between his days in her presence and his nights alone was forcing him to see that "the well-read apostle of reason, who thought he had control over his existence, didn't have any control over anything."9 He began to read the works of Steffans, Goethe, Schelling, and Fichte, and of other figures in the emerging romantic tradition. Throwing away his older, unexamined convictions, he began what was to be a series of movements in and through nearly all of the major intellectual and spiritual trends of his time, a restless, unceasing development that was to last for the rest of his life.

A voluminous writer who penned by hand, he left behind a collection of letters, diaries, and entire finished books, which if published would comprise more than 120 volumes. It is for this reason that his positions and changes of position are quite well known. For the same reason, one can sometimes cite him quite correctly in support of opposing sides on the same issue. He was skeptical about the introduction of democratic government in 1849, yet one of its glowing defenders when it was threatened by the forces of reaction in 1866.10 He was a radical hater of privilege who on many occasions sounded like a bastion of proper conservatism. When he had formulated his revolutionary conception of a new kind of school, the first thing he did was ask for the help of the *Danish king* in getting it started! Perhaps strangest of all, as Niels Højlund has pointed out, is the fact that he filled all of these dozens of thick bound volumes with written words in order to convey the essential message that printed words are dead and that it is only the spoken word *(det levende ord)* that is truly alive. As if in silent testament to the truth of his own insight, the theological and historical volumes are written in an archaic and convoluted prose that is difficult to understand and even more difficult to translate. Yet many of his poems, written for the quite astounding number of hymns that are still today sung everywhere in Denmark, seem to have been written by quite another hand. Their clarity, freshness, and insight are as perennial as the summer flowers that bloom in the Danish countryside.

His personal energy was monumental and bordered at times on the superhuman; he paid a psychological and emotional price for it in the form of several nervous breakdowns during the course of his life. The following description of him in the 1830s, however, is not without its amusing side:

> It has been calculated that in the course of a single year he wrote on the average one hymn a day. . . . He permitted himself only the barest minimum of necessary rest. When he was once at a baptism in Sorø and needed to remain overnight, Frau Hauch asked, "Pastor Grundtvig, do you sleep with a feather quilt or a blanket?" Grundtvig became quiet and self-conscious. Then Ingemann gave Mrs. Hauch a nudge, pulled her to the side, and whispered "But my dear Frau Hauch, how could you have asked

Grundtvig that question. Don't you know that he never goes to bed?" It was only those closest to him who were allowed to know that he remained sitting in his horse-hair sofa all night long and worked. When he was tired, he screwed the petroleum lamp down a little and dozed—but after a few hours he would turn the lamp up again.[11]

There is neither time nor space here to go into all the twistings and turnings of his life's development. He went, for instance, through his Nordic mythology period, in which, after rejecting his earlier rational view of life, he looked back in time to the heroes of the old Norse myths to find deeper meanings that could light up the darkness of the present (his *Nordic Mythology* was published in 1832). This led him to a concern with what he called "universal history," which he saw not as a series of unrelated and fortuitous contingencies but as guided by divine agency. A famous passage provides insight into his views:

> Humanity is not a kind of monkey, condemned to imitate first the other animals and then itself until the world's end, but a matchless, miraculous creation, in whom divine forces shall proclaim, develop and survive through a thousand races and generations, a divine experiment that shows how spirit and dust can interpenetrate and be explained in a common divine consciousness.[12]

What were some of the major biographical events taking place in Grundtvig's poststudent life? He was called back to his father's parsonage in Udby in 1810, and it was there that he became engaged to his first wife, Lise Blicher, in 1811, but upon his father's death in 1813 he was drawn back to Copenhagen.[13] In 1815 he experienced the first of many episodes of self-doubt, and it brought him to lay down his priest's robe and immerse himself in philosophy. He started a magazine *(Dannevirke)*, which he edited from 1816 to 1819; its philosophical articles were supplemented by poems and translations of old texts. It consists of four volumes, each about four hundred pages. Because he received no other contributions, the first two volumes were written in their entirety by Grundtvig himself.[14] In 1818 he received a grant from the Crown to help with his translation of the ancient chronicles; this modest windfall made it possible for him to conclude his seven-year engagement to Lise with a marriage ceremony.

One of the consistent threads in Grundtvig's development is outspoken radical critique of those who he believed held mistaken views on major questions. Back in 1810 he had given for his trial sermon a talk entitled "How Has the Lord's Word Vanished From His House," attacking what he saw as the ignorance of contemporary priests about the real meaning of Jesus' preaching. When he overplayed his hand by having it published, six

Copenhagen priests complained, and Grundtvig received an official reprimand from the university. He became a marked man in the eyes of powerful
Copenhagen church figures, which probably explains why he was unable to
take over his father's position in Udby in 1813. Subsequent inquiries after
a priest's position in the next seven years were to prove equally fruitless. It
was not until 1822 that he was able to find a good position, that of curate
in the Church of Our Savior in Copenhagen. But his jousting and ferocious
temperament were soon to cost him dearly; it was a position that he would
occupy for less than four years.

When the noted theologian Professor H. N. Clausen came out in 1826
with his "Church Doctrine, Teaching and Ritual in Catholicism and Prot-
estantism," a large and learned work on the meaning of ritual in Christian
thought, Grundtvig was enraged.[15] Less than two weeks later his reply was
ready, a forty-seven-page pamphlet immodestly entitled, "The Church's
Reply to Professor of Theology Dr. H. N. Clausen by Nik. Fred. Sev.
Grundtvig, Curate of the Church of Our Savior."[16] Not only did he identify
himself with the church (a contention that must have infuriated his theological opponent), but he went on to accuse the learned professor of teaching
and spreading false doctrines. Clausen, he said, must either publicly acknowledge his error and repent or else resign from office.

Instead of the lively public debate he had anticipated, Grundtvig
found himself dragged into court and sued for personal injury. What is more,
in the ensuing legal battle, Grundtvig was decisively defeated. Even before
the case was decided, he was forbidden by church authorities to preach at
the Pinse holiday and to use the three hymns he had written specially for
that occasion. He had to use the existing hymn book; in addition, it was
specified that the occasion was not to be marred by any preaching on
Grundtvig's part. When attempted negotiations with the provost and the
bishop failed, Grundtvig took a course of action that went against all the
warnings he had received from friends. He gave up his position just before
Pinse in 1826. A half year later in October, he lost the case in the courts.
His expressions against the professor were found to be baseless and offensive.
He was ordered to pay all court costs plus a large sum of money (1,000
rigsdaler) as a fine. Perhaps most significantly, he was set under official
censure. From then on nothing of his could be published before a stamp
from the police chief reading "May Be Printed" had been conspicuously
placed on the title page.

Grundtvig was not to be freed from censorship until eleven years later
in 1837. It wasn't until 1839 that he was given another ministry, in Vartov
in Copenhagen. But no one could have known this at the time. These events
of 1826 left a man apparently on the way to becoming an outcast, one whose

Grundtvig in 1820. Painting by C. F. Christensen (from Thaning, N. F. S. Grundtvig, 1972: 25, reprinted by permission of Gyldendal).

future looked dim and obscure. He was forty-three years old at the time and a family man whose oldest child was just four years old. He had given up a secure position to return to the independent writer's uncertain existence, though now he lived under the added disadvantage that everything he wrote had to be cleared first with the police censor. Yet the public humiliation, censure, and poverty that followed these events did not end his fame but marked its beginning. In the eleven years that he was under censorship, he continued to travel, write, and preach. His fame began to spread, and it was not long after that the expression Grundtvigianer ("follower of Grundtvig") began to be heard. Perhaps the final judgment to remember is that of history. His hymns, once banned, now fill the pages of the church hymnal and the Folk High School Songbook. Although few other than Grundtvig scholars and historians of theology are familiar with the name H. N. Clausen, everyone in Denmark knows about Grundtvig. He is admired and respected even by people who have never read a single word he wrote.

Returning to Grundtvig's situation after censure, he was once again helped by an act of royal dispensation. During an audience with King Frederic VI in 1828, the king asked him in a friendly way, "What are you doing now?" (*Hvad bestiller De nu?*) Grundtvig, who was never at a loss for words, replied, "Nothing, Your Majesty, and I don't know of anything to do at the moment, unless it could please Your Majesty to let me travel to England and make a closer examination of the Anglo-Saxon manuscripts. They are an important source of information about Denmark's ancient history, but have been completely neglected in their place of origin."[17] Just as Reventlow's casual conversation with Frederic VI forty years earlier had expedited the passage of the Land Reforms, this exchange between Frederic VI and Grundtvig was to have a major consequence: they would set in motion a series of events that led to the founding of the Danish folk high schools.

Grundtvig's Views on Education

With royal support Grundtvig was able to travel to England in the summer of 1829. He made two additional voyages in 1830 and 1831 and spent the total of a year's time busy with his studies in the English libraries. His scholarly contribution to the knowledge of these ancient manuscripts was to be considerable, but something that was to prove of equal importance was his encounter with English society. To put this into perspective, we must recall that the years of the immediate past (1814–30) had been crisis years

Grundtvig in 1831. Painting by C. A. Jensen (from Thaning, N. F. S. Grundtvig, 1972: 65, reprinted by permission of Gyldendal).

in the Danish society, years pervaded by a sense of stagnation and retreat. Grundtvig's encounter with the developments in England was to be a source of great inspiration in his life and work. He was not unaware of the negative side of industrialization, of the exploited workers who were treated as mere extensions of the machines they tended, of the factories that the poet and engraver William Blake described as "dark, satanic mills." He saw the evil as well as the good that accompanied the industrial revolution. Yet he was, in spite of himself, greatly impressed by the signs of enterprise and energy that were to be seen everywhere. They presented a striking contrast to the static life that he knew in Copenhagen, a life where people's concerns were limited to "cooking and pastimes." All of the people in England "from the ministers to the pickpockets" appeared equally busy. The manifestations of the English public spirit, which ranged from the debates in the House of Commons to the impassioned orators of Hyde Park, he found enormously impressive. "What do you do?" everyone asked him, and it was a question no one would have asked back in Copenhagen. Fourteen years later, back in Denmark, he recalled his embarrassment on being asked this question:

> In a country where a great deal is always being done [i.e., England], of which a certain amount is wrong, not infrequently very wrong indeed, yet also a fair amount that is good, and not infrequently astonishingly good, there, where you are asked what you do at home, having to answer "Nothing!" is not so easy, and I wriggled like an eel to avoid having to make this answer. . . . But no matter how I twisted and turned, this Englishman continued to stick to his point, an old habit of the English, and the more I found to criticize in English activities, the more persistently did he ask me, "Well, what do *you* do then?" That confounded "What do *you* do?" is something I shall never forget if I live to be a hundred![18]

Grundtvig's cross-cultural experience was illuminating in many areas, but perhaps most of all in the field of education. His own education proceeded apace during his visits: he was continually frustrated, surprised, and delighted with the skepticism the cheeky English displayed toward even his most cherished ideas. Whenever he raised objections "on the basis of what I had learned as a child" or argued that circumstances in England were "contrary to advanced theories," the English would always coolly reply: "Well, it seems to work quite well." Grundtvig then found himself forced to consider the proposition that there might be something wrong with the theory he had learned. Perhaps his most decisive experiences came as the result of a two-week visit to Trinity College, Cambridge, in the summer of 1831. He encountered there an educational system different from any he had ever known, one where conversation between student and teacher was the dominating theme. The teachers lived at the college, and it was the custom for students and teachers to take their meals together. Grundtvig saw that the dialogue between them was open ended, continuous, and intense. When he returned to Denmark after his third voyage to England in 1831, he was on the verge of some momentous personal insights and discoveries. Let us briefly outline some of the ideas that came in these and later years to mark Grundtvig's mature thought.

Kaj Thaning has written that "1832 marked his conversion to 'life'— immediate, real, human life. He said himself that it had dawned on him 'as if by a miracle.'"[19] The English experience seems to have served as a catalyst through which the decades of searching and sifting through the Christian tradition culminated in what could be called a "peak experience" (he was about fifty at this time). The first tenet of Grundtvig's new enlightenment can be summarized in the expression "the living word" *(det levende ord)*. Down through all the ages of history, it was the words that men actually spoke, the words that came from their lips, that had revealed and constituted the essence of their being. Without this spoken word, there could be no life. He saw himself as having been a "book worshipper" in the past, as having lived too much of his life inside the yellowing and withered pages of a book. Yet books had to be regarded now as secondary. His new revelation demanded an emergence from the frozen darkness of print into the bright sun of the living word. This new doctrine for schooling and education would have profound implications.

Another critical tenet of Grundtvig's new faith was the idea of Enlightenment for Life *(livsoplysning)*. What he meant by this was that an understanding of the real and deepest truths that constitute Enlightenment never comes from rote study of classroom texts. One can learn the facts and theories of received tradition in the classroom, and these might prove useful, but they can be no substitute for Life's Enlightenment, which can only be taught by life itself. Herein lies a paradox for educators: it is and must be the deepest task of our lives to acquire this Enlightenment for Life, for only through its realization will we be able to distinguish light from darkness, truth from lies, and the cause of death from that of life. Yet this liberating insight is something that no schoolroom lesson will ever teach us.

A third and related concept is that of the People's Enlightenment *(folkeoplysning)*. Due to the depth of Grundtvig's commitment to all things Danish, it is easy to see why some foreign authors have mistakenly labeled his views as chauvinistic. Yet his lifelong work as a universal historian, which culminated in an immense three-volume treatise on the history of mankind, was not written from the point of view of a narrow nationalism. He was convinced that each people, each tribe, each nation on earth had a valuable

Grundtvig in maturity, 1844. Drawing by J. Vilh. Gertner (from Grundtvig og Danmark, *1983, reprinted by permission of the Nationalhistorisk Museum, Frederiksborg Castle).*

role to play in the unfolding of world history. This unfolding was taking place in its own time and its own way in accordance with God's plan of creation. Grundtvig had a high degree of respect and admiration for the other cultural traditions of the world and looked down his nose at none of them. There is love for Denmark in his writings, but nothing at all about Danish superiority to the other peoples of the globe. Nor is there a belief that *all* grass roots movements were necessarily good or right (a naive position that has been attributed to him by several foreign observers).

There is thus a dual thrust to his concept of *folkeoplysning*. On the one hand, it argues that all humans everywhere are born into a particular *folkelig* and historical context, and it is within this framework that their own personal drama of Enlightenment must be played out. Hanne Severinsen writes that "for Grundtvig it was a fundamental condition of human life, that it unfolds itself in a definite people, who have their own character created through history."[20] On the other hand, it suggests that there is a collective as well as an individual aspect to the experience of Enlightenment, and that it must be the goal of a society to create, through wise and farsighted policies, the conditions that will facilitate *folkeoplysning,* the People's Enlightenment.

A fourth of Grundtvig's key ideas, the notion of *vekselvirkning,* speaks to the question of how to create the preconditions for this enlightenment within society. After a good deal of thought, I would suggest the following translation: "a balance between two things that remain different, but that should fertilize each other in their differentness." Grundtvig was only too aware of the tendency for both the people within a society and the different social institutions to attempt to dominate and control each other. Between state and army, church and state, state and school, each is always attempting to take over the other and create a situation where the power flows in only one direction. The same can often be observed in the classroom, where the teacher attempts to dominate the students in order to fill them with his or her knowledge and views.

Grundtvig was opposed to domination in a way that stands outside of the European emancipation tradition, with its emphasis on liberal individualism.[21] Influenced in particular by his reading of the French Revolution, he was on guard against the idea that the way to obtain freedom is to dissolve the power structure. What you will get, he says, is most often another form of power that is worse than the one just replaced. He wanted to substitute for violent revolution a peaceful transformation of all elements in society based on a mutual recognition that all had the right to exist. Yet his views on *vekselvirkning* went further than the mere tolerance of diversity. He was really insisting upon a mutual recognition that each institution, each power center, and indeed each individual could both teach and learn in a dialogue predicated on mutual respect. Furthermore, such dialogue would create in the long run a society with widened social and individual perspectives, constituting the type of fertile soil in which the experience of Enlightenment could best grow.

A fifth central concept is Grundtvig's unswerving belief in the wisdom of the ordinary people over and above the educated and the elite (*folket overfor de dannede*). It was the ordinary people, and not those he contemptuously referred to as "the learned ones" (*de lærde*), who would be the source of enlightenment, if only they were given a chance. The theme is one that permeates his writings. An excellent statement of it can be found in 1871 when, at the age of eighty-eight, he would react to the first violent conflict between labor and capital in Danish society by warning against "overvaluing the physical work at the expense of the spiritual work—and the reverse. The two views give rise to a danger, which can only be prevented by a People's Enlightenment, *which in contrast to the Academic arises from the People itself* [italics added]."[22]

Grundtvig's life after 1832 was divided along two different paths, the religious and the cultural.[23] Although his approach to religion would never again be the same, he remained an active minister who would preach without a break for the remaining years of his life. His religious commitment would be reflected in the writing of countless hymns and the stream of theological dissertations and religious articles that would continue to pour forth from his sleepless nights of work. Yet the universal vision he had received, which led him to make his controversial statement "First man, then Christian," would not let him limit his concern to the welfare of those who, like himself, were Christians. He made a conscious distinction between religion and culture and insisted that above both had to be placed "the needs of human life," which he often expressed in breathtaking oppositions of Light and Darkness, Life and Death, Truth and Lies. Witness, for instance, his use of metaphors of light in these two verses from the poem "Enlightenment":[24]

> Is the light only in the planets found, that can neither see nor speak?
> Is not the word in our mouth a light for all souls?
> It gives the vision for our spirits, as the sun our body's light,
> It blasts our souls alive, like lightning come down from the skies.
>
> Is the light under certain conditions only to be halfway enlightening?
> Doesn't it always, everywhere do us good?
> Isn't the light the eye of life?
> Shall we for the sake of misuse rather see darkness and blackness
> Than the sun's white light on the arching sphere of heaven?

One of his major contributions in the realm of culture was the idea for a new type of school, which culminated in the 1838 publication of his *School For Life and the Academy in Søer.* When one recalls his breakthrough insights of the 1830s—the living word, life's enlightenment, people's enlightenment, balanced and equal dialogue, the ordinary people over the learned ones—it is not difficult to understand the extent of his fury at the schools he saw around him in Denmark. His ideas were simple and powerful, and he expressed them in a series of ringing metaphors that bring to his polemic a kind of high dignity. He saved his special anger and contempt for the classical Latin Schools, which, through the rote learning of texts written in Greek, Latin, and German, dutifully prepared the children of elites to assume their parents' privileged positions in society.[25] His scorn for them knew no bounds: "the black schools," he called them, and "the schools for death." They were "workplaces of dissolution and death, where the worms live high at the cost of life."[26] The following citation captures something of the spirit behind his proposed new school (I have tried to preserve the original character of his syntax and metaphors):

> Now I have my eye on something that unfortunately would be completely new among us, namely an institution of Enlightenment, where the People could gradually wake to self-awareness, and where the leaders would learn just as much from the youth as the youth from them, a kind of living *Vekselvirkning* and mutual instruction, through which a bridge could be laid over the yawning abyss that hierarchy, aristocracy, *Latineri* and social ambition have built for the people on the one side, and its leaders and teachers, with a handful of so-called educated and enlightened ones on the other side, this yawning abyss, which if it is not bridged, then all of our middle class society and all possibilities for peaceful, historic progressive development must soon fall into its precipice.[27]

It is impossible to understand the depth of Grundtvig's dislike for "the learned ones" without knowing his feelings about Danish language and culture. One must not forget that in Grundtvig's day Danish was considered an ignorant, rude tongue, the proper language for peasants and farmers, perhaps, but not for an educated person. It was part of the classical Latin School tradition of that time to instruct and give the students competence in the languages of European high culture: French, German, Greek, and Latin. The outstanding men discussed in the previous chapter, the Bernstorffs and the Reventlows, normally wrote their letters not in Danish but in French or German. Not a single word of Danish can be found in the surviving manuscripts of the elder Bernstorff, regardless of how well he served Denmark as a diplomat and statesman. It is interesting to note that the extensive personal library of Thomas Jefferson at this time contained volumes in Latin, Greek, French, Spanish, and Italian, all of which Jefferson read.[28] Only later in life did Jefferson recognize Germany as a country of scholarship: Danish almost certainly did not exist either for him or for the other learned men of his day.

These sociolinguistic facts speak to a deep division that remained in Danish society, and one must be aware of them in trying to understand the intensity of Grundtvig's views. A lover of his native tongue, he could not sit still at the snobbery of the Latin Schools and their misguided teachings reinforcing the centuries-old feeling—both in the country and abroad—that Danish was the language of ignorant peasants. The implication was that Danish was by its very nature an inferior language, unsuited to a consideration of the themes of high culture. The fact that the young students who went to such schools would become the future officials and power holders in Denmark angered him even more. These are some of the subtle threads in the tapestry of Grundtvig's thought.

The new school he envisioned was not to be just for the sons and daughters of farmers, but for those in all the different classes and occupations. It was to be a national or folk high school, an institution to be attended by "self-owners both large and small, handworkers of all kinds, seamen and tradesmen." It would serve the needs of "those behind the plow, in the workplace, at the top of the ship's mast and in the market stall," and its very existence would bring to an end the monopoly on education possessed by the university. The need for such a school, he believed, was now particularly acute. In 1831 the first "consultative provincial assemblies" (*stænderforsamlinger*) were allowed to meet, and these assemblies provided the first official forums in which elected representatives of the people could advise the king on the affairs of the country.[29]

Grundtvig was pleased at the life and strength that came out of these first movements toward parliamentary democracy, but he was also afraid that those who would eventually rule in the name of the people would be unable to see beyond their own narrow interests. He watched the mounting pressures for abolition of the absolute monarchy in the 1830s and 1840s with reluctance and mixed feelings, afraid that the proposed democratization would lead to a war of all against all carried on by egoistic pressure groups lacking any conception of the common good. Only through the establishment of a *folkelig højskole* (Grundtvig's term for the new school), where the young people from all regions and classes met and lived together to study their mother tongue, their country's history, and its present condition, would the young people of the future be able to acquire the foundations for Life's Enlightenment. (Grundtvig did not believe that any school, including the new school he proposed, could teach Life's Enlightenment, that being something that could only be taught by life itself.)

Taking up his pen in the early 1830s, Grundtvig began to write about his new idea and continued his efforts tirelessly, year after year. It looked as though his efforts were to be brought to fruition when in 1847 he succeeded

To the left: Grundtvig in 1862. Painting by Wilhelm Marstrand. To the right: Grundtvig's third wife, Asta (both pictures from Thaning, N. F. S. Grundtvig, 1972: 165, reprinted by permission of Gyldendal).

Søren Kierkegaard (1813–55), a contemporary of Grundtvig. Pencil drawing by H. P. Hansen (reprinted by permission of the Nationalhistorisk Museum, Frederiksborg Castle).

in interesting King Christian VIII in his proposal. What Grundtvig had in mind was a single school, a *folkelig højskole,* that would be built in Sorø on the site of an ancient academy where there were already many fine historical monuments. The king decided to lend his support to Grundtvig, and a royal resolution was issued on the last day of 1847. The resolution was hailed by Grundtvig in a poem that to their joint satisfaction was read aloud to the king on his sickbed. It looked as though the school at Sorø was an idea whose time had come, but then a few days later King Christian VIII passed away. Two months later both the absolute monarchy and the king's Sorø resolution were dead in the water: D. G. Monrad, the new minister of education, would have nothing to do with a state-run *folkelig højskole.*[30]

Let us leave the historical narrative at this point (we shall return to it shortly). What are we to make of Grundtvig? He has been called a romantic, a revolutionary, a reactionary, an anarchist, a liberal, a nationalist, a conservative, and a mystic. This state of affairs obtains partly because of his thought, which is both dialectical and full of nuances, and partly because he cannot really be identified with any single position. He was always—or nearly always—in movement from one position to another. P. G. Lindhardt has written of him:

> The competent interpreters have unquestionably revealed for us various sides of who Grundtvig was, but these sides of Grundtvig stand as monuments over the interpretations given. . . . It is beyond question that he was in a steady showdown with himself, had to battle to find himself, and the preacher of the living word more than anyone else had in his pen the best tool for "writing himself to clarity." Time after time he "found himself," and proclaimed it every time with a loud cockcrow that both amused and provoked his contemporaries. But his latest reversal never meant the decisive break with the past that he himself thought it was.[31]

His influence is very much alive in Denmark today. K. B. Andersen writes of him: "Grundtvig talked so strongly for freedom in the school, that it has had decisive effects on Danish primary schools and schools for youth that day as well as today. We have larger possibilities for local influence and for parental influence than is the case in many other lands."[32] Indeed, Danish parents today are the beneficiaries of a long-standing tradition: they do not have an obligation to send their children to school *(skolepligt).* What they have instead is an obligation to instruct their children *(undervisningspligt),* which can be fulfilled in many different ways. Two examples may be cited. First, Bertel Haarder, the present Minister of Education, was raised in a Grundtvigian milieu and received no formal schooling until he went to the university. Second, the freedom of choice that permeates the Danish school system has obliged the state to support an openly Marxist series of free schools "even though the explicit intention of these schools was to bring down the existing political and social order. As long as the parents come up with 10% of the funding, the state is compelled by law to provide the rest."[33]

This situation is a direct reflection of Grundtvig's inheritance, but it is assuredly not the only one. It is worth mentioning that when the German Occupation of Denmark was half a year old in the autumn of 1940, author and Grundtvig scholar Hal Koch began a noteworthy series of lectures at the University of Copenhagen. Grundtvig's ideas served as a central core in this lecture series, both to remind the Danes of their traditions and to unite them in opposition to the occupying power. Koch once put the question from the speaker's platform: "Can one in any other land find a single person, who has set so deep a mark on the life of his people?"[34]

Like the poet Walt Whitman who heard America singing, N. F. S. Grundtvig heard the songs of his native Denmark, the songs of the Danish people. He heard not only their songs, but their myths, their legends, and their deepest aspirations as well. He succeeded in freeing the Danish language from the undeserved stigma it had long suffered at the hands of the learned Latin pedants and served as a major source of inspiration for a cultural renaissance that was able to create, in the ashes of historical catastrophe, one of the most peaceful and productive societies the world has ever known. It is given to few men to be the mythmakers of their era. Such men both create and reflect the times that they live in, and their heritage is something that lingers long after the man himself is gone.

Two remarkable eyewitness accounts of Grundtvig on the preacher's platform near the end of his life make it clear that by that time the transition from outcast to icon was almost complete. Edmund Gosse, in his visit to Denmark in 1872, was fortunate enough to hear Grundtvig preach one of his last sermons. Although his Danish host and hostess had warned him that "you must not expect us to countenance such a dangerous schismatic," they relented and decided for their visitor's sake to go. This was what they saw and heard:

> The congregation began to sing hymns of his composition in a loud, quick, staccato manner invented by the poet, which was very little like the slow singing in the State churches. Suddenly, and when we had given up all hope, there entered from the vestry and walked rapidly to the altar a personage who seemed to me to be the oldest human being I had ever seen. Instantly an absolute silence prevailed throughout the church. . . . He wandered down among the ecstatic worshippers, and stood close at my side for a moment, while he laid his hands on a girl's head, so that I saw his face to perfection. For a man of ninety, he could not be called infirm; his gestures were rapid

and his step steady. But the attention was riveted on his appearance of excessive age. . . . From the vast orb of his bald head, very long strings of silky hair fell over his shoulders and mingled with a long and loose white beard. His eyes flamed under very beetling brows. . . . His features were still shapely, but colourless and dry, and as the draught from an open door caught them, the silken hairs were blown across his face like a thin curtain. While he perambulated the church with these stiff gestures and ventriloquist murmurings, his disciples fell on their knees behind him, stroking the skirts of his robes, touching the heels of his shoes. Finally, he ascended the pulpit and began to preach; in his dead voice he warned us to beware of false spirits, and to try every spirit whether it be of God. . . . Had I missed hearing and seeing Grundtvig then, I should never have heard or seen him, for he took to his bed a few days later, and in a month the magnificent old fighting man was dead.[35]

Johan Borup, author of one of the many works dealing with Grundtvig, wrote this reminiscence of the time when he experienced Grundtvig's personal presence in a church:

> I remember one Sunday, when I stood in the central aisle of a beautiful little church. The sermon had been given and the hymn singing had died down. In the stillness I suddenly heard the hard sound of iron against stone, and in the same instant he stepped quickly with his staff in hand, down across the church to the baptizing fountain. That was the only time I saw him up close. Before that he had stood distant and elevated up there on the pulpit, and it was only now that I got to see that he was a real human being just as we others. But I have never in all my days seen or even imagined something so ancient and immemorial. His long white hair and beard flowed down over his shoulder and chest, the high forehead marked by deep furrows, the large clear eyes under lion eyebrows, the broad harsh mouth, and as he now, stocky, heavy of body, supported by his staff that made a heavy sound against the tiles, strode past, a little bent, he resembled most in his incredible antiquity a giant from the heathen times who, full of his days, hastens toward the distant hills.[36]

For all of his vaunted fury and anger, there was a gentler side to Grundtvig's personality. Karl Otto Meyer writes, "It may well be that the experts will maintain that Grundtvig really wasn't a democrat, because democracy means the power of the people, while Grundtvig wanted *folkelighed,* which is something other than the people's power. *Folkelighed* builds on love of language and culture."[37] When he was writing of love, and of *folkelighed,* the bitter words of the critic could suddenly give way to the lyrical celebrations of the poet. Nowhere is this better illustrated than in the words of Grundtvig's poem on *Folkelighed,* Hymn 156 in the Folk High

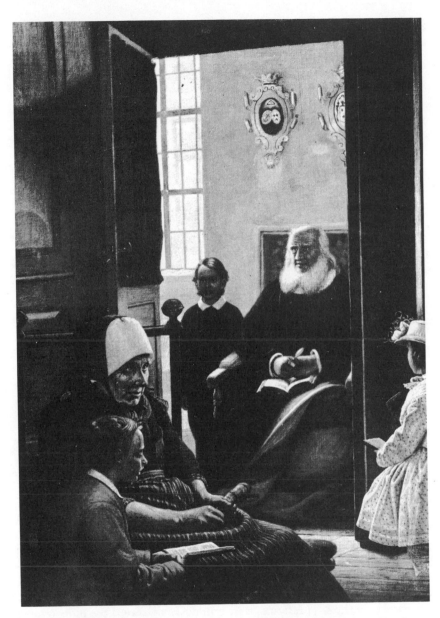

Grundtvig in old age. This painting by Christian Dalsgaard shows him during hymn singing at Vartov Church, Copenhagen. He was the minister at this church from 1839 until his death in 1872 (from Thaning, N. F. S. Grundtvig, 1972: 145, reprinted by permission of Gyldendal).

School Songbook,[38] from which the concluding fifth through seventh stanzas follow in a prose translation:

> 5. If one class regards itself as superior to the spirit of the common people,
> Then the head, the hands and the feet will part ridiculously on their own.
> Then the nation is torn apart. Then the history has come to an end.
> Then the people have been put to sleep,
> And you cannot wake them up again.

> 6. If we get legislation or laws in the Danish spirit,
> If we get these new Danish schools,
> Danish thoughts, Danish plows,
> Then we regain our old reputation.
> The Danes, happy and clever,
> Living with peace and joy on the sea.
> Then we see the people's deeds and poetry,
> Then is everything *folkeligt*.

> 7. *Folkeligt* is here in this lush countryside
> Still one more thing stemming from the depths of the heart.
> *Folkeligt* is the song of love, true Danish at all times,
> Neither at home nor in the senate assemblies
> To look down on children or women,
> No matter what goes up and down,
> Danish is always love!

II. THE RISE OF THE FOLK HIGH SCHOOLS

Change and Betrayal: The Farmers in National Politics

We have reviewed N. F. S. Grundtvig's proposal for a new *folkelig højskole*. What were the major developments in the situation of those who were to take up his call? When Grundtvig was inundating the country in the years after 1830 with his plea for a *"folkelig"* high school, what was happening to the new class of self-owning farmers? Many of the self-owning farmers, well aware of the role King Frederic VI had played in facilitating the passage of the land reforms, were still positive toward the monarchy in 1830. In the later years of that decade and the next, however, the relationship between the farmers and the monarchy would worsen. This process intensified when his successor, Christian VIII, began to adopt policies more favorable to the large landowners.

On 8 November 1845 an infamous document was issued *(Bonde-cirkulæret)* that encouraged local police to keep a close eye on those persons who were traveling around the countryside to speak to the farmers about politics. Furthermore, it forbade public meetings dealing with the rights of the farmers unless special permits were obtained from the police in advance, and individuals who did not reside within the local district were forbidden to take part. Because of these developments, the mounting political pressure for constitutional government and basic civil rights that was coming from the bourgeois middle class—from tradespeople, university professors, and city officials—found a quick acceptance among the self-owning farmers. Aided by them, the representatives of the bourgeoisie were able to success-fully press their demands for overthrow of the absolute monarchy, and on 21 March 1848 yet another peaceful revolution took place in the streets of Copenhagen. Skovmand has given this description of the events:

> In a peaceful and calm mood the procession of people began to go forward. . . . The procession reached the square in front of Christiansborg castle. All of the streets, roofs, ships, wharfs and opened windows were filled with people, somewhere between twelve and fifteen thousand people. Some had climbed up on ropes or were hanging in the masts of the ships on the canal. A soundless tension dominated while the leaders of the procession were inside the castle. One who participated later wrote "It was a gripping sight: this huge, peaceful crowd, borne by one and the same thought. Suddenly I thought, what if now, as in Berlin a few days ago . . . there were a pair of fatal shots fired into this peaceful crowd, what then? Then we would have here as there a revolution. . . ." The waiting time seemed endlessly long, but finally the door of the castle opened.[39]

What the watching crowd quickly learned as their representatives came through the door was the wonderful news that the government of King Christian VIII had acceded peacefully to their demands. Upon hearing this, the crowd shouted "Long live the king" *(Kongen leve!)*, and there was general celebration and embracing on the part of many who had participated. Although the Constitution *(Grundlov)* would not be signed until 5 June 1849, the day of the last absolute monarch had already come in Denmark. It was a peaceful day whose proceedings took place in the complete absence of violence (interestingly enough, not a single one of the city's policemen could be seen in the crowd's vicinity during these events).

The farmers had given their support to the democratic forces whose actions brought about this significant event. Yet they were to find them-selves quickly set out of this fine company, their alliance with the represen-tatives of the urban middle class disintegrating almost as quickly as it had been formed.[40] The urban and commercial elites were concerned with free

Peaceful revolution in the streets of Copenhagen, 21 March 1848. Grundtvig looks on from the window, upper right (artist unknown, from Skovmand, Danmarks Historie, *Vol. 11, 1978: 240, reprinted by permission of Politikens Forlag).*

trade and the free movement of labor. It was in their interest to increase the extent to which laissez-faire economics and politics prevailed in the commercial arena. To accede to the farmers' demands (e.g., the abolition of tenancy for landed farmers) would require changes in property rights, a development the ascendent middle class found itself opposed to on principle. It was painful enough for the farmers to see themselves being pushed out of the saddle just after the conclusion of a race that could not have been won without their support. But of the justifications given, by far the most painful was the condescending dismissal based on the claim that the farmers lacked the necessary education and background to participate in the politics of the state. And even worse, in the eyes of the merchants and the urban middle class, the farmers' manners and ways of speaking were often a source of great amusement.

"I can't tell what it is we ate, except for the very first dish—it was soup. . . . How many flasks and glasses there were on the table, it is impossible for me to describe that either. . . . God knows what it was we ate, but it all tasted good" was the plainly overawed reaction of a farmer serving on the consultative provincial assembly to his first dinner at the royal commissary.[41] A cleric serving on one of these assemblies in 1838 wrote home in amusement to a colleague: "The farmers are all as dumb as a school of trout."[42] To add injury to insult, the broken alliance between the farmers and the urban middle class enabled the nobility and estate owners to begin winning back some of the ground they had lost in the constitutional crisis of 1848–49.

In spite of the difficulties made clear by the above account, the situation of the self-owning farmers in Denmark was one that gave grounds for optimism. There were many new possibilities. Freed from the limiting constraints of the feudal bond, the nature of the reward system had been fundamentally changed. Unlike a century earlier in 1750, the more they produced, the more they could earn. Cultivation was no longer a collective affair, but something for which the individual farmer was personally responsible. A farmer and his family, functioning as a social unit, enjoyed or suffered the consequences of their enterprise. These changes toward a life based on individualism brought in their wake the need for a whole new code of ethics and values. If the farmers were going to take advantage of their new opportunities, laziness would have to give way to industry, slovenliness to order, and drunkenness to sobriety. When an entire group experiences intense social mobility over time, it is not uncommon for their religious beliefs to change profoundly as well. The following comment by P. G. Lindhardt suggests that this was in fact the case:

> The religiosity that came to be significant in the 19th century for the steadily more independent farmer, had to speak to his new sense of personal worth and to the new social groups in which he lived; it had to be a personal revival Christianity . . . a modern individualistic religion that united free personalities in the strength of common religious experiences and common socio-economic conditions or political efforts. Therefore the farmers began to doubt after 1800, that the state church was what it said it was: the true Christianity.[43]

A wave of revival movements swept the Danish countryside in the early years of the nineteenth century, bringing new forms of religious observance with them.[44] Although they cannot be treated here in greater detail, their very existence suggests that the possibilities inherent in the newly liberated situation of the self-owning farmers had not yet been fully achieved. But there was much activity in the countryside, and a movement in support of the farmers was coalescing. Members of this diverse group, many of whom were from nonrural backgrounds, came to be known as *Bondevennerne* (the friends of the farmers). The independent self-owning farmers were casting their eye out for new possibilities in all of the affairs that concerned them: in religion, in agriculture, in community affairs, and in national politics. The pragmatic members of this new class, heirs to the political vision of Reventlow and Colbjørnsen, had their eyes open. They wanted to find ways of consolidating the advances already made and to prepare as well for the needs of the future. Something of their mood is captured in the remarks made in 1845 by an independent farmer from Udby, the town where Grundtvig was born and spent his youth:

> Back in those days when I first became a farmer, we talked about our horses and cows, about our soil, about our farming techniques when we got together. Our thoughts didn't go any farther. We still talk about those things, and it wouldn't be good any other way. But now I seldom meet with other farmers, when we don't also talk about self-ownership or equal taxation. And someone always asks what can be done to advance the condition of the farmers, and how it will be for our children. . . . A new life has awakened in us.[45]

The farmers were neither cowed nor subdued by their former masters. A new type of school would soon appear.

The Earliest Schools

The better one comes to know Denmark, the more one is impressed by the unique qualities of each of its regions. The southern part of Jutland, known as *Sønderjylland,* has long had a special relationship with the rest of Denmark because of the Slesvig-Holsten question.[46] It is here that one can find Danish areas with German-speaking minorities (though the farther south one goes, the more the reverse situation obtains). It is here that the Danish border with Germany has been defined and redefined over the course of three wars in the last 150 years. It is often said that the Danish patriotism and national feeling are most intense in this region, where over a long period of time its Danish inhabitants could not take for granted their Danish national identity. It was in this region of Denmark that the first folk high school opened its doors at Rødding in North Slesvig on 7 November 1844.

The founding of the school was intimately connected to the political struggle of the Danish population in North Slesvig to keep the area within the Danish monarchy. Supported financially by the National Liberals in Copenhagen, it was a professor from Kiel, Christian Flor (1792–1875), who took the initiative of starting a new school to be based on Grundtvigian principles. At the opening of the school its first principal declared that the goal we have set ourselves is to found an institution where farmers and other citizens can receive useful instruction—not so much with regard to technical operations as with regard to his position as a son of the country and a citizen of the state. . . . We call it a *højskole,* because it is not to be a usual school for boys, but an institute of instruction partly for young people after the age of confirmation, and partly for full-grown men and workers—and we call it a *folkehøjskole* because members of every group in society can gain entrance to it, even though it is most intended for farmers. . . . The young people will be able to learn here to think, speak and write in a clear and healthy manner, sensibly and correctly: but this teaching will be given in a national and *folkelig* way.[47]

The twenty pupils who showed up for the schools's first session in 1844 in a modest farmhouse were not exactly what Grundtvig had in mind when he had written about a state-run folk high school at Sorø. The subjects taught were to include Danish language and literature, geometry, drawing, surveying, German and Swedish, natural sciences, singing, and gymnastics. The school's entire course was to last two years, with a separate section completed every six months. Its instruction was specifically aimed at the sons of self-owning and independent farmers. The goal of the school and the others that followed was specifically *not* to prepare them for a university education or a position in the bureaucracy. It was well understood that after the course of instruction a pupil would return to his work as a farmer. Had it been otherwise, there would have been little reason for the independent farmers to send their sons to these schools.

It is one thing to write idealistic programs and quite another to live them out in practice. Johan Wegener, the first principal of Rødding Højskole, wrote to Flor that "it was a whole course of study to talk in such a dumb and childlike way that he could be sure he was being understood."[48] Although he maintained that he became so close to his students that on their departure all "cried as if they had been whipped," the fact that he abandoned the school after the first winter tends to make one skeptical about this claim. Faced with a rudderless institution, Flor left his home and university position in Kiel and succeeded through his own personal influence in breathing life back into the little school in the countryside.

From the outset one major dilemma was how much weight to place on technical agricultural subjects and how much on general education and the quest for "spiritual enlightenment." One of the teachers at the school wanted to emphasize agriculture and as an "extra" put a little humanistic education into the instruction. Flor objected to this line of reasoning on the following grounds: The farmer is oppressed because he is unable to participate in the life of society. Excluded from the councils of government, he sits fearful and dejected, believing that he knows nothing outside of his narrow sphere of competence. To teach him to sow and plough his fields more effectively will not by itself be sufficient to overcome this lack of knowledge and self-confidence. What he must learn in these schools is a point of view that unites him with common human experience and draws its strength from exposing him to all of life's different areas.

The words Flor used to express these ideas could have been written by Grundtvig himself: "The most important thing about the instruction at our *højskole* is not the positive knowledge and accomplishments that we try to impart to the students, but more the spiritual life that is waked and nourished in them, so that their understanding becomes sharper, their judgment more mature and their hearts more open."[49] The late Roar Skovmand, the foremost Danish authority on the high school tradition, writes that "luckily for the Danish *højskole* and for the youth that sought it, it was Flor's thinking that won out here."[50]

Another area in which Flor's point of view came to characterize the school was the question of examinations. The students at a folk high school were young lads straight from the farms. The new school simply would not work if they were forced to greet each new day with the oppressing thought, "Here is another burden being laid upon you." They were to be taught instead in such a way that each day at the school made them feel, "The light is going up for me!" In accordance with Grundtvig's thinking, the teaching of facts and techniques was adjudged secondary to the wakening of the spiritual life of the student. Flor was one of the many early high school figures who could enthrall a roomful of young students with spellbinding and instructional tales that drew from the rich source of Nordic mythology. A student later wrote: "How I felt that the 'living word' was more important than the written! . . . I forgot everything around me, and when I came home, I wrote down the whole lecture, as much as I had been able to understand and receive it."[51]

The folk high school movement had begun. The school at Rødding was soon joined by other schools at Uldum (1849), Hindholm (1852), and Viby (1857). There was no unanimity of outlook in these early schools, and by no means did all of them look to Grundtvig as a source of inspiration. The school at Uldum was connected to the religious revival movement that had swept over Denmark in previous decades. The school at Hindholm was started by a group of radical farmers who wanted to use it as an instrument in the ongoing political struggle against the educated middle class. And the school at Viby did not even call itself a folk high school but a "higher school for farmers" (*højere Bondeskole*). Its director, Lars Bjørnbak, was openly hostile to Grundtvig's ideas. He labeled what he called "Grundtvig's ravings" as the worst sort of pie-in-the-sky idealism.[52] His school was to be based on "the power of knowledge," its goal to give students practical skills in agriculture and a fundamental understanding of society so that they could become leaders in it. The rivalry between these different approaches was to continue (indeed, a new *højskole* at Testrup was established in 1866 with the explicit goal of providing a Grundtvigian alternative to the school at Viby[53]).

Grundtvig, as we have seen, wanted a "romantic and historic-poetic" perspective to prevail in the folk high schools. Yet his program for the folk high schools had in another sense left a vacuum, and the debate that came to mark the folk high school movement during the 1850s and 1860s moved squarely into the resulting empty space. For all his thunderous preaching about the need for these schools, Grundtvig had not been terribly specific about what their curricula or classrooms would look like. He had said little or nothing about who should run them, how the teachers should be chosen, how the teachers should teach, or what the living conditions at the school should be. Of course, Grundtvig could always say (and did so) that it was not for him to decide such things, that the school must serve the needs of life, and in doing so life itself would teach all with a good heart the best solutions to specific problems. For Grundtvig it lay in the very nature of the endeavor that life at a folk high school couldn't be planned in advance.[54] The relationship between Grundtvig and the early folk high schools, then, is more complex than one would initially imagine.

One thing to bear in mind is that Grundtvig's initial conception of a folk high school as an institution that would reach all classes of society had come to naught. Or more precisely, it would be realized not in the single, centralized, and government-supported school that Grundtvig had envisioned but by a large number of smaller schools that were closely connected to a single class and interest group, the landed farmers. The folk high schools arose as an authentic grass roots institution "along the country road" *(hen ad landevejen)*. The pattern of their early development did not depend on any one man or philosophy, even that of Grundtvig himself. A second thing to bear in mind is that many of the early schools were led by educators openly unsympathetic to Grundtvig's point of view. It was also the case that many of the farmers who sent their sons to these schools did not exactly fall all over themselves in admiration for Grundtvig's teachings. P. G. Lindhardt has given this pragmatic description: "Grundtvig's point of view was not particularly noticed, but the farmers understood in any case that if they were to acquire the ability to represent themselves adequately in the debate with the other classes in society, they had to be made more educated and more competent. Therefore they were instrumental in setting up and maintaining the first schools."[55]

Rødding Højskole, established in 1844, was forced to close for three years of war with Germany (1848–50). When it opened again on land that was to remain a part of Denmark only until 1864, an internal struggle began that continued throughout the next decade. One dispute was the familiar one between those who believed that practical agricultural instruction should be the dominant element in the curriculum and those who favored the more Grundtvigian approach: inspiration drawn from myth and world history with the goal of "enlightenment." The question of whether or not it was proper to give examinations was also hotly debated. Rødding had other problems as well. Its high fees and its two-year duration had made its course a difficult one for the typical young farmer to attend. Not only did it take him away from his work for an extended period, but it also made demands on him in the summer season, the time when he was most needed at home. Consequently, its main clientele had become the sons of ministers and prosperous independent farmers. The numbers of students seeking entrance to Rødding dropped at the end of the decade, just at the time that a new approach to folk high school instruction was achieving its reputation elsewhere.

Christen Kold: A Man of the People

In 1851 a new folk high school had been established at Ryslinge, on the island of Fyn. The founder of this school, Christen Kold (1816–70), was a figure who "has come to exercise an even greater influence on the Danish Højskole than Grundtvig or Flor."[56] Ole and Poul Christensen and Peter Warrer state in their scholarly treatise that "it is hardly an exaggeration to regard Kold's højskole endeavors as a pioneer work, because the later højskole movement took over many of the forms that Kold developed in his own work."[57] Niels Højlund writes that Kold's work was of "the greatest significance for the future højskole movement."[58] Its program was based on a new pattern that was to become the usual one in the future: "School for the young fellows in the winter, a girl's school in the summer, common dining such that teachers and students eat together."[59]

The details of his life history are remarkable. Kold was born in 1816 in Thisted in north Jutland, the son of a shoemaker. After his confirmation, he served briefly as a tutor on an estate. Not yet eighteen, he was "awakened" by the devotional sermons of Peter Larsen Skræppenborg, a traveling revival preacher with a strongly Grundtvigian message. Grundtvig's religious style has been called "the happy Christianity" *(den glade Kristendom)*, and Kold said later that the blinders fell from his eyes when he suddenly understood that God loved him. "I thought earlier that God was a police master, a strict schoolmaster, who watched over us and gave us a good box on the ear when we were bad," he wrote. But when he suddenly understood the simple truth of God's universal love, it gave him, in modern terms, a memorable peak experience: "I have never experienced anything like the life, the joy, the strength and power that suddenly arose in me. I was so happy over that discovery, that I didn't know which leg I should stand on."[60]

After his awakening, Kold became strongly identified with the revival movement. His organizational activity in support of the movement led to his being blacklisted. Unable to find work, he moved to West Slesvig, where he found temporary work as a teacher in the house of a prosperous farmer. But even in this early period his views on education were radical. He was strongly opposed to compulsion and rote learning and refused to make his pupils learn the catechism by heart. Soon he was jobless again. Disappointed over the blacklist that was keeping him out of the public schools, he decided to accompany a Danish missionary priest down to Smyrna in Turkey. He spent five years there, working initially for the priest but later establishing himself as an independent handworker, specializing in bookbinding. On the way back to Denmark he sailed first to Trieste in Italy, where he bought a wagon for his possessions; in this way he walked on foot the seven hundred miles to Denmark.

When he returned, his own path had become clear. He would start his own school. Influenced by Grundtvig's teaching, he succeeded in obtaining a personal meeting with the pastor himself. Grundtvig was so impressed with Kold that he raised half of the money Kold needed for his new school. Taking the other half from what he had saved in Turkey, Kold purchased a small plot near Ryslinge and built—partly with his own hands—the little thatched cottage that still stands there. In November 1851 he was ready to begin his first session. Before the school started, he journeyed around the countryside to find pupils. His school had fourteen students the first year, sixteen the second. Although he was to move in 1853 to Kerteminde to establish a "free school" for children and in 1862 to Dalum to establish another *folkehøjskole,* these movements were not due to any failure on Kold's part. On the contrary, all of his schools were successful; they were able both to attract students and to send them away feeling that a new spirit had begun to breathe in them. Though there is no mention of reading, writing, and arithmetic (which were also taught), the following excerpt from his original plan of instruction gives some insight into what Kold would try to do at his school:

a. an oral lecture on World History as the foundation;

b. oral narrative *(fortælling)* of Bible history;

c. a selection of church history, especially selected to shed light on the different sects;

d. Nordic mythology and Danish history, primarily based on oral narrative;

e. global geography, followed by a description of the people and countries (for instance, the novel *The Last of the Mohicans* would be used to sketch life in the U.S.A.);

f. selected Danish writers will be read in the form of Evening-entertainment three evenings a week;

g. song, especially the long ballads.[61]

One of the reasons for Kold's success was the Spartan life-style maintained at his schools. Everyone ate the same food. Neither coffee nor tea was served. The school's combined use of sugar during one winter was just over two pounds. Each person got only one raisin in his soup. Kold and his fellow teacher slept in the common sleeping room, and it was not uncommon for two or three students to share the same mattress. All members of the school were together throughout the entire day sharing the extended fellowship of a family. Kold himself wore the plain homespun clothes of a farmer, but he made sure that his pupils got used to cleanliness and order. And in order not to separate them unduly from their own homes, he limited the school session to the five winter months, during which they could best be taken away from the work in the fields. Kold's school was also the first one to begin to hold summer school for the young farm girls.[62]

The strong emphasis on a Spartan existence reflected Kold's background in the religious revival tradition. "If life is to be true," Kold said, "it must be simple and direct. So is everything that comes from God."[63] Many in this tradition believed along with Kold that a simple and humble life-form was pleasing in God's eyes. Another potential justification was that the resulting minimal fees (about one-fourth those of Rødding) would enable the less prosperous farmers to send their children as well. With this in mind Kold was even able to persuade some of the wealthier farmers to contribute a yearly sum so that each winter four or five pupils from less prosperous backgrounds could attend the school without cost.[64] He wanted all his pupils to think of their school experience in these terms: "We are a group of young farm lads, who are staying for some months at the home of the farmer Christen Mikkelsen Kold in Hjallese. We are helping him a little with his work, we have conversations both inside and outside, we hear talks, we become better in writing, arithmetic and such things, and when these months are over, we go each his own way, take hold of our business, and are the same plain lads we were before."[65]

Kold's original opinion was that students at the school should be young, fourteen or fifteen years old. Grundtvig, on the other hand, held firm to the belief that the schools would best serve those eighteen years and older. After the very first session it was necessary for Kold to revise his opinion. He wrote in a letter to a contemporary, "We have as you know had students of different ages from thirty-three to fourteen, and I owe Pastor Grundtvig a recognition that his view is the right one, that the oldest are the best, that is, the ones from whom the best can be brought forth."[66] This seems to have been one of the infrequent occasions when Kold openly admitted he was wrong. He wrote once of himself, perhaps not without conscious or unconscious irony, "I have always been sure of my case, even when I was wrong."[67] (*Jeg har altid været vis i min sag, ogsaa naar jeg tog fejl.*) What one can truthfully say of him is that he was a deeply religious man driven by his own sense of mission. The purpose he saw behind it is perhaps nowhere better stated than in this evaluation he once made of the competition:

> Yes, we have Rødding and Hindholm and a few others. . . . Rødding came first, that one was to be a border fortification against "Germanness" (*Tyskheden*). Hindholm lies on Sjælland, where the estates and the nobles have great power. That school was created by friends of the farmers to battle against the aristocracy, the farmers want to liberate themselves and attain control over their own lives, that is also a good and useful work. Then there's my school. The enemy I have set my sights on is Death, and that enemy is closer to us than either the Germans or the Estate owners, because it lives in our hearts, side by side with Life. All other battles are lost in the ripple of time's waves, but this battle lasts for all time, and to prepare oneself for it, this is the one that really counts.[68]

For better or for worse, Kold had what could be called a Lone Ranger approach to education. He seldom discussed school questions with anyone, let alone fellow teachers. And although the everyday subjects of reading, writing, and arithmetic *were* taught at his school, they were typically left in the hands of a group of more or less undistinguished fellow teachers. The real task of the other teachers was to do something to fill up the time when Kold himself wasn't giving a talk. He seems to have regarded their presentations as something on a lower level than what he himself did. It would be natural to attribute this neglect of fellow teachers to an overdeveloped ego, but one must exercise care in this regard. Kold wrote almost nothing, had no desire for public recognition, and is known first and foremost by the overwhelming impression he made on his students and on visitors to his school. He did not in any way seek fame. Nevertheless, he would come to serve as a role model for the young university students who were to become the leading high school men of the next generation. One of the foremost in their ranks, Ludvig Schrøder, made these observations of life at his school in a letter written in the 1860s. They testify to Kold's genius as a teacher:

> It is a kind of Socrates, who sits in his chair surrounded by a crowd of boys and girls from the farms. They have come a long way to be at the school, and the whole day he talks with all these people in such a way that he always awakens something in them. When he holds an hour or an hour and a half lecture every morning, the school's living room is filled with students and guests. It is usually World History that he is discussing a chapter from, but the main thing is its practical application for life, and he has a really good grip on this. What he wants to awaken is "a heart for the spirit," that we may open our hearts to the spiritual, so that it can come to use us as willing instruments to advance the task that belongs to our people and to all of humanity.[69]

Kold's instruction was always aimed at "awakening," and this inner perspective on education imbued his teaching with its own unique character. It is a perspective that can be seen quite clearly in the few written statements of his that survive. Witness what he says about the teaching of reading, writing, and arithmetic to children:

> The three skills of reading, writing and arithmetic, which should comprise the second half of instruction for children, take up nearly the whole at the present time. These skills have in reality only a small value, because they are only means or instruments for the service of the spirit. . . . We have brought things so far, that all Danish children can read— but there are only a few who can really use it, because all the others are sleeping. And it doesn't help a sleeping man to have so many good tools.[70]

Kold was in total accord with Grundtvig that the teaching of history is an enterprise central to the task of *folkelig* instruction. Even in his brief statements one feels Kold's gift for language. How can instruction at the schools be made *folkelig?* The answer is given in a single well-formed sentence:

> But we ask: how can this be made to happen—without waking the spirit of the people to clear and living consciousness, and teaching the people to know its own peculiarities so that it can understand itself and its development—without setting the people in a living connection with its past, so that its present will not appear as a disconnected and therefore unintelligible fragment, but as a link in the large chain that is the magnificent career of the Danish people?[71]

The only known portrait of Christen Kold (1816–70) is reproduced here from a lithograph. Kold was a key figure whose approach to education came to characterize not only the folk high school but also much of the spirit of children's education in Denmark (from Skovmand, Danmarks Historie, Vol. 11, 1978: 393, *reprinted by permission of Politikens Forlag).*

Kold returns again and again to his fundamental themes. All instruction must take into account the nature of children and their real needs. Children must be allowed time to develop the capacity for feeling before they are taught facts, to develop appreciation before they learn skills. In an essay entitled "An Instruction Suited to Children's Needs and Abilities," he makes an indictment: "The children's school has been guilty of the mistake, that it almost exclusively has tried to talk to *understanding* and only partly to *feeling,* while *fantasy,* the power of the imagination, has been as good as forgotten."[72] Both children and adolescents receive too much of the wrong sort of written instruction, he argues. It deadens and desensitizes their minds and hearts, turning them into enemies of both the school and its learning. What they need instead is the right kind of oral instruction, one that will bring them to life and widen their feeling for the world in which they live.

Grundtvig held that the aim of the folk high schools was enlightenment *(oplysning).* For Kold this goal was equally important, but he maintained that enlightenment could only come once a student had been brought to life: the task of the schools was to stimulate, brighten, and encourage them *(oplive),* and this was a necessary precondition for enlightenment. Near the end of his life he said of his *højskole,* "I wanted to enlighten and encourage, but first and last to encourage." When he was once asked by one of his students what he really wanted to accomplish with his *højskole,* he answered by asking the student a question in turn: "What's that you have in your vest pocket?" "A pocket watch, that can be wound up," answered the young farmer. "That's exactly what I want to do," replied Kold. "Wind you up so that you never stop ticking."[73]

Although it was Grundtvig who envisioned "the school for life," it was Kold who first showed how Grundtvig's ideas could be brought to fruition. It was Kold who founded and ran the first successful schools and in doing so left behind him a model for the future, the "Grundtvig-Kold" *folkehøjskole.* And it was Kold as well who brought to life what Grundtvig had preached about the centrality of "the living word." Peter Manniche writes of him that "by the power of his words, in virtue of his inspired personality, he made all that he touched living. He spoke till his students became part of the world of gentleness, peace and beauty into which he carried them. And they felt that this world was reality, because he lived as he spoke."[74] There were differences between Kold and Grundtvig: Kold's school had a distinctly "religious" emphasis; Grundtvig preferred a more subtle approach to the question of religion. And Kold can perhaps be criticized for running a one-man show, for it is certain that no one else could have stepped in and taken his place. He did not bother to think about training successors. Yet when Christen Kold died in 1870, he had not only instructed more than thirteen hundred students at his *folkehøjskoler* but had also left behind him a living source of inspiration for future schools.[75] Three of the most prominent high school principals of the next half century, Ludvig Schrøder, Ernst Trier, and Jens Nørregaard, had made extended visits to Kold's school. They would now utilize what they had learned in their own work. The breakthrough period of the Danish folk high schools was about to begin.

Breakthrough Time: The New School's Triumph

The year 1864 is one of the darkest in Danish history. Deluded by a sad mixture of patriotic arrogance and short-sighted miscalculation, the ruling National Liberals allowed Denmark to be drawn into war with Bismarck's Prussia in that year. Slesvig had been controlled by the Danish king since 1720, its southern neighbor Holsten since 1773; the result of this devastating war was to be the loss of both Slesvig and Holsten to Prussia. Yet in one of history's odd juxtapositions, it is in this same dark year, 1864, that the breakthrough period of the folk high schools begins.

Even before Kold's death in 1870, the *folkehøjskole* was an idea whose time had come. The period 1864–76 saw a veritable explosion of the new schools over the entire Danish countryside. In 1862 there were still only fifteen schools with barely five hundred students attending. But in just the four years between 1866 and 1869, forty-four new *folkehøjskoler* were established. In 1869 approximately two thousand students were enrolled in the winter courses. By 1875, only six years later, there were nearly four thousand students attending fifty-five schools. From this time on and through the next decade, it has been calculated that, on the average, 15% of the yearly age group of young people from the agricultural districts had attended or were in the process of attending a folk high school.[76]

When peace was finally reached in 1864, the area of south Jutland in which Rødding Højskole was located had come under German rule. After some discussion, a decision was made to move the school to Danish territory. In 1865 it was established at its present site at Askov, near the town of Vejen. The principal of the new school was Ludvig Schrøder (1836–1908), a young theology student who was a disciple of Grundtvig. In spite of difficult conditions, poor buildings, and insufficient funds, Askov Højskole quickly blossomed. By the mid-1870s it was already recognized as the center of the high school movement. Its experimental teaching of natural sciences in a Grundtvigian spirit after 1878 only reinforced this preeminent position. But it was essential to the new school's success that Schrøder was not alone. He belonged to a circle of intense young theologians who, influenced by Grundtvig, had decided to dedicate their lives to the development of the new schools for farmers. Ernst Trier (1837–93) established a school at Vallekilde on Sjælland in 1865, Jens Nørregaard (1838–1913) a school at Testrup near Aarhus in 1866. These three—Schrøder, Trier, and Nørregaard—were representative of a new type of person in Danish society: the "high school man." Often urban and university educated, frequently theologians in their training, such men were to form the backbone of the emerging folk high school movement over the next three decades.

What was life like at one of these schools in 1880? It was generally Spartan, though not as much as had been true of Kold's schools. But those who came to such schools as students were used to doing with little. They were not likely to be bothered by the fact that six to ten students often slept in the same room, two to a bed, sharing the same mattress. The young men came for the five months from November to March, the time between the end of the harvest and the beginning of spring planting. The young women came between May and July, leaving the farm after their spring work but returning to it in time for the autumn harvest. A daily course schedule from 1881 gives some idea of how their time was spent:

> 8:00 Morning song; 8:25–9:00 Lecture over different Subjects (Myth, Legend, Proverbs, History of Literature, Biographies, Bible History); 9–10 Reading aloud of Poetic Works; 10–10:30 Free; 11:00–12:00 Lecture over the History of the Fatherland [i.e, Denmark]; 12:00–2:00 Dinner; 2:00–3:00 World History; 3:00–4:00 Orthography; 4:00–5:00 Free; 5:00–6:00 Geography or Physics; 6:00–7:00 Arithmetic and Calculation; in the Evening Hours now and then Instruction in Reading.[77]

The emphasis on group singing was not a casual afterthought but a basic part of folk high school life. The "Morning Song," which in the above schedule marks the official beginning of the school day, would typically be followed by additional songs. There was group singing both at the beginning and the end of each class hour, and at meals. There would often be an Evening Song as well. The songs frequently had an educational function, requiring the singers to recount the phases of a major historical event or to give firm voice to themes of uplift and character building ("Lift your head, you strong young fellow," began the first verse of one such song).[78] The act of singing in a group encouraged the emergence of communal fellowship, even though the quality of the singing was not high: it was typically monotonous, unaccompanied by piano or other instrument. The level of choral achievement was higher at Askov Højskole, where the skilled composer Nutzhorn guided and led the singing. As Ludvig Schrøder makes clear, the emphasis on group singing had another function as well: "The young people really enjoy it, and we place a high value on it, because it educates song leaders, something we would like to see many of our students become after the end of their high school stay."[79]

A second element in the højskole plan was the *foredrag,* a type of classroom learning guided by Grundtvig's concerns for the primacy of "the living word." The dictionary meaning of the Danish word *foredrag* is "a lecture, paper, or talk," but the mode of instruction at the *folkehøjskole* was something quite different from what one ordinarily thinks of as a lecture.

Themes in mythology and world history were taught in such a way that the audience of young farmers not only hung on every word but could easily relate the message of the talk to what was happening in their own lives, here and now, in Denmark. Jens Nørregaard, the principal of Testrup, exemplified this tradition in the teaching of history. The point was not merely to teach the facts of history but to show that God Himself was an active agent in the process and thus to strengthen the religious belief of his listeners.

Roar Skovmand has given us a vivid picture of him in the act of giving a *foredrag*.[80] When Jens Nørregaard stood before an audience of young people and described the destruction of the Spanish Armada in 1588, it was as if the thunder of that distant catastrophe came alive and they could hear it all: the wind of the Lord shrieking and howling along the canal and the mighty ships of the Armada blown like a handful of wooden shavings from a carpenter's workbench to the destruction that awaited them on the rocky cliffs. This was not the dry and lifeless history that scholars bury in their dusty tomes but history taught by "the living word" in the very sense that Grundtvig had called for. Not all could speak with the intensity of a Nørregaard (Schrøder, for instance, was more subtle and indirect though equally effective in his teaching). But behind all of their presentations was the same thoroughly Grundtvigian message: the history of Denmark was filled with heroes who had battled to improve the lives of their people, and they had been placed by history in a direct line of inheritance to this grand tradition. The teachings made it clear to them that *they* were a part of this tradition. *They* had been called by history to the completion of certain tasks, and they were told that they would find in themselves the ability to do whatever was needed to bring these tasks to fruition. They were not dumb farmers who had to feel inferior to the learning of priests or professors. They would accomplish and overcome just as the heroes of old had done (and more than they themselves had ever dreamed was possible). And this accomplishment was something that had to begin at the high school: a weekly course plan from Askov in the 1880s shows that a student who took part in everything would come up with fifty-two hours of instruction.[81]

A third element of fundamental significance was the shared experience of the communal life itself (*fælleslivet*). Both students and teachers lived at the school, ate at the same tables, and were in continuous contact. The communal life that developed, however, went much further than mere physical proximity. During a stay at a *højskole* one was not merely a student but came to feel in a profound way that one had become part of a new family. The fact that the wife of the principal was called the "high school mother" is indicative of the way in which the entire school came to function as a family with the principal himself as its patriarch. The school's patriarchal structure was in perfect accordance with the life back on the farm, where the male head of the farm functioned as a patriarch with final responsibility for nearly every question that arose. Thus the early folk high school was an experiment in pure free enterprise: the buildings of the school were usually either owned or leased by the principal and his wife; when a new principal took over a school, he and his wife actually bought and assumed ownership of the property and its buildings. Often the old teachers would be fired summarily and new ones brought in when this happened. But if principals were accorded a great deal of power, it is also true that they were the ones who took the most risk. If there was insufficient demand for a school on the part of students, it soon shut its doors. There was a lot of competition between the new schools; many lasted only a few years and then had to close down. A successful school was almost always one to which large numbers of students had been attracted through widening general knowledge of a principal's personal charisma. The principal and his wife were very much the backbone of the school.

This intense primary group formation made a stay at these schools a time when one's whole self-conception could easily be altered. It was not at all unusual for a student to feel himself transformed and reborn during the stay at the *folkehøjskole*. Perhaps just another farm lad before attending the winter session, one's vision was altered: one now saw oneself as a proud and respected member of a new elite. And this new self-conception would be confirmed by events both at the school and afterward. The network of intense personal connections developed with present, past, and future students (as well as those with teachers and with the principal's family) provided a framework in which the dual themes of uplift and self-respect could be further realized after the school stay had been completed.

Gymnastics was often taught together with such "skill" subjects as reading, writing, and arithmetic. But in the spirit of the Grundtvig-Kold folk high school, these subjects remained secondary. The attitude toward them is summed up in a speech given by Jens Lund, principal of Vejstrup Højskole from 1870 to 1911, at the fifty-year jubilee celebration for Askov Højskole in 1894:

> Grundtvig has taught us that "where the most life is, there is the victory." Along these lines our main purpose has not been to teach factual knowledge *(Kundskabsmeddelse)*, but Life's Awakening, even though we had a high respect for knowledge. The school should be for Life, for the spiritual and that which is of the heart, and we were of the opinion that the necessary skills in all of the good conventional pursuits would in time spring forth out of this Source.[82]

A collection of letters in Ernst Trier's private archives shows how the *folkehøjskole* came to function as a far-flung social network with the principal and the school at its center.[83] Written between 1865 and 1893 by former students at Vallekilde Højskole, the letters show them in transition from youth to adulthood. Although most letter writers come from rural Denmark, they are of both sexes, live in different regions of the country, and represent different social classes. The matters that come up in these letters are many and various according to Margarethe Balle-Petersen, who studied the archive material. Is it possible that a brother or friend can be accepted for the next winter school? Will Trier himself come and hold a lecture at their school? Will he write a wedding song for good friends who are also former students? Can he help with money for a hospital stay? Write a letter of recommendation for a free school teacher who is seeking a position? Or, as in the following letter, help with fruit trees:

Dear Trier.

I have finally got the letter from the Heath Society that I can get the last windbreak trees for half price for our new garden. So I am reminding you about your words to me last summer in Bregninggaardskov that I shouldn't give out money for fruit trees but just write a little letter to you and then you will send me fruit trees That is my wish if you could send some for the spring and if possible some fruit bushes also.

You are greeted now with love from me and my wife. Please greet Bentsen, Peter Mortensen and his wife from us. (Kristian G.)

Some of the letters deal with personal difficulty. They mention disappointments, poor economy, and bad health. But many glow with the joyful optimism of those who feel that they have been truly awakened by their high school stay. The resulting gratitude and good feelings are often expressed in deeply religious metaphors, as in the following letter:

Dear Trier.

I am saying it still another time, many thanks for the stay at Vallekilde, it was light and wonderful days that flew by, but I can still if God be permitted say that it wasn't just the momentary gladness and joy, but I received a Light to see that now eclipses my whole life. I was raised in a wonderful christian home, but when I listened at morning confession and prayer I was filled with a peace and a rest that I cannot describe to anyone. (Katherine G., 1884)

Another insightful letter is written by a former student who has just become engaged and contemplates the prospect of married life. It is not difficult to detect the influence of the high school stay on his thinking:

> Yes Dear Trier I have become engaged with a girl who is young and poor. I hope it is with God's Will that we have gotten to be close to each other and I am hoping that when the Time comes that we will live in our own home no matter how small it may be. Not just to be a place where we eat our food and sleep our sleep and have a shelter against weather and wind but a house where warm hearts beat and noble thoughts are born, where Life's best forces are strengthened and developed, because such a home would I wish and ask God to set port in. (Niels A., 1885)

These letters and many others like them testify to the personal transformation that had taken place in the lives of Trier's students. Envisioned by Grundtvig and then brought to life by the work of Kold and others, the Danish folk high school had begun to set its mark on the quality of rural life. The following decades would see many new developments, but in its essential outlines the type of school described here would build on these traditions. It would serve primarily the children of Danish farmers until the postwar decades of the 1950s and 1960s.

Ernst Trier holding a foredrag for the young women at Vallekilde, 1888. The prevalent pattern was that the young women came in the summer, the young men in the winter (from Grundtvig og Danmark, *1983, reprinted by permission of the Nationalhistorisk Museum, Frederiksborg Castle).*

A Day at Askov Højskole in 1900

At seven o'clock in the morning the bell over the main entrance rings; the school awakens. Doors and windows are thrown open, and the students make up their beds. As a rule there are two in a room and everyone brings his bedding from home. The students fetch water from the pump, sweep the floor, and clean up their rooms. Everything must be finished by half past seven. Then the bell rings a second time for breakfast in Dagmar Hall. You hear the clattering of wooden shoes and heavy boots. The young fellows pour out of the "White House," the main building, and the other dormitories and are soon seated on benches at the long tables in the large hall. After breakfast there is a morning service at which attendance is voluntary. The service begins with a hymn played on the harmonium by Frau Ingeborg Appel, the wife of the director, which all join in singing. Then a prayer is read.

At eight o'clock comes the first lecture in the large lecture hall, before which they all join in a song. Singing, singing, continual singing might be the motto of the school. Songs by Grundtvig, Richardt, Bjørnson, and folk songs predominate. At the morning lecture both men and women are present; the subject matter varies. Either Dr. Marius Christensen lectures on philology, Professor La Cour on the history of physics, or Professor Ludwig Schrøder tells some Norse myths and sagas.

As soon as the lecture is over, the young fellows rush to get into their gymn suits, and by nine o'clock they are in the gymnasium. They are directed to run around the track a few times to get limbered up. After that the setting up exercises are gone through very carefully. Then the students form in separate sections and are soon occupied with a great variety of exercises. Some turn somersaults or do Swedish bending movements;

others practice on the horizontal bar or vaulting the horse. Every man is as active as can be, and at the end of the hour they are dripping with perspiration. The order is given to "quit work," and like a flash the boys rush into the dressing rooms to take showers. There isn't a lot of heat: the gymn is cold and the shower is cold, but no one becomes ill. Immediately thereafter, the bell for the second breakfast rings.

At half past ten all the students reassemble in the large lecture hall. This time either Professor La Cour or Director Appel gives a lecture on natural science following the historical method originally developed by La Cour; or Axelsen, the history teacher, speaks on the history of the world in modern times. After this the students divide up, going to separate rooms where instruction in arithmetic, needlework, hygiene, history, and geography is given until two o'clock. Then comes dinner. The food at Askov is not the least of the school's achievements. It is grown on the lands that surround the high school.

It requires a high degree of economy and efficiency to provide four meals a day at 25 kroner a month, which is what the pupils pay for their board. The dinner is simple and good, consisting of two solid dishes such as soup and roast beef or eggs in some form, with dessert and some special Danish delicacies. At Askov, as in all the other high schools, this is the business of the director's wife. She plays an important part in the management of the school, besides occasionally teaching courses in home economics. After dinner there is a recess until 3:15, during which time the students, if they care to, take part in some sport—football, or if the weather serves, a winter sport.

At 3:15 old man Nutzhorn, one of the early teachers, appears in the school yard with his baton under his arm; the students all assemble in the gymnasium and soon the great room resounds with hundreds of lusty voices.

From four to six o'clock there are lessons for the men in Danish, German, and English, while the women take gymnastics under the direction of Frau Ingeborg Appel. Since 1885 Askov has had a women's department. The girls do not live in the institution but with the teachers or in other homes of the little town that has grown up around the school. They attend the chief lectures with the men; in other studies they are taught in separate classes. Besides this department for women in the winter, there is also the general high school course for women in the summer.

At six o'clock the students all reassemble in the large lecture hall for the last lecture of the day, which is again devoted to history. Fenger, a divinity school graduate, may speak on early Danish history; or Director Appel on some subject dealing with the history of other countries, such as England or Russia; or Professor Schrøder on Grundtvig's ideas of nationality or on some other historical or philosophical subject.

Another astounding thing—especially if one remembers college scenes where one went to the library because one had to—was the library at Askov at night. Anyone who comes to Askov Højskole in the evening, any evening, even in the dark of winter, will most likely find the library filled until nine or ten at night with students who are reading and studying on their own. These students are proud and self-motivated. *All* of the lectures are attended. There are no disciplinary threats needed to get people to go; everyone just comes. Alcohol is officially forbidden and virtually nonexistent in student life. The statistics in 1906 will show that 31% of the young people of the country districts between the ages of twenty and twenty-five are attending either the agricultural or the folk high school. In 1927, about every third man or woman in the rural districts will go to a folk high school. In 1928 there will be from four to five hundred students in attendance during the winter course at Askov, and the staff will include thirteen full-time teachers. By this time, in the first three decades of the twentieth century, the folk high school has become "one of the great cultural forces in Denmark—a fact of great significance in the life of the country, since the country people are now among the leaders in political as well as economic affairs."[84]

III. Summary and Conclusion

In reviewing the historical material of the last two chapters, two concluding arguments need to be made. The first is more narrow and specific, summarizing the developments that have been traced in Danish society over time. The other, of a somewhat broader nature, will be put in the form of a question. Let us begin with the former.

In the years following the breakthrough period of 1864–76, the folk high school became a familiar sight on the Danish countryside. The schools accomplished a dual task. First, they provided a type of education that lifted the self-owning farmers above the limitations of their social class background and enabled them to transcend the provincialism of the village and the small town. Second, they facilitated an intense interpersonal experience that functioned "to harmonize inwardly the separate individual interests of the independent farmers by establishing a common ideological understanding."[85] When a student completed a stay at a *folkehøjskole* and returned to his or her home district, it was only natural to join a circle of people who had been transformed by the same experience. Many former students deliberately chose to live near a high school so that they could participate in its public meetings. They would come to listen when teachers or guest speakers held forth on topics of interest. In this way they not only reinforced their ties with the folk high school community but continued their personal education as well. In the last four decades of the nineteenth century, the new type of school became the effective social instrument of a single, relatively homogeneous group of the rural elite, a class of self-owning farmers whose existence was made possible by the Land Reforms of the late eighteenth century. Although the liberation of the rural underclass would have to wait until the early years of the twentieth century, the members of this independent class of self-owning farmers could already see their lives being transformed.

The institution of the *folkehøjskole* was an essential element in this successful transformation, yet viewed in context it is only one of a number of "secondary agents of transformation." Many who once attended a folk high school were instrumental in the formation of the cooperative movement (*andelsbevægelse*) that radically transformed the face of Danish agriculture in the 1880s. Its growth was rapid to the point of being explosive: in 1882 the first cooperative dairy was established; in 1903, just twenty-one years later, the cooperative dairies were handling milk from 80% of all the cows in Denmark.[86] The two movements are distinct yet related, the role played by the folk high schools most likely an important but indirect one.[87] The nature of the connection between them is suggested by these comments made by a former female *folkehøjskole* student:

> These enthusiastic *højskole* people . . . transformed the whole district. The battle for freedom and *folkelig* self-control brought new forms of social gathering: the political meetings, the target-shooting parties, the hunting clubs. . . . Dairies and cooperatives were built. It was the force of the people that sprang out among us, a social conduit in which old social barriers crumbled and new forms of fellowship bound people together. But up over that, lines were lifted that pointed up over one's class and that of the social, and in toward *folkeligheden* and personality.[88]

The rural culture of the self-owning farmers would be transformed in other ways during these years. Agricultural schools were established *(landbrugsskoler,* 1849), and agricultural instruction made available at the university level as well *(landbohøjskolen,* 1856).[89] New legislation gave independent congregations the right to choose their own ministers *(valgmenigheder,* 1867). Local meetinghouses made it possible to sustain and encourage an active group life *(forsamlingshuser)*; it has been estimated that at least seventeen hundred were built in the course of the last century.[90] The establishment of Grundtvigian free schools *(friskoler)* enabled the self-owning farmers to educate their children in the way that they saw fit. Many felt that formal education was detrimental and chose to educate their children at home. When the time came for the children to take the formal exams, they did so often with just one year of schooling; many went on to high achievements.

In the decades that followed, the members of this group came to constitute that rare and valuable human resource, a class of democratically educated, independent farmers possessing its own distinct tradition and culture. Although the existence of this class is increasingly threatened by contemporary developments, it is a class that still exists in Denmark today. What kind of people are they? The following lines, written by a Danish rural historian, are concise and to the point (as are the people of whom he speaks):

> For someone coming from the outside, it could almost be moving to meet these people. There was often a natural carriage, a secure, matter-of-fact sense of one's own worth, that clearly flowed over into openness and broadmindedness. There were many books on the shelves, there was often fine art in the local tradition on the walls, and as well, something that could be perceived as their own musical tradition.[91]

We must recall the previous chapter's descriptions of the general wretchedness of Danish rural life under the feudal system before the real achievements of the Land Reforms become clear. C. Wright Mills has posed the following as fundamental questions in any systematic study of social change: "What varieties of men and women now prevail in this society and in the period? And what varieties are coming to prevail?"[92] We are now in a position to address these questions. At least two new social classes have been created in rural Denmark, and in connection with their creation two new types of personality can be seen: the farmers and their wives who, when young, had been touched by the Grundtvigian dream of enlightenment and the "high school men" who willingly dedicated their lives to serve as instruments of the old pastor's vision. The ascendancy of the self-owning farmers would have pleased Reventlow. Hopelessness has been replaced by optimism, helplessness by independence, and indifference by competence. The modernized rural sector has followed a unique Danish path to capitalist development. The primary agents of transformation were the Land Reforms (1784–99), followed a half century later by the end of absolute monarchy and the achievement of constitutional democracy (1848–49). The secondary agents of transformation were located in a complex of grass roots social movements, including the central focus of this chapter, the folk high school movement.

What was to happen to these schools? In 1892 the first High School law (*Højskolelov*) was passed. It provided the following forms of state support: a fixed yearly subsidy of 300 kroner to each high school; a support of ten kroner for each pupil per year; coverage of up to one-third of the expenses for staff salaries and instruction; and a special subsidy for poor students seeking to attend a school session.[93] The passage of this legislation marks the conclusion of the initial period of the folk high school, a time when the schools belonged to a decentralized grass roots social movement that gave the independent landed farmers a vehicle of social and personal self-trans-formation. The same school, however, would show itself capable of playing other and quite different roles in the future. This issue, perhaps implicit in Grundtvig's original vision, was addressed in a prescient and earthy comment made by Ludvig Schrøder in 1872: "We have a saying in Denmark: stick your finger down into the soil and smell where you are! *There* is where the needs of the people are found, which can be different in different places and times. Where this meets the abilities of the teacher, there lies the *højskoles*' calling."[94]

The way ahead for the independent farmers was not to be an easy one, for in the period after 1860 Danish society was to move generally to the right. The fiasco of 1864 brought more conservative forces to power and resulted in a right-wing alliance between the estate owners and what was left of the National Liberals. This right-wing alliance *(Højre)* was to remain more or less in power all the way to the mid-1890s, and it was not until 1901 that a system shift would bring the new party of the self-owning farmers (the *Forenede Venstre,* or United Left) to national power.[95] In the meantime the farmers would be forced to wage an extended battle against the dominant alliance to protect their own interests. This right-wing alliance would attempt in 1866 to drastically limit the Constitution, and in 1872 it would try to deny the farmers' United Left party the right to exercise its elected majority in the Parliament *(Folketing).* It regarded many of the folk high schools as subversive institutions, as "political nurseries," and would attempt to deny many of them the state support that even as early as 1872 was becoming increasingly common.

In spite of the fact the folk high schools belonged to no particular creed, they were never completely apolitical. As Trier himself wrote with a touch of irony the same year: "I am not a politician and speak seldom of politics at my school. But yet every last young man that goes out from my school is an enthusiastic supporter of the United Left party."[96] In the 1880s the forms of confrontation between the farmers and the old guard elite would be extreme, almost coming to open armed conflict. But no matter how intense the efforts to crush the farmers, they did not succeed. The goal of cultural revitalization had been achieved for a significant minority of the Danish rural community. And the outbreak of social violence on a mass scale was somehow avoided. But how and why were the Danes able to accomplish this major transformation of the rural sector without recourse to violence?

Having considered the more narrow of the two concluding arguments, let us again face the broader and central question that guides this inquiry: What is it about the Danes that has made it possible for the process of modernization to take place among them in the virtual absence of political repression and widespread social violence? Why are there no lynchings, guillotines, mass executions, death squads, unmarked graves, or even a single real reign of terror during these episodes of crisis-driven social change? One must look at geopolitical factors—at the relevant details of climate, resource base, demography, geographic setting, social class structure, the changing world economy with its markets, wars and alliances, and the long- and short-run historical trends resulting from the interaction of all of the above. But I would like to argue that these trends and developments will in the end prove necessary but not sufficient to account for the Danish ability to conduct major social transformations in the absence of mass social violence. Indeed, all of these factors *have* been reviewed in previous chapters, and there is *nowhere* in the material presented a clear solution to this dilemma. On the basis of long-term ethnographic fieldwork, I believe that no coherent answer to this question can be given without an examination of the topic to which we now turn—Danish national character.

It seems fitting to end this chapter with several reflections about Grundtvig. The first is a judgment made by Danish historian Uffe Østergård: "It seems as if the series of thoughts formulated by Grundtvig in the middle of the previous century have a validity far exceeding the epoch and the class they were formulated in and for."[97] The truth of this judgment can be seen in the fact that the folk high schools of today play an equally important, though much altered role. Østergård's analysis, however, suggests that Grundtvig's real impact goes far beyond the single case of the folk high schools, influencing such wider cultural patterns as Danish nationalism and the manner of its acceptable expression (the next chapter will draw on Østergård's insights in fashioning an interpretation of Grundtvig's influence on Danish national character).

The second statement was not made with Grundtvig in mind. It is a remembrance of Dante offered by the English poet Andrew Marvell. Written in a Shakespearean language that Grundtvig himself doubtless would have appreciated, it celebrates the poet as the savior of his people in times of national crisis:

> When the Sword glitters o'er the Judges head
> And fear has Coward Churchmen silenced
> Then is the Poet's time, 'tis then he drawes
> And single fights forsaken Vertues cause.
> He, when the wheel of Empire whirleth back
> And through the World's disjointed Axel crack,
> Sings still of ancient Rights and better Times,
> Seeks wretched good, arraigns successful Crimes.[98]

But it is perhaps these lines written by Jørgen Bukhdal that provide the most fitting tribute to Grundtvig, in whose fertile mind the Danish folk high schools were first envisioned:

> By far the most of his opinions and ideas are broken against time's coast, wash ashore in the wreckage that is gathered like relics. He belonged to a definite time and echoed it completely: Late Enlightenment, Romantic, late Romantic time. He was always on the move, acting or reacting. That is natural. The man who is not time's child can bring us no message from eternity.[99]

PART IV

THEMES IN THE DANISH NATIONAL CHARACTER

CHAPTER SIX

Democracy and Egalitarianism

I. GRUNDTVIG AND DANISH NATIONAL CHARACTER

THE PAST TWO CHAPTERS have traced some of the fundamental historical events connected with modernization in Denmark. A distinction was made between the *primary agents of transformation,* which included both the Danish Land Reforms (1765–99) and the acquisition of constitutional democracy (1848–49); and *the secondary agents of transformation,* a complex of grass roots social movements that included the folk high schools, cooperatives, agricultural schools, local meetinghouses, independent congregations, rural religious revival movements, the society to reclaim the heath in Jutland, the landless farmers' movement, and the beginnings of social welfare institutions. These events were part of the process of modernization and capitalist development in Denmark. Parallel processes were taking place in France, England, Italy, and the other nations of Europe during this historical period, as well as in the United States. And yet the process as seen in Denmark has its own unique features, perhaps the most interesting of which is that the far-reaching and fundamental social transitions connected with the modernizing process took place in a generally non-violent manner. The demonstrated ability of the Danes to make these peaceful social transitions is what the following analysis seeks to clarify.

History, Gibbon once wrote, is little more than a "register of crimes, sorrows and misfortunes." It is, equally often, a study in personal and collective self-deception, in the black ironies of tragedy, and in the fatal excesses of greed. Only rarely does it enlighten and inspire by revealing a narrative of events that demonstrates the potential for human wisdom. It is my contention that the pattern of events described in the previous two chapters provides an example of just such a narrative. Indeed, this is part of the significance of these events and one reason they ought to be of interest to those outside of Denmark. Let us recall some of the distinctly unusual features of the Danish case: A class of feudal landowners that voluntarily undergoes a diminution of its power by relinquishing control over nearly

50% of the rural peasantry bound to its estates? A minority of this same class of elite landowners that not only willingly surrenders this authority but is found in the very vanguard of the political process by which this end is accomplished? One king who consistently aids and abets these rural reforms, and another who allows a nearly two hundred-year-old tradition of absolute monarchy to be ended by the people without firing a shot? Any discussion of Denmark and the Danes, whatever its conceptual approach, must be able to shed some light on the cultural factors behind these unusual actions and policies. A number of Danish authors writing in the 1980s and earlier have seen a connection between the Danish path to modernization and the life and work of N. F. S. Grundtvig. They have argued that Grundtvig's influence went far beyond any of his specific contributions, beyond his writings on education, or his prophetic vision, which proved instrumental in the founding of the folk high schools. To understand this line of reasoning, it is necessary to look at the relationship that exists between Grundtvig the man and the philosophy or social ideology that came to be called *Grundtvigianisme.*

Uffe Østergård has pointed out that the philosophy of *Grundtvigianisme* belonged to neither a system nor a party during Grundtvig's own life. In fact the initial use of the term *Grundtvigianer* was not by those to whom this term referred but by the conservative opposition, and the intent behind it was not at all complimentary. It was meant to communicate the snide contempt felt by members of an old guard for the odd collection of priests, principals, farmers, and professors who were foolish enough to think that there was meaning in Grundtvig's madness. The matter is further complicated because Grundtvig was not necessarily a Grundtvigian and did not subscribe to everything that was preached or practiced in his name. The situation is perhaps best put into perspective by Anders Pontoppidan Thyssen's remark that after 1870, "Grundtvig was taken prisoner by the Grundtvigians."

Nevertheless, the developments that took place after Grundtvig's death confirmed that there had been a meaning behind his madness. They further suggested that its influence was to be of a more subtle and pervasive form than anyone (including Grundtvig himself) could have anticipated. We have seen that Grundtvig's ideas were quickly taken up by the folk high school movement that served for the most part a single incipient rural elite, the self-owning farmers. His ideas were instrumental in the political education, personal development, and social ascendancy of their particular subgroup in rural Denmark. An institutional sociologist anticipating the future at this point might well have predicted the following: "Such fanciful ideas as the People's Enlightenment and *Folkelighed* will tend to remain the

Grundtvig as icon. "To battle against 'the bite of death,'" reads the caption in this contemporary lithograph by Thomas Kruse, 1977. The top section shows a range of contemporary grass roots movements in non-violent protest. Note the supporting presence of Grundtvig located between the oppressive figures and the liberated dancers in the bottom section (from Grundtvig og Danmark, *1983, reprinted by permission of the Nationalhistorisk Museum, Frederiksborg Castle).*

exclusive property of this rural elite, and as the class consolidates its position in society over time, the ideas themselves will become more and more rigid as they become increasingly identified with a particular and limited set of class interests."

What happened, however, is that precisely the opposite development took place. Instead of continuing to act as the vehicle of a single group, Grundtvig's views were gradually absorbed into the general fabric of Danish society. From its initial role as a specific class ideology of the independent self-owning farmers, the philosophy advanced in Grundtvig's name slowly reached out its *folkelig* tentacles to all of the other major institutions of

Grundtvig as a
working man. This lino-
cut by Herman Stilling,
1972, shows Grundtvig
in work clothes, helping to
build the new folk high
school in Kolding
(from Grundtvig og
Danmark, *1983, re-*
printed by permission of
the Nationalhistorisk
Museum, Frederiksborg
Castle).

Danish society, and one by one it engulfed and devoured them. First the schools, then the church, next the political party of the self-owning farmers (*Forenede Venstre*). These were in turn followed by the newly significant urban working class, the labor unions that sought to advance their interests, and eventually nearly all Danish politicians, whatever their narrow party allegiance. When the church service for the two hundredth anniversary of Grundtvig's birth was held in September 1983, the panning camera showed representatives from almost every side of Denmark's economic, political, and cultural elite in dutiful attendance. The heritage of Grundtvig belongs unquestionably to everyone in Denmark today. It is no longer the property of a single social class but has succeeded in infiltrating most segments of Danish society. Thus Thomas Bredsdorff, a folk high school principal until his death in 1922, wrote that "all Danes have met the effects of Grundtvig's life struggle in our people, consciously or unconsciously."[1] Østergård has spoken of "the establishment of the cultural hegemony of Grundtvigianism as the dominating national ideology." It is a judgment in which many other Danes would concur.

Still, upon learning the exceedingly broad and diverse affiliations of those professing to express Grundtvigian sentiments, the first response of our institutional sociologist might well be to explain it away on the following grounds. "What we see is only a rhetorical and outward show of loyalty and consensus that has been artificially manufactured for the purpose of public ritual," he could easily conclude. "It represents the final conversion of a living man into a dead totem, and is made possible by the fact that anything really controversial in Grundtvig's original vision has been smoothed over, ignored, or forgotten." I would not want to argue that this indictment is entirely false. The many ritual ways in which the specter of Grundtvig is invoked in contemporary dialogue can be a source of irritation, amusement, or even profound boredom to a Danish audience. But to reduce Grundtvig to the level of a lifeless icon fails to take into account the subtle way in which part of his original vision has become transformed into Jung's "collective unconscious," or what the poet William Anderson has called "the Great Memory," thus becoming part of the unconscious social fabric of the Danish nation. It is perhaps this that is hinted at when Danes say wisely of Grundtvig, "You meet him at the border." The subtle nature of Grundtvig's influence has been thus encapsulated by Østergård:

> If one defines Grundtvigianism in a very broad way, one can say that the ideology of the self-owning farmers triumphed over the urban middle class. Not in a formal and institutionalized way, but really, in actual fact. It was namely their premises that came to be the foundation of the political culture and education in this country. *The Grundtvigians succeeded in influencing their opponents in a manner that went "behind the back" of their opponents' self-understanding* [italics added]. It looks to me as though their class ideology became something preconscious, something "natural," something we don't think about. This is true not only for all of the present ruling political elite but also for the elite in the labor movement, in spite of the fact that they received a very different education and socialization.[2]

One of the tasks of this discussion of national character will be to detect the influence of Grundtvig on that part of Danish national character that helps account for the ability to undergo massive social transitions and upheavals without recourse to institutionalized violence. There is, of course, considerably more to this pattern of events than the life and work of Grundtvig. Perhaps the single most important instance of non-violent transformation, the passage of the Land Reforms, had nothing whatsoever to do with him. The Land Reforms were written by Reventlow, Colbjørnsen, and others at a time when Grundtvig was quite young, well before anything he did or said could have begun to influence his contemporaries. It is furthermore clear that Grundtvig himself must be seen as having been formed in part by the Danish culture that would subsequently be so influenced by his own life and work. Yet even with all these qualifications, the influence of Grundtvig is a profound one that must be taken into account in any discussion of Danish national character.

II. NATIONAL CHARACTER AND CORE VALUES

The concept of national character used here is "symbolic interactionist" rather than psychoanalytic.[3] Based on nearly three years of observant participation in Danish society during the 1980s, this discussion will treat some of the major values underlying Danish cultural life. A range of questions must be considered: What are some of the ideological bases of Danish social institutions, and what kinds of social interaction are found in particular settings? What types of people does one meet in Denmark, and—given their individual differences and uniqueness—is it possible to see and identify in them something that is specifically "Danish"? In other words, what are the systematic commonalities in mode of thought, feeling, and social behavior that distinguish Danes from non-Danes? How are these commonalities related to important present and past themes in Danish history, in particular the demonstrated ability of the Danes to carry out fundamental social change without recourse to organized social violence? What are the most important Danish social rules, and how do the Danes practice or avoid practicing them? What are the consequences of each kind of behavior? How does the author's point of view differ from the way the Danes themselves would be likely to view these matters?

This task has been approached using the concept of *core values*. A core value may be defined as a principle or set of related principles that is deeply cherished as part of a coherent cultural tradition. Like any value, it will not be capable of realization in each and every instance. Indeed, individuals *do not* always embrace these values; on the contrary, they may even be seen resisting and expressing hostility toward them.[4] A core value, it may be said, is one that is usually honored more in the observance than in the breach. The significance of the core values, however, is not that all individuals slavishly conform to them but that they form a set of powerful background expectations that constantly play on the actions and judgments of members of a society. The criterion used in choosing "core values" in this study was simply that people in Denmark could be seen orienting themselves and relating to others in terms of the value a significant proportion of the time and on a wide range of occasions. For that reason I believe these values are critical in any discussion of the Danish national character.

The following four chapters will focus on the positive side of these core values: (1) democracy and egalitarianism; (2) balance and moderation; (3) the Danish art of sociability as reflected in the concept of *hygge*; and (4) welfare and social responsibility. Each core value involves a number of related attitudes and practices. Taken together, these four value areas constitute a positive and specifically Danish functional complex of values that it is hoped will provide some insight into the Danish capacity for non-violent social transitions. Yet it behooves an ethnographer to have some respect for the people of whom he writes. To portray Danish culture in an exclusively positive light would be intolerable to Danish readers; it would violate the balance principle, the second of the above core values. In the interest of making a more balanced presentation, Chapter Ten provides a look at the dark side of the same core values.

III. MOVING THROUGH THE ANTHROPOLOGIST'S WINDOW OF TIME

Our focus moves now from the past to the present. We must leave behind the triumphant optimism of the self-owning farmers and the folk high schools. We are no longer in an age of cooperatives but in one of multinational corporations. Most of the local meetinghouses are empty. The prevailing turn to agnosticism, cults, Eastern religions, or to mere indifference has made the church significantly less of a social vehicle for the achievement of community than it was in past times. There is no need today for a special school to serve the children of farmers. For one thing, the rural segment of the population has shrunk so drastically that it constituted only 7% of the total in 1988. In addition, a series of educational reforms, particularly the reform law of 1937, has created a balance between education in the urban and rural sectors. The greater effectiveness of rural public education makes it much less necessary for the folk high school to play its traditional role. The landed farmers do not need to hear uplifting themes these days; they are already part of a ruling conservative elite. The old rural proletariat has vanished, but a new and disturbingly large underclass can be seen hanging out in the streets of cities and towns. Many are young and under the influence of narcotics or some other form of nihilism. Beginning in the postwar years of the 1950s and 1960s, Denmark began the transition from a modern to a postmodern society.

There is a revealing expression in Danish about the decade of the 1960s: *de glade tressere* (the happy sixties). It was a decade that began with the Danish Great Leap Forward (1958–62), a four-year period in which the national product at fixed prices increased by a total of 26%, a rate never before or since equalled. One of the factors behind this sudden jump toward prosperity was that the terms of international trade had swung in favor of Denmark again. As a partial consequence of the subsequent expansion it stimulated, unemployment fell from seventy-five thousand in 1957 to a mere twenty-five thousand in 1962, providing a full-employment economy. An added development of considerable importance took place midway in the decade as the emerging worldwide youth movement, much like Sandburg's fog, arrived from California on little cat feet. Armed with beads, trip glasses and hallucinogens, many were aroused by the heady mixture of new music and old ideals to make demands for personal and social liberation. Some (mainly but not exclusively the young) watched it all with glad rejoicing. Others could only watch with consternation.

But there were even then a number of disturbing signs in the air. For one thing the 1960s were a decade of soaring taxation. Indirect taxes on cars, alcohol, and tobacco were substantially increased; a 10% value-added tax (VAT) was introduced in 1967. Late in the decade the income tax system was further restructured in a way that made Danes some of the highest taxpayers in the world. As the economic expansion took place, significant numbers of immigrant workers from such countries as Turkey, Pakistan, and Yugoslavia were invited into the country to meet the rising labor demand. Two decades later the relationship between members of these minority groups and the general Danish population has become a major unsolved problem. Moreover, it is one that has been exacerbated by the increased unemployment of the 1980s.

Danish foreign policy in the postwar decades has reflected the attempt to reach a difficult balance among a number of competing themes. It has pursued the general goals of national security, international coexistence, and economic cooperation. These goals led Denmark to become a member of NATO in 1949, after negotiations for a common defense alliance with Norway and Sweden had fallen through. The theme of Nordic cooperation remains an important one for Denmark. In 1952 Denmark, Finland, Iceland, Norway, and Sweden formed the Nordic Council, an assembly that works to promote closer relations between the Nordic countries. Yet its lack of raw materials and its dependence on outside trade links were critical factors inhibiting the further extension of Nordic cooperation. These factors eventually facilitated the Danish entrance into the European Economic Community (EEC).

In both economic and political terms, the year 1973 was a significant one for Denmark. When Britain—a major trading partner—decided to become a member of the European Economic Community, Denmark did so as well. Together with the U.K. and Ireland, Denmark became an active member of the EEC on 1 January 1973. Entrance into EEC that year earned the country higher prices for its farm exports and better terms of trade. But the first oil crisis in the autumn of that year not only fed the flames of inflation but largely canceled out the favorable effects of EEC membership. With no alternative energy sources available and therefore forced to import all of its energy needs, the Danish economy absorbed a 300% increase in oil prices between 1972 and 1974. During the period of 1973–75, a worrisome inflation took place; wages rose by about 20%, prices more than 15%.

The deepening of the international recession hurt both the terms of trade and the balance of payments situation (the latter a critical index that had begun to show signs of deterioration as early as 1969). All of these developments in turn had consequences on the political party system and the voting behavior of the Danish electorate. In December 1973 the country held its twelfth general election since the war. The results pointed to a high degree of internal ferment and change. There had been five parties in the *Folketing;* suddenly there were ten. These changes portended a more complicated political process than ever before, one in which coalitions and minority splinter parties would play an increasingly important role. To some Danes, it was all beginning to look like chaos.

In the meantime, there were further developments. The impact of the second oil crisis (1978–80) served only to intensify these difficulties. The balance of payments situation had become intolerable, if not to the average Dane, then certainly to the community of international bankers. By 1982 *The Wall Street Journal* could snidely point out that *some* countries in western Europe had spent themselves into such a corner that the international financial community was threatening to include them in the same category as Mexico, Poland, and Brazil. Denmark was specifically mentioned as one of "them," a prime and pampered offender whose triple-A credit status was clearly jeopardized by its spendthrift life-style.[5] Some bankers talked openly about a bailout by the International Monetary Fund; others even whispered the dreaded word "default." The Danes were living too well on borrowed money. They were going to hell, but they were going *first class.* They had financed their better health care systems, higher unemployment benefits, and new child care centers by increasing the national debt from $2 billion to $16 billion in the course of a single decade. The bankers in London and New York from credit-granting institutions like Chase Manhattan and Standard & Poor were very upset. Something needed to be done.

And something was. The ruling minority government from 1975 to 1982 had been formed by the Social Democrats, who had been in control for the better part of many decades. As the burden of foreign debt became increasingly heavy, and the evident alternatives more and more unpalatable, the government led by Anker Jørgensen did a completely unprecedented thing. In September 1982 it resigned and surrendered power, without an election, to a new and nonsocialist government led by Poul Schlüter. Although the new government almost fell apart from internal dissension even before assuming power, a series of timely compromises were made and for the first time since 1901 Denmark had a Conservative prime minister. On 10 September 1982, Poul Schlüter formed a coalition government (nicknamed *Firkløveret,* the "Four-Leaf clover") consisting of four parties. One of them, his own party, was the direct descendent of the old right-wing alliance. Originally known as the party of the Right *(Højre),* it had been renamed the Conservative People's Party *(Konservative Folkeparti)* in 1915.

Their main partner in the new coalition, ironically enough, was the Left party *(Venstre,* conservative in spite of its name). This party, a descendent of the old farmers' party, the United Left, was now united with the former enemy against which it had struggled a century ago (a political development indicating, among other things, that the farmers were once again a strongly conservative force in society). Two other small parties, the Center Democrats *(Centrum Demokraterne)* and the Christian People's Party *(Kristelig Folk Parti),* joined them in this coalition. With only sixty-five seats this new government was a minority government that could not get any legislation of real significance passed without support from outside of its own ranks. Such support had in most cases to be obtained from the ultra-right-wing Progress Party *(Fremskridts Parti)* and the somewhat hard-to-characterize Radical Left *(Radikal Venstre),* a critical swing party that is neither radical nor left. On rare occasions the needed support could be obtained from some element of the determined and vocal left-wing opposition. This opposition was made up of Denmark's single largest party (the Social Democrats) and two independent socialist parties, the Socialist People's Party *(Socialistisk Folkeparti)* and the Left Socialist Party *(Venstre Socialist Parti).* This new political constellation, with its two opposing alignments and key swing parties, would characterize Danish politics for most of the 1980s.

An American landing at Kastrup airport for the first time and driving into Copenhagen feels at home and yet a little distant. Such party coalitions and alignments as those described above, common in European politics, are foreign to Americans; discussions of Danish politics, even when they take place in English, are difficult for Americans to follow. Another thing that must be faced with some bravery is the Danish sense of humor. Upon landing in Copenhagen last summer, I shoved what I confidently proclaimed to be a brand new passport down into the hands of the young customs official in the glass booth. As he studied it, a perplexed expression slowly came over his face. My confidence turned to surprise and then to dismay as I watched him. "This passport is not valid," he said sternly to me when he finally looked up. I became excited, and just as I was about to launch into an indignant speech, he quickly broke into a delighted grin. "You forgot to sign it," he said, and shoved it back out at me for the signature. This kind of leg-pulling is not the sort of communication one expects to receive from customs officials, but at the time I recall that I grinned ruefully back, thinking only that I had to remember I was once again in Denmark.

Denmark in the 1980s. The country has a respected queen and a popular royal family. The entire country is served by an effective network of public transportation. Bicycle lanes are everywhere, as are bicycles with riders of all ages, including men in suits coming home from work. Most teachers at all levels wear jeans to class, and students call them by their first names. Gun control is stringent and enforced. Public gatherings of thousands of people can take place with virtually no police in evidence and no resulting violence. Nudity is tolerated on beaches, in public parks, and on the front pages of major newspapers. The number of officially recognized political parties fluctuates somewhere between nine and thirteen, with at least three or four others attempting to gain recognition. Policemen do not carry guns. There are no commercials on the Danish national television station, and even its new competitor (TV2) does not show commercials in the middle of a program. In addition, the purchasing of space for commercial advertisements does not give companies the right to control the content of programs. There are a great many beautifully kept public parks, even in the urban bustle of downtown Copenhagen. I have never seen a child openly abused or even severely scolded in a public place. There is a kind of school called a Danish folk high school, but it differs greatly from the schools treated in the previous chapter. Welcome to Denmark in the 1980s. Our investigation of Danish national character has begun.

IV. Democracy and Egalitarianism

By taking this as the first of the four core value complexes to be treated, I do not mean to imply that all Danes are unfailingly egalitarian. Nor do I mean to suggest that their society is in every respect a democratic one. "A man's reach should exceed his grasp," wrote the English poet Robert Browning, and it is in this sense that the Danish commitment to these core values must be understood. It is nonetheless true that at the heart of the Danish national character there can be found a strong belief in democracy and egalitarianism. To an extraordinary degree their ideal aspirations, their social attitudes, their political institutions, and even their humor reflect a belief in these two fundamental principles.

The terms require some definition. By "democracy" I mean that state of affairs in which the right to exercise political power is widely distributed and made available to the broadest possible spectrum of those who live in a society. By "egalitarian" I mean the belief that social stratification should be minimized rather than maximized and that individuals, regardless of their wealth or social status, ought to be treated as possessing equal human value. The two are seen as intimately related, the presence of the one usually implying the presence of the other as well.

To suggest that democracy and egalitarianism are fundamental values is not at all to deny that Danish society possesses its own internal system of social class. Even back in 1969, well before the onset of the present social crisis, the sociologists Svalastoga and Wolf distinguished within it nine different strata.[6] If anything, the crisis of the past two decades has added to and exacerbated these previously existing class divisions. What is at issue here, then, is not the existence of class divisions, but how the Danes themselves perceive and evaluate them. Rank and class distinctions are and remain explicit within Danish society, but my observations suggest that their importance as well as their extent is continually minimized and challenged by the presence of a democratic, egalitarian ideal. This ideal is given vigorous and frequent expression; both the context and the manner of its expression typically bring into question the assumptions and attitudes of privilege.

Anthropologists have frequently emphasized that it is not enough to study formal social rules; one must go beyond them to understand how rules function in specific cultural contexts. Rules may be sidestepped, covertly broken, or followed for the wrong reasons. In each of those cases one will want to know something of how the actor's private world intersects with the public consensus reality on the stage of everyday life. The concept of ethos has been a useful one: it refers to the underlying mood, spirit, and sentiment that accompanies the social behavior of performers in a culturally defined situation.[7] The expression of the core values of democracy and egalitarianism will be examined in a range of situations, using the concept of ethos. These situations include labor, everyday sociability, authority relations, gender roles, linguistic change, education, and the Danish monarchy.

Sanctioned Egalitarianism

The Danish attitude toward social stratification can be summed up in the well-known aphorism "A man's a man for all that." A satirical description cited by Svalastoga and Wolf is particularly revealing of the ethos of labor found in Denmark: "If one implies to excavator-and-concrete worker Hansen that there is a difference between him and count Rosenskjold, he will become red in the face and say that that's absolute nonsense, and point out that the count is a fine man, whom one must respect."[8] The humor of the story comes from what it shows about Hansen's basic premise.

Excavation-and-concrete worker Hansen regards himself as a good person possessing excellent human value despite the fact that he is an excavation-and-concrete worker (and not a count). His sense of his own self-worth is so unshakable that the only response he can make to the assertion that there is a difference between him and the count is to fly angrily to the defense of the count, whom he assumes must have been impugned by the implied comparison. This is a man whose dignity is unassailable. Judith Friedman Hansen has perceptively observed that "a Dane will tend to consider any other person as neither better nor lesser than himself, while acknowledging, for example, that the other person may incidentally have more money or a lower status."[9] I should add here that I met quite a few "excavator-and-concrete worker Hansens" during my time in Denmark. Included among them were sandwich makers, public bathhouse attendants, butcher's apprentices, train conductors, hot dog vendors, and folk high school teachers—in short, members of a wide range of occupational groups.

Like all good satire, this little story provides a world of insight. It points to a more general conclusion: in spite of the fact that both are democracies, the ethos of labor in Denmark differs in subtle ways from that found in the United States. This situation is in part due to structural factors in the Danish society that influence the socialization and training of workers. For instance, those employed in many of the occupations considered unskilled in the United States must receive some kind of formal training in Denmark. Cooks in institutions, professional sandwich makers, and agricultural workers will often take lengthy courses as part of their apprenticeship. The experience of Birgitte Toft, the current expert in open-faced sandwiches (smørrebrød) at a Scandinavian restaurant in New York city, is probably typical. Ms. Toft, who can complete a complicated sandwich in thirty seconds, underwent a two-year apprenticeship back in Denmark before coming to work in New York. One thing she learned during her apprenticeship was how to prepare all of the many ingredients from scratch. A proper sandwich is not made in just any old way: "One important rule is that the bread must not show. It must be completely covered with ingredients to suggest abundance. It has to look much bigger than it is. . . . If you can't butter and cut the bread in three quick motions you're not a real professional."[10]

Typically members of a union, those in these occupations are encouraged (more so than in the United States) to develop a sense of competence and self-respect *vis-à-vis* their work roles. It is perhaps only in Denmark that an unskilled worker could be chosen, not once but twice, to serve as prime minister (Anker Jørgensen, who headed a Social Democratic government in 1972–73 and again in 1975–82).[11] Perhaps as a consequence Danish workers, whether in so-called menial jobs or in service occupations, do not lightly tolerate being treated as social inferiors during the performance of their jobs. Whether the formal interaction is between waiter and guest in a restaurant, shopkeeper and customer in a business establishment, or driver and passenger on a downtown bus, the potentially hierarchical implications of the relationship are (or had better be) downplayed by guests, customers, and passengers alike. Putting on any sort of airs before a Dane with whom one has a service relationship is an excellent way to provoke irritation and outright annoyance, often followed by very poor service.

Not only work situations but the more informal focused interactions of everyday life are marked by what Hansen calls "sanctioned egalitarianism." The cardinal sin is to appear to take oneself too seriously and to indicate thereby that one has an inflated view of one's own self-worth. When an individual seems to be setting herself on a pedestal, others will be only too quick to knock it out from under her. If an individual displays pretentious behavior and fails to quickly move to censor his own presentation in the direction of greater social humility, it will usually be done for him by others present. Open boasting made in such a way that it is apparently to be taken seriously violates this informal social code. Through such devices as teasing, joking, and sarcasm, corrective sanctions are effectively brought to bear on an errant individual.

In most cases such an errant individual will quickly "collapse" his or her offending presentation and be taken back into the good graces of those present. Ritual interchanges like these are so stylized that the entire sequence often occurs as a unit within a special "play frame" in informal sociability, both the claims of the "sinner" and the correcting maneuvers of the group being advanced in a nonserious fashion. In this case it is jest and wit offering mutual appreciation of verbal spontaneity that are the goals of the interaction. As I can say from personal experience, "putting on airs" is not something that the Danes allow each other (or anyone else) to get away with for very long.

One of the strongest and clearest manifestations of the egalitarian spirit can be seen in the manner in which those who hold high office are treated. There is a great readiness on the part of nearly everyone to criticize all forms of authority. The statements and actions of public officials are under constant scrutiny by the population at large. A process is thus set in motion through which those who hold public office are never allowed to be complacent about either their popularity or the degree of respect in which they are held. They know that they will become the frequent objects of ridicule and satire, expressed with equal pungency whether in newspaper articles, media programs, or everyday gossip. This Danish attitude has been nicely summarized by Bo Bøjesen: "Although sworn adherents of the democratic system, we do not hide the fact that every popularly elected representative strikes us as a lying, intemperate, sexually maladjusted swindler whose mental faculties are incomprehensibly poorly developed."[12]

The natural suspicion about authority implied in these comments is an integral part of the Danish national character. This suspicion extends beyond the perceived degree of basic competence possessed by the authority to include its intentions and goodwill. In the United States there is a tendency to at least *begin* by imputing to some authorities greater knowledge and superior ability ("if we only knew what they knew," "you've got to trust the President," etc.). In Denmark there is on the whole a much quicker and deeper sense of suspicion about the actions of an authority. If an individual citizen is hit by a policeman, it will more likely be the policeman, not the citizen, who is called on the carpet. If a politician is felt to have expressed contempt for the people or a sense of superiority, that politician will be mercilessly flayed in the press soon afterward. Nor are the political parties themselves exempt from such treatment.

Thus the comedians on a Sunday morning radio program brightly announced, as if doing a soap commercial, "Seven out of eight politicians use the Radicals!"[13] When a minister allegedly commented that the recent parliamentary criticism of her policies was an unjustified interference in her work, one paper ran a cartoon that showed her contemptuously tossing the Danish constitution into a garbage can. The caption read "My Will—The People's Law."[14] When the prime minister's coalition attempted to negotiate further cuts in welfare funding, the same newspaper showed on the cover a picture of the prime minister's smiling face, placed above a body in the form of a huge slot machine. The headline was "The Machine that Crushes The Poor." It is true that sharp political satire can be found in the United States, but in my experience there is nothing that matches the truly savage tone of the above Danish commentary. Danes do not mince words when taking their leaders apart in public, and there is not much these leaders can do in response other than try to keep their wits about them and their dignity intact.

Suspicion as to the limited competence of authority is not restricted to Denmark. On the contrary, it extends well beyond Danish borders. Foreign dignitaries and even heads of state are not exempt from treatment aimed at diminishing what is felt to be their excessive public image. Thus in one prime-time Saturday night TV variety program, a fake news broadcaster suddenly appeared with an interpolated news bulletin: "We interrupt to bring you news of this emergency: a fire has broken out in the American White House, and [after a moment of coy hesitation] we regret to tell you that *both* of the President's books were burned." Two minutes later the simulated news broadcast reappeared and the same "broadcaster" announced with a worried look on his face: "The tragedy was even worse than we thought—he had only colored one of them in."[15]

The same irreverent distrust of authority is often in evidence when televised documentaries treat social problems. Interviews with administrators about their agency and its policies are typically either preceded or followed by interviews with recent clients who have had dealings with them. One memorable program dealt with the problem of old people separated from their pets when forced to enter nursing homes. Interviews with administrators officiously justifying the practice on health grounds were juxtaposed with shots of old people and their beloved pets. These scenes were followed by moving conversations with the older people themselves, which made obvious their deep bond with the pets. The program then administered the *coup de grace;* it showed an interview with the head of an agency that allowed old people to keep their pets. This administrator maintained with a cheerful smile that the policy was not only carried out without any great difficulty but that its adoption had caused their institution no health problems at all. The program concluded with shots of happy old people together with their equally happy pets. By that time the authoritative-sounding claims of the previous administrators had been effectively discredited for those viewers with even a speck of compassion and humanity left in their hearts.

Gender Roles

No type of authority is being examined more critically in Denmark than the well-known one that has to do with gender roles. Both the unquestioned domination that the male *Homo sapiens* is able to assert over females elsewhere and the doctrine of male superiority that is used to legitimate it are under severe siege in Denmark. In public forums as well as in private relationships, there is a powerful trend toward questioning "the rights of man." Much of this is unquestionably due to an active and influential feminist movement, especially in the larger urban centers such as Aarhus and Copenhagen, Odense and Aalborg (though it is by no means restricted to these cities). Its influence is felt even in the lives and experiences of many Danish women who would never think of calling themselves "feminists."

One general trend is illustrated by the fact that there are now more single than married adults in Denmark. This situation can in part be explained by the relatively large numbers of those living together "without benefit of paper," for it has long been acceptable for a couple in Denmark to live together without marrying.[16] The resulting "consensual unions," often viewed as part of courtship itself, are preferred by many. Asked why they do not want to get married, young Danes will say something like "to be married is the wrong way to stay together," and they will emphasize that they are more concerned with the *quality* of a relationship than its legality. Yet in the past decade a new dimension to this trend has become evident: greater numbers of women than ever before have decided to have one or more children without the presence or long-term participation of any male partner whatsoever. Often desiring at least one child and sometimes more, these women anticipate performing the tasks of child-rearing as much as possible on their own, or with the help of other women. Perhaps this is one of the reasons for the increasing numbers of personal advertisements in major newspapers that come from women looking for other women to form or be part of larger collectives or the smaller living cooperatives (*bofællesskaber*) that make such life-styles a viable option.

Journalists Inge Methling and Christine Cordsen suggest that in order to grasp the meaning of these trends, it is necessary to revise the traditional concept of "single mother."[17] The older view of her as an unfortunate and passive victim of circumstance must be amended, for the single mother's way of life can also be the result of conscious choice. As one of those women who spoke to them remarks, "Damn it, I'm not a 'single mother.' I'm a reasonably sensible, adult human being with two children, and I've chosen this way of life for myself." How is the father of the child picked? Possibly an extreme instance of female strategy is Methling and Cordsen's case of a woman who when younger had decided that she would have a child by thirty at the latest. Not having achieved a stable relationship at that age, she deliberately picked out a man she found handsome, and on the basis of his presumably "good genes," seduced him and had a child. He was never told either the purpose or the result of her actions.

Although few would openly approve such procedures, they may be practiced more often than is generally admitted. The significance of the above case, however, is not the frequency of its occurrence but the testament it provides to a more general statement: that men and women in Danish society today quite possibly stand farther away from each other than ever before. The demography of the post–World War II decades provides an objective counterpart to this mood. One of its critical features, a decline in fertility, which first made its appearance in 1967, is of such magnitude that, if it continues, "an absolute decrease in the population size at the end of this century is to be predicted."[18]

One achievement of the active and determined feminist movement in Denmark is that women have begun to write their own history. In doing so they can place the lives of earlier generations of Danish women in a larger historical perspective. Some have begun to examine the settings and contexts in which mythical images of women were formed as a means of more effectively challenging these images.[19] One of their harsh and unsettling conclusions is that the history of women has been in large measure a history of survival. On a personal level, such insights and perspectives often lead women to redefine the rules of relationships. For a woman whose primary orientation is women's concerns and the problem of gender inequality, even the slightest weakening in a man's apparent acceptance of her as a strong and independent woman can be a very serious concern. This is frequently true for women with a purely emotional (and not ideological) orientation to the feminist perspective. I do not have any neat set of statistics to prove this, but my conclusion is that the high incidence of such orientations (especially in the urban milieu of Copenhagen and the larger cities) leads to a more widespread, frequent, and higher-intensity questioning of traditional gender role patterns by Danish women than by women in most other Euro-American societies.

Aside from the fact that such a strategy permits women the kind of sexual freedom usually thought of as the prerogative of men, a woman permitting herself such freedom will often be engaged in more or less conscious experimentation. She may view the entire process as a stage of her own development rather than as an ideologically inflexible mode of operation. One of the most perceptive and at the same time amusing accounts of just such a personal evolution is found in the writings of Suzanne Brøgger, whose collection of essays "Free Us From Love" (*Fri os fra kærligheden*) first appeared in the early 1970s. Some of her writings have attained near-classic status among urban audiences in Danish society. Ms. Brøgger is a liberated child of the sixties who, while artfully chronicling the details of her own rich passage to enlightenment, manages to fill in some of the gaps between giggles and sobs with trenchant and lucid commentary on everything from the trials of love to the terrors of nuclear devastation.

The breadth of her concerns is indicated in several of the subtitles of this early volume: "Monogamy: The Cannibalism of our Time," "Let's Do Away with Private Life," "From Nuclear Family to Nuclear War." The latter essay, an ironic commentary of extraordinary breadth, states her scholarly position in the very first paragraph: "The nuclear family gave me cold sweat, and I read and read in order to find support for my theoretical aversions." While sharing her insights, a few of the themes she deals with along the way in this one essay include marriage, pairs without marriage, loneliness, suffering, communication, comradeship, Tolstoy, Marx, Erich Fromm, collectives, child-rearing, the patriarchal nuclear family, empirical science, capitalism, advertising, production, and nuclear war. Here is one provocative passage about men, women, and the nuclear family:

> But the primary reason that the man accepts this form of life is that no other is offered. It is family life or no life. The mismatch between the individualized economy in production and the pseudo-communistic economy in the nuclear family has traumatic implications for both sexes. Naturally the man never thinks that he gets enough for his hard earned money. But it is even harder for the woman, because she has to justify to herself the whole time that she doesn't earn anything. She feels herself deep inside rendered powerless, because she lives in a society which defines individuals on the basis of the role they play in production. One knows here these letters to the editor—either masochistically signed "yours truly, a ordinary housewife," or aggressively "yours truly, an *extraordinary* housewife." The housewife is the first to realize that she is without social identity. She seeks to compensate for her unproducing role by identifying herself with her husband's producing—and push him forward and up. She is called the producer's female inspiration *(inspiratrice)*. It is symptomatic of the female inspiration, the secondary producer, that she energetically tries to appropriate the maximum part of her husband's income. The explanation is her economic dependence, and that she earns nothing herself. Her only possibility for intervening in the economic life is to buy.[20]

Her stylistic skills puts Brøgger's writings in a class by themselves. One of their sources is a determined refusal to separate her analysis of society from her own personal situation. Her ability to fuse the two often provides a richly comic interplay focusing on the conflict between the demands of ideology and the demands of the flesh. She has traveled extensively not only in Europe and America but to numerous third world countries as well, to

Laos (1965), Vietnam (1966), and Afghanistan (1969). These experiences are reflected in both her fictional and nonfictional writings. She is able to combine humor with a serious perspective in her never-ending exploration of the dilemmas presented by the new gender freedoms. Although she identifies herself (and is identified) as one of the sixties' rebels against strait-laced sexual conventions, her message is by no means a simple one. "Everything we liberate, disappears," she has said. "Whatever we set free, is lost to us." The new freedom to do everything has not necessarily aided Eros, she argues, but has rendered it wingless: "Its wings have been bound—for the sake of medicine, psychology, sociability and therapy. Eros was anonymous, but so is bureaucracy as well. For this reason bureaucracy has been able to absorb Eros as a matter of course. Eros is now the law, hired by the state and given a pension."[21]

Suzanne Brøgger's dissident and questioning voice is one among many. The frequent women's conferences are a good measure of the gender issues that stand in the wings awaiting their call to center stage. At a recent conference in Göteborg, the new parameters being suggested for debate were evident in the article that reported on the event. "The man's place is in the home," a ten-character headline crushingly announced in bold black letters. Speakers at the conference were making it crystal clear that the role of men, not that of women, would be the primary problem for the next ten years. Helle Degn, a Social-Democratic member of the Danish Parliament, put it in a nutshell: "In the sixties we lacked work force in the labor market, and women came in. Now we lack work force in the home. And women can't do any more there than they're doing. So the men must look it squarely in the eyes, that it's them who's going to be the reserve labor force on the home front."[22] The calls for men to spend more time at home are accompanied by demands that women be permitted to enter occupations previously regarded as for men only. These demands are often met. Thus, although the armies of Denmark, Belgium, and the Netherlands allow women in theory to receive any kind of assignment, it is only Denmark that has moved to impose full equality in all armed services branches. It is an experiment that has produced—in addition to teamwork at sea—five pregnancies and a marriage. One interesting result of the four-year experiment is that when they are allowed enough time to overcome initial problems, male-female crews outperform single-sex units of either gender.[23]

Though it is important to acknowledge these critical trends, it is equally important to acknowledge that the traditional marriage based on the nuclear family is far from disappearing. It is very much alive if not in perfect health. Young women without advanced formal education or economic security may well choose an early marriage based on the traditional pattern. Those who come from a secure, protected, and prosperous family tradition may also opt for the traditional pattern. Still a third category is made up of those women who have married farmers and chosen a rural way of life. These cases are neither mutually exclusive nor do they exhaust all of the possibilities. In any case due weight must be given to women's experiences that run counter to the trends mentioned and to those women who do not approve of parts of the feminist agenda.

Few would contest the proposition that women in Denmark have made considerable progress toward full social participation since they were first given the vote in parliamentary elections in 1915. In 1908 they were first permitted to hold office in community government. Equal pay for men and women in the public services was enacted in 1919; equal entry to government employment in 1921. In 1966 all women, regardless of age, were given the right to obtain advice and guidance about methods of contraception.[24] In 1973 every woman was given the right to abortion up to the end of the third month of pregnancy. The Danish Sex Discrimination Act prohibits employment advertisements from stipulating a particular sex. Since the first women were ordained as ministers in 1948, many others have followed in their path. Women in Denmark have not only entered the ministry but may well come to be the dominant force in its future. In the autumn of 1990 nearly two-thirds of the entering 272 theology students at the universities of Copenhagen and Aarhus were women.[25] It is also significant that the early campaigns for women's emancipation in Denmark never encountered the degree of violent opposition met with by suffragettes in other countries (which provides still another illustration of the central theme of the inquiry).

Danish television carries a children's program (*Fjernsyn for dig:* television for you) that is in many ways a good Danish version of "Sesame Street" on American television. It consistently presents an egalitarian view of gender roles and gender identity. In one typical program, two young adults, a strikingly handsome man and woman, are discussing this topic. It is strongly argued and demonstrated that all can do what each can do: girls are seen playing football and taking apart machines, boys are seen playing with dolls and ironing clothes. The program concludes with a series of scenes in which an act usually associated with one or the other sex is shown in a way that it is impossible to say the sex of the person doing the act. The young man looks at a typically masculine activity and says "he!!" It turns out to be a girl. The young woman looks at a typically feminine activity and says "she!!" It turns out to be a boy. This motif is repeated up to the last shot, in which the doer of the act turns out to be a dog.[26]

Many would nonetheless agree with the proposition that there is still a long way to go before women in Denmark have achieved true equality.[27] One remaining problem area is in scientific education: there is evidence suggesting that Danish schoolgirls are systematically disadvantaged by the kind of mathematics and physics instruction given in the schools.[28] There is still a widespread view that mathematics and physics are not suitable subjects for women and that "language studies" would be more appropriate for them. Instruction is further biased by the fact that boys are encouraged to take an early interest in electronics and technology; girls are in most cases not at all encouraged to do so. Two other problem areas for women are wage discrimination and the right to maternity leave (barselsorlov). New studies suggest that the disparity between men's and women's wages is much higher than previously recognized,[29] and that nearly a fifth of the women with little education who take advantage of their legal right to maternity leave are dismissed by employers who give other reasons.[30]

But Danish women do not have to look very far to find encouraging models for the future. Vigdis Finnbogadottir is Iceland's head of state; in neighboring Norway not only Prime Minister Gro Harlem Brundtland but nearly half of the present cabinet members are women. In 1983 the Norwegian Labor Party decreed at its annual congress that at least 40% of each sex must be nominated in all party elections and nominations.[31] The preceding analysis leads nevertheless to the conclusion that the egalitarian ideology has been and continues to be a powerful force for culture change in the area of Danish gender roles.

Linguistic Change

In addition to the previously mentioned contexts, this egalitarian theme can be seen in some details of recent linguistic change. Just as its German neighbor to the south, the Danish language possesses two variants of the second person pronoun: a polite form (DE) and a more informal one (DU). Unlike in Germany, the use of the formal variant (DE) (the polite form used to express distance and hierarchy) is restricted in its everyday usage. One would have thought ten years ago that it was passing out of the Danish language; it may now be in the process of making a small comeback. Still, in everyday speech its use is generally restricted to those over fifty years of age, though it continues to survive as the language of commerce in advertisements, sales, bank forms, and the radio-TV media. But those who use it in everyday discourse risk making great fools of themselves, as I found during my first two weeks in the country in 1982. Not sure of what to do, I followed the instructions of an otherwise excellent language text from the early 1960s and used the polite form to people I didn't know. Typically, those who had been so addressed either laughed in my face or looked at me in a puzzled way, searching for signs of irony. It didn't take me long to give up the DE form completely except on those rare occasions with older people when its use seemed appropriate.

Although most Danes have given up the DE form without so much as a backward look, there are those among the older generation for whom the change has been traumatic. Numbered among them is the retired female high school principal for whom supermarket lines became a difficult experience. On at least one occasion when a much younger checkout girl asked her for another kroner using the familiar DU form of address, she fixed the young woman with the same stony and disapproving stare that had worked on generations of former pupils. But the checkout girl, concentrating on her work and oblivious to either the stare or its meaning, simply repeated her demand. When this happened, the elderly woman marched off in a huff without paying, leaving her filled shopping cart in the checkout line. It is questionable whether the checkout clerk so treated ever understood the reasons for the old woman's behavior. "Just another crazy old woman" is what she probably thought upon witnessing the older woman's sudden departure.

Another person apparently left behind by this shift in terms of personal address is an older professor of physical sciences at Copenhagen University. A favorite colloquial exclamation during my initial stay in Denmark was the expression *"Hold kæft"* (it means "shut up," or literally "hold your jaw"). This expression had acquired a secondary meaning among young Danes, who would often use it as an expression of astonishment, outrage, or approval. They would say *"Hold kæft, man"* or *"Hold kæft, Du"* with an exclamatory intonation that did not constitute a command to shut up but expressed instead a variety of evaluative meanings. These evaluations could be positive (Wow! You don't mean to say! No, really!!) or negative (Oh, my God!).

One of this professor's colleagues was a woman in her sixties with grown children. From them she had become familiar with this secondary usage of *"Hold kæft,"* so much so that one day in a faculty meeting she unconsciously let it slip while talking to him and said *"Hold kæft, Du"* in the informal evaluative context of a longer sentence. Although she didn't mean it at all, he was absolutely horrified at her words and immediately took great offense. "Do you say 'shut up' and 'Du' to me?" he asked, "after we have been colleagues here together for so many years?" Only after she had apologized profusely and tried at length to explain did he begin to understand and take a more lenient attitude toward her strange misbehavior.

Until the post–World War II decades, the DE form was universally observed for elders, superiors, and strangers. It was also used for those who, though they were not strangers, remained outside of a particular individual's sphere of intimacy. The mere fact of its use indicated neither disdain nor superiority but only social distance. Thus the owner of a business establishment might be on DE terms with long-term customers for many years. As one of my informants emphasized, two people could use DE with each other for thirty years and still be very good friends in this more formal sense. Signifying mutual courtesy and respect, the DE form could be part of the context of a stable and satisfactory relationship. (A significant exception to this pattern was out in the country, where DU was always used rather than DE. It did not do for one farmer to be "finer" than the one on the neighboring farm.) There was even a special ceremony, called literally "drinking Dus" with each other, for going from the DE to the DU form of address. It was a real event and not something to be taken lightly.

I am not clear on the precise timing, but it seems that by the late 1950s and certainly in the 1960s the DU form gained its present ascendancy. Although not so long ago it was proper for young people to address friends of their parents formally while being addressed themselves with the familiar form, the use of DE (in this as in similar settings) has declined almost to the point of disappearance.[32] A reason often given by younger people for the original decline of the DE form is its implied inequality and its connections to a hierarchical model of society. Its decline is seen as part of a general democratization of society: the view, as one girl summed it up, that "we should all be friends." It is tempting to speculate that this linguistic trend has some connection to the years of student activism in the sixties.

Some recent developments must be noted that force one to qualify the preceding argument. A poll taken in the summer of 1988 indicated that the group wishing to preserve the DE form had increased from 24 to 31% in the course of the preceding two years. In the same two years the number of consistent DU users had fallen from 36 to 29%. The desire to bring back the use of the DE form was most seen among Copenhagen residents (42%), women, and political conservatives.[33] The apparent comeback of the DE form witnessed in the last years of the 1980s is a trend that must be noted; its extent is not yet clear and may not be until well into the 1990s. The long-run change from reliance on the formal DE to the informal DU nevertheless appears to provide another illustration of the expression of egalitarianism in Danish cultural life.

Role of the Monarchy

The political system of Denmark is a parliamentary and democratic monarchy whose roots can be traced back a thousand years to Gorm the Elder. Gorm's descendants have ruled Denmark ever since. One can chart for the monarchy a historical continuity of over a thousand years, more than five times the age of the United States. Its status as the oldest monarchy in Europe is supported by the famous Jelling stone, whose richly ornamented runic inscriptions attest in a blunt, no-nonsense fashion to the events of unification and Christianization: "Harald the King [King Harald Blue-tooth, d. c. 985] ordered this monument to be raised in honor of Gorm his father and Thyra his mother, the Harald who won all Denmark and Norway and made the Danes Christians."

The period of nearly two hundred years that Danish kings ruled as absolute monarchs (1660–1848) seems to pose an exception to the themes of egalitarianism and democracy. Yet a closer look reveals what by now will come as familiar themes. The first king in the era of absolutism (Frederic III) did not so much usurp power as have it thrust upon him by an uneasy coalition. King Frederic III was only one member of a coalition that included the army and the citizens of Copenhagen. What was the background to these events, and how did they transpire?

In 1660 Denmark was a country from which foreign armies had just withdrawn after a disastrous two-year siege. The land was in the words of one Danish historian, "humbled and mutilated, ravaged by acts of war and epidemics."[34] There was a profound distrust of the government in large parts of the population. Both before and after these tragic events the members of an aristocratic council, anxious to maintain their tax privileges, had pushed matters beyond their limits. The tripartite coalition (clergy, crown and middle class) formed as a response to the council's abuses succeeded in carrying out a semimilitary coup. The gates of the city were closed and the army stood prepared to fight. Faced with these threats, the representatives of the nobility capitulated. They agreed to revoke the charter signed at Frederic III's accession, and when this was done, all parties concerned signed a new agreement. This new document, which was aimed at limiting the power of the nobility, created instead a royal absolutism. Denmark was "the only country to get, in the Act of Royalty, a written absolutist constitution, under which in theory the king was bound solely by his own conscience and responsibility before God."[35]

But just as the Catholic Church fell without a real struggle in 1536, the aristocratic regime was installed in the autumn of 1660 without the firing of a single shot. And though some of the succeeding kings who ruled as absolute monarchs were unwise, eccentric, or even just plain crazy, not a single one of them proved to be a tyrant on the grand scale. Moreover, when the handwriting was on the wall for this system in the late 1840s, the Danish kings surrendered their absolute power in the same way they had been given it, peacefully, without turning to politically inspired mass violence to defend their interests. The official motto of the last absolute king, Frederic VII, was "the people's love, my strength" *(Folkets kærlighed min styrke).*[36]

Those days and events are now part of the distant past. The chief function of the monarchy today is to serve as a cheerful symbol of continuity and collective identity. Theoretically, the queen does appoint the prime minister and the ministers. But this grand ceremony is only carried out with the advice and consent of elected officials: all real political power remains in the hands of the voters and the political party leadership. The powers of the present queen, Margarethe II, consist largely of recognizing newly elected governments, signing already-passed bills into law and making a televised speech to the nation on New Year's Eve. This speech is one that is and must be above the clamorous squabbles of political gamesmanship (that being delegated to the capable hands of the fifteen or sixteen political parties contending for electoral office).

How, one may ask, do the egalitarian Danes respond to the existence of royalty in their midst? One American observer's conclusion was that "the respectful awe in which the English royal family is held is foreign to Denmark."[37] Their unannounced public appearance does not cause a riot, for the Danes, who place a great value on privacy, accord it as well to the royal family. If the queen and her husband decide to eat at a restaurant, other Danes avoid staring at them or in any way interfering with their privacy. A cartoon shows a waiter in a restaurant who passes by a coat rack, looks up, and notices the royal robes and crown. Judith Friedman Hansen's perceptive comment is "the king has hung them up and become a private person, eating his supper like anyone else. . . . In this way royalty is permitted to become human, while its desire to become human is a levelling quality which endears it to egalitarian Danes."[38]

Members of the royal family are supposed to behave as any other Danes would: gracefully, naturally, and without pretension. If they didn't, if they began to take themselves too seriously, they would be subjected to the same sanctions other Danes receive. The attitude toward them is indicated in some comments made to me by academic colleagues. "We've got a good one now," one man said seriously, speaking of the queen. "She's clever and well educated." There was not the slightest suggestion of blind adulation in his words, nor was there any hostility. They were spoken more with the implicit assumption that "she's just one of us." From the tone he used it was clear

Waiting for the royal family, south Sjælland, 1979.

that in his eyes the queen, like any other civil servant, would be given a fair evaluation on the basis of her abilities, character, and performance. "She's a clever girl" *(en kloge pige)* was the similar, fond description given to me by a female colleague who is about the same age as the queen.

The present queen is a fine public speaker and in addition a talented artist and illustrator. I witnessed personally her popularity (and that of the royal family) when I went on Monday, 16 April 1984 to Amalienborg castle together with a crowd of several thousand people to exchange greetings and congratulate her on her forty-fourth birthday (this exchange of greetings is a yearly celebration in Copenhagen). As a properly democratic American I didn't really want to go to this event. In fact I was dragged there quite against my will by a former folk high school classmate who correctly realized that it was something I needed to see. There is no real equivalent to it in American social or political life. When the clock struck noon, the queen and her husband Prince Henrik and two small princes stepped out on the balcony. Nine times the crowd chanted "Long live the Queen" *(Drønning leve)*. By chance the queen's birthday fell that year in the middle of the Easter school holiday, which meant that the children lost part of a vacation day. Nevertheless, I saw no unhappy faces among them. I went there with a chip on my shoulder, but found myself charmed anyway by the whole event, by the crowds of mostly mothers and children happily waving their red and white flags, and by the simple and sincere comments made by the queen.

Succession to the Danish throne was once limited to males, but the 1953 constitution recognized female succession as well in the case where there is no male heir. Interest in this modification was enhanced because Frederic IX, the reigning monarch, had three daughters but no son. On his death in 1972 the throne passed to his oldest daughter, Margarethe II. Another clause of the 1953 constitution is that "the King shall not marry except with the consent of the *Folketing* [parliament]." This clause symbolizes well the relationship between present-day monarchs and their people, one in which the monarch, while revered as a proud symbol of present and past continuity, is like all other Danes subject to the action of the core values of democracy and egalitarianism.

Some Further Instances

In education the egalitarian ideal has been expressed in historical time by the gradual democratization of school as an institution. The Reform Act of 1814 signed by Frederic VI made public education compulsory for both boys and girls from the age of six until confirmation (at age 13–14). Vagn Skovgaard-Petersen, who has traced the developments that led to major subsequent educational reforms (1903, 1937, 1958, 1967, and 1973), concludes that "in the democratization process that the Danish society has experienced in the last 150 years, all forms of school and instruction have played a significant role."[39] Grundtvigian attitudes reflected in the Danish national character were also learned in part at Danish schools. Ministers, teachers, and urban intellectuals with Grundtvigian views have been influential at every level of Danish education in the hundred and twenty years since his death. More of this in later chapters, but my observations indicate that students in Denmark today will play and expect to play a greater role in the decision-making processes than one sees in most other cultures. Upon presenting to one professor the syllabus of a course I hoped to teach as a visiting lecturer at the University of Copenhagen, I was surprised to find that the decision would be made by a committee of three faculty and three students.

When the minister for cultural affairs planned to appoint to the National Theatre School a new principal with avowed plans to make radical changes in the education of theater professionals, a coalition of students, teachers, and other hired personnel wrote an open letter to the minister. One member of the school community was cited as saying, "We are not against the new director personally, but we are protesting against the minister's one-sided decision to make changes in the school that we don't agree with her about."[40] Of more concern than the substance of the disagreement here is the assumption made by the members of the school community that they had the right to challenge publicly the policies laid down by legitimate authority. This kind of public protest in the area of education is not an unusual event. It is merely one out of many that could be cited. Protest, I might add, is a familiar and accepted Danish theme. To take part in demonstrations is probably as Danish as the making of open-faced sandwiches (indeed, the two forms of action are by no means mutually exclusive).

In many ways the most profound expressions of democracy and egalitarianism can be found in the Danish political system, but discussion of this crucial topic is postponed to Chapter Nine. I conclude this treatment of the core values of democracy and egalitarianism with four further instances of its expression. The first can be seen in two features of the institutional structure of the Danish Lutheran Church. The Danish church has since 1867 had the tradition of *valgmenigheder*, or congregations with the right to choose their own pastor rather than having one appointed by a central ecclesiastical authority. This downplaying of centralized authority is further indicated by the fact that the Danish Church has no archbishop.[41] In contrast to neighboring Sweden, where the bishops are under the authority of an archbishop, there is no controlling centralized authority in the Danish Lutheran Church.

The second instance of its expression is an open letter by a seventeen-year-old Danish girl to the Danish prime minister. Appearing in the "Positions Sought" section of *Politiken* (8 Feb. 1984), it caught my eye and I read it with amusement and some astonishment.

> Dear Mr. Prime Minister (he is mentioned by name):
> The undersigned has now for three months, with among other things the help of the telephone yellow pages, applied for about 60 positions—no possibilities. According to Your [polite form] cityboy [she names a prominent member of parliament], there aren't any poor people in Denmark—in spite of this I'm about to become one of them. Will You [polite form] help me?? Possibly with the help of Your cityboy—all work has interest—except out on Halmtorvet [a well-known pick-up corner in Copenhagen's red light district]. I am 17 years old and you can contact me at telephone. . . . my work clothes are laid out. Sincerely, author's name.

It is not clear if the prime minister ever received her letter, or, if he did, whether or not he chose to help her. The point is that the letter writer is an unemployed seventeen-year-old and its intended recipient the Danish prime minister. Nevertheless, the fresh, uppity, and even insulting tone of the public letter makes it very clear that she does not consider herself to be in any way his inferior. Her use of the polite form is in this case almost certainly meant to be ironic, a mocking salute to the pretensions of aristocracy and gentility. The use of this kind of mocking humor is a traditional and much-used Danish put-down of those in authority. It is almost unnecessary to point out that she apparently has no fear of the repercussions of publishing such a letter, even though it is written to deliberately embarrass a powerful public figure.

The third example comes from World War II. When German soldiers during the Nazi Occupation marched in patrol behind a barrier that made them invisible from the waist down, Danes hung a sign on the barrier that read, "This Nazi is wearing no trousers." Part of the Danish strategy was to deny the Nazi occupying force its legitimacy by constant ridicule and the performance of small acts of disdain. Those with pretensions to greatness today run the risk of being cut down to human size by similar ego- and image-shrinking techniques, devices that the great majority of Danes, whatever their education and social class, are able to employ with great skill and precision. As the American author John Steinbeck once remarked, "If I were a dictator I wouldn't occupy Denmark for fear of being laughed to death."

As the fourth and final example shows, these motifs belong to the past as well as to the present. In Edmund Gosse's memoirs describing his 1874 visit to Denmark, a familiar theme and mood can be observed in his description of an evening at Tivoli:

> When the night was fully fallen, the place assumed the illusive fairy appearance proper to such gardens in such weather. And now the extremely democratic character of Danish life asserted itself. Here a workman stopped the Minister of Foreign Affairs that he might beg a light from his cigar. Here a small tradesman and his family shared the amusements of an ambassador. . . .

These momentary, apparently incidental vignettes took place in Tivoli Gardens more than a century ago. The spirit of democracy and egalitarianism that was visible in Danish society when Gosse wrote remains there today. It is manifest in a certain quality to Danish life, a widespread mood, an underlying orientation, all of which have been noticed by a series of foreign observers. Class and status divisions are very real in Danish society, but as I have attempted to show in this section, it is part of the Danish ethos to attempt in ways large and small to transcend, minimize, belittle, and contest them. An ongoing public critique of power that uses skepticism, humor, and irony as its chief weapons creates an atmosphere not at all conducive to the raw exercise of power. A formal political system in which as many as sixteen political parties contend for the right to attempt to govern is a further indication of strongly democratic and antiauthoritarian sentiment. Denmark, in short, is not a place where totalitarian practices of any sort can flourish long unchallenged.

CHAPTER SEVEN

Balance and Moderation

O NE CAN OBSERVE in Danish society a set of attitudes and ways of acting that constitute a balance principle. Combined with what is in general a marked preference for choosing moderate courses of action over extremes, this core value of balance and moderation can be expressed in a number of ways. Its influence leads Danes to view with tolerance the expression of a wide range of competing points of view regardless of the particular issue or context. It tends as well to bring potentially disruptive and divisive social events back into a less contested middle ground. Yet this action entails something of a paradox. Although this balance principle may sound like a device to bring about conformity and conflict management, in some situations its effect is just the opposite. Its general function is unquestionably to promote and maintain a high level of social tranquility. Nevertheless, on other occasions it can represent a form of inner direction, a balance weight working against external forces threatening to compromise deeply held ethical and moral standards.[1] In the latter situation, its operation may encourage rather than discourage conflict.

The operation of the balance principle can be seen in the small events of everyday social interaction as well as in many of the major events in Danish history (though the principle does have its limits, as an unfortunate evening in the wrong bar in Copenhagen might quickly demonstrate). The following analysis of the balance principle includes examples selected from Danish literature, politics, and the world of everyday encounters or focused gatherings. Judith Friedman Hansen defines balance as "the tendency to seek a stable harmony," and she goes on to note that neither the traits that bring about this state of harmony nor the assumptions that underlie them have been made sufficiently explicit in most prior discussions of Danish character.[2]

Let us begin again with history. When the decision was made toward the end of the fifteenth century to build a university in Copenhagen, it was necessary to ask the permission of the pope before work could begin. Letters and high-ranking emissaries from the Danish crown were sent to Rome to accomplish this purpose. The religion of Denmark has since become so identified with the Danish Lutheran Church that it is difficult even to remember that it was once a strict Catholic country. At the time of the Reformation in Denmark (1536), the Catholic Church owned one-third of all Danish land.

The Protestant Reformation in the early sixteenth century (1517) was accompanied by great bloodshed in neighboring countries as the Church lost not only many of its members but much of the land it had traditionally owned. Yet these events, just as the early transition to Christianity some centuries before, took place on the whole peacefully. We have already reviewed the critical series of Land Reform acts that began in 1788 and the transition from absolutist monarchy to parliamentary democracy some sixty years later. It is not true that there was *no* violence connected with these events. Indeed, this is not my point; it is rather that in each of these three cases a major transformation of power took place in Denmark without the mass violence and large-scale breakdown of social order that has so often accompanied such transformations in human history.

I do not want to present a naive and oversimplified picture of Danish history. Its record includes bloody power struggles that took place both with neighboring kings and within the palace walls of Copenhagen. These political conflicts were most often fought among monarchical rulers and their powerful advisers. They could have bitter and lethal consequences. To take one example, on just the first day of what has come to be known as "the Stockholm Bloodbath" in 1520 (in circumstances that are not clear even today), eighty-two opponents of a Swedish archbishop were summarily executed. The archbishop, Gustav Trolles, had previously aligned himself with the Danish king and aided the latter's military campaign in Sweden. This campaign resulted in the Danish king's short-lived coronation as king of Sweden. It is generally thought that Christian II, in Stockholm at the time of these executions, stood behind them with his own authority. He may even have been the one primarily responsible for them.[3] Numerous other similar examples of the violent pursuit of power could be cited.

Danish history has certainly had its fair share of war and violence. Yet if one looks at the larger picture, one can see in recent centuries a pattern of declining incidence of the appearance of these two apocalyptic horsemen. And in a strange and suggestive historical coincidence, it is particularly since the last years of the eighteenth century, the period of the major Land Reforms, that organized political persecutions have been conspicuous by their absence. There have been no large-scale imprisonments and inquisitions, no lynchings, and by the same token no civil wars. Curiously enough, in all its long history there does not seem to have been a single violent social revolution in Danish society.

Such patterns can be cited as first-order evidence for the existence of a balance principle that operates within Danish society. The same balance principle that can be seen in these features of Danish history is reflected in an intricate code of values that influences the social organization of everyday life. What follows focuses on some typical attitudes and ways of acting that are part of this balance principle (these include a cultural code of modesty and humility, together with a complex of values including skepticism, caution and independence, a cheerful willingness to engage in "bending the rules," and a high tolerance of political and social diversity).

I. THE CULTURAL CODE OF MODESTY AND HUMILITY

I found out about the code of modesty the hard way. When I first arrived in Denmark, a number of Danes asked me why I had become interested in their country. "What made you, living in America, decide to come and study our little country?" was the essence of their question. Denmark's smallness was frequently emphasized or exaggerated; it would often be referred to not just as a small country but as "our speck" or "our little spot" (*vores lille plet*). The answer that rolled off my tongue to the first wave of questioners was a truthful and sincere one. I would mention the Holocaust and the rescue of the Danish Jews and duly recite the litany of praise for what they and their parents had done forty years ago. I then said that by studying the folk high school I hoped to come to a better understanding of the people who had been responsible for this action, adding that it was one I had long admired.

Their response to my answer was an interesting one. I was not in the least prepared for it. My questioners became uniformly embarrassed at this straightforward endorsement of Danish heroism. They shrugged it off, doing the best they could to minimize it. They claimed that what the world thought of them grossly exaggerated what they had actually done. They also endeavored to point out historical facts about the Danish Occupation that would undercut my oversimplified positive point of view.

"We did nothing when the Nazis first invaded. We just tried to keep to ourselves and lead our private lives as though nothing had happened," said one of my questioners who had himself lived through the period. "It wasn't until 1943, when things began to go bad for the Germans elsewhere, that our Resistance really began to be active." Another friend reminded me that anti-Semitism was not absent in Denmark, and that there had once even

been an actual *pogrom* in Denmark in 1819. When I looked into it, I found
that he was right. A mob *had* gathered in 1819 in connection with a
carpenter strike and student riots. There seems to be no question but that
anti-Jewish feelings were found among some of the hundreds who gathered
in the streets. True enough, its expression had been comparatively mild. A
few stones were thrown, and after some properly ritualized conflict the mob
dispersed. I wasn't even sure that it could properly be called a real persecution, a *pogrom*. Placards and posters from that time have been found with the
slogan "Down with the king," but they say nothing about the Jews. Bent
Blüdnikow, a historian of the period, has given the events a more exact
characterization: "the Jewish controversy" (*jødefejden*).[4] But they had happened, and my questioner wanted me to know about them.

Each time I responded to their questions by raising the issue of the
Danish Jews, I was given a similar response. To my surprise and initial
consternation the respondent in every case refused to take any credit for my
imputation of virtuous action. There was no modest head nodding ("yes, we
really did a beautiful thing for those Jews"). The reaction was instead one
that emphasized the negative. They said things like this: Our heroism has
been exaggerated. Why did it take us so long to become active? We wanted
to look good in the eyes of England and the other allied nations. Many of
us, who had insisted on living totally private lives, were in effect collabo-
rating with the Nazi Occupation. All this and more I heard.

I did not realize it at the time, but this was a first socialization into
Danish ways. After the same unsatisfactory conversational sequence had
been repeated three or four times, I began to sense that there was more at
issue here than the mere possession of wrong information. I began to feel
that in speaking as I had spoken, I had committed a subtle but nonetheless
real *faux pas* in Danish eyes. Not a single one of those to whom I spoke took
my positive words about Denmark without going to some pains to point
out my errors of fact and interpretation. They did not seem to be angry, but
they still needed to let me know that what I had said was somehow wrong
and in need of correction.

What informal convention had been violated by my uncritical remarks? I had given an evaluation of events that, by touching on questions
of Danish nationalism and national identity, had triggered deeply felt
"behavioral codes" influencing belief and expression. I believe that these
codes guide, limit, and constrain the way in which one can talk about such
things as nationalism and patriotism in Denmark. At the risk of losing my
anthropological mask of objectivity, I have to say that the existence of this
code strikes me as a beautiful thing, and I wish many of the other peoples
of the world could learn something from the Danes in this regard. It is only

when we remember the arrogant and ethnocentric spirit in which patriotic nationalism is expressed in most of the world's nations and ethnic groups that we can appreciate how unusual the peculiar form of Danish nationalism is. Unlike most others, it must be kept free of simple-minded jingoism; moreover, it requires a limited and partial statement of the nation's worth. Denmark is not to be seen blindly and foolishly as number one. One simply does not hear speeches by Danish politicians reminding the listener that theirs is the land with the best people, the most moral history, the greatest natural beauty, the richest economy. The theme of Danish limits is constantly emphasized at the same time that tolerance and even admiration for other nations and peoples of the world are expressed. Pompous expressions of national pride are seen as hilariously stupid and strongly discouraged. A Dane who violates these codes even in small ways will be quickly deflated. It is probably in this spirit that one should read these lines written by Poul Sørensen:

> As every Dane knows, Denmark is the center of the universe. Should anyone doubt this, let him stand in the middle of Town Hall Square in Copenhagen. Here, with his own eyes, he will be able to confirm that the world revolves around this square. The further from this spot anything lies, the more insignificant it appears. The many things beyond the horizon will therefore pass quite unnoticed.[5]

The influence of this behavioral code is so deep that in many cases it will be embedded in the discussions of nationalism and national feeling. Thus Uffe Østergård's provocative analysis criticizes Danish nationalism even while stating its main features in language similar to that I have just used:

> That gentle and understated kind of unshakable superiority is a typical expression of the peculiar Danish self-understanding. This self-understanding is a particular form of nationalism that expresses itself in refusing the designation of nationalism. Nationalism is something ugly, something the others have, while we are better because we are not(!) nationalistic. This lack of nationalism causes the unique result that we alone, of all nations, can hang our national flag up in our Christmas trees without any feelings of shame. What kind of commentaries would it be the occasion for, if the Germans suddenly decided to do the same thing?[6]

Østergård goes on to make guarded but enlightening comparisons between the militaristic chauvinism of the British and French national anthems and the Danish national songs. The imperialistic message of the British "Rule Britannia" (1840), he argues, is obvious, as is the chauvinistic

"Marseillaise" of the French. The Danish national song to which he compares them is one written, of course, by Grundtvig. It is one of Grundtvig's best known and loved hymns, "Denmark's Consolation" (*Langt højere bjerge,* Hymn 216 in the Folk High School Songbook). Østergård's analysis suggests that it is an example of false modesty masking feelings of national superiority. He points out correctly that the *last lines* of each of its six stanzas constitute an enthusiastic affirmation of Denmark and Danes. Yet if one looks carefully at the words to Grundtvig's hymn, one will see that the *first two lines* of each of the same stanzas illustrate the required theme of balanced moderation. Each stanza begins by modestly comparing features of Denmark to similar features in other countries. I cite the first two lines from each of these six stanzas:

1. Much higher mountains so wide on earth are found
   than here where mountains only are hills,
2. Much more beautiful regions, we would like to believe,
   can strangers in other countries find,
3. Much larger enterprises for honor and pay
   one may have seen foreigners achieve,
4. Much wiser people are there surely on the earth
   than here between channel and sea,
5. Much higher, nobler and finer language
   can be found in foreign tongues,
6. Much more precious ore so white and so red
   have others received in mountains or trade,

Balance is achieved in this hymn by the lines following those I have cited. In every stanza the succeeding lines give a positive statement of what Grundtvig felt were some of Denmark's excellent and redeeming features. In the second stanza, for instance, his initial two-line ode to the beauties of other lands is counterbalanced by these memorable lines:

But the Dane has his home where the beech trees grow,
near the coast with its fair sweet memory
and most wonderful we find, in cradle and grave,
the flowering field in the flowing sea.

In the sixth and final stanza he goes on to say:

Among Danes the daily bread is yet
not smaller in the poor man's hut;
and thus have we gone far in wealth
when few have too much, and fewer too little.

These last lines have given rise to a great deal of critical discussion. One might have thought that Grundtvig had expressed himself here with sufficient attention to the cultural code of modesty and humility. Yet at least one contemporary Danish historian has taken their measure and found them wanting:

> In his fatherland's song "Denmark's Consolation" from 1820 Grundtvig congratulated Denmark for its lack of industry. . . . There were quite probably only a few who had too much, but the number of those who had too little had become more than before. Among them were the landless farmers and day laborers who were so poor that their daily bread was not to be found in the hut of which Grundtvig spoke, because it wasn't their own. It had to be found in the poor houses or by begging.[7]

The modest, self-critical tone of Danish patriotism contrasts strongly with the complacent arrogance that so often characterizes such expression in other countries (particularly, perhaps, in the larger nations of the world). There are of course historical reasons for this. Villy Sørensen has looked into history's mirror and given us this provocative interpretation of Danish national self-image: "There are limits to what a little nation can allow itself, and there are limits to the harm that it can do to others. . . . Danes are less fixated on their past than other nationalities, both because there isn't so much to be proud of and because there isn't so much to regret."[8] Sørensen's statement is both balanced and insightful; yet the reason why Danes may be "less fixated on their past" than other nationalities may have just as much to do with the fact that there is so much of it (i.e., the time depth of their long and unbroken historical continuity) than with any lack of things to be proud of or to regret. Certainly the expressions of national feeling in Denmark tend to be more ironic and self-critical than those in neighboring Norway, which in contrast received its national independence as recently as the first decade of this century.

The contrast that most quickly and easily comes to mind, however, is with American culture. Everyone knows that it is an accepted and fundamental part of our ethos to beat your own drum and extol your virtues in a loud voice (this was particularly true in the decade of the 1980s). We Americans are taught to think that others will not believe in us if we do not continually try to sell ourselves. It is undoubtedly the case that, as drama critic Martin Esslin has remarked, "the image of the U.S. that is presented on television is a false one: more violent, shallow, vulgar than reality; and above all, pervaded by the hysterical tone of a perpetual hard sell quite unlike the far more relaxed atmosphere in American life."[9] That does not, in my view, prevent American commercial television from being a relentless mirror both of and for the American character. The quality of our patriotism is equally driven. In focusing on our presumed national greatness, we can deny both our individual insecurity and the collective errors forced upon us by our history. Perhaps this is why Americans, unlike Danes, are so shamefully comfortable in the presence of foreigners (such as refugees from Eastern bloc countries) who express flattering views about American excellence. Unlike Danes, many Americans not only do not like to hear their country criticized but often become very upset when its limitations are openly discussed. Citizens of a global and imperial power, they are for the first time in their history face-to-face with a pattern of multiple constraints on American action. They do not like it and find it easier to deliver and hear reassuring speeches on the supremacy of the American way of life.

In postimperialist Denmark matters are different. Judith Friedman Hansen comments that "the attitude common to many segments of the American population that patriotism precludes criticism of one's country and that the virtues of American society outweigh and negate its faults, contrasts sharply with the Danish outlook."[10] Thus when Hansen pointed out to a Dane who was criticizing her own society that these were minor flaws in comparison with the major faults plaguing other societies, and thus implying that she should acknowledge the virtues of her own, the woman responded, "Why should we compare ourselves with the USA or any other country? If something is wrong, it is wrong, and it should be changed."[11]

Perhaps the Danes I spoke with *were* secretly pleased to hear their country's virtues extolled by a foreigner. If so, this did not prevent them from being deeply bothered by the naive and oversimplified manner of its expression in my case. I found, the longer I stayed in Denmark, that the way most Danes view themselves is in large part framed by this code of cultural modesty. An unhappy reaction is likely to be felt by Danes who find that too much virtue is being assumed or implied by others. They are led to oppose both morally and aesthetically any pronouncements that reek of one-sided self-aggrandizement (a prime example of which would be unreserved bragging about the virtues of one's own country).

A cultural code of modesty and humility is expressed in the more self-critical orientation of Danish patriotism and nationalism. The operation of the same principle can also frequently be observed in the ethos of everyday life. One of its interesting manifestations is in the Danish response to a direct compliment. Compliment an American on his or her house, car, or appearance, and the response is usually a warm "thank you." Americans savor and appreciate compliments. Pay such a direct compliment to a Dane and the response will typically be one that disregards, deflects, or downplays its implications. A common response is to turn the compliment on its head, thus in effect "de-acknowledging" its factual import. In response to being told that his home was truly majestic, a Dane might reply along these lines: "What, this old house? No, it's falling apart. The attic is leaking, the paint is cracking in the other room, and the plaster is falling out all over the place." (The initial "no" would be said in a longer and more drawn out form than its English equivalent). Compliment a Dane on her car and the response might be: "That car? It's barely running, and besides, you know, one of the front doors fell off just yesterday." Another difference is that a Dane directly complimented in this way does not feel obligated to smile in a pleased way and say "thank you," as would an American so complimented.

A point raised earlier could be expanded into an objection to this line of analysis. Do Danes really mean it when they express self-critical sentiments about Denmark? Are they *really* being so modest when they do not acknowledge direct compliments? Or is this just a facade masking quite different kinds of feelings? After many months of watching, listening, and thinking, I came to doubt that this was something that could be explained on the basis of a clever facade. Sometimes it is altogether too easy to discount what the people in a given situation are actually saying. Let me cite a parallel from my earlier research on an Israeli kibbutz.[12]

When asked to serve in powerful positions, kibbutz members almost uniformly said that they couldn't do it: they were not qualified for the position, they were in the middle of another job, they had health and family problems, etc. Taking a purely cynical view of these claims, one could easily argue that these kibbutz members were offering *pro forma* objections that they did not mean in the slightest. Organizational elites form, and candidates are attracted to them, runs this view; individuals only express these modest views because they are following a set of social conventions and do in fact aspire to these positions.

Applied to the kibbutz, such analysis sounds both elegant and convincing. The trouble with it is that it is also quite wrong. Members actually *do* mean what they say in most instances because they know only too well the difficulty and stress that accompany such elective offices, the performance of which is (as is all kibbutz work) unpaid. It is in many cases only the diligent application of "moral blackmail" and sustained appeals to collective responsibility that weaken potential candidates just long enough for them to be appointed to one of these offices. The candidates surrender to a fit of civic virtue they knew in advance they would later come to regret. As with the Danish code of cultural modesty, this small example from a different social context provides concrete support for the injunction that one should not always debunk the words that come out of people's mouths.

Sometimes, as in the case of surprisingly unambitious kibbutz members and culturally modest Danes, they may mean exactly what they say.

Listen to a random newspaper sample of the answers given by three Danes to the question "do we treat tourists well enough?"[13] A young man from Odense replies: "Not if they are colored. I think that we Danes still discriminate against people who are different. We show them no helpfulness, and what's even worse, some people just plain bother them. That's not a decent thing to do."

An older man from Odense answers: "We Danes are much too reserved when it comes to tourists. We think we have enough in ourselves. We only need to go down to West Germany to find a friendlier population. I have asked a policeman down there the way in the middle of a big city, and after that the police drove in front of me showing me the way all the way until we got out of the city."

A young man from Bellinge says: "We have good material conditions to offer the tourists, but having said that, you've said everything. We Danes are cool and hold ourselves very far from tourists, even though we discover that they may need a helping hand. When it comes to how to handle tourists, we have a lot to learn from poorer lands."

Though a prevalent mood, this modesty is not something that Danes obtrusively and commonly reveal as a deliberate ploy. It is more, one feels, a part of their inner being that one is privileged to witness on occasion. And it is a code affecting not only evaluations made of country but of self. Thus when a prominent Danish female journalist was told that a Gallup poll showed only the queen and the prime minister above her in personal popularity, this was her very Danish response: "It is so sweet, if people can like me. But I can't really relate to it, or conduct myself according to it. I am neither glad nor the opposite, and I am certainly not proud of such a study, because what does a Gallup poll mean anyway?"

In spite of the fact that he was one of the world's most renowned physicists, Niels Bohr exemplified this principle of cultural modesty. It is perhaps one of the reasons why he was so fine a teacher. He left a memorable personal legacy:

> Bohr lacked, as his pupil Weizsäcker put it, two qualities which usually distinguish most heads of a school. He was neither a pedagogue nor a tyrant. He showed no signs of offended pride when his ideas were sternly or even rudely criticized. . . . Bohr's true greatness was most evident to his pupils in private practice. When a new piece of work was first submitted to him, his first comment was usually: "Magnificent!" But it was only newcomers who exulted prematurely over this exclamation. By asking certain questions,

occasionally speaking at length, or else remaining silent for some minutes, the great thinker would gradually persuade the young physicist who had come to him for advice to realize for himself that perhaps his work had not yet been quite thoroughly thought out. Such an interview might last for several hours and be prolonged until late at night . . .

In the end the pupil would not only begin to discover the faults in his work, but also would start remorselessly tearing it to pieces himself. At this point Bohr would check him, warning the young man against indiscriminate rejection, since even errors contained something which might later turn out to be useful.

"When, after a few years, one left his Institute, one knew something about physics which one didn't know before and couldn't have learned in any other way," Weizsäcker once said in talking of Bohr. It was no wonder that so many eminent natural scientists emerged from his class.[14]

Several small expressions of this principle in personal encounters may be cited. On one occasion after a fine dinner I commented at length on the excellence of the new potatoes that had been served. It got to be too much for the hostess. "Steve, they were just potatoes!" she said to me with amusement and a touch of annoyance in her voice. Another time I was riding on a train with a Danish friend I had known in the United States. It was spring, that time in early May when the first green leaves wave and shimmer high in the ancient beech forests in and around Copenhagen. We were on our way to such a forest for an afternoon's walk. I gestured toward the wonderful scenes passing outside of our train and remarked on their beauty. My friend said in an offhand way as he waved toward the window, "Well, it's not much compared with the leaves in New England in October." His words were sincere; I could detect no irony or false modesty behind them.

A third incident took place when visiting an older man, a noted historian. I mentioned to him in passing how much I had enjoyed reading one of his major works. He shrugged, and his polite reply was, "Well, it's really out of date now." He was not being coy. He was (or so he thought) just being realistic. These are a few incidents out of many that illustrate the particular mood of modesty, sometimes combined with humility and quiet dignity, that I found among the Danes. Remarks like these made a great impression on me at the time, and I still believe they are worth thinking about. In the end they gave me only a deeper feeling and respect for Danish ways, although I learned quickly enough to avoid causing embarrassment by making direct and public expression of these feelings.

II. Skepticism, Caution, and Independence

The cultural code of modesty is one component of the balance principle. A second component is a complex of values and character traits that are
highly valued by Danes. Among them can be included skepticism, caution,
and independence. Skepticism, defined here as the tendency for debunking
and critical disbelief, can be commonly observed among Danes of every
region and social class. Among both intellectuals and nonintellectuals, the
quickest way to arouse skeptical disbelief is to give an unbalanced presentation of facts when dealing with a complex issue. To express a simplistic
point of view and ignore competing evidence is to invite challenge by a
Danish audience. In this case the operation of the balance principle may
cause them to become upset by what they regard as a one-sided, *negative*
evaluation of Danish ways. Herbert Hendin recounts an example of this in
his colleagues' response to his study of Danish suicide:

> Although the Danes have been accustomed to speaking humorously
> about their suicide rate, they are sensitive to any attention given it by a
> foreigner. When talking before Danish colleagues about my work, I was
> interrupted on two occasions with the non-sequitur "What about homicide
> in the United States?" I subsequently learned to mention at the outset that
> the homicide figures were high in the United States and low in Denmark.
> Assured that their country was not about to be criticized, the audience was
> willing to listen with relaxed attention.[15]

What may have been at issue here is not so much mere criticism from
a foreigner but the fact that Danish skepticism about one-sided accounts
requires such discussions to give formal expression to the balance principle.
As soon as the high U.S. homicide figures were recognized and pointed out,
Hendin's audience was willing to listen to the rest of his argument.
Remember also that discussion of a topic such as suicide rates touches
unavoidably (by implication at least) much broader questions such as quality
of life and national character. The same balance principle that required some
Danes to question my one-sided assumptions of Danish virtue led others to
question the equally one-sided negative implications of Hendin's suicide
research. And while admitting the value of Hendin's study, it is difficult to
disagree with Judith Friedman Hansen's observation that "an accurate
description of the range of Danish character must rest on a more varied
sample than the suicidal patients and the members of the medical profession
with whom Hendin talked."[16]

In addition to simplistic and unbalanced accounts, any presentation
demonstrating pompous or bombastic qualities in the speaker is likely to

be unpopular. Initial expressions of disbelief will often be followed by ridicule and derisive irony unless the speaker quickly makes conciliatory statements absolving him of pomposity, a primal sin in Danish eyes. The resulting social sanctions are well known to Danes, who usually do their best to regulate and modify their own conduct so that wrong-sounding presentations will not be made in the first place. Danish author Leif Panduro writes that "it is a little coolly observant troll which keeps us informed of it when we occasionally act more pompously than we can justify."[17] A Dane who in so acting has "overdrawn his merit account" will often recognize at once that he has done so. Joking self-criticism is one measure frequently taken. If done in time, it will avert the need for others present to feel themselves responsible for initiating the correction process.

A classic expression of this theme of correction can be found in the play *Erasmus Montanus* by the eighteenth-century Norwegian-Danish author Ludwig Holberg (1684–1754). The play, a light comedy much loved by Danish audiences, shows a young man both before and after the phases of correction. It is a grand satire, focusing on the empty egoistic pedantry of the learned and on the self-abasing credulity of ordinary people before them.

When the play begins, the young hero Erasmus Montanus is due back in his peasant village after years of learning and engaging in philosophical "disputations" in Copenhagen. His parents, brother, and fiancée await eagerly his return, but not so the uneducated deacon of the village, who has been using his six or so words of Latin to impress the local farmers. When he hears of Erasmus' impending return, he becomes afraid that Erasmus will unmask him as the ignoramus that he is. In those days much educated discourse revolved around the knowledge of Latin, and as the deacon tells us with great satisfaction in an early monologue, he has made good use of this in his business dealings. The peasants used to believe that one funeral song was as good as another, but under his tutelage this lamentable ignorance has been corrected. They have learned to bargain and negotiate when he asks, "Which hymn will you have? This one costs so much and this one so much?" Similarly, he has taught them to pay more for fine sand than common dirt, in the belief that this shows a higher degree of respect for the departed family member. He confides smugly to the audience that the peasants' respect for him comes chiefly from their mistaken belief in his mastery of Latin: "I tell you, Latin helps a man a great deal in every sort of business. I wouldn't give up the Latin I know for a hundred rix-dollars. It has been worth more than a hundred rix-dollars to me in my business; yes, that and a hundred more."

It is precisely at this point in the play that Erasmus shows up in town. From his first moment on stage, it is clear that life at the University has turned him into a dandied fool. His stockings are falling down around his ankles (a sure indication that his mind is occupied with more profound matters). Lighting his pipe, he puts the bowl of the pipe through a hole he has made in his hat, commenting sagely that "it's a pretty good invention for any one who wants to write and smoke at the same time." His main concern is that there will be no one in the entire village worthy enough to engage him in "disputation." His brother Jacob, a farmer, has earned with his hands the money that has been used to support his academic studies in Copenhagen. Yet he is insulted when Jacob greets him warmly with "welcome home again, my Latin brother!" He insists that Jacob, in due deference to his learning, must now address him as "Monsieur Montanus."

Holberg's language ridicules the pretensions of scholastic knowledge. When Jacob asks his brother, "What is it then, that Mossur disputes about?" Montanus answers, "I dispute about weighty and learned matters. For example: whether angels were created before men; whether the earth is round or oval; about the moon, sun, and stars, their size and distance from the earth; and other things of a like nature." When their parents return, Erasmus is beating his brother for not complying with his request to be addressed as "Monsieur Montanus." Their mother then asks, "What does this mean? He wouldn't hit you without good reason." When Erasmus continues to complain, their father turns angrily to Jacob, saying, "What a devil's own rogue! Don't you know enough to respect such a learned man? Don't you know that he is an honor to our whole family? My dear and respected son [said to Erasmus], you mustn't pay any attention to him; he is an ignorant lout."

Unappeased, Erasmus retorts, "I sit here speculating about important questions, and this *importunissimus* and *audacissimus juvenis* comes and hinders me. It is no child's play to have to deal with these *transcendentalibus*. I wouldn't have had it happen for two marks."

In the action that follows, the folly of each of the characters is revealed: the parents who bask in stupefied admiration at the learning of their pedant son, the deacon who must publicly defend his unearned reputation as a master of the Latin language, and Erasmus himself, an ignorant peacock of a youth in love with his own empty words and phrases. A suitable denouement is prepared, and a much-humbled Erasmus appears at the drama's end, crying, "Oh, alas! I lament my former folly, but all too late." In a speech that expresses the main point of the play, he is informed and made wiser by the chief agent of his correction:

> Listen, my friend, your parents have spent much money on you in the hope that you would become an honor and a comfort to them in their old age. But you go off a sensible fellow and come back entirely deranged, arouse

the whole village, advance strange opinions and defend them with stubborn-
ness. If that is to be the fruit of studies, then one ought to wish that there
never had been any books. It seems to me that the principle thing a man
ought to learn in school is just the opposite of what you are infected with,
and that a learned man ought to be distinguished from others in that he is
more temperate, modest and considerate in his speech than the uneducated.
For true philosophy teaches us that we ought to restrain and quiet disagree-
ments, and to give up our opinions as soon as we are persuaded, even by the
humblest person, that they are mistaken. The first rule of philosophy is,
Know thyself; and the further one advances, the lower the opinion one should
have of himself, the more one should realize what there remains to be learned.

It is a much-chastened Erasmus Montanus who replies at the play's
conclusion: "Oh, my good sir, I will follow your advice, and do my best to
be a different man from now on." Holberg, who produced books on
international law, finance, and history as well as satires, biographies, and
moral essays, stands as a major figure in Scandinavian literature. A number
of authors have suggested that the form his plays took was of great importance not only for future Danish and Norwegian theater but for the cultural
life of these two countries.[18] Their emphasis on skepticism, clear-sighted-
ness, and the necessity of keeping both feet on the ground may have acted
over time to reinforce these central themes in the emerging social character
of the two peoples.

Though he was no stranger to the Danish university life of his time,
Holberg is most beloved and remembered for his comedies. The literature
of a people, especially their perennial favorites, can reveal much about their
world and its values. The moral lesson of *Erasmus Montanus* can be summed
up in one critical injunction: to be skeptical of all pretentiousness, especially
that of learned men. And by simple extension, do not fail to exercise your
capacity for independent skeptical judgment no matter what the context.

One can frequently observe Danes exercising their capacity for skeptical disbelief. It is even taught by some teachers in the schools, as an
American girl who attended a Danish *gymnasium* for a year found out. She
worked long and hard on a difficult assignment in statistics, only to find
that the answers didn't come out right and that the statistics given couldn't
be related to the conclusions stated in the problem. When she went to see
the Danish teacher, she was angry and frustrated. The teacher, however, was
pleased. He smiled approvingly and then told her, "Good, you got the point
of the assignment. You should never naively trust any scientific arguments
just because they claim to be based on statistics." She was furious at him
even a year later, but she got the point. It was one she probably would never
forget.

A modern example of the same theme is found in the review of a television astronomy program.[19] The writer, after pointing out that faraway galaxies can reflect light from ones even farther away, goes on to say that "astronomers can use them as 'extra lines' in their telescopes. And they may also be used to decide the age of the universe; *but about that there is not yet complete agreement among the learned ones*" (italics added). This dry reference to "the learned ones," with its residue of doubt as to the capacity of the astronomers to figure out the age of the universe, expresses a theme present in the writings of both Kierkegaard and Grundtvig. It is one that, as we have seen, can be traced even farther back to Holberg. The latter's play, *Erasmus Montanus*, provides an excellent object lesson in Danish skepticism, making a whole evening's entertainment out of a corrective ritual process that can occur within a few minutes during ordinary Danish social interaction.

What can be seen in literature is also expressed in Danish politics and international relations. Skepticism is often combined both with caution and the ability to follow an independent course. This aspect of the balance principle has shown itself recently in several important matters. First, there is the history of Denmark's recent relationship to NATO and its NATO allies. This relationship is highlighted by some statements made at a 1987 post-Summit conference in Copenhagen by then American Secretary of State George Shultz.[20] Shultz took the unusual tack of publicly criticizing Denmark for its defense allocations. Denmark currently spends 2.3% of its gross national product on defense, the lowest percentage of any NATO country apart from Luxembourg and Iceland. To understand the force behind Shultz's remarks, one must understand that of the sixteen NATO countries, Denmark has been the sharpest and perhaps most consistent critic of the deployment of American Cruise and Pershing 2 missiles at bases in Britain, West Germany, Italy, Belgium, and the Netherlands. Indeed, for the past eight years the Danes have distanced themselves even further from mainstream NATO policy by insisting on the addition of a series of disagreeing footnotes to NATO communiques on a variety of subjects. While having little or no direct effect on any policy, these footnotes have nonetheless taken their subtle toll (somewhat like a flea nibbling on an elephant), rendering it impossible for the organization to present a unified facade. For its actions, Denmark has come to be called by some "the footnote nation."

What are the ideological bases for these actions of protest? Although clearly more sympathetic to NATO than to the Soviet bloc, and deeply tied to it as a member of the Western alliance, many Danes profess a constellation of attitudes that might be labeled "Scandinavian neutralism." The essence of this informal doctrine is that smaller nations such as Denmark, Sweden, and Norway must remain capable of standing in equal moral opposition to both of the superpowers whenever necessary. This line of thinking rests on the assumption that it may not always be in the interest of Denmark or of world peace to uncritically support each and every NATO policy. These independent attitudes are exemplified in a speech made by former Prime Minister Anker Jørgensen before the Socialist International in Luxembourg (1984):

> It is natural that Europe has become the center for progressive points of view when one considers the behavior of the [two] superpowers. Out of their own interests both of them have invaded independent countries that were on the way to some kind of development not approved by the super-power in question. In contrast to the superpowers, most political parties in Europe have made an independent evaluation, one that is colored neither by exaggerated fear of communism nor by doctrinaire Marxist-Leninism. When Europe and the Common Market countries adopt a different position, it shows that the democratic system has been strengthened, especially com-pared with the rest of our history in this century.[21]

The same Scandinavian neutralism was reflected in a number of Swedish and Norwegian policies of the last few decades. The late Olof Palme excoriated the American involvement in Vietnam, advocated nuclear disar-mament, and envisioned a nuclear-free Europe. Even as prime minister he was not above actively participating in street demonstrations against Ameri-ca's Vietnam policies. It is easy for Americans to misunderstand the cultural roots of such actions. As a Swedish diplomat suggests in an interview with an American reporter, "When you say you're neutral, you have to prove your innocence every morning. Especially with you Americans. You think a small country must be with you or against you."[22]

For the governing conservative coalition, the influence of this "Scan-dinavian neutrality" and its acceptance by a large part of the political opposition turns international policy-making into an area of continual confrontation and debate. The decision to bar nuclear-armed ships from Danish ports, pushed through by the left-center opposition in April 1988, led Prime Minister Poul Schlüter to call for new elections in May of that year, only eight months after the last national election.[23] Foreign Minister Uffe Ellemann-Jensen warned that the United States and Britain were about to curtail military cooperation with Denmark unless the decision was changed. These issues are much debated within Denmark itself and cannot be considered here on their merits. Rather what is relevant here is the Danish ability to insist on steering an independent course even above the publicly stated objections of its close allies, a group that includes some larger and

VI KAN SELV
- UDE AF EF

"We can ourselves; out of the Common Market." This 1982 poster by Marianne Østergård was used by the People's Movement Against the EEC (Folkebevægelsen mod EF) to protest continued Danish membership in that organization. Forgetting for the moment its partisan message, the poster captures in a single image the Danish values of skepticism and independence essential to the operation of the balance principle (from Uffe Østergård, 1984, reprinted with permission).

much more powerful nations. It is critical to point out that in this case the operation of the balance principle, far from ensuring tranquillity, could result in systematic diplomatic conflict between Denmark and its NATO allies. Indeed, one suspects from the tone of some of the public utterances by Schultz and others that it has already done so. Britain, for instance, not only assailed the Danish action but moved to postpone all naval visits to Denmark before the election.

A second instance where the operation of the balance principle led not to tranquillity but to an increased risk of conflict was in the rescue of the Danish Jews. A third instance can be found in the organized movement in opposition to Danish membership in the European Economic Community. Although it has not been able to determine actual policy, the very existence of this movement demonstrates the action of this component of the balance principle. A final example of the operation of the balance principle can be seen in Denmark's energy policies. While more than a hundred nuclear plants were rushed into construction in the United States, and many of its European neighbors also went quickly ahead making large investments in such plants, the cautious Danes began a debate that has continued to the present day. Though a vocal minority pressed for nuclear power, a larger and

equally vocal minority has been able to prevail, at least in the sense that no
nuclear plants have ever been built in Denmark. Now, in the wake of Three
Mile Island, Kyshtym, Chernobyl, and other nuclear catastrophes, the
Danish decision seems a prudent one to many observers. Even neighboring
Sweden, which had invested in nuclear plants, has now decided to phase
them out by the end of the century. Another fact worth citing is that through
much of the 1980s Denmark was a world leader both in energy conservation
and in the search for alternative, renewable, and nonpolluting energy
sources.[24]

The outcome of this national debate over energy policy provides yet
another example of a major theme: the Danish capacity for skepticism,
combined with caution and the ability to pursue an independent course of
action. It was a child in the H. C. Andersen fairy tale who plainly saw that
the Emperor had no clothes; a little of that child survives in many of the
adult Danes I came to know.

III. BENDING THE RULES

A third dimension of the balance principle is the ever-present Danish
capacity for "bending the rules." This implicit attitude about social rules
and regulations is one that sharply distinguishes the Danes from their
immediate neighbor to the south. It is not a part of Danish culture to act as
if rules in themselves are absolutes, to be mindlessly obeyed in any and all
circumstances. In fact, the very idea would be laughable to most Danes.
Rules are enforced, but the manner of their enforcement will typically leave
an area of discretion for considerations of a more human kind. Danes usually
act with a clear knowledge that all social rules are made in the last analysis
by frail and fallible human beings, and that the person enforcing the rule in
a given situation as well as the person to whom the rule applies must both
be included in that modest category, "only human." Furthermore, although
rules are general, contexts are unique; general rules must therefore be
interpreted to suit the needs of particular contexts.

Military parades are common in Denmark. A company of the Queen's
Guard can often be seen marching through the streets of downtown Copenhagen resplendent in their finest uniforms. Police as well as train conductors
wear uniforms (although public school teachers commonly do not wear the
tie and jacket required of American teachers). Yet somehow in Denmark,
knowing the Danes, the uniforms aren't taken as seriously as they might be
in some other places. Whether it's a marching band, a soldier's parade, or
just two policemen on patrol, one always has the feeling underneath the

insignia it's just some Dane, a guy perhaps from Copenhagen, Fyn, Jutland, or one of the islands. One simply assumes that he'll be a human being first and an official second. The general feeling is that he's someone who can be talked to, someone who won't let the uniform blow him up into a self-important ass who blindly enforces the rules without looking at the essentials of the situation.

This feature of the core value of moderation and balance is one that I learned from personal experience. I cite three personal examples of this Danish capacity for "bending the rules." During the months that I taught at the University of Copenhagen, a colleague who was on leave that semester had loaned me his office. Before going away he had instructed me to use the office in any way that I saw fit, with a single exception. "Don't ever sleep there," he told me. "They come in every night checking and no one's allowed to do it." I followed his instructions religiously for most of the semester, but there inevitably came the Sunday night when I felt so exhausted after working late that I decided to sleep there anyway. I rationalized to myself that it was Sunday, and they would never check on a Sunday evening.

At about one o'clock Monday morning, the door to the office was suddenly opened, and in came a security guard with a heavy-duty flashlight. It was embarrassing, to say the least. Trying to make the best of a bad situation, I quickly managed to communicate to him that I wasn't an intruder but a foreigner teaching at the Institute that semester. He was skeptical at first. Fortunately I had my hiring letter with me and could show it to him as well as personal identification. He took the time to listen to me. Then he quickly cooled down and told me with a wry and understanding smile, "Well, just don't do it again. And make sure to be out of here early in the morning."

By the rules he ought to have ordered me to leave at once. He could have called for the police as well. Yet he could see that no harm was being done and that it was a very cold winter night outside. He could also surmise that it was a first offense and that I really meant what I said about it not happening again. He had been understandably upset at first encountering me, but after seeing the situation in its entirety, he was able to bend the rules and act as humanely as possible under the circumstances.

A similar event took place when I returned to Denmark from a train trip to Germany. My visa had expired, and knowing this, I took all my Fulbright papers along, as well as various letters of recommendation. I had prepared what I thought was a convincing story to tell if I ran into trouble. When the train came off the ferry into Denmark at the little town of *Rødby Færge*, it wasn't long before the Danish conductor came into my compartment. Handing him my passport, I prepared for the worst. He studied me carefully and looked at my passport for a long time. As I mentally rehearsed my lines, he smiled and handed the passport back to me, leaving the compartment. The only thing he said was, "I can see that you've been here before." Ten minutes later he came back to offer me a stick of chocolate.

On a third instance in the summer of 1988, the baggage allowance had been changed between my arrival in Denmark and my departure seven weeks later. The Danish clerk working for British Airways listened to my sad story, decided that the rule wasn't a fair one, and turned his eye in the other direction. I did not have to pay the excess baggage charges that the new rules would have required. In all of these cases I was fortunate enough to encounter the Danish capacity for bending the rules, a tendency I observed to be not in the least uncommon. A Dane usually turns out to be someone you can talk to, someone with a degree of reasonable flexibility about applying rules, someone who just might be able to see the wisdom of relaxing abstract principles in order to let things run more smoothly for flesh-and-blood human beings.

IV. TOLERANCE

Another expression of the balance principle is the Danish capacity for tolerance of dissenting points of view. This underlying tolerance can be seen in issues that involve individual life-style, politics, education, and religion. One can observe it in the Danish folk high school movement, where a single umbrella organization is able to contain schools with philosophies ranging from Marxist-Leninism to right-wing Christian fundamentalism. In neighboring Norway, by comparison, the folk high schools with a more doctrinaire religious orientation split off to form their own separate movement; they did not want to remain in the same movement with schools they felt were too secular in orientation. One can observe it in the political system, where a large number of both left- and right-wing parties receive unquestioned official recognition and work peacefully (if contentiously) together when elected to the Danish parliament.[25] And one can observe it in the treatment of gay couples, who are allowed to form "registered partnerships" that give them all but a few of the rights of married heterosexuals (this measure, passed in May 1989, was the culmination of a forty-year campaign by gay-rights advocates).[26]

A far broader spectrum of political opinion is represented in the Danish parliament than in either of the American legislative bodies. The subtle influence of Grundtvig may have something to do with this greater Danish tolerance of competing points of view. Ejvind Larsen, a contemporary writer who has done much to extend and clarify the meaning of Grundtvig's original vision, suggests that the idea of "the living word" is ultimately more than a pedagogy for the classroom. It is the program for a type of politics that strongly favors both tolerance of ideological diversity and peaceful conflict resolution. In discussing the Grundtvigian conception of political debate, Larsen has cited these words of Ove Korsgaard, a folk high school principal:

> Such a duel requires in the meantime that one has an opponent who at the same time is a partner, a fellow player. The living word demands that one not only respects his opponent, but also sees him as necessary, yes in the deepest sense as a friend. For the individual person just as for a people it is important that the truth not fossilize into dogma. Therefore it is of critical significance to recognize the value of a (word) battle with an opponent. In this way the concept of rights and the concept of freedom are indivisible for Grundtvig. He who wants to be free must let his neighbor be free with him; this is Grundtvig's fundamental perception. Therefore it is not liberation from but *vekselvirkning* with the neighbor, that is the central idea in his view of freedom.[27]

One consequence of this tolerance is that the rigid, hysterical anti-communism that has sometimes characterized American political life is rarely seen in Denmark. The Danish Communist party has slipped from the popularity of its postwar years, but most Danes still regard it as a legitimate party. They will probably tell you that anyone who votes communist is a fool, but they will *not* tell you that such a person is a devil or has been led astray by devils. Nor will they question the right of the party to exist. In Danish politics there has been neither a Senator Joseph McCarthy nor a Danish equivalent of the House UnAmerican Activities Committee. The most successful Danish Communist politician seems to have been Axel Larsen, who in the years after World War II left that party to found the Socialist People's Party. When his new party had acquired twenty seats in Parliament, enough for him to receive a minister's seat, which one did this lifelong and dedicated communist ask for? Axel Larsen demanded (and received) the Ministry of Traffic, an action that left the members of his own party and everyone else equally bewildered.

An interesting example of Danish tolerance is the existence of the "Free State of Christiania," founded during the late years of the hippie era when a suite of vacant military training barracks in downtown Copenhagen was occupied by a group of squatters (1971). Refusing to leave when asked to do so, the squatters formally banded together and established their own "free state." They stayed with the announced aim of turning its eighty acres of barracks and woodlands into their own permanent homes. They claimed the right to conduct themselves in accordance with their own moral principles, which included such newly conceived freedoms as the right to set up public stands for the selling of marijuana and hashish. The original vision of the early squatters was a peaceful society based on the elimination of weapons, violence, cars, and hard drugs. There are many problems now nearly two decades later; some of them include drugs, violence, and the relationship between older and newer generations of inhabitants.[28] But viewed from an outside perspective, it is a miracle that Christiania continues to exist at all.

When I walked through the pleasant anarchy of its streets last summer I looked with my American eyes at the peddlers hawking their contraband drugs and at the runaways, the derelicts, the rebels, the artists, the hip crafts people, the children, the members of ethnic minorities, and the tourists like myself who filled its streets and meeting places. I saw the stands where everything from *falafel* to waterpipes was being sold, and I could not help thinking about what would have happened if the same series of events had taken place in the United States. It would have been followed in all likelihood by a SWAT commando attack, perhaps an invasion by the National Guard as well. There would have been clouds of billowing tear gas, clubs and truncheons, scenes of hate and mob violence followed by the immediate restoration of civic "order." Nothing like this happened in Denmark. No, that would not have been the Danish way of settling the problem. Instead, there was a great deal of debate and now, sixteen years later, the enclave of Christiania still stands, a monument to Danish official patience and tolerance (or as some Danes would say, official confusion and irresponsibility). The whole thing is even more extraordinary from an American point of view when one considers that the occupied land is valuable and could be used for parks or expensive private dwellings. More-over, the Free State of Christiania is located not out in some obscure rural area but only a few blocks from the site where the Danish Parliament meets.

In sum then, the balance principle in Danish life operates in a way that is not always predictable. Though its functioning typically leads in all of the ways that have been specified to a greater tendency toward social tranquillity, it may also lead to exactly the opposite result. It provides one possible explanation for why Danes are leery of fanatics, while at the same time it suggests reasons for the Danish ability to act in unified and nonconforming ways when it is their belief that this is what the occasion demands. Perhaps the best visual metaphor is that of a powerfully spinning gyroscope, one that appears to be fragile but is surprisingly resistant to all attempts to knock it off course.

Bo Bøjesen has written of his fellow Danes, "The ability of the Dane to banish from his mind all troubles, domestic and world alike, is a gift from the gods but one which must be paid for by a somewhat sheepish expression."[29] In spite of the undeniably sheeplike expressions of which Bøjesen complains, the operation of the balance principle ensures an underlying cultural integrity. When they feel that matters are getting out of hand, many Danes are capable of making strong and principled stands on important issues, regardless of the consequences. The mood that underlies these commitments, however, is an ironic one, perhaps best expressed in the following short poem by Piet Hein:

The Only Right Ones

When the time is 11 in Denmark, it's 5 in the U.S.A.,
10 in London, and 17 in China, and about 13 in Moscow.

How fortunate it is that we Danes are a chosen people,
that we are the ones lucky enough to have been born in
just the one little blessed land, where the time is 11,
when it is 11.[30]

CHAPTER EIGHT

Hygge and the Art of Celebration

H YGGE IS THE NAME for a quintessentially Danish social value, one that must be addressed in any account of Danish life and character. Gregory Bateson has written that "zero, the complete absence of any indicative event, can be a message . . . the letter that you do not write, the apology you do not offer, the food that you do not put out for the cat—all these can be sufficient and effective messages."[1] The principle of *hygge* effectively pervades Danish informal social interaction, so much so that both its presence and absence can be meaningful features of an event. An analysis of its many moods will extend the scope of the ethnography beyond the large-scale themes of history and public events, enabling it to show something of the character of family and private life in Denmark.

I mentioned in an earlier chapter an observation that was surprising to me at the time, namely that parties in our volunteer quarters on the kibbutz were more fun when there were two or more Danes present. Similar observations have been made by others. The anthropologist Michael Seltzer, who worked as a seaman, noticed that Danish sailors stood out from other nationalities in their ability to laugh and have a good time. When depressed in port, he would sometimes try to seek out Danish seamen, knowing that an evening with them would succeed in lifting his spirits.[2] Both my kibbutz experience and Seltzer's observations of Danish seamen point to the same underlying pattern in Danish culture. The meaning of this pattern thoroughly eluded me until I came through living in Denmark to understand something of the nature of *hygge*.

Any discerning treatment of *hygge* must begin by making clear its connection to a closely related Danish value, that of *festlighed*, or the festive orientation. The latter has been defined as "the tendency to define occasions festively and the readiness to exploit even minor aspects of a situation to gain maximum enjoyment."[3] *Hygge* and *festlighed* are paired values, the former representing the warmth of successful informality, the latter more connected to the formal feasts and ceremonies that mark the flow of the annual cycle. Coming at particular junctions in this cycle, these feasts provide break points in day-to-day activities and opportunity to mark the passage of the seasons. At these times members of families, communities, and sometimes even entire cities will celebrate publicly the holiday in question.

It can be said without great fear of contradiction that the long centuries of Danish history are both advantageous and disadvantageous for Danish schoolchildren. On the one hand, there are many more names and events that must be learned in studying more than a thousand years of history. On the other hand, there is some consolation in the fact that all of the holidays that have developed over this extended period of time must be appropriately celebrated. Some of the occasions embraced by this tradition involve religious themes. These include (but are not limited to) Christmas *(jul)*, Easter *(påske)*, Shrovetide *(fastelavn)*, Pentecost *(pinse)*, and Prayer Day *(store bededag,* the fourth Friday after Easter). Rites of passage are often celebrated by feasts: these include such events as baptism, confirmation, engagement, marriage, birthdays, funerals, wedding anniversaries, graduations, and success on the early summer student exams *(studenterexamen)*. This short enumeration does not begin to exhaust the list.

Although not technically the occasion for a feast, the granting of independence from the crown *(Grundlovsdag)* is given a warm public celebration each year on the 5th of June. Similarly, the 1st of May is invariably the occasion for a grand holiday with noisy parades to celebrate workers' day. The birthday of the queen on April 16 is an occasion on which thousands meet at Amalienborg Palace in Copenhagen to exchange friendly greetings. *Pinse* in recent years has been celebrated by a riotous carnival, celebrated in Copenhagen alone by between 400,000 and 600,000 people. Although many Danes regard it with less than positive feelings, the idea is so popular that it has been successfully copied by some smaller Danish cities and towns.[4] The Roskilde festival is only one of the many rock festivals that dot the summer landscape. The summer solstice itself is celebrated by the burning of a cloth-and-paper witch on the evening of Saint Hans in mid-June. Even the successes of Danish football teams have been known to become the occasion for festive celebrations. The existence of these festivals testifies to the active character of *festlighed* in Danish life. But although related, the value of *festlighed* embodied in these grand occasions and that of *hygge* are still distinct from each other.

Etymologically, the word *hygge* is derived from Old Norse and was borrowed from Norwegian toward the end of the eighteenth century. It is a concept rich in connotative meaning. The American anthropologist Judith

Friedman Hansen has this to say of it: "Briefly, *hygge* denotes comfort, coziness, cheerfulness, and friendliness. To be in a situation characterized by *hygge* is to be in a state of pleasant well-being and security, with a relaxed frame of mind and an open enjoyment of the immediate situation in all its small pleasures."[5] Sometimes a concept can be brought more clearly into focus by stating its opposite; the antithesis of *hygge* has probably never been more clearly expressed than in these lines by Søren Kierkegaard:

> My soul is so heavy, that no thought can support it any more, no stroke of wings lift it up into the ether. If it moves, then it sweeps along the earth like the birds' low flight when the fierce winds show that a thunderstorm is on the way. An oppression is brooding over my inner being, a fear, an *angst* like the foreboding of an earthquake.[6]

Although the concept may seem simple at first glance, further analysis reveals a range of unexpected complexities in its everyday meanings and applications. Let us begin with its use in actual speech. It may be used as a common noun to refer to an abstract quality or mood *(hygge)*. It may be used as a verb, occurring most often as part of a reflexive pronoun *(vi hygger os:* lit. "we *hygger* ourselves"; or as it is sometimes heard, *lad os nu bare hygger os,* meaning something like "let's go and really have a good time now"). It can appear as an adjective *(hyggeligt)* and is frequently used in connection with the colloquial expression "to have it *hyggeligt*," or to be in a situation where *hygge* is present. It is sometimes heard as a kind of rhetorical question, a joyful exclamation made at the beginning of an encounter to communicate positive anticipation *(Skal vi ikke rigtig hygge os?* which means literally "Shall we not *hygge* ourselves, or have it *hyggeligt?*"). There are even those purists who go so far as to refer to their own residence as *Hyggebo* (lit. "house of *hygge*").[7] The negative form of the term *(uhyggeligt)* provides a range of contrasting meanings, among which are uncomfortable, cheerless, dismal, alarming, sinister, and uncanny.

This profusion of grammatical transformations bears witness to the term's extensive and common use. The principle of *hygge* must be looked in the eyes and squarely confronted; an understanding of it is essential to any treatment of cultural patterning in Danish informal social interaction. Part of the problem comes from the fact that it belongs to a class of terms that cannot be given a simple translation because they are deeply embedded in a rich and complicated system of symbolically elaborated cultural meanings. Parallel terms abound in other languages. I have been told that it is not a simple matter to translate the English term "feminism" into Japanese. The Hopi word *tunatya* is most often translated as "hope," but this simple English translation does not do justice to a non-Indo-European southwest

American Indian language in which most words having to do with meta-
physics are verbs, not nouns: thus, "it is in the action of hoping, it hopes, it
is hoped for" are among the other meanings suggested.[8] Another example
of this class of terms would be the Spanish *pundonor,* which as Hemingway
explained can be translated with the English word "honor" but means a great
deal more:

> Bullfighting is the only art in which the artist is in danger of death
> and in which the degree of brilliance in the performance is left to the fighter's
> honor. In Spain honor is a very real thing. Called *pundonor,* it means honor,
> probity, courage, self-respect and pride in one word.[9]

Admitting the difficulties inherent in simple item-to-item translation, the question must still be asked: what are some of the literal and
connotative meanings of the term *hygge?* It is often inadequately translated
by Danes themselves as "cozy." But to give such a simple translation may
well be to mistake an effect for a cause, as well as to fixate on only one of its
many possible meanings. As we have seen, the term can connote a state of
relaxation, enjoyment, light-heartedness, friendship, or positive feelings. It
resembles in some ways the German *Gemütlichkeit,* with its implications of
comfortable, satiated satisfaction. Like the latter, it has an oral component
and is strongly (although not exclusively) connected with the experience of
eating and drinking in a convivial social setting:

> *Hygge* is at home with a plurality of people, specifically Danes. One
> Saint Hans Eve two or three of us brought out food to one of the small open-air
> cafes on Pilealle and got a bottle of snaps. Our children played about
> nearby—swings, gazebo roofs, see-saws—but they ran out of things to do
> and came to us, not knowing what to do next. From the gazebos rang the din
> of good humor, toasts and *hygge*; warmth virtually poured out from these little
> shrines of noisy *hygge*: "Go over there and watch the Danes."[10]

Many Danes would probably agree that *hygge* is something most often
achieved with those who are a part of one's own social network—with family,
extended family, and friends. The home itself, as the center of private life,
is a primary source for it. What is it that makes a home *hyggeligt? Hygge*
comes from neither an obsessive attention to cleanliness nor an uncontrolled
tolerance of disorder. It is more associated with the middle ground of a home
that is lived in and the feelings of the real people who inhabit it. Excessive
order as well as disorder discourage *hygge*; neither provides an ideal soil in
which it can grow. Perhaps this explains why *hygge* is not the exclusive
property of any particular region, age, or social class in Denmark but seems

to be distributed evenly and widely among all groups, though practiced somewhat differently in each.

But this discussion has already run into difficulty, just as I knew it would. Rather than tack on more names or characteristics to an already expanding list of generalities, let me begin with a humble example of personal *hygge* that occurred while I was a dinner guest at a home in North Sjælland. It was in December, just a few days before Christmas. We were sitting at a large dining room table beautifully decorated with candles, dried flowers, and freshly picked roses. As I looked around after my first glass of wine, I couldn't help noticing that matching color themes and the subdued candlelight brought out the deep brown color of the venerable oak table. The table itself had been lovingly set with antique China, porcelain serving dishes, and cotton napkins in wooden rings at each place. Bottles of red and white wine stood inconspicuously among the serving dishes. Our hostess, a lively and energetic woman in her sixties, prepared and served the meal herself.

I was there because I had known her son in the United States. He and an aunt had been out for a walk with the family dog just before dinner that evening. We sat down at the table, drank the *skål* and *velkommen* toast that often begins such an occasion, and then commenced eating. It was at about this point that a small problem of identity cropped up. While they were out walking the dog some nice woman had waved to them from across the street. Now just who was this woman? Whoever she was, she owned a cocker spaniel. The small talk continued, and as we enjoyed the excellent food, the informal atmosphere, and the elegant setting, I remember someone asking, "Was it the pharmacist's wife?" "No," answered our hostess, "it couldn't have been her—they have a beagle now."

It is difficult for me to explain exactly why, but just at that moment something about the juxtaposition of all the elements in the situation caused me to experience a sudden and unmistakable flush of *hygge*. There was no doubt about it. Some of it may have been from the sudden and unexpected contrast between the grandeur of the setting and the down-to-earth nature of the conversation. It may in part have been the role played by the small dogs in the conversation as well as the very large Newfoundland that insisted on sitting under the table and mostly on my foot during the course of the dinner (many Danes have pets and include them in nearly all their social events). I should add that the hostess' son had been my Danish teacher in the United States several years earlier, that I had just finished three months at my first folk high school, and that I could (to everyone's surprise) actually speak and understand a small amount of Danish. A glance out the window would have revealed the desolate landscape of a dark and cold December evening, yet an observer glancing in would have seen a group of people enjoying a warm and pleasant evening, clustered around the cheerful, subdued lighting of a fully stocked table.

This example, however modest, can be used to illustrate some of the significant features of *hygge*. However much one may try to prepare for it, it always emerges in a somewhat unpredictable fashion. Furthermore, it is a creature of the moment, closely tied to the social situation immediately at hand. Both the attributes of the setting and the behavior of the participants combine to generate an overall mood. The mood that emerges is critical to the proper experience of *hygge*. Indeed, it is well known to Danes that *stemning* (mood) is the first cousin of *hygge* and its frequent table companion. A good host is one who "has gotten the *stemning* to blaze like the fire in the hearth."[11] The mood that gradually emerges will ideally serve to guide and constrain the flow of interaction into successive multiple channels of *hygge*. Yet the image of a blazing hearth may be not quite the most appropriate one to use in this connection. The image it suggests is perhaps one of too much bright light; it fails to include the subtle balancing influence of shadows. "It is strange," observes Jens Kruuse, "that *hygge* is found in half-light."[12] This author views *hygge* as an island in the stream of life that must hold the surrounding darkness at bay.

But up to this point we have explored only the bare bones of *hygge*. It is true that one of its important components is the setting in which the human interaction takes place. The Danish reputation in constructing elegant things for use in such settings has long been an excellent one, as the presence of Scandinavian Designs outlets in virtually every North American city suggests. Yet it must be emphasized that the emergence of *hygge* depends neither on the elegance of the material setting and its details nor on how much brute economic force has been expended in their acquisition. Furthermore, it does not depend on how new and shiny they happen to be. Indeed, newness, perfection, and ostentation are not at all *hyggeligt*. Karlsen has aptly remarked: "Just as there is nothing as 'un-hyggelig' and impersonal as people who always appear in new clothes, so is nothing as *unhyggelig* as visiting a home with completely new things. . . . The unused is distant, a bit unfriendly. *Hygge* first emerges after mutual adjustment between people and things."[13]

As the previous example suggests, *hygge* is not a creature of grand formality. One would not be advised to look for it in the faultless splendor of an ice palace or under the vaulted dome of a majestic cathedral. On the contrary, in spite of the fact that it is everywhere sought after, it has not lost its head and remains a surprisingly humble creature. It thrives best when surrounded by small talk and simple pleasures. Pomposity and arrogance, indeed all forms of conspicuous display, will not only fail to bring it to the table, but can only serve to frighten it away. When two or more people cluster together in the intimacy of a small focused gathering in order to eat, drink, and celebrate life—it is at these kinds of occasions *hygge* may come to grace a social encounter. Thus Kruuse writes: "Tonight we'll have a really *hyggelig* evening. We'll be alone. Buy some nice food. Just a little. There'll be a fire in the fireplace. The dog will lie quite still and listen to imaginary sounds. We'll have a cup of tea."[14]

The foregoing discussion of *hygge* suggests a more general point about the social interaction necessary to sustain it. The worlds that emerge when people are in each other's presence are a product of joint symbolic activity. In order for these small worlds to be created and maintained for the period of the encounter, a ceremonial division of labor is required among those immediately present. Erving Goffman once wrote that "the individual must rely on others to complete the picture of him of which he himself is allowed to paint only parts. Each individual is responsible for the demeanour image of himself and the deference image of others, so that for a complete man [or woman] to be expressed, the individual must hold hands in a chain of ceremony, each giving deferentially with proper demeanour to the one on the right what will be received deferentially from the one on the left."[15]

When applied specifically to *hygge*, Goffman's lines point to one of its essential requirements: it is a joint creation, a product of group ceremonial effort. Such effort begins ideally even before the encounter takes place. Thus when visiting a Danish home as a dinner guest, one comes to know that it is not enough just to show up at the doorstep at the appropriate time. A thoughtful gift, perhaps some wine or a bouquet of flowers, should be brought for the host or hostess. When the door is opened and greetings are exchanged, this small gift can be presented. Both the giving of a gift and its grateful reception can set a positive tone for the entire evening. The guest is then invited in and often welcomed into the living room for a drink and a small chat before dinner. Or the guest may be invited directly to the dinner table, which in a middle-class home will have been set before the guests begin to arrive.

This small detail points to an interesting feature of the behavioral code around which Danish (and Scandinavian) hospitality is organized. For when one really examines it, the ease and informality that at best characterize the flow of social interaction during a *hyggeligt* occasion are bounded by a curious kind of formality. When contrasted with the casual style of American hospitality, this formality of expectations on the part of Danes can easily lead to intercultural misunderstanding. Thus Judith Friedman Hansen quotes the surprise of a Dane who had lived in the United States for two years:

"Why, frequently the table isn't even set when we arrive. That would never happen in Denmark." Similarly a Norwegian woman remarks, "In Norway when you go to someone's house you know they really look forward to your coming. The work they've put in to make things as nice as possible is evident. They will use their nicest things—there will be an embroidered tablecloth on the table and special food. They won't just make the easiest thing possible, like steak and baked potatoes."[16]

Such decorative elements as flowers (dried and live), hand-painted vases, candles and candleholders, embroidered tablecloths, a symmetrically well set table, subdued lighting, art objects, antique furniture, beautifully prepared and served food, together with fine wines, after-dinner coffee, a choice of sweets and liqueurs, pleasant music, and a fire burning in the fireplace—any and all of the above can serve as conventional props for the realization of *hygge*. They are important at least in part not only for what they directly bring to an occasion but for what they indirectly imply about the amount of time, effort, and care that someone has expended in preparation. But the complexity of the discussion must be further compounded. As all Danes know, not even the successful provisioning of an occasion with the most tested and decorative props can guarantee the emergence of *hygge*.

For *hygge* is neither a commodity that can be bought and sold, nor is it some kind of a chemical compound that can be produced infallibly by the mere mixing together of all of its elements in the correct proportions. It is not a matter of formulas and recipe books (though one would never understand this from a perusal of the large-circulation women's magazines that clutter up the Danish newsstands, filled with the latest hints and suggestions about what women should buy to have it *hyggeligt* with their families and the men in their lives). Neither is it in the last analysis a matter of having access to opulent settings, as the minimalist performances of my former Danish kibbutz comrades with candles and inverted orange crates convincingly show. The minimalist theme must be emphasized because it conveys an important insight into *hygge*. Consider this description given by an actress of her younger days on tour with an actor husband:

> One of the young actresses understood how to create *hygge* wherever she was with just a few possessions. A pretty silk spread decked the table on which stood a bouquet of flowers and a bowl of fruit. On the night-table, the white cold marble top of which had also been covered with silk cloth, stood a photograph. These small things had transformed the room from a grim and impersonal space to a *hyggelig* place to spend time.[17]

In the final analysis there is nothing at all mechanical about *hygge*. "Like its cousin happiness," writes novelist Tove Ditlevsen, "*hygge* is a fickle guest which comes when it suits it and most often when no one has called for it." It is, as another commentator has said, "a retiring creature which cannot be forced." To go overboard in attempting to create the perfect setting in which *hygge* must emerge is to invite it never to show up in the first place. And to talk about it during the course of an occasion, to say "Oh, how *hyggeligt*" we're having it *(Ih, hvor har vi det hyggeligt),* may well result in its quick departure (if indeed it was ever there at all). As Hansen notes, this kind of comment during an ongoing interaction "implies a degree of evaluative detachment which is antithetical to the involvement which generates *hygge.*" Thus for all its modesty and humility, *hygge* behaves in some ways like a stubborn and aesthetically minded purist. It will linger only where there is an uncontrived, spontaneous involvement in the events of the here and now.

No matter how much sincere effort an individual, a pair, or the participants in a larger gathering may expend on "having it *hyggeligt,*" it may still be conspicuous by its absence. When this happens, it is a common strategy to continue to invoke the word even though the mood to which it refers is plainly absent. The motivation in such cases might be formal politeness or a sincere attempt not to hurt the feelings of one or more of the participants. But the word might also be invoked in one of the countless shades of irony available to a typical Dane, communicating everything from boredom and impatience to comic relief. Life being what it is, this kind of illegitimate usage is understood by all Danes. Fondly or bitterly memorialized in their literature, the resulting false or empty *hygge* is a type of situation with which they are only too familiar.

A convincing instance of false *hygge* is found in the poem "What do you think that I think?" by the contemporary Danish poet Vita Andersen in a volume entitled *Security Addicts.*[18] The poem begins with these lines: "I've been invited out for dinner by a guy. . . ." It then goes on to recount with deeply ironic insight the double-edged pleasure and pain of a night out on the town in Copenhagen. The poet and her male companion both try to conceal their personal insecurity and impress the other with how fantastically desirable and sought after they are by the opposite sex:

> you pick me up at six o'clock
> we take a whisky first (ballantine 12 year old Master Card)
> we converse *hyggeligt*
> you praise my apartment
> that I've carefully cleaned up
> because you are coming . . .
> you decide what we will eat . . .
> we sell ourselves the best we can

you tell about your job your house your career
and I let you know discreetly what a sought after lady I am
you mustn't think you're out with just anybody . . .
we have it *hyggeligt*
we both laugh at the right moments . . .

The poem astutely portrays the multiple levels of ambiguity and misunderstanding that lie behind the facade of spontaneous enjoyment presented by a sophisticated, smart young pair out on the town. In the context of the revelations that emerge, it is clear that the repeated uses of the term *hygge* ("we converse *hyggeligt*," "we have it *hyggeligt*") are at best rhetorical statements that provide a kind of ironic camouflage. The truth is that the occasion is not *hyggeligt* for any of its participants in spite of painstaking mutual pretense to make it seem as if it were.

In addition to this "false *hygge*," where all present are alienated from the interaction and merely trying to maintain a successful front, there are other potential problems. There is the problem of the once *hyggelig* situation that has somehow lost its good spirit *(hvor blev hyggen af?)*. There is the related problem of "split or partial *hygge*," in which what is *hyggelig* for some participants is definitely not *hyggelig* for others. This problem can occur in a range of situations, one man's meat often being another man's poison. Differences in taste and values stemming from rural-urban divisions, political ideologies, social class perspectives, or intergenerational boundaries are some of the things that may be at issue here. Thus when my folk high school experience brought me into contact with farm families in Jutland, I was present on some social occasions in rural settings that provided great *hygge* for me as a visiting anthropologist (these included both church services and festivals in private homes). The same occasions might have seemed utterly ridiculous to some of the folk high school students from the Copenhagen area (especially those who thought of themselves as sophisticated city people).

In addition to rural-urban differences, perhaps the classic occasion for split *hygge* is family gatherings. What is *hyggeligt* for the older generation may be quite *dødkedelig* ("deadly boring") for members of the younger. The *hygge* observed by many members of the older generation includes a code of politeness that younger people no longer observe, or observe only in part. Thus in describing his own upbringing a folk high school teacher remarks:

> I learned that when I visited some people, the next time I saw them I said thanks for the last time *(tak for sidst,* lit. "thanks for last"). If you were to a party, then you wrote back, or called, and said "thanks for a good party." I think there are more Danes who do this than other people. But if students

have been out to visit me, then they say thanks when they leave *(tak for i aften)*, but it's very rare that one of them says, the day after, thanks for the last time, or thanks for yesterday. It's unusual, if you meet it today, but that's the way it was earlier.

Although it does not come across clearly in these words, I believe that the failure of most members of the younger generation to observe these small social details was something that left him feeling very sad. An instance of split *hygge* seen from the point of view of the younger generation is provided by Danish novelist Tove Ditlevsen:

> Often my mother said, "This evening don't be running down to the street. Uncle Peter and Aunt Agnete are coming over, and we're going to have a *hyggelig* time." They came with my cousins close behind, and we sat all nine of us around the coffee table. No one could get up and breathe without everyone getting up to make room. I couldn't breathe, my heart pounded, I felt queasy, and flushed and upset, along with an unbearable need to go to the bathroom smack in the middle of *hygge*.[19]

I have tried to demonstrate that *hygge*, like true love, is not always smooth sailing. There can be too much wind, or no wind at all. And even if the wind is fine, there can be those who wish they were on another boat, surrounded by a different set of companions, steering an alternate course. The discussion to this point, however, has always assumed a need for the existence of companions. It is good at this point to ask a question: Is *hygge* something that requires the presence of others? Or can one have *hygge* alone? There appear to be differences of opinion on this matter. Although some argue that it is scarcely possible for one person to have a *hyggelig* time, others maintain that they have had a perfectly *hyggelig* time while quite alone. When I asked two teachers at Silkeborg Højskole about this, their first response was to say that this was impossible, but after quick reflection they had second thoughts. They finally answered in the affirmative. Long walks in the country or evenings alone doing just what one wants at the desired pace—most of those I talked to agreed that the possibility of private *hygge* does exist.

One place where a Dane may be able to find *hygge* alone is in bed, with the quilt *(dyne,* rhymes with English "soon") drawn up about the ears on a winter evening. A woman resting on her bed after a day's work in the garden writes, "It is warm and *hyggelig* in the half-dark room and I am pleased with myself and feel surrounded by affection and solicitude."[20] Perhaps the key prerequisite for *hygge* is that one must be relaxed and totally alive in the present moment. If this is the case, the presence of others may in fact not be an absolute requirement for its emergence.

The Danish *dyne,* or feather quilt, is all that now remains of the elaborate peasant beds of the sixteenth century. The beds of those days resembled a true refuge from worldly existence. Overflowing with quilts, they could be ascended by means of a little stairway. Such beds were constructed with paneling, sliding doors, and even overhead canopies.[21] And though the reduced model that constitutes the modern-day quilt can be a source of great pleasure for a Dane, its first use on the part of an untrained foreigner may be quite a bit more stressful than anticipated. The ordeal experienced by the Irish-born journalist Francis Hackett is a vivid illustration:

> That night I found myself in bed with a strange animal. This was a feather bed, what the Danes call a *dyne.* At first it was one of the most benign and fondling beasts I had ever become introduced to. It warmed me up so gratefully and rubbed against me so thoughtfully that I thought the *dyne* and I were going to be lifelong friends. It had all the qualities one demands— pliability, gentleness, insinuating warmth, passivity and devotion. Safe in the arms of this comforting monster I fell asleep. Perhaps an hour went by, or two hours, and then I began a terrible struggle that nearly ended me. I was in hell-fire. I could feel hot fire on my breath. Determined not to be annihilated without a blow, I lunged out with all my might, but instead of making an impression on the enemy I wasted all my efforts and was borne down by a suffocating, overwhelming mass that tried to asphyxiate me without uttering a sound. The battle was all the more fierce because it was wordless. I was dumb. At last, summoning all my strength, gritting my teeth, purple in the face with effort, I decided either to die or to conquer, and I woke up, gripping the *dyne* by the throat.[22]

Hackett's near demise at the hands of a Danish *dyne* is probably an exceptional case. The *dyne* itself, a light, soft quilt filled with down and encased in a cotton cover, doubtless wished him no harm. This garment, which serves as a combination sheet and blanket, is part of the indoor heritage of a cold-climate people. Most non-Europeans do not fully appreciate how far north northern Europe actually is. New Yorkers, for instance, tend to think that their city and London are at roughly the same latitude, yet London is farther north than any of the fifty states except Alaska. The Scandinavian countries are in turn a good deal north of London. They are far closer to the North Pole than most of the other populated regions of the world, and it is only the moderating influence of the Gulf Stream that has made them habitable. The sharp Scandinavian swings "between the nearly continuous daylight in summer and the grudging few hours in winter represent the most pronounced example of the considerable seasonal changes in light that occur throughout northern Europe."[23]

It has often been suggested that the code of *hygge* is primarily an adaptation to the long dark nights of the Scandinavian winter. If this is the case, one would not be surprised to find equivalent versions of it in other Scandinavian countries. During eight months in Norway I heard the term *hygge* used in all of the ways that I had come to know so well in Denmark. And as if not to be outdistanced by the Danes on this (or anything else), the Norwegians even had a second expression *(koselig)* that they used in a way utterly synonymous with their own (and the Danish) *hyggeligt*. Most Norwegians that I talked to, however, graciously conceded a special excellence in the theory and practice of *hygge* to the Danes (in this area as well as the field of Grundtvig scholarship one would have to be foolhardy to question Danish supremacy).[24]

At this point a non-Scandinavian reader may be beginning to think along the following lines: "So what if Danes have a good time at parties? People all over the world do exactly the same thing, and even if the Danes have a special word for it, that doesn't mean they're doing anything different from anybody else." Although there is some merit to the objection, I would reply to such a reader that the Danish practice of *hygge* is more than just the having of a good time. After all, some people can have a good time at a lynching.[25] *Hygge* as practiced by Danes has special characteristics. First, it depends on the complete and positive participation of all present in the encounter (the inclusion principle, discussed in the next chapter). Second, it requires an evenness of flow, a sustained back-and-forth dance of involvement that encourages and even demands this level of participation. And third, the achievement of these goals is made possible by a range of positive social skills, including teasing (a national pastime), quick repartee, the telling of stories and jokes, patience, sensitivity, and the ability to be an enthusiastic audience as well as performer. The ability to participate easily in social encounters that bring this principle to life is a part of the Danish heritage that others can well regard with envy.

A fine example of appreciation for the quick repartee of successful *hygge* comes from Edmund Gosse's reminiscence of his visit to Denmark in 1874. He is describing a series of events that took place one evening at the home of a prominent Danish theologian:

> Dr. Fog [another guest] had been dwelling, as foreigners in those days used to, on the vileness of the coffee they were given in England. Mrs. Martensen (always addressed as Bispinden, or "the Bishopess") asked me in rather a rhetorical tone, "Does not Mr. Gosse think it wonderful that an English lady cannot make a good cup of coffee?" expecting me to be crushed. But I instantly said, unconsciously imitating her tone of voice, "Does not the bishopess think it wonderful that a Danish lady cannot make a good cup of

tea?" The repartee may seem primitive, although as a fact it was just, and we were all in a mood to laugh at anything. But the effect on Bishop Martensen was excessive, since, delighting at the tables being turned on his wife, and happening to be swallowing something at the moment, he giggled, and then gurgled and then choked, and had to be shaken and finally laid out at length.

Learning the informal skills that facilitate subsequent competence in *hygge* is an important part of the socialization process. Everywhere in Denmark one can see young children being taught these skills, frequently through enactment by adult role models. Consider the theme of the following scene witnessed on the evening TV program for children, *Fjernsyn for dig:*

> A young adult woman is seen escorting a group of expectant five year olds out to the beach for a birthday party. But this is not going to be any rushed affair of grabbing for the cake and eating it. Such a thing would be most lacking in *hygge*. On the contrary, I watched in fascination as the young woman was able to get the children first to sit in an orderly circle around the cake by using a series of skillful techniques. Responding to her cues, they interacted with each other in a pleasant and relaxed manner while still sitting in the circle around the cake. Eye contact was maintained, and all the children present were encouraged to be actively involved in playing, singing and talking. They even got up and left the cake for a brief, casual saunter down to the water (someone may have been delegated to remain behind and guard it). Things went on like this for quite a while before the candles were blown out. By the time the cake—with its candles and its red and white Danish flags—went the way of all cakes, the children present and those watching at home had seen a respected adult role model enacting some basic elements of the Danish code of *hygge*. They had learned something about teamwork and cooperation, and in the process ample opportunities had been provided for what psychologists call "observational learning."[26]

I watched this program on TV while at a folk high school. The patterns of social learning taking place on the screen were so obvious and charming that I broke out in laughter. Some of the Danish students in the room glanced at the program to see what I was laughing at and then looked at me in complete puzzlement. Being totally within the culture of *hygge*, they had no idea at all what I was laughing at even after I tried weakly to explain it to them. But such scenes of instruction are common not only on the streets but in the schools, parks, and museums, as well as in the home. *Hygge* is a fundamental part of the behavioral code of Danish informal social organization. As such, it is an area in which most Danes receive effective instruction during childhood. Something this important cannot be left to chance in any culture.

A basic part of the *hygge* of the past several decades has been the shedding by significant numbers in the population of body-image taboos prevalent in most other Euro-American nations. Thus an observer walking through the Royal Gardens *(Kongens Have)* in downtown Copenhagen during periods of warm weather is likely to see women of all ages enjoying a few moments of topless sunshine. The beaches around the country have become places where the human body can face whatever sun there is to find in an unclothed state. A good number of Danes would probably agree with the statement that the most dangerous form of pornography is not mere nudity or for that matter sexuality, but the constant repetition of scenes of violence. Perhaps not surprisingly, what is often censored on Danish television is the high level of violence in so many American media productions.[27] High-speed chases, beatings, explosions, gun battles, knife fights—to many Danes American television programming has a contrived and almost pornographic preoccupation with violence. They notice with dismay, as did I upon my postfieldwork return to the United States, the ceaseless, unconscious glorification of acts of violence.

In contrast, nude human bodies and the facts of human sexuality and reproduction are much more explicitly recognized and accepted for what they are in Denmark. The Danish public tends not to become as upset by these things as its American counterpart. Consequently their showing is more generously permitted in the public media such as movies, TV, and even daily newspapers. Major Danish newspapers, for instance, will accompany a second-page article about warm weather with a picture of a topless couple frolicking in the surf (see opposite page). One can also find uncensored views of human genitals of both sexes in mainstream Danish papers, something that would be unthinkable in the United States. I am not speaking here of pornography, which though legalized since the 1960s, is still the subject of frequent debates.

What lies behind the Danish code of *hygge?* Is it merely, as some have suggested, a cold-climate adaptation to long winter nights? The very least one can say of it is that it reflects a skill, talent, and concern for the values of conviviality and "positive sociality." And though the rituals, styles, and decorative traditions facilitating it may seem to require an inordinate effort for the attainment of quite superficial goals, this view of it is in my judgment almost certainly incorrect. The American sociologist Erving Goffman wrote these lines at the conclusion of one of his most elegant essays on the subject of informal human interaction: "As far as gaming encounters and other focused gatherings are concerned, the most serious thing to consider is the fun in them."[28] One has the feeling that the kernel of Goffman's message has been understood in Denmark for a long time.

The headline for this picture reads, "Sweat, sweat, and more sweat. The warm weather continues interrupted by thundershowers." Anywhere else this weather forecast would not be a good one, but in Denmark it is (as the picture above convincingly shows) cause for hygge *and general rejoicing. The caption reads, "Enthusiastic water-lovers disregarded the meteorologist's prophecies of a late bathing season." (Politiken, 28 May 1985. Photo: Lars Hansen. Reprinted by permission of Politikens Press Photo.)*

It is my contention that the deepest understanding of *hygge* cannot be found in the vacuous consumerism of the daily women's magazines, but in the voices of the Scandinavian poets and writers, where joy is often balanced with grief and happiness with sorrow. I stated in an earlier chapter that there was something about this very real Danish melancholy that made its joyous celebrations only deeper and more significant in my eyes. Something of this Scandinavian mood is captured in a short poem, "A Poem for the House," by the Norwegian poet Arnulf Øverland (the poem can be found engraved on a plate in many a Norwegian house):

> There is one happiness in life
> which cannot be changed to sorrow:
> This, that you gave joy to another,
> that is the only happiness.
>
> There is one sorrow in the world
> That no tears can lighten:
> This: that it was too late
> when you understood this.
>
> No one can take the rest of the time to
> stand before a grave and lament.
> The day has many hours.
> The year has many days.[29]

Whatever else it is that lies behind the behavioral code of *hygge*, it has its sources in another aspect of the Danish national character that I have found nowhere better described than in the following lines by Judith Friedman Hansen:

> There is an Epicurean strain in Danish culture, an absence of ambivalence with regard to enjoyment, which is reflected in the Danish ability to savor the most commonplace of things as something special, as an experience. That Danes enjoy trips to the south or new automobiles or Tivoli or even towering open face sandwiches is scarcely surprising. What is remarkable to an outsider is that a very similar delight may meet a slice of Danish salami or of liverpaste (which a sizeable number of Danes eat every day) or a fresh breakfast roll or a tree just beginning to burst into leaf or birds suddenly breaking into song. One comes to feel that there is an abiding respect for simple natural things running deep in Danish culture, perhaps part of the rural heritage which is retained even by urban Danes.[30]

Or as it has been said by Danish folklorist Iørn Piø:[31] "Every time there is the slightest occasion for it, people celebrate. And so it has always been."

CHAPTER NINE

Welfare and Social
Responsibility

THE FOURTH CORE VALUE ORIENTATION is one for which the Danes are already well known in other lands. In the political idiom of mainstream America, the term "welfare state" has long been associated not only with Danes but with Scandinavians in general. It is commonly used as a term of opprobrium, derogation, abuse, and condemnation. Anyone who doubts this is encouraged to bring up the topic of Scandinavian welfare systems to a group of Americans in an informal setting and see what happens. The results are likely to be the same whether the setting is a posh cocktail party in Scarsdale or a hot dog and Polish sausage cookout in Southwest Philadelphia. A heated discussion based on little or no knowledge will follow. What is likely to emerge is a general consensus that the welfare state is an impediment to free enterprise and individual initiative. It hasn't worked in Scandinavia, wouldn't work anywhere else, and is therefore something to be avoided at all costs.

Let us pause for a moment and reflect on the fact that the term welfare state has acquired such a heavy ideological load in the American political mainstream that any clear and open-minded discussion of the issues behind it is nearly impossible. That the term has become such an emotionally loaded label in American political life gives convincing testament to the rhetorical skills of the legions of journalists, academics, politicians, and preachers who, enamored of their free market ideology, have for decades been inculcating a silent, woolly minded, and unprotesting American majority with their own dark images of the welfare state and its alleged destructiveness. One hesitates to interject a note of unhappy doubt into an area where so many have already made up their minds (or had their minds made up for them). Nevertheless, I would like to propose a counterinterpretation to the familiar stereotype about welfare (some of the evidence to support it has been presented in earlier chapters).

This counterinterpretation is based not on aggregate economic indicators viewed in isolation but on how they appear when seen in their human context. Its central theme is that the Scandinavian cultures should be seen not as failed welfare states but as vanguard, postimperialist societies with a long history of utilizing legitimate "people-intensive" strategies in their economic development. The development and implementation of these "people-oriented" strategies, based on a wide range of secondary institutions, has allowed the Scandinavian nations to benefit from the unquestioned dynamism of capitalist free-enterprise economics *while at the same time avoiding some of the worst social and human disfigurements that inevitably follow from its unrestricted operation.* The state of affairs that results from a failure to curb the excesses of capitalism has been summed up succinctly by J. K. Galbraith: "private opulence and public squalor." Viewing the American scene today, even the conservative journalist George F. Will was moved to write that "nothing that happens in Bangladesh should be as interesting to Americans as the fact that a boy born in Harlem today has a lower life expectancy than a boy born in Bangladesh."[1]

It is unfortunate that the term welfare state has come to function as a label that frames and negatively stereotypes most discussions of Scandinavian experiments with people-intensive social institutions and strategies. Those who hold such simple stereotypes will never be able to consider with detachment, much less learn with positive appreciation, what it is that the Danes have to teach us. They might think it strange that generous stipends and loans *(statens studenter uddannelsesstøtte)* are available to all Danish university students whatever their course of study, and that no university student is required to pay tuition. Perhaps they would also object to other, related Danish welfare policies: that all under the age of eighteen receive free dental care paid for by the state, that rent control is strict and in force, that those who finish a university degree and do not obtain jobs can still receive state support for extended periods of time. Yet such policies, far from destroying personal initiative, will often facilitate its survival. Consider this example of an academic researcher who became unemployed after completing her examinations:

> She nonetheless remained active in a wide range of professional connections: held lectures, wrote articles and books, went to meetings. Regardless of her unemployed status, she was busy throughout this whole period developing and improving the qualifications she had achieved through her studies. This was also one of the reasons that she achieved her present position.[2]

When Americans think of welfare, it is almost a conditioned reflex for them to point to its abuses. Abuses certainly do exist. Welfare policies are administered through bureaucratic structures with their well-known, inevitable shortcomings. It is demeaning for anyone to have to stand in line and wait for an interview with a harassed social worker to whom one may be no more than a case and a number. And the relationship to the social worker takes on an especially demeaning character when economic dependency is involved. These regrettable facts are as true for Denmark as for the rest of the world. The system also has other kinds of abuses: an American working man—let us say a journeyman carpenter—might be shocked to find that his opposite number in Denmark is able to earn close to 90% of his full salary over a period of five years just by reporting for work at certain key periods for several months each year.[3] Yet there is a wider dimension to the notion of welfare found in Danish culture than the one conjured up by these negative images of the welfare state.

Those who doubt this should pause a moment to reflect upon the previously cited study by Richard Estes, based on a longitudinal research design that made use of detailed statistical information at the beginning and end of the 1970s. When the data from Estes' forty-four indices were tabulated and the countries of the world placed in rank order, the statistics told a surprising story. Who would have thought that in terms of social welfare, the United States belongs in the fourth (1979–80) or fifth (1969–70) tier of nations, grouped together in the 1979–80 scoring with such countries as Mexico, El Salvador, South Korea, and Turkey?[4] Recall that the Index of Social Progress used in the Estes study rated Denmark as the nation with the world's highest quality of welfare-related social provisioning at both the beginning and the end of the decade (the sample size included 107 nations).[5] If there is even the slightest bit of validity in his research, then both the welfare state and the people who live in it deserve a second and more open-minded look.

It is of course true (as the Danish *gymnasium* teacher discussed in the last chapter showed his American student) that statistics are normally manipulated and chosen to fit a preconceived aim. Thus many American institutions have recently begun to measure comparative national GNPs in terms of "purchasing power parities" rather than current exchange rates. The Japanese GNP, measured through current exchange rates, seems to be nearly 60% of the size of the American economy, but a much nicer figure of 40% is obtained by measuring purchasing power parities.[6] Through the judicious application of similar techniques, data can be manufactured to support desired conclusions in any area where instructive comparisons are required (the precise level of the Soviet Union's military investments and capabilities *vis-à-vis* our own has long been inflated dramatically by Pentagon statisticians).

Yet the significance of the Estes study for this inquiry goes beyond any questions of statistical interpretation. It suggests a number of issues that I do not believe can be answered (or even addressed) through the mere citing of statistics. Recall the lack of natural resources that acts as a fundamental geopolitical constraint on the Danish economy. In light of this fundamental constraint, at least three qualitatively oriented questions must be asked: How have the Danes been able to achieve these successes in the field of social welfare? What are the nonmaterial bases behind the overall Danish achievement in social provisioning and quality of life? What are the distinctive value orientations that make this achievement possible?

These questions are ones with fundamental implications for the study of national character. We must recall that the Danish society of the 1970s and 1980s was not built on a westward migration into a new continent with untapped material wealth, but on a far from ideal landscape containing few material resources. The history of Denmark in the nineteenth century was neither a triumphant expansion from sea to shining sea nor a largely untrammeled movement along an apparently endless frontier. On the contrary, it was a national experience characterized for the most part by severe retrenchment and loss. What factors, then, are responsible for the Danish achievement in the field of social welfare? How, in short, did the Danes do it?

Faced with both an absence of material resources and a series of historical calamities that had deprived them of a significant role in international power politics, the Danes shrugged their collective shoulders and turned inward. They began cultivating their own gardens as best they could: "Outward loss, inward gain," in the words of the Heath Society's nineteenth-century slogan. Seen in the long term, the Danish response has enabled them to successfully transcend the material and geopolitical limitations of their history. Certainly one critical element in this success has been their ability to develop a rich network of people-intensive strategies for investment in the human quality of the labor force.[7] Denmark has made a series of concentrated investments in its people—in the maintenance, education, training, and personal development of its human population. The distinction made in earlier chapters between the primary and secondary agents of transformation revealed some important features of the Danish case. A matrix of social movements, unfolding over the course of more than a century, facilitated a high level of social cooperation and welfare planning. These long-term developments have beyond question played an integral role in the non-violent Danish path to modernization.

The growth of welfare institutions in Denmark and the details of their functioning have been treated elsewhere in great detail.[8] I therefore do not focus here on the institutional mechanics of the welfare state but rather on the related concepts of welfare and social responsibility that permeate Danish society at many levels. It is part of an anthropological perspective to focus on the pervasive, implicit, and underlying orientations that are the lifeblood of any system of formal rules and institutions. The ability of the Danes to envision, formulate, and establish institutions based on people-intensive social reconstruction is closely connected with their orientation toward the core value complex of welfare and social responsibility. The critical nature of this fourth core value is apparent.

I will treat three components of this orientation toward welfare and social responsibility: (1) the function of the inclusion principle as it is demonstrated in informal social interaction, formal welfare policies, alternative grass roots welfare efforts, and the Danish political party system; (2) the Danish social conscience with its quick readiness to criticize perceived social injustice; and (3) the notion of *folkelighed*, which can be traced back to the writings of N. F. S. Grundtvig.

I. THE INCLUSION PRINCIPLE

To my knowledge it was Judith Friedman Hansen who first drew attention to the critical importance of the inclusion principle in Danish society.[9] By the inclusion principle I refer to the strong tendency to try to structure a wide range of social situations in such a way that people are brought together into a common unit rather than polarized into insiders and outsiders.

The operation of the inclusion principle is striking in most Danish informal social interaction. Danes are good at doing things together. For one thing, everyone knows that it is difficult to find *hygge* unless each of those present agrees to carry his or her share of the ceremonial burden. Although the task appears to be a minor one, the consequences of failure are noticeable to all. *It just will not do* for someone to sit off in a corner looking lonely and dejected. Nor will it do for a person in the center of an encounter to remain sour, angry, or withdrawn. Great effort is not infrequently extended to make sure that all persons present in a social gathering are sitting loosely oriented to each other and included within a single interaction, governed by a relaxed and positive mood.

After one has learned to look for it, it is not at all difficult to see the operation of the inclusion principle in the spatial clustering behavior of

Danes abroad (Uffe Østergård, 1984: 98, reprinted by permission). Østergård remarks that every Dane's photo album is full of similar or even better examples of behavior influenced by national character. In this visit to North Italy in 1982, note how the inclusion principle has resulted in a "cluster effect" in which people come together even in a relatively large group for informal social provisioning and exchange.

Danes in Denmark. I have taken this informal Copenhagen street scene from my own photo album. Note how Danes of different ages and social backgrounds, in this case probably strangers, sit casually in close proximity while they listen to a group of street musicians. They are enjoying a late afternoon beer and the relaxing ambience of the music.

Danes in public places. In his thoughtful and stimulating analysis of Danish character, Uffe Østergård presents a picture from his private photo album that shows fifteen members of "some undetermined European nationality" on tour in North Italy. He quite rightly points out that if taken individually, it is impossible to decide what European country each person comes from. Yet when one looks at the group as a whole, the national identity of its members would be obvious to any Dane. Time after time I observed Danes doing what can be seen in Østergård's picture. All present would be encouraged to draw together into a common cluster. No one would be allowed to remain indefinitely in a mood or posture communicating separateness or isolation. Individuals remaining separate were often invited, cajoled, or persuaded to join in the center of an encounter. Teasing is one kind of corrective strategy that frequently works in this situation because by the very act of responding to it an individual cannot help effectively becoming part of an interaction.

I first noticed this pattern of behavior at the folk high schools I attended. These schools function today as special and in a sense privileged settings where the Danish capacity for light-hearted sociability is allowed to flourish in an environment freed from the normal sanctions of a daily routine in civil society. It was a setting with special advantages for my research, because when the operation of the inclusion principle became clear in that environment, I was able to see it in many other places as well. Gradually, as I was forced to take notice of how it prevailed across many different cultural domains, the centrality of the inclusion principle dawned on me. Its influence is not limited to the sphere of informal sociability, for it can be seen as well in the operation of formal institutions.

Formal Welfare Policies

Consider first the area of formal welfare policies. It has been estimated that every year 1 million Danes between the ages of eighteen and sixty-seven run into some form of social hardship such as illness or unemployment.[10] The social welfare supports available to them are based not only on sheer human goodness but on the practical recognition that protracted periods of hardship will ultimately be more expensive for the State than short periods. This legitimate insight provides both sensible and humane motivation for the provision of social aid. Whether their clients are young, elderly, handicapped, emotionally disturbed, temporarily or long-term unemployed, substance abusers, or accident victims, the ideal task of welfare institutions is to bring these citizens back into the normal sphere of society through the allocation of various forms of aid. The ultimate challenge of social welfare is to develop cooperative strategies with which to face the universal and inevitable problems of the human condition. These include conflict management, division of social wealth, education of the young, and care of the old and sick.

What are some of these forms of aid, and how are they dispensed? Family allowances are granted to families with incomes under a certain level (with payments made directly to the mother). Rent subsidies are available to those who need them on the basis of a means test. A major differentiating factor in the Danish housing market is the existence of tight rent controls. Not only does this ensure lower rents, but it gives tenants options and a degree of control rarely if ever found in the United States. Virtually all expenses connected with illness are covered by the State, including hospitals and medical services. Those wage earners who have paid into a variety of union and government funds receive extraordinarily high unemployment benefits; those who have not paid into such funds are eligible for public assistance *(bistand)*. There are generous benefits for victims of industrial accidents, up to and including total disability. The legally guaranteed maternity benefits include job protection and an automatic twenty-four-week leave after a woman has given birth to a child (women with less education are not always able to exercise these rights, in spite of the fact that they are written into the public law). A universal retirement pension *(folkepension)* is given to everyone over the age of sixty-seven, irrespective of means.

One of the most innovative welfare programs is the home-help service *(hjemmehjælp)* available for old people or others during illness, maternity, or convalescence. This service also provides relief for persons caring for a handicapped child or adult. If agreed on by the evaluating team of a registered nurse and a social worker, an individual will receive not only home help from a young man or woman but home medical care *(hjemmesygpleje)* in the form of regular visits by a trained nurse. The number of weekly hours and visits is determined by the decision of the evaluating team after a home visit. In many cases this service permits those who are old and infirm to remain in their own homes, receiving both social and medical aid in this familiar environment rather than having to move into a nursing home. The goal of this service is to ameliorate the demands made on nursing home facilities and to save the human dignity of older persons by allowing them to remain in their own homes longer than would have otherwise been possible. Large funding cuts during the 1980s have by all reports considerably reduced the effectiveness of the *hjemmehjælp* and other Danish welfare programs; the demography of a rapidly expanding older sector of the population is another complicating factor.

Danish social security legislation differs from that of most other countries in that it is financed largely by government revenue. An added feature is that in most cases there is no stipulation of membership in an insurance scheme or payment of fees or premiums. One has merely to be a resident of Denmark in order to receive the benefits. Some major areas of expenditure in 1979 were old age and service to the disabled (42%); illness (30%); families with children (15%); and unemployment (9%). Many of these policies involve wealth redistribution via income transfers. The goal of such policies is to ensure that Denmark will remain a land where, in Grundtvig's words, "few have too much and fewer too little." Whether this cheerful little Grundtvigian epigram provides a fair or reasonable picture of contemporary Denmark is another question. It is one that has given rise to a great deal of painful debate among the Danes themselves. The reason for this is that in spite of the considerable retrenchment affecting many welfare programs during the past decade, social welfare remains a fundamental Danish value.

Grass Roots Welfare

A second manifestation of the inclusion principle in the area of welfare is the frequent appearance in Denmark of alternative grass roots welfare institutions. Whether created to fill an unmet need or to improve on the substandard performance of a traditional welfare institution, these alternative institutions resemble each other in many ways. They are usually small, and they offer an unusual sampling of innovative, experimental techniques. If the particular innovation represented by such an institution gains a general and widespread acceptance, it may subsequently become part of the more traditional welfare apparatus.

A successful example of such grass roots welfare was reported in the town of Horsens in Jutland. Rather than treating clients on the usual individual basis, a number of social workers experimented with the idea of treatment in support groups. A total of forty clients and eight social workers participated (one group, for instance, concentrated on problems of single mothers, another on problems faced by divorced men). The participants reported increased clarity about their own lives and a greater sense of self-worth. They indicated as well a substantial number of training courses begun and new jobs found.

Two other examples come from Copenhagen. Members of a new group called the Volunteers from the People's Movement Against Hard Drugs (*Frivillige fra Folkebevægelsen mod Harde Stoffer*) announced at the opening of their own crisis center that the established system had utterly failed to aid sufferers from the most severe drug-related traumas. Their announced goal is to specialize in helping only the oldest and most seriously injured addicts work toward a life without drugs.[11] With only two permanent staff members and a support group, they seem to make up in drive and vision what they lack in resources. A parallel program is offered by the Kofoed School, which specializes in reeducation of those young people who have given up hope and renounced further participation in normal civil society. "I hate the label 'social loser,'" remarks Ole, one student at the school, "but the people around me will probably think that that label fits me perfectly."[12] Now thirty-eight years old, he went on an early pension in 1984 after twenty-five years as a alcoholic and smoker of hashish. The harsh reality of his situation is reflected in the life choices made by increasing numbers of young people who, unable to find a place in the postmodern industrial society of the 1980s, turn to more destructive alternatives. For him and others like him, the Kofoed School offers an alternative route to the road they have chosen, a road that leads nowhere.

The Western world's first torture-rehabilitation center was opened in Denmark in 1982. Copenhagen's International Rehabilitation and Research Center for Torture Victims (*Rehabiliteringscenteret for Torturofre*), which treats seventy to seventy-five torture victims annually, is probably better known than any of these three fledgling grass roots welfare efforts.[13] The center combines the efforts of psychologists, psychiatrists, physical therapists, and others in a multi-disciplinary form of treatment. Patients at the center typically exhibit symptoms of a standard psychiatric condition called post-traumatic stress disorder, experienced by victims of war, sexual assault, severe accidents, or natural disasters. Torture has been practiced in ninety-eight countries during this decade, according to Amnesty International. The goals of the Center are to help those who have suffered torture in prisons and concentration camps to lead normal lives again. It is one of the few such centers in the world.[14]

An alternative grass roots welfare program that succeeds in gaining mainstream acceptance may eventually become an established institution. The folk high schools themselves exemplify this process. Once an alternative grass roots welfare institution regarded as radical or even revolutionary in their first decades of operation in the previous century, the schools are now thoroughly accepted. In making alternative forms of education potentially available to the entire adult population of the country, they can be seen as a further extension of the inclusion principle in public education. And although the Danish folk high schools occupy a unique position in Danish society today, they serve (as do the above grass roots welfare programs) to carry out the social imperatives of the inclusion principle. These imperatives are based on the firm Danish belief that it must be made possible for all to enjoy the benefits of full participation in society and that remedial action should be taken in those cases where an individual or a group has been excluded from full participation.

The Danish Political Party System and Elections

The operation of the inclusion principle has been reviewed in informal social interaction (*hygge*) and in traditional and grass roots welfare programs. It is not surprising that the same principle is reflected in the Danish political system. Virtually the entire political spectrum from right to left is able to participate in the ongoing political debate. As a result the range of opinions and philosophies available to voters far exceeds what can be found in the United States. Moreover, there seem to be few if any points of view that are "beyond the pale." The operation of the inclusion principle in Danish politics is worth exploring in greater detail. In the 1984 election, I watched while thirteen officially recognized political parties vied for power. They included Conservatives of the moderate and far right, Social Democrats, Radical Socialists, and Communists (as well as every shade of opinion in between). All of these points of view, including those of the Socialists and the Communists, were made fully available to the public. Over and above this broader political inclusion, the nature of the Danish political campaign was structured in a way that differs greatly from American campaigns.

Let me introduce a small parenthesis. The last American Presidential campaign (1988) was begun more than *two years* before the day of the election. It is common knowledge that all politics in America must be waged through electronic media, a situation that gives those backed by greater wealth an immediate advantage. The long period of time before the election, together with the media domination, inevitably combine to turn such elections into a three-ring circus. In this American political environment the differences between the parties sometimes seem minimal and chiefly cosmetic, the campaign politics extraordinarily depoliticized by Danish standards. Real political issues are almost by definition barred as beyond the attention span of voters whose tolerance is thought to be limited to a succession of thirty-second commercial messages. Personal issues loom disproportionately large in this political wasteland of democracy. For both the candidates and their wives, nice smiles, neat grooming, photogenic families, and a talent for finding new and memorable cliches may prove to be more important than whatever they know or do not know, understand or do not understand, about world or domestic affairs. As one candidate would later write, "The lessons are clear: be vague but sound informed. The media focus on non-issues. Money plays too big a role."[15]

Viewed through Danish eyes, there is little real debate in American politics. Indeed, there was much Danish commentary at the time on the destructive use of the media in American politics.[16] Those in America who correspond roughly to the Social Democrats and Socialists (not to mention the Communists) have been effectively ostracized from American political life, their points of view rarely if ever heard in the sanitized and oddly truncated version of the political spectrum permitted expression in American political campaigns. The operation of an implicit system of ideological self-censorship confines all legitimate political debate within the boundaries imposed by a sanctified and much revered two-party system. This type of *de facto* political discrimination is simply not found in the Danish political system. Nor does a Danish election campaign usually become the kind of personality contest familiar to Americans.

In Denmark, political power is exercised in most cases not by a single party, but by a coalition. The "Four-Leaf Clover" *(Firkløveret)* was the coalition of four independent conservative parties that governed Denmark through the greater part of the 1980s (1982–88). The single largest member of this coalition (in terms of seats in the *Folketing)* was the Conservative People's Party, the party from which the current Prime Minister, Poul Schlüter (in office since September 1982) was chosen. This party was joined by three others: its main partner, the Left *(Venstre)*[17]—also a large party— and two smaller parties, the Christian People's Party *(Kristelig Folk Parti)* and the Center Democrats *(Centrum Demokraterne).* It is a crucial feature of Danish politics that both the mandate of this coalition and its power to enact policy were seriously limited, for even when taken together, its parties held less than a majority of the seats in the Danish *Folketing* or parliament. What are some of the parties that stood in opposition to the Four-Leaf Clover?

The Progress *(Fremskridts)* Party, with its strong views on taxation, immigration, and public policy, stood somewhere to the right of the governing coalition. Immediately to the left of center were the Social Democrats *(Social Demokraterne),* which remained the largest single party in terms of representation even though it was unable to form a governing coalition. Many of its positions resembled those taken by moderate or liberal Democrats in the United States, while others tended to be more in the direction of moderate democratic socialism. Standing still farther to the left on most issues were two parties that provided an independent socialist perspective: the Socialist People's Party *(Socialistic Folk Parti)* and the Left-Wing Socialist party *(Venstre Socialister)*. On the basis of this brief description one would predict that the four conservative parties, occasionally joined by the right-wing party, would have to vie with the left-wing parties for effective political power. Although not false, this description is dangerously incomplete because it fails to mention the existence of a crucial factor: the Radical Left party *(Radikale Venstre)*. One must be clear about the role played through most of the decade by the Radical Left in order to grasp the dynamics of the Danish political system today.

The first key provided by the Radical Left is its name, which is misleading. When founded in 1905, it was both a radical and a left-wing party; today it is (I believe it is fair to say) neither. Like the conservative Left party *(Venstre)*, its name testifies more to its history than to any of its present or recent political positions. A second key to the Radical Left is its present political positions, which are difficult to characterize. It is sometimes said that this party tends to be economically conservative while remaining liberal on ecological and peace issues, though the party is famous (or infamous) for its unpredictability.

A third key provided by the party is perhaps the most important of all. The Radical Left was a crucial swing party whose support was required on most issues in order for legislation to pass. When matters reached a decisive stage, two variant outcomes were often seen in Danish politics: (1) the Four-Leaf Clover coalition succeeded in having a piece of legislation enacted; or (2) a temporary coalition (frequently made up of left-wing parties) was able to block this legislation. *In either case* the result frequently depended on the ability of the two competing coalitions to line up the support of the coy, slippery, and often unpredictable Radical Left.

Thus Danish politics for much of the 1980s resembled a seesaw with this single, small party sitting in the middle. By merely shifting a little from one side to the other, it often exercised a decisive voice in the making of parliamentary decisions. "The Traffic Minister [a member of the governing coalition's Center Democrats] can cancel his order for a pair of gold scissors to give to the Queen in 1992 to cut the ribbon inaugurating the bridge over the Large Belt," ran a news story in *Politiken*.[18] The Radicals in the Finance Committee had put another temporary stop to the bridge, this time by undermining the minister's attempt to begin a formal investigation of its potential sources of finance—yet another policy squelched by the Radicals (a not uncommon theme in Danish politics). Toward the end of the decade, however, the Radicals did something that astonished everyone, even those who thought they knew the depths of treachery to which the Radicals could sink. When the Four-Leaf Clover crumbled in 1988, the Radical Left joined the Conservatives and the Left Party in a new three-party governing coalition. This new "KVR" coalition remained in power from 1988 until the election of December, 1990 (discussed in the final chapter).

Let us turn from this narrow consideration of the party system to a broader consideration of some of the details of the election campaign. How does the operation of the Danish electoral system reflect the inclusion principle? First, the Danish electorate (as we have already seen) samples a far wider band of the available political spectrum than that allowed in the American political system. Second, through the proportional representation found in the Danish electoral system *(forholdstalsvalg)*, each new Parliament shows almost perfectly the results of each election, even to the point of reflecting the minute movement of votes in one direction or the other. The precise dynamics of this system of proportional representation are said to be so complex that there are no more than forty people in the entire country who actually understand how it works.[19]

Third, since a party only needs 2% of the total votes to ensure representation in the Parliament, it is relatively easy for new points of view not only to be heard but to gain a forum. Fourth, the procedures by which a new political party can gain recognition are relatively simple, thus enabling those who are sufficiently unsatisfied with all existing parties to try to establish one of their own. Concrete evidence that this can be done comes from the 1973 election, in which three newly formed parties (Center Democrats, Christian People's Party, and the Progress Party) won between them 49 of the 179 seats in the *Folketing* (175 seats from Denmark, 2 each from Greenland and the Faroe Islands). In the course of the next decade they would be joined by another new party, the Left Socialists *(Venstre Socialister)*.

The actual election campaign shows a further cascade of the inclusion principle and its influence. Danish election campaigns differ significantly from their American counterparts in the amount of time that is allotted for them. I was fortunate enough to be present for the parliamentary election that took place early in 1984. From an American point of view perhaps the most shocking thing about the campaign was its brevity; there were only three weeks from the time the election was first called until the day of voting. This short campaign effectively eliminated many of the worst "cult-of-personality" features found in the interminably drawn-out American presidential campaigns.

Possibly the most interesting feature of the Danish election, however, was not its brevity, but the fact that equal media space was made available to *all* political parties qualifying to stand for election. Perhaps even more extraordinary, this space was made available to them *regardless of whether or*

not they were currently represented by voting members in the Parliament. Thirteen
political parties stood for this election. Beginning about two weeks before
election day, *each* party had its evening on the national television station.
The smallest parties were the first to present their points of view. As election
day drew closer, the larger and more established parties were interviewed,
each in turn.

Regardless of the party being interviewed, the evening's format was
the same. Each program began with a short, self-serving film made by the
party itself. Short introductory statements given by each of the three party
delegates followed the showing of the film. These statements tended to
elaborate on the themes presented in the film and explained in each case why
their party alone possessed both the understanding and the moral fiber
needed to solve Denmark's pressing problems. Up to this point one had
heard only the party's own unchallenged point of view, expressed and
embellished with no lack of self-serving superlatives. But for the remainder
of the program, four hard-bitten and knowledgeable political journalists
subjected the party spokespeople to a searching and in some cases almost
devastating cross-examination.

It was obvious that the journalists had researched both recent and past
party policies. It turned out that they were also embarrassingly familiar with
speeches given by the particular party members being interviewed. This
remarkable procedure led to a lively dialogue. Evening after evening,
political party after political party, the interviews and discussions took place
up to election day. In my estimation they facilitated a level of political debate
and exchange broader, deeper, and more searching than anything I have seen
during a comparable American political campaign. One important reason
for this conclusion is that the entire political spectrum—from the right-
wing Progress Party to the Danish Communist party—was included in the
pre-election discussion (the inclusion principle at work again). Each party
received full and equal time on television regardless of how many seats in
Parliament it possessed. Moreover, when the questioning began, each party
seemed to be treated about the same. All were regarded with polite but firm
skepticism. All were in addition forced to answer a large number of searching
and potentially embarrassing questions.

Members of the Communist party, for instance, were questioned along
these lines: "So you say you want to nationalize the banks—but what will
that do to our international image as a debtor nation? Won't it have a
negative effect on our balance of payments and make our situation even
worse in the long run?" Members of the governing Conservative People's
Party were asked these kinds of questions: "So you say that you want to raise
the minimum level of income for welfare eligibility by so much—we have

calculated the results, and don't you realize that even by your own standards this will bring another 10% of the population below the poverty line? Isn't that an arrogant, inhumane, and egoistic policy?" In the way this last line of questioning is phrased, we see the appearance of the Danish social conscience.

In summary, the Danish political system provides yet another context for the operation of the principle of inclusion that exists in Danish society. The spread and number of the Danish political parties reveal a high level of tolerance for the diversity of political programs represented among the Danish population. The speedy timing of the election and the full media empowerment given to each political party regardless of size and previous electoral success reflect what must be read as a high level of confidence in democracy. The operation of the inclusion principle is an essential part of the Danish core values of welfare and social responsibility. It is a force that works strongly to promote both democracy and tolerance. Indeed, one could go even farther than this. If the essential problem of democracy is how to control and limit those who have power, the checks and balances ensured by the broadest possible spectrum of participating voices provide a key to its successful operation. Viewed in these terms, the inclusion principle is not of secondary importance. On the contrary, it is a prerequisite to any real and functioning democracy.

II. THE DANISH SOCIAL CONSCIENCE

When actual or potential violations of the inclusion principle occur, an aroused social conscience often leads Danes to react with strong public criticism. Its critical sanctions can in a sense be viewed as attempts to extend and ensure the operation of the inclusion principle. Yet the Danish social conscience must be treated in its own right as a second important element in the core value orientation of welfare and social responsibility. Exemplified in the last of the preceding questions asked by a TV journalist, it combines a quick readiness to protest perceived injustice with a high level of sensitivity to the social exploitation of the innocent and helpless. It should be emphasized that it is *perceived mistreatment of the downtrodden* that most angers Danes; the Danish social conscience is particularly concerned with the fate of the underdog. Indeed, even if the matter at hand concerns animals rather than human beings, an expectation will be strongly communicated that the animals must be treated with humane standards.

Chronicled by a stream of newspaper articles, a bitter controversy over the exploitation of caged hens took place in 1984. A series of articles invited

The caged hens. "The rules say that every hen must have at least 480 sq. cm," reads the caption. See text for discussion. (Politiken, 5 *February 1984. Photo: Erik Friis. Reprinted by permission of Politikens Press Photo.*)

readers to see the world from a hen's point of view. "The sun is a neon pipe," read the caption for one picture that showed hundreds of hens crowded into a mechanized feeding space. "Here the hens are forced to lay 'fresh land-eggs,'" the article continued, and went on to reveal that what was advertised as a "back-to-the-land" milieu for the hens was in reality a large, rebuilt loft with no daylight.[20] In the public outcry that followed these articles, the loudest voices did not appear to be those of the hen owners or their supporters.

A group of poultry farmers eventually mounted a campaign to try to counteract the bad publicity they were getting. As a final tactic they staged a public debate on the national television station.[21] Among their supporters was a female politician who refused to express even the slightest sympathy for the caged hens during the debate. In the public response to the program she was (I believe it is fair to say) roasted and broiled in her own juices. I cite from three representative letters to the editor: (1) "Set her in the cage, together with four others of her type. Then let's see how they look after a month, without any skin on their body. It isn't easy to move about much in a little cage." (2) "We really must look at these poor caged hens again; it was a harrowing experience." (3) "This program about the poor caged hens ought to make every Dane stick to 'land-eggs.' Let us begin a campaign to get rid of this organized filth."

When human beings are felt to be the victims of unjust treatment, Danes are again likely to respond with outrage. There is much active protest against both domestic and international violations of basic humane principles. To take a domestic example, the frequent protests against Danish police actions are often accompanied by a barrage of critical commentary aimed at the criminal justice system. In Copenhagen a group of young squatters who called themselves the BZers was in frequent conflict with the city police. One article criticizing police actions quoted Henrik Stevnsborg, a criminologist: "Now the police really have to relax a little. The BZers aren't going to change themselves, therefore it's up to the police [to change]."[22]

The arrested girl crying. "Many of the young cried when they first came under police treatment, and later were driven off to their arraignment," reads the caption. See text for discussion. (Politiken, 13 January 1984. Photo: Ole Steen. Reprinted by permission of Politikens Press Photo.)

Stevnsborg appeals to the police to try more constructive methods such as "at least one time going out without their battle equipment of helmets, shields, billy-clubs, dogs and cars." He points out that if an ordinary citizen demonstrates without a permit, the police come up peacefully and disperse it; when it is BZers, the police show up in full battle gear. "Why?" he asks. The picture accompanying the article shows a disarrayed young girl in tears.

The implication is plain: the methods used by the police are too harsh. These are, after all, young people. In spite of previous battles with the BZers (in which some policemen were injured), it is the responsibility of the police to soften their attitudes. Yet the attitudes expressed here by Stevnsborg are positively mild when compared to some of the other criticisms made by Danes of the Danish criminal justice system. My files are full of articles attacking this system in the harshest terms. Listen to a brief sampling from January 1984. One article in a mainstream newspaper begins with these lines: "Social justice and the idea of a human criminal politics are myths, illusions maintained by that entire part of the population that has no direct relationship to it in practice."[23] "The Myth of a Human Criminal Politics" is the title of a second article,[24] "The Stigma of our Justice System" of a third.[25]

There is an extraordinary sensitivity to the real and potential abuses of police power. When government agencies decided against the claims of a Turkish woman whose husband had been fatally injured in a confrontation with two police officers, a front-page headline screamed out the news: "Turkish widow with five children doesn't get a penny: two policemen released."[26] The rights of the squatters are carefully scrutinized and defended: "Police people forced the BZers to give fingerprints; three have filed suit against the police after the house-occupation."[27] When two members of the Copenhagen police force mistakenly accused Christiania's cycle-smith of receiving 90% of all the city's stolen bicycles, their written apology in the magazine *Danish Police* was duly noted in other newspapers.[28]

I was constantly surprised by the light sentences given criminals, a practice justified on the grounds that the longer the period of incarceration, the more difficult it is for the offender to resume his or her place in society upon release. Yet many Danes write and speak of their own justice system as though it were a totalitarian fascist juggernaut. What are the reasons for this? It may be that this constant criticism is partially responsible for ensuring that police activity *is* on the whole more mild and less violent than in many other societies (there is unquestionably much less police violence in Denmark than in the United States). Perhaps the Danes really understand what Edmund Burke meant when he wrote that "eternal vigilance is the price of liberty."

Another frequent target of an aroused social conscience in Denmark today is proposed budget-cutting policies that entail worker layoffs, firings, and reduced funds for public institutions. Most often suggested by the ruling conservative coalition, these proposals reflect the unpleasant dilemma around which much of Danish domestic politics is presently structured. The planned budget cuts are put on the table with the goal of improving Denmark's international balance of payments. Yet their social cost is high: "Cancer hospital closed as link in planned savings" (16 March 1984); "Thirty deaf children hit by the savings knife" (14 Feb. 1984); "Thousands fired in county and regional government" (26 Feb. 1984); "Tightened budget demands can lead to firings at universities" (2 March 1984). "Open your eyes now, politicians" reads an appeal from the parents whose handicapped children have been served by a school now about to lose its funding.[29]

The critical commentary offered by the Danish social conscience can be scathing. Take the case of the two high-ranking hospital administrators who recommended cuts in hospital funds even though their own doctors testified that the cuts might be "life-threatening."[30] Shown in a political

OPERATION SPAREKNIV

— Jamen, operationen lykkedes jo.
Nu har den patient ikke brug for mere pleje.

Operation Sparekniv (at spare = *to save*). *A protest against cuts in the health sector, aimed at the politicians responsible for making them. The two bedside figures in white are, respectively, the director of a hospital and the chief of the medical association. The caption reads, "Yes, but the operation did succeed. Now that patient doesn't need any more care."* (Extra-Bladet, *30 May 1984. Reprinted by permission of Anne-Marie Steen Petersen.)*

cartoon entitled "Operation Savings-Knife," the two administrators are dressed in white laboratory jackets while standing at the bedside of an obviously moribund patient. They hold between them a gigantic knife pointed at the patient, while one of them gestures toward the mummified figure in the bed. The very least one can say is that they do not seem to have the patient's best welfare at heart. Labor disputes over wages, strikes, worker safety, and proper representation are another kind of social question frequently brought into the public forum by picketing, distribution of leaflets, and demonstrations. The science of ergonomics, which reverses the usual order of things by studying how technology can be adapted to human needs to design safer work environments, is much better known and more widely accepted in Denmark than in the United States.

The Danish social conscience extends beyond Danish borders into the world at large. It is hard to find a better illustration of this internationalist theme than the life and work of the famed Danish physicist Niels Bohr. One of Bohr's many achievements is represented in the series of far-sighted objections he voiced about the nuclear arms race that began in the years immediately after the Second World War. As he watched the Cold War unfolding, his good Danish social conscience could not let him be silent. He wrote these prophetic lines in a 1950 Open Letter to the United Nations:

> Humanity will, therefore, be confronted with dangers of unprecedented character unless, in due time, measures can be taken to forestall a dangerous competition in such formidable armaments and to establish an international control of the manufacture and use of the powerful materials. . . .
>
> The development of technology has now reached a stage where the facilities for communication have provided the means for making all mankind a cooperating unit, and where at the same time fatal consequences to civilization may ensue unless international divergences are considered as issues to be settled by consultation based on free access to all relevant information.
>
> The very fact that knowledge is in itself the basis for civilization points directly to openness as the way to overcome the present crisis. Whatever judicial and administrative international authorities may eventually have to be created in order to stabilize world affairs, it must be realized that full mutual openness, only, can effectively promote confidence and guarantee common security.[31]

This was not the first of his public stands on an important issue. In 1939 Bohr (who was half-Jewish) spoke out openly against the Nazis' pseudoscientific credo of Aryan racial superiority at an International Conference of Anthropological and Ethnological Sciences held at Elsinore Castle (the German delegation got up and walked out before Bohr finished speaking).[32] It was the same internationalist social conscience that led Bohr to his personal crusade against the nuclear arms race. His views, put forth in the late 1940s and early 1950s, were unfortunately voiced decades ahead of their time. He spoke out publicly against the nuclear arms race at a time when the American political mood was dominated by the Stalinesque crusades of Senator Joseph McCarthy and the House UnAmerican Activities Committee. It is not surprising that Bohr came to be seen (at least in the eyes of many American cold warriors) as an unwanted pariah, his views regarded as a great danger to national security. Nevertheless, he insisted on continuing his campaign for openness on every possible occasion. In addition to continually warning about the unique dangers posed by nuclear weapons, he was one of the first to point to the growing dangers posed by bacteriological and biochemical warfare.[33]

The preoccupation with international issues of war and peace represented in Bohr's life is very much alive in Denmark today. Contemporary Danish skepticism leads to the asking and re-asking of many uncomfortable questions (e.g, whether a flock of geese impinging on an arctic radar network could lead to a terminal thermonuclear exchange).[34] In the narrower sphere of party politics, the internationalist theme finds expression in the main party congress of the Danish Social Democrats. Many Americans might be shocked to learn that the party congress of this mainstream Danish political party, the single largest party in the Danish political system, is traditionally opened by the singing of the Communist "Internationale."[35] Former Prime Minister Anker Jørgensen is quoted: "Taking from the poor and giving to the wealthy must be stopped." Such views are often expressed in Danish politics by those left of the political center. Though they are difficult to implement in actual practice, this comment nonetheless reflects something of a Danish obsession.

When the discussion turns to questions outside of Europe, a greater unanimity is sometimes found. Far more than the American press, the Danish media reflect a preoccupation with the present vast scale of international suffering. Stark pictures attest to the death by hunger and thirst of refugee children in Ethiopia and Mozambique. These articles, often found on the front page, reflect editorial policies that make it difficult for a Dane to forget what is going on in the rest of the world. Programs like this are also frequently found on the national television station. One such program juxtaposed the theological pomposity of a Vatican campaign against liberation theology in the third world with lengthy footage of Brazilian children shown rooting around in garbage dumps for food.[36] Shots of naked and terrible human suffering that would appear only for a brief moment or be

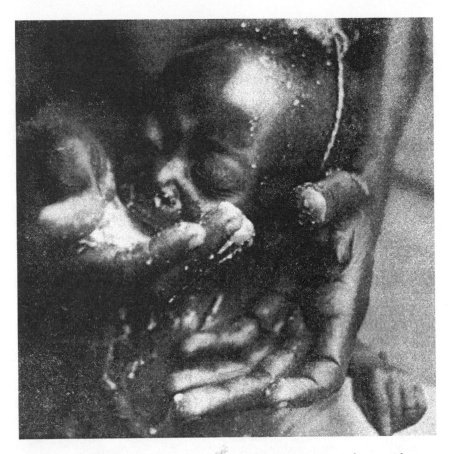

The picture shows a desperate mother in Mozambique trying to force porridge on a small child who is so starved that it cannot take in food. ("Refugee children are dying of hunger and thirst," Politiken, 28 February 1984. Reprinted by permission of Politikens Press Photo.)

censored from American TV programs are not similarly censored in Denmark. Neither are films that show such things as nudity or live human birth. On the other hand, high levels of interpersonal violence tend to be unacceptable to Danes and are either censored, shown infrequently, or not shown at all.

The question of censorship is an exceedingly interesting one. Both the direction in which the censorship cuts and the type of human situation it seeks to edit out are proper topics for ethnographic inquiry. The themes of censorship richly illustrate the kinds of cultural patterning a particular culture uses in developing its version of a social conscience. In order to further develop these arguments, let us focus on a single televised documentary film entitled "The Best Milk."[37] A newspaper previewing the program showed a picture that would have unquestionably been cut out of its American equivalent. The picture showed a close-up of the topic in question, mother's milk itself, seen squirting directly from a woman's nipple onto the face of a crying infant. The publication of such a picture is in itself a telling comment on Danish attitudes toward the human body. What this image and others like it suggest is a greater acceptance of the natural functions of the body, among which are birth, nursing, and the drama of sexuality itself.

The documentary began with an ugly story. It showed how a giant multinational corporation had influenced a group of African peasant women to become dependent on the company's baby formula, and as a result to stop breast-feeding their infants. It then traced in detail the destructive public health consequences that followed this campaign of public "education." Company representatives gave out initial "free samples" to naive and uneducated women. They relied on the women's blind belief in the superiority of Western technology to get them to try the product. Once the women had

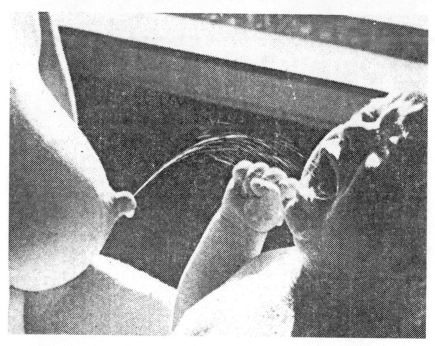

Preview of the documentary program, "The Best Milk." See discussion in text. (Politiken, 4 June 1984. Reprinted by permission of Politikens Press Photo.)

used it a few times, they became psychologically "hooked" (meaning that they now perceived the bottled formula as a felt need). They discovered at this point to their surprise that the samples were no longer given without a charge. Even though the cost might be as much as half of a young African village mother's monthly income, the women shown in the film were adamant in their desire to purchase the formula. All believed that what they were doing was "Western" and therefore best for their babies.

The resulting cultural and economic exploitation was bad enough, but it was only a small part of the story. Far from benefiting the infants, the introduction of the bottled milk resulted in serious public health problems. Correct preparation of the bottled formula required that a complicated set of instructions be followed each time to the letter (for instance, an exact proportion of formula had to be used each time). Clean water as well as sterilized instruments and utensils were essential. In these villages this meant that water had to be boiled for each and every infant feeding. Yet these women faced constant fuel shortages, and they lacked even a basic understanding of the reasons for modern sanitation. Understanding neither the necessity for sterilization nor its required procedures, they began to take short cuts. Some began to interpret the instructions to mean that the bottles needed boiling only the first time they were used. Others believed that they could make the precious formula last longer by diluting it. After all, it was the same white milk that they could see in their baby's bottle. They could not understand why their babies grew sick and weak, began to suffer from diarrhea, and in many cases died right before their eyes.

After reviewing this pattern of events, the program went on (in true balanced fashion) to treat the movement that, in reaction to these events, had sent its representatives around the world to praise, glorify, and sell the breast-feeding of human infants. The process of birth itself was included in the discussion; not only that, but a completely uncensored live birth was shown on camera. With a midwife and the father present, the mother's labor and baby's eventual birth seemed the easiest and most natural thing in the world.

Another question posed by the documentary was just how long a mother should be permitted and encouraged to nurse her child. To view one end of the spectrum, the case was presented of a woman who still nursed her five-year-old girl. This woman was shown in full view nursing the child after kindergarten, while the two of them talked about what sort of a day the girl had had in school. Asked if other children criticized her child, the mother answered in the affirmative but added that the child didn't seem to be bothered by it. I remember being struck by how peaceful and calm both mother and child appeared to be and thinking to myself that such a program would in all probability never be allowed to air on American television.

Representing the voice of the Danish social conscience, the documentary first forced its viewers to confront these African women whose human rights had been violated. It then introduced a range of issues connected with the physical and emotional nurturance of human infants. In its refusal to censor any of the physical and sensual aspects of the process of breast-feeding, the documentary provided support for the contention that Danish culture has a different view of the body and its natural functions than that found in the United States. The Danish view, I would argue, tends to be more accepting and far less puritanical than the American one. In the breadth and scope of its concerns, this program came to embody for me the international dimension of the Danish concern for welfare and social responsibility. (Though let me emphasize here that it was only one of a good number of Danish books, magazines, and television programs that forced me to look at the world through a different set of cultural lenses.)

III. The Concept of *Folkelighed*

In addition to the inclusion principle and a social conscience quick to protest its perceived violations, a third manifestation of the Danish core values of welfare and social responsibility is bound up with the notion of *folkelighed*. This term, a multidimensional one, cannot be simply translated (in that respect it resembles the previously discussed concept of *hygge*). Let us nevertheless record some of the attempts. "This is a *folkelig* hymn from the Middle Ages," announced the Lutheran priest at the Easter service in the provincial town of Vordingborg in South Sjælland. He did not have to define what he meant by the term "folkelig"; the meaning of the term is quite clear to any Danish audience. It is used in a way that might smack of socialism or communism to a conservative American audience, but it is nonetheless used approvingly in that way by all Danes. Whether due to wisdom or cowardice, my own Danish dictionary takes the easy way out and refuses to give any definition at all for the term (although it does define *folkelig*, the adjective from which it is constructed, as "popular, simple and unassuming"[38]).

Grundtvig scholar Kaj Thaning writes that *folkelighed* is "a Danish word normally applied to that which has a popular, democratic, unassuming quality or character."[39] Uffe Østergård tells us that it "refers to enlightened, responsible and tolerant participation in the exercise of power."[40] Vagn Skovgaard-Petersen has discussed its close connection to the problematic ideal of equality, a connection reflected in the etymology of the word itself (when split, its two elements (*<folke-lighed>*) *can* be respectively translated as "the people" and "equality," though the word can also be very loosely translated as "the quality of being of the people," or just plain "people-ness").[41] On the death of King Olav V of Norway in January, 1991, the Norwegian artist Håkon Bleken wrote of him: "He was easy to talk with, and could combine *folkelig* sociability with royal dignity in a fantastic way. He was a king to be properly happy about."[42] As even this brief review indicates, the concept of *folkelighed* possesses a range of meanings and connotations.

The idea of *folkelighed* was initially formulated by Grundtvig in his attempt to work out the conflict between freedom and equality in the years immediately prior to 1848, at a time when pressure was mounting to do away with the institution of absolute monarchy. "*Folkelighed* will be our watchword in the North, and gently solve the riddles of equality," he predicted in a famous passage *(Folkelighed være vort Losen i Nord, lempeligt løser den Lighedens Gaade).* The concept of *folkelighed* that came out of his writings reflected, among other things, a concern with the welfare and freedom of *all* of the groups living in society, as opposed to a concern with the interests of only a single group. Since these issues are complex, what will be posed here is not the abstract question "What is *folkelighed?*" but two more concrete queries: "What is it like to live in a society where *folkelighed* is an important concern?" and "In what ways does this concern reflect the core values of welfare and social responsibility?"

First, it must be said that to live in Denmark is to live in a child-centered society, one in which there is an intense public and private concern for the rights of children. This view of Danes is one that runs counter to their frequently expressed opinion of themselves. The high level of concern over the rights of children is seen in the continual debate over the best way to educate and socialize them (sexual education, for instance, begins early in the primary schools, where one recently debated issue was whether a teacher may consciously and deliberately use pornographic material as part of this education). Though this may be more apparent to foreigners than to the Danes themselves, my impression was that there is *on the whole* an astonishing absence of discipline problems with Danish children. I am not a psychologist, but one of my special fields is the observation of behavior in public places. My fieldwork methods enabled me to gain a prolonged exposure to a variety of Danish social class and regional contexts. The resulting observations made during a period of well over two years lead me to strongly question Hendin's dependency hypothesis. I would emphasize instead the extent to which self-reliance and independence are both the expressed and achieved goals of child training. Unlike in the United States and Germany, I never saw a single child slapped, shouted at, or humiliated in public places such as supermarket lines, playgrounds, or amusement parks.[43] On the contrary, it is common to see children treated everywhere with extraordinary care, affection, and concern.

In recognition of the needs of children, a group of institutions exists to supplement the care given by parents and primary schooling agents. Although some sound familiar to American ears, others have no real equivalent in the United States. The nursery school (*vugggestuen*) is set up to provide toys and positive social experience for the very young (birth to three years). The kindergarten (*børnehaven*) differs from its American equivalent; physically and socially separate from the grade school, it brings together a much wider age group (three to seven). Danish children are not pressured to learn how to read in kindergarten; they may wait until the age of seven or even longer before acquiring these skills (by the age of nine or ten they typically read just as well as children from nations where reading is introduced earlier).[44]

A special institution called a *fritidshjem* (lit. "free time home") exists to provide care to older children (seven to fourteen) both before and after school. The provision of this care can be especially important in families where one or both parents work long hours. Other kinds of clubs (*fritids- og ungdomsklubber*) make available free meeting places for older schoolchildren and adolescents (ten to eighteen). A number of scouting groups (*Spejder, FDF, FPF*) teach everything from camping to sailing; on a summer trip a fourteen-year-old Danish sea-scout may sail in a small boat with others around the nearby islands or in longer trips all the way to Poland.

What would it be like for an American family to send its children to school in Denmark? An American woman who lived in Denmark for a year as a Fulbright Scholar watched as her children went to Danish schools and caretaking institutions. Her perceptive reminiscence contains insights both about Denmark itself and the effects of the year on her family:

> I have tried, many times, to explain the apparent lack of discipline problems with Danish children. When they are very young, Danish children are often restrained. They are strapped into strollers or on to bicycles for shopping trips with their mothers or snapped securely into their prams and put outside for a daily dose of afternoon sun. . . . A small automobile with a large pram attached to the top is a common sight on Danish highways. . . . Other possible sources of explanation might be the lack of commercial television, especially the non-existence of "hard sell" ads directed at children, or the more secure place given children, as consumers, in Danish society. Denmark is a small country, with few resources except people. Therefore,

children are valued. All of these factors may contribute to the behavior of
Danish children, but, personally, I think the nature of the society itself offers
the most plausible explanation. Danish children obey their parents because
Danish adults, for the most part, obey the state. *{After giving a series of everyday
examples, which include the largely unsupervised operation of the mass transit system
and the self-regulated use of cardboard clock parking timers kept in vehicles, she
continues.}*

I do not mean to imply that the regulations imposed by the state are
oppressive. They are not. Most legislation is intended with the well-being of
the many clearly preferred over the personal convenience of the few. At times,
the strict adherence to laws and customs was troublesome to us as foreigners,
but our Danish friends did not seem to mind. In fact, they hardly seemed to
notice. For both children and adults, compliance in some areas results in
greater freedom in others. Adults trade off high taxes for social services (child
care, medical care, old age security); frequent, and rigid, car inspections for
safer highway travel; taxation on use of radios and televisions for commercial
free programming; installation of appliances only by professionals and mandatory twice a year chimney sweeping for a low incidence of fires in a city
filled with buildings that are often several hundred years old, some with
thatched roofs. Children trade off unacceptable public behavior for the
opportunity to be welcomed at public places; short, intensely academic school
days for the freedom to explore at the *fritidshjem;* and greater respect for adults
for the privilege of being included in more family activities. The result is a
rather formal, ordered life style in which both adult to adult and adult to
child interactions become more enjoyable.[45]

A second important point is that the concept of *folkelighed* is found in
a society that highly values the ideal of social cooperation (which is not the
same thing as saying that all Danes are always socially cooperative). Two
reflections of this cooperative ideal can be seen in the way that terms familiar
to native speakers of English are used in a slightly different sense by Danes.
Consider the simple English word "pedagogy" *(pædagogik)*. Simple translation fails to communicate the subtle difference in cultural connotation
between the Danish term and its American equivalent. The Danish term
has a more positive sound and is much more frequently used. It does not
have the same stuffy connotation as its American equivalent "pedagogy," a
word that sounds like some rare and dangerous tropical disease.

I was first struck by this difference in usage when trying to translate
the phrase "professor of education" into Danish. I translated it as professor
of *uddannelse* (a term literally meaning "education"). I was told firmly that
the man was a professor of *pædagogik* and not of *uddannelse*. Used as an
adjective *(pædagogisk)*, the term is commonly found in a range of situations
that have to do with instruction, training, and learning. When commenting

on someone's teaching or instructional methods, a Dane would often say, "That wasn't at all pedagogical" *(Det var ikke spor pædagogisk).* This positive usage of the term "pedagogical" differs greatly from any American usage of the term. My interpretation is that this usage reflects the intense and specific Danish concern for how best to work with people in the teaching and quasi-instructional settings found both in schools and in caretaking institutions.

A second differing usage of easily translated English equivalents has to do with the critical language that is commonly brought to bear on politicians. Critics of a Danish politician are quite likely to remark that he or she is egoistic *(egoistisk)* or arrogant *(arrogant);* these appear to be fairly common terms of abuse in Danish politics.[46] Thus in an article accusing a politician of arrogance, his picture appears together with the interpolated caption, "I answer only those questions, that suit ME." When a Danish critic calls Denmark "the society of egoism," he is not being complimentary.[47] The motivation for using terms like "egoistic" and "arrogant" here comes from the fact that the objects of criticism are felt to have departed from the proper ethic of social cooperation, of *folkelighed,* that good Danes should feel obliged to live up to. This type of criticism is one I have never heard used in American political or cultural debate (where the ultimate political condemnation is probably to be called weak, indecisive, or "wimpy"). Parenthetically, I do not think that these Danish tactics would be effective in the United States. To call an American politician "arrogant" or "egoistic" would not only fail to tarnish that politician's image but in the present climate might even improve it.

The society in which *folkelighed* appears as a basic value is one that regards militarism, violence, and the use of force with considerable dismay. The Danish dislike for contributing to NATO is by now legendary in some circles. When NATO recently held its most extensive winter maneuvers ever, the events were reported in Danish newspapers not with admiration but with great concern.[48] Denmark is a society where the values of militarism are held in very low regard. The parades given by the resplendent Royal Guard are one of its few public celebrations, yet a closer look will show that even these are more for the sake of tradition and tourism than any emotional attachment to the field of battle. Denmark, like the other Scandinavian nations, seems to have evolved into a fundamentally post-imperialist, non-militaristic society. Of course, one could correctly argue that this dislike of militarism is in part due to the small land area and flat terrain that render Denmark virtually indefensible against the technology of postmodern warfare. There is some truth to this, and it does not take a genius to see that Denmark's rejection of military values has some relation to its size. Yet size alone does not lead to an absence of militarism (consider Israel, for instance, with its even smaller land area and total population). We must look not at size alone, but at the total experience of Danish history (in particular the experience of contraction and loss) in order to understand how the rejection of militaristic values came about.

In addition to its overwhelming rejection of militaristic values, a society characterized by *folkelighed* is on the whole a peaceable and safe place to live. The Danish crime rate is very low compared with the United States. Even though Copenhagen is a city of well over a million inhabitants, I felt safe traveling the city streets at any hour of the day or night. The existence of strict gun control laws makes it much more difficult for Danes to own firearms. At the numerous public mass gatherings I attended (ranging from rock concerts to National Independence day, *Grundlovsdag*), I was struck by the simultaneous absence both of individual acts of violence and of blue-uniformed police with their guns and riot clubs (I suspect there is a causal factor and not mere correlation operating here). If there was sun, clothes were often taken off, sometimes a lot of clothes, and no one seemed to mind. There was frequently a relaxed feeling in the air, even though many thousands of people had gathered. Listening to good music with a group of friends and acquaintances, sitting on the grass with a bottle of beer in your hand, who could possibly get upset about someone else's having a little bit of *hygge?* I suspect that this mellow ambience is another of the faces of *folkelighed*.

As the above reference to *hygge* suggests, the themes discussed in this last section on welfare and social responsibility must be viewed as part of the framework of a larger cultural stage on which *hygge*, egalitarian inclinations, and the balance principle often dance together. The separation between the core value orientations as they were treated in the preceding sections is of necessity analytical and artificial; it cannot do justice to their rich and subtle interplay in real situations, such as the mass public gatherings described above. And yet it is my contention that, whether viewed separately or as part of a larger constellation, these core value complexes (democracy and egalitarianism, moderation and balance, *hygge*, welfare and social responsibility) do reflect some of the basic positive themes found in the Danish national character.

One final point needs to be made, especially for American readers. Many Americans will assume that a nation believing in social welfare must be guided by impractical and idealistic considerations. But as I lived in and moved through a succession of schools, towns, and regions, learning to know a rich variety of people, it slowly became clear to me that the Danish concepts of welfare and social responsibility are not based on any soft-minded soapbox idealism. I came in fact to see the Danes as an eminently practical people. "Stick your finger down in the earth and smell where you are," was the earthy and practical advice given by Ludvig Schrøder in 1872. The Danish concepts of welfare and social responsibility are based on an implicit cultural recognition of two deep human truths. The first is a familiar theme from American history: *it is the moral postulate that minimum social, economic, and political rights are to be extended to all members of society.* The idea of equality is part of the mythical charter of both the United States and Denmark; even though it may be in the process of becoming little more than a slogan trotted out for ceremonial occasions, it is nonetheless part of our sacred political folklore.

The second insight behind the Danish commitment to welfare and social responsibility is one to which many Americans might take exception. It is simply this: *life is at best full of hardship, and this hardship is most effectively borne by some degree of social sharing between the haves and the have-nots.* The Scandinavian perception of this basic truth is perhaps best suggested by a Norwegian Labor party campaign poster from the summer of 1987. It had not been taken down even though the election was long since past. A picture of the Labor party candidate, Gro Harlem Brundtland, was located in the center of the billboard. To one side there was a very young child, and to the other an old man. The caption said simply, "Because we need each other."

Forgetting for the moment its partisan message, this Norwegian poster expresses a fundamental Scandinavian insight into the existential reasoning behind the provision of adequate social welfare policies. What messages did it communicate? First, it implied strongly that interdependence is perhaps even more fundamental than independence. Second, it suggested as well that the distinction between the haves and have-nots is not always one of money. Third, it reminded its viewers that being counted among the have-nots is something that sooner or later will be part of the experience of every human being. This is true if for no other reason than the fact that aging is a universal human experience. The moral imperative for providing adequate welfare is thus based not only on idealistic but on eminently practical grounds: everyone needs to be cared for as an infant and child. And everyone will grow old and sick sooner or later in the course of a lifetime. Shouldn't society as a whole guarantee aid to all the individuals and families that need it?

I have attempted to make clear in this section the high positive evaluation of certain Danish social values that resulted from my fieldwork in Denmark. In the interests of full disclosure it has to be recorded that the Danes with whom I lived and worked could not always return the compliment. As they looked at my peripatetic life-style, with a guitar and tape recorder in one hand and a suitcase in the other, always on the move from place to place, what they saw sometimes seemed to worry them. "It's good to have both feet on the ground *(benene på jorden),*" I was frequently told. Repeated in a kindly but didactic fashion, this line would usually be accompanied by a plainly paternal look from the speaker that conveyed that there was a special message in these lines meant for my ears to hear. "Your own foot under your own table *(Foden under eget bord),*" was another favorite motto often quietly but firmly repeated for my benefit. "You live like a millionaire, Steve" was the quiet comment of the old Danish farmer on whose land the stone tools had been found when he heard of my planned itinerary for the next six months. I remember that at the time I was flattered and took it as a compliment. Looking back, I can now see that it was said in a tone of voice that brings to mind the old fable of the grasshopper and the ant (and it was perfectly clear which one he thought I was).

As these and other similar sayings imply, the Danish view of life is hard headed, practical, and down-to-earth. The Danish Land Reforms were not passed by impractical dreamers but by practical men of this world. The first folk high schools were expressions of earthy wisdom, not airy idealism. This view of Denmark is beautifully suggested in the first stanza of one of Grundtvig's most popular and enduring songs: "We [Danes] are not created for majesty's refined quest, to stay in earth's fellowship is what serves us best"[49] *(Vi er ikke skabte til højhed og blæst, ved jorden at blive, det tjener os bedst).* Remembering the results of the Estes study, one can only conclude that the Danish achievements in the field of social welfare are at least in part a realization of Grundtvig's prophetic insight into the Danish character. As we have already seen, it was by no means the only one of Grundtvig's insights.

CHAPTER TEN

Through A Glass Darkly: A Counterperspective on Danish National Character

AFTER SOME THOUGHT, I decided to make no attempt to disguise the highly positive view of Danish culture that lies behind the writing of this book. The preceding chapters in Part IV have treated Danish national character by focusing on the operation of four core values. In making their positive and optimistic interpretation, I spoke not only for the Danes but for myself, communicating a vision of Denmark deeply congruent with what I myself have seen and experienced. But an ethnography must also deal with the dark side of an investigated culture. In this chapter I do not speak for myself. I attempt rather to speak for the Danes, for what they say when they come face-to-face with the dark side of their own culture. And to look deeply at this dark side, at the negative "shadow" image of their culture and its achievements, is precisely what the Danish people have been forced to do in the 1980s and early 1990s.

One finds a widespread mood of extreme self-criticism and doubt among them. It is a type of doubt that has not been seen or heard much in Denmark's recent history. Its many caustic expressions are increasingly accompanied by a widespread fear of growing individual helplessness in the face of the harsher social and economic conditions now coming to prevail in Denmark. Even those who are adequately protected from the new, harsher set of conditions often feel that there is something very wrong with what is happening and find themselves strangely helpless in the rapidly changing Danish society. These personal expressions of dissatisfaction with the domestic situation are intensified by a concern for the nation itself, based on a widespread perception that a gradual erosion of Danish national autonomy on the international scale has been and is continuing to take place. Such fears, driven by an average rate of unemployment that in December 1990 stood at an even 11%,[1] are also a part of the Danish experience.

Each of the four core values previously treated has its dark "shadow" side in contemporary Danish life; in each case the shadow value pursues and is in conflict with the positive core value. For the core value of democracy and egalitarianism, it is the relentless leveling principle all Danes know as the *Jantelov* (the law of Jante). For the core value of balance and moderation, it is the accelerating cultural collision between Danish society and the increasingly large pockets of non-Western "guest workers," immigrants and political refugees who have come to live and work in Denmark. For the core value of *hygge*, it is the growing measure of economic insecurity represented in what has been called "the invisible poverty," accompanied by an ever-widening circle of those whom the traditional welfare institutions are unable or unwilling to reach. For the core value of welfare and social responsibility, it is a widespread mood of powerlessness and anxiety connected to the general economic and social uncertainty in one of the world's smaller nations, combined with a deep ambivalence toward recent international developments (such as the proposed European integration of 1992–93 and the prospect of a new Europe with a reunified German state at its center). Many fear that Danish culture and national identity will be submerged, perhaps even lost in what seems to be an emerging "United States of Europe."

I. *JANTELOVEN* (THE LAW OF JANTE)

The operation of the Danish core value of democracy and egalitarianism is one reason why Denmark does not provide fertile soil for a political dictatorship. Checks and balances on the exercise of power are not only written into the Danish constitution but are part of the ethos of everyday life. It can be taken for granted that those Danes who become powerful will be systematically ridiculed, their smallest corruptions and human failings serving as legitimate excuses for mocking deflation. This does not prevent the existence of would-be tyrants, but it forces them to dance carefully on the head of a pin if they wish to avoid public ridicule. One aspect of this continual debunking of the powerful is an open willingness to critique the values and life-styles of the wealthy. Thus the folk singer Trille begins a stanza of one of her most popular songs with these lines:

> We drive slowly into the next town
> I think the streets of the rich are so ugly
> And while we are here I see it again
> That it's not here I live.[2]

The dark side of this positive core value is expressed in the action of a leveling principle which many Danes feel works systematically against the more creative and the gifted members of their society. The Danish-Norwegian writer Aksel Sandemose (1899–1965) has articulated this principle as the Jante Law (*Jantelov*). Sandemose, a Dane who spent most of his adult life in Norway, conceived of the Jante Law in his novel *En Flygtning Krysdser Sit Spor* (A fugitive crosses his track, originally published in the early 1930s). In my many conversations with Danes it was repeatedly cited and explained in depth. Most who spoke of it could and often did quote sections of it by heart. Sandemose's *Jantelov* has become so widely known that it can legitimately be regarded as a part of Danish and Scandinavian folk culture.

The term *Jantelov* refers to the ten negative commandments that govern interpersonal relationships in the fictional town of Jante. The central figure of Sandemose's novel, Espen Arnakke, commits murder when still a young man. In a series of glimpses from the past, present, and future, it is made clear that Espen's character has been profoundly shaped by the hammering of the Jante Law. Much of the novel depicts his subsequent attempts to escape its influence, but even after he leaves Jante to travel in the Western world, he carries with him a deeply internalized sense of guilt and failure. After a closer look at the Jante Law, one is not very surprised at this. I reproduce it here in full from Sandemose's novel:

> This is The Jante Law:
>   1. You shall not believe that you *are* somebody.
>   2. You shall not believe that you are worth as much as *we* are.
>   3. You shall not believe you are more clever than *us*.
>   4. You shall not try to fool yourself by thinking that you are better than *us*.
>   5. You shall not believe you know more than *us*.
>   6. You shall not believe you are more than *us*.
>   7. You shall not believe that *you* will be good at anything.
>   8. You shall not laugh at *us*.
>   9. You shall not believe that anybody fancies *you*.
>   10. You shall not believe that you can teach *us* anything.[3]

The same leveling principle that so effectively limits the inappropriate individual exercise of power can have another, more troubling function. It can work to keep talented people "in their place" and to discourage the development of their individuality. This is the other and darker face of egalitarianism, set forth with pompous rectitude in the informal ten commandments of the Jante Law. These commandments, with their smug air of self-righteousness, have been described by the Norwegian psychologist Willi Railo as a set of rules on how to be second best.[4] "Don't be different," is their underlying message. It does not take a licensed psychoanalyst to see that the primary mood behind them is a concealed envy fueled by a deep sense of personal insecurity. "You shall not think that you know more than us." This is the ethic of the small-town closed society at its worst. It has been brilliantly depicted by the Norwegian artist Edvard Munch (1863–1914) in paintings such as "Village Street" (*Landsbygate,* 1905), which shows a grim, faceless crowd dressed in black glowering hatefully at the viewer.[5] Its ethic is heard in the jeering voices of parents and teachers who believe they have nothing to learn from their children, of repressive peer groups that want their members to fit in no matter what the cost, of all those who somewhere along the way have surrendered their autonomy and now demand that their children do the same. One can easily imagine some of its many faces: the county construction official who ignores what local teachers have to say about the architectural plans for a new school, the teacher who ridicules the student for whom the lessons do not make sense, the parent who humiliates sons and daughters in the fear that they might become independent personalities.

At its worst, the operation of the Jante Law is a clear prescription for mediocrity. One early and vociferous critic of Danish society was the English diplomat Robert Molesworth, who lived in Denmark shortly after the establishment of the absolute monarchy (1660). Molesworth wrote these unflattering lines as long ago as 1694:

> To conclude: I never knew any Country where the Minds of the People were more of one calibre and pitch than here; you shall meet with none of extraordinary Parts or Qualifications, or excellent in particular Studies and Trades; you see no Enthusiasts, Mad-men, Natural Fools, or fanciful Folks; but a certain equality of Understanding reigns among them: every one keeps the ordinary beaten road of Sence, which in this Country is neither the fairest nor the foulest, without deviating to the right or left.[6]

Molesworth (1656–1725), who served as British ambassador to the Danish court, did not find much in Denmark worthy of praise. He seems to have developed an intense loathing for the entire country and its people—for the absolute monarch and his court, the arrogant and pompous aristocrats, the petty and scheming merchants, the drunken and inept peasants. It should be pointed out that Molesworth was writing a century before the Danish Land Reforms and 150 years before the transition to parliamentary democracy. And much of what he said was unfair and exaggerated even when seen from his own time. For in the very same years that the British diplomat was preparing to pen his venomous critical comments, the Danish astronomer Ole Rømer (1644–1710) was in the process of discovering the finite velocity of light, which he measured by observing the eclipses of Jupiter's satellites. Carrying on a Danish tradition of accuracy in astronomical observations begun a century earlier with the work of Tycho Brahe (1564–1601), Rømer subsequently developed accurate new methods of determining the position of stars. And Ole Rømer was not the only Dane of that time who was making important contributions to the emerging corpus of modern scientific knowledge.[7] The physician Thomas Bartholin (1616–80) was the first to observe that the chyle vessels did not go to the liver as previously thought but went along the spine to the neck, ending in large blood vessels. This finding led to the discovery of the lymphatic system.[8]

Yet in spite of its exaggerated quality, Molesworth's accusations contain a haunting prefiguration of the Jante Law that is probably not without some measure of accuracy. If we permit ourselves only a modicum of imagination, we can see in it an earlier version of the same law that sanctions humiliation and ridicule for those who dare to stand out from the prevailing midrange of achievement today. Danish writer Albert Naur, after noting the existence of schools for gifted children in the United States to speed their development, remarks that in Denmark it is considered "undemocratic to give prominence to anyone—to tell the gifted, so to speak, that they are singular."[9] It would similarly be undemocratic to provide children recognized as gifted with special educational opportunities. "What about all the other students?" it would be asked. "Don't they deserve the same treatment?" This view of the Danish educational system brings to mind the striking observation of the French writer Jean Bailhache that "it is contrary to the instincts of the Danes to have great men."[10]

It is common for those gifted in a skill or profession to find they must leave Denmark to attain recognition. The classic example is Hans Christian Andersen; long after he was recognized in other European countries as a major literary figure, he still was not taken seriously in Denmark. In Denmark today, a young professional conductor who received many invitations to conduct orchestras abroad reports that his Danish colleagues began to stereotype him as a man who "runs around conducting all over the place." The result of this criticism was that he began to concentrate on work offered him outside of the country. A young Danish trapeze artist trained by a leading school in Paris found it almost impossible to get circus engagements after returning to Denmark. The special skills she had learned during her training were simply not recognized at home. She came to express considerable regret that she had declined an offer from the prestigious Folies-Bergere to come back to Denmark and seek employment.[11]

These examples are only a few of the many that could be cited. Actors, authors, ballet dancers, scientists, and business entrepreneurs are among those who have left Denmark for similar reasons. Pia Degermark, a Danish actress in the 1960s, once said that in Paris she was a movie star; back in Denmark she could only be the girl next door. A Danish actor who made his career in the United States remarked, "If I had never left Denmark, I would never have reached my present position, even had I been Peumert's equal. In a little country competition is—strange as it sounds—far harder than in a big country."[12] And even for those who have left home and become a spectacular success abroad, the Jante Law remains part of one's personal drama. One can feel it hovering in the background in this short extract from Norwegian actress Liv Ullman's autobiography, *Changing:*

> Lunch. A Swedish journalist sits waiting for me on the lawn outside the canteen. Not having read this week's papers, he thinks I am still going with last week's Film Hero. Fifteen minutes of the precious lunch break are spent on him, so the papers at home will not report that I have become "stuck up."[13]

Those who do well in Danish competitive situations are likely to be reminded that the Jante Law applies also to them. Thus in the examination for entrance to the program in communication at the Roskilde University Center in a recent year, the minimum qualifying score was an unbelievable 10.2 (in American terms this would be something like an average score of 750 on both the Verbal and Quantitative Scholastic Aptitude Tests). Nevertheless, the director of the admissions committee, a civil engineer, gave the successful applicants an appropriate Jante Law welcome: "It doesn't mean a great deal, the fact that these new students with a high test score are a little popular just now. They shouldn't believe that they are anything special. If people begin to perceive themselves as an elite, they can well be disappointed. Nothing magical has happened to a person, even if that person is accepted with an average score of over ten."[14]

This civil engineer's comment can perhaps be justified as a legitimate warning to bright entering students not to take their test results too seriously. Sometimes, however, the expressions of the Jante Law can be just plain mean spirited. This harder mood of the Jante Law is encapsulated in a common Danish figure of speech, the term *Lille Ven* (Little Friend). When spoken in a sharp, cutting, and denigrating tone of voice (*What do you think you're doing, Little Friend?*), it can be used as an effective tool for sanctioning children, employees, students, or just anyone. It is a term of address that, while seeming to convey extreme civility on the part of its user, manages to suggest a sad mix of incompetence and poor behavior on the part of the one to whom it is addressed.[15]

Many Danes believe that the operation of the Jante Law discourages those who are potentially at the higher end of the spectrum of human abilities. It tends to make it difficult for gifted individuals to realize their talents in Denmark. The climate that results is one in which creative people are often faced with the choice of leaving Denmark or finding that their unusual talents go unrecognized and undeveloped. As stated earlier, it is not unusual for creative Danes to receive their first recognition abroad. Some return or at least maintain their connection with Denmark. Others do not. In part this is a function of size: one expects that there will be more opportunities in a larger country (other things being equal). In part, however, this exit abroad is a consequence of the Jante Law.

The Jante Law functions in Danish society as a powerful social code ensuring conformity to the midrange of established custom. In doing so, it can come to act as a set of boundaries working against the attainment of an integrated sense of self, against the processes of individuation and self-realization. One can hear its echoes in a bitter comment made by Danish author Karen Blixen: "The Danish character is like dough without leavening. All the ingredients which supply the taste and nourishment are there, but the element which makes the dough able to change, to rise, has been left out."[16] The Jante Law is an obstacle to that attainment, an oppressive part of one's own culture that must be fought and contested in the difficult struggle for self-realization.

II. Cultural Collisions

The Danish core value of balance and moderation is maintained through an extraordinary tolerance toward competing political, social, and sexual life-styles. Denmark remains a remarkably free and open society characterized by the same high level of tolerance. Yet in one major area, the operation of this principle is seriously threatened. The way in which the Danes helped their Jewish fellow citizens escape from the Nazis in the fall of 1943 cannot be forgotten. But the reality of the 1980s is that racism, formerly thought to be something found in places like the United States and South Africa, has been discovered to exist in Denmark as well. It can be found not only in the streets of Copenhagen but in the small towns of Jutland and Fyn.

Until the 1960s the population of Denmark was remarkably homogeneous. Most of the non-Danes residing in the country were either other Scandinavians (who could easily assimilate Danish custom) or other Europeans. It was in that decade that Turks, Yugoslavs, Pakistanis, and members of other non-Western societies came to Denmark as foreign workers. For the most part they settled initially in an urban milieu, either in Copenhagen or in several of the larger towns. Often they had little or no desire to assimilate. Their primary reason for coming to Denmark was an economic one; they hoped to earn wages that could be sent back home immediately or saved over time to purchase something deemed desirable (perhaps a plot of land) back in the country of origin. For the most part they lived in isolated enclaves, small islands of non-Western culture surrounded by a sea of Danes. The typical pattern was that the men worked and the women remained in the home. It was usually the men who learned enough Danish to get by, and some of them became fluent. Frequently, however, the women or the grandparents spoke little or no Danish at all. Danish women wear jeans and shorts (weather permitting). The women of Turkey and Pakistan, who follow a different dress code, would never dream of engaging in such barbaric behavior. Their dress, customs, and isolation as a speech community made them conspicuous whenever they left their homes.

As long as the economy was expanding, the problems were minimal. But when the Danish economy began to contract in the early 1970s, the situation of the foreign workers changed. Unemployment, practically unknown in Denmark before that time, began to be a problem. In 1971 Danish unemployment was at the extremely low level of 1.55%. In 1974 it was 2.95%: by 1977 it had become 7.65%, and by 1978, 8.30%.[17] In the 1980s the figure would at times exceed 10%. A high level of structural (as opposed to temporary) unemployment has remained an unsolved economic and social problem ever since. The problem is compounded because the most severely affected segment of the population is made up of marginally educated and inadequately trained young men between the ages of sixteen and twenty-five, especially those from working-class neighborhoods or from neighborhoods called "slums" by other Danes. Perhaps predictably, it has been among members of this group that the most clear and overt expressions of racist, antiforeign sentiment have been seen. In 1987 it was estimated that there were thirty-five thousand guest workers and their families in Denmark.[18] The problem has been further intensified by the arrival in Denmark of large numbers of political refugees from countries like Lebanon, Iran, and Sri Lanka. Although the doors are now closed to foreign guest workers, nine thousand refugees were expected to arrive in 1986 alone.[19]

Let us look more closely at one racist and antiforeign youth group, the Green Jackets (*grønjakker*), or Confederates (*sydstatsfolk*), of Copenhagen's Østerbro section.[20] The nucleus of the group is seven or eight young men eighteen to twenty years old, all of whom have spent their formative years in a section known for its violence, vandalism, and alcoholism. It is a neighborhood where nearly 50% of the inhabitants have had extended contact with social authorities such as the police or the welfare system. The full membership of the group is twenty-five boys and young men sixteen to twenty-three years old. Most come from badly split or dysfunctional families, sometimes with large numbers of children. Their schooling was typically broken off in the fifth or sixth grade. Many have been in and out of locked psychiatric wards, foster homes, and special boarding schools since the age of ten. Their excursions into criminality have included burglary, armed robbery, violent assault, and attempted murder. Among the leaders in the nucleus, it is a common pattern to have been incarcerated in prison for two years by the age of nineteen. Knives, teargas, and baseball bats are never far out of their reach.[21]

Flirtations with various forms of extreme right-wing ideology are accompanied by a profound psychic identification with violence. The Green Jackets have taken the Confederate flag of the American Civil War as their symbol of white power. "The South Will Rise Again" is the slogan printed on their T-shirts, armbands, and belts. They read with approval books on Nazism and the Ku Klux Klan and would like to see a chapter of the Klan formed on Danish soil. Occasionally they meet to burn a symbolic cross in some nearby garden or to engage in acts of violence against minority groups (taking care first to make sure that the numbers are on their side). What kinds of things can such disaffected young people do? In April 1984 five Danes about twenty years of age forced an eighteen-year-old Pakistani-born youth to undress before more than a hundred witnesses in a local commuter train, throwing each piece of clothing out of the train window. When the train reached the next station, the Pakistani youth fled in terror.[22] One can only theorize that these acts and others like them provide grim ritual compensation for an underlying sense of powerlessness and social isolation.

Members of this subculture usually do not work. They will rise between ten and noon. If they have scored on the streets the night before, they will spend their money quickly on beer, cigarettes, and pornographic videos. Sooner or later they will wind up at a local tavern (*værtshus*). Foreign workers, Jews, gays, and left-wingers are seen as their main enemies. They burn with anger. Yet their sporadic acts of vengeance are—at least to date—not part of any wider political strategy. They drift helplessly and angrily through life on the margins of respectable Denmark, trying desperately to carve their initials on something or someone. They have their own poorly articulated vision of a counterworld to traditional Danish values, a dismal little world of racism and white supremacy. The Jews and the intruding foreigners (referred to disparagingly as *perkere, krullere*, and *fejlfarver)* will be forced to leave, and Denmark will once again belong to them. They are a tinderbox of frustration waiting to be set aflame by the right demagogue.

A different segment of Danish society with a high potential for individual and social violence consists of the motorcycle gangs—with names like the Hell's Angels, the Morticians, and Bullshit. Members of these groups are a step above the Green Jackets economically (they own their own motorcycles). At present their hostility is mostly focused on each other. Thus when three members of Bullshit drove a car in the vicinity of the Morticians' clubhouse in Vanløse (a section of Copenhagen), the inevitable happened: they encountered a member of the Morticians. They left their car to have words with him. He took out a revolver and shot them, one critically, the other with wounds in the thigh. The police showed up quickly, ransacked the Morticians' clubhouse, and arrested seven gang members.[23] Such events are frequently chronicled in the Danish newspapers.

Members of these gangs and their hangers-on are not known for their chivalrous treatment of women. But it is not only gang members who are responsible for violence against women. Many fear that this kind of violence is widespread. As of 1984 there were fifteen crisis centers in Denmark to protect women who were victimized by violence. One woman psychologist has estimated that at least ten thousand Danish women are continually and repeatedly subjected to violence by their marriage partners.[24] When one considers the frequent use of hard narcotics in certain urban subcultures[25] and the fact that many violent crimes, both against women and men, are committed by boys fifteen years and younger,[26] it is easy to understand the quiet desperation that many in respectable Denmark feel about these developments.

From the point of view of the immigrants and "guest workers," it is not only the actions of hostile Danish youth that cause alarm. Even the most sincere attempts of the Danish welfare system to aid them can violate symbolic boundaries taken for granted in their own cultures. Such routine Western medical procedures as the taking of X-rays and blood samples can be threatening to those whose culture defines disease as something that comes from an evil eye or the actions of the spirit world. When a Danish doctor attempts with the best of intentions to praise a Turkish child, the child's mother may perceive such praise as a direct invitation to the evil eye to do the child harm. Amulets and talismans, facial painting, keeping secret a child's real name—all these are part of an alternative strategy aimed at controlling the onset of illness. Even though a Turkish family with a sick child will as a rule hedge their bets by trying to get help from the Danish health authorities, they frequently misunderstand the nature of the treatment the child receives. And not many Danish doctors are able to explain it to them in terms that they can understand.[27]

The question of immigration has become a major political issue in Denmark (as well as in neighboring Norway and Sweden). Populist groups that once centered their appeal on taxation and the welfare state have done well by adding the issue of immigration to these concerns. In the Danish elections of September 1987, the ultraright Progress Party (*Fremskridtsparti*) jumped from four to nine seats in the 179-member *Folketing* after campaigning hard against an influx of asylum seekers from Iran and Lebanon. "We are not a wealthy country, and it costs a lot to take care of these people, who come from countries that are culturally very different from Denmark," said Pia Kjærsgaard, the leader of the Progress Party. She added, "Compared to twenty years ago, there are many fewer reasons today to be proud to be Danish."[28]

Even the enclave of Christiania, which stands as a symbol of Danish tolerance to dissenting philosophies and life-styles, can be the scene of violence and racism:

> On a recent sunny day, a young black man peddled his bicycle past the teen-age hashish dealers who hang out under the white bird of peace sign marking the entrance to Christiania's 80 acres of barracks, woodland and handmade houses. A slender blond girl in tight jeans kicked the tires of the visitor's bike to try to turn him away. A blond boy called him the Danish equivalent of "black s.o.b." In an instant they were fighting. The white youth pulled a pistol and bashed the black youth in the face. An older white man, one of the aging hippies from the nearby bars, intervened and allowed the black man to get away. . . . Within moments the teen-age dealers were hawking again.[29]

Established in 1971 as an Aquarian experiment in utopian living, the community began with four cardinal rules: no hard drugs, no violence, no weapons, no cars. Unfortunately, they have proved impossible to enforce. Drug addiction, alcoholism, disease, and pollution are part of its present reality. Yet it also has its successful businesspeople, some of whom export cabinetry, wood-burning stoves, and bicycles to Europe and the United States. Approximately a hundred of the residents are original hippie settlers from 1971, who do the best they can to enforce the law against hard drugs and unregulated building. But the fact remains that a dark-skinned person may be subjected to attack on the streets of Christiania today, something that would have been unthinkable not much more than a decade ago. Klaus Blomquist, a welder at one of Christiania's successful bicycle companies, has summed it up in these words: "You have a new generation coming around. They're not based on flower power. They're facing a worse economic situation than we had in the 60s and 70s. It's not just Christiania. You see it all around. It's probably the same in the States."

III. THE INVISIBLE POVERTY

When a knowledgeable American observer is shown what in Denmark is called poverty, it is impossible for the most polite American not to laugh. It is true that even the worst instance of poverty in Denmark seems at first glance almost genteel when compared to certain sections of North Philadelphia, the Bronx, or Boston's Roxbury district. Yet this discounting response misses a central point because it fails to make the important distinction between absolute and relative poverty.[30] The poverty that begins about ten blocks north of Market Street in Philadelphia is more extreme in absolute terms than any poverty one is likely to see in Denmark. Yet if one wants to understand the psychological dimension of poverty in Denmark, it is necessary to use another frame of reference than that of poverty in American cities. The most relevant comparison to the Danish case will not be found on the streets of Philadelphia, but in Denmark itself. It is necessary to begin by formulating a definition of poverty relative to the particular context of Danish society. The most relevant statistic, if one could be formulated, would be the minimum income, residence, and life-style it takes to be able to escape poverty relative to its Danish definition. Such a formulation inevitably involves not merely economic questions but psychological, sociological, and cultural ones as well. The attempt to specify the parameters relevant for the definition of poverty is an area of intense and bitter debate among Danish specialists, a fact that in itself reinforces the centrality of the issue.[31]

Estimates of those living in poverty in Denmark during the 1980s have been as low as 3% and as high as 13%.[32] The basic fact remains the same at whatever point between these extremes one chooses to draw the poverty line: beneath the apparent general high level of prosperity, significant numbers of the Danish population are, by virtue of their economic situation, denied anything like a *hyggelig* life-style. What are the psychological consequences of being poor in Denmark? An extraordinarily compelling portrait relevant to the psychological dimension of Danish poverty is given by author Knud Sørensen in the person of Jens, the central character in Sørensen's short story "When Ones Like Us Go on Strike" *(Naar saadan nogle som os strejker)*. Jens is an older man who has spent most of his life as a hired farmworker on a prosperous family's land. One day he has a sudden, desperate feeling that life is passing him by. He himself belongs to no union. Yet he is driven to such desperation that when he hears on the radio of workers striking in the nearby town, he announces to his quite astonished employer that he is going to join it. He, Jens, will also go on strike:

> He [Jens' employer] sat on the sofa and got more control over himself. Then he said, in that voice he used to announce decisions, "You can't do that."
> Jens stood and held his eyes fast. "I'm going on strike," he said, and then turned around and went out of the living room and closed the door after him, but a minute later he knocked carefully, opened the door and stuck his head in and said, "I'll set the tractor in before I go," and then he closed the door again, quietly, and the man looked confusedly at his wife, who had come in from the room opening to the garden. She asked, "What was it?" and he answered: "I don't know," and she asked, if he had been drunk, and he said that he knew very well that Jens didn't drink. They went over to the window and stood and watched Jens walk through the courtyard, saw him get up on the tractor and start it and drive it around to the machine-house, and they saw him come walking back, saw him take out the bicycle, and the wife said, "What do you think he wants?" and the man shook his head as if it wasn't his at all, and Jens got up on the cycle and drove out of the entrance and disappeared.
> They stood a little and peeked out at the empty courtyard. "Why don't you ask Karen?" asked the man, "she probably knows something."
> She looked at him. "What happened? What did you say to him?" and the man still looked very strange and now also a little irritated. "I haven't said anything," he said, "I haven't even seen him, since I saw him one time this morning," and he added, mostly for himself: "And there can't have been anyone here."
> They stood a little while in mutual silence. "I have always said he was a little strange," said the wife, "It was your father who wanted us to keep him on."[33]

Jens rides his cycle along the rural highway, a familiar figure to local residents because he is the only adult male who still depends on a cycle to get him from place to place. He relives a journey through his past, peddling all the while on his old, used woman's cycle. "That's where Laurits lives, he was good enough even though it hurt him to get up in the mornings," he thinks as he passes one farm, or as he passes another, "Thomas got that property even though he never could plough straight." He thinks of the past, "of the time when there was life in the meeting halls in the evening, and there was always someone to play cards with, or to tease a little or someone to go home and dream about a little." He is lost in his own world of private reminiscences. As Jens continues peddling, Sørensen gives a powerful and evocative description of the town he is gradually approaching:

> It wasn't a big town. Its inhabitants liked to talk about it as an enterprising town, and for centuries it had made a tolerable living from the surrounding land, had been burned down a few times as once was the fate of such cities, had gotten a few factories during the time when industrialization together with the railroads was spreading out over the land in past centuries, but it still had been the trade and the surrounding land that had been its reputation and legitimacy. It was only when the surrounding area changed, when the people's meeting rooms were emptied of people, when the small farmers began to give up and their small farms were sold in large, combined units, that the city became just like any other, a place where one began to dream more of industry than of trade, and there came more factories, drawn by regional subsidies and the willing and stable work force that could be brought in from the fields for quick and effective retraining.[34]

Jens is lost, marginalized, trapped between two worlds. He exists somewhere between the disappearing world of the small rural farmer and the industrialized work force (rural and urban) that is taking its place. He is not really needed at the farm, where he is kept on mainly by the charity of his employer. But when he arrives in the city to join the strike he heard about on the radio, he discovers to his surprise that he is equally estranged from the striking workers. He follows along behind them, repeating a few of their slogans, and a few of them greet him in a friendly way. Yet at the crucial moment he is unable to join them and gives up, knowing that he will never become part of their world. In the end he leaves them to go sit on a bench, where his thoughts begin to dwell on his own failure. Sadly, he gives up his fantasy of rebellion and plans to return home quietly, so as not to cause a fuss:

> "If I had only moved that time when I was 30, I would be one of them now." But that time he was 30, there were still many out there on the land, and no one had thought that it would be otherwise, and everything had become easier with tractors and other machines. And so the time went and he was 40, and it was easiest just to stay, and he was 50 and they gave him a television, so that he wouldn't feel so alone in the evenings.
> "It just couldn't have been any other way," he thought. "The time just went." He thought, "I better go to the movies. It's best that I don't come home until after they're asleep."[35]

Sørensen's portrait of Jens, a man passed over by time, is in many ways a tragic one. But at least Jens is employed and has a modest, comfortable place to live. There are many in Denmark who lack even these amenities. The growing number of those who suffer from involuntary long-term unemployment have been placed apart in an even more fundamental way. First, they have been excluded from the common working life of society and denied the self-esteem that comes from pride in work. Second, their inadequate income prevents them from even minimal participation in the social life surrounding them. The *bistand* (social aid) that they receive from the Danish government generally enables them to live only at a bare economic minimum, to survive without really existing.[36] Many Danes close to the welfare system believe that it has been unable to mount an adequate response to the challenges brought on by the social and economic dislocations of the 1980s. Short-term unemployment turns into long-term unemployment after a year or two. Long-term unemployment provides a fertile breeding ground for social and individual pathology. Some of its ugly faces include alcoholism, drug abuse, depression, crime, racism, and broken families.

Let us take a closer look at Denmark's invisible poverty. It is clear that individual or family annual gross income is one useful criterion for defining and understanding poverty. Another and perhaps more relevant indicator is the amount available to an individual or family after all fixed expenses have been paid. For this second criterion it has been suggested that the line might be drawn at a figure of 1,000 kroner a month (currently about $150).[37] This proposal has been severely criticized on the grounds that such an amount ensures only mere physical survival and does not facilitate an adequate or positive social existence in Danish society.[38] Long-term qualitative research on the situation of the chronically unemployed done at the Sociological Institute at the University of Copenhagen led investigators to conclude that even a slightly higher figure does not suffice. Thus a single mother with two children living in supported housing, who has 1,110 kroner a month for each person in her household, remarked to them in an interview: "I am just as surprised each month that there isn't very much money [left]. But it's probably because the budget doesn't take into account that day when the bike goes to pieces, or the washing machine needs to be repaired, or the kids need new football shoes."[39]

For those who must live on state-mandated relief *(bistand)*, the margin of survival is measured in whether or not such unexpected events occur and, if they occur, how to get through the month until the next check arrives. Should I buy a new mattress for the child's bed or get the toilet fixed? Just when I was planning to buy a used cycle, there is a problem with the stove. When one of the children has lost his only warm coat, what shall I do? It goes without saying that given so small a margin of safety, there is little or nothing left for subscribing to a newspaper or for buying the children the birthday presents one really wants them to have. A life lived at this level has profound symbolic implications for both older and younger generations in a way that transcends the mere fact of economic deprivation. Birthe Mørck, a social worker with ten years' experience in Copenhagen's Vesterbro, has pointed clearly to this further dimension of the problem:

> Think how it feels, in this affluent, overflowing Denmark, to be kept out of all these areas of life. Think how it feels, when there isn't enough money to buy your infant a new pair of clothes. Understand, that when a mother feels that there is simply no way she can give the child what it needs, that this perception of the mother will color in a fundamental way the atmosphere in which the child is raised. Understand, in other words, that economic poverty over a long period of time leads to isolation, diminished self-confidence and resignation.[40]

What is it like to be completely dependent on welfare in Denmark? What do some of those caught in this negative spiral of state-sanctioned relief *(bistandshjælp)* say about their situation? Hans, a divorced fifty-nine-year-old man, is a former salesman and teacher in a business school. Once at an earlier time he was unemployed for three years; at the present time he has been out of work for a year and a half. Although he is both physically and mentally fit, many employers do not want to hire a man his age. After his fixed expenses have been paid (including a contribution to his two children), about 1,600 kroner (about $230) remain. As a result of long-term unemployment, he has given up his car, TV, small pleasure boat, vacations, trips abroad, theater trips, and movies. One of the worst things about being unemployed, he says, has to do with sexuality:

> Your sex drive doesn't disappear just because you have become unemployed, but you don't have a chance with the female sex, when you are nobody. Try to read the contact and marriage advertisements: "Woman seeks man in good economic circumstances" or "I have a wonderful and exciting job, that I am involved in, and expect that you will as well." You don't ever see an announcement from a woman who writes, "I am unemployed."[41]

Sara, a divorced thirty-two-year-old woman, has a nine-year-old son and a ten-year-old daughter. Unemployed for half a year, she has 1,100 kroner per person when all fixed expenses have been paid. Her daughter gained more than forty pounds immediately after the trauma of the divorce and began to suffer from asthma and bronchitis. After medical examination a special diet based on fresh fruit and vegetables was recommended. She cannot afford this at her present support level and says:

The situation is hopeless. I must have work and earn more in order to take care of our economy. At the welfare office *(bistandkontor)* I had a sweet social worker, but now I've gotten a new one, and it's like doing battle every time. And when I ask down at the employment office whether they have a job for me, they look up surprised and say that I can just try to find one myself. I'm trying for whatever there is.[42]

Vibeke, an unemployed nurse of forty-three, is single and has been out of work for nine years. Her level of support has recently been cut. She still gets 63 kroner a day (about $10), which must pay for food, clothes, transport, personal hygiene, recreation, and excursions. Her comments vividly illustrate how long-term unemployment can affect every aspect of an individual's psychological and social identity:

Existence becomes a desert-wandering, trying to save. But one doesn't live by bread alone, and I can't be satisfied with eating and sleeping. I also have intellectual needs. People can talk about free pleasures, but just to be together with other people costs money. I don't like to eat together with others who have more money than I do, because I feel that I am a scrounge or a sponge. And I hear that often enough, that it makes me very easily hurt. One's friends get tired of always hearing: I can't afford it, I don't have the money, it costs too much for me. When I get invited out, I often say no, because I don't have respectable clothes to wear. I never thought I would come to envy retired people their reduced-price cards, but I do today.[43]

In the years between 1980 and 1986, the institutions that specialize in providing care to the poorest groups in Danish society experienced a 60% rise in the number of people requesting help.[44] The earlier pattern was that men in their forties or older formed the bulk of their clientele, but they report that increasing numbers of younger men and women with children now come to them for aid. The Kofoed School provides a program of instruction where former alcoholics, drug users, and panhandlers can receive forty hours a week of intensive instruction in academic subjects as well as a full measure of encouragement and support from a committed staff. The school's principal, Jens Aage Bjørkøe, is highly critical of the *bistandssystem:*

One could almost say that the Danish *bistandssystem* is organized to produce social losers. The system leaves the clients as passive and psychically-broken down charity recipients, who along the way have received surprisingly little aid and encountered a shocking amount of passivity. The way the system functions today, by far the most amount of effort is used to decide the size of the support level, while the active, setting-in-motion contribution is neglected. As a result, the clients are kept hovering in a vacuum.[45]

The effect of poverty is felt not only by those who have been reduced to it but by those who can see its shadow not far behind them in their present lives. Among them are the large numbers of Danish workers affected by increased cutbacks in the work force, whether these cutbacks have already been carried out or are in the planning stage. Schools and libraries have been closed. Teachers at all levels have been fired, their institutions closed. Hospital staffs have been cut. Research budgets have been tightened or eliminated. Women's crisis centers and institutions for handicapped children and adults have seen their funding disappear. Workers at all levels of government live in a climate where the elimination of their jobs is being seriously considered and intensely debated. For young people just out of school, the hunt for a job is likely to be bitter and prolonged. It may be necessary to make more than fifty applications to private and public employers before finding a job (and not even this many applications guarantees that one will be found).[46] Serious housing shortages in major cities mean that it may be difficult or even impossible for those in their late teens and early twenties to leave the parental nest. As a result many families are forced to make do with makeshift sleeping arrangements and conflicting life-styles far longer than is best for anyone. The same heavy metal rock that a teenager and his peer group believe to be "outrageous" and "awesome" may drive one or both parents into early cardiac arrest.

Taking all of these developments into consideration, one critical aspect of the situation has yet to be reviewed. It is that the experience of poverty in Denmark is further intensified because, in Birthe Mørck's words, "the worlds of the rich and poor have no connection with each other." In such a situation, it becomes necessary to hold lengthy hearings on poverty merely to prove that it exists. The poor, together with their helpers and experts, have an exceedingly difficult job. They must try to prove to official Denmark that the povertization process at work in Danish society today is dangerous and systematic, that much larger numbers of people are affected by it than are generally known or admitted, and that its consequences will ultimately affect the lives of all Danish citizens, not just those immediately touched by it. For the long-term poor remain not only stigmatized but isolated, invisible, and untouched. At the end of the day, the rich and poor, the prosperous and the poor, the comfortable middle class and the poor, the stable working class and the poor, all go back to their separate worlds. Part of the degradation of being poor is a sense of their own private shame at the invisible world in which they live. It is a world to which they alone must return, day after day.

When viewed in this light, the celebrations of Danish *hygge* may seem somewhat less appealing. "We are hard and cunning under our nice Danish smiles," Judith Friedman Hansen was told by one of her informants. "There must be no unpleasantness," one woman told me in explaining how *hygge* is ordinarily practiced, "no talk about refugees." I think again of another woman's cutting remark: "Danes love to throw a brick, as long as it's made of papier mâché." Perhaps a good deal of Danish *hygge* does have an artificial, papier mâché quality to it, based on a need to keep from awareness things one would rather not see, such as the unpleasant realities of the invisible poverty. Even Christiania can be interpreted in this less charitable light as a good way to keep the social losers off the street by sweeping them under the carpet.

"The future is after you," warned an anonymous spray painter on a city wall. It was an eloquent expression of the fears of a generation that is being raised to expect the worst.[47] An American who has lived in Denmark for more than twenty years writes this: "*Hygge* always has its backs turned on the others. *Hygge* is for the members, not the strangers. If you want to know what is Danish about Denmark, ask first a Greenlander and then a guestworker. . . ."[48] Perhaps the most damning indictment of all was given by a Vietnamese refugee: "In Denmark it is sad and lonely. It is so quiet here, because people don't talk with each other. Denmark lives behind a locked door."[49]

IV. THE GERMANIZATION/THATCHERIZATION/AMERICANIZATION OF DENMARK

Denmark is one of twelve European nations (along with Britain, Ireland, the Netherlands, Belgium, Luxembourg, West Germany, France, Portugal, Spain, Italy, and Greece) that have approved nearly half of a far-reaching program to end barriers to travel, trade, employment, and investment—barriers that have separated them for centuries. Regardless of whether the projected amalgamation of nations turns into a free-trade market, a federation, or something in between, it will significantly alter the face of Europe. Its aim is to establish a uniform environment for business, labor, and economic development, a new "supernation" that would extend over a single giant region reaching from Scotland to Spain, from Portugal to Greece. With 322 million consumers, this newer version of the EEC (European Economic Community) would become the largest single market in the developed world.[50] The sense of paralysis, confusion, and vulnerability that many Danes feel in the face of the proposed European integration has been a major expression of the shadow side of Danish culture in the 1980s and early 1990s.

The first response of an American to the news of European integration is likely to be positive. My own initial response certainly was. After all, two terrible world wars were fought on this continent during this century. Nationalism was one of the driving forces in each case. Wouldn't the proposed continental federation be a sensible development working against the possibility of another such conflict in Europe? Aren't the predicted economic advantages for each of the member countries powerful reasons for enthusiastic national participation? There is probably something to be said for each of these arguments, yet they do not allow insight into the just fears that the citizens of a small country may have about the proposed federation. Consider these facts: Denmark has just over 5 million inhabitants, while the population of Britain is 57 million; of France 56 million; of West Germany 60 million.[51] The population of Holland is nearly three times that of Denmark; even the population of Belgium and Portugal is twice the Danish size. Denmark is the tenth largest country in the twelve-member EEC; only Ireland (3.5 million) and tiny Luxembourg (0.4 million) are smaller. When one realizes the extent of these size discrepancies (mirrored to a large extent by similar discrepancies in the aggregate economic statistics), one can better understand the basis for the insecurity and anxiety expressed by many Danes about the proposed federation. For many centuries Denmark has lived in the shadow of bigger nations like Germany, France, and England. Is it possible that the proposed European integration will spell an end to even this marginal independence?

It is important to understand that the Danes have been ambivalent about the EEC virtually since their entrance in 1973. The Danish agricultural sector was one of the interest groups most strongly in support of EEC membership; yet in subsequent years a sizeable opposition to Danish membership has developed among this sector. The tasty and delicious carrot of EEC subsidies and markets has not made as deep an impression on many Danish farmers as the fierce and slashing stick of EEC quotas, rules, and red tape. Danish fishermen are another occupational group deeply affected by EEC quotas and fishing prohibitions. In at least one case (White Sands, a village of 3,400 on Jutland's west coast), it has been claimed that EEC rules spelled not mere difficulty but outright ruin. When their pleas for help to the prime minister and the governing coalition were not met with a quick response, the mayor of the city, himself a member of one of the parties in that coalition, remarked: "It's apparently just as far from White Sands to Copenhagen as it is from White Sands to Brussels. It's absolutely mysterious to me that such decisions can be made without so much as asking what harm they will cause in a small, local society like ours."[52]

The action of a grass roots pressure group, the People's Movement against the EEC (*Folkebevægelsen mod EF*) kept the issue of Danish EEC membership alive through the decade of the 1980s. Some of their objections have included the following: (1) The EEC has morally objectionable ways of dealing with food surplus: it stores thousands of tons of unsalable butter, milk, meat, and grain and destroys huge amounts of edible fish, tomatoes, and other foodstuffs in a world where hundreds of thousands die each year of starvation. (2) The EEC has lower standards for protecting consumers both from low-quality foodstuffs and from food dyes and other additives: Denmark as an EEC member cannot exclude these potentially dangerous wares from coming into the country. (3) The EEC provides heavy subsidies to nuclear fission reactors and nuclear energy. Denmark has no nuclear reactors; would participation in an integrated European economy oblige it to give *de facto* support to the building of a nuclearized Europe? (4) The EEC is a centralized bureaucracy that supports the vested interests of bank directors and the barons of industry; both the ordinary working person and those marginalized by poverty will be victimized and exploited by its policies.[53]

It is easy to understand why many Danes are upset by and vehemently opposed to the proposed European integration of 1992–93. The Danish fears are grounded in their unique history. Between the loss of Norway to Sweden in 1814 and Bismarck's Prussian conquest of Slesvig-Holsten in 1864, the prevailing national experience in the nineteenth century was sustained, long-term territorial loss and contraction. Denmark was reduced in the course of that century from a third-rank European power to one of the smallest nations in Europe. The analysis made in earlier chapters traced the positive response to catastrophe that enabled the Danes to overcome the disintegrating forces of their history. It explored some of the cultural roots of a revitalization process that enabled them to build one of the most remarkable and successful societies the world has ever known (symbolized in such achievements as the folk high school, advances in general public education, and the cooperative movement). Yet the achievement represented in these successes is at best a partial one, for Danish national identity is not only focused on but, I am tempted to say, obsessed with the country's small size. And Denmark's small size is an unquestioned heritage of the events of the nineteenth century, the same century that in so many other ways saw the Danes respond with an extraordinary degree of determination and ingenuity to the challenges forced on them by their history.

I wish I had a dollar for every time that I heard the expression "Oh, but we're such a small country" and similar references to Denmark's insignificance and unimportance in the scheme of things. I have little doubt that

I would be able to treat myself to an excellent dinner at a fine restaurant. "Our little spot" or "this little speck" it would be called, often in a tone of sad self-dismissal. "We are aah, such a little bitty land" *(vi er aah, så lillebitte et land)*, the Danish critic Elsa Gress unmercifully expressed it in an essay entitled "The Special Danish Cult of Mediocrity."[54] During nearly three years of living in Israel, a nation whose population is smaller than that of Denmark, I never heard a single similar reference to the country's size. An American singing the American national anthem can take quite seriously the idea of bombs bursting in air and the twilight's last gleaming. But a Dane singing the royal anthem of Denmark may be forgiven if it is difficult to repress a grin, especially when singing some of the lines about King Christian:

> King Christian stood at the High Mast
> In smoke and damp
> His weapon hammered so steady
> That the helmet and brain of the Goths was smashed
> Then sank every enemy sail and mast in smoke and damp
> "Flee," they screamed, "Flee, those who can.
> Who can stand against Denmark's Christian?
> Who can stand against Denmark's Christian in battle?"

There is on the one hand something healthy in a diminished national identification with the grandiose, self-centered projections of large-state nationalism. It did not make me unhappy, for instance, that the Manifest Destiny of Denmark was never suggested as the necessary basis for all international relations. Nevertheless, there was another side to these utterances that disturbed me deeply. For there is no inevitable relationship between Denmark's size and the presence of what Danish writer Martin Hansen has called "the littleness and insignificance philosophy," which has been preached by many Danes, especially after the tragic events of 1864.[55] "Our little land, we are so small," argues Hansen, is a continually repeated mantra that sits like a cloudy film over most Danish eyes. Flemming Bergsøe writes of the Danish inferiority complex, remarking pointedly that "feelings of national inferiority are quite general among small nations that live in sentimental memory of a vanished greatness."[56] As Uffe Østergård points out, the problem with the above national anthem is that the Swedes actually did "stand against Denmark's Christian," roundly defeating him and subsequent Danish kings in the wars of the seventeenth century.[57]

Taking these considerations into mind, perhaps the greatest fear that the Danes have about European integration is that it will render them unacceptably dependent on Britain, France, and Germany, the three large powers. Of these three, I believe that the changing Danish relationship with Germany is by far the greatest source of concern. "The Germans are going to accomplish through European integration what they were unable to do through war" is a frequently heard remark. Something that is less well known but never far from Danish national self-awareness is the conflict that has taken place in that part of the country sharing a land border with Germany, South Jutland (Sønderjylland). These national borders changed several times in the course of recent history (1864 and 1920). There has been a long and intense history of the struggle of Danish minorities for recognition both in parts of South Jutland and further south in what is now the German province of Slesvig.

A series of incidents that took place around the turn of the century gives a vivid picture of this struggle.[58] Recall that as a result of the war in 1864, areas with significant Danish minorities (or even a Danish majority) were ceded to Germany. On 16 June 1903, some forty years later, an election took place in Germany. The Danish editor of the Flensborg Avis, Jens Jessen, was elected as a representative to the German parliament from the Haderslev-Sønderborg area. When several days later he led a political meeting of Danish speakers in the Danish-language singing of a patriotic song, "High North, Home of Freedom" (Høje Nord, friheds hjem), the room was immediately entered by a German policeman who demanded that the gathering be dissolved. In the court proceeding that followed, Jens Jessen was required to pay one fine of thirty marks for singing the Danish song and another fine of ten marks for having suggested that it be sung in the first place. The policeman himself did not escape: he was reprimanded by his superiors for having allowed the song to be sung to its conclusion before marching in to break up the meeting.

The case eventually went to the Prussian Supreme Court. After the legal debate had run its course, a large number of Danish songs were officially banned on the grounds that they contained politically inciting themes (e.g., expressed a desire for reunification with Denmark). Included on the list was one song that began with the apparently inoffensive lyric "I am a simple farmer" (Jeg er en simpel bondemand). After some discussion, a decision was made that the latter song could be sung in German translation; nevertheless, it was still forbidden to sing it in the original Danish. In the town of Aabenraa in South Jutland, fourteen people were arrested and put on trial for singing this song. The German authorities persisted in their attempts, and the fines levied on Danes for the singing of forbidden songs grew to as much as 100 marks. It became possible to be punished just for playing the melody of such a song, even though none of the words had actually been sung.

These events are not without a certain humor when seen from the vantage point of our time. I cite them merely to show that the cultural conflict between Denmark and its larger southern neighbor long precedes the events of the Second World War. I do not know what this heritage looks like from the German side, but seen from the Danish side there is a large measure of anxiety, fear and a sense of helplessness. The essence of the Danish fear is that full economic integration into the emerging European Union will facilitate the slow growth of German hegemony in Denmark. The giant German economy will set in motion a process of economic strangulation, and the result will be the slow cultural absorption of Denmark into the German state. The large numbers of Germans who have purchased summer homes in parts of Denmark are thus part of a wider development that many Danes regard at best with profound ambivalence, at worst with shock and disbelief.

There are other considerations behind the Danish fears of proposed European integration. The dismantling of the British welfare system proceeded apace under Margaret Thatcher in the 1980s. There are some in Denmark who have watched this development in admiration; many, however, regard it with great uneasiness. For the Danish welfare state as it exists today includes not only the problematic relief aid *(bistandshjælp)* discussed in the previous section but a wide range of other services that few Danes would want to do without. Even those bastions of individualism, the Green Jackets—who consistently support the Progress Party because of its anti-immigration stand—know as if by instinct where to draw the line. As one of its leaders remarked: "But that stuff about paying for your own hospital stay, they can just stick it you-know-where."[59]

The problem is that the Danish welfare system is financed by one of the highest progressive income taxation systems in the world. It has been predicted that once the borders of Europe are opened to the free movement of firms, labor, and capital across national boundaries, there will have to be a series of drastic realignments in the Danish tax system. When alternative taxes (such as the value-added tax) are cut back to the same level found in other EEC lands, the burden of supporting the Danish public sector (the sector that carries out the various recognized welfare functions) will fall increasingly on an already overburdened personal income tax system. The public sector in Denmark is much larger in proportion to the population than it is in other EEC countries, and of course the money to support it must come from somewhere. An attempt to continue the present high level of taxation might be an unwise policy that would keep promising foreign businesses from deciding to locate in Denmark. Moreover, it could even come to be expressly forbidden as legislation enacted in Brussels removes the power to set tax levels away from Copenhagen to EEC headquarters in the south.

What is the reaction of the Danish financial community to these events? It has been for the most part to proclaim their inevitability. A Danish banker makes the following prediction: "Denmark has 10–12 years to change the system of public expenditure. It is completely unrealistic to maintain the tension in regard to taxation that today exists in relation to the other EEC lands."[60] The chief officer of the Danish Industrial Council (*Industrirådet*) makes a more general, if equally unsettling comment: "It is not the Inner Market's fault. The Inner Market has just made it more apparent for us, how much we have to adapt ourselves to the world around us."[61] The National Bank director's views are along the same lines. Denmark can do little itself to improve the land's economy: the only hope is that foreign growth, the growth of the global economy, will pull the Danish economy along with it in a positive direction.[62] Danes must learn to tighten their belts at the same time that Danish companies figure out how to sell more Danish products abroad. The bankers, of course, see themselves (and are seen by others) as a group that will benefit handsomely by European integration.

A different set of questions is being asked by those who feel that they might not be so handsomely benefited by what seems to lie ahead. What will it be like to carry not a Danish but a European Community passport? Isn't the proposed Inner Market nothing more than a convenient cover for a life-threatening environmental vandalism that will have catastrophic social and environmental effects not only in Europe but all over the globe?[63] Will Denmark and the other small countries be able to protect their legitimate rights of national self-determination? How will the relatively high present wage levels of Danish workers be affected by European integration? Will labor conditions (salaries, fringe benefits, safety of the workplace) be reduced to some European average, and what will that mean for the Danish worker? Will large numbers of foreign workers (especially from southern Europe) come to Denmark, drawn by the prospect of higher wages? What strains will this put on an already overburdened public sector?

The possible dimensions of the new situation become clear when we consider some of the wage differentials in member European countries. The average hourly labor costs—wages and benefits—in 1988 were $15.88 in Denmark; by comparison they were $8.75 in Spain and $2.73 in Portugal.[64] As industries like trucking are deregulated, will Danish trucking companies be driven out of business by Portuguese companies that pay their workers $2.73 an hour, less than one-fifth the Danish average? How will the Danish workers and their unions be able to compete in this deregulated marketplace? Will the same pattern occurring in other industries bring about massive unemployment in Denmark, followed by the destruction of unions as workers desperately compete for whatever low-wage jobs are available?

Will some faceless committee of European bureaucrats in Brussels ultimately decide on such issues as the subjects to be taught in the Danish schools, the size of Danish classrooms, and the level of Danish educational spending? If the Danes decide to resist decisions made in Brussels, can they expect to see a European Community police force (perhaps one with a large German contingent) flown into Denmark to enforce the ruling? A Danish traffic minister defends the controversial building of a bridge between Sjælland and Fyn by appealing to these deep-rooted fears in Danish history. Failure to build the bridge immediately will mean that Jutland becomes a part of Germany in the 1990s ("therefore the bridge must be built, and it must be built now").[65] How will European integration change the shape of domestic politics and even the very framework of internal political debate?

All of the Danish achievements connected with the core value of welfare and social responsibility presuppose an independent, autonomous Denmark. The thought that history may be running against them, that they are a small people caught in the grip of powerful forces against which they struggle in vain, is the dark side of the Danish cultural autonomy. It was a stubborn cultural autonomy that made it possible for the people of a small nation with limited natural resources to respond effectively in the last century to a series of catastrophic events. The people of that country are challenged now as never before. What will be the fate of the uniquely Danish vision of society on which their peacefulness and prosperity up to the 1980s has been built? Will it be abandoned to the abstract rulings of the microeconomic balance sheet, reduced to the framework of narrow cost/benefit logic, and surrendered to the goals of deregulation and short-run profitability? Will major economic decisions be taken regardless of their social and psychological consequences? And if so, what will these social and psychological consequences be?

Lacking a crystal ball, I cannot provide an answer to these painful questions. I have raised them only because they are relevant to an understanding of the present dilemmas facing Denmark and its people. The question may legitimately be asked: what is it that the Danes fear most? Anthropologists have used the term "culturally constituted fantasy" to make the point that even an individual's private fantasy life is deeply tied to the culture within which that individual is located.[66] I have tried to make the point in this section that those with the Danish identity share a culturally constituted fantasy relating to the dissolution of Denmark as an independent national entity. It is often the writers and humorists of a culture who give deepest expression to such themes. The Danish writer and poet Benny Andersen has written a short piece entitled "When Denmark Was Abolished," from which the following is cited:

> I dreamed that Denmark was closed down.
> I had been far up north in Sweden for a month in order to finish a book, and in all that time I hadn't read a newspaper. On the way home, I visited my friend Jan Maartenson, who lives in southern Sweden. I asked if I could stay overnight and take the Malmø Ferry the next day. "You had better move in with us for the time being," he said. "The Malmø Ferry has been shut down." He said it in Swedish, of course; here I've just translated it. "Shut down?" I burst out. "But they can't just shut down the Malmø Ferry."
> "Here, have a beer and a little brandy," he said with a strange awkward glance that wasn't at all like him. "And just relax, while I tell you what has happened—because I can see that you haven't heard about it."
> "Heard about what?" I asked, but he didn't answer before we had had a strong shot of brandy and a few sips of beer. "Denmark has been closed down. All the Danes have been thrown out of the country. . . . You came to owe so much money abroad, that the European council declared you bankrupt. The only way that your country could be made profitable was to evacuate all the people and convert it to an exercise area for the military games of the European army and a center for the Northern European nuclear power industry, as well as the main storage dump for nuclear waste from all over Europe."
> "That's a lot of crap," I said. "Where is my family, then?" "I don't know," answered Jan. "You Danes have all been evacuated and spread out in small groups over the whole EEC area, so that you can better be integrated into the other societies."
> "The hell with that!" I shouted, and Jan hurried to fill the glasses. "How will I get my book published?" Jan smiled nervously at me: "I am your friend, you know that. I'll translate it into Swedish and make sure that a Swedish publisher takes it. By the way, what does it deal with?"
> "It deals with Denmark and the Danes, Danish lifestyles and such." "Oi, oi!" said Jan. "That is going to be much more difficult. You must understand, that the Danish language has been forbidden until further notice, just as the terms Denmark and Danes have been harmonized. The land is now called North Prussia, and the earlier inhabitants, have received immediate citizenship in the other countries. . . . You have to be careful, there are EEC agents also in Sweden to track down and take away possible deserted—um—ah . . . North Prussians."[67]

The late Jules Henry wrote that each culture has its own distinct nightmare, its own vision of failure.[68] The humorous mood taken by Benny Andersen should not blind us to the fact that his innocent and guileless little sketch directly confronts a distinctly Danish cultural nightmare: a vision of social collapse and failure based on the loss of national autonomy. It is only partial consolation that later in the sketch the narrator awakens to find that it was all a bad dream, that he shouts crazy endearments at his wife in five languages and then goes back to sleep. For the vision of his bad dream, no matter how humorously told, has brought us face-to-face once again with the same underlying dilemma that has shaped Danish existence since the time of the Bernstorffs. The perennial question is this: how can the people of a small nation conserve their culture and their tradition in a world where they are surrounded by powerful and dangerous giants?

V. CONCLUDING REFLECTIONS

In these five chapters I have presented some themes in the Danish national character. What I have tried to do in these chapters is to specify a complex configuration of cultural forces whose expression can be seen in a range of everyday social situations. It is hoped that the preceding analysis in terms of the positive core values (democracy and egalitarianism, moderation and balance, *hygge,* and welfare and social responsibility) has provided some insight into the roots of the Danish capacity to make non-violent social transformations even during times of crisis-driven social change. The present chapter's focus on the dark side is aimed at providing a greater balance to the perspective presented in earlier chapters.

What experiences led to this view of Danish national character? And why has this section been entitled "themes" in national character rather than the more scientific-sounding "model" of national character? A picture of "the Danish character" is in the last analysis only an abstraction drawn from looking at living individuals, and perhaps from literary and historical records as well. Like a character on any stage, including the stage of real life, whatever picture emerges must be taken with a grain of salt. Any generalization about national character runs a great risk of being partial and inadequate. And yet, like a good stage character, if it is successful, it can show us something we have never seen before or remind us of something important that we have forgotten.

The answer to the question at the beginning of the last paragraph is that I am under no illusions that my knowledge of Danish national character is deep enough to present a clear "model" of that character. Let me say in my defense, however, that this was not due to any lack of effort on my part. The construction of such a description is in part scientific analysis, and yet in equal part it requires a kind of artistic perception. It also requires persistence and luck. Danish national character will never be found in a laboratory or a test tube; it is a jigsaw puzzle whose pieces are to be found in classrooms, in village churches, in train stations, and in ancient documents. It is there in the faces of the living if you can see it; it also lies buried in the written testimony of the dead.

Like a true anthropologist, I went looking for it everywhere—in homes, in churches, in open fields, in taverns, in the eyes of children and old people, and in the crowded night streets. I went looking for it in what people said, in what they didn't say, in how they moved and looked at each other, in how they dressed and how they shook hands. I went looking for it in the faces of the living and in the transcripts of the dead ("the communication of the dead is tongued with fire beyond the language of the living," wrote T. S. Eliot in *Little Gidding*). I went looking for it in all these places, helped and hindered by twists and turns of fate. There were unexpected triumphs and equally unexpected setbacks, and in the end I found the pieces of it that came to me, I think, almost in spite of my methodology. Indeed, I almost didn't survive the clever methodology that guided my original research plan. In the end I was saved by luck and a few friends. It was a little like the Magic Theater in Herman Hesse's *Steppenwolf*: "Enter, ye who wish to lose your minds. . . ." Or as Bob Dylan has put it in one of his songs: "Are you willing to risk it all, or is your love in vain?"

What options are open to citizens of Denmark in these troubled times? A blue pamphlet available at the welfare office shows a picture of young men in their twenties sitting in a classroom. The lines on the cover read: "Unemployed? Go to a folk high school. The folk high school can give you new knowledge and will." The next chapter contains an account of my year in three Danish folk high schools.

"Unemployed? Go to a folk high school. The folk high school can give you new knowledge and will" (from a pamphlet available at the welfare office).

PART V

THE DANISH FOLK HIGH SCHOOLS
IN THE 1980S AND BEYOND

CHAPTER ELEVEN

A Year in Three Danish Folk High Schools

I N THE SPRING OF 1982, just two months before receiving my Ph.D. for a study of an Israeli kibbutz, I received news that I had been awarded a Fulbright grant for the following year to study the Danish folk high schools. I decided in advance that I would try to maximize my connection with the folk high schools during this year. Rather than attend one or two of them, I would try to be a student at three different schools in the course of this year. At the time there seemed to be an unbeatable logic in this procedure. I had learned by then that the folk high schools offered both long and short courses.[1] The long ones, which generally last between three and seven months, would provide the in-depth, firsthand experience that I needed to carry out the study. I sat there in California working it out. If I chose schools with classes lasting between three and four months, I would have time to study at three schools. As soon as I finished the first course, the second one would begin. As soon as the second one was completed, I would be ready to start the third. I had no way of knowing it then, but this procedure was based on a complete misunderstanding both of what the folk high schools were and of what it would be like to attend them.

It is not for nothing, that old maxim about fools rushing in where angels fear to tread. In retrospect it seems that folly is frequently rewarded in the initial stages, the devil hoping to further commit the fool to his folly and to make his fall that much longer when it comes. No Dane in his or her right mind would ever dream of attending three long courses at three different folk high schools in a single year. Undeterred by my lamentable ignorance, I wrote exploratory letters in unconvincing pidgin Danish to fifteen Danish folk high schools whose names I had picked out of the folk high school catalogue. I received about ten replies. Some were encouraging, others were openly skeptical. They asked how much Danish I really understood and reminded me that classes, discussion, and social life would all be conducted in Danish. Such a format, of course, was exactly what I had in mind.

I read through all the answers, and after some thought I selected Kolding Højskole in Jutland for my first folk high school stay. Kolding's literature made clear that it was an alternative folk high school with a system-critical, left-wing perspective. I was particularly intrigued by the fact that a course in wind energy was being offered. The school itself had several windmills generating electricity for its internal energy needs. I wrote back to the school, was accepted, and began to pack my bags. Influenced by prior knowledge of its age and tradition, I had already made a decision to attend Askov in the spring of 1983. I had not yet decided which school to attend for my second stay. I was determined to choose schools located far from Copenhagen to improve the chances of total immersion in the language (in retrospect, I need not have worried so much).

On 1 September 1982 I arrived in Denmark with my fifty words of Danish, ready to begin a study of the folk high schools. I spent the first month in Copenhagen, trying out my pathetic attempts at speaking the language on those few virtuous souls who didn't walk away quickly or begin grinning widely as soon as they heard me. Some, such as a succession of postal clerks, were virtual captive audiences, but that didn't prevent them from suddenly switching to English after the first five words had come out of my mouth. I knew elementary Danish grammar but hadn't yet learned to talk as if I was trying to chew a mouthful of potatoes while suffering from a bad cold (which is what you must learn to sound like if you want to speak proper Danish and be understood). In spite of its many redeeming features, Denmark is a nation of mumblers, and Danish, as someone once remarked, is not a language at all but a disease of the throat.

I took the train to Kolding on 4 October 1982. My journey was about to begin.

I. KOLDING HØJSKOLE: THE VIEW FROM A WINDMILL

The Crisis of the Traditional Folk High School

The decision to include both Kolding and Askov seems in retrospect to have been a clear stroke of genius; as time goes by I find that it takes more and more willpower for me to remember what actually happened. The truth is that I chose Kolding for two reasons and two reasons only: it was far from Copenhagen and had windmills. Luckily for me, it turned out that the school was ideal for an initial folk high school experience. To put the icing on the cake, its choice could even be later justified on impeccable theoretical grounds. For Kolding Højskole had been founded by a group of dissident teachers who broke away from Askov in 1970. The two schools were united by a long and intricate history, and a knowledge of the relationship between them provides an excellent introduction to the folk high schools of the last two decades.

In order to trace these recent developments, let us recall how the earlier folk high schools functioned. It was made clear in Chapter Five that one reason for the success of the early folk high school was its ability to function as a patriarchal equivalent of the family farm. The role of the principal and his wife at the school directly paralleled the role of farmer and his wife at home. By the very act of attending a folk high school, a student became a member of an extended family composed of graduates of that high school. A student thus became part of a community held together often over decades by (at least in part) the charisma of a *højskole* principal. When a student married and had children, they frequently went as well to a folk high school. In this way an informal tradition was built up in many rural families, and the resulting continuity in the nature of the clientele became an established feature of most folk high schools.

This patriarchal tradition continued unchallenged from the founding of the first folk high schools in 1844 until the post–World War II decades. It remained customary for folk high school principals to exercise control over such critical matters as the definition of acceptable student behavior and the hiring and firing of teachers. But by the late 1940s and the 1950s the surrounding Danish society had undergone a radical transformation. This transformation, representing a late phase of the modernization process, saw a large-scale migration out of agriculture, an explosive growth of industrialization, and a new concentration of population in the urban sector. Another relevant factor was that the quality of primary and secondary education available in the rural areas had by this time become equal to that found in the rest of the country.

Keeping these facts in mind, it is possible to understand two key developments. The high school's traditional clients—the young farmers— became a group that was reduced (1) in absolute numerical terms and (2) in their degree of distinctness with respect to other groups in the population. The percentage of folk high school students from traditional rural backgrounds fell steeply just as the proportion of those from urban backgrounds was sharply rising. Suddenly there was a newer group of students coming to the folk high schools, and they came with a quite different set of norms and values than the traditional clientele, the sons and daughters of farmers.

Often they were older and had little or no previous connection with what these schools had always stood for in Danish society. They were in every sense strangers to the schools' traditions.

A further dimension to this postwar problem was created by well-meaning Danish social workers, who began especially in the 1960s to encourage individuals with severe social and emotional problems to attend folk high schools. The hope, of course, was that exposure to the folk high school milieu would help these individuals to solve their problems, that it would "put wind in their sails" just as it had done for generations of young Danish farmers. But however well intentioned these actions were, they failed to take into consideration the fact that the folk high schools were never set up to dispense psychotherapy. A folk high school was not equipped with the facilities nor did its staff possess the training necessary to deal with individuals suffering from drug or alcohol addiction, from clinical or subclinical depression, or from a range of equally serious problems. When many such individuals began to show up for the long courses, the problem of integrating them into the school's activity further contributed to the generation of a crisis mood among folk high school principals and teachers. When the principal of Askov Højskole stated publicly that the school normally did not accept students who in the past year had received psychiatric treatment at a state hospital, a number of critical psychiatrists went so far as to accuse the school of practicing a form of apartheid through its admission policies.[2] The resulting atmosphere of guilt and recrimination made things even more difficult for those in the folk high school community.

All of these factors taken together created a potentially explosive mixture. When principals and teachers at the high schools continued to treat the newcomers as they had treated earlier generations of students, frustrations began to mount. Matters came to a head in June 1968 at Ryslinge Højskole in Fyn. Ten students decided to leave the school, dropping out of courses they had been attending for several months. One of them said, in the typically self-undercutting way that a Dane will announce a declaration of principle, "It should be no secret that our decision to leave has not exclusively sprung out of anything as sublime as the efforts toward democratization. It should be seen primarily as a protest action against the principal's daily treatment of students."[3] Note that this student's declaration is influenced by the balance principle (both a positive and a negative are stated), by the commitment to democracy and egalitarianism (true in spite of the initial disclaimer), by the code of cultural modesty (we're not such great democrats even though we may appear to be in others' eyes), and by the Jante Law (we're not so fine and special). What were the specific forms of maltreatment against which these students were so vehemently protesting? It was the enforcement of rules that up to that point had been normal and accepted in Danish folk high schools: boys and girls mustn't come into each other's hallways; drinking beer at the school is forbidden; the lights must be put out at a certain hour, etc.

The protest action of the departing students was backed up by a majority of those still in attendance. It had as well the open support of five teachers. In the beginning of July, the students took the further step of boycotting instruction, substituting for the planned instruction a series of organized discussions. Their goal was to formulate a list of demands to be presented to the school and its leadership. Out of this process arose an ultimatum: the school had to be further democratized at once, and the principal would have to change his authoritarian style. The teachers quickly followed this student ultimatum with one of their own that included the demand that the principal and his wife resign. Perhaps not too surprisingly, the school's governing board *(bestyrelse)* supported the principal. Several days later the principal fired all the teachers.

I do not know of anything that symbolizes the crisis of the traditional folk high school better than these incidents at Ryslinge. About a hundred years earlier Ryslinge had been the site for the pathbreaking folk high school of Christen Kold (1851). The difference between the harmonious atmosphere that prevailed at Kold's school and the atmosphere of recrimination during these events of 1968 is extraordinary. But the times had been changing. These events took place during the late 1960s, when protest actions resounded throughout the Western world against the Vietnam War and other failures of democratic government. It was a period when many Danes, among them folk high school people, were actively reexamining their cultural heritage. Looking closely both at the world and at their own society, they did not like what they saw. Some began to question whether the traditional Danish folk high schools could meet the new set of social challenges. As one of these critical high school people has written:

> Our society will in the future be more and more characterized by the split between a relatively small number of experts in the service of the state and private business, who understand and control the complicated machinery of society based on a view of society derived from the natural sciences, and a large majority of powerless and manipulated citizens, who don't understand very much of what is going on in their society and function only as cogs in an effective machine.[4]

Propelled by this vision of a negative and declining future, many educators began to ask urgent questions about the relevance of the school form in which they themselves were participating. Debates on these wider issues as well as on the more narrow grounds of the Ryslinge controversy became a familiar part of the Danish scene in these years. In the fall of 1970 a bitter debate over these issues took place at Askov Højskole. The significance of the debate and its resolution are highlighted by the fact that Askov is a direct descendent of the first folk high school founded at Rødding in 1864. A number of important trends, including the teaching of natural sciences in a folk high school curriculum, were pioneered at Askov during the last century. Its prestige and influence have remained considerable. For this reason the outcome of the debate at Askov is of particular interest.

The group in opposition, which included the principal and eight teachers (one-third of the teaching staff), supported radical change. They demanded more socially relevant critique in the curriculum and more student democracy. The majority of the teachers at Askov argued that the school should continue along its traditional lines, and this view of the majority was supported by the governing board. In the aftermath of this debate a new principal was appointed. The minority in opposition decided to leave the school and to build their own based on new principles. Kolding Højskole was constructed in the following years as a direct result of these events (its first courses were offered in November 1972). It thus occupies a position of unique interest and importance to those interested in the evolution of these schools.[5] What are the dimensions of its theory and ideology today? How do they work out in actual practice?

What follows is the description of a year in three Danish folk high schools. It includes the long courses at Kolding (the autumn of 1982), Silkeborg (the winter and spring of 1983), and Askov (the summer of 1983). The three schools will be contrasted in history, ideology, curriculum, course offerings, architecture, living conditions, food policies, student social life, faculty, and classroom experience. I will also seek to make clear some of the underlying similarities that exist despite differences in design and philosophy.

The potential difficulties that exist in attempting to give this kind of description must be pointed out. My experience was limited in duration. How accurate is a brief snapshot of a single session of such a school taken during part of a single year? Who are the people one *didn't* talk to from whom one could have learned important information, information that might have altered the conclusions one reached? How *typical* was my experience in these folk high schools, one might ask? How *actual,* how real or accurate was it?[6] These descriptions are meant to provide an ethnographic record of what the three schools were like in 1982 and 1983. Much has happened in each school since then. Yet it is hoped that the following description will provide some valuable insights into problems, trends, and solutions in their history even for those familiar with the schools today, however much they may have changed. For those who do not know these particular schools or have no acquaintance with folk high schools whatsoever, its aim is to present an introduction both to them and by extension to the situation of the Danish folk high schools in the 1980s.

First Impressions

It was a beautiful and windy day, that first train ride across Denmark in early October of 1982. When I got off the train in the town of Kolding, I didn't know what to do. I stood there with my suitcase, backpack, typewriter, and guitar, looking around in confusion, and my eyes fell on a young man with a backpack. After a brief conversation, we established that we were both bound for Kolding Højskole. We were soon joined by a woman in her mid-thirties, and the three of us hired a taxi for the trip. The woman was attending the school for a weekend conference; I never saw her again. I am still in touch with the young man seven years later, and he has become one of my dearest friends. His name is Axel.

We watched with a sense of mounting anticipation as the taxi drove through the clean streets and parks of a medium-sized provincial town. The trip was a short one, and we soon arrived at Kolding Højskole. There we saw a small group of buildings and some people dressed in jeans going about their business. It was the two windmills that caught my eye, one of them quite large. I couldn't wait for our course to begin. We stood there with our bags in front of a small building, which we were told housed the offices, dining room, and kitchen, waiting for someone to acknowledge our existence. I thought that perhaps the principal or one of the teachers would come out to meet us. But no one did. People walked by, and we asked them what we should do. But they were busy and no one paid much attention to us. We waited and waited. We asked and then we asked again. But nothing happened. It was the Jante Law ("and who do you think *you* are?") in operation. Just because we were new students, the school seemed to be telling us in a quiet way, we shouldn't get the idea that we were anybody important. I remember how frustrating this nonreception was to me. To my relief the two Danes with whom I had come were experiencing the same intense emotion. Finally, Axel could stand it no longer. "Come, Steve," he said in a determined way, and we marched off in the general direction of the other buildings, which turned out to be dormitories. "Dormitories," however, is probably the wrong word to describe them.

The residential housing units at Kolding (photo: Axel Nielsen).

All of them were simple and elegant ground-level houses. They possessed the same compound architecture: a center rectangle connected on two sides to structures that looked like downward-slanting irregular parallelograms. The center rectangles in each house turned out to be the communal space (*fællesrum*), a communal kitchen and dining room together with a living room. Each kitchen was supplied with a refrigerator, stove, oven, and expertly constructed dining-room table, built and braced in the Danish manner. These tables were big enough to seat more than a dozen people. Each living room was similarly graced by a large hardwood table surrounded by chairs and elongated benches with pillows.

The net effect of this arrangement was to create a natural social space for work, play, leisure, eating, drinking, and discussions. The structures shaped like irregular parallelograms turned out to be the site for individual rooms, the higher level containing on each side a double room with one bed below and the second in a loft. The lower level contained single rooms on each side. In the outer ends of the house were the communal bathrooms and rooms for showering. I later learned that the houses had been built with volunteer labor donated by the many Danes who were sympathetic to the idea of what Kolding Højskole would come to stand for. There were impressive pictures of this initial construction in the office hallways. I also learned that all of the sturdy hardwood furniture in the houses had been built in the school's carpentry shop.

Somehow Axel had learned that there were two rooms vacant in one of the houses and that these rooms had been allocated to arriving students in our course, "Wind Energy: Theory and Practice." The other students in the house did not go out of their way to welcome us. Indeed, some of them were not hospitable at all. They had already been at Kolding for periods of up to a month and had become involved with their own courses, activities, and social life. It was only after some animated discussion, of which I could not understand a single word, that Axel apparently convinced them that we had a right to move into the empty places in this house and were damn well going to do so whether they liked it or not. At any rate, we would be able to stay for the night. The whole thing was a terrible letdown for me. I felt even worse when my attempts to speak Danish fell on deaf, indifferent, and almost patronizing ears. It was a hard beginning.

The next day we finally began to make contact with the school. After eating a breakfast prepared in our house by other students, we met the instructor for our wind energy course. There were seven students, including Axel and myself. They were an interesting mixture. Three of them (Christian, Peter, and Axel) were eighteen or nineteen years old. Poul, slightly older, had worked as a machinist, and another, Lars, was a plumber's apprentice. The sixth member of the class was Dorthe, a very determined-looking journalist. And then there was me. Our teacher, Henrik, was a gentle and soft-spoken man with advanced technical training. We spent the whole morning discussing our goals for the course, what we hoped to accomplish and how we would go about doing it. Or rather *they* spent the morning discussing these goals. I spent the morning (as I was to do for most of the next two months) looking back and forth from speaker to speaker, trying hard to understand even a few words of what was being said. Yes, this was going to be a challenging experience.

In the end it was to prove more than just challenging. It was to be inspiring, broadening, and at the same time bitterly disappointing. We in the wind energy course would gradually come to know each other better, perhaps too well. And yet in a sense we never came to know each other at all. None of us could have predicted this at the time. A quick look at the school program for the month of October was enough to show that nearly all of our mornings and afternoons would be spent in each other's company.[7] These sessions were called "workgroups" *(arbejdsgrupper),* instead of classes, a fact that reflects the school's consistently critical attitude toward academic knowledge as well as its socialist identification with the working class. Similarly, those attending the school are not referred to as "students" *(elever),* a term felt to have negative bourgeois associations with alienated learning, but with the more neutral term "course-taker" *(kursist)*. If, however, I had expected that the school's forthright left-wing perspective would attract a student body made up mainly of committed left-wing socialists, I would have been surprised at what I saw. Committed party goers? Yes, there were many of those. Committed socialists, on the other hand, were a very small minority.

It is misleading in the extreme to take the wind energy course as a simple barometer of what was happening at Kolding Højskole. Nevertheless, let us begin with this course, for it is the one that I came to know best. Our teacher could best be characterized as an extreme exponent of nondirective teaching. He seemed to know a lot about how windmills worked, but it was difficult to drag small pedestrian details out of him. His approach reminded me of a Rogerian therapist: "Well, what do you think you'd like to do with windmills this week?" We had a lot of excellent and challenging literature, but the one who was supposed to be our guide was encouraging us to sink or swim while giving us precious little guidance of his own. He had a great fear of seeming authoritarian because he possessed more knowledge than we did, and this fear led him to avoid taking an active role in our group discussions of the theory and the practice of wind energy. It used to drive me nearly crazy because I felt that I had the chance to learn something about windmills and it simply was not happening.

We spent a lot of time sitting around in a relatively unstructured way, waiting for something to happen. For instance, we spent weeks discussing whether or not we could build a new type of hydraulic windmill. Finally we realized that it was simply beyond our capabilities. Dorthe was justifiably angry. Why, she asked, did the whole group have to discuss this idea for weeks, wasting our time and boring us to death when possibly Poul and certainly our teacher could have told us at once that it would not work? And after that it took us many weeks of disorganized, unfocused discussion just to decide on what we were going to do for our smaller group projects. In spite of all the time we were to spend together in the coming months, we remained a collection of individuals who never came together as a group. Although at times we seemed to be making progress, people in the class got up late, did not come back from weekends on time, did not do what they said they were going to do, and in general could not be relied on. And our teacher did not push us. The same unfortunate combination of youth, inexperience, inertia, and personality conflicts that hindered us from the beginning was to sink us in the end. Our teacher's commitment to nondirective guidance, which perhaps in another context would have been productive, facilitated a series of small but significant catastrophes. But before describing in more specific terms the nature of our group's failure, let me say a few more words about Kolding Højskole. The reason for doing this is that the problems in one course should not prevent the discussion from focusing on other pertinent issues, some of which will show the very real strengths and achievements of Kolding Højskole. Among them are the school's general ideology and philosophy, its "food politics," its main areas of coursework, and its social life.

The Ideology and Philosophy of the School

The teacher explained about the employers [lit. "work-givers"].
A student asked:—What do they give away?
The teacher explained that the class struggle was a thing of the past.
A student asked:—Who won?
The teacher shouted:—If you want to learn more about democracy, then sit still and be quiet!

—"The Situation," Carl Scharnberg[8]

The founders of Kolding Højskole wanted the school's primary identification to be with the working class. Their vision of the school was as a center in which the interests of this oppressed class, as well as society at large, would be served through an exploration of the diverse aspects of the present world crisis. This diversity of focus would enable the school's curriculum to deal with the crisis on both the national and the international levels, to deal with the problem both within Danish society and at the level of the global system. And in terms of the course offerings at the school, their vision has at least in part been realized. Course offerings are supplemented by an active program of speakers and artists. During my stay the poet Carl Scharnberg was only one of the many creative writers, musicians, and social critics who graced the school with their presence.

The courses offered during the year that I was in attendance and the two subsequent years (1982–84, the tenth through twelfth years of the school's operation) fell into five general areas: (1) energy and ecology (exemplified by courses entitled "Nuclear Power or Renewable Energy," "Ecological Agriculture," and our wind power course); (2) culture and media politics (two courses entitled, respectively, "Theater and Video" and "Who Makes the News?"); (3) gender and child politics ("Women and Violence," "Children and Housing"); (4) labor and the labor market ("The Workplace of the Future," "Furniture-Making," "Unconscious Consumers: Is That Us?"); and (5) international politics (the "Nicaragua Brigade," "Hunger and Overconsumption"). A further illustration of the school's critical and egal-

Former students at Kolding sometimes return to do voluntary maintenance work around the school. These two women were among a group of ten who returned in August, 1986, after taking part in a spring course, to help renovate one of the houses (from a Kolding Højskole publication).

itarian ideology is its principle of "collective leadership." Although a principal is formally appointed from among the teaching staff to satisfy the formal demands of government bureaucracy, this office rotates and its possessor has none of the traditional powers of a folk high school principal. Decisions are made by the teachers as a group, in combination with the governing board *(bestyrelse)* made up of former teachers, students, and influential ideological supporters of the school's special purposes and ideals.

One of the central innovations made by Kolding Højskole is in its food politics *(kostpolitik)*, a series of arrangements in which the practical details of food preparation and consumption are beautifully integrated with the school's guiding philosophy. It is a central principle that there are no hired "servants" or "cooks" either to prepare the food for the course-takers or to clean up after them. The members of each course (such as those in our wind power group) are asked to function not only as a course grouping but as a work unit. The responsibility for these jobs is assumed in turn by each course group, an arrangement that gives a practical basis to the use of the term "workgroups." One staff member is hired as a specialist in this area, but his or her job is merely to introduce the members of each workgroup to the various machines in the kitchen and to make sure that they observe established kitchen procedures. The actual food preparation and cleanup is done by a workgroup composed of the students taking a particular course together with their teacher. (There is often a further rotation within the workgroup between those responsible for preparation and those responsible for cleanup, thus maximizing the free-time possibilities available for workgroup members).

This arrangement has the disadvantage of taking some time away from the course itself, because during the week or so of each month that the workgroup is responsible for the kitchen, the responsibility for preparing two meals a day (lunch and dinner) for somewhere between fifty and a hundred people can become heavy and time consuming. Breakfast is eaten not in the central dining room but in the individual houses, and it is prepared on the basis of a rotation system within each house. The advantages gained by this adherence to principle, and the consequent exposure of all at the school to the often onerous work of food preparation and cleanup, are felt to outweigh the disadvantage of reduced coursework time. For me it was a new and exhilarating experience to bake bread, and even though such communal food preparation was not new to me, I believe that doing this work gave all of us a certain grounding and connection to the earth. It was an invaluable part of the stay at the school in spite of our occasional complaints.

A second principle behind the food politics of Kolding Højskole is that the food served should be prepared with a full awareness of the existence of starvation in other places in the world. The raising of animals for meat production requires that vast acreages be devoted to raising grain to feed these animals. The school holds (in accordance with the work of international nutritionists such as Frances Moore Lappé[9]) that if we in the West would learn to eat less meat, we could free some of this acreage for the raising of vegetable crops. The grain from these crops could then be used to ameliorate the problem of world starvation. Consequently, meat or fish are eaten only once or twice a week; the emphasis is on the preparation of vegetarian meals.

A third principle is that the food served should be healthy and of high quality. In practical application, what this means is that the school serves a

Communal dining at Kolding (from a Kolding Højskole publication).

good selection of salads and raw vegetables in addition to more traditional Danish foods. The attempt is made to obtain as much as possible of the school's food from its own small, well-cultivated vegetable garden, or from ecologically responsible producers. Similarly, an attempt is made to obtain food free of chemical additives.

A fourth principle is that the kitchen is not locked; it is open at all times to any member of the school. For one thing, this allows food for breakfast and individual snacks to be taken from the central kitchen back to the houses. For another, it breaks down the split between students and staff, encouraging all to feel responsible for looking after the common food supply. Anyone can come in and open the large refrigerators, either for a specific purpose or just to see what is there. Groups often make use of this accessibility to prepare the pot of coffee or tea that will facilitate a more *hyggelig* discussion. In treating every person as a fully grown and responsible adult, the school encourages social maturity and gives all its members the experience of freedom and responsibility in this important area of life.

The wide range of critical course offerings, the system of decentralized collective housing, and the ecologically focused food politics are three examples of how the ideology at Kolding Højskole is realized in practice. The specific course one takes becomes the dominant focus of activity; one spends four mornings and four afternoons a week fully involved in its activities. The fifth morning is taken up with another aspect of the school's concern with democratic values, the weekly collective meeting (*fællesmøde*).

Found in all folk high schools, collective meetings are held for both individual houses and for the school as a whole. The house meetings took place at 8:30 on Tuesday evenings; the all-school meetings on Wednesday mornings at 8:30 after breakfast. Through this arrangement, issues that had come up in house meetings the night before could be brought to the attention of the entire school. It also made it easier to discuss some particular issue in all the houses in order to gain a schoolwide perspective on it in advance of the following morning's general meeting.

An attempt to give balance to the curriculum is provided by the choice of an independent elective *(valgfag)* taken one afternoon a week. Although there were offerings in music, art, and drama, the facilities for such activities at Kolding were rather limited in 1982. I decided to take an elective offering that was simply called "Renewable Energy," taught by Benny Christensen. Having once written a column on ecology for the Stanford Daily, I was sure that I was an expert on this subject and did not expect to learn very much. But Benny Christensen's course proved to be the high point of my stay at Kolding. Benny is a highly trained, professional civil engineer who publishes regularly in the Danish media on energy issues.[10] His expertise enables him to take even the most cleverly formulated arguments against renewable energy and reframe them to show how relevant data are being ignored or concealed. When the chairman of the Danish Electrical Utility System (ELSAM) was asked whether Denmark could survive without nuclear energy, he replied, "It's a question of dollars and cents. The Swedes have cheaper electricity than we do because they have nuclear power." Benny's response (complete with supporting statistical data) is worth citing because it shows how his agile mind works:

> We are going to hear that argument many times in the coming months, and it's no coincidence that the example of Sweden in particular is pulled out. In the *ELSAM Post* [the utility journal] of December, 1983, the price of electrical consumption to big consumers (i.e., industry) was compared in a number of European countries. *{After explaining the nature of the chart, he zeros in for the kill.}* It can be seen that Sweden and Finland, nations that both produce a large amount of electricity with the help of nuclear power, have lower prices than Denmark. And this is the basis for ELSAM's claims about the economic advantage of nuclear power. But on the other hand, the *other* European countries that have nuclear power (Belgium, Germany, England, France and Switzerland) have *higher* electricity prices than Denmark. This is true, for example, for countries like Belgium and France that have a higher percentage of electricity produced by nuclear power than Sweden or Finland. When ELSAM uses the Swedish example to maintain that nuclear power will give lower electricity prices, it would be possible with equal correctness —and using a greater number of countries as "evidence"—to claim that

nuclear power would give higher electricity prices. Naturally, neither of the arguments is worth anything, but these figures at least say something about the level of argument used by the electrical utilities.[11]

Benny's criticism of the conventional wisdom in the field of energy use was consistently knowledgeable, penetrating, and clear. He is one of the many longtime activists in the grass roots pressure group OOA (Organization for Information about Atomic Energy) that successfully opposed the introduction of nuclear power in Denmark. His approach to energy issues exemplifies the deep-rooted skepticism in the Danish character that made Denmark wait for two critical decades, until after the partial meltdown of the 1,000MW reactor at Chernobyl,[12] before making its national decision about nuclear power. Not only did Benny give us his own enlightened critique of Danish energy politics, but he introduced us to the work of Niels I. Meyer and others in Denmark whose work suggests the need for sustainable (rather than conventional) economic growth. Benny was also one of those active in running the Energy Office (*energikontor*) at Kolding Højskole, a local center for the dissemination of information relevant to individual, local, regional, and national energy planning. He once led a course whose members traveled with him to Germany to study the problems of nuclear power firsthand. Some of Benny's energy courses have resulted in articles

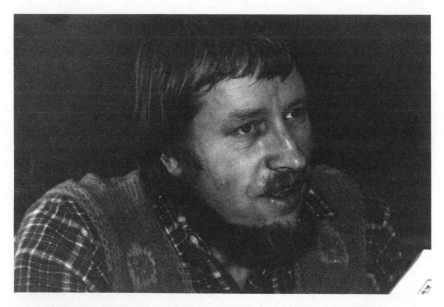

Benny Christensen, acting principal at Kolding, 1982–83 (photo: Axel Nielsen).

and even entire issues of *Tryk,* Kolding Højskole's regularly published magazine.

I return now to a description of some of the events that occurred during my stay in autumn 1983.

Social Life

I stayed in a state of shock for most of the first six weeks. The humilation of not being able to speak or understand more than an occasional word of Danish even after two years of study was bad enough. It meant that I became a useless appendage to the active life around me. In the collective house where Axel and I had succeeded in declaring squatter's rights, it meant that I remained at best a tolerated stranger who peered nearsightedly at everyone as if that would help him better understand what they were saying. In the wind power course, it meant that I could not participate meaningfully

A student preparing to work on the large windmill, nicknamed "Holger Danske 2."
An experimental prototype constructed in 1978, it was taken down and sold in 1985, but
much was learned along the way. By the time it came down not only were windmills a common
sight on the Danish landscape, but windmill parks were being planned, more than fifteen
hundred Danes were fully employed in the burgeoning windmill industry, and exports had
risen to more than a billion kroner a year. The pioneering era of which this windmill was a
part had ended, and it was no longer necessary to go to a folk high school to learn about them
(photo: Axel Nielsen).

in any of the group discussions. When it came time for the group to be divided up to do two-person projects, I learned to my consternation that the rest of the group had decided by unanimous consent—without informing me—that my work partner would be Dorthe, the determined journalist. When our group was responsible for meal preparation, communicating the nature of my responsibilities became an extra task for everyone.

I remember one time when Axel was trying to explain what a portion was (the Danes use the French pronunciation, por*tión*, accent on the second syllable). It took him fifteen minutes. "Portion, Steve, portion!!!" he kept shouting at me, pointing to the one he had already cut. When I finally understood that we were having all this trouble with a word that also existed in English, it was the occasion for an outburst of laughter. The struggle to understand the language was continuous. It took such precedence that I decided on the ambitious policy of refusing to speak English. "Sink or swim," I thought to myself. That was perfectly okay with all the other course-takers; they just went about their business, leaving the strange American to wonder what was happening. Yet even in the midst of more or less continuous confusion, I could see that there was a slow movement in the direction of understanding. And I began to see that I was not the only one who was to some degree estranged from what was going on. It turned out that there were subtle forms of social stratification that existed despite the best efforts and excellent principles of the school.

One problem was that the other course-takers all came from different backgrounds, were of different ages, had different values and ideals, and did not necessarily communicate well with each other. A second problem, which intensified the effect of the first, was the policy of beginning the different courses at different times. The net effect of this was that when a new course began, its arriving members came into a situation where social relations in the school were to a surprising extent already laid down in well-established groups and cliques. Needless to say, this was precisely the opposite of the school's intentions.[13] During the period of the wind energy course, another critical factor was that the social life of the entire school was totally dominated by a single course, the "Nicaragua Brigade," made up of about twenty-five adults and two children who were energetically preparing for a five-month stay in that Central American country. They had been at the school longer, had a higher morale and group spirit, and a deeper sense of mission about their project. The domination of the Nicaragua Brigade was so complete that even they could be heard complaining about it from time to time.

Once during a farewell party in our house for the people in one course who had finished and were leaving, Elisabeth, who came from a good-sized provincial town in central Jutland, expressed feelings of real disappointment. "Everything in the house between people was just surface experience," she said. "We didn't get to know each other, because everyone was too joking and casual all the time." She said it openly, to everyone present. I was surprised, because I had thought that the joking style gave a nice light touch to the house social life, even if I could only understand the smallest part of the humor. Kurt, a house resident who was a member of the Nicaragua Brigade, pointed out that the members of his group were so busy with their courses—which included practical carpentry and electrical work, arrangements, negotiations, and fund-raising—that when they got back to the house at night they didn't have the energy to do anything other than rest, recuperate, and joke around. They didn't have the strength or will to begin thinking about "deep relationships" with those outside their own course. Another factor I could see was that Kurt and at least several others in our house were native Copenhagen residents; the same type of unceasing banter that they were used to because they had grown up with it might strike a girl from central Jutland as superficial and evasive.

Nevertheless, this minor incident points to the split that existed at Kolding between what I came to call the Big Commune and the Little Commune. The idea of the whole high school existing as a single Big Commune did facilitate work arrangements, but it did not facilitate people's getting to know each other better. In our case, the Nicaragua group so completely dominated Kolding during this time that the members of the other groups felt invalidated, even shoved rudely into the background. This perception of mine was consistently confirmed by a good number of others there at the time, and I am quite confident that it is more than merely a visiting anthropologist's-eye view of things. The way things were, one came not into the open community that one had expected to find but into a community that was to some extent closed to outsiders (among whom were even new arrivals to the school!). I remember one collective meeting at which the point was firmly made that people were not getting to know those in other houses. The suggestion was made that on each Thursday a different residence would hold "open house" so that all others would feel free to come and visit with its inhabitants. The reply to this by experienced teachers present at the meeting was a sophisticated one. Yes, it was good that the point had been raised, but many of those complaining had only been at the school two weeks, and it is natural to get to know the people in your own house first. Nevertheless, I believe that these complaints addressed a real and underlying problem in the social life of the school.

The Big Commune, then, served as a framework for organizing work assignments, the Little Commune (by which I mean the separate courses, houses, and informal cliques) as a framework for pursuing social interaction and beginning personal relationships. And the Danish capacity for *hygge* being what it is, a great deal of social interaction was pursued and many personal relationships were begun! There were many parties held in each house, and everyone from any other house was always made to feel welcome. If you walked past and looked in, generally someone would smile and invite you to join them. The inclusion principle operated mainly in terms of the Little Commune, the Big Commune being perhaps something a little too abstract for it to reach in spite of everyone's best efforts.

How It Ended

After a rocky start, our wind energy course seemed at last to be going somewhere. Well, it is true that getting to class on time was sometimes a problem. Take breakfasts, for instance. The first few days we were up bright and smiling (well, not exactly, but at least all were up). Whoever was supposed to rise a few minutes early that day and get the food on the table did not fail to do so. Then, about five weeks later, I suddenly began to notice that breakfast preparation was no longer taken so seriously. We straggled in one by one, at the last moment. We ran out to class late, grabbing a few pieces of bread to chew on the way. Sometimes we didn't get there at all. Of course by this time a further fissioning of the house group had taken place into smaller cliques, interest groups, and couples. We were interested in what was happening in our courses, but we were even more interested in what would happen afterward, in the late afternoon and evenings when the coursework for the day was done. An entry in my field notebook for 20 November 1982 reads as follows:

> Finished six plus weeks at Kolding. It's odd, though I have several times been down to utter despair, I have developed a great fondness for the place and an unwillingness to leave it. Maybe it's the beautiful wooden tables in the *fællesrum,* so pleasant to put your feet up on. Maybe it's the casual atmosphere of the communal structure generated by the structure of the houses. Maybe it's the slanting wooden ceilings, or the other myriad details of its excellent construction. At any rate, I feel better, am beginning to understand a little of what's going on around me, and am enjoying life much more.

I had begun to relax and to feel at home. In retrospect, I am glad that I experienced that brief moment of contentment, for the remaining four weeks of the course were to prove much more difficult than I could have known at the time. I will try to tell the story of these final events briefly and succinctly, though even now when I think of them my blood pressure rises and my stomach begins to churn.

The initial competition in our wind energy course seemed at that point to have given way to a more cooperative attitude. Take my work placement with Dorthe. Our job was to improve the platform of one of the two small windmills, which required some welding and some carpentry. I am neither a carpenter nor a welder, but have done a little work both with wood and with steel, enough to see that Dorthe's determination to take control of our mutual task was not guided by any superior knowledge of the materials or the task at hand. The Little Herr General, I called her privately, and I deeply regretted that I had not been able to speak enough Danish to get out of having to be her work partner.

Our two-person job was to replace a flimsy wooden platform on the smaller windmill with one that had a welded frame. The platform had two sides. "Steve, take both sides down," the Little General ordered. "Steve, do this. Steve, do that." I tried to point out to her that if we took both sides down and welded them simultaneously, we would then have to break our backs when we got around to re-attaching them to the windmill. If, on the other hand, we took down *one side at a time,* welded it, finished the drilling, *and then put only that side up,* we would be able to use the unfinished side as a support while we attached the finished side. *Then* would be the logical time to take the second side down for the welding and drilling that it required. I could see that my attempts to explain to her in Danish why we had to do the job this way were not working. So I broke my cardinal rule. For the first time in many weeks I began speaking in English to her. I spoke quick, fluent, precise, annoyed English to her, explaining why we had to put the platform up this way and not that way in order to do a good job. I managed to communicate to her as nicely as I could that I thought she was behaving like an idiot. She was a little shocked. Slowly, the reasonableness of what I was saying became clear to her once she heard it in English. She saw that I wasn't the complete fool I often appeared to be. We wound up doing it my way, which really was the best way under the circumstances. And the other members of the group seemed to be making similar progress on their small projects and in their personal relationships.

Alas, it was all an illusion. Dorthe and I soon began quarreling again. Axel nearly got into a fight with Poul, the self-proclaimed expert machinist in our group. One or two of the younger men in the group had by this time more or less faded out of the picture, at least as far as I was concerned. Our teacher, whom I had initially thought to be the picture of detached, Taoist wisdom, proved unable or unwilling to take effective action: he watched helplessly as everything began to unravel. Poul's apparent technical dominance did not help us very much because he kept whatever knowledge he had to himself. Dorthe's attempt to dominate others in the group resulted in great antagonism toward her and from her on more than one occasion. We suggested a Friday afternoon talk to clear the air, but it never happened.

One of our key projects had been to hook up a small secondary generator to the large windmill so that it could generate electricity even at smaller wind velocities. Because we had been late getting started, we were rushing to complete this project in mid-December, the day before the final festival marking the end of all autumn courses and the departure of all course-takers. Finally, the generator was installed high up on the windmill, and the electrical coupling to the control room, with its complicated array of relays, bridges, capacitors, and connectors, was completed. The secondary generator was coupled to the electrical circuits in the control room, and we watched with great anticipation while the wind blew the wings of the large windmill faster and faster. Then it happened. There was a series of sudden conflagrations in the control room. Sparks flew, wires ignited, and all the components in the electrical system burned quickly to a sizzled black mess. Those of us who had been standing outside rushed into the control room. It was obvious from the very first glance or smell that this project was finished, a total and complete failure.

Humpty Dumpty had taken a great fall, and since we were all leaving the next day, there would be no one left to try to put Humpty Dumpty back together again. I had this fantasy all along that it was going to work out in spite of our problems, that we would leave the school with two functioning and improved windmills. Instead we left the school with no windmills working at all. Ironically, one of our few accomplishments was the improved platform that Dorthe and I had built. How could it have happened? Didn't our teacher know that either our components or the way we had been putting them together was fundamentally flawed? I remembered the death rattle in the relays when the system had first been hooked up. It didn't sound like an improved version; it sounded more like the Titanic going down. I had been too blind to notice it at the time. The late physicist Richard Feynman once wrote that "for a successful technology, reality must take precedence over public relations, because Nature cannot be fooled."14 We had asked Nature a question, but—taken in by our own public relations—we were shocked at the definitive, mocking answer we received: burned-out condensers and relays with an evil, sickening chemical smell, a mass of twisted wires all tattered and burned, the end to our efforts and hopes.

For me there was another lesson. I had thought the crisis of our group wouldn't touch me, that I was here as an anthropological observer, but in the end I was deeply touched, and distressed, and disturbed by the failure of our course to achieve any of its goals. In the end I was so furious with myself, with our teacher, and with everyone else in the course that I walked away into the darkness of a winter afternoon with my eyes full of tears. I was sickened by what I had seen and by everything that had led up to it. "You bloody fools," I raged to myself. "How could you have let it happen?" I was most furious at our teacher. He must have known. Didn't he see what we were doing? How could he not have intervened?

I had spent a fair number of hours freezing up there on both of the functioning windmills. I had cut my teeth in Danish, so to speak, reading descriptions of wind energy, and in the process I had learned something. Wind energy represents renewable energy, unlike the nonrenewable energy of the planet's limited oil reserves. Once oil is burned, it is gone, but the wind's energy is constantly being renewed by solar and global climatic patterns. Wind energy represents a viable form of energy with the potential to create many jobs, and it is happily compatible with just that kind of small-scale, local, decentralized development that the first folk high schools themselves represented. The people of those nations and regions that learn to use it will achieve a higher degree of independence from the oil-producing cartel and the insecurity of Middle East politics. Wind energy does not generate byproducts that contribute to ozone destruction, to the greenhouse effect, or to the danger of acid precipitation. Furthermore, its utilization (unlike nuclear energy) produces no dangerous long-term wastes that have to be stored in complete isolation from the biosphere for a quarter of a million years.[15]

In spite of these clear advantages, the governments of the world (including the Danish government) have removed many of its research subsidies. The deeply rooted cultural attitude that Jules Henry (1963) referred to as "technological drivenness" leads to an uncritical acceptance of large-scale mega-projects and a belief that such small-scale enterprises as windmills are suitable only for naive amateurs and idealists. "Those rotten, democratic little windmills, why nearly *anyone* can build them!" seems to be the condescending attitude of the official energy specialists, although they use the language of economics to support their policy decisions. In Denmark, which is endowed with many places that have high wind energy potential, the removal of industry subsidies seems to me to be particularly shortsighted.[16] I write these lines to make explicit my firm belief that wind power remains a practical technology of enormous importance in the world's energy future and to dissociate any discussion of wind power from the idiotic consequences of our poorly organized and pathetically ineffectual course at Kolding Højskole in the fall of 1982.

I remember how bitter I felt on that day. We called a crisis meeting for that evening. Poul the Great Hydraulic Expert showed up, but when the phone rang, he left to answer it. It was one of his girlfriends. "Just what I've been waiting for," he squealed with delight, and we didn't see him again. Axel was as depressed as I was. His cold turned into a flu, and he had to go to bed. Other survivors from our course were wandering around in various states of anomic confusion. I lost patience with it all and took another long walk down to the town of Kolding. When I got back, everyone from the entire school had gathered in one of the houses. I walked past the crowded scene to our house, where I was quickly grabbed by a housemate and escorted back to where everyone was. Lars, the apprentice plumber from our course, was having a birthday party. He was surrounded by a mob of drinking, happy people. The afternoon's meal preparation had fallen through. Even the entertainment planned for the evening had fallen through. But everyone was happy just the same. There were candles, children, dancing, laughing, drinking, music. Everybody was happily kissing and embracing each other on the last night of the session.

It was all too much for me. I found my mood slowly changing to match that of the party and woke up to find that I had at last really arrived in Denmark. There I was, surrounded by a group of happy, laughing people, all the failures and misunderstandings and bitterness forgotten. There was Axel, and Morton, and Susanna, and Henrik, and Lars, and Jan, and Dorthe, and Ole, and Connie, and half a dozen others whom I had come to know in the months that had passed. Soon I had a beer or two and was dancing and laughing along with the rest of them.

From the description I have given of my stay at Kolding, some readers may be tempted to conclude that a folk high school is not really an educational institution but a state-supported adult camp, a place where people make friends and have fun. Yet several important facts suggest the need for a more complex reading of these events. First, keep in mind that a series of earlier wind energy courses not only built several functioning windmills out of scrap material but succeeded in coupling them to the school's electrical energy supply. Second, many other courses at Kolding were highly successful in accomplishing their project goals. The Nicaragua Brigade, for instance, went on to complete numerous construction projects during its five-month stay in Central America. The finely crafted wooden furniture that stood in all the houses had been built by previous course-takers in the school's carpentry workshop. These things must be remembered so that the failure of our one course does not lead to an unbalanced evaluation either of Kolding in particular or folk high schools in general.

The next day I took the train back to Copenhagen, but this time I was not alone. I traveled together with Axel, and Susanna, and Lars. It was good to have their help with my giant suitcase, backpack, guitar, and typewriter, and it was even better to have their friendly company. Long before we reached Copenhagen, we had exchanged addresses and telephone numbers, and the goodbyes we said to each other when we parted were not at all sad. It seemed more like a beginning than an end.

II. SILKEBORG HØJSKOLE: THE EXISTENTIAL NECESSITY

Mixed Feelings, Second Thoughts

While at Kolding, I chose Silkeborg Højskole in central Jutland for my second folk high school stay. One factor behind this choice was the school's connection with the liberal wing of the Danish Lutheran Church. It had been explained to me on a visit to Silkeborg that religion was one of the school's strong course areas but that there was no mandatory attendance at any religious services and no feeling that prospective students would be stigmatized if they didn't accept the kind of religion the school offered as part of its curriculum. In short, the school had a thoroughly Grundtvigian approach to religion. It was in a section of the country renowned for its natural beauty, a place where gently rolling hills alternated with numerous lakes and ponds. One day in mid-January I took the same journey from Copenhagen to Jutland, only this time the train turned north after passing through the town of Fredericia and continued northward. After one change of trains, I reached the town of Silkeborg. I didn't know it then, but I was to get off to an equally rocky start at Silkeborg, for completely different reasons.

My first impressions were positive. Everybody seemed so friendly. It was a younger crowd than Kolding; the median age was closer to nineteen than twenty-six. My command of the language had improved, which made everything easier. On our first night we met together and were given a welcome to the high school by Bent Martinsen, the principal. It was a fiery speech, all about good and evil being in each of us and our need to strive for wholeness and to find something in which we can believe. He meant every word of it; you could almost hear the rafters rattle as he spoke to us. He emphasized that the rules would be strictly enforced. A reprimand, then a warning, but a third offense in lateness or class absence and you would be asked to leave the school. No ifs, ands, or buts. Just one offense would be sufficient in the area of illicit substances. He explained that we would meet together every morning for group singing. It was so different from Kolding. "Hey," I thought to myself, "this is great. This is a real folk high school." As in Kolding I had taken a single room, and I went back there happily to get my things in order.

My problems began the next morning, when I was rudely awakened out of a deep sleep by a roaring buzzer that sounded like an antiaircraft siren. It played for what seemed like endless minutes over the school's intercom. True, no student would ever be able to sleep through such a noise, but was this really necessary? Was this what I had to look forward to every morning? My sense of unease began to intensify after I had eaten two meals, breakfast and lunch, in the school's dining room. The food was nowhere near as good as it had been at Kolding, and there was a very different atmosphere connected with its serving. *This* kitchen was completely off-limits. I was suddenly overcome by all the new faces, and the new situation, and the need to go through all the introductions and chats and casual small talk again. It got worse in the afternoon, and by the next day I was absolutely miserable. I knew that Axel, and Susanna, and Lars, and Morton, and some of the others I knew at Kolding the previous term had returned to the school for the winter term to take different courses. I decided to call them, and after we exchanged happy greetings on the phone, they told me that there was a big party planned for the next night. As soon as I heard this, I decided that I would have to travel there (some two hours away by train) for that party to see my friends.

So, when the next day came, I took the afternoon train down to Kolding. I was not disappointed. When I went to the house where my friends had moved in as a group, I was glad to see that there was even a big sign on the door welcoming me. The sign announced that they were working in the kitchen. I greeted them happily and joined in cutting cabbages for the meal. It turned out to be a fantastic dinner in the best Kolding Højskole style. Everyone came in costume. There was a group dressed as Maoists, rising periodically to read from their little red books. Another group came as clergymen, dressed in black. I remember that Børge, the carpenter, who was one of the original teachers at Kolding, came dressed as a priest. Although I knew him to be a good Communist, he more than any of the others really succeeded in looking like a priest, with his sharp pointed beard and his finger stabbing the air to make points. It was a source of great merriment.

The general theme of the evening was a mocking, ribald look at capitalism and Danish middle-class values (much fun was also poked at doctrinaire Maoist ideology). Afterward, a local band played the best music I ever heard at a Kolding Højskole party. They played on and on; there was continuous dancing. Everyone felt good. People greeted me, coming up and saying, "It's great to see you! How's the other high school?" They were expecting me to say "fantastic," but the response I found myself giving was "not so good." They were quite surprised. "Well, are you thinking of coming back here?" they asked. The thought hadn't even occurred to me. I found myself saying, "I'm not sure—tomorrow I'll think about that."

The next day was agony, hideous agony, all day long. Breakfast wasn't too bad. I had gotten to bed at two, rather earlier than most people. When I woke up I was sleeping in an empty room, and when I opened the door and stepped outside to look for the others, the house was empty. Everyone had gone off, presumably to their courses. I didn't know what to do, so I decided to go for a walk through the town of Kolding. I spent the morning and most of the afternoon doing just that, admiring the town and thinking how nice it would be to come back here to high school with all my friends. But I couldn't make a decision. The tension in me mounted until I was shaking like a leaf. Every time I decided to stay in Kolding, the thought of all I would be missing in Silkeborg ran through my mind. But every time I decided to go back to Silkeborg, I thought of the friends I would miss, the beautiful wooden tables, the houses, the good food. I returned to Kolding at about four in the afternoon, still undecided.

I went to the dining room and saw Morton. I grabbed him and said, "Please talk to me." I was able to get him temporarily relieved from kitchen duty. We went back to his room, where he gave me a severe lecture. I sat in his room all the while, crying. "I think this is what happened," he said. "You went to a bad high school, one with terrible food, where you can't even make a cup of coffee when you want to. I think you should come here, where all your friends are, and where you want to be." "Keep talking, Morton," I told him. In the end he convinced me. I got in even deeper, because when I decided to stay at Kolding we had to find a course for me. The theater course was the only one open. The next morning I announced my intention to join this course if they would accept me. I told my story, and all the members of the class voted "yes." The instructor was very sympathetic. There were no problems! I was free to come back to Kolding; all I had to do was go back to Silkeborg and pick up my baggage. I joined the theater course that day, and it was wonderful (it was only the third or fourth day of class). The instructor was very professional. We did warming-up exercises, and the class discussed two pieces of Bertolt Brecht about villages that went to war. I felt completely convinced. I had made the right decision. It only remained now to return to Silkeborg and pick up my baggage.

I was very tired at the end of that day. One of the children in the house helped me fix up my new room. I woke up having overslept because the batteries failed to work in the alarm clock I had borrowed. I was anxious to get to class on time. I tried to get the other people in the house up, but they were either nowhere to be seen or in no manner to be roused from their beds. I came to the theater class five minutes late. Half the house was missing from class. The instructor was angry and frustrated. Here he had taken the time and trouble to put together such an excellent course, and only half the group showed up in time. What was wrong with them? I began to remember the strictness that Bent Martinsen at Silkeborg had emphasized just a few days ago. And suddenly, things were no longer going well for me at Kolding. By lunchtime I felt so bad that I couldn't even go to eat in the dining room. I packed my things, even though I still hadn't clearly made up my mind, and I waited for Connie, the only one to whom I had confessed my new misgivings. How ironic. Only the day before Morton and Connie had offered to come up to Silkeborg and help me bring my baggage down to Kolding. We walked through the forest down to the station at Kolding. It was then that I told her that I had decided to return to Silkeborg. It was the first time that I knew it myself. I asked her to tell the others, and then I took the train back to Silkeborg knowing, at least, that this time I had really burned my bridges behind me. In the most existential sense, I had made a choice. Whether I liked it or not, I was going to have to find out what Silkeborg Højskole was all about.

Silkeborg Højskole.

Ideology and Philosophy of the School

At a formal level, the ideology of Silkeborg Højskole differs greatly from that of Kolding. The curriculum is also quite different. During my session in 1983, the four-month period was divided into two equal portions (Period A and Period B: the coursework requirement was 24 hours per week). The general subjects (*fællesfag*), intended to facilitate a better understanding of human life and society, formed the cornerstone of the curriculum. The courses in this category fell into three categories: literature, social studies/history (*samfundsfag/historie*), and the study of Christianity (*kristendomskunskab*). A student was required to choose one of the many course offerings in the study of Christianity during either Period A or Period B; the same student was required to take a course in either social studies/history or literature during the alternate period.

In addition to these required areas, students could choose electives from the following five areas: (1) Leadership subjects (*lederfag*), intended to aid students in becoming leaders or counselors. Parents, teachers, youth workers, and athletic coaches are examples of those social roles where leadership training is felt to be of great benefit. Courses in this category included psychology, pedagogy (which does not sound so stuffy in Danish), sociology, religion instruction, and the psychology of religion. (2) Creative subjects, including drama, pictorial arts (drawing, graphics, painting, and art orientation), weaving, batik, ceramics, photography, and music (choir, advanced choir, music theory, group musical activity, individual instruction in guitar, flute, piano, trumpet, etc.). (3) Athletic subjects, including ballplaying (volleyball, soccer, basketball, handball, and badminton), swimming, athletic gymnastics (with conventional gymnastics equipment), and rhythmic gymnastics (movement to music). (4) Self-sufficiency (*selvforsyning*), including ecological agriculture, animal husbandry, and clothing production. (5) Outdoor life (*friluftsliv*), including sailing, canoeing, and hiking. In addition there was a one-week study trip abroad, required of all students. During my stay a student could choose between Norway, Sweden, England, Holland, and Poland. Offerings in film and English language instruction rounded out the curriculum.

An individual was required to take courses in all four primary areas during the four-month stay at the school. One advantage of this curriculum in comparison to that at Kolding is that it makes it possible for an individual student (*called* a student at Silkeborg, not a "course-taker") to encounter a diverse sample of course offerings rather than spending all (or nearly all) of one's time on a single course.[17] Another is that it provides a greater strength in key areas, such as music, art, and outdoor life, where the possibilities at

Music and choir practice. Silkeborg has a tradition of excellence in music instruction (photo: Silkeborg Højskole).

Volleyball game in progress (photo: Silkeborg Højskole).

Kolding were limited. With respect to the outdoor life, the emphasis on experiencing the natural beauty of the surrounding area is a natural consequence of the school's relationship to FDF and FPF, two of the Danish scouting organizations for young people. There is of course the additional question of religion and instruction in Christianity: it is in this area where the split between the two schools was probably the sharpest. But in spite of these areas of contrast, there was a remarkable underlying continuity in their political perspectives. Both were strongly critical of personal materialism and the ethics of consumption in Denmark and around the world. Both were painfully conscious of the worldwide conflicts that have resulted in mass migrations, deculturation, and starvation in our time. They sought to make students confront social and economic inequality, racism and discrimination, and the painful reality of global environmental destruction. And they criticized American as well as Soviet foreign policies in the nuclear age.

Indeed, exactly a year after my stay at Silkeborg, I received a Christmas card from Terkel, one of its teachers, showing a photo of a bent and broken guided missile with both American and Soviet signatures. The missile had an American flag and "USAF" clearly written across its fuselage, but it was decorated by the Soviet flag and military lettering as well. Why was the fuselage cracked? Had the Danish students just vented their hostilities and smashed the thing? No, the truth was more subtle than that. On a Theme

Terkel's Christmas greeting, with its symbolism of peace (see discussion in text).

Day in the beginning of December, the subject chosen had been "Peace."[18] The joint US-USSR missile had been constructed by students as part of that day's activity. During a subsequent morning gathering (*morgensamling*), when the cardboard guided missile was moved, it was decided to hang on it some white peace doves and joint "US-USSR hearts" that students had made as well. The moment this was done, the center of the missile had collapsed and twisted in upon itself. This unusual sight was then made into a Christmas card, with the written message, "Merry Christmas," in large letters under the picture of the inoperative missile. As Terkel explained in his card, "You can surely understand the symbolism." The deep concern with peace and greater international understanding was a bond uniting Kolding and Silkeborg in spite of their ideological differences. For all the fun that the people at Kolding were wont to poke at organized religion, the equal and overriding concern with peace issues at the two schools meant that the spirit of instruction found in them was not as different as one might otherwise be led to believe.

I took a number of excellent courses at Silkeborg. For a social studies course, I took one from Leif Skipper entitled "How Does Denmark Function?" In this course I came for the first time to grasp something of the complicated coalition-formation behind the Danish political system, including the special role of the Radical Left party that is neither radical nor left. For a leadership course, I took from Leif Rasmussen "What Should We Be Socialized For?" (*Hvad skal vi opdrage til?*) In this course we contrasted behaviorist, Christian existentialist, and transpersonal perspectives on human nature. I took from Erik a course called "Crisis in the Middle East," (he quickly identified my special area of competence and used it to encourage informed and lively class discussion when the treatment turned to Israel and the kibbutz). I took from Vibeke "Rhythmic Gymnastics," where I ran around in circles to music until I thought my heart would give out. I even allowed myself to become the star of a dramatic production, in which I played the character of Ezekiel, a Nigerian student in Denmark who faces racism and ridicule while trying to learn the Danish language. For my study trip abroad, I chose Norway, and the winter week I spent with other students from Silkeborg at Haugtun, a rural retreat center near Lillehammer, has since led to five return trips and a deepening personal identification with this northern Scandinavian land.

Faced with no way out of taking a religion course, I chose one entitled "Human Life and Christianity." It was taught by Bent Martinsen, the principal. Bent had just returned from a six-month sabbatical in England, where he had retraced Grundtvig's steps to Trinity College in Cambridge. Bent, like many high school principals, is a deeply knowledgeable Grundtvig scholar. Like Grundtvig he had a beard, although it wasn't yet as long, white, or Whitmanesque as Grundtvig's had been. And like Grundtvig, he had a ferocious intensity that both attracted and inspired fear in his onlookers. Even in our small class of half a dozen students, his intensity impressed us. Sometimes it even overpowered us.

In the first class session we discussed the question: how can one keep from being crushed in modern society if one has no religion? "I think it's important that we learn to see a wholeness in our lives, and not just a bunch of separate pieces," he told us. If we don't have any religious faith, how can we survive the disintegrating, anomic effects of modern industrial society? The second session he asked us, "How do we usually relate to suffering?" And then he told us: we are afraid of it, we think of it as something negative, and we try to avoid it. He suggested that there was another way, that we could learn from our suffering. In later sessions we discussed the gospel of St. Matthew and tried to relate it to contemporary non-violence, to the preaching and actions of Martin Luther King. We learned to distinguish between passive and active non-violence: "You will not be able to force us to be brutal and dehumanized, even if you yourselves behave in that way toward us." We discussed Paul's letter to the Romans. We debated the true nature of peace. We criticized the empty consumerism of modern industrial societies and the spiritual supermarket mentality that discourages any deep form of commitment.

We listened raptly to his lectures. They usually started out as a series of questions, and then when none of us could answer any of them, gradually turned into a monologue. I remember once looking around after a lengthy monologue by Bent. The class seemed a little awed. There was a long and respectful silence. Only the knitting continued busily, uninterrupted. "Are there any others who want to say anything about this?" he would ask, and it would be followed by a deafening quiet. On the last day he could not contain himself. "Why didn't some of you say anything?" he remonstrated with us in a hurt and angry tone of voice. "Was it that you weren't interested?" We sat there for a minute like so many silent lumps of clay, and then one girl spoke well for the class when she said, "There are so many things going on, you say so much at one time, that it's hard for us to formulate even a sentence, anything, to say back." To this one of the boys added, "It's not necessarily negative when people are not saying anything. There's a lot happening, it takes time to digest your words and think about them." I could see from Bent's face that he wanted to believe this but still had his doubts.

I was fortunate enough to have an extended interview with him in which he gave eloquent expression to the ideology and philosophy of

Silkeborg Højskole. Although the following citation from this taped interview cannot do full justice to his remarks, it gives at least some impression of their content and direction:

> The world is something more than that which can be weighed or measured or described. The world is more than that, there are other dimensions in life that affect us, that mean something to us. We must have another perspective than the narrow scientific one. You can say it in another way, you can say that the school here should be the bearer of a poetic perspective. We have to go into it, go into life and take hold of it. But there is something bigger than us in life. That is the dimension which gives a place for God, or the transcendent, whatever one will call it. People should have a possibility to relate here to that perspective. Not forced. They shouldn't be forced. But if there are some who want to meet it? They can come, but they do not have to. There isn't to be any forcing. You can find some of the religious high schools so narrow that they force their students. Every day of the week they are required to meet for a morning song, for prayer and preaching. But I think this is wrong. One can only relate freely to such a deep spiritual question. Either it means something to you or it doesn't. You can't say to people, "Now this here is going to mean something to you." You just can't do that. . . . I love my work here. It's a colossal challenge, and you have to say that it's a privilege to be allowed to use your daily life to debate essential questions with young people, both those having to do with society and with human character.

Social Life

Unlike the *hyggelig* and decentralized houses at Kolding, Silkeborg Højskole consisted of a single, large, L-shaped concrete structure. It contained the classrooms, the bedrooms, the library, the gymnasium, the kitchen, and the dining room. There was a long series of straight hallways with right angles and no interesting curves or breaks in the architectural monotony. You could spend days in there running around from place to place, and not get out unless you made a point of doing so. It probably weighed more heavily on me than it did on most of the others, first because they were younger, and second because they had nothing to compare it with. Still, it suggested in some ways a total institution, and this fact was not lost on the students. I can remember the day I was sitting at the dinner table, and Martin, looking out the window, remarked, "If we ever have a war, I bet they'll use this place as a prison." And Kirsten, looking up, joined in: "It's so ugly. Ugly, ugly, ugly! How could they build such an ugly building in such a beautiful place?"

What weighed most heavily on me during the time at Silkeborg, however, was the kitchen and meal policies. The woman in charge of the kitchen had fixed and traditional ideas about what food should be served and how to serve it. Cold and unappetizing bread was always served for breakfast, in the hopes that someone would eat it. Ice cold to the touch, it was. True, there were oat flakes and boiled eggs, but you couldn't get either skim or lowfat milk at any of the meals. It was not breakfast I minded most, however; it was the other two meals. The dining room doors opened at twelve sharp for lunch. At 12:06, the tiny plate or two of potatoes put out for a hundred people would be gone. "Are there any more potatoes?" I ask her. "No, there aren't today," she smiles with phony warmth. "Try tomorrow." My stomach groans and I have beatific visions of what the tables at Kolding used to look like. It didn't take long before there was a line at the door of the dining room by 11:55. There would be friendly jostling, until the bell rang at 12:00 and the door opened. Once that door opened, there was a race, an honest to goodness race, past all the dining tables to those food counters with the tiny plates waiting for us. The first four people would finish a plate, and then there would be what seemed like an hour's wait while the plate was taken back into the kitchen and refilled. Back and forth, back and forth, the kitchen workers scurried like busy ants to bring us the refills on the same small plates. This procedure further pressurized eating in a not very subtle way.

Neither in kind, quantity, nor access did the food policy of the school agree with me. I was sick several times during my four-month stay. I lost twelve pounds, even while some of the Danish students, who were perhaps more used to the heavy and traditional foods served, gained weight. But even though only the vegetarians among the Danes suffered as I did, there was a widespread dissatisfaction with the food policy. Several times we brought our complaints to the collective meeting. Jakob stood up once with a reasonable and well-thought-out suggestion that the students help with the food planning. But the woman in charge of the kitchen dismissed the idea out of hand: "When they do that, too often it's just because they want to have their favorite meals served to them." She sounded like an estate owner talking about unruly tenant farmers. We decided to put all our effort into getting skim milk, and we did eventually succeed in this. At first it was put out in a corner, but before the end of our stay its use had become much more widespread among the students. I guess there's no stopping an idea whose time has come.

But in spite of the concrete building and the restrictive food policies, the students at Silkeborg created for themselves the same *hyggelig* social life that I had seen at Kolding. They were insatiable socializers who would throw a party at the drop of a hat. It would begin with two or three people sitting in a room. The doors would be left open, and as people walked by they would be invited to come in. The opportunity to be social was irresistible. First the chairs, then the beds, and even the floors would become filled with people as the inclusion principle was allowed to operate in an atmosphere virtually free of constraints. In a room two doors down the hall from mine, one of the female residents kept asking the boys at such gatherings if any of them wanted to learn how to knit. Finally, one expressed an interest. They were married a week after the last day of our session.

Svend has become a special friend. He is a tall, slim, and handsome young man who has just graduated from the *gymnasium*. Next year he will begin to study engineering at the University in Aalborg. Svend is a ladies' man. I take the train from Silkeborg down to Tønder in south Jutland. It leaves at 2:49 in the afternoon. I come ten minutes early. Svend comes exactly at 2:49, just managing to squeeze through the train doors a few seconds before they close. He meets me in the car; later we switch in Skanderborg. He is looking for his girlfriend and can't find her. Maybe she has taken the wrong train. I tease him. "It's nothing to grin at!" he says to me seriously. The recognized technician of our group, Svend has assembled the custom-built stereo speakers in his room all by himself. He has decided that I should listen to Danish music and makes some superb tapes for me. He does the lighting for the plays and the recording as well. "Dolby or without Dolby?" I hear him talking to himself out loud one time. Finally he decides without. Another time a number of us have gone out to a party and suddenly we find there are no candles. Everyone's looking for candles. "I've got candles," Svend announces calmly and reaches into his pocket for them.

So many parties. Someone says: "Did Flemming come?" Someone else: "No, I said it was a *good* trip." Laughter. When someone had a birthday, there would be a special birthday table set up for breakfast, with Danish flags, flowers, and candles. The usual friendly rivalry between those from different parts of the country. "Copenhagen? That's Denmark's name!" says Alan. A boy from Jutland holds his nose. Parties, parties, and more parties. Cigarettes and beer. Smoky rooms. Waiting for class to end so life can begin.

From the teachers' point of view, the students' emphasis on good times can come to be a source of frustration:

> Vibeke: [complaining] But that's the problem today, it shouldn't only be *hyggeligt*. There's really too much *hygge*.
> Terkel: [unhappily] It leads to a situation in which we high school teachers are like some prop necessary so that the students can have a good time. If we weren't here and giving instruction, then it wouldn't be possible for them to go out and *hygge* themselves.

Vibeke: [with laughter] Life begins after 4:15!

Terkel: We are absolutely necessary so that one can get the best *hygge* possible. And that's a little sad, isn't it? [he chuckles at the thought][19]

The Teachers' Point of View

My distinct impression is that another difference between Silkeborg and Kolding Højskole was in their teaching staff and its relation to the school. At Kolding, the teachers were in many cases younger; they were single and more transient. There seemed to be a high burnout factor; only one of the original founders remained after ten years. From what I could tell, it was not uncommon to arrive, stay at the school for a year or two, and then depart. The advantage to this pattern was a continual flow of new faces, some of whom were extraordinarily competent and talented. The drawback, however, was the absence of a settled, long-term group of committed teachers. At Silkeborg, in contrast, there was precisely such a core of experienced teachers, settled in the area with their families and committed to staying there.

Terkel, who had been at Silkeborg for fifteen years when we spoke, expressed his feeling for the area in this way: "Where I come from in North Sjælland we have a great deal of natural beauty, but here it's even nicer. You don't have to drive long here before you're out into the heath, or the small forests, and the lakes. I won't leave here by choice. It could be that I will find some other work, even though I'm glad to be a folk high school teacher, but I hope to be living here to my days' end." Vibeke, who comes from North Jutland, remembers that she once told her mother on a childhood outing that she would live in Ry, a town only a few kilometers from Silkeborg. Eric and Leif, two other veteran teachers whom I came to know well, both live with their families on farms that they manage to work in addition to holding full-time positions at Silkeborg. Their wives are also fully employed, Erik's as an elementary school teacher, Leif's as a nurse. It is a busy and challenging life, the life of a folk high school teacher.

There is no specific course of study that prepares one to be a folk high school teacher. Nor is there an official state credential required for those who teach in these schools. One must keep in mind the extraordinary diversity demanded of today's folk high school teachers. Terkel, a specialist in athletics, has taught volleyball, gymnastics, swimming, and orienteering. Yet among the fields he has also taught are Christianity, Danish literature, written Danish, club leadership, anatomy, and physiology. Erik teaches not only all of the courses related to self-sufficiency (biodynamic agriculture, animal husbandry, fence building, etc.) but in addition ceramics, art, art

Erik Lindebjerg in the ceramics workshop (photo: Silkeborg Højskole).

appreciation, Danish literature, ecology, crisis in the Middle East, and a special course in drawing for the blind. No single course of study could prepare an individual for all those specializations. A folk high school teacher must be flexible, talented, and ambitious enough to be able to cover all of these areas when necessary, as well as sensitive enough to divine the direction in which changing demands are heading.

The days when a principal could hire and fire teachers at will are gone. What typically happens today is that an informal consensus develops among the principal and faculty in making these decisions. Although a principal will usually try to ensure the "advise and consent" role of the faculty in particular decisions, this is not universal. It is unquestionably best for a school, however, if the principal and the faculty maintain a harmonious and collegial relationship. In this connection, the development of skills in diverse teaching areas serves not only students but the teachers themselves, for the field of potential students for which more than a hundred folk high schools must compete is large but limited. It is a difficult and changing market. A common reason for a teacher's being "let go" these days is that the school is attracting fewer students. If a teacher comes to have a steady pattern of declining enrollment in his primary classes, his continued employment may be endangered. Given such a situation, there is a greater probability that the teacher who has developed the appropriate secondary areas of instruction will remain employed.

One principal from a nearby school told me with sadness of having to let go a teacher whose special field was ecology. His interpretation of the pattern of declining enrollment in this area was that many students have deep-rooted fears and do not want to hear things that may disturb them. They come to the school in a sense to escape harsh reality, not to encounter it. When I spoke with Erik recently, he affirmed that he no longer teaches self-sufficiency courses because the student demand isn't there anymore. But Erik has developed so many other skills that the loss of this one area isn't crucial. His technical skills, for instance, include interior design; the implementation of his detailed plans to remodel the main student area resulted in both a more functional and more attractive use of the available space.

Regardless of how many specializations they possess, folk high school teachers face some unique challenges. The tendency to treat teachers as necessary window dressing whose daily ministrations must be tolerated in order to obtain good *hygge* has already been mentioned. A second challenge is that many students bring with them a negative perception of schools and schooling. Whether this attitude has resulted from ten to twelve years of sitting in uninteresting classrooms or a personal history of having dropped out at the seventh-grade level a decade ago, the result can be the same: a teacher appears as an authority figure who is neither to be listened to nor trusted. With such students there is a communication barrier a teacher must break through to form a relationship with them.

A third challenge comes from having to teach in a single class those from very different educational backgrounds. It is not at all unusual to teach a class on crisis in the Middle East or on foreign policy to a mixed group of university students and seventh-grade dropouts, to a group that ranges from bright-eyed young graduates of a rural *gymnasium* to unemployed thirty-year-olds from a down-and-out section of Copenhagen. Some, because of their former education, find it easy to read and formulate ideas. For others this is difficult if not impossible; exchanging serious ideas may be something they have rarely, if ever, done. The classroom is initially a foreign land in their eyes.

A fourth challenge comes from having to confront the mood of the students in this decade. "In the 70s they were all ideological, and they knew everything," remarked a former principal. "In the 80s it's better because they *don't* know, they're even more confused. You can work with them." Terkel and Vibeke were not as optimistic. When I asked them to talk about the operation of the collective meeting during my stay at Silkeborg, they replied as follows:

> Terkel: I think it's been unusually tame. There hasn't been much life in it. There was much more debate and discussion in other groups.
> Vibeke: I think there's been a change; the students who come today are not as politically conscious as before. If one is going to characterize them, then I'd call them the "I" generation, the culture of narcissism. The concern is all with their own experience, their own development. It is a generation that to a very large extent thinks, how do I get my desires and my needs met. It's not very political; there aren't many political discussions. It was just the First of May, and there wasn't even one student in the class I had who said anything about it. This is the first time that's happened.
> Terkel: We have had groups who, when we were going on a trip at that time, they had a big problem because they thought they should be going to the First of May demonstration. But this year there weren't any like that.[20]

A fourth challenge, then, is how to deal with a generation that tends to be depoliticized, careerist, and anomic, a generation for whom the folk high school stay may be little more than another stab in the darkness. The Danish author Finn Abrahamowitz, who teaches at a folk high school, has given a sensitive portrait of the kind of young person one is likely to meet at these schools today:

> —You'll see, you'll be pleased with it, said the woman. They overtook a tractor pulling a cart filled with straw.
> —At least you get out of having a social worker on your butt all the time.
> —That's also one of the advantages. . . .
> He had the job ready, for when he came home from the high school. That was great. And maybe then he would also come home with a girl. Niels had found his girl friend at the high school. They all fall in love, he had said. You'll get a lot of action. But he wasn't so sure of that. He was always blocked at the last moment. There wasn't much to find in Skjern, but it wasn't just because of that. But maybe it was that it always went better when he got to know them slowly. As a soldier he had had Inge. She had gone. He wasn't so handsome, or anything like that. He always became weird and couldn't think of anything to say. The others were better at it. It goes easier when you're in a group. Then you can just grin at what the others are saying. They were also older and more experienced. The hell with it. Now he would take a look, and see if there was anyone at all he was interested in. And of course there were

the classes and all that. And parties. You had to be able to dance. Dancing, that wasn't him. But maybe there would be someone who played sports. There was gymnastics and handball and volleyball and table tennis. And on Wednesday you could go over to a center and swim. He sat and dreamt and forgot the way. It was here he had to turn.[21]

"At least you get out of having a social worker on your butt all the time." It is an extraordinary commentary on the difference between older and newer generations of folk high school students. A final challenge of the folk high school teacher is that there is no extrinsic reward that can be held over the students' heads during their stay. Although class attendance is mandatory, students receive no grades, write no papers, and take no examinations during their course of study. They receive no diplomas or transcripts when they graduate, merely a brief confirmation that they have attended a particular session. I am reminded of what an American I met at Askov told me about his experience during the winter course of 1948. He came from a Danish-American family, and after serving as a sailor in the Second World War he decided to return to Denmark with a friend to attend Askov. When the term was nearly over, he went to Arnfred, the principal, and asked if he and his friend could have a diploma to take back with them to America. The response to this request was very revealing: "Arnfred looked at me, and he scratched his head, and he thought a while, and he said, 'No, I'm sorry but we don't give diplomas in these schools. Whatever you have learned here you can take away in your head, or in your heart perhaps, but not on a piece of paper.'"[22]

The folk high school is an experiment in freedom, and as such it must allow the student the right to fail, to misuse that freedom if that is what happens. Otherwise the freedom was not real. Besides, who is to say what failure is in such a context? Perhaps at that point in life what this student needs is a period of "cultural decompression" in which all forms of subject learning are secondary to a positive social experience in a secure and peaceful environment.[23] On the other hand, who is to say what seeds have been planted at the time unbeknownst even to the student, seeds that will mature in a year, in two years, or in ten? What new role models have been taken that will influence the student's life in a positive way after he or she leaves the school? What is the long-term, unquantifiable value to a democratic society of supporting an institution in which members of all sectors and classes of that society can meet peacefully and positively for a period in their lives to explore their own possibilities, unencumbered by the competitive struggle for survival? What invisible and intangible benefits in social cooperation are encouraged by the existence of such schools? I cannot give definitive answers to such questions, but remembering the results of the

Estes study, I am tempted to conjecture that the development of the folk high school is a factor that has played a major role in the peacefulness and high level of social cooperation that have characterized the Danish path to modernization.

Is there any connection in this respect between the folk high schools of today and those of the past? In spite of the considerable differences between the folk high schools of the last century and those of today, they are linked by a common thread. That thread is the teaching of confidence both in oneself and one's people. The folk high schools of the nineteenth century taught the children of farmers that history had given them a mission. It also inspired them with a faith that they had the ability and talent necessary to carry that mission out successfully. The folk high schools of today have what looks at first like a different role, for they must deal with a diverse and unpredictable clientele in a period characterized by retrenchment, doubts, and diminishing expectations. To teach and communicate faith will not be an easy task in today's crisis-dominated, postmodern society. But it remains the same task, the deepest and most essential assignment of the folk high school teacher.

How It Ended the Second Time

It happened again. I had sat through another folk high school session and learned to love and care for another group of people. I had survived the crazy buzzer in the morning, and the food, and the race to the food, and the concrete halls, and the noise, and the parties every night until four. It had been a long, hard winter. The trip to Norway had been worth it, though. I had been back to Kolding at least two or three times to visit Axel and the others. And now there were more people I was going to miss: Svend, and Hanne, and Niels, and Flemming, and Martin, and Birgit, and Steen, and Morten (a different one), and Helle, and Anette, and Jakob. . . . We had taken courses together and traveled together and gone on nature hikes around the hills and lakes of Silkeborg. We had sat in taverns and at parties together drinking beer. My Danish was getting better all the time. And now I was going to have to do it all again. In fact, it was already starting to happen. The school's session was due to end on May 6, but I suddenly realized that I signed up for a session at Askov that was due to start on May 1. How had I managed to shoot myself in the foot like this? It is a question I still ask myself sometimes.

III. Askov Højskole: The Grand Old Tradition

Another New Beginning?

I left Silkeborg shortly before the end of April and spent a few days wandering aimlessly in Copenhagen. When the first of May arrived, I was once again on the same train to Jutland, this time turning south at Fredericia and taking a line that led toward the west coast of Denmark. The town of Vejen lies in that direction, and Askov Højskole is located several kilometers outside of the town. And again it was strange faces, a different room, and another set of buildings to learn. More new people and the endless who-are-you, let's-get-acquainted-with-each-other conversations. By this time I was becoming fairly competent in Danish, and when the details of high school life at Askov were explained, I was so familiar with the general procedures that it was hard to keep from yawning. And even though I sometimes had to grit my teeth at going through the whole thing again for a third time, at least this time it came as no surprise. I was surprised at my equanimity. In spite of the fact that I was a foreigner, I felt like a smug and clever know-it-all when it came to high school life.

I spent most of the first week physically present at Askov, but my heart was back in Silkeborg. I was looking forward with great anticipation to the concluding festival (afsluttningsfest). I smiled a lot and pretended to be happy, but I wasn't at all. I knew that by the time the three months were over, I would have another set of friends and acquaintances from among these people, but I wasn't ready to open up to anybody else just yet. I knew that I could get away with distancing myself for a while if necessary. I also knew that the folk high school culture was so powerful that everything would work out in the end no matter how hard I tried or didn't try. On the day of the Silkeborg festival I woke up late, forgot my wallet, and had to walk the three kilometers back from the town of Vejen to get it. But when I finally got on the train, and after shifting twice was let off in Silkeborg, the whole thing began to happen again. I met Svend and Birgitte on the street. A dozen others from the high school were sitting in a tavern, socializing and having fun. I looked at them and remembered how they had been during the first week. Later, back in the high school, there was a small gathering together in someone's room just before the farewell dinner. One boy in particular was laughing and having a good time. I remembered how painfully shy he had been in the beginning, withdrawn and almost unable to speak. "Hey Steve, Lisbeth really has hips to grab on to, don't you think so?" Now here he is, a naughty flesh puller with a glint in his eye. Lisbeth is protesting in mock outrage, but all around the room there is only good feeling.

The final dinner is real food for a change, and everyone is up on their feet many times during the meal, proposing toast after toast. Jens rises and toasts all the teachers and staff, saying, "Thanks for our stay." We toast Bent and many of the teachers individually. We even toast the woman in charge of the kitchen for her "great food." Am I seeing Christianity in action here, I ask myself? It's hard to say. I have a good conversation with Erik, whom I have hardly known during these months. He invites me to come to the family farm and makes sure to write down his address and telephone number. All I can think of is the time at Askov, and I am not sure I will want to come back to Silkeborg once the session is finished. But Erik is sly. He casually mentions that his house has a straw-thatched roof, guessing correctly that an American of my type will be drawn by romantic curiosity to see what kind of a Rousseauian existence can be carved out in the Danish countryside. Later, after the time at Askov, I will spend several weeks with him and his family.

Bent's final speech is powerful and moving. After some initial jokes and pleasantries, he tells us about the two faces struggling in each of us, good and evil. He urges us to strive for wholeness in our lives. He talks for fifteen minutes. We listen to every word and are touched by what he has to say. At least we are touched by it until after dinner, when the dancing and partying begin. It is wild, as I knew it would be. I dance closely with one young lady for ten minutes. A few minutes later I notice that she is passionately kissing Svend. "What about your girlfriend, Svend, your beautiful blond girlfriend from Aarhus?" I think to myself. Svend seems a little sheepish afterward, but still quite proud of his existential response to Anette's enthusiasm. There is music and drama the last night as well. I notice that Benny, someone who has come to the school with a very troubled past, does an act and a song with real confidence in front of the whole group. He has spent much of the stay locked within himself, very shy and withdrawn. It doesn't matter how good you do it, what matters is that you have participated and given of yourself, and it is this that the enthusiastic applause is recognizing. Everyone is given enthusiastic applause. I get up there with my sunglasses and steel-stringed guitar and give my Bob Dylan imitation; they love it and I feel great. It goes on and on. I get to bed somewhere around three.

The next morning there is a final meeting (morgensamling). After singing a few songs, something happens. We all break down and start crying. We walk around, and around, and around. Everybody hugs everybody else and expresses deep feelings. I have never seen such love freely flowing. It goes on and on. Later, when I speak to my teacher friends, they say that they have never seen anything like it before at the school. Then when we go outside, we discover that it is a warm spring day. Life is awaiting us. I say goodbye to Alan, Flemming, Tina, Peter, Per, Anette, Svend, and a dozen others. As we leave, they continue to cry, but I am no longer crying. I am amused by it, because by now I've been through this sort of thing before. I know that it is not an end but a beginning. I hear them planning a reunion in Aalborg. See? It has begun. I feel old and wise. I get on the train to go back to Askov, to the new classes and new faces of my third high school experience.

I arrive back in Askov on Friday, feeling great after the fantastic concluding festival at Silkeborg Højskole. And then, over the course of the weekend, I sink down into a terrible depression. Both physically and psychically, I am in a state of near collapse. I lie there on the bed seeing all the faces of those I had come to know at Silkeborg, just what had happened to me last time at Kolding. I miss them and want to see them again. I feel as burned out as the wires of our failed windmill project. I try to go for a walk but am put off by this small town, Vejen. It's flat as a pancake. None of the hills or lakes of Silkeborg, or even the lovely parks of Kolding. There is a drizzling gray rain that lasts the entire day. And the rain continues, day after day. Do I have the strength to do this one more time?

Helle

One day in the middle of the second week I meet Helle. We have both gone to a meeting of those who are interested in playing an instrument for possible group singing. Like me, she has a guitar. She is wearing a sweatshirt and black jeans. She is thin and nervous and she has a nice smile. Blue-green eyes, red-brown straight hair, turquoise earrings. I sense that there is some kind of a bond between us, and so does she. I see her every so often during the first month or so of classes, sometimes at the library, or between classes. We have friendly and sincere conversations. She has a girl of six and must spend a lot of time looking after her. After a series of casual conversations, I begin to think that it was just my fantasy. Then on Thursday, the 23rd of June, it is the Evening of Saint Hans, the summer equinox celebration. The days have been getting longer and longer all during May and June, although it is hard to appreciate the lengthened daylight because it rains just about every single day, the worst May in Danish history. I had heard all through the autumn and dark winter at Kolding and Silkeborg about the wonders of the Danish summer. Now I have begun to write the whole thing off as a cultural myth. "There is no such thing as summer in Denmark," I begin to tell myself. "That's why there are so many stories about it. It's all collective fantasy and wish-fulfillment." But in the first week of June the daily drizzle that we have become accustomed to suddenly holds up. We actually see the sun during the day. The students at Askov can't throw off their clothes fast enough to lie in its warmth. The cultivated fields that begin a few short blocks from the high school are beginning to turn green. And the whole countryside becomes alive with wildflowers. Suddenly there are long summer evenings of a kind I have never before experienced. So *this* is the Danish summer they have all been telling me about!

By the time we get to the evening of Saint Hans the sun doesn't set until somewhere near eleven o'clock. For the last ten years, everyone says, it has rained on this day, so don't expect things to be different. But this year we are pleasantly surprised. Tonight there is no rain at all. The air is clear and the sky is lit by a full moon. Energy vibrations of early mid-summer. There is a sense of anticipation shared by everyone. We have been together at Askov for six weeks now. Whispers and promises, first names pronounced with affection. Earth pipe on a green lawn. Eyes meeting, people embracing, music, singing, laughter. The paper-and-cloth witch is burned over a big woodpile in the flames of a giant bonfire. I sit by the side of the circle of people watching the burning witch, looking at the faces of the children. Suddenly Helle is beside me. We talk a little. She motions to me to follow her. We walk away, past the crowd. We go out to the cemetery by the small church. We sit down on the grass near a tombstone and she begins talking. After a little bit of small talk, she opens up. She tells me about herself for the first time, who she really is.

She tells me about the other Denmark. She *is* the other Denmark. I won't go into any detail about her past lives. She has seen very rough times. She knows the streets of Copenhagen and those who live in the shadows; she once lived in those shadows herself. Now she is running from her past. The Denmark that she knows has little or nothing to do with the Denmark I thought I was beginning to know. "Did you choose Askov because it was the first and oldest folk high school?" I ask her. She grins at me: "I took a pin, closed my eyes, and put it down somewhere in Jutland. It landed here. That's why I came to this school." This is the first time in her twenty-five years that she has been to Jutland. *She has never even heard of Grundtvig.* She tells me about her past, story after story. People in prison and on drugs, living their lives in the shadow of official Denmark. I sit and listen. I don't know what amazes me more, the content of her stories or the fact that she is telling them to me.

"One is diplomatic when one comes to a high school," she tells me once. She keeps to herself and doesn't allow many people to get close. She is not as social as the rest. People sense she is different. There is a mystery about her. She is one tough lady. No one can tell her what to do. "Hey, you're not allowed to take that out of the dining room!" a matronly looking woman in the library says fiercely, seeing her with a bowl of food. "I'll bring it back at lunchtime," she says coldly, continuing on her way, brushing the woman off without an apology. The woman stands there in open-mouthed astonishment. "What do you think of the high school?" I ask her once. "Askov?" she says. "It's an open prison." By the look on her face I can see she knows this is not really a fair characterization, but she has made her point. This old boyfriend is now in jail; that one is still dealing. She doesn't want to see them anymore. She wants to make a new life for herself. Sometimes she is not sure she can do it. The shadows pursue her; they will not let her go. They remind her, torment her, threaten her. To be so far away from that street, those apartments, and those people. It is the first time she has dared to come so far away. She doesn't want her daughter to live like that. She doesn't want her daughter to know them. After I know a little of who she is, of what she has seen and experienced, I begin to see a side of Denmark I have never seen before. I have never seen it through my own eyes, but she makes it come alive for me. Even after I leave Askov to live in Copenhagen, I will see Denmark in part through the filter of her dark vision. She tells all her stories with the same wit and style, and although she would never admit it, she has a great gift for language. She is full of sharp, pungent, bittersweet observations on high school life and all the other faces of official Denmark. The shadows are never far away; they are only out of sight for the moment. I wish her success on the difficult and dangerous journey that she is trying to make.

Classes, Social Life, and Afterward

The course offerings at Askov are more numerous and diverse than Kolding or even Silkeborg. There are the familiar staples of a general folk high school curriculum: literature, psychology, art and music appreciation, media studies, international politics, and milieu studies. There is a great depth in the offerings that teach one or another form of crafts: drawing, painting, ceramics, the making of plant dyes, pottery, woodworking, and several kinds of weaving. But there are also more unusual offerings: a course in yoga, for example, and courses in mathematics and astronomy (which remain from Askov's early experimentation with natural science subjects in the folk high school curriculum). There is also instruction in foreign languages (English, German, and French) as well as a course in Danish for foreigners, which happily I no longer need.

For me the time at Askov turns out to be by far the easiest and most pleasant of the three field experiences. It is summer. We spend a lot of time under "the large and melodious trees," the giant beech trees that stand on the central lawn, trees that in their vast age could not help symbolizing (to us in the summer course as well as to generations of former students) something of the age, the continuity, and the tradition of Askov Højskole. The sense of tradition is everywhere: in the large paintings of scenes showing the famous high school men who have served Askov in earlier years, in the bell tower that has become a national symbol, in the bookstore across the street from the school operated by two former students. The area that surrounds Askov, especially around the King's River *(Kongeaaen)*, is beautiful in these high summer days. Possibly one has to be born a Dane to feel the significance of its name; the King's River is not an ordinary stream but one that is rich in Danish history, in particular the history of South Jutland *(Sønderjylland)*. "No man can know Denmark unless he know Ribe," wrote Hilaire Belloc, and I make the sixty-kilometer round-trip journey to Denmark's oldest city many times by bicycle during these weeks, to linger by its mill stream, its fountains, and its aged buildings.[24]

By this time I am able to understand most of what goes on around me and in classes. I take from Finn a class in Danish literature that introduces me to the work of Knud Sørensen, Tove Ditlevsen, and numerous other important writers. I take a course in modern art from Karen; in it we discuss everyone from the early impressionists to Picasso and Chagall, as well as a range of Danish artists. I take a course in music understanding from Mogens; we listen to selections from the work of Schubert, Beethoven, Brahms, Schumann, and numerous others, learning as well about their personalities and often tragic life histories. I emerge from all of these courses feeling that they have been both enjoyable and of great value. I am popular with the kitchen staff because I am constantly complimenting them on their food (at first they think I am being ironic; they soon come to accept me as an eccentric but well-meaning foreigner). It is more traditional than the food at Kolding, but there is a lot of variety and it is served in generous quantities. The students at Askov are hungry, but no one here finds it necessary to do a fifty-yard dash to get to the food.

The housing situation is more like Kolding than Silkeborg. Students live in one of a number of dormitory-like structures bearing names like Apple Farm, Forest Farm, Blue Farm, and West Farm (the fact that I was assigned to one called the White House occasioned much joking commen-

Ludvig Schrøder giving a lecture at Askov, about 1900 (reprinted by permission of the Nationalhistorisk Museum, Frederiksborg Castle).

Listening to a lecture at Askov today (photo: Askov Højskole).

tary). Although these older houses are not as elegant as the units at Kolding, they facilitate social interaction in much the same way. And as at the other schools, the social life among the students at Askov can best be described as *hygge* and informality run amuck. It is easy to meet people, and conviviality is the reigning mood. I happen upon Hanne, who I barely know, ironing her clothes in the halls of the White House. "Hey, what's that you're doing?" I ask. "Now Steve," she replies, "let's not fight about who does the ironing until we get married." Later she and I will hitchhike together to Aalborg, and from there I will visit Skagen, the northernmost point in Jutland.

One must not get the impression from this description that a folk high school stay is one happy party after another. Particularly at Askov, I encountered a number of students who expressed serious reservations about the constant high intensity of the social life.[25] A girl who had been popular and outgoing in our house life once confessed to me, "Sometimes I have a feeling of drowning in people. If I play volleyball so that I can go to bed thinking 'I've done something,' just because I've been with the group, it's crazy. It's okay if we're *doing* something together, but just to sit down in the tea kitchen of the house to be with someone and drink a cup of tea, it's too much." Another girl in our house spoke of the conflict between a need to be alone and a feeling that it is wrong not to participate in all group activities. Given the intensity of the group life, my own opinion is that it is not only normal but virtually necessary for students to occasionally withdraw into their private selves. Some, however, felt a great deal of guilt about doing this. I know that this was sometimes a burden for me: I remember feeling that it was somehow wrong of me to have chosen a single room, that I should have lived in a double like nearly everyone else. At such moments, the second chair and the empty bed in my room would gaze at me like silent accusers, and I would shrink inside myself, horrified at my selfishness and ego-centricity. As on the Israeli kibbutz, the pull of the group life can be at times overwhelmingly powerful. One will always encounter both pleasure and pain at a folk high school.

Perhaps in part as a response to the incessant sociability, a form of spontaneous social stratification could be observed at mealtimes among the students at Askov. It was not as if hard-and-fast lines could be drawn, but after a few weeks even a cursory glance would show, for instance, that one table was composed of single parents with children at the school. In part, it was natural for them to eat together because of their common child-care responsibilities, and the children enjoyed eating at tables with other children. It was at this table where Helle ate, and I began to eat there often myself. Those who were likely to eat at this table were not only single parents but city people in their late twenties or thirties from Aarhus or Copenhagen.

Mogens Melbye leading a group of singers on the lawn.

Informal discussion over coffee (photo: Askov Højskole).

There were commonalities in their vocabulary, experience, and worldview that made it easier for them to talk to each other than, say, to a nineteen-year-old from a small rural town. After a short time it was a rare and unusual event for someone who did not belong to this group to eat at their table.

Many of the students are older, meaning that the median age is somewhere in the mid-twenties, and quite a few are in their thirties (a pattern similar to what I saw at Kolding).[26] The students are the usual mix of personality types and social backgrounds. Some come secure in the belief that they are in control of their lives; they merely want to see what a folk high school experience can add to their life experience. Two frequent examples of those in this category are university students taking time off from their studies and *gymnasium* graduates who want a break in their formal education. Others, however, come to a folk high school because they feel they have lost control; they may be fleeing a traumatic divorce, the breakup of a significant relationship, alcoholism, drug addiction, a recent job layoff, or the hopelessness that comes from long-term unemployment (these categories are not mutually exclusive). They come hoping that the folk high school will enable them to build a new life, or at the very least a new set of relationships.

The existence of a noncompetitive school atmosphere and a supportive peer and staff group makes the folk high school a place where people are very often willing to reach out and help others; such positive peer responses, and the words spoken by a caring teacher or principal, may make it easier for an individual to deal with a crisis that has suddenly and painfully manifested itself. That this has long been a part of the folk high school tradition is illustrated in the following description given by Roar Skovmand of J. Th. Arnfred, a legendary high school man who served as Askov Højskole's principal for twenty-five years (1928–53):

> He wasn't one for small talk. You didn't chat with Arnfred about the weather; on the other hand you could very well ask him, for example, what the difference was between cumulus and cirrus clouds. But it was not difficult to go to him if you had something on your mind. There are more than a few young people who in some difficult situation sought him out and found a most gentle, understanding and helpful counselor. His role as a high school man has to be evaluated not only on the basis of his classes and lectures (which could range from Wegener's theory of continental drift to Einstein's theory of relativity), but keeping in mind what he gave to young people who asked for help from him, and received it.[27]

The short-term response to a personal crisis is facilitated by the folk high school environment and will often be a positive one; the ability of the high school to help in the long term, however, is much more questionable. And even in the short term, an individual can come to feel that it is impossible to get help. One woman who I knew was going through great difficulty at the time made this remark about human relations at the high school: "We don't come too close to each other. There's no engagement. We have our own problems, and that's all we can deal with." Many students experience moods of bleak depression when they contrast the positive social life and elevated life expectations that are part of the culture of the folk high school with the hard reality of what it is they must go back to once the folk high school stay is over. They wonder in their deepest selves if there is really something to all this stuff they are hearing, or if it is all just rhetoric accompanied by empty promises. "What will it be like for me when I have to leave the high school?" As one woman student with a university education commented:

> Three months are just too little time. You just have time to learn to know each other well, and be secure with each other, and then it's time to go. And there come more and more those who have problems, and that's difficult because you yourself maybe don't have the surplus to help these people out. That can give you a bad conscience; it can be that you don't think you have done enough for these people. There are so many who have serious problems. I don't know how many will get their problems solved at a high school.

Partly as a response to this dilemma, it is not unusual for some of those who have taken the same high school course to stick together once it is finished. All high schools encourage active alumni organizations and frequent return visits to the school. But some small groups of former students go even further. They move to a new city and try to establish one or more housing cooperatives. They travel together on Interrail youth passes to explore the countries of southern Europe. They publish informal newsletters to ensure that those who have moved to the same city or region will get together regularly. All want to keep intact the positive atmosphere that has been generated during the folk high school stay. At Askov, our group decided to hold a reunion on a farm in North Jutland just a month after our course had finished; at that reunion it was decided to make this an annual event. There is no question in my mind that these support groups function effectively during the first year or two after a high school stay. My impression is, however, that these networks begin to attenuate after a few years. Almost everyone, however, remains in contact with a handful of others who in many cases will be friends for life. I know a woman in her late sixties who went to Askov during the Second World War: she has a group of four friends, all of whom were together at Askov more than forty years ago. They meet several times a year to keep in touch. The legacy of these friendships is one of the richest parts of the high school experience.

A Class That Fails (And One That Doesn't)

The subject of the class was psychology, taught by a temperamental yet fragile older woman who probably deserved better than she got at the hands of the students in her class. Somewhere about the second week it became obvious that things were going downhill. The basic cause of the problem was that the teacher consistently communicated to the class an attitude that *she* was the authority and that they were there to listen and learn. Her style was to ask a few leading questions, which, when nobody answered them, served as a transparent excuse for her to launch into a long, endless analysis, which she did at each class session. "What do you think about Freud's theory?" was the much too general form in which nearly all her leading questions were asked. When she did this the first time, we gave her the benefit of the doubt. There was silence, followed by boredom and indifference when she held court. But when she continued to play the role of authority figure by lecturing continuously at each session, the displeasure felt by members of the class grew. The tone used by some of those in the class when speaking with her became less and less civil.

She could feel this gradual withdrawal of respect and responded to it with a rebellion of her own that was meant to shock us. One day she came into class, and when there was no response to the usual perfunctory questions, she took aim at us and fired with both barrels: "A lot of people haven't read the article I assigned," she said. "This is not only an insult to me but to the others in the class who have read it." She then threatened to end the class: "If this class is to continue, you must be willing to work. This means reading the material." A lot of genuine anger was coming through in her presentation. She assumed that our silence meant that we hadn't read the material. Many had tried, but found it to be as incomprehensible as her lectures. They were very interested in the subject but felt that her way of presenting it made no sense. Her anger was met head-on by the anger of the class. In the subsequent discussion, someone suggested that the class be broken down into groups. She asked at one point, "Should we do something else, in groups next time?" "Yes," came back the answer. "Shall we divide it up into groups now?" "No, let's do it next time," one of the girls in the back states definitively. Once her posture of authority had cracked, it became a broken dam through which a torrent of thinly veiled opposition began to stream.

The next time we break up into groups. Our group decides to hold its own separate class in one of the houses. Of course, a trip to the local baker is in order first, and so the group meeting turns into a grand social event with fresh bread, gourmet tea, and Danish pastry. The subject is Freud, and with these sources of oral gratification within easy reach, we have a pleasant and excellent discussion among the five of us. It is so stimulating, in fact, that when ten o'clock comes and we are supposed to go back to her classroom, we stay right where we are. The free-flowing discussion of Freud proves so hilarious, and we are having such a good time, that we stay until the end of the period and continue through most of the next, missing whatever classes we are supposed to attend. "The Dragon, " one of the students calls her jestingly, and the name sticks. Later we find out that the Dragon is understandably annoyed at us for not coming back to class on time. But by this time we do not care.

When we come to class for the next meeting, she suggests that we form new groups, breaking up the old ones. "You're not acting like grown-up people," she tells us, when we tell her we want to keep our orally gratified discussion group intact for the rest of the course. We refuse to recognize her authority and keep meeting according to our own schedule. Members of the class begin to sit spontaneously in small groups around the school and discuss what is happening in this class. Once she walks past the reading room while half a dozen of us are having a loud discussion of what to do about her. "Naughty children," the expression on her face communicates. Another time she actually comes out to visit us in our group discussion in the Apple Farm kitchen. She manages to look disapproving and wistful at the same time as she glances quickly at the full plates, the piles of pastry, and the teacups.

After the first few weeks, the class number begins dropping. It goes quickly from about twenty down to ten, and eventually there are only three or four left. At that point, she decides to call off the class. I believe that in setting herself up as an authority, she violated a number of informal principles in the behavioral code of Danish culture, among them egalitarianism, the balance principle, and the Jante Law. She had unconsciously given double messages to the class, saying one thing verbally ("say something; what do you think about this?") and another nonverbally ("keep quiet; I want to do the talking"). The fact that this happened in a class in psychology made the students even more impatient and offended. Many of them were genuinely interested in the topic and would have been quite willing to do the work if it had been presented in a different way. Another consideration is that we had somehow spent all of the first three weeks on Freud, and a number of class members were anxious to go on to the work of other figures in modern psychology, such as Carl Jung, A. H. Maslow, and Stanislav Grof. The interest was so intense that when the class had been officially canceled, some decided to hold their own "alternative psychology class." After a few false starts, it finally met in the same old place, and there were interesting and provocative discussions of some of the themes class members were really interested in: mythology, ESP, *The Tibetan Book of the Dead,* Grof's LSD research, and other topics that required going beyond the writings of Freud.

What is the lesson to be learned? Perhaps the worst thing a folk high school teacher can do is to stand up and communicate, verbally or nonverbally, to a class, "I am the authority." If this teacher had begun by asking, "What questions in psychology interest you, and whose work would you like to consider in this course?" the outcome might have been completely different. Even if she knew nothing of Jung, Maslow, and Grof, I believe it would have been a far better strategy for her to say, "Great! I don't know too much about their work myself, but we can learn together. Why don't we talk about Freud this week, and then for next week why don't those of you who want to discuss Jung look into it and suggest to us what readings of his we might consider for the week after? Or come in and talk to me about it and we'll decide together." A class of excited collaborators is much more fun than a mob of silent, sulking critics.

Hans, on the other hand, was a smart folk high school teacher who knew his audience better than they knew themselves. I took a class in international relations and foreign policy with him in which the student backgrounds ranged from university level to long-term dropout. It did not faze him in the slightest. He began by assigning a short piece by the American diplomat George Kennan, one that had been translated into Danish and published in a major newspaper that very week.[28] There were many unclear terms in the article, but a more fascinating and relevant short introduction to the subject could hardly be imagined. We discuss it in groups. People come back from the groups saying it was interesting, but that the meaning of terms like MIRV (multiple independently targeted reentry vehicle) and the distinction between "tactical" and "strategic" nuclear weapons were giving them serious problems. Well, it just turned out that Hans had another short article that defined all of the terms in question; would they be interested in perhaps reading that for the next class period? It turned out that they would, and what do you know—he had already prepared enough copies to hand out to the class before they left. The

Hans Møller Christensen at the conclusion of an afternoon class in the summer session (he is the one with the most clothes on).

next day when they come, he asks, "Should I talk a little about the whole history of this and give some background?" "Yes," they say, that would be a great idea. He has introduced them to the material, succeeded in getting their honest response to it, and given them a context in which the class can begin to treat the topic. Moreover, he has significantly empowered them by making them part of the classroom decision-making structure. They are not reading something Hans handed them and then told them they had to read. On the contrary, they are reading something they want to find out more about.

Consensus, participation, power sharing, and contextualization: it was all done so smoothly, by a balding, red-faced man with a quietly excited voice and a soft, encouraging smile, that the clear agenda and the focused, positive mood had taken shape after the first twenty minutes of the class. It was equally stimulating for all of us, regardless of our previous level of formal education—we read a succession of short, relevant, and interesting articles and then struggled to clarify them in a cooperative way. I still have the sheet he handed us for our discussion group the first day. At the top he had written, "Discuss the Kennan chronicle any way you want to. The following questions are just thought of as a help." The following four samples are from his list; in my opinion *any* discussion of such questions would result in members of the class learning more about the topic:

1. Are nuclear weapons suited to the waging of war?
2. Are the tactical nuclear weapons in West Germany the biggest danger?
3. What is the significance of the French and English nuclear weapons?
4. What is a false and a real zero option?

IV. A Brief Comparison of Kolding, Silkeborg, and Askov (1982–83)

Although many of the details have been covered earlier in this chapter, I include the following brief summary as a guide toward systematic comparisons:

1. Food and labor policies: Only at Kolding were the food and labor policies consciously integrated into the school's ideology and social philosophy. The emphasis on vegetarian diet, the open kitchen, and the all-student labor force were effective instruments of instruction and experience. At Askov and Silkeborg, students were served food by a hired staff, which created a very different social atmosphere surrounding mealtimes. Dining and meals at Askov were relaxed; as earlier discussion made clear, the food policies then in effect at Silkeborg were the least successful of the three schools.

2. Class organization: Kolding's innovative focus on a single course was fine if that course worked out, but potentially disastrous if it didn't. The fact that courses began at different times at Kolding led to some confusion and posed strains for newcomers. Silkeborg and Askov both had more traditional forms of class organization, as well as more course offerings from which to choose.

3. Housing: Kolding's small decentralized houses were ideal. Essentially the same system was found at Askov, though the houses were older and not quite as innovatively designed. Silkeborg's single concrete structure with its fusion of separate functions within one building represented a different, highly centralized design.

4. Age-group: Both Kolding and Askov seemed to attract many in their late twenties and thirties as well as the younger crowd (mean age somewhere in the mid-twenties). Silkeborg had fewer in this age range during my stay and more in the late teens and very early twenties (mean age about twenty or twenty-one).

5. Class size: This was typically small, between five and fifteen—a fact which tended to counterbalance the difficulty of working with students from a wide range of social and educational backgrounds.

6. School enrollment: Most folk high schools are small, with the capacity to board between fifty and a hundred students. Askov, the largest

of the folk high schools, has room for about 250 students. Many schools depend on a combination of short courses (one to two weeks) and long courses to achieve near capacity enrollment, especially in the summer. During my stay, Kolding had seventy students in residence, Silkeborg and Askov approximately a hundred.

7. Facilities for families and single parents with children: Both Kolding and Askov had child-care facilities and encouraged parents to bring their children to the school. Silkeborg was set up for single students only.

8. Philosophy and social ideology: Kolding and Silkeborg were both relatively new schools, still struggling to achieve self-definition. Both were succeeding in different ways. Kolding offered a radical critique of Denmark and global capitalism, while ridiculing organized religion. Silkeborg, on the other hand, offered a Christian existentialist critique of the values of modern consumer society. These two approaches have many intersection points. It is harder to pin down Askov in any one-sentence characterization. It had the widest selection of course offerings. Elements of both Kolding's and Silkeborg's philosophies were represented, but as part of a more settled and stable tradition. I did not fully appreciate the relative newness of Kolding and Silkeborg until after I had been to Askov. There are advantages, of course, in both types of schools.

Unlike Kolding, both Silkeborg and Askov can be characterized as "Grundtvigian" folk high schools. Perhaps this difference is best illustrated by the traditional custom of morning group singing found at Silkeborg and Askov (though not at Kolding). The students were required to meet as a group after breakfast and before the beginning of classes. This meeting (*morgensamling*) would begin and end with collective singing. Someone, usually a teacher, made a brief presentation (a poem, a reading from a myth) in between the songs. Then the meeting was over. The singing was as a rule not very impressive.

I remember thinking when I first came to Silkeborg, what kind of dumbness is this with a group of half-asleep zombies singing out of tune and so low you can hardly hear them? "Wake up and exert yourself, sing to me beautifully and strong / O dear soul, stand up from your bed, and make with gratitude a heavenly song."[29] This was one of our morning songs, but the words were barely audible. Day after day we sang religious songs, patriotic songs, international folk songs, and hymns—all in the same out-of-tune, zombielike manner. I didn't realize until much later what a subtle form of cultural learning it was. The same songs that seem ridiculous at the time come to be regarded with affectionate nostalgia once the school stay is finished. Just to hear the opening lines of some of them years later is enough to bring a tear to a good Dane's eye. This will be equally true even if that person hardly remembers the words and only mumbled them as a student years before at a folk high school. These songs, especially the hymns, are frequently chosen from among the more than 1,500 that Grundtvig composed during his lifetime. In later years many of these same songs are sung at parents' meetings, union meetings, political meetings, and other social gatherings; to have some familiarity with them is one of the earmarks of the Danish identity.

9. Faculty and principals: The teachers at Kolding were a younger, less settled, and more mobile group. The teachers at Silkeborg and Askov were as a rule more settled; these two schools appeared to have a much larger core of older, long-term, stable faculty. Kolding's policy of collective leadership meant that the school had no permanent principal. During my time there Benny Christensen, a civil engineer, was acting principal. Bent Martinsen, a Lutheran minister, was Silkeborg's principal. The principal at Askov was Hans Henningsen, a former teacher at the school, a calm, peaceful man who, like Bent Martinsen, is a Grundtvig scholar. I had written Grundtvig off as some kind of a Nordic culture quack before my interview with Hans Henningsen; in our conversation I gained a whole new respect and insight into what Grundtvig represents both for the folk high schools and for Danish culture.

10. The folk high schools and the university: It is not the role of a folk high school to provide in-depth courses in such subjects as engineering, mathematics and physics. The type of courses offered at all three folk high schools are aimed more at enjoyment and the development of one's human potential than at promoting a professional level of competence in technical fields. This fact should be kept in mind when evaluating folk high school courses.

In spite of the real ideological differences between the three schools, there were—as I have been at some pains to emphasize—profound areas of continuity. One final image I will use to illustrate this is a festival at Askov. On this particular evening we were singing halfheartedly as usual, when Hans Henningsen suddenly and quite uncharacteristically started going from table to table to encourage everyone to do a better job. "Shout out the number!" he told us when he came to our table. "Really sing it!" he told those at the next table. The next song we sing turns out to be the "Communist Internationale" (which together with the ballads "John Henry," "Swing Low Sweet Chariot," and "Where Have All The Flowers Gone?" is in the Folk High School Songbook). In the beginning we show great role distance, laughing at the strident militancy of the text. But toward the end, our role distance collapses. We stand arm in arm at our table and some others follow. In the end we sing it seriously and there is loud cheering when we finish. The mood at that moment—of shared experience, of spontaneous involvement, of focus not just on Denmark but on international peace and solidarity—is one that I have experienced at all three schools, regardless of their differences in social ideology.

When the time came for the concluding festival at Askov, I had no desire to be part of it. I knew it would be too much for me. I left Askov on the afternoon the festival was scheduled, taking a train to North Jutland to visit Niels, a friend from Silkeborg who still lived at his father's farm. One odyssey had ended, and another had begun. I had come to Denmark ten months earlier as a stranger speaking a few words of Danish. Now I could speak the language well. I came knowing just a handful of people. Now I could see that I had touched many lives, and many lives had touched mine. I had come thinking that a folk high school was primarily an academic institution. Now I had seen that a folk high school was an experience in community and in personal growth, one in which academic learning plays a definite, if circumscribed role. But during the course of the ten months of high school life, something else had happened to me. Beneath the joys and sorrows, beneath the perpetual journeying, the growth and the learning, I felt that through the time spent in the folk high schools I had been privileged to touch deeply the sacred core of wisdom of another culture. I knew that the folk high school was only one expression of that wisdom, and that is one reason why this book, although it addresses the question of these schools, is careful to locate them in their greater social and historical context.

All of my subsequent research, which led to the Estes report and to nineteenth-century Danish land reform, to Grundtvig, Kold, and the origin of the folk high schools, and to the peculiar configuration of Danish national character as I have perceived and described it, was motivated by the ten months of lived experience that I have tried to describe in this chapter. I could have written about this experience objectively and clinically, in the cold, detached prose of my profession, pretending that I was never confused and that everything I did was scientifically immaculate. Yet I believe that to do so would have been a mistake. I did not want to round off the edges, force the experience to fit the professional model, or pretend that all was a straight path to discovery and insight. I wanted to communicate something of the experiential process behind the perspective taken in this book and, in doing so, to put the reader more directly in touch with the folk high school tradition. I believe that this way of doing things gives a more accurate reflection of the spirit and philosophy that guides these schools, as well as of the experience of those who come to live, work, and learn in them.

CHAPTER TWELVE

A Critical Reappraisal

I. THE FUTURE OF THE FOLK HIGH SCHOOLS: A NECESSARY TENSION

I BEGAN THE PRECEDING CHAPTER by outlining the crisis of the traditional folk high school in the immediate postwar decades. There were even those who predicted at the time that since there was no longer a current need for these schools, they had outlived their usefulness and would most likely soon die out. But all of these predictions of impending demise were based on mistaken assumptions. They underestimated the degree of flexibility inherent in the idea of a folk high school, and they did not envision that this flexibility would allow the schools to respond to a different set of social conditions by coming to perform a new set of social functions. It is true that the transformations from the old to the new folk high school were not always made easily or gracefully. It is also true that in making the adaptations necessary to carry out these altered functions, a perplexing new set of problems was created. The preceding chapter's description of a year in three Danish folk high schools touched on many of these problematic areas. They do exist, and it is because of them that even in the 1980s one could hear about "the crisis of the folk high schools." Yet the overall pattern of my observations is congruent with the comment made by Arne Andresen, director of the Folk High School Sekretariat: "The folk high school is not in crisis. Quite the opposite. There have never been so many high schools as there are now, and there have never been so many students."[1]

Indeed, the folk high schools have never been as popular as they are now. Just after the Second World War there were 60 folk high schools in Denmark. In 1975–76 there were 81 such schools, with 10,000 students on the long courses (at least four weeks in length) and 21,000 on the short courses. Five years later, in 1980–81, there were 88 schools with 10,000 on the long courses and 35,000 on the short courses. In 1984–85 the number of high schools had reached 105, with 11,000 on the long courses and almost 42,000 on the short courses. In 1987, it was estimated that there would be 43,000 coming to attend the short courses. While the number of those attending the long courses has remained relatively constant since 1975, there has been a doubling of those attending short courses and nearly a 25% increase in the number of schools. One fact to keep in mind (when considering the long and short courses together) is that more than 50,000 people (in a nation of just over 5 million) are taking a residential course of study at a folk high school each year.

Using these statistics as an initial measure, it is difficult to reach any conclusion other than this: the folk high school tradition is alive and well in Denmark. A closer look at the reality behind these statistics reveals a paradoxical situation: the high school tradition is *so* alive and doing *so* well that some of the most knowledgeable high school supporters have expressed concern with its rapid growth. Among them is K. E. Larsen, a former principal who as folk high director for the Ministry of Education was responsible for acting on applications made for permission to start a new school. Larsen pointed out in 1984—when there were 101 schools—that there were at the time forty-two additional applicants hoping to begin their own new folk high schools! On the one hand, the fact that so many plans to establish new schools were submitted shows the strength and vitality of this educational tradition. On the other hand, total student demand is not sufficient to support this many new schools. The competition is already very keen; it is virtually certain that some of the now-existing folk high schools will "go out of business" due to failure to attract sufficient numbers of students. Faced with such a situation, the official response has been to tighten the regulations and standards for approving new schools. Thus only four of the forty-two applications have been approved, and it is unlikely that even half of the new applications will be approved in the future. Even stronger measures were considered but rejected:

> It is very important that we do not destroy the as-yet unknown grass roots contributions. For this reason a temporary stop to recognition of new high schools—and this was a theoretical possibility—would have been a very bad thing. Many fresh seeds would have been destroyed. It would have been difficult for them to make the start up effort again.[2]

Many of the rejected applications are for the establishment of special schools aimed at those with a particular handicap. Although the license-granting officials believe strongly that such individuals deserve the best care that society can give them, their feeling is that a folk high school must be for everyone, and not for just one group or one type of student (no matter how legitimate their special needs are). In spite of this emphasis on maintaining the folk high school as an instrument of general education in the widest sense *(almendannelse)*, one recognizable tendency during the past two decades has been for folk high schools to appeal to a steadily narrower group. Typically, a school will offer a program specially tailored to fit this group's needs and interests. Thus one now finds in the folk high school catalogue an amazingly diverse collection of course offerings: yoga and Eastern meditation, biodynamic agriculture, athletic training, fundamentalist Christianity and system-critical ecology, feminism, language study, and international travel exist side by side in its pages. There are also a good number of schools that continue in the generalist Grundtvigian pattern. Silkeborg exemplifies this type of school. Yet even its liberal connection with religion would be rejected by many of the Grundtvigian schools, based on their interpretation of Grundtvig's famous statement, "First man, then Christian." Askov belongs to this older, well-established Grundtvigian tradition; yet in contrast to Silkeborg, there are no formal religious services at the school. Viewed from this perspective, Kolding can be seen as one of the newer schools whose main appeal is to some extent aimed at specific groups within the population.[3]

In summary, the folk high schools have been able to adapt to a new set of conditions in Danish history, changing as the society around them has changed. Created as a school for the children of farmers, they faithfully carried out that task for more than a century with extraordinarily successful results. In the postwar decades they have been forced to adapt to the new demands placed on them in a postmodern industrial society undergoing stressful culture change. The response of those in these schools was to redefine their task in order to carry out the altered set of social and educational functions implied by the new challenge. In view of these developments, how can we best sum up the changed role of the Danish folk high schools in the 1980s?

One answer to this question is suggested by a concept found in the work of E. H. Erikson. The existence of these schools constitutes an institutionalized experiment permitting the citizens of a postmodern crisis society to have, in his terms, "a psychosocial moratorium." Erikson, an anthropologically oriented psychoanalyst, defined this kind of moratorium as "a period of delay granted to somebody who is not ready to meet an obligation or forced on somebody who should give himself time."[4] Embedded in a treatment of identity confusion in individual life history (*Identity: Youth and Crisis,* 1968), his discussion shows how each society has institutionalized a different type of moratorium for the majority of its young people, ranging from "horse-stealing and vision quests, a time for *Wanderschaft* or work 'out West' or 'down under,' a time for 'lost youth' or academic life, a time for self-sacrifice or pranks—and today, often a time for patient-hood or delinquency."

Erikson's perceptive discussion of the psychosocial moratorium focuses on its role in the adolescent period. Yet it is hard to dispute the observation that the adults in a complex postmodern society may come to need a psychosocial moratorium just as much as its youth and adolescents. Economic instability and devastating social change are now characteristic features of life even in these outwardly prosperous and protected societies. Their adult members can therefore frequently experience the same life cycle discontinuities often primarily thought of as belonging to the adolescent stage of the life cycle: problems of insecurity and self-definition, substance abuse, lack of direction, traumas in personal relationships. At least in Denmark, a potentially positive and non-stigmatized solution to these developmental dilemmas is provided by the popular Danish institution called "a stay at a folk high school" *(folkehøjskoleophold)*. What the Danish folk high schools do that is different is to offer the possibility of a socially sanctioned moratorium not only to those in late adolescence but to those in varying phases of adulthood. Moreover, the high level of state and local support for the idea of a stay at a folk high school is concretely manifested in the existence of generous subsidies that make the schools financially available to any Dane who really has made the decision to attend one.[5] In summary, these schools are based on an insight that further extends Erikson's perspective by pointing to the need for a moratorium even after the early life phases of youth and adolescence.[6]

The existence of the folk high schools allows the Danish citizen to undertake a direct personal experience in free education. For a limited period in his or her life, any Danish citizen can come away from the normal routine of life in order to sustain a free encounter with new ideas, people, and places. In the open and relatively unconstrained space of the folk high school environment, an individual may look again at career choices, personal relationships, or questions of faith and belief. Yet one feature of this moratorium sharply distinguishes the type of learning and achievement that occurs at a folk high school from most other kinds of schools. At a Danish folk high school all present are forced to work through problematic life history questions in their own inward and individual way, and not in terms that are conveniently and externally defined for them by the agency of the school itself or by society at large.[7] Students at a Danish folk high school receive no grades, certificates of merit, or diplomas to hang on their walls when they return home. There are no trophies or framed indulgences awaiting them at graduation, nor do they receive symbols attesting to their success or failure in any of the customary areas of personal competition. The fact is that a student must struggle with success or failure in strictly personal terms, stripped of the reward hardware around which competitive schools crystallize the social and personal identities of those who move through them. It all amounts to a simple paradox: the folk high school has become a forced, conspiratorial experiment in free education. The students at a folk high school discover to their joy and sorrow, as I did, that they are—in Sartre's phrase—condemned to freedom.

It is a special time, the living out of this paradox, one with its own challenges, trials, and learnings. It is a time for quiet reappraisal of what one has done in life up to that point. It is not a time without disappointments and frustrations. For many, even for most, it is a time of personal growth. But subtle issues differentiate what happens in a folk high school from the learning provided by other kinds of educational institutions. From the point of view of the wider society, the experience made available to those who come to these schools represents a form of social investment in human beings whose dividends cannot be calculated on a quarterly basis; they have to be understood from the perspective of the long-term individual life cycle (an area that I believe has not been adequately studied). The life cycle of a Danish citizen, viewed as a whole, may be just a little different because of the existence of these schools.

I am thinking here not only of the specific long- and short-term personal growth that I believe is facilitated among many of those who attend them. I am thinking as well of what it means to live in a society in which the positive, optimistic, and far-sighted views of human nature expressed by Grundtvig have become part of the fabric of Danish educational institutions.[8] What does it mean for a democratic society to have a school where those with university backgrounds and those who never finished the seventh grade can meet in a noncompetitive setting and encounter each other as real persons, stripped at least in part of external credentials? And even though (as at Askov) the older Copenhagen crowd and the nineteen-year-olds from the rural districts may wind up eating at separate tables most of the time, I believe from having shared their experience that few of them did not acquire a changed and broadened understanding of fellow Danes from backgrounds different from their own. I do not have any statistics to prove this, but the very existence of the folk high schools may contribute to the cohesiveness of the surrounding Danish society through the positive experience of friendship, learning, and social cooperation that they engender for a substantial pool of the population. Their beneficial effect on the wider society can be visualized as the circle of ripples spreading outward from a stone thrown into a pond (an apt metaphor for Grundtvig's *folkeoplysning*). It is easy to see the initial splash (the stay at the school), but it is these invisible ripples and patterns generated by them that are the most enduring heritage of the folk high schools.

There is a certain irony in the fact that the newer version of the Danish folk high school is probably closer to Grundtvig's original vision than the single-clientele school that existed during the last century. One could almost say that Grundtvig's idea was so enlightened, that there was so much life in it, that the school he envisioned was able to adapt to a radically transformed set of social conditions and still serve Denmark well. In making such a conclusion, however, I do not want to draw attention away from the many difficulties that have come with serving the new generation of students. The following two citations,[9] the first pessimistic, the second less so, can serve to remind us of them:

1. Most high school teachers know that the pupils' motivation for a high school stay is diffuse and many sided and that a large number of them regard a high school stay as a vacation, recreation or a half a year driving on one of society's side paths. Why not admit it—that for young people who come to a high school there is only seldom a clear goal behind their decision to come? Vague conceptions of getting your eyes opened up, meeting new people, finding yourself, taking a pause, getting an idea about an education . . . but all passive according to their nature: hope that something will happen for me or with me, much more than conceptions about something I must do.

2. It's unreasonable to believe that grown adults, who come of their free will to a high school, need first and foremost to be motivated and activated. Isn't the truth of the matter quite the contrary: that the high school is sought primarily by well-motivated students who have the goal of coming to a high school, that they seek clarity about some essential questions in life, and that they hope some months living together with teachers and comrades can be meaningful in this situation? The high school will be wiser if it regards this as a taken for granted assumption.

Somewhere in the necessary tension between these two points of view, the contemporary Danish folk high school can be found As the ethnographic description of the previous chapter should have made clear, these schools remain in the best and deepest sense schools for life.

II. SOME IMPLICATIONS OF THE DANISH PATH TO MODERNIZATION

The Danish modernization process, which began to accelerate in the decades after 1750 with the Land Reforms, was essentially completed by the time of the Second World War. By that time even the *husmænd* had been set free from their chains. A rural, largely preindustrial society had been transformed into an urbanized, industrialized one, its overall demographic patterns showing (for instance) the lower infant mortality and increased life expectancy that are predicted to come with modernization. It is significant that throughout the period in question there were no violent revolutions or civil wars, nor does there seem to have been any systematic police or military action by the Danish government against the Danish population. What has been seen in Denmark in the decades since 1945 comprises a distinct but related set of problems perhaps best referred to as "postmodern." In this way the modern and postmodern periods can be analytically separated for purposes of discussion.[10]

Of what relevance are the folk high schools and the Danish path to modernization for developing nations in today's postmodern world? Both the recent anthropological literature dealing with cross-cultural education and a series of older studies in acculturation show that the attempt to transfer institutions across culture is difficult and frequently fails.[11] The folk high school is nothing else if it is not Danish. On the other hand, it is clear that the Danish society of the late eighteenth and nineteenth century had many features in common with today's third world cultures (rural poverty, dominant landowner class, etc.). Two other things are also clear: (1) it would be to the advantage of many contemporary third world cultures if they could undergo some local variant of the relatively peaceful and non-violent modernization process that took place in Denmark; and (2) democracy (as Asmarom Legesse points out) is not a unique Western institution: many third world cultures have viable, non-Western democratic traditions of their own, forming a preexisting base to which parts of the Danish experience could be adapted if favorable conditions arose.[12] The latter restates an important point: the take-off period for the Danish Land Reforms was a time of rising expectations and increasing economic general prosperity. Keeping the above reservations in mind, I believe that it is nonetheless possible to abstract some universalistic principles from the history of the Danish path to modernization. In my judgment these principles speak to the problems of human development both in "modernizing" and postmodern societies.

The first of them is that the institution of the folk high school was built on a deep faith in people and in their ability to intelligently alter and improve their situation as a result of their education. It is of critical importance that the type of education offered in these schools was not conceived of as any positivistic set of data points to be learned by rote and committed to memory for an examination. On the contrary, the inner core of meaning of this type of education involved a deep transformation of character and self-identity. The goal of this transformation was to facilitate the growth of a new set of positive attitudes toward self and society. The prediction was made that the learning of data points will come later (and in the Danish case it certainly did, a conclusion richly attested to by the development of the successful cooperative movement in agriculture). This is the first lesson the folk high school taught: real education begins by communicating to its students a deep sense of mission and purpose. Along with this sense of personal mission, it teaches them that they have within themselves the ability to acquire whatever specific skills are required for its achievement.

One could say in response that the education of the SS in Hitler's Germany also communicated a deep sense of personal mission. But there was a significant difference in the form education took in Denmark, and the difference is probably due most of all to the meaning that Grundtvig's concept of *folkelighed* has come to have in Danish society. This is the true meaning of *folkelighed*: it teaches a form of patriotism that steadfastly refuses to devalue other cultures. Unlike most forms of nationalism, which build up self at the cost of other, the principle of *folkelighed* that Grundtvig taught in his poems, hymns, and histories repeatedly emphasized that "the others are just as worthy as we are." *Folkelighed* thus stands adamantly opposed to the strident demands of nationalism. It is true that the young farmers who attended an early folk high school were taught to believe in themselves and their own destiny, but by the same token they were never taught to find scapegoats among other nations or ethnic groups. They learned (as do the students in folk high schools today) to respect the diversity and wisdom of the world's other cultures and to see what can be learned from them. A style of education more in contrast to the ideology of the SS can hardly be imagined. This is the second lesson of the folk high school; the principle of *folkelighed,* functioning as an alternative to nationalism, aided the peaceful transformation of self and society.

A third lesson of the folk high school is its long-term continuity in the entire life cycle. One of the most remarkable features of these schools was the social network that grew up around them. Often connected with the activities of a popular and respected principal (recall the letters from former students to Ernst Trier in Chapter Five), this network made it possible for someone who had once attended a folk high school to continue for decades—or even a lifetime—the process of learning and personal uplift that had begun while a student there. New forms of community (such as the meetinghouses and the Grundtvigian free schools) were also created. It was in this sense that the schools by all accounts seem to have met the challenge of Grundtvig, embodied in the old man's angry call to create in Denmark "a School for Life."

A fourth lesson of these schools is that those connected with them shared not only a national identity, but a value system based on revitalization and self-improvement. First, it was equally true of both educators and

educated, of the "folk high school men" and the young farmers who went
to their schools, that all were Danish. But this common cultural origin
provided in itself no necessary protection from educational imperialism.
Indeed, many folk high school people were from a different and more
privileged social class than the farmers they taught. Nonetheless, they did
not act as cultural imperialists imposing their own values on a passive or
hostile student population (the latter are two frequent signs that suggest
the presence of educational imperialism).

Although they had a deep sense of mission and viewed their work in
Weberian terms as a quasi-religious "calling," those who lived and taught
at these schools could not be called missionaries, if by this latter term we
mean to imply the possession of patronizing, condescending feelings toward
their students. Their educational role was given added strength due to the
fact that they and their students possessed a common purpose. The goal of
this education was to be the improvement of the life of the farmer; this was
their common spiritual center. The fortunate confluence of roles seen here
reflects the fact that the movement which gave rise to these schools was local,
decentralized and grass roots. It was not imposed from above or from without
as a "development strategy," nor was its success something that could have
been purchased by an outside agency for a given price. For development
theorists, the history of the folk high school provides a valuable case study
of a successful and enduring grass roots movement in adult education.

A fifth consideration is that the type of folk high school relevant to
the needs of a developing country might well be closer to the original
pattern, that is, to a school for one particular group in the population that
aims at building pride and self-confidence among the members of that group
without teaching them to hate or to feel superior to anyone else. Such a
school could either be allied with specific institutes for technical training
(following the Danish pattern, in which the agricultural high schools that
gave technical training were kept separate from the folk high schools), or
the two types of education could be combined in a single school. The type
of folk high school found in Denmark today is a response to crisis in a
technologically advanced, industrialized nation; it seems doubtful to me
that a developing country would be able to spare the resources to allow its
citizens the "socially sanctioned moratorium" that today's Danish folk high
schools make possible. Whether other nations sharing with Denmark the
postmodern condition could benefit from its experience, and might attempt
to create parallel institutions supplying such a moratorium to their own
citizens, is a rhetorical question that must at least be posed here.

Crucial as the folk high schools are, an analysis that has them as its
exclusive focus leaves out a fundamental feature of the Danish path to

modernization. To understand its true meaning let us look again at the two primary agents of transformation, the Danish Land Reforms (1784–97) and the peaceful surrender of absolute royal authority (1848–49). The most significant feature of these reforms was that they represented an enlightened surrender of destructive social power and privilege. Moreover, in both cases the surrender was made by representatives of a social elite to members of social classes over which they had long exercised virtual absolute rule.

In the case of the Land Reforms, the leading members of the landed elite had two related goals, an idealistic and a practical one. It was their ardent desire both to correct existing social injustice and to increase the general prosperity of Denmark. Not being bound by the short-run micro-economic thinking that has a stranglehold on nearly all contemporary discussions of development (a style of argument that E. F. Schumacher has aptly labeled "the religion of economics"), these men were clear-sighted enough to discern that the two goals were not mutually exclusive. In fact, the achievement of the one depended on the achievement of the other. It is precisely this kind of farsightedness, I am tempted to say, that was conspicuously missing from most social policy discussions both in America and elsewhere during the 1980s.

In passing the Land Reform legislation, the social elite to which Reventlow and his compatriots belonged set in motion a long series of positive developments that would benefit Danish society long after they themselves were gone from the scene. The fact that their wisdom was both idealistic and practical can be seen, for instance, in their insistence on a gradual transformation of the law regarding *stavnsbaandet*. By giving all concerned twelve years (1788–1800) before the legislated loosening of the law would go into effect, they succeeded both in reducing general fears and in giving everyone involved time to cope with the projected changes. This wise policy encouraged the creation of an altered social environment in which those who had been at odds with each other could now try to figure out how to become partners benefitting through mutual cooperation. Its results were evident in the description of the physical and social reorganization of agriculture *(udskiftning* and *udflyttning)* that took place in the town of Fjellerup in 1794 (Chapter Four, p. 143). Of special interest is the fact that this difficult, lengthy, and complicated process was begun on the initiative of the estate owner.

It would take well over a century before the full meaning of these farsighted legislative reforms would become evident. Their long-term impact could then be seen in such developments as (1) the flourishing of the folk high schools, (2) the successes of the agricultural cooperatives, and (3) the emergence of the other social movements that acted as "secondary agents of transformation." One of the central conclusions of this inquiry is that the prior history of the Land Reforms accounts for much of the generally peaceful and non-violent Danish modernization process. Its predominantly peaceful character was further enhanced by the non-violent surrender of absolute power on the part of a Danish king a half century later.

These events imply that the Danish model of social and economic development imposes as its initial precondition the (more or less) voluntary and peaceful surrender of destructive social privilege by dominant elites. This requirement does not mean that dominant elites must give up all their power, but that the possession of unreasonable social and economic power must be non-violently replaced by a more limited set of privileges (the question of what is "unreasonable," of course, goes to the very heart of the matter). The net effect of reform, in any case, must be a greater sharing of available resources during an era of crisis-driven social change. This is the first step in the Danish path toward modernization. An interesting parallel to the Danish case may be found in neighboring Finland, where in sharp contrast to the Baltic lands a Finnish nobility that "actively promoted the development of Finnish autonomy" was willing to freely abandon its privileged status during the revolution of 1905.[13]

In conflict situations where some equivalent to the Danish solution is not found, uglier and more painful outcomes can frequently be seen. The 1990 Yearbook of the Stockholm International Peace Research Institute documents thirty-two major armed conflicts during 1989 alone, with a brutal war in Liberia too new to make the list. A conservative estimate is that more than 20 million people, most of them civilians, have died in armed conflicts around the world since 1945.[14] It was a multitude of unresolved smaller conflicts in the region that led the nations of the world to the incendiary war in Iraq and the Persian Gulf in 1991. Peaceful conflict resolution such as that seen in Denmark provides at least in theory an alternative pathway to this epidemic of organized destruction, with its repetitive cycles of protracted civil war, violent revolution, expansionist militarism, and police state terror.

Behind much of this conflict lies the significant but rarely discussed issue of "failed modernization." Speaking for his own country, the Mexican anthropologist Roger Bartra has encapsulated the relationship between its social classes by using the image of the axolotl, the amphibian that reproduces in its larval state without reaching adulthood.[15] With all due respect to the real animal, its life history—used as a metaphor for human society— suggests a frozen pattern of development, a failure to mature, a fundamental incompleteness. I would like to extend Bartra's metaphor and use the image of the axolotl to speak of the pattern of failed modernization. Many of the world's ostensibly "modernizing" societies appear to be going nowhere, caught up in cycles of bitter violence, defense of extreme privilege, and failure of compromise and conflict resolution. It is well to remember that the Estes study includes, in addition to the three principal categories of Developed Market Economies, Eastern Bloc, and Developing Countries, a fourth category called Least Developing Countries (LDC). Many of the countries belonging to this category have in recent decades moved in the direction of greater poverty and social instability (in 1975, the list of LDCs included Chad, Uganda, Ethiopia, and Upper Volta).[16] I believe that these late eighteenth-century words of solicitor Oluf Bang have as much relevance for the situation of those in today's third world, for those in contemporary India and El Salvador, as they did for the tenant farmers of his day:

> Where this exists, the Farmer is utterly oppressed, [and] an oppressed man can neither desire nor act well; the concern that all Created Beings have for their deeds, which is their own welfare, is lacking in him. He may do as he will, he sees nothing other than Poverty and Oppression; he may finally stop wanting his own Best [interests]; because he sees that he can't attain it. This despair is the first thought that each upcoming generation drinks in. It sets roots, propagates itself, and becomes a source of corruption to entire generations. . . . I find this mode of treatment both completely destructive and completely unjust.

Or recall these words of Colbjørnsen: "The tenant farmer's rights should therefore be decided by a law. This law, which shall protect a poorer class against a mightier, must therefore be given such strength and constancy, that neither the might of the one nor the weakness of the other will be able to shake it, or hinder its serious enforcement." The Danish path to modernization is encapsulated in these words. It is a topic that deserves further serious scrutiny. Both the spirit and philosophy of its major reforms and the practical measures by which they were implemented are of great relevance in today's world. Further study of these events in Danish history could throw light on two major contemporary problems: the failed modernization that plagues many third world nations and the internal social disintegration that plagues the prosperous, postmodern Western democracies. These are unresolved problems of enormous significance.

III. Concluding Reflections

On 22 November 1990 a national election was announced in Denmark. The minority government that had been in power since 1988, a coalition made up of the Conservative, *Venstre* (Left), and *Radikal Venstre* (Radical Left) parties (the KVR government), was forced to call the election ostensibly over a narrow question of taxation. Several weeks of intense negotiation between the economic ministers of the three coalition parties and the Social Democrats (the largest opposition party) had failed to produce a compromise agreement. When the negotiations broke down even after the personal participation of the prime minister, an election was called for the twelfth of December, three weeks later.

In typical Danish fashion, the politicians from all parties were not allowed to think that they were anything special. "An election without content" was the conclusion in one editorial.[17] "An election campaign without respect for the sound sense of the voters" was the abrasive comment of a columnist.[18] "Shameless," commented another editorial writer. A pre-election poll showed that only 11% of the voters believed the politicians' promises that lighter taxes were on the way.[19]

When Prime Minister Poul Schlüter and Social Democratic Chairman Svend Auken held their first public debate of the campaign at Askov Højskole a week before the election, a panel of four højskole students was selected by *Politiken* to evaluate the debate. The students unanimously agreed that it had been a flop, that the politicians had only given them time to ask a few of their questions.[20] In contrasting the relative appeal of these two major politicians (both of them central figures in contemporary Danish politics), one political commentator cited the dictum of movie actress Mae West: "When I'm faced with two evils, I choose the man I haven't tried before."[21] The implication about the respective merits of the two men was clear if not flattering. Nevertheless, when election day came, in spite of the pouring rain and pre-Christmas stress, more than 82% of the adult population turned out to vote.[22]

The results of the election were not simple to decipher. A net of six seats in the *Folketing* had been transferred from the right to the left bloc. But within each bloc there were complications. Of the parties on the right, the Left had gained seats, but most likely at the expense of the Conservative, Radical Left, and Progress parties, all of which lost seats. Of the parties on the left, the Social Democrats gained hugely, but much of this gain may have been at the expense of the left-wing Socialist People's Party. A handful of small parties on both the left and the right were probably the biggest losers, failing to record enough votes to gain representation in the *Folketing*.[23] But there were also a number of well-known faces from the political mainstream who did not gain reelection.

If there is anything truly shameless about Danish politics, it is the round of intense post-election maneuvering that is necessary to form a government when no single party or bloc has been given a clear majority to do so. A mad dance of promises, treachery, accusations, flirtations, wooing, cuckoldry, and desertion follows, all telescoped within a week or ten days' time and reported in grisly personal detail by the press. Finally, a government emerges from this stressful chrysalis of democracy. I followed the election on Norwegian television, reading the Danish newspapers a day later. The coverage of the Danish election in Norway was quite good. To my surprise, Prime Minister Poul Schlüter (the longest governing conservative prime minister of the century) succeeded in doing the impossible: he put together a new minority government consisting only of his Conservative and the Left party (the KV government). More than his two previous coalition governments (the Four-Leaf Clover and the KVR), this one seemed to be walking a political tightrope right from the beginning. Yet as some Danish commentators were quick to point out, the fact that the whole framework of political debate had changed with extraordinary speed made predicting the future more difficult than ever before.

For one thing, 1990 was the year when a significant segment of the Danish political elite, previously critical of the proposed European Union, came instead to strongly support it. Some leading Social Democrats in particular decided that their former opposition to European Union was isolationist and could no longer be justified after the recent events in eastern Europe and the Soviet Union. Thus a proposed Union declared "stone-dead" by Prime Minister Schlüter as recently as 1986 now seems to have carried the day.[24] Interestingly enough, in spite of its overriding critical importance for Denmark's future, the detailed pros and cons of this issue do not seem to have been much discussed by the representatives of the major parties in the election of 1990. Some observers even felt that the major parties had studiously avoided the difficult issues of European Union in a narrowly pragmatic campaign lacking principled ideology and oriented toward the rhetorical simplification of television. When the Conservatives begin to preach ecology and the Social Democrats financial responsibility, who then is one to believe? Can one trust the assurances of the major politicians that the coming European Union will be both inevitable and on the whole benign? Or should one listen to minority voices such as the defeated *Folketing* candidate Ebbe Klovedal Reich, who predicts that the European Union will do away with the Danish democracy just as easily as the absolute rule of Danish kings was abolished in its time?[25] And if Ebbe Kløvedal Reich is correct, what alternative Danish decisions could delay, alter, or transform the face of European Union?

Seen through the eyes of a foreign anthropologist, part of the problem may be that the movement to European Union is simply taking place far too quickly given the magnitude of the proposed changes. It may be relevant to recall in this context that part of the genius of the Danish Land Reforms was the steady and gradual pace of their enactment. Just one step at a time, with frequent tea pauses; in this way their successful impact on the wider society was spread over many decades. One could argue that this pace of life was only possible in a bygone age, one before automobiles, jet planes, computers, and even radio. Yet to do so would constitute a serious failure of the imagination. There is no reason why we in the postmodern present cannot learn from the workable past of our own societies, and try to adapt this knowledge to the problems of our present.

Kierkegaard, writing more than a hundred years ago, made a strange and unusual observation about the future: "He who fights the future, has a dangerous enemy. The future is not, it borrows its strength from the man himself, and when it has tricked him out of this, then it appears outside of him as the enemy he must meet."[26] If the consequences of European Union are to be as bad as many Danes fear, then the dictum of Kierkegaard needs to be amended. Perhaps the future will come to be an even more dangerous enemy if one does *not* fight against it. Seen in this light, did the dominance of the large parties in the 1990 election represent a victory for pragmatic clear-thinking, or were the smaller parties bearing a terrible truth to which most people simply turned a deaf ear? Even for those in favor of it, wouldn't the European Union be better conceived of and deliberately planned as a process that will take place in the course of decades rather than a few quick years? Shouldn't it be tied to a more gradual timetable, allowing all parties to adapt to and overcome the problems of each new phase before moving on to the next?

To speak of the Danish Land Reforms in today's political context suggests an obvious question: where is Denmark now in terms of its history? From the last half of the nineteenth century the Danes began a sustained movement down their own alternative pathway to modernization. Some of its major themes have been (1) the predominantly peaceful surrender and sharing of absolute power by established social elites; (2) the abandonment of external military conquest and interference in the internal affairs of other countries as ways of solving the nation's problems; and (3) the flourishing of people-oriented, cooperative solutions facilitated both by a complex of grass roots social movements and a generally benevolent and permissive state. In the area of rural modernization, a movement over time based on these trends made it possible for the Danes to develop one of the world's most productive systems of agriculture. Although not rich in natural resources, they became at the same time one of the most prosperous and genuinely democratic nations the world has ever known. But Denmark stands at a crossroads now, its older vision challenged by the harsh realities of a postmodern age.

One question many Danes are asking today is whether these older progressive strategies can work in today's relentlessly competitive global economy. Faced with such new problems as the demands of European Union and the balance of payments deficit, many argue that they are in fact irrelevant. In his own day Grundtvig grappled with the problem of Denmark's decline. Its fearsome prospect was very real to him, and the need to formulate strategies that would avert it and preserve the special enlightenment he felt would someday be Denmark's gift to the world was one of the things that drove him through the long sleepless nights of selfless labor and creation. Yet it remains an open question: will the vision of which his work was an integral part survive, or is that vision doomed to disappear? Will Grundtvig's vision serve to inspire new Danish "people-oriented" solutions to pressing problems, or is it really nothing more than the outdated vision of a nineteenth-century Nordic culture quack, inadequate to the needs of the postmodern era and soon to be relegated to the deserved obscurity of the Folk High School Songbook?

It is difficult to say whether Grundtvig's vision will survive. It is not difficult to identify the alternative vision that would replace it. I wrote earlier of European Union and the "Germanization/Thatcherization/Americanization" of Denmark. Even more than images of Thatcherized social services and German-owned Danish coasts, I would argue that the energy of the new vision that seems to be taking hold in their society is coming from another place. The real direction of this projected change is nothing less than the Americanization of Denmark. If it continues, some of the developments will include a further transformation to the politics of individualism, the gradual loss of a welfare-state ethic, and the inevitable emergence of a highly stratified society with entrenched and ever-widening patterns of social inequality. Denmark, in other words, will come more and more to resemble the United States.

An anthropologist probably shouldn't take sides on this question, particularly an American one. A good number of Danes offer convincing, well-reasoned arguments that given the present situation this is the only way that Danish problems can be responsibly solved.[27] Yet I cannot resist making an observation: it is ironic that this increased identification with America and the American way of life comes precisely at a time when American models of modernization and economic development need to be questioned more than ever before. A good number of voices (both American and other) have expressed deep concern with the American model of development in recent decades.

I cannot conclude these reflections without mentioning two of the most eloquent among them. To cite the first completes a circle by making clear some long-term consequences of the Oklahoma Land Rush (discussed in Excursus Two). Less than thirty-five years after the overnight rush to grab land in Oklahoma, on a day of high wind from the west, a strange dark cloud hung over the city of New York and the coast north and south of it. In the words of Edward Hyams: "The cloud was dust, and the dust was the topsoil of the Middle West, including vast areas of Oklahoma, on its way to be lost in the Atlantic. A combination of monoculture, dust-mulching, a couple of drought years in succession and a couple of weeks' high wind, had had its inevitable result. The soil of the Middle West was blowing into the Atlantic at a rate which, combined with water-erosion in other parts, could reduce North America to a barren Sahara in a matter of about a century."[28]

Hyams remarks that the thousands of farmers who flocked to Oklahoma between 1889 and 1900 must have thought at the time that they were founding a new agricultural civilization that would endure as long as Egypt. Yet only a few short decades later they were forced to trek from their ruined farms "with the dust of their own making in their eyes and hair, the barren sand of a once fertile plain gritting between their teeth." Failing to understand the limitations of their ecosystem, they unwittingly became "a disease of their soil" and were forced westward in single families, in groups of families, to pick fruit in California. They became the unfortunate and despised "Okies," immortalized in American literature by the work of John Steinbeck. The connection between the people who became the Okies and the earlier Oklahoma Land Rush is not generally known. It is an open and relevant question whether the dominant pattern of large-scale capitalist development, a pattern that until recent years was most identified with American methods and technology, is driving us toward a similar disastrous outcome on a global scale.

From a larger perspective, what I have called "the American model" blends indistinguishably into the larger global capitalist culture. At the level of the single interconnected world system, it is a culture whose terrifying dynamic the American anthropologist Loren Eiseley has instructively compared to the life cycle of a slime mold:

> It came to me in the night, in the midst of a bad dream, that perhaps man, like the blight descending on a fruit, is by nature a parasite, a spore bearer, a world eater. . . . Modern man, the world eater, respects no space and no thing green or furry as sacred. The march of the machines has entered his blood. They are his seed boxes, his potential wings and guidance systems on the far roads of the universe. The fruition time of the planet virus is at hand. It is high autumn, the autumn before winter topples the spore cities.[29]

Do the writings of Grundtvig have any relevance for this shared and confusing present, or is he a figure whose thoughts and ideas have meaning mainly for the past? It is easy enough to point to Grundtvig's excesses, to ridicule his often impenetrable prose, his unending tilting at windmills, perhaps even his naive passionate belief in the possibilities of the common person. Many Danes have done so with justification both during and after Grundtvig's time. Yet for all his idealistic preoccupations the old man sometimes showed himself to be worldly and clever in the extreme. When he got it right, he could be remarkably prophetic. Take these lines from the fifth verse of his poem "Folkelighed," in which he is describing in the awkward metaphors of his nineteenth-century language one of the deepest sources of the present social crisis in America and elsewhere:

If one class regards itself as superior to the spirit of the common people, then the head, the hands and the feet will part ridiculously on their own. Then the nation is torn apart. Then the history has come to an end. Then the people have been put to sleep, and you cannot wake them up again.

There is much to be gained from reinterpreting Grundtvig. Yet a deeper treatment of these issues must be left for another occasion. Let us now ask what these general reflections on America and the postmodern condition imply for an analysis of Denmark and its folk high schools. The first thing that must be said is that E. F. Erikson's "identity confusion" is not an uncommon phenomenon, especially among youth in today's Denmark. The purpose of the welfare state is to provide a secure life for Danish citizens. For most of them it succeeds in this goal, at least insofar as this can be shown by outward statistical measures. Yet under all the achievements and the prosperity, and underneath the impressive statistics, there is a widespread mood of doubt, of emptiness, and of futility. In my judgment this dark mood is the greatest threat of all. When all the institutions seem to be breaking down, what then? Or when all the institutions function, and everything is going well on the outside and you still feel a sense of emptiness, of something missing, what then? I have heard a prominent educator speak of "the failure of the social democratic vision" that has guided Denmark for more than half a century. Is the vision with which it shall be replaced the Americanization of Denmark?

Even in an Americanized Denmark, the institution of the folk high school will survive. But under such circumstances the already present tendency for Danish society to be sharply divided into winners and losers could well be intensified. The "winners" will be those who take the most practical, short-run, instrumentalist approaches to education: don't ask what the meaning of anything is, just take the courses and get the training that will—you hope—ensure your private economic security. In an American-ized Denmark, these young people will not come to the folk high schools to ask questions about life and its meaning; indeed, they will be likely to think of a folk high school as a place where the social losers go because no one else will have them. One could envision a gradual decline in folk high school attendance as more and more people begin to regard education in a purely pragmatic and short-term way. The important question to ask in such a society might be, "Who goes to a folk high school and who *doesn't* go?" If the folk high school becomes a dumping ground for social losers or comes to be widely perceived as such a school, serious consequences for the role it plays in Danish society will most likely follow.

My own estimation is that Grundtvig's general vision for Danish society and the specific institution of the folk high school will survive even these difficult times. I am not able to convince myself that they are on the way out in spite of the logic of these gloomy ruminations. It is a prediction based not on any intellectual analysis of trends and directions in Danish culture, but on a certain feeling for the country and its history. It is hard to talk about these things objectively. What is the nature of Grundtvig's influence? You can see it in the laughter and self-respect of the Danish working man, and in the egalitarianism that is today, in spite of existing stratification and inequality, a fundamental Danish value. There is a large and impressive statue of Grundtvig outside of the Marble Church in downtown Copenhagen, but Grundtvig's heritage is far more than a thing of stone and marble.

Ole Wivel has suggested an apt metaphor. There is a famous painting that hangs at the National Museum in Frederiksborg: Constantine Hansen's monumental rendering of the Assembly that drafted the first Danish constitution in 1848. Grundtvig appears in that painting to have been brought in as an afterthought, occupying a minor and modest place off to one side. Yet a closer examination reveals that the painter placed Grundtvig exactly in the perspective vanishing point of the picture. Wivel quotes a comment by museum director Povl Eller: "Grundtvig has been put in the main position. All of the room's lines meet directly over the crown of his head. It's not something that hits you in the eye, on the contrary, there's actually no one who discovers it."[30]

There are places in Denmark where Grundtvig's picture hangs, and where his translations of hymns from the Latin are often sung. Yet it is this image of Grundtvig that in my estimation best captures his importance to Danish culture. He appears as the background figure that makes everything come together. Thus Ole Wivel writes of his own upbringing: "Grundtvig's

Den grundlovgivende rigsforsamling (*The session of the constitution-granting assembly*) 1848–49, painting by Constantine Hansen, finished in 1864. See discussion in text (reprinted by permission of the Nationalhistorisk Museum, Frederiksborg Castle).

name was seldom mentioned at home. He was in the background, in the perspective vanishing point just as in the great painting." When the *folkehøjskole* songbook is brought out, whether at high school gatherings, labor union meetings, or private parties, it is often Grundtvig's words that are the music's text. There are, on the other hand, places in Denmark where his name would never be mentioned. Indeed, if it were, it would be met with hostility, polite shrugs, or even outright indifference. It is all the same. Grundtvig's place is somewhere off in the background—in the perspective vanishing point—as in the monumental painting of Constantine Hansen. It is there that the true legacy of his visionary idealism can be found.

In an earlier chapter I briefly compared Grundtvig to Walt Whitman. I believe that some interesting comparisons could be made between the role played by Grundtvig in Denmark and Whitman in the United States. To explore these in any depth would go beyond the boundaries of this discussion. Yet it is possible that the spirit of Grundtvig's legacy to Denmark has never been given better expression than in these lines with which Walt Whitman concluded his epic poem, "Song of Myself:"

> I bequeath myself to the dirt to grow from the grass I love,
> If you want me again, look for me under your bootsoles.
>
> You will hardly know who I am or what I mean,
> But I shall be good health to you nevertheless,
> And filter and fibre your blood.
>
> Failing to fetch me at first keep encouraged,
> Missing me one place search another,
> I stop somewhere waiting for you.

When I knew Bent Martinsen at Silkeborg Højskole, he had just returned from a half year's leave of absence during which he studied at Trinity College, Cambridge. He had chosen to retrace the exact steps of Grundtvig at Cambridge 150 years earlier. While there, he carried on an investigation of Grundtvig's English experience. He described the results in these words:

> I read all of his school writings and diaries while I was there, and some after I came home. I also read his letters from England, and those he wrote after coming home. He was a fantastic personality [short but significant pause]. There's nobody that knows him in England, that's something I'd like to tell you. I asked about him in some places while I was there. They shook their heads and said, "We never heard of him." But we're used to that, such a little country as Denmark, we're used to it, that there's no one who knows

and appreciates something we think is fantastic. If he had been born in England or Germany, the whole world would know about him.[31]

For too long a time Denmark has had to exist in the shadow of its larger neighbors. It is my hope that this book will make available to a wider audience something of contemporary Denmark as well as some insight into the Danish past. Few know of Grundtvig outside of Denmark, and the figure of Reventlow (whom one is tempted to call a Danish Tolstoy) is virtually unknown. Yet the alternative Danish modernization process to which they contributed included not one but a number of "people-oriented" experiments and solutions; it is a topic of great potential interest to those concerned with third world development today. Similarly, the Danish philosophy of consistent non-violence and non-interference in the internal affairs of other nations could usefully be studied by citizens of larger nations. The goal of this book has been both to describe the pattern of these Danish achievements and to make clear some of the challenges faced by Danish society today. Only the future will make clear the pattern of their resolution.

*Entitled "Militarism," this sculpture by the Danish artist Niels Hansen Jacobsen
aptly symbolizes the contemporary Danish (and Scandinavian) perspective on war and
the abuses of militarism. Note the skulls in varying states of decomposition at the figure's
feet. This prophetic sculpture was completed in 1899, well before the two world wars of
our century. Vejen, Denmark. (Slide courtesy of Karen Holst, Askov Højskole).*

EXCURSUS SIX

The Land of The Living
—N. F. S. Grundtvig (1824)

I know a land,
Where hair never grays, and time has no teeth,
Where the sun never burns, and the waves do not harm,
Where the autumn embraces the blossoming spring,
Where evening and morning go always in dance,
With the light of midday's radiance.

O wonderful land,
Where no tears run in the hourglass sand,
Where nothing is missing that is worth wishing,
Where the only thing lacking is what causes pain!
We seek with longing again that which we remember most
Your smiling coast.

Promised Land!
You are greeted in morning's mirror-clear shores,
When the child takes as real your bright image there seen
And dreams you are found where the forest is green,
The child shares your smile with the flowers of spring
That grow in a ring.

O, transient dream
Of eternity's island in the stream of time,
Of the temple for joy in the valley of tears,
Of half-divine life in the room of the dying!
From the long sojourn of generations giving
The land of the living.

O, disappointing dream!
You shining bubble on the stream of time!
The poet in vain with mouth and pen,
From shining shadows would create you again
When likeness comes nearest, the little ones weep
This vision to keep.

O, spirit of love!
Let me childlike kiss your shining hand,
That reaches from heaven to earth's rich mould
And touches our eyes with fingers like gold,
Rising like heaven from a spire of blue waves
The wonderful land.

O, heavenly name,
That opens in us your holy embrace,
So spirit unfettered can touch human dust,
Resurrect the withered leaf from its rust!
O, bowed low in my clay kneeling down may I be
That God can see.

O, wonderful faith,
Whose swaying bridge bears us over the depths,
Defying the roaring sound of the icy river below,
From death's home to the land of the living!
Sit lower beside me, o high-born guest!
As you like it best.

O, love
You peaceful source for the river of all strength!
He calls you father, who loosens our bonds,
All life in the soul, a spark of your spirit,
Your kingdom is there, where one overcomes death
It comes in each breath.

O Christian faith!
You give to our heart what the world does not know,
What's only seen faintly when seen with the eye,
And yet lives within us, we feel its deep cry
My land, says life, is on heaven and earth
Where love has its hearth.

Notes

CHAPTER ONE

[1]The following is a partial list: Paul Kennedy, *The Rise and Fall of The Great Powers* (New York: Vintage, 1987); David P. Calleo, *Beyond American Hegemony* (New York: Basic Books, 1987); Mancur Olsen, *The Rise and Decline of Nations* (New Haven, Conn.: Yale University Press, 1982); William Pfaff, *Barbarian Sentiments: How the American Century Ends* (New York: Hill and Wang, 1989); Lester Thurow, *The Zero-Sum Solution: Building a World-class American Economy* (New York: Touchstone, 1985); E. Rothschild, "The Costs of Reaganism," *New York Review of Books* (15 March 1984); and Ezra Vogel, *Japan as Number One* (Cambridge, Mass.: Harvard University Press, 1979). A recent counterwave of works opposed to the thesis of decline includes: Henry R. Nau, *The Myth of American Decline: Leading the World Economy into the 1990's* (New York: Oxford University Press, 1990) and Richard Rosecrance, *America's Economic Resurgence: A Bold New Strategy* (New York: Harper & Row, 1990). For reviews of "the school of decline," see S. P. Huntington, "The U.S.—Decline or Renewal?" *Foreign Affairs,* vol. 67, no. 2 (Winter 1988–89): 76–96; and Paul Kennedy, "Can the U.S. Remain Number One?" *New York Review of Books* (16 March 1989). The recent wave of opposition to the thesis of decline is reviewed in Paul Kennedy, "Is the U.S. Going Downhill?" *New York Review of Books* (28 June 1990).

[2]Kennedy (1987), Chapters 5–7.

[3]Vogel (1979), vii.

[4]Cross-cultural perspectives on education can be found in George Spindler, ed., *Education and Cultural Process: Anthropological Approaches* (Prospect Heights, Ill.: Waveland Press, 1987) and Colin Turnbull, *The Human Cycle* (New York: Simon & Schuster, 1983). A classic volume, still relevant, is Jules Henry's *Culture Against Man* (New York: Random House, 1963).

[5]See E. F. Schumacher, *Small Is Beautiful: Economics As If People Mattered* (New York: Harper & Row, 1973), 146. I have paraphrased here Schumacher's eloquent call for a "technology with a human face."

[6]A flourishing folk high school tradition once existed in the U.S. (1870–1930). Brought by Danish immigrants after 1864, its primary locus was the Danish-American community in the American Midwest. See Jonathan Matthew Schwartz, "The *Folkehøjskole* Movement in Appalachia, USA," in *In Defense of Homesickness: Nine*

Essays on Identity and Locality (Copenhagen: Akademisk Forlag, Kultursociologiske Skrifter No. 26., 1988) and Enoch Mortensen, *Schools for Life* (Solvang, Calif.: Danish American Heritage Society, 1977). At least one folk high school exists in France, founded by Erica Simon. Her historical analysis can be found in *Réveil national et culture populaire in Scandinavie, La genèse de la Højskole nordique 1844–1878* (Copenhagen: Gyldendal, 1960).

[7]Jan Diament, "Højskoler afløser sol, sprut og grisefester: de korte højskolekurser mere populære end nogensinde" (Folk high schools replace sun, spirits and barbecues; the short high school courses more popular than ever), *Søndagsavis* 3 (26 July 1987): 1. The past decade has seen the number of short courses jump from 270 to 809, a clear sign of their growing popularity and significance.

[8]This is the closest European equivalent to the American high school: it provides education at the advanced secondary level and prepares the Danish student to take the university entrance examinations.

[9]Thus Brøndby's mayor, Kjeld Rasmussen, complained, "We are not going to pay for a *højskole* stay in which citizens learn to become better at throwing stones at the police." At issue was a brochure from the Red Højskole in Svendborg, which allegedly promised that participants in a new course would be tutored by former activists in an urban squatters' movement (the "BZers"), some of whom were known for their skill in stone throwing. The mayor emphasized that there was no talk of censorship: "All who want to teach how to break society down are free to do it. It's just that in the future they must pay for it themselves." K. B. Jørgensen, "Nej til kursus i stenkast" (No to courses in stone throwing), *Berlinske Tidende,* 11 March 1983. This type of conflict is unquestionably the exception rather than the rule.

[10]There are a number of problems connected with the uncritical use of the term "third world." It suggests an oversimplified dichotomy of wealth distribution (the situation in Costa Rica and Singapore can hardly be equated with that in Ethiopia and Guatemala); it conceals the fact that "third world" poverty can be found in inner-city areas of most cities of the industrialized Western world; and it provides no satisfactory framework to talk about the disintegrating situation of stateless indigenous "fourth world" peoples, such as the Yanomamö of Ecuador and Brazil. I have unhappily used the unsatisfactory conventional term "third world" only in the interests of providing a quick gloss for this initial discussion. See Nigel Harris, *The End of the Third World: Newly Industrializing Countries and the Decline of an Ideology* (Harmondsworth, England: Penguin, 1987).

[11]The review of Danish history is based primarily on the following works: (1) Roar Skovmand, *Danmarks Historie,* Vol. 11, Folkestyrets Fødsel (The birth of the people's government): 1830–70 (Copenhagen: Politikens Forlag, 1978); (2) Vagn Skovgaard-Petersen, *Danmarks Historie,* Vol. 5, 1814–64 (Copenhagen: Gyldendal, 1985); (3) Palle Lauring, *Danmarks Historie* (Copenhagen: Carit Andersens Forlag, 1968); (4) Jens Vibæk, *Danmarks Historie,* Vol. 10, Reform og Fallit (Reform and bankruptcy): 1784–1830 (Copenhagen: Politikens Forlag, 1964); (5) Sven Skovmand, *Den Danske Historie,* Fra 1700-tallet til 1918 (Copenhagen: Forlaget Notat, 1984); (6) Peter Ilsøe and Johs. Lomholt-Thomsen, *Nordens Historie 1* (The

history of Scandinavia) (Copenhagen: Gyldendal, 1966); (7) Ole Feldbæk and Ole Justesen, *Danmarks Historie: Kolonierne i Asien og Afrika* (The colonies in Asia and Africa) (Copenhagen: Politikens Forlag, 1980); (8) Steward Oakley, *A Short History of Denmark* (New York: Praeger, 1972); (9) Lord Acton et al., *The Cambridge Modern History*, Vol. VI, The Eighteenth Century (New York: Macmillan, 1934); (10) Erik Kjersgaard, *A History of Denmark* (Copenhagen: Danish Ministry of Foreign Affairs, 1974); (11) Kenneth E. Miller, *Government and Politics in Denmark* (Boston: Houghton Mifflin, 1968); (12) John Danstrup, *A History of Denmark* (Copenhagen: Wivels Forlag, 1947).

[12]The complex of social movements treated here could well be described as "revitalization movements," defined by Anthony Wallace as the "deliberate, organized attempts by some members of a society to construct a more satisfying culture by rapid acceptance of a pattern of multiple innovations," in "The psychology of culture change," in his *Culture and Personality* (New York: Random House, 1961), 143–44. They succeeded in accomplishing most of their aims and left a deep imprint on the structure of Danish society down to the present day.

[13]I am thinking here primarily of the events connected with the regime of J. B. S. Estrup ([1825–1913], minister in 1865–69 and 1875–94), including the Constitutional Revision of 1866 (protested by Grundtvig among many others) and the Provisional Finance Bill of 1876. In the latter case Estrup responded to the defeat of his budget proposals in the *Folketing* (parliament) by raising funds through what amounted to personal decree based on his claim that a state of emergency existed. Treated in Roar Skovmand (1978), 500–508; Oakley (1972), 198; Kjersgaard (1974), 60–64.

[14]The metaphor of a river has been suggested by Danish historian and Grundtvig scholar Hal Koch in his essay "Bidrag Til Vurdering af 19. Aarhundrede" (Contribution to an evaluation of the 19th century), in *Festschrift til J. Th. Arnfred* (Dansk Udsyn, 1953). J. Th. Arnfred, who served as principal at Askov Højskole from 1928 to 1953, was one of the foremost "high school men" of this century.

[15]Frederick Howe, *Denmark: The Cooperative Way* (New York: Coward-McCann, 1936), 1.

[16]Though the slogan is sometimes attributed to Dalgas himself, the real author was the Danish poet H. P. Holst. See Roar Skovmand (1978), 508–23. This concise translation of the Danish phrase is found in the American social reformer Frederick Howe's *Denmark: A Cooperative Commonwealth* (New York: Harcourt, Brace, 1921).

[17]An exception to this generalization can be found in the years between 1864 and 1870. At this time a desire to revenge the defeat suffered at the hands of Bismarck's Prussia was widely expressed even among folk high school students. When the loss of Slesvig was officially accepted in 1870, the bitter mood gradually gave way to acceptance.

[18]For reviews of nineteenth-century nationalism: A. J. P. Taylor, *The Struggle for Mastery in Europe, 1848–1918* (New York: Oxford University Press, 1954); F. R. Bridge and R. Bullen, *The Great Powers and the European States System 1815–1914* (London: Longman, 1980).

[19]The classic treatment of the folk high school during this period is found in Roar Skovmand, *Højskolen Gennem 100 Aar* (The Folk High School Through 100 Years) (Copenhagen: J. H. Schultz, 1944), 95–160.

[20]Quoted in Thomas Rordam, *The Danish Folk High Schools* (Copenhagen: Det Danske Selskab, 1980), 21.

[21]Niels Højlund, *Folkehøjskolen i Danmark* (The folk high school in Denmark) (Copenhagen: Aschehoug, 1983), 33.

[22]The recent two hundredth anniversary of the French Revolution was the occasion for a bicentennial celebration, but as Louis Pauwels, editor of the conservative *Figaro Magazine,* commented, "I do not know anybody on the right who is an enemy of 1789. But we should be careful in the way we celebrate it. It was necessary to reform the ancient regime, but we lost a great chance for a liberal order—and we ended up with the dictatorship of a general." The use of the guillotine and the massacres of insurgents in the Vendee between 1793 and 1795 are part of a heritage that the modern French must regard with ambivalence. See Olivier Bernier, *Words of Fire, Deeds of Blood: The Mob, the Monarchy and the French Revolution* (New York: Little, Brown, 1989); William Doyle, *The Oxford History of the French Revolution* (New York: Oxford University Press, 1989). See also James Markham, "A Calm, Ambivalent France Looks Back to 1789's Fervor," *New York Times,* 9 July 1989 (the citation from Pauwels is from this article).

[23]For a history of the decades before the revolution see Hugh Seton-Watson, *The Russian Empire, 1801–1917* (New York: Oxford University Press, 1967). For analyses of the revolution itself see E. H. Carr, *The Bolshevik Revolution, 1917–1923* (New York: Macmillan, 1951); a perspective based on newly available documents can be found in Robert Conquest, *The Great Terror: A Reassessment* (New York: Oxford University Press, 1990). See also Roy Medvedev, *The October Revolution* (New York: Columbia University Press, 1979).

[24]A superlative case study can be found in Charles Drucker, "Dam the Chico: Hydropower Development and Tribal Resistance," in *The Ecologist,* vol. 15, no. 4 (1985). See also John H. Bodley, ed., *Tribal Peoples & Development Issues* (Mayfield, Calif.: Mayfield Publishing Co., 1988); Eric Wolf, *Europe and the Peoples Without History* (Berkeley: University of California Press, 1982). Up-to-date accounts can be found in any issue of the journal *Cultural Survival Quarterly* (Cambridge, Mass.: Cultural Survival).

[25]E. F. Schumacher, *Small is Beautiful: Economics As If People Mattered* (New York: Harper & Row, 1973).

[26]Thomas Rordam, *The Danish Folk High Schools* (Copenhagen: Det Danske Selskab, 1980), 9.

[27]Ole Christensen, Poul Christensen, and Peter Warrer, *Højskolebevægelse og Almendannelse, Skitse til en forståelse af højskolens dannelsesverden* (The High School Movement and General Education: Sketch toward an understanding of the formative world of the high school), Institut for Statskundskab, Aarhus Universitet (Aug. 1981), 125.

28George E. Marcus and Michael M. J. Fischer, *Anthropology as Cultural Critique: An Experimental Moment in the Human Sciences* (University of Chicago Press, 1986). See also James Clifford, *The Predicament of Culture: Twentieth-Century Ethnography, Literature and Art* (Cambridge, Mass.: Harvard University Press, 1988). For a critique of the position taken by Marcus and Fischer, see Steve Sangren, "Rhetoric and the Authority of Ethnography," *Current Anthropology*, vol. 29, no. 3 (June 1988), 405–35. A review of Scandinavian anthropology can be found in Marianne Gullestad's "Small Facts and Large Issues: The Anthropology of Contemporary Scandinavian Society," *Annual Review of Anthropology*, vol. 18 (Oct. 1989). See also Michael Herzfeld, *Anthropology Through the Looking Glass: Critical Ethnography in the Margins of Europe* (New York: Cambridge University Press, 1987).

29Gordon A. Craig, "Getting along with Hitler" (a review of current trends among German historians), *New York Review of Books* (16 July 1987): 32.

30Hayden White, "The Burden of History," *History and Theory* 5 (1966), 132, quoted in Peter Novick, *That Noble Dream: The "Objectivity" Question and the American Historical Question* (Cambridge, England: Cambridge University Press, 1988), 599. See also by Hayden White, *Metahistory* (Baltimore: Johns Hopkins Press, 1973) and *The Content of Form: Narrative Discourse and Historical Representation* (Baltimore: Johns Hopkins Press, 1987). I am grateful to Bob Bannister for bringing this debate to my attention and for his enlightening comments regarding it.

31Jacques Derrida, *Disseminations* (University of Chicago Press, 1972). Some recent trends are discussed in Stanley Fish, *Doing What Comes Naturally: Change, Rhetoric and the Practice of Theory in Literary Studies* (Durham, N.C.: Duke University Press, 1989). Reviewed by Perry Meisel, "The Kingdom of Doublethink," *New York Times Book Review* (21 May 1989). The connections between anthropology and literary theory are reviewed by James Clifford, "Introduction: Partial Truths," in James Clifford and George Marcus, eds., *Writing Culture* (Berkeley: University of California Press, 1986), as well as many of the other contributions to this volume.

32An excellent discussion of the work of Edmund Husserl (1859–1938) can be found in Roger Poole, *Towards Deep Subjectivity* (London: Allen Lane, Penguin, 1972): see in particular Chapter 4, "Subjective Objections to 'Objectivity.' " Husserl's classic work, written between 1934 and 1938, is *The Crisis of European Sciences and Transcendental Phenomenology*, transl. David Carr (Evanston, Ill.: Northwestern, 1970).

33Niels Bohr, "Discussion with Einstein on Epistemological Problems in Atomic Physics," in P. A. Schilpp, ed., *Albert Einstein: Philosopher-Scientist* (Evanston, Ill.: The Library of Living Philosophers, 1949), 209–10 (italics in the original). For contemporary Danish interpretations of Bohr's life and work, see Tor Nørretranders, *Det Udelelige* (The Indivisible) (Copenhagen: Gyldendal, 1988) and Niels Blaedel, *Harmony and Unity: The Life of Niels Bohr* (Madison, Wisc.: Science Tech Publishers, 1988). See also Dugold Murdock, *Niels Bohr's Philosophy of Physics* (New York: Cambridge University Press, 1987).

34A good introduction can be found in Heinz R. Pagels, *The Cosmic Code* (New York: Simon & Schuster, 1982). For a more complete historical review see A. P. French and P. J. Kennedy, eds., *Niels Bohr: A Centenary Volume* (Cambridge, Mass.: Harvard University Press, 1985). Parenthetically, this volume's focus on Grundtvig should not detract from Kierkegaard's central importance in Danish intellectual history. Two examples of the latter's influence: Bohr's theory of complementarity had its roots in Kierkegaard's stress on discontinuity between incompatibles, his emphasis on the "leap" rather than the gradual transition. See Gerald Holton, "The Roots of Complementarity," in his *Thematic Origins of Scientific Thought: Kepler to Einstein* (Cambridge, Mass.: Harvard University Press, 1973), 144–47. It is quite clear that Bohr was profoundly influenced by Kierkegaard. On a more contemporary note, the Danish scientist Niels Jerne, who fundamentally altered the thinking of immunologists on two occasions with the natural selection theory (1955) and the network theory (1973) of immune response, has described how reverberations of Kierkegaard's thought contributed to his idea of the selective mechanism of antibody formation (cited in E. S. Golub, *Immunology: A Synthesis* [Sunderland: Sinauer, 1987], 9–10. Golub, p. 379, referring to Jerne's 1985 Nobel Prize, writes that "his contributions have been so extensive that it must have been a very difficult task for the committee to decide which of them to cite in the award.") For an exposition of Jerne's network theory, see his Nobel acceptance lecture, "The Generative Grammar of the Immune System," *EMBO Journal*, vol. 4, no. 4 (1985): 847–52. I am grateful to Scott Gilbert for pointing out this connection between Kierkegaard and the extraordinary scientific work of Niels Jerne.

[35]For a moving account of how subjective emotional experiences led an anthropologist to a radically new understanding of the motivations behind the practice of headhunting, see Renato Rosaldo, "Grief and a Headhunter's Rage: On the Cultural Force of Emotions," in E. Bruner, ed., *Text, Play and Story* (Seattle: American Ethnological Society, 1984).

[36]C. Wright Mills, *The Sociological Imagination* (New York: Oxford University Press, 1959), 6.

[37]These maps do not cover Denmark's earlier colonial holdings overseas in Africa, Asia, and the East and West Indies (which included Tranquebar in south India, several forts on West Africa's Gold Coast, and the Danish Virgin Islands—the latter sold to the U.S. in 1917). The history of the Danish holdings in Africa and Asia is covered in Feldbæk and Justesen (1980); the Danish Virgin Islands in Jones (1970), 243–45.

Maps 2 through 6 have been adapted with permission from Johan S. Rosing, *Gyldendals Historiske Atlas* (Copenhagen: Gyldendal, 1973). Other sources used in preparation include Rolf M. Hagen et al., *Norges Historie* (The history of Norway), Bind 15: Historisk Atlas (Vol. 15, Historic Atlas) (Oslo: J. W. Capellans Forlag, 1980); Ilsøe and Lomholt-Thomsen (1966); Vibæk (1964); Skovmand (1978); Skovgaard-Petersen (1985). I thank Jeff Case and Linda Maxwell for their skilled computer work in adapting the maps, and Vagn and Inge Skovgaard-Petersen for their very helpful introduction to the complexities of medieval Danish history and the relationship between Denmark and Sweden in the seventeenth century.

38Judith Friedman Hansen, "Danish Social Interaction: Cultural Assumptions and Patterns of Behavior" (Unpublished Ph.D. thesis, Department of Anthropology, University of California at Berkeley, 1970).

CHAPTER TWO

1The Norwegian actress Liv Ullman reports in her autobiography, *Changing* (New York: Knopf, 1977), 162, that she was greeted one time on her return to Hollywood at Christmas by friends who "have brought colored balls and long strings of Swedish flags—but this is not an uncommon mistake in Hollywood, where Norway is thought to be some province in Scandinavia." Scandinavians living in America must get used to such experiences.
2Sir Edmund William Gosse, *Two Visits to Denmark*, (London: Smith, Elder and Co., 1911), 98–99.
3Given the cultural code of modesty (discussed in Chapter 7), it would not be easy for a Dane to make the glowingly positive evaluations of Denmark that I express here. Two Danish authors who have nonetheless dared to make many of the same connections are the rural agricultural historian Fridlev Skrubbeltrang in his English-language pamphlet "Agricultural Development and Rural Reform in Denmark," Food and Agricultural Organization of the United Nations (Rome, Italy, 1957) and more recently historian Uffe Østergård, "Hvad er det 'danske' ved Danmark?" (What is the "Danish" about Denmark: Thoughts on the Danish way to capitalism, Grundtvigianism and the "Danish" mentality), *Den Jysk Historiker*, Nr. 29–30 (1984). See also Uffe Østergård, "Peasants and Danes: Danish National Identity and Political Culture." Working paper (Center for Cultural Research, Aarhus University, 1990).
4Paul Lewis, "In Oslo, Blessings for 733 Who Kept the Peace," *New York Times*, 12 Dec. 1988.
5Samuel Rachlin, "Danes–Some of the World's Biggest Doubters," *New York Times*, 30 Nov. 1986.
6B. W. Andrzejewski and I. M. Lewis, *Somali Poetry: An Introduction* (New York: Oxford University Press, 1964), 144.
7Numerous discussions of this theme can be found in Melford E. Spiro, ed., *Context and Meaning in Cultural Anthropology* (New York: Free Press, 1965) (a *festschrift* volume for A. Irving Hallowell). See also Peter Berger and Thomas Luckman, *The Social Construction of Reality* (New York: Doubleday, 1966).
8See the essay "Frontier Thesis and American Foreign Policy," in William A. Williams, *History as a Way of Learning* (New York: New Viewpoints, 1973). A voluminous literature exists concerning Turner's work. In addition to the above, see the work of such historians as Charles Beard, James C. Malin, Walter P. Webb, and the critiques of Turner by Benjamin Wright, George W. Pierson, Earl Pomeroy, Arthur Schlesinger, Jr., and Fred Shannon. The utility of the frontier concept is certainly not limited to American and Canadian history; three other examples that

can be cited are the relationship of Australians to the aborigine population; that between Israel and the Occupied Territories; and that of modern Brazil to its rain forests. The concept has also proved useful in African studies. Using a radically revised version of Turner's frontier hypothesis, one suggesting that the frontier "may also be a force for culture-historical continuity and conservatism," Igor Kopytoff has been able to throw new light on such previously puzzling phenomena in African ethnology as the widespread occurrence of divine kingship. See his "The Internal African Frontier: The Making of African Political Culture," in I. Kopytoff, ed., *The African Frontier* (Bloomington, Ind.: Indiana University Press, 1987). Another use of the frontier concept in African history is found in Howard Lamar, *The Frontier in History: North America and Southern Africa Compared* (New Haven, Conn.: Yale University Press, 1981). Lamar, a Yale historian, laid the foundations for a revisionist view of the American West with his *Reader's Encyclopedia of the American West* (New York: Crowell, 1977). This new view emphasizes greed, environmental plunder, racial strife, and sharp dichotomies between rich and poor. See, for instance, Patricia Limerick, *The Legacy of Conquest: The Unbroken Past of the American West* (New York: Norton, 1987).

[9]The quotes, taken from Turner's 1893 paper, "The Significance of the Frontier in American History," are cited in Forrest McDonald's excellent review, "Rugged Individualism: Frederick Jackson Turner and the Frontier Thesis," in *The World and I* (Washington Times Corporation, May 1990), 539. For a biography of Turner, see Ray Billington, *Frederick Jackson Turner: Historian, Scholar, Teacher* (New York: Oxford University Press, 1973). The discussion in this chapter emphasizes the negative features of the frontier heritage; to adequately cover its positive features, what Turner perceptively called the legacy of frontier idealism, would require a separate and lengthy treatment of its own.

[10]Paul Kennedy, "Is the U.S. Going Downhill?" *New York Review of Books* (28 June 1990): 37.

[11]Elizabeth Hardwick, "The Fictions of America," *New York Review of Books* (25 June 1987): 12.

[12]C.Vann Woodward, *The Future of the Past* (New York: Oxford University Press, 1990). See his essay, "The Age of Reinterpretation," and the excellent review by David Brion Davis, "The Rebel," *New York Review of Books* (17 May 1990).

[13]Noam Chomsky, *The Culture of Terrorism* (Boston: South End Press, 1988), 18.

[14]Edward Hyams, *Soil and Civilization* (New York: Harper & Row, 1976), 146. See also Angie Debo, *And Still the Waters Run: The Betrayal of the Five Civilized Tribes* (University of Oklahoma Press, 1980) and Stan Hoig, *Land Rush of 1889* (Oklahoma City: Oklahoma Historical Society, 1984).

[15]Many good examples of the early American mood can be found in Richard Hofstadter's *Social Darwinism in American Thought* (Philadelphia: University of Pennsylvania Press, 1944).

[16]An unfortunate example of American blindness that had tragic consequences was the Challenger space shuttle disaster. For a devastating account of the accident itself and the official investigation that followed, see the account by Nobel laureate and

physicist Richard Feynman, "An Outsider's Inside View of the Challenger Inquiry," *Physics Today* (Feb. 1988), 26–37.

[17]Christopher Tilghman, *In a Father's Place* (New York: Farrar, Straus & Giroux, 1990). Reviewed by Michiko Kakutani, "Going Home Again, and Finding You Can't," *New York Times*, 3 April 1990: C17.

[18]Thomas Wolfe, *The Hills Beyond* (Garden City, N.Y.: Sun Dial Press, 1935), 174–75.

[19]For a personal account of the adoption of an Indian boy suffering from fetal alcohol syndrome, see Michael Dorris, *The Broken Cord* (New York: Harper & Row, 1989). In "Uranium Miners Tell Panel Radiation Caused Ailments," *New York Times*, 14 March 1990, it is reported that "for nearly 25 years, Navajo Indian miners dug uranium ore without protection or warnings from their employers or the government, breathing in radioactive dust, eating their lunches deep in the mineshafts and even drinking contaminated water that seeped through the walls of the mines." This picture of their working conditions, presented before a U.S. Senate subcommittee, emerges from testimony that has been collected over eleven years. Many of the miners have developed health problems believed to be related to their years of exposure to ionizing radiation; yet to date they have been unable to obtain benefits under state workman's compensation.

[20]Garry Wills, "What Happened?" *Time*, 9 March 1987, 21.

[21]P. Shabecoff, " U.S. to Back Fund to Protect Ozone," *New York Times*, 16 June 1990.

[22]John Holusha, "Some Smog in Pledges to Help Environment: Companies Claims Found Misleading," *New York Times*, 19 April 1990.

[23]W. D. Ehrhart, "Who Will Apologize for Vietnam?" *Philadelphia Inquirer*, 4 July 1989.

[24]See John Holusha, "Are We Eating Our Seed Corn?" *New York Times*, 13 May 1990, Business section. For discussions of the frontier legacy of wastefulness in American life, see Marc Reisner, *Cadillac Desert: The American West and Its Disappearing Water* (New York: Viking, 1986) and Donald Worster, *Rivers of Empire: Water, Aridity and the Growth of the American West* (New York: Pantheon, 1985).

[25]Jonathan Yardley, "Throwaways Begin with Diapers," *Philadelphia Inquirer*, 30 June 1989.

[26]Herbert J. Muller, *The Uses of the Past* (New York: Oxford University Press, 1952), 25.

[27]Rubén Darío, "To Roosevelt," in *Selected Poems of Rubén Darío*, transl. Lysander Kemp (Austin, Tex.: University of Texas Press, 1965).

[28]See note 1 in the first chapter. For an overall study of the theme of limits, see Lester R. Brown et al., *State of the World: A World Watch Institute Report on Progress Toward a Sustainable Society* (New York: W. W. Norton, 1990).

[29]Poul Sørensen, introduction to Bo Bøjesen, *Dagligliv i Danmark* (Daily life in Denmark) (Copenhagen: Hans Reitzel, 1960), 12–13.

[30]The quote is from an interview in *Scanorama Magazine* (June 1984), 105. Estes' research summarized here is contained in *The Social Progress of Nations* (New York:

Praeger, 1984). In a more recent volume by Estes, *Trends in World Social Development* (New York: Praeger, 1988), Denmark continues to score at the top of the national rankings. None of the interpretations suggested here are brought into question by the results of the more recent volume (Richard Estes, personal communication). Thus two reports published in 1990 (OECD's most recent six-month report and the English *Winners and Losers in the New Europe*) portray Danish development in a less favorable light. Yet both of these reports, based solely on conventional economic indicators having to do with GNP aggregates and averages, tell little about relative social provisioning, the central topic of the Estes study. For two studies which, like those of Estes, focus on long-term sustainable development and life-quality issues, see Brown et al. (1990) (listed in note 28) and the Human Development Report, published for the United Nations Development Program by Oxford University Press (1990).

[31]Estes (1984). It should be noted that on the related Index of Net Social Progress (INSP), Denmark scored second at both the beginning (191) and the end (194) of the decade. Sweden (201) had the highest score at the beginning of the decade, Norway (196) at its end (table 5-3, 106–109). What this means, of course, is simply that all three of these countries score very highly in the field of social welfare; the real significance is probably not in their individual ranking *vis-à-vis* each other, but in the existence of the highly ranked "Scandinavian cluster" indicated by the statistics.

[32]Estes (1984), table 5-7, 117–18.

[33]I would like to thank Ward Watt for pointing out the connection between these developments in Denmark and the idea of Jeffersonian democracy. I first heard the felicitous phrase "failure of the imagination" (used in the final chapter) in one of Ward Watt's unforgettable Bio 40 lectures at Stanford University.

[34]Herbert Hendin, *Suicide in Scandinavia* (New York: Doubleday, 1965).

[35]The increase has been sudden and sharp. Researchers at the Regional Hospital in Trondheim, who have been studying suicide in the South Trøndelag region of central Norway, report that the number of suicides and attempted suicides has quadrupled since 1982. In general most severe in the under-thirty group, the sharpest rise has been seen among two distinct groups: men in rural districts where traditional employment in both agriculture and fishing is threatened and women in cities between the ages of forty-five and forty-nine. G. Isern, "Selvmord skal forebygges—Ta truslene på alvor" (Suicide must be prevented—take the threats seriously), Trondheim *Adresseavisen*, 3 Dec. 1990 (a review of the work of Petter T. Jørgensen and Tarjei Rygenstad).

[36]I am grateful to Otto Larsen for his discussion of the Scandinavian suicide statistics with me. Any errors of fact or interpretation are my own responsibility.

[37]Donald Rubenstein, personal communication.

[38]The familiar "du," or you, said this way before a proper name, is generally a term of endearment, a colloquial way of expressing affection in the Danish language (it may also be used in other, less complimentary ways).

[39]*Folkehøjskolens Sangbog*, 1982 ed., Song #299, Otto Mortensen (1932). I am grateful to Marie Andersen of Vordingborg for pointing these lines out to me.
[40]Martin A. Hansen, *Dansk Vejr* (Danish weather) (Copenhagen: Hasselbach, 1953), 89–91. I thank Anne-Lise Malter for aid in the translation of this passage.
[41]For a contrasting view of Danish attitudes toward death, see Hendin (1965), 45.
[42]Johannes Møllehave, "Troldmanden og sproget" (The magician and the language), Chronicle in *Politiken*, 9 Dec. 1986.

CHAPTER THREE

[1]The concept of modernization is treated in a world system perspective by the historian Immanuel Wallerstein in *The Modern World System I: Capitalist Agriculture and the Origins of the European World Economy in the Sixteenth Century* (New York: Academic Press, 1974). Two useful and challenging anthropological perspectives can be found in Eric Wolf, *Europe and the Peoples Without History* (New York: Columbia University Press, 1982) and Michael Taussig, *The Devil and Commodity Fetishism in South America* (Chapel Hill, N.C.: University of North Carolina Press, 1980). For a study of the psychosocial implications of modernization see Peter Berger, B. Berger, and H. Keller, *The Homeless Mind: Modernization and Consciousness* (New York: Vintage, 1973).
[2]Hilaire Belloc, *Return to the Baltic* (London: Constable and Co. Ltd., 1938), epigram from the last page.
[3]There are eighteen islands covering 1,399 sq km. Volcanic in origin, they consist of high, rocky mountains, deep valleys, and long, narrow fjords. The present population of the islands is about 45,000; the capital is Torshavn, with about 14,000 inhabitants. Fishing provides about 90% of the export, supplemented by shipbuilding, textiles, and knitted garments. (See Factsheet Denmark, Tryggvi Johansen, "The Faroe Islands," Royal Danish Ministry of Foreign Affairs, 1983.)
[4]Otto Andersen, *The Population of Denmark* (Copenhagen: Cicred, 1977), 77.
[5]For an illuminating discussion of these features of Danish geography, see Kenneth Miller, *Government and Politics of Denmark* (Boston: Houghton Mifflin, 1968), 1–5. The chief source for the discussion of Danish geology, climate, and soils is the useful compendium *Denmark: An Official Handbook*, Press and Information Department, Royal Danish Ministry of Foreign Affairs (1970). I have also drawn on P. V. Glob, *Denmark: An Archeological History from the Stone Age to the Vikings* (Ithaca, N.Y.: Cornell University Press, 1967) and Erik Kjersgaard, *A History of Denmark* (Copenhagen: Danish Ministry of Foreign Affairs, 1974).
[6]T. H. Van Andel, *New Views on an Old Planet* (London: Cambridge University Press, 1985), 70.
[7]T. Douglas Price and Erik Brinch Petersen, "A Mesolithic Camp in Denmark," *Scientific American*, March 1987.
[8]Until recently it was generally thought that agriculture was brought to Denmark by immigrants from the south, but a number of Danish archeologists now believe

there are good grounds to conclude that it was developed by the indigenous population. Roar Skovmand, personal communication.

[9]Peter Manniche, *Living Democracy in Denmark* (Westport, Conn.: Greenwood Press, 1970), 23.

[10]As the owner of a nursery, he would call himself a gardener *(gartner)*, not a farmer *(landmand)*; nevertheless, I have taken the liberty of using the term farmer, which I believe provides a more accurate reading for the English-speaking reader.

[11]Karen Blixen, *Winter's Tales* (New York: Random House, 1942), 29.

[12]Hackett (1940), 9–10. See also Judith Friedman Hansen (1970), 86.

[13]Hannah Arendt, *Eichmann in Jerusalem: A Report on the Banality of Evil* (Viking Press, 1964), 172; see also 170–75.

[14]Leni Yahil, *The Rescue of Danish Jewry: Test of a Democracy,* transl. from the Hebrew by Morris Gradel (Philadelphia: Jewish Publication Society of America, 1969). Preface, p. xii. This book contains an extensive bibliography on the Danish Resistance Movement.

[15]Norman Melnick, "Great Danes Who Saved Jews from the Nazis," *San Francisco Examiner,* 15 July 1983.

[16]Martin Gilbert, *The Holocaust* (New York: Hill and Wang, 1978), 32. In Norway, unlike Denmark, the Nazis were able to find enthusiastic and for a time effective support in the person of Vidkun Quisling. For a detailed account of the National Socialist movement in Norway, see H. F. Dahl, B. Hagtvet, and G. Hjeltnes, *Den Norske Nasjonalsosialismen: nasjonal samling, 1933–1945* (Oslo: Pax Forlag a.s., 1982).

[17]A popular legend has it that the Danish king, Christian X, made it a point to perform personal acts of resistance on learning of the first edicts of Jewish persecution. Specifically, he was said to have attended with due pomp and ceremony a service in Copenhagen's finest synagogue and to have worn in public the yellow armband with the Star of David that the Jews had been ordered to wear. From the historiographic point of view these stories apparently cannot be corroborated and they may well be mythical. Yahil (1969) nevertheless remarks (p.63) that the premise put forth by some people, that the king's character was such that he might well have said and done such things, is correct. It has been established that the king did express solidarity with Jewish citizens during a time when Danish National Socialists were trying to stir up unrest as a prelude to action against the Jews.

[18]This topic is explored in depth by the philosopher Larry Axel in his "Christian Theology and the Murder Of Jews," *Encounter Magazine* (Spring 1979). Additional insights into Luther's character can be found in E. H. Erikson, *Young Man Luther* (New York: W. W. Norton, 1958) and Alan Dundes, "Life is Like a Chicken Coop Ladder: A Study of German National Character through Folklore," *Journal of Psychoanalytic Anthropology,* vol. 4, no. 3 (Summer 1981), esp. 299ff.

[19]Quoted in K. B. Bardakjian, *Hitler and the Armenian Genocide* (Cambridge, Mass.: The Zoryan Institute, 1985), Introduction, 1.

[20]*New York Times,* 25 April 1988: 2. See also Stephanie Strom, "Armenians Observe a Grim Anniversary," *New York Times,* 30 April 1990. An outsider's account by the

U.S. consul in Harput in eastern Turkey from 1914–17 is Leslie A. Davis, *The Slaughterhouse Province: An American Diplomat's Report on the Armenian Genocide, 1915–1917,* ed. Susan Blair, pub. Aristide D. Caratzas (1990). Reviewed by David Corn, "Report from the Inferno," *The Nation,* 28 May 1990.

[21]Amnesty International, *Political Killings by Governments* (London: AI, 1983), 69–77.

[22]T. B. Millar, *Australia in Peace and War* (Canberra: Australian National University Press, 1978), 539.

[23]Noam Chomsky, *Towards a New Cold War* (New York: Pantheon, 1982), 341,470, citing Father Vierra do Rego and Father Francisco Maria Fernandez.

[24]"Bitter and Cruel. . . ." (Report of a mission to Guatemala by the British Parliamentary Human Rights Group, Oct. 1984); C. Krueger and K. Enge, *Without Security or Development: Guatemala Militarized* (Report submitted to the Washington Office on Latin America, 6 June 1985).

[25]Robert Pear, "Mozambicans Fled Rebels, U.S. Says: Many Thousands of Civilians Were Brutalized or Killed, Refugee Study Alleges," *New York Times,* 21 April 1988, sec. A 11.

[26]Arendt (1964), 171.

[27]Yahil (1969).

[28]Danish agriculture is generally regarded within Denmark as being in a crisis state. How can this observation be reconciled with the positive evaluation given here? When I say that Danish agriculture is one of the most sophisticated and successful in the world, I am thinking in the historical long term and referring primarily to the system's high potential productivity, that is, its potential yield per unit of land, labor, and resource input. It is true that political and economic factors extraneous to questions of productivity *per se,* such as quotas placed on Danish farmers (and fishermen) by the EEC, have put Danish agriculture into a state of crisis. The existence of the crisis is in this view a matter of international economics, and however difficult it has made life for Danish farmers, it does not give grounds for abandoning the generalization that Danish agriculture is one of the most sophisticated and successful in the world (when viewed in terms of potential productivity per unit output). Two recent Danish books attest to the devastating effects of this crisis: Knud Sørensen, *Bondeslutspil* (The last act of the farmer) (Aarhus: Modtryk, 1983) and Palle O. Christensen, *En Livsform på Tvangsauktion?* (A life form up for forced auction?) (Copenhagen: Gyldendal, 1983).

[29]Birger Thøgersen, "Danmark er en krydset gris" (Denmark is a crossed pig), *Information,* 4 May 1984.

[30]Britte Schall Holberg, "Dansk landbrug i en brydningstid" (Danish agriculture in a period of convulsion), *På Herrens Mark* (In the fields of the lord) (Copenhagen: National Museum, 1988), 110.

[31]The population figures are taken from Otto Andersen, *The Population of Denmark* (Copenhagen: Cicred, 1977).

[32]The mortality statistics are taken from Vagn Skovgaard-Petersen, "Skolens Danmark: 1814–1920," in H. Haue et al., eds., *Skolen i Danmark fra 1500 tallet til idag*

(The school in Denmark from the 1500s til today) (Herning, Denmark: Forlaget Systime, 1986).

[33]Niels I. Meyer, K. H. Petersen, and Villy Sørensen, *Revolt from the Center* (London: Marion Boyars, 1978), 30. This popular critique of the 1970s and early 1980s presented an early view of how to build a "sustainable society" based on alternatives to the conventional paradigm of economic growth.

[34]Some additional sources for the information and facts cited here are the following: Eric S. Einhorn and John Logue, *Welfare States in Hard Times: Denmark and Sweden in the 1970's* (Kent, Ohio: Kent Popular Press, 1980); Hans Edvard Teglers, "Denmark—A Bit of the World," Joint Export Council of Denmark (undated); Tage Kaarsted, "Danish Politics After 1945," Factsheet Denmark, Royal Danish Ministry of Foreign Affairs (1984); and Anders Olgaard, "The Danish Economy After 1945," Factsheet Denmark, Royal Danish Ministry of Foreign Affairs (1983).

CHAPTER FOUR

[1]Anthony Wallace's classic discussion (1961) distinguishes between two types of change: (a) the steady state baseline "equilibrium fluctuations," which are always occurring in any ongoing society, and (b) the potentially revolutionary change that accompanies sustained periods of intense social crisis. The difference between the two types of change is not always obvious at the time. Thus ruling elites who mistakenly interpret the initial manifestations of true "crisis-driven" social change as merely another inconsequential set of baseline fluctuations may live long enough to witness their own decline. Revolutionaries guided by false hopes who make the opposite misinterpretation may live to experience bitter subsequent disillusionment. The material presented in this chapter suggests that the Danish Land Reforms were a response to an episode of true "crisis-driven" social change.

[2]F. W. Reddaway, in Lord Acton, ed., *The Cambridge Modern History, Vol. VI, The Eighteenth Century* (New York: MacMillan, 1934), 735. It is interesting to see an English historian's evaluation of the role played by the elder and the younger Bernstorff in this period of European history.

[3]John Chester Miller, *The Wolf by the Ears: Thomas Jefferson and Slavery* (London: Free Press, 1977), 12.

[4]Karl Peder Pedersen, "Vi fejrer et bluffnummer" (We celebrate a bluff number), Chronicle in *Politiken* about the land reforms, 18 May 1988. For a reply to Pedersen's critique of the meaning of the 1788 reform of stavnsbaandet, see Claus Bjørn, "Da stavnsbaandet brast kom de nye friheder" (When stavnsbaandet broke the new freedoms came), *Politiken,* 25 May 1988.

[5]This figure is taken from Jens Vibæk's masterful discussion of the major land reforms in *Danmarks Historie, Vol. 10,* Reform og Fallit, 1784–1830 (Copenhagen: Politikens Forlag, 1964), 56–101. Additional major sources include Torben Hansgaard, *Landboreformerne i Danmark i det 18. århundrede: problemer og synspunkter* (The Land Reforms in Denmark in the 18th century: Problems and viewpoints) (Copenhagen: Landbohistorisk Selskab, 1981) (this very useful work includes much

of the original legislation, letters, and documents of the time); *På Herrens Mark* (In the fields of the lord) (1988), the National Museum's edited collection for the two hundred-year celebration of the loosening of *Stavnsbaandet;* Fridlev Skrubbeltrang, *Det danske Landbosamfund 1500–1800* (The Danish rural society, 1500–1800) (Copenhagen: Den Danske Historiske Forening, 1978); J. A. Fridericia, *Aktstykker Til Oplysning om Stavnsbaandets Historie* (Selected documents providing information about the history of *stavnsbaandet*) (Copenhagen: Selskabet for Udgivelse af Kilder til Dansk Historie, 1973, orig. 1888).

[6]An estate could also be owned by the Crown itself, by a monastery or convent, a school (such as the University of Copenhagen), or a provincial town *(købstæd).* A few farms were independently owned, but their number was so small (less than 2%) that it had little or no effect on the system as a whole.

[7]Hansgaard (1981), 15.

[8]Jens Holmgaard, "Landmilitsen" (The land-militia), in *På Herrens Mark,* (1988), 43.

[9]Numerous examples are given in Hansgaard (1981).

[10]Vibæk points out that this highly functional, utilitarian, and economic motive for marriage was a general feature of the period and not limited to society's lower ranks. It was the responsibility of a new priest, for instance, to marry his predecessor's widow.

[11]Vibæk (1964), 60. For both the details of estate life and the interpretation of their significance, I am greatly indebted to Vibæk's analysis.

[12]Vibæk (1964), 60.

[13]Skrubbeltrang (1978), 465 (Gårdforsiddelse 1720–1807). The figure was lower for Jutland (between 10–15%) and lowest for Fyn (averaging about 10%). See also Hansgaard (1981), 19, and Vibæk (1964), 61.

[14]Possession of 1–12 tdr. land is generally regarded as signifying *bonde* or gaardmænd status; possession of between ¼ and 1 tdr. land as signifying *husmænd* status (1 td. = 1.36 acre). There were, of course, also many of the latter who owned no land. For a recent historical review, see Palle Ove Christiansen, *Husmandsbevægelse og jordreform i Danmark* (The cottar *{husmand}* movement and land reform in Denmark) (Copenhagen: Etnologisk arbejdsgruppe for nordiske og europaeiske studier, 1975). See also Hansgaard (1981), 13–22.

[15]Karin Kryger, "Kvinderne bag reformerne" (The women behind the reforms), in *På Herrens Mark* (Copenhagen: National Museum, 1988), 56.

[16]Vibæk (1964), 64.

[17]F. Skrubbeltrang, *Agricultural Development and Rural Reform in Denmark,* Food and Agricultural Organization of the United Nations (Rome, Italy, 1957), 13.

[18]Joan Rockwell, "The Danish Peasant Village," *Journal of Peasant Studies,* 1(4) (1974): 450.

[19]Evald Tang Kristensen, *Gamle folks fortællinger om det jyske almueliv som det er blevet ført i mands minde, samt enkelte oplysende stykker fra øerne* (Old people's narratives on the life of the common people in Jutland, as it has been transmitted in man's memory, together with a few enlightening pieces from the islands) (Copenhagen: i

Commission hos Gyldendalske boghandel, 1891), bk. 2, chap. 1, 15. Cited in Rockwell (1974), 451 (hereafter referred to as ETK).

[20]ETK, bk. 2, chap. 6, 66.

[21]Rockwell, (1974), 451.

[22]Eric Berne, *What Do You Say After You Say Hello?* (New York: Bantam, 1972).

[23]ETK (1891), bk. 2, chap. 1, 12, cited in Rockwell (1974), 449–50.

[24]Vibæk (1964), 64.

[25]W. F. Reddaway, in Lord Acton, ed. (1934), 736.

[26]Hansgaard (1981), 13.

[27]Grith Lerche, "Hjulplov og Svingplov," in *På Herrens Mark* (1988), 32–37. For a more general view see Lynne White, Jr., *Medieval Technology and Social Change* (New York: Oxford University Press, 1962).

[28]Vibæk, (1964), 65.

[29]Reddaway, in Lord Acton, ed. (1934), 737.

[30]The private reform efforts of the elder Bernstorff are reviewed in Hansgaard (1981), 35–42. It is clear that private reform efforts took place as early as 1759 on Horsholm, the estate of the widowed Queen Sophie Magdalene. Intense public discussion about the situation in agriculture was well underway by 1750 (see pp. 26ff).

[31]Although not yet legally king, Crown Prince Frederick VI had obtained for all practical purposes a good measure of royal authority because his father, Christian VII, was incompetent to rule. Confirmed as crown prince in April 1784, he did three amazing things on his first royal council meeting. He declared to an astonished group of relatives and supporters that A. P. Bernstorff must be brought back into power. He influenced the king to sign this order (after which the latter is reported to have fled the room). And after engineering the downfall of the previous government, he was able to obtain another signature from his father that made him, for all practical purposes, regent (see Reddaway, in Lord Acton, ed. [1934], 754–55).

[32]Kryger, in *På Herrens Mark* (1988), 58. See also Vibæk (1964), 75.

[33]This is in all probability a reference to the crown prince.

[34]Cited in Hansgaard (1981), 92.

[35]Cited in Hansgaard (1981), 110.

[36]Cited in Hansgaard (1981), 110.

[37]Cited in Hansgaard (1981), 111.

[38]Vibæk (1964), 72.

[39]Hansgaard (1981), 77.

[40]Fridericia (1888), 206.

[41]The tendency to reduce social inferiors to childlike status reinforces structural socioeconomic disadvantages with a stigmatizing attribution of a lower status in the age-grading system. There is often an effective exclusion from normal adult status, based on a powerful and frequently covert psychocultural proscription against functioning as a normal and competent adult. Discussed at length in Erving

Goffman, *Stigma* (Englewood, N.J.: Prentice-Hall, 1963) and *Asylums* (New York: Doubleday, 1961).

[42]Fridericia (1888), 227.

[43]Vibæk (1964), 69.

[44]Amtmand Frederik Hauch (1768), cited in Hansgaard (1981), 119.

[45]Cited in Hansgaard (1981), 121–22. The ability to read and write was restricted to a small minority throughout the eighteenth century in Denmark; thus the farmers' oral complaints were doubtless written down for them by some literate member of the community, probably a priest or teacher.

[46]These and other forms of pathological communication are discussed in the work of R. D. Laing, Gregory Bateson, Don D. Jackson, Jay Haley, Paul Watzlawick, and Eric Berne. See, for instance, the essays in Part III, "Form and Pathology in Relationship," in G. Bateson, *Steps to an Ecology of Mind* (New York: Ballantine, 1972).

[47]Hansgaard (1981), 121.

[48]With the exception of Colbjørnsen and Bang, the citations just given come from the period 1765–70. During the so-called Guldberg period (1772–84), the debate over rural problems receded into the background. It emerged again in full force after the system shift of 1784 that brought A. P. Bernstorff and Reventlow back to power.

[49]Hansgaard (1981), 113.

[50]Vibæk (1964), 79.

[51]Hansgaard (1981), 96.

[52]Hansgaard (1981), 96.

[53]Hansgaard (1981), 97.

[54]Vibæk (1964), 79.

[55]Hansgaard (1981), 98.

[56]Hansgaard (1981), 101.

[57]Hansgaard (1981), 102.

[58]Skrubbeltrang (1978), 315.

[59]Hansgaard (1981), 142.

[60]Hansgaard (1981), 144.

[61]Alexis de Tocqueville, "The Old Regime and The French Revolution" (1856).

[62]Hansgaard (1981), 160.

[63]Karl-Erik Frandsen, "Landboreformerne" (The land reforms), in *På Herrens Mark* (1988), 120.

[64]Peter Michelsen, "De store forandringer: landboreformerne i kulturhistorisk sammenhæng" (The big changes: The land reforms in their culture-historical context), in *På Herrens Mark* (1988), 12.

[65]Grith Lerche, "Hjulplov og svingplov" (Wheel plough and swing plough), in *På Herrens Mark* (1988), 32–37.

[66]Vagn Skovgaard-Petersen, "En ny skole" (A new school), in *På Herrens Mark* (1988), 102. See also by Vagn Skovgaard-Petersen, *Dannelse og Demokrati* (Education

and democracy) (Copenhagen: Gyldendal, 1976) and Vagn Skovgaard-Petersen, Tage Kampmann, Ingrid Markussen, and Ellen Norgaard, ed., *Et folk kom i skole: 1814–1989* (A people came to school) (Copenhagen: Danmarks Lærerhøjskole og Undervisningsministeriet ved Institut for Dansk Skolehistorie, 1989).

[67]Vibæk (1964), 92.

[68]Michelsen, in *På Herrens Mark* (1988), 11.

[69]Vibæk (1964), 84.

[70]Einar Reventlow, "Christian Ditlev Reventlow," in *På Herrens Mark* (1988), 73.

[71]Vibæk (1964), 85.

[72]Cited by Jens Engberg, "Dansk Guldalder eller . . ." (1973), in Hansgaard (1981), 205.

[73]Claus Bjørn, "Store reformer, lange virkninger" (Large reforms, long effects), in *På Herrens Mark* (Copenhagen: National Museum, 1988), 106.

EXCURSUS FOUR

[1]Cited in Roar Skovmand, *Danmarks Historie*, Vol. 11, Folkestyrets Fødsel (The birth of the people's government): 1830–70 (Copenhagen: Politikens Forlag, 1978), 42. I wish to acknowledge a deep professional and personal indebtedness to the late Professor Skovmand, who on numerous occasions shared his knowledge both of this period and of the history of the folk high schools with me.

[2]Skovmand (1978), 48.

[3]Skovmand (1978), 52.

[4]Skovmand (1978), 43.

[5]Skovmand (1978), 34.

[6]Skovmand (1978), 51.

[7]Vibæk (1964), 85.

[8]There were two further grounds for Danish pessimism. Czar Alexander I of Russia, a country traditionally friendly to Denmark, had signed an agreement in 1812 with Crown Prince Karl Johan of Sweden. And it was clear that Karl Johan hoped to secure Swedish occupation of the Danish islands; he had expressed this goal on many occasions.

[9]Vagn Skovgaard-Petersen, *Danmarks Historie*, Vol. 5, 1814–64 (Copenhagen: Gyldendal, 1985), 21.

[10]Christensen et al. (1981), 51.

[11]The characterization of the *husmænd* as "landless" must be qualified. Sometimes their houses did have a little land attached, but the size of the holding was so small that in most cases it supplied only enough food to feed a single family. A *husmand* was in essence one without sufficient land to use it for commercial purposes. Members of this group were hardly ever self-sufficient and had to earn their living by work as day laborers on the fields of the landed farmer or estate owner (or as servants, crafts workers or fishermen).

[12]Skovgaard-Petersen, *Danmarks Historie*, Vol. 5, 1814–64 (1985), 117–20.

[13]Palle Ove Christensen, *Husmandsbevægelse og jordreform i Danmark* (The cottar {*husmand*} movement and land reform in Denmark) (Copenhagen: Etnologisk arbejdsgruppe for nordiske og europaeiske studier, 1975), 4.
[14]Vibæk (1964), 81.
[15]Vibæk (1964), 7.
[16]Vibæk (1964), 92.
[17]These population figures are taken from Skovgaard-Petersen (1985), 111; and O. Andersen (1977), 80.
[18]Cited in Skovmand (1978), 72.
[19]Cited in Hansgaard (1981), 23.
[20]Skovmand (1978), 74.
[21]Skovmand (1978), 206.
[22]Skovmand (1978), 73.

CHAPTER FIVE

[1]For a discussion of the connection between Grundtvig and Marx, see Ejvind Larsen, *Det Levende Ord* (The living word) (Copenhagen: Rosinante, 1983), 45–48.
[2]Paul Hammerich, "Kronik-uge om Grundtvig og det levende ord" (Chronicle-week on Grundtvig and the living word), *Politiken*, 2 Sept. 1983.
[3]Bo Green Jensen, "De levendes land" (The land of the living), *Berlinske-aften Weekendavisen*, 2 Sept.–8 Sept. 1983: 14.
[4]Uffe Østergård, "Hvad er det 'danske' ved Danmark? Tanker om den 'danske vej' til kapitalismen, grundtvigianismen og 'dansk' mentalitet?"(What is the "Danish" about Denmark? Thoughts on the "Danish way" to capitalism, Grundtvigianism and the "Danish" mentality), *Den Jysk Historiker*, Nr. 29–30 (1984), 100.
[5]Kaj Thaning, *N. F. S. Grundtvig* (Copenhagen: Det Danske Selskab, 1972), 160.
[6]Finn Slumstrup et al., eds., *Grundtvigs Oplysningstanker og Vor Tid* (Grundtvig's enlightenment thoughts and our time) (Nordisk Folkehøjskoleråd, 1983). See esp. Finn Slumstrup, "En Skitse af Grundtvigs liv"(A sketch of Grundtvig's life). Another sourcebook, available in English, is Christian Thodberg and Anders Pontoppidan Thyssen, eds., *N. F. S. Grundtvig: Tradition and Renewal* (Copenhagen: Det Danske Selskab, 1983).
[7]Hal Koch, *Grundtvig* (Copenhagen: Gyldendal, 1944).
[8]Cited in Slumstrup et al. (1983), 12.
[9]Slumstrup et al. (1983), 12.
[10]Hanne Severinsen, "Grundtvig—80ernes græsrod"(Grundtvig—the grass root of the 80s), Chronicle in *Politiken*, 7 Sept. 1983.
[11]Skovmand (1978), 116.
[12]Cited in Skovmand (1978), 115.
[13]He was to remain married to Lise until her death in January 1851. In October of the same year he married the widow Marie Toft, whom he had known for many years. Their marriage was an extremely happy one, until her death in the summer

of 1854 (just two months after giving birth to their son). It took him some time to recover from this loss, but in the autumn of 1858 he married another widow, Asta Reedtz, who loyally supported him for the remaining fourteen years of his life. Apparently his busy career did not stand in the way of an active family life.

[14]Peter Kemp, "Det levende ord på dataskærmen"(The living word on the computer screen), Chronicle in *Politiken*, 5 Sept. 1983.

[15]Much of the dispute centered on the true meaning of the ceremony of baptism. See Slumstrup et al. (1983), 19–22.

[16]There is an interesting parallel in the life of Søren Kierkegaard (1813–55), who like Grundtvig was both guided by a deeply personal view of religion and not afraid to speak out regardless of who might be antagonized by his comments. At the funeral of Bishop Mynster, whose successor he would become, the Danish prelate H. L. Martensen (1808–84) called the late bishop "a witness to the truth." Kierkegaard was so incensed at this oration that he published an angry reply in which he claimed that no man can be a witness for the truth because we are all sinners. Kierkegaard went on to argue that the late Bishop Mynster, a man who had been honored and esteemed in the country, least of all could be called "a witness for the truth"; in fact, he had been someone for whom the preaching of Christianity was a good livelihood. See Sven Erik Stybe, *Copenhagen University: 500 Years of Science and Scholarship* (Copenhagen: Royal Danish Ministry of Foreign Affairs [transl. Reginald Spink], 1979).

[17]This conversation is described in Skovmand (1978), 112.

[18]Cited in Thaning (1972), 79–80. All citations from Grundtvig's English voyages are from this source.

[19]Thaning (1972), 69.

[20]Severinsen (1983). See note 10.

[21]These views of *vekselvirkning* are influenced by a series of discussions with Hans Henningsen, principal of Askov Højskole, in the spring of 1983. I thank also Bent Martinsen, former principal of Silkeborg Højskole, for his help in understanding Grundtvig's ideas and philosophy. I wish to acknowledge an indebtedness to both men though I alone must take responsibility for the views expressed here.

[22]Cited in Christensen et al. (1981), 111.

[23]Thaning (1972), 83.

[24]I would like to thank Peter Winsløv of Copenhagen for his help on this joint translation of the second and third stanzas of this poem.

[25]These schools were a form of *gymnasium*, the closest European equivalent to the American high school; they prepared students for university entrance examinations.

[26]Cited in Slumstrup et al. (1983), 40–41.

[27]N. F. S. Grundtvig, *Skrifter i Udvalg* (Selected writings), 125, cited in Christensen et al. (1981), 31–32. Grundtvig's collected writings on education appear in K. E. Bugge, ed., *Grundtvig's Skole Verden i tekster og udkast* (Grundtvig's school world in texts and draft), Vol. I and II (Copenhagen: Gads Forlag, 1968). For an English translation see Knudsen, ed. (1976) and Niels Lyhne Jensen et al. (1984).

[28]Herbert Mitgang, "Document Opens a Window on Mind of Jefferson," *New York Times,* 1 June 1988.

[29]Allowed to meet only every other year, they could give nonbinding advice on such questions as personal rights, property questions, and taxes.

[30]These events are described in Skovmand (1978), 388–89.

[31]P. G. Lindhardt, *Grundtvig* (Copenhagen: Gads Forlag, 1964). See Slumstrup et al. (1983), 27.

[32]K. B. Andersen, "Grundtvig, grundtvigianisme and lønarbejdere," in Henrik S. Nissen, ed., *Efter Grundtvig: hans betydning i dag* (After Grundtvig: his meaning today) (Copenhagen: Gyldendal, 1983), 90.

[33]Østergård (1990), 38. As of this writing, the state has not yet been overthrown.

[34]Hammerich (1983).

[35]Gosse (1911), 85–87.

[36]Johan Borup, *N. F. S. Grundtvig* (Copenhagen: C.A. Reitzels Forlag, 1943), cited in Slumstrup et al. (1983), 34.

[37]Karl O. Meyer, "Det nationale—blev det noget særlig i Danmark?" (The national—did it become something special in Denmark?), in Nissen, ed. (1983), 37.

[38]This beautiful translation was made spontaneously by Erik Lindebjerg, who teaches at Silkeborg Højskole.

[39]Skovmand (1978), 239–40.

[40]The interpretation of these events given here follows Christensen et al. (1981), 52–57. See also Martin Zerlang, *Bøndernes Klassekamp i Danmark* (The farmers' class struggle in Denmark) (Copenhagen: Medusa, 1976).

[41]Skovmand (1978), 152.

[42]Skovmand (1978), 181.

[43]Cited in Christensen et al. (1981), 60.

[44]The traditional stereotype is that Grundtvig's "happy Christianity" was particularly well suited to the new and improved situation of the self-owning farmers, whereas their landless counterparts chose the more dour and pietistic Indre Mission movement. The adequacy of this simple dichotomy has been questioned. See Margarethe Balle-Petersen, *Guds folk i Danmark* (God's people in Denmark) (Lyngby: Etnologisk Forum, 1977), 107–15, (English version: "The Holy Danes," *Ethnologia Scandinavica* [Lund, Sweden, 1981]).

[45]Cited in Skovmand (1978), 207.

[46]Lord Palmerston once declared that only three people had ever understood the Slesvig-Holstein question. The first was a German professor who had gone mad, the second was Prince Albert, the Prince Consort, who was unfortunately dead, and the third was Palmerston himself, who had forgotten all about it. As Kjersgaard (1974), 59, justly remarks, one can feel in these observations the contempt that a powerful statesman from England might feel for an irritating but minor Continental issue.

[47]Johan Wegener, "Tale ved Folkehøjskolens Indvielse i Rødding 1844," in Valdemar Stenkilde, *Den Grundtvigianske Folkehøjskole.* Cited in Christensen et al. (1981), 83.

[48]Højlund (1983), 25.

[49]Højlund (1983), 26.

[50]Roar Skovmand, *Højskole Gennem 100 Aar* (The højskole through 100 years) (Copenhagen: J. H. Schultz Forlag, 1944), 19.

[51]Skovmand (1944), 20.

[52]Skovmand (1944), 41.

[53]Christensen et al. (1981), 115.

[54]Dan Christensen, "Grundtvig går igen i Sorø 1950" (Grundtvig goes again in Sorø 1950), *Politiken,* 2 Sept. 1983.

[55]P. G. Lindhardt (1957), cited in Christensen et al. (1981), 30.

[56]Skovmand (1944), 23.

[57]Christensen et al. (1981), 119.

[58]Højlund (1983), 27.

[59]Ludvig Schrøder, principal of Askov from 1862, cited in Christensen et al. (1981), 91.

[60]Christensen et al. (1981), 29.

[61]Christensen et al. (1981), 118.

[62]Skovmand (1944), 27.

[63]Peter Manniche, *Living Democracy in Denmark* (Westport, Conn.: Greenwood Press, 1970), 111.

[64]Christensen et al. (1981), 119–20.

[65]Højlund (1981), 29.

[66]Letter from Kold to P. C. Algreen from 26 March 1852, cited in Christensen et al. (1981), 120.

[67]Højlund (1981), 27. For an English-language treatment of Kold, see Thomas Rordam, *The Danish Folk High Schools* (Copenhagen: Det Danske Selskab, 1980), 35–43.

[68]J. Th. Arnfred, ed., *Danske Folkehøjskole,* 1844–1944, 427, cited in Christensen et al. (1981), 122. Roar Skovmand (1944), 29, has critiqued Kold's views: Rødding Højskole, for instance, was concerned with quite a bit more than just opposing the Germans and "who gave Kold a patent on the battle against Death?"

[69]Cited in Skovmand (1944), 25.

[70]Christen Kold, "De tre færdigheder: læsning, regning og skrivning"(The three skills: Reading, writing and arithmetic), in *Om Børneskolen* (On the school for children), ed. Lars Skriver (Friskolebladet: Faaborg, 1981), 8.

[71]Christen Kold, "En folkelig undervisning" (A *folkelig* teaching), in Lars Skriver, ed. (1981), 6.

[72]Christen Kold, "En undervisning afpasset efter børnenes evner og trang" (A teaching adapted to children's needs and abilities), in Lars Skriver, ed. (1981), 2.

[73]Højlund (1983), 31.

[74]Manniche (1970), 111.

[75]Christensen et al. (1981), 122.

[76]These statistics are taken from Skovmand (1944), 43–44, and from E. Borup and F. Norgaard, ed., *Den Danske folkehøjskole gennem 100 aar* (Odense, 1939), 306–15.

77Christensen et al. (1981), 128.

78Christensen et al. (1981), 132.

79Christensen et al. (1981), 132.

80Skovmand (1944), 42.

81Højlund (1983), 48.

82Christensen et al. (1981), 133.

83All of the material from Trier's letters is taken from Margarethe Balle-Petersen, "Højskole, Vækkelse og Hverdagsliv" (High school, revival and everyday life) (Paper given at a symposium on religious revival in Scandinavia during the eighteenth and nineteenth centuries, Lund University, 14–15 May 1984).

84This description is adapted from an anonymous pamphlet, "A Winter at Askov Højskole," written by a former student. It is included in A. H. Hollman's "The Folk High School," in Sherman F. Mittell, ed., Democracy in Denmark (Washington, D.C.: National Home Library, 1936), 97–98. Initially published in German in 1909, Hollman's study is one of the best early foreign expositions of the developing folk high school.

85Christensen et al. (1981), 141.

86Østergård (1984), 111.

87This point is made in Christensen et al. (1981). See also Claus Bjørn, Folkehøjskolen og Andelsbevægelse (The folk high school and the cooperative movement) (Copenhagen: Årbog for Dansk Skolehistorie, 1971).

88Christensen et al. (1981), 145. For the farmers to establish their own shooting clubs was a revolutionary act that shocked and alarmed the landowners. This was especially true in the 1880s, a time when it seemed that violent social conflict could well be imminent.

89Rordam (1980), 168–69. I am indebted also to Roar Skovmand for his clarification of the differences between these institutions. An admiring description of the Ladelund Agricultural School can be found in H. Rider Haggard, Rural Denmark and Its Lessons (London: Longmans, Green and Co., 1913), 13–18.

90Margarethe Balle-Petersen, "Forsamlingshuskulturen—oprør og tradition" (The meetinghouse culture—rebellion and tradition), Humaniora 4 (1979–80).

91Claus Bjørn, "Landbrug og landbosamfund anno 1983—og så 'det grundvigske'" (Agriculture and the rural society in 1983—and then the Grundtvigianske), in Nissen, ed. (1983), 100.

92Mills (1959), 7.

93Christensen et al. (1981), 190.

94Christensen et al. (1981), 141.

95Østergård (1990), 30, remarks that the departing members of the ruling elite proclaimed after this election that they would never return to seats "soiled by the manure of peasants." The tenor of this remark vividly illustrates the political antagonisms faced by the farmers during the initial period of the folk high schools.

96Christensen et al. (1981), 179.

97Østergård (1984), 100.

98"Tom May's Death," lines 63–70, from *The Poems of Andrew Marvell*, ed. H. MacDonald (London: Routledge, 1952), 80. See also William Anderson, "Poetry, Myth and the Great Memory," in *Parabola: The Magazine of Myth and Tradition* (Summer 1989): 16–26.

99Cited in Slumstrup et al. (1983), 9.

CHAPTER SIX

1Cited in Peter Manniche, *Living Democracy in Denmark* (Westport, Conn.: Greenwood Press, 1970), 91.

2Østergård (1984).

3The concept of national character used here stems both from symbolic interactionism and from the emphasis on viewing culture as "configuration" and "constellation" found in the older culture and personality tradition in American anthropology. The concept of national character has fallen out of fashion in anthropology. Yet used with appropriate caution, it provides a framework ideally suited for a discussion of the Danish case because of three factors: (1) Denmark's relatively high degree of cultural homogeneity; (2) the fact that it has acted as a single social, political, and economic unit for a period at least five times longer than the existence of the United States as a nation; and (3) its relatively small size, which tends to minimize the geographic and cultural variation that can complicate explorations based on national character. I view national character not as some mystical expression of a people's "essence," but as the contingent result of a socially constructed reality, one influenced by culture, geography, and history.

4Cf. the discussion of commitment, embracement, and attachment in the essay on role distance in Erving Goffman, *Encounters: Two Studies in the Sociology of Interaction* (Indianapolis: Bobbs-Merrill, 1961), esp. 88–110. See also Goffman's discussion of "rules of conduct" in "The Nature of Deference and Demeanour," in *Interaction Ritual: Essays in Face-to-Face Behavior* (New York: Pantheon, 1967), 48ff.

5David Brand, "Paying the Piper. . . . How Danes Got into a Mess," *Wall Street Journal,* 14 Dec. 1982.

6Kaare Svalastoga and Preben Wolf, *Social Rang og Mobilitet* (Social rank and mobility) (Copenhagen: Gyldendal, 1969).

7The concept of ethos was formulated by the anthropologist Gregory Bateson. See Bateson's classic, *Naven* (Cambridge, England: Cambridge University Press, 1936). A more recent discussion can be found in "Bali—The Value System of a Steady State," in his *Steps to an Ecology of Mind* (New York: Ballantine, 1972).

8This anecdote is cited in Hansen (1970).

9Hansen (1970), 80.

10Florence Fabricant, "Smørrebrød: Danish Way with Bread," *New York Times,* 30 Dec. 1987.

11Anker Jørgensen had been a member of *Folketing* for eight years and chairman of the country's largest labor union for four years when named prime minister in 1972.

12Bo Bøjesen, *Dagligliv i Danmark* (Copenhagen: Hans Reitzel, (1960), 90.

[13]The Radicals *(Radikale Venstre)* were then the swing party whose votes were needed both by the governing and opposition party coalitions. These comments reflect a popular belief that they occasionally took advantage of this position by behaving in an unbecomingly opportunistic manner.

[14]*Ekstra Bladet,* 9 May 1984: 2. It is true that this example comes from the "boulevard press," but I still believe it is significant that this type of focused political critique often appears in such newspapers in Denmark. Its American equivalent would most likely focus on a politician's alleged alcoholism or extramarital affair, without bringing his or her political views into question.

[15]*Eldorado,* 10 Jan. 1984.

[16]Such choices are facilitated in Danish society by a 1937 law that gives children born of unmarried parents equal status with children of married parents (this includes the rights to name and inheritance).

[17]Inge Methling, "Kvinder vælger mændene fra: flere og flere kvinder får børn uden ønske om en samlever" (Women chose to live apart from men: More and more women have children without wanting a male companion), *Politiken,* 6 May 1984, sec. 3: 7.

[18]O. Andersen (1977), 134.

[19]See L. Frost and A. Berg, ed., *Kvindfolk—en Danmarkshistorie fra 1600 til 1980* (Women—a history of Denmark from 1600 to 1980) (Copenhagen: Gyldendal, 1984), reviewed by Inge Methling, "Kvindfolk har skrevet kvindfolkets historie" (Women have written the history of women), *Politiken,* 15 April 1984, sec. 3: 3. See also Lene Koch, ed., *Hendes egen Verden* (Her own world), Tiderne Skifter (1984).

[20]Suzanne Brøgger, *Fri os Fra Kærligheden* (Free us from love) (Copenhagen: Rhodos, 1985), 44.

[21]"Man må vælge" (One must choose), interview with Suzanne Brøgger, *Politiken,* 28 Sept. 1980.

[22]Quoted in Inge Methling, "Mandens plads er i hjemmet" (The man's place is in the home), *Politiken,* 8 May 1984, sec. 2: 3.

[23]Karen DeYoung, "In Denmark's Navy, There's Nothing like a Dame," *Washington Post National Weekly Edition,* 5 Oct. 1987.

[24]The source for these and the other laws cited in this chapter resulting from the women's movement is Hanne Budtz, "The Status of Women," in *Denmark: An Official Handbook,* Royal Danish Ministry of Foreign Affairs (Copenhagen, 1970), 191–93.

[25]Hans Jørgen Poulsen, "Piger vil i præstkjole" (Girls want to wear the minister's robe), *Politiken,* 14 Oct. 1990.

[26]This program was seen on 28 May 1984.

[27]For instance, unemployment increased more among women than among men in 1983 (from 10.6 to 12.2% among women, from 10 to 10.8% among men), from Equal Rights Council statistics cited by Inge Methling in "Kvindernes ledighed steg mest" (Unemployment among women rose the most), *Politiken,* 2 May 1984, sec. 1: 9.

[28]Lene Susanne Andersen, "At lære fysik kræver en stærk psyke—hvis man som pige vil hævde sig i timerne" (To learn physics it takes a strong mind—if as a girl you want to hold your own in the classes), *Berlinske Tidende,* 15 April 1984. Ms. Andersen was sixteen years old at the time.

[29]Michael R. Lindholm, "Kvinder diskrimineres langt mere end hidtil antaget" (Women discriminated against much more than previously supposed), *Information,* 3 Jan. 1991.

[30]Inge Methling, "Hver 10. fyres ved graviditet og barsel" (One of every ten is fired with pregnancy or maternity leave), *Politiken,* 3 Jan. 1991.

[31]James M. Perry, "A Distressed Norway Counts on Its Women to Set Things Right: Prime Minister Is a Woman, So Are Seven on Cabinet; Doing Dishes After Party," *Wall Street Journal,* 7 May 1987: 1.

[32]A high school friend tells me that when first meeting older people he still listens for cues that they would rather be addressed with the "DE" form.

[33]"Flere og flere går over til DE" (More and more go over to DE), *Politiken,* 12 July 1988. The poll had surveyed 1,254 adults.

[34]Kjersgaard (1974), 45.

[35]Kjersgaard (1974), 46.

[36]Kjersgaard (1974), 303.

[37]Hansen (1970), 84.

[38]Hansen (1970), 87.

[39]Skovgaard-Petersen (1976), 12.

[40]Ulla Nielsen, "Teater elever protesterer mod Lone Hertz' planer" (Theater students protest against Lone Hertz' plans), *Politiken,* 8 Feb. 1984.

[41]I am grateful to Margarethe Balle-Petersen for pointing this out.

CHAPTER SEVEN

[1]The term "inner direction" is here used in the sense of a gyroscopic metaphor for internally rather than externally driven character development. See David Riesman, *The Lonely Crowd: A Study of the Changing American Character* (New Haven, Conn.: Yale University Press, 1953).

[2]Hansen (1970), 95.

[3]Palle Lauring, *Danmarks Historie* (Copenhagen: Carit Andersens Forlag, 1968), 102–05; Erik Kjersgaard, *A History of Denmark,* Royal Danish Ministry of Foreign Affairs (1974), 33.

[4]Bent Blüdnikow's work is reviewed in Birger Thøgersen, "Vist var der oprør i Danmark" (Probably there was insurrection in Denmark), *Politiken,* 31 Jan. 1983.

[5]Poul Sørensen, introduction to Bøjesen (1960).

[6]Østergård (1984), 94–95.

[7]Skovmand (1978), 95.

[8]Villy Sørensen, "Det indre Danmarksbillede" (The inner Denmark-image), in Thorkild Borup Jensen, *Danmark og Danskere* (Denmark and the Danes) (Copenhagen: Gyldendal, 1979), 35.

9Martin Esslin, *The Age of Television* (Stanford, Calif.: Stanford Press, The Portable Stanford, 1981).

10Hansen (1970), 110.

11Hansen (1970), 110.

12Steven Borish, "Stones of the Galilee: A Study of Culture Change on an Israeli Kibbutz" (Unpublished Ph.D. thesis, Department of Anthropology, Stanford University, 1982).

13Torben Larsen Foto, "Behandler vi turisterne godt nok?" (Do we treat tourists well enough?), Carsten Reenberg, *Berlinske Tidende,* undated, probably 1988.

14Robert Jungk, *Brighter Than a Thousand Suns: A Personal History of the Atomic Scientists* (Harmondsworth, England: Penguin, 1960), 45–48.

15Hendin (1965), 162.

16Hansen (1970), 9.

17Leif Panduro, *Av! Min guldtand* (Copenhagen: Steen Hasselbachs Forlag, 1969), 144–45.

18See the essay by Georg Brandes, "Ludwig Holberg and the neoclassical spirit," in Evert Sprinchorn, ed., *The Genius of the Scandinavian Theater* (New York: Mentor, 1964). See also Østergård (1984), 91–92.

19Review of "Den Kosmiske Kikkert" (The cosmic telescope), *Kristelig Dagblad,* 2 Dec. 1987.

20Elaine Sciolino, "Shultz Asks NATO to Raise Spending on Non-Atom Arms," *New York Times,* 13 Dec. 1987: 1.

21Cited in *Politiken,* 10 March 1984: 9.

22Richard Reeves, "Sweden Sticks to Its 'Maddening' Neutrality," *San Jose Mercury,* 2 Feb. 1987.

23Serge Schmeman, "Danes Divided on Nuclear Resolution," *New York Times,* 26 April 1988.

24One frequently sees in the international press articles such as G. Yerkey, "Denmark Saves on Energy with Waste Energy," *Christian Science Monitor,* 15 June 1981. A systematic early attempt to think through the transition to a sustainable society can be found in Niels I. Meyer et al., *Energi for fremtiden: alternativ energiplan 1983* (Copenhagen: Borgen).

25At last count between thirteen and sixteen.

26Sheila Rule, "Denmark Permits Gay 'Partnerships,'" *New York Times,* 2 Oct. 1989.

27Ejvind Larsen, *Super Bowl som samfundsmodel for SF* (The Super Bowl as a model of society for the Socialist People's Party), *Information,* 26–27 Jan. 1991.

28Søren Østergård Sørensen, "Christiania 1987: en parentes i normal samfundet" (Christiania 1987: A parenthesis in the normal society), *Information,* 30 July 1987; Lars Hedegaard, "Bjørneudsigten," *Information,* 29 July 1988.

29Bøjesen (1960), 58.

30Piet Hein, "Den eneste rigtige," in *Kumbels Lyre* (1950).

CHAPTER EIGHT

[1]Gregory Bateson, *Mind and Nature* (New York: Bantam, 1980), 51.

[2]Cited as personal communication in Hansen (1970).

[3]Judith Friedman Hansen, "Danish Social Interaction: Cultural Assumptions and Patterns of Behavior" (Ph.D. thesis, Department of Anthropology, University of California at Berkeley, 1970). The following discussion of *hygge* owes much to the pathbreaking work of the late Dr. Hansen, to my knowledge the most sensitive and perceptive American student of Danish informal social patterns.

[4]For a dissenting note on the value of the carnival festivities, see Palle Nielsen, "Monsterkoncerten, eller: 1 kron for en torn på næsen" (Monster concert: Or one kroner for a thorn in the nose), Chronicle in *Politiken,* 5 Oct. 1984.

[5]Hansen (1970), 49.

[6]Søren Kierkegaard, *Either-Or* (1843), cited in Skovmand (1978), 216.

[7]It must be kept in mind that Danes are much more likely than Americans to have a name for their home.

[8]Benjamin Lee Whorf, "An American Indian Model of the Universe," in *Language, Thought and Reality* (Cambridge, Mass.: MIT Press, 1956), 61.

[9]Ernest Hemingway, *Death in the Afternoon* (New York: Scribners, 1932), 91.

[10]A. Naur, "Hygge—ved fjender," *Om Hygge* (1965), 31, cited in Hansen (1970), 49.

[11]Lis Byrdal, *Små Fester, Glade Gæster* (Small parties, happy guests) (Copenhagen: J. Fr. Clausens Forlag, 1964), 9.

[12]Jens Kruuse, "En Ø i et Menneskeliv" (An island in a human life) *Om Hygge* (1965), 41–46.

[13]Arne Karlsen, "Noter om *Hygge*" (Notes on *hygge*), *Om Hygge* (1965), 83–84.

[14]Kruuse (1965).

[15]Erving Goffman, *Interaction Ritual,* (New York: Pantheon, 1967), 84.

[16]Hansen (1970), 40.

[17]Ulla Poulsen Skou, *En Efterarsdag* (A fall day), *Om Hygge,* 1965: 16–27.

[18]Vita Andersen, "Hvad tror du jeg tror" (What do you think I think), in *Trygheds-narkomaner* (Security addicts) (Copenhagen: Gyldendal, 1982).

[19]Tove Ditlevsen, *Digte i Udvalg* (Selected Poems) (Copenhagen: Steen Hasselbachs Forlag, 1965), 9–10.

[20]Cited in Hansen (1970), 54.

[21]Hansen (1970), 63, citing the Danish historian Troels-Lund.

[22]Francis Hackett, *I Chose Denmark* (New York: Doubleday, 1941), 46.

[23]Steve Lohr, "In Summer, the Swedes Think Bright," *New York Times,* 25 June 1989: 9. In the bright nights the suppression of melatonin can make it difficult to sleep, but one fairly typical comment is that of a Swedish woman who remarks, "Personally, I couldn't stand living in California, where it's sunny all the time. I need the swings of season from light to dark and back. We are dependent on the sharp changes in Sweden." The same can probably be said of most Danes with respect to seasonal light changes.

24One Norwegian analyst suggests that the concepts of peace and quiet (*fred og ro*) play a central role in Norwegian everyday life. See Marianne Gullestad, "The Meaning of Peace and Quiet in Everyday Norwegian Life" (Paper presented at the symposium on Nordic national and regional stereotypes, American Anthropological Association Annual Meeting, Phoenix, Ariz., 16–20 Nov. 1988).

25See James Baldwin's short story "Going to Meet the Man," in his volume *Going to Meet the Man* (New York: Dial Press, 1965).

26From the author's field notes.

27Although this did not keep "Dallas" from being very popular with Danish audiences, including many at the folk high schools.

28E. Goffman, *Encounters* (Indianapolis: Bobbs-Merill, 1961), 80.

29I am indebted to Trygve Natvig for his help in making this translation. Øverland is one of the outstanding Norwegian poets of the twentieth century, known for his use of symbols and metaphors drawn from the Pietistic tradition of the Norwegian Lutheran Church in making a bitter critique of that same tradition. He was an early and active anti-Nazi during the Second World War and was in fact imprisoned during the Nazi Occupation of Norway.

30Hansen (1970), 25.

31Iørn Piø, "Folk fester," in A. Steensberg, ed., *Dagligliv i Danmark i det nittende og tyvende aarhundred* (Daily life in Denmark in the nineteenth and twentieth centuries), Bind 2 (Copenhagen: Arnold Busck, 1964), 49.

CHAPTER NINE

1George F. Will, "Who Will Stoke the Fires?" *Newsweek*, 9 April 1990, 78. Cited in Paul Kennedy, "Is the U.S. Going Downhill?" *New York Review of Books* (28 June 1990): 31. Will points out that nineteen nations, including Jamaica and Costa Rica, have lower infant mortality rates than the United States; the rate of infant death in Japan is less than half the American rate.

2G. Nelleman, ed., *Dagligliv i Danmark i vor tid* (Daily life in Denmark in our time) (Copenhagen, 1988), 81; cited in Viveca Liventhal, "Hvad er supplerende dagpenge?" (What is a supplementary maintenance allowance?), *Information*, 23 Nov. 1990.

3This situation was possible in 1983. My chief informant was a fellow folk high school student, himself a journeyman carpenter.

4Estes (1984): 119, table 5-7.

5The statistics for 1979–80 show Denmark, with a score of 201, as having the highest Index of Social Progress among the nations of the world. The statistics for 1969–70 show Denmark and Sweden, each with a score of 198, tied for the leadership. A related index, the Index of Net Social Progress, shows Denmark as second to Sweden in 1969–70, and second to Norway in 1979–80. See Estes (1984): 106–9.

6Discussed in Paul Kennedy, "Is the U.S. Going Downhill?" *New York Review of Books* (28 June 1990).

[7]Recall, for instance, the greater Danish emphasis on education and training for those in a range of occupations that include those described as "menial" in the U.S. (discussed in Chapter Six).

[8]Kenneth E. Miller, *Government and Politics in Denmark* (Boston: Houghton Mifflin, 1968); Erik V. Mortensen, "Social Security, Danish-style," Department of the Ministry of Foreign Affairs (Copenhagen, 1979). For a more general review see Peter Flora, ed., *Growth to Limits: The Western European Welfare States Since World War II,* European University Institute Series C, Walter de Gruyter, vol. 1, Sweden, Norway, Finland, Denmark, (1988).

[9]Hansen (1970), 126.

[10]Erik V. Mortensen, "Social Security, Danish-style," Department of the Ministry of Foreign Affairs (Copenhagen, 1979).

[11]Eva Schulsinger, "Krisecenter for narkomaner på harde stoffer: det etablerede system har spillet fallit " (Crisis-center for addicts on hard drugs: The established system has not functioned), *Politiken,* 26 Feb. 1984.

[12]Jacob Juhl, "Kofoed elever: ja til flere krav" (Kofoed students: Yes to more demands), *Berlinske Tidende,* 23 Aug. 1988.

[13]Kaj Spangenberg, "Minister: Vi er stolte af center for tortur-ofre" (Minister: We are proud of the center for torture victims), *Politiken,* 6 May 1984.

[14]Other centers have since been built in Toronto, Paris, and Minneapolis. See M. Satchell, "For Ultimate Survivors, a Place to Heal," *U.S. News & World Report,* 19 Dec. 1988.

[15]Paul Simon, "What I Learned: Reflections on My Run," *New York Times Magazine,* 3 July 1988.

[16]Cf. the Chronicle in *Politiken,* 25 July 1987, by author and media researcher Ralf Pittelkow, "Stop engang, hr. præsident" (Stop for once, Mr. President).

[17]The Left Party (Venstre) is in fact a conservative party reflecting the interests of the established agricultural community. As with the Radical Left (Radikal Venstre), its name can be misleading.

[18]Mogens Gahms, "De radikale bremser bro-planer" (The radicals put the brake on plans for the bridge), *Politiken,* 15 March 1984: 9.

[19]Mogens N. Pedersen, "Electing the Folketing," Factsheet Denmark, Royal Danish Ministry of Foreign Affairs (Copenhagen, 1984).

[20]"Solen er et neon-rør" (The sun is a neon pipe), *Extra-Bladet,* 15 May 1984: 12.

[21]The debate was aired on 13 May 1984.

[22]Kaj Spangenberg, "Krimi-forsker: Nu må politiet slappe lidt af " (Criminologist: Now the police really must back off a bit), *Politiken,* 13 Jan. 1984: 3.

[23]Ole Schierbeck, "Afsløring af magtens medløbere" (Exposure of power's followers), review of Gretelise Holm, *Lov og ret, magtens medløbere* (Forlaget Vindrose, 1984), *Politiken,* 8 Jan. 1984: 7.

[24]Ole Espersen, "Myten om human kriminal politik" (The myth of a human criminal-politics), review of Gretelise Holm (see previous note), *Politiken,* Jan. 1984.

[25]P. Bruun Nielsen (a Danish judge), "Vort rets-sytems skamplet" (The stigma of our justice system), *Politiken,* 28 Jan. 1984, sec. 2: 5.

[26]*Politiken,* 15 March 1984.

[27]*Politiken,* 16 Feb. 1984: 7.

[28]"Politi unskylder anklage mod Christiania" (Police apologize for accusations against Christiania), *Information,* 29 Feb. 1984. It is duly announced that the Danish police "give him an unreserved apology, because they now think, in spite of everything, that there isn't any foundation to the accusations they made against him." I am trying in vain to remember the last time I read about an American police department making a public apology to someone unjustly accused.

[29]Eva Schulsinger, "Luk nu øjnene op politikere" (Open your eyes now, politicians: An appeal from the parents of handicapped children), *Politiken,* 10 Feb. 1984.

[30]*Extra-Bladet,* 30 May 1984: 2.

[31]Cited in A. P French and P. J. Kennedy, eds., *Niels Bohr: A Centenary Volume* (Cambridge, Mass.: Harvard Univ. Press, 1985), 288–96.

[32]Ruth Moore, "Niels Bohr As a Political Figure," in French and Kennedy, eds. (1985), 255. The full text of Bohr's address, "Natural Philosophy and Human Cultures," is reprinted in Niels Bohr, *Atomic Physics and Human Knowledge* (New York: Wiley, 1958).

[33]John Wheeler, "Niels Bohr and Nuclear Weapons," in French and Kennedy, eds. (1985), 276.

[34]Bent Sørensen, "En flok gæs kan udløse tredje verdenskrig" (A flock of geese can start a third world war), Chronicle in *Politiken,* 18 Jan. 1984.

[35]*Søndags-Aktuelt,* 16 Sept. 1984: 10

[36]The program was shown on 14 Oct. 1984.

[37]The documentary was shown 4 June 1984.

[38]Herman Vinterberg og Jens Axelsen, *Dansk-engelsk Ordbog* (Copenhagen: Gyldendal, 1979), 116.

[39]Kaj Thaning, *N. F. S. Grundtvig* (Copenhagen: Det Danske Selskab, 1972), 99–100.

[40]Østergård (1984), 122.

[41]Vagn Skovgaard-Petersen, "Lighed i skolen—mulighed eller illusion?" (Equality in the school: A possibility or an illusion?), in Ingrid Markusson, ed., *Dansk Skoleproblemer: før og nu* (Danish school problems: Before and now) (Copenhagen: Gjellerup, 1978), 44.

[42]Cited in supplement to Trondheim *Adresseavisen,* 19 Jan. 1991.

[43]At least one pilot study that compares Danish, German, and Italian playground behavior reached similar conclusions. See Leopold Bellak and Maxine Antell, "An Intercultural Study of Aggressive Behavior on Children's Playgrounds," *American Journal of Orthopsychiatry,* vol. 44:4, July: 503-11.

[44]This permissive policy has come under debate in recent years.

[45]Sharon Thomas, "Remembering Denmark, a Child and Family Centered Society," in *American Examiner,* special issue, International Year of the Child: Cultural Perspectives (Fall-Winter 1979–80), 31–32.

[46]Typical, for instance, is the critical commentary on a high-ranking politician in "Den mand er utrolig arrogant" (That man is incredibly arrogant), *Extra-Bladet*, 30 May 1984: 10. This newspaper is a "boulevard press" publication. An example of the same theme in a more mainstream paper was the article by former Minister Kjeld Olesen, "Magtens arrogance" (The arrogance of power), *Politiken,* 23 Jan. 1984. It is a common theme in Danish newspapers.

[47]Kurt Bælsgaard, "Den ustyrlige stat" (The uncontrollable state) (1975), in T. B. Jensen, *Danmark og Danskerne* (Denmark and the Danes) (Copenhagen: Gyldendal, 1979), 41.

[48]Erik A. Wold, "NATO indleder hidtil største vinterøvelse" (NATO holds its largest winter maneuvers up to the present time), *Information*, 26 Feb. 1984.

[49]*Folkehøjskole sangbog* (1982), Song #216.

CHAPTER TEN

[1]Kim Schaumann, "Ledighed rammer folk hårdt," (Unemployment hits people hard), *Berlingske* (Erhverv), 15 Dec. 1990.

[2]*Altid har jeg længsel* (Always I have longing), title song of album.

[3]Aksel Sandemose, *En Flygtning Krydser Sit Spor* (Viborg: Norhaven, 1972). English version: Eugene Gay-Tifft (transl.), *A Refugee Crosses His Track* (New York: Knopf, 1936).

[4]*Scanoroma Magazine* (April 1987), 97.

[5]This painting can be seen in the Munch Museum, Oslo.

[6]Robert Molesworth, *An Account of Denmark As It Was in the Year 1692* (London, 1694). These lines, widely known in Denmark, are trotted out affectionately whenever Danish character is being seriously discussed. It is almost obligatory to cite them. Molesworth has thus succeeded in achieving an odd sort of fame in the land that he did not love.

[7]Some other major Danish contributors to early modern science include Rømer's teacher Rasmus Bartholin (1625–98), who discovered the double refraction of light in Iceland spar; Ole Borch (1626–90), a chemist whose work with noninflammable but fire-nourishing gas generation puts him on the line leading to the work of Scheele, Priestly, and Lavoisier; and Niels Steensen (1638–86), also known as Nicolaus Steno, who was one of the first to perceive the true nature of fossils and crystals. See *Denmark: An Official Handbook*, Royal Danish Ministry of Foreign Affairs (Copenhagen, 1970), 562–70.

[8]Reported in Sven Erik Stybe, *Copenhagen University: 500 Years of Science and Scholarship,* Royal Danish Ministry of Foreign Affairs (transl. Reginald Spink) (Copenhagen, 1979), 75. Bartholin was so excited by his discovery that he composed an epitaph to the liver. Its main theme was that the liver—which up to then had been seen as the ruler of the organism—was now deposed, but nonetheless deserved our gratitude for long and loyal service. Rømer seems also to have been a man of intense emotion. When he once criticized a student for lack of knowledge during

an examination, the student retorted in Latin, "Non-omnis omnes possumus" (We can't know all about everything). Rømer was reportedly so enraged that he failed both that student and all the following examinees.

9Cited in Hansen (1970), 83.

10Cited in Hansen (1970), 82.

11Peter Thygesen, "Artisterne er sure" (The artists are sour), *Politiken*, 4 May 1984.

12Cited in Hansen (1970), 82–83.

13Liv Ullman, *Changing* (New York: Knopf, 1977), 164.

14Hans Jørgen Poulsen, "Studenter i benhård kamp om 26 pladser" (Students in bonehard battle for 26 places), *Berlinske Tidende*, 29 July 1987.

15I have heard a variation on this term of address, namely "Little Brother" *(Lille Bror)*, used in a more friendly way.

16Judith Thurman, *Isak Dinesen: The Life of a Storyteller* (New York: St. Martin's Press, 1982).

17*Yearbook of Nordic Statistics* (1977), 74–75. See also the discussion in E. Einhorn and J. Logue, *Welfare States in Hard Times: Denmark and Sweden in the 1970's* (Kent, Ohio: Kent Popular Press, 1980), 20–21.

18This estimate is found in Howell Raines, "Copenhagen Journal: In Utopia, Bad Seeds Take Root," *New York Times*, 14 Sept. 1987.

19Samuel Rachlin, "Danes—Some of the World's Big Doubters," *New York Times*, 30 Nov. 1986.

20The name comes because so many of them wear green pilot jackets from army surplus stores.

21Lars Villemøes, "Danmark er for danskere" (Denmark is for Danes), in Offside, magazine section of *Information*, 31 May–6 June 1985. An excellent and in-depth article on the Green Jackets, whose place of origin is Studsgaardsgade in the Østerbro section of Copenhagen.

22"100 Tavse vidner til terror i S Toget" (100 silent witnesses to terror in the S train), *Extra Bladet*, 16 April 1984. There was no indication that the Green Jackets were responsible for these particular events; the incident is cited as an example of the kind of thing for which they are known.

23Helle Lyster, "Blodigt rockeropgør tæt på at slutte med drab" (Bloody rocker battle close to ending in murder), *Politiken*, Jan. 1984.

24Else Christensen, "Vold—ties ikke ihjel" (Violence: Isn't ended by silence) (Copenhagen: Nyt Nordisk Forlag, 1984). Reviewed by Inge Methling in *Politiken*, 23 March 1984.

25Jens Skaarup, "139 døde af narko i 1983" (139 died of narcotics in 1983), *Politiken*, 29 March 1984. The police adviser interviewed states that these are minimum figures. They do not include, for instance, addicts who died in a hospital and were not given an autopsy.

26Jens Skaarup, "Knivrøver på 15 år trængte ind hos ægtepar" (knife robber 15 years old broke into the home of a married couple), *Politiken*, 4 Dec. 1986. Three boys 17, 15, and 14 terrorized a couple in their home and made off with 4,000 kroner.

[27]Inge Methling, "Indvandrere frygter lægens ros" (Immigrants fear the doctor's praise), *Politiken*, 28 Feb. 1984. The article is based on the work of anthropologist Petrea Højlyng.

[28]"European parties spring up to oppose immigrants," *New York Times*, 22 Nov. 1987.

[29]Howell Raines, "Copenhagen Journal: In Utopia, Bad Seeds Take Root," *New York Times*, 14 Sept. 1987.

[30]J. Andersen, J. P. Henriksen, P. Abrahamson, J. E. Larsen, and H. Hansen, "Fattigdom er en følelse" (Poverty is a feeling), Chronicle in *Politiken*, 18 Nov. 1986.

[31]Cf. the review of Erik Jørgen Hansen, "Danskernes levekaar 1986 sammenholdt med 1976" (Danish living conditions in 1986 compared with 1976) (Copenhagen: Hans Reitzel, 1986), in the source cited in the previous note. The other articles cited in this section present arguments that are part of the same ongoing debate.

[32]The 3% figure is given by Erik Jørgen Hansen (see previous note); the 13% figure by a European Economic Community Commission. A similar high estimate (600–700,000, in a land of just over 5 million people) is given by Birthe Mørck, a social worker with ten years of experience in one of Copenhagen's most difficult settings, the social center Enghave in Vesterbro. From her minichronicle, "Fattigdom gøres usynlig" (Poverty is made invisible), *Nørrebro Avis*, 29 June 1985.

[33]Knud Sørensen, "Naar saadan nogle som os strejker" (When ones like us go on strike), *Bondeslutspil* (The last act of the farmer) (Aarhus: Modtryk, 1983), 200–201. I first read this story in a class in Danish literature taught by Finn Thrane at Askov Højskole.

[34]Sørensen (1983), 204–205.

[35]Sørensen (1983), 208.

[36]State-mandated relief *(bistand)*, treated in this section, is only one part of the Danish welfare support net. Those who belong to a union or professional group and have paid into a so-called *A-kasse* receive a different and much more generous form of aid *(arbejdsløshedsunderstøttelse)* when unemployed. It is the state-mandated relief *(bistand)* to those who fail to qualify for the other form of support that seems to have problematic and even serious consequences.

[37]Erik Jørgen Hansen (1986) (see note 31).

[38]J. Andersen et al. (1986) (see note 30).

[39]J. Andersen et al. (1986).

[40]Birthe Mørck (1985) (see note 32).

[41]Eva Schulsinger, "Fattigdom er et liv uden haab" (Poverty is a life without hope), *Politiken*, 3 June 1984.

[42]Schulsinger, 3 June 1984.

[43]Schulsinger, 3 June 1984.

[44]Keld Broksø, "De fattiges tomrum" (The void of the poor), *Politiken*, 30 July 1987.

[45]Broksø, 30 July 1987.

[46]Anna Vinding, "Den bitre jagt på et job" (The bitter hunt for a job), *Politiken*, 12 Feb. 1984.

47Malin Lindgren, "Fremtiden er efter dig" (The future is after you), *Politiken*, 19 Feb. 1984.

48Jonathan Matthew Schwartz, " Letter to a Danish historian," in *Den Jyske Historiker* 33 (1985), 123–24.

49Jørgen W. Sørensen, "Danmark bor bag en lukket dør" (Denmark lives behind a closed door), Chronicle in *Politiken*, 2 May 1987.

50Robert J. McCartney, "The United States of Europe," *Washington Post National Weekly Edition*, 27 March–2 April 1989.

51McCartney (1989). These are 1986 figures.

52Aksel Jeppesen, "Hvide Sande: Katastrofe-stemning in den lille fiskerby" (White Sands: A mood of catastrophe in this little fishing village), *Politiken*, 15 May 1984.

53I have summarized these objections from two pieces of campaign literature from the People's Movement Against the EEC, both of which were designed to influence opinion before the election of the Danish contingent to the EEC Parliament that took place on 14 June 1984.

54Cited in Thorkild B. Jensen, *Danmark og Danskerne* (Copenhagen: Gyldendal, 1979), 109.

55Martin A. Hansen, *Dansk Vejr* (Danish weather) (Copenhagen: Steen Hasselbachs Forlag, 1953), 55.

56F. Bergsøe, from the essay "Den lille nisse" (The little pixy) (1948), in Thornkild B. Jensen, ed., *Danmark og Danskerne* (1979).

57Østergård (1990), 27.

58I am indebted to Mogens Melbye of Askov Højskole, who described these events as part of his course in music appreciation!

59Villemøes (1985) (see earlier section on the Green Jackets).

60Jakob Groes, "Indre market er en bombe under dansk skattesystem" (Inner market is a bomb under the Danish tax system), *Information*, 21 July 1988.

61Groes, 21 July 1988.

62Groes, 21 July 1988.

63Else Hammerich, "De Grønne og euro-chauvinismen" (The Green and Euro-chauvinism), in *Information*, 16–17 July 1988.

64Steven Greenhouse, "Workers Want Protection from the Promises of 1992," *New York Times*, 25 June 1989.

65"Trafikminister: Indre marked vil dele et Danmark uden bro" (Traffic minister: The inner market will split a Denmark without the bridge), *Information*, 22 Aug. 1988.

66The concept comes from the American anthropologist A. I. Hallowell. See his remarkable collection of essays, *Culture and Experience* (Philadelphia: University of Pennsylvania Press, 1975).

67Benny Andersen, "Da Danmark blev nedlagt" (When Denmark was abolished) (1976), in Thorkild B. Jensen, *Danmark og Danskerne* (1979), 48–49.

68Jules Henry, *Culture Against Man* (New York: Random House, 1963).

CHAPTER ELEVEN

[1]The following description is limited to the long courses. Although approximately 80% of those who attended a folk high school in the decade of the 1980s came for a short course, these courses are, however successful, a more recent innovation. A description of the folk high school must begin with the long courses.

[2]*Kolding Avis,* 27 May 1976, cited in Højlund (1983), 74.

[3]Christensen et al. (1981), 326.

[4]Christensen et al. (1981), 333.

[5]Kolding is only one of a number of folk high schools that take a left-wing, system-critical view of Danish society and the surrounding world (among the others are the school at Store Rejstrup, the Red Højskole, The Little Højskole, the Women's Højskole, and the schools of the Tvind movement—the Traveling Folk High Schools).

[6]These questions were posed by cultural sociologist Jonathan Matthew Schwartz in recounting his own experience at a Danish folk high school. See his article, "En beslutningsproces' struktur: et bidrag til hojskøledebatten" (The structure of a decision process: A contribution to the high school debate), *Højskole Bladet,* 16 (1971). I wish to thank him for generously making his knowledge and expertise available to me, especially during the early phases of my own research.

[7]The number of weekly instructional hours recommended for folk high schools by the Ministry of Education is twenty-four, though this figure is flexible and subject to some interpretation. At Kolding, for instance, collective meal preparation replaced some of the assignments and meetings of daily coursework for the two weeks that the members of our course had that responsibility. During my subsequent stay at Askov, where students were required to have a program that contained at least twenty formal hours of coursework, it was understood that the other four hours would come from a combination of attendance at lectures, house meetings, excursions, and other offerings.

[8]Carl Scharnberg, *Udvalgte digte* (Selected Poems) (Copenhagen: Forlaget Tiden, 1977), 11.

[9]See, for instance, Francis Moore Lappé and Joseph Collins, *World Hunger: Ten Myths* (San Francisco: Institute for Food and Development Policy, 4th ed., 1979).

[10]Benny Christensen, (1) "Farvel til atomkraften—og hvad så?" (Farewell to nuclear power—and so what?), *Information,* 24 Feb. 1984; (2) "Et farvel til atomkraften må også betyde et farvel til energiplan 81" (A farewell to nuclear energy must also mean a farewell to Energyplan 81), *Information,* 27 Feb. 1984.

[11]Christensen (1984), "Farvel til atomkraften—og hvad så?"

[12]S. Goldstein, "Report Documents Early Deaths Among Chernobyl's Survivors," *Philadelphia Inquirer,* 11 Oct. 1989. Chernobyl was not the first major Soviet-bloc nuclear disaster: others probably occurred at Turnov, Czechoslovakia (1983); the Semipalatinsk Test Site (1972); the Tallin Naval Base (1976); and the nuclear waste storage facility at Kyshtym in the Cheliabinsk region (1958). The total contaminated area of the latter accident was approximately 8,000 sq km. See Z. A.

Medvedev, *Nuclear Disaster in the Urals* (New York: W. W. Norton, 1979) and D. Kaplan, "Was Chernobyl an Isolated Incident?" *S.F. Chronicle,* 12 Nov. 1986.

13This policy has since been abolished at Kolding Højskole. A look at the school's autumn 1988 brochure shows that its four long courses (media, theater, ecology, and a Ghana study course) all began on September 26.

14This is the concluding sentence of Feynman's minority report to the Commission investigating the explosion of the Challenger rocket in January 1986. See his partly autobiographical *What Do You Care What Other People Think?* (New York: W. W. Norton, 1988), 220–37.

15The half-life of plutonium is 24,400 years; it will emit dangerous ionizing radiation for ten times that period.

16The Danish Electrical Utility (DEF) announced in December that it would soon be more difficult to connect private windmills to the public net (*Information,* 28 Dec. 1990: 7). At the same time the energy chairman of the Social Democrats, Denmark's largest single party, came out against any state support to the small windmills (*Politiken,* 7 Jan. 1991: 5). According to the windmill trade association (Foreningen Danske Vindkraftværker), this could mean a halt to all new windmill projects by 1991. Although the wind energy industry was apparently rescued soon afterward by a so-called green majority consisting of the Social Democrats, the Radical Left and the Socialist People's Party (SF), the new situation requires them to negotiate their own future with the much larger electrical utility (DEF). Hans Bjerregård, the director of the Organization for Renewable Energy, commented that "the Social Democrats, SF and the Radicals should have put out some clear signals about what they believe should be the substance of such an agreement. Otherwise it is like setting a dwarf up against a giant" (*Information,* 8 Feb. 1991:7). In 1990 the nearly 3,000 Danish windmills produced pollution-free electricity in an amount sufficient to supply the electrical needs of 330,000 people (*Information,* 2 Jan. 1991).

17A teacher at Kolding could defend its single course policy on the grounds that these courses are of greater political relevance and more concentrated in their organization.

18A year before my stay the subject for the Theme Day had been Ghana, and the whole school had tried to live like Ghanese villagers, aided by a teacher who had been involved in a development project in that country.

19Transcription from taped interviews.

20Transcription from taped interviews.

21Finn Abrahamowitz, *Solskin for det sorte muld: roman om en højskole* (Sunshine for the black loam: A novel about a folk high school) (Copenhagen: Gyldendal, 1981), 7, 14.

22Wil Larsen, personal communication.

23The concepts of cultural compression and decompression were formulated by George Spindler to sharpen our description of how particular cultural contexts influence the learning process. I have made use of these concepts in discussing the school difficulties of kibbutz adolescents (See Borish 1988, English bibliography).

24Hilaire Belloc, *Return to the Baltic* (London: Constable and Co. Ltd., 1938), 47.

[25]I suspect that the reason I encountered more expressions of this feeling at Askov is merely that by that time I was better able to understand what people said, and that it was therefore easier for people to speak to me. I am quite sure that those at Kolding and Silkeborg were having the same kind of experiences.

[26]In succeeding years groups with a higher mean age, more like the pattern I experienced at Kolding and Askov, were commonly seen at Silkeborg (personal communication, Erik Lindebjerg and Leif Rasmussen).

[27]Roar Skovmand, *Arnfreds Blaa Bog* (Arnfreds blue book), in *Festskrift til J. Th. Arnfred: Forstander for Askov Højskole 1928–1953* (Festschrift for J. Th. Arnfred: Principal of Askov Højskole) (Dansk Udsyn, 1953), 9. Skovmand's reminiscence is given even greater authority by the fact that he was a teacher at Askov for seven years while Arnfred was the school's principal (1938–45).

[28]George F. Kennan, "George F. Kennan om en virkelig nulløsning" (George F. Kennan on a real zero option), *Politiken,* 3 May 1983. In 1991 Hans Møller Christensen is retiring after 33 years of teaching at Askov Højskole.

[29]Hymn #10, Th. Kinko, Folk High School Songbook (1982). The translation is very loose.

CHAPTER TWELVE

[1]Poul Erik Petersen, "Folkets populære skole" (The people's popular school), *Berlinske Magasin,* 13 July 1987. See also the useful collection of short essays edited by Arne Andresen, *The Danish Folk High School,* (Copenhagen: Folkehøjskolernes Sekretariat, 1981).

[2]Lisbeth Skov Larsen, "Alle vil lave deres egen højskole" (All want to make their own folk high school), *Weekendavisen,* 15–21 June 1984.

[3]One would not, for example, be likely to find a person deeply committed to Christianity at Kolding.

[4]E. H. Erikson, *Identity, Youth and Crisis* (New York: W. W. Norton, 1968).

[5]In order to be eligible for state support a pupil must have reached seventeen and a half years of age before the beginning of the projected high school stay. Both state and local support are calculated according to complicated formulas that consider an applicant's yearly income, degree of dependence on parental income, condition of nuclear family (e.g., if the applicant has younger siblings who are dependent on parental income). There are in addition several types of support available for unemployed people who are seeking a high school stay.

[6]I am indebted to Jonathan Matthew Schwartz for making the connection between the folk high schools and Erikson's concept of the socially sanctioned moratorium. See Schwartz (1971, 1986).

[7]This is true in spite of the ever-present *hygge* and sociality.

[8]Grundtvig's influence on Danish education apart from the folk high schools has been a profound one. This is illustrated by the Grundtvigian "free schools" of the last century, the development of Grundtvigian educational complexes for post-free school education (especially in the rural areas), and the emphasis on "instructional

duty" rather than "school attendance duty" that has emerged as the basis of Danish school law.

9Christensen et al. (1981), 336–37. In the first citation I have combined the views of two separate individuals who take the same position; the resulting citation better expresses their common point of view. The second citation is from Hans Henningsen, principal of Askov Højkole.

10In the search among competing candidates for signposts to justify the distinction between "modern" and "postmodern," I concur with Arthur Koestler's conclusion that 1945 is the boundary year. It was in this year that the Second World War ended and the postwar era with its Cold War began. It was also in this year that atomic weapons were first used on a human population. "After such knowledge, what forgiveness?" wrote T. S. Eliot, and the dilemma is not Denmark's alone.

11A good introduction to cross-cultural education can be found in Spindler (1987) and the journal *Anthropology and Education.* For acculturation studies see Hallowell (1955).

12Asmarom Legesse, "Self-sustaining development and African pastoralists," testimony presented to the Joint Economic Committee, United States Congress, 27 February 1990. See also Legesse's ethnography of an East-African nomadic democracy with a long history of successful functioning in *Gada* (New York: Macmillan Press, 1973). A parallel argument for India may be found in Vandana Shiva, " Forestry Myths and the World Bank," *The Ecologist,* vol. 17, no. 4/5, 1987: 142–49.

13Osmo Jussila "Finland from province to state," in Max Engman and David Kirby, eds., *Finland: People, Nation, State* (London: Hurst & Co., 1989), 94.

14Robert Epstein, " At Least One Day of Worldwide Peace," *International Herald Tribune,* 2 Jan. 1991.

15Roger Bartra, *La Jaula De La Melancolía: identidad y metamorfosis del mexicano* (The cage of melancholy: Mexican identity and metamorphosis), Editorial Grijalbo, S.A., Calz. San Bartolo Naucalpan num. 282, Argentina Poniente 11230, Miguel Hidalgo, Mexico, D.F. 1987. For a critical review of land reform in Mexico and Latin America see Alain de Janvry *The Agrarian Question and Reformism in Latin America* (Baltimore: Johns Hopkins Press, 1981), especially chapter 6. I thank Miguel Diez Barriga for introducing me to the work of Roger Bartra.

16Estes (1984), 119 (table 5–7).

17*Information,* 3 Dec. 1990.

18Torben Krogh in *Information,* 12 Dec. 1990.

19*Politiken,* 9 Dec. 1990, sec. 1: 4. The low percentage of voters believing the politicians claims of future lower taxation was remarkably constant across the recognized political spectrum. It ranged from 10% (Social Democrats) to 16% (the KVR parties).

20Henrik Groes-Petersen, "Ungdommen gik skuffede fra mødet" (The young people went disappointed from the meeting), *Politiken* , 5 Dec. 1990, sec. 2: 1.

21Ejvind Larsen, "Vampen og valget" (The vamp and the election), editorial in *Information,* 23 Nov. 1990.

[22]Svend Auken, "Regeringen må glemme valglofterne" (The government must forget its campaign promises), *Politiken,* 30 Dec. 1990.

[23]Those on the badly fragmented left wing included a newly organized Green party as well as a "Red-Green Unity List" (Enhedsliste) made up of three small parties: the Danish Communist Party (DKP), the Socialist Workers Party (SAP), and the Left Socialists (VS). Those on the right included veteran Mogens Glistrup's new Common Course (Fælles Kurs) party. The Left Socialists (VS), a small but potent political force in the early and mid-1980s, did not gain reelection to the *Folketing* in 1988.

[24]Prime Minister Schlüter's remark cited in lead editorial "Europa-året" (The year of Europe), in *Information,* 2 Jan. 1991.

[25]Cited in Hans Drachmann, "Sidste EF-chance for de rød-grønne" (Last EF chance for the red-green), *Politiken,* 7 Dec. 1990: 7.

[26]Cited in Loren Eiseley, *The Firmament of Time* (New York: Atheneum, 1962), 117.

[27]See, for instance, the interview with leading Left party politician Anders Fogh, entitled "Skatten sætter samfundet i stå" (Taxes make a society stagnate), Berlinske Magasin, 22 July 1988.

[28]Edward Hyams, *Soil and Civilization* (New York: Harper Colophon, 1976), 149 (see Chapter X: Oklahoma, Death of a Soil).

[29]Loren Eiseley, *The Invisible Pyramid* (New York: Scribners, 1970), 53.

[30]Cited by Ole Wivel, in H. Nissen, ed., *Efter Grundtvig* (Copenhagen: Gyldendal, 1983), 23.

[31]Transcription from taped interviews.

A Select English Bibliography

Andersen, Otto
 1977 *The Population of Denmark.* Copenhagen: Cicred.
Andresen, Arne, ed.
 1981 *The Danish Folk High School.* Copenhagen: Folkehøjskolernes Sekretariat.
Balle-Petersen, Margarethe
 1981 "The Holy Danes." *Ethnologia Scandinavica.* Lund, Sweden.
Bellak, Leopold and Maxine Antell
 1974 "An Intercultural Study of Aggressive Behavior on Children's Playgrounds." *American Journal of Orthopsychiatry* Vol. 44:4, July: 503–11. [A comparison of Danish, German, and Italian playground behavior.]
Belloc, Hilaire
 1938 *Return to the Baltic.* London: Constable and Co., Ltd.
Borish, Steven
 1988 "The Winter of Their Discontent: Cultural Compression and Decompression in the Life Cycle of the Kibbutz Adolescent." In Henry T. Trueba and Concha Delgado-Gaitan, eds., *School and Society: Learning Content Through Culture.* New York: Praeger.
Brown, Lester R. et al.
 1990 *State of the World: A World Watch Institute Report on Progress Toward a Sustainable Society.* New York: W. W. Norton.
Burrows, John
 1984 "Grundtvig: Prophet and Pioneer of Modern Denmark." *History Today,* April, special supplement.
Campbell, Olive Dame
 1928 *The Danish Folk High School.* New York: Macmillan.
Danstrup, John
 1947 *A History of Denmark.* Copenhagen: Wivels Forlag.

Davis, C. D.
   1970   *The Danish Folk High School: An Experiment in Humanistic Educa-tion.* Ann Arbor, Mich.: University Microfilms Ltd.
Einhorn, Eric S. and John Logue
   1980   *Welfare States in Hard Times: Denmark and Sweden in the 1970's.* Kent, Ohio: Kent Popular Press.
Erikson, Erik H.
   1968   *Identity, Youth and Crisis.* New York: W. W. Norton.
Estes, Richard
   1984   *The Social Progress of Nations.* New York: Praeger.
   1988   *Trends in World Social Development.* New York: Praeger.
Flora, Peter, ed.
   1988   *Growth to Limits: The Western European Welfare States Since World War II.* European University Institute Series C, Walter de Gruyter, vol. 1, Sweden, Norway, Finland, Denmark.
Glob, P. V.
   1967   *Denmark: An Archeological History from the Stone Age to the Vikings.* Ithaca, N.Y.: Cornell University Press.
Goffman, Erving
   1967   *Interaction Ritual.* New York: Pantheon.
Gosse, Sir Edmund William
   1911   *Two Visits to Denmark: 1872, 1874.* London: Smith, Elder & Co.
Grundtvig, N. F. S.
   1976   *Selected Writings.* Edited by Johannes Knudsen. Philadelphia, Pa.: Fortress Press.
   1984   *A Grundtvig Anthology: Selections from the Writings of N. F. S. Grundtvig (1783–1872).* Niels Lyhne Jensen et al., eds. Cambridge: James Clarke & Co.
Gullestad, Marianne
   1986   "Equality and Marital Love: The Norwegian Case as an Illustration of a General Western Dilemma." *Social Analysis* No. 19, August, 40–52 (describes a parallel cultural code of modesty in Norway).
   1989   "Small Facts and Large Issues: The Anthropology of Contemporary Scandinavian Society." *Annual Review of Anthropology,* October.
Hackett, Francis
   1941   *I Chose Denmark.* New York: Doubleday.
Haggard, H. Rider
   1913   *Rural Denmark and Its Lessons.* London: Longmans, Green & Co.
Hallowell, A. Irving
   1955   *Culture and Experience.* Philadelphia, Penn.: University of Penn. Press.

Hansen, Judith Friedman
1970 "Danish Social Interaction." Ph.D. thesis, Department of Anthropology, University of California, Berkeley.
Hendin, Herbert
1965 *Suicide in Scandinavia.* New York: Doubleday.
Henry, Jules
1963 *Culture Against Man.* New York: Random House.
Howe, Frederick
1921 *Denmark: A Cooperative Commonwealth.* New York: Harcourt, Brace.
1936 *Denmark: The Cooperative Way.* New York: Coward-McCann.
Human Development Report
1990 Published for the United Nations Development Program by Oxford University Press.
Jones, W. Glyn
1970 *Denmark.* London: Ernest Benn Limited.
Kennedy, Paul
1987 *The Rise and Fall of the Great Powers.* New York: Vintage.
Kjersgaard, Erik
1974 *A History of Denmark.* Copenhagen: Royal Danish Ministry of Foreign Affairs.
Knudsen, Johannes
1955 *Danish Rebel: A Study of N. F. S. Grundtvig.* Philadelphia, Pa.: Muhlenberg Press.
Lindhardt, P. G.
1951 *Grundtvig: An Introduction.* Oxford: Cowley.
Manniche, Peter
1970 *Living Democracy in Denmark.* Westport, Conn.: Greenwood Press.
Meyer, Niels I., K. H. Petersen, and Villy Sørensen
1978 *Revolt from the Center.* London: Marion Boyars.
Michelson, William
1968 "From Religious Movement to Economic Change. The Grundtvigian Case in Denmark." *Social History* 2, 283-301.
Miller, Kenneth E.
1968 *Government and Politics in Denmark.* Boston: Houghton Mifflin.
Mittel, Sherman, ed.
1936 *Democracy in Denmark.* Wash., D.C.: National Home Library.
Mortensen, Enoch
1977 *Schools for Life.* Solvang, Calif.: Danish American Heritage Soc.
Oakley, Stewart
1972 *A Short History of Denmark.* New York: Praeger.

Price, Douglas, and Erik Brinch Petersen
  1987   "A Mesolithic Camp in Denmark" *Scientific American*, March.
Rockwell, Joan
  1974   "The Danish Peasant Village." *Journal of Peasant Studies,* 1(4).
Rordam, Thomas
  1980   *The Danish Folk High Schools.* Copenhagen: Det Danske Selskab
          (now the Danish Culture Institute).
Sandemose, Aksel
  1936   *A Fugitive Crosses His Track.* New York: Knopf (transl. Eugene
          Gay-Tifft).
Schumacher, E. F.
  1973   *Small Is Beautiful: Economics As If People Mattered.* New York:
          Harper & Row.
Schwartz, Jonathan Matthew
  1988   *In Defense of Homesickness: Nine Essays on Identity and Locality.*
          Copenhagen: Akademisk Forlag, Kultursociologiske Skrifter N. 26.
Skrubbeltrang, Fridlev
  1953   *The Danish Folk High Schools.* Copenhagen: Det Danske Selskab
          (now the Danish Culture Institute).
  1957   "Agricultural Development and Rural Reform." Rome, Italy:
          United Nations Food and Agricultural Organization.
  1961   "Developments in Tenancy in Eighteenth-century Denmark as a
          Move Towards Peasant Proprietorship." *Scandinavian Economic History
          Review,* 165-75.
Spindler, George
  1987   *Education and Cultural Process: Anthropological Approaches.* Prospect
          Heights, Ill.: Waveland Press.
Stybe, Sven Erik
  1979   *Copenhagen University: 500 Years of Science and Scholarship.* Copen-
          hagen: Royal Danish Ministry of Foreign Affairs (transl. Reginald
          Spink).
Thaning, Kaj
  1972   *N. F. S. Grundtvig.* Copenhagen: Det Danske Selskab (now the
          Danish Culture Institute).
Thodberg, Christian, and Anders Pontopiddan Thyssen, eds.
  1983   *N. F. S. Grundtvig: Tradition and Renewal.* Copenhagen: Det
          Danske Selskab (now the Danish Culture Institute).
Thomas, F. Richard
  1990   *Americans in Denmark.* Carbondale, Ill.: Southern Illinois Univer-
          sity Press.

Thurman, Judith
   1982   *Isak Dinesen: The Life of a Storyteller.* New York: St. Martin's Press.
Turnbull, Colin
   1983   *The Human Cycle.* New York: Simon & Schuster.
Wallace, Anthony F. C.
   1961   *Culture and Personality.* New York: Random House.
Wåhlin, Vagn
   1980   "Bourgeois and Popular Movements in Denmark 1830–1870."
           Scandinavian Journal of History 5, 151–83.
Yahil, Leni
   1969   *The Rescue of Danish Jewry: Test of a Democracy* (transl. from the
           Hebrew by Morris Gradel). Philadelphia, Pa.: Jewish Publication
           Society of America.
Østergård, Uffe
   1990   *Peasants and Danes: Danish National Identity and Political Culture.*
           Working paper, Center for Cultural Research, Aarhus University.

A Select Danish Bibliography

Abrahamowitz, Finn
  1981   *Solskin for det sorte muld: roman om en højskole* (Sunshine for the black loam: A novel about a folk high school). Copenhagen: Gyldendal.
Andersen, J., J. P. Henriksen, P. Abrahamson, J. E. Larsen, and H. Hansen
  1986   "Fattigdom er en følelse" (Poverty is a feeling). Chronicle in *Politiken*, 18 Nov.
Balle-Petersen, Margarethe
  1977   *Guds folk i Danmark* (God's people in Denmark). Lyngby: Etnologisk Forum.
  1979–80   "Forsamlingshuskulturen—oprør og tradition" (The meeting house culture—rebellion and tradition). *Humaniora*, 4.
  1984   "Højskole, Vækkelse og Hverdagsliv" (High school, revival and everyday life). Paper given at a symposium on religious revival in Scandinavia during the eighteenth and nineteenth century, Lund University, 14–15 May.
Bjørn, Claus
  1971   *Folkehøjskolen og Andelsbevægelse* (The folk high school and the cooperative movement). Copenhagen: Aarbog for Dansk Skolehistorie.
Brøgger, Suzanne
  1985   *Fri os Fra Kærligheden* (Free us from love). Copenhagen: Rhodos.
Bugge, K. E., ed.
  1968   *Grundtvig's Skole Verden i tekster og udkast* (Grundtvig's school world in texts and draft), Vol. I and II. Copenhagen: Gads Forlag.
Bøjesen, Bo
  1960   *Dagligliv i Danmark* (Daily life in Denmark). Copenhagen: Hans Reitzel.
Christensen, Benny
  1984   *Farvel til atomkraften—og hvad så?* (Farewell to nuclear power—and so what?). *Information*, 24 Feb.

Christensen, Ole, Poul Christensen, and Peter Warrer
1981 *Højskolebevægelse og Almendannelse, Skitse til en forståelse af højskolens dannelsesverden* (The High School Movement and General Education: Sketch toward an understanding of the formative world of the high school). Specialopgave, Institut for Statskundskab, Aarhus Universitet.
Christensen, Palle O.
1975 *Husmandsbevægelse og jordreform i Danmark* (The cottar {husmand} movement and land reform in Denmark). Copenhagen: Etnologisk arbejdsgruppe for nordiske og europaeiske studier.
1983 *En Livsform på Tvangauktion?* (A life form up for forced auction?). Copenhagen: Gyldendal.
Feldbæk, Ole and Ole Justesen
1980 *Danmarks Historie: Kolonierne i Asien og Afrika* (Denmark's history: The colonies in Asia and Africa). Copenhagen: Politikens Forlag.
Festschrift til J. Th. Arnfred.
1953 Askov: Dansk Udsyn.
Folkehøjskolens Sangbog (The folk high school songbook).
1982 16th ed. Odense: Foreningens Forlag.
Fridericia, J. A.
1973 *Aktstykker til Oplysning om Stavnsbaandets Historie* (Selected documents providing information on the history of *stavnsbaandet*). Copenhagen: Selskabet for Udgivelse af Kilder til Dansk Historie (orig. public. 1888).
Hagen, Rolf M. et al.
1980 *Norges Historie* (The history of Norway), Bind 15: Historisk Atlas (vol. 15, historic Atlas). Oslo: J.W Capellans Forlag.
Hansen, Martin A.
1953 *Dansk Vejr* (Danish weather). Copenhagen: Hasselbach.
Hansgaard, Torben
1981 *Landboreformerne i Danmark i det 18. aarhundrede: problemer og synspunkter* (The Land Reforms in Denmark in the 18th century: Problems and points of view). Copenhagen: Landbohistorisk Selskab.
Henrikson, Alf
1987 *Nordens Historie: et illustrert overblikk* (The history of Scandinavia: An illustrated overview). Oversatt fra Svensk av Leif Toklum. Den norske Bokklubben.
Højlund, Niels
1983 *Folkehøjskolen i Danmark* (The folk high school in Denmark). Copenhagen: Aschehoug.

Ilsøe, Peter, and Johs. Lomholt-Thomsen
    1966   *Nordens Historie 1* (The history of Scandinavia). 10th ed. Copen-
           hagen: Gyldendal.
Jensen, Thorkild Borup, ed.
    1979   *Danmark og Danskerne* (Denmark and the Danes). Copenhagen:
           Gyldendal.
Kold, Christen
    1981   *Om Børneskolen* (On the school for children). Lars Skriver, ed.
           Friskolebladet: Faaborg.
Larsen, Ejvind
    1983   *Det Levende Ord* (The living word). Copenhagen: Rosinante.
Lauring, Palle
    1968   *Danmarks Historie* (The history of Denmark). Copenhagen: Carit
           Andersens Forlag.
Meyer, Niels I. et al.
    1983   *Energi for fremtiden: alternativ energiplan 1983* (Energy for the
           future: Alternative energy-plan). Copenhagen: Borgen.
Mørck, Birthe
    1985   "Fattigdom gøres usynlig" (Poverty is made invisible), mini-
           chronicle in *Nørrebro Avis*, 29 June.
National Museum
    1988   *På Herrens Mark* (In the fields of the lord). Copenhagen.
Nissen, Henrik S., ed.
    1983   *Efter Grundtvig: hans betydning i dag* (After Grundtvig; his mean-
           ing today). Copenhagen: Gyldendal.
Rosing, Johan S.
    1973   *Gyldendals Historiske Atlas.* Copenhagen: Gyldendal.
Sandemose, Aksel
    1972   *En Flygtning Krydser Sit Spor* (A fugitive crosses his track). Viborg:
           Norhaven.
Schwartz, Jonathan Matthew
    1971   *En beslutningsproces' struktur: et bidrag til højskøledebatten* (The
           structure of a decision process: A contribution to the high school
           debate). *Højskole Bladet* 16.
Shiva, Vandana
    1990   *Livets ophold. Kvinder, økologi og udvikling.* Oversat af Lene Sjørup.
           Copenhagen: Rosinante/Munksgaard.
Skovgaard-Petersen, Vagn
    1976   *Dannelse og Demokrati* (Education and democracy). Copenhagen:
           Gyldendal.
    1985   *Danmarks Historie,* Vol. 5, 1814–64. Copenhagen: Gyldendal.

Skovgaard-Petersen, Vagn, Tage Kampmann, Ingrid Markussen, and Ellen Norgaard, eds.
  1989 *Et folk kom i skole: 1814-1989* (A people came to school). Copenhagen: Danmarks Lærerhøjskole og Undervisningsministeriet, Institut for Dansk Skolehistorie.
Skovmand, Roar
  1944 *Højskolen Gennem 100 Aar* (The Folk High School through 100 years). Copenhagen: J.H. Schultz.
  1978 *Danmarks Historie, Vol. 11, Folkestyrets Fødsel: 1830–70* (The history of Denmark: The birth of democratic government). Copenhagen: Politikens Forlag.
Skrubbeltrang, Fridlev
  1978 *Det danske Landbosamfund* (The Danish rural society) 1500–1800. Copenhagen: Den danske historiske Forening.
Slumstrup, Finn et al.
  1983 *Grundtvigs Oplysningstanker og Vor Tid* (Grundtvig's enlightenment thoughts and our time). Copenhagen. Nordisk Folkehøjskoleråd.
Svalastoga, Kaare, and Preben Wolf
  1969 *Social Rang og Mobilitet* (Social rank and mobility). Copenhagen: Gyldendal.
Sørensen, Knud
  1983 *Bondeslutspil* (The last act of the farmer). Aarhus: Modtryk.
Vibæk, Jens
  1964 *Danmarks Historie, Vol. 10, Reform og Fallit: 1784–1830* (The history of Denmark: Reform and bankruptcy). Copenhagen: Politikens Forlag.
Zerlang, Martin
  1976 *Bøndernes Klassekamp i Danmark* (The class struggle of the farmers in Denmark). Copenhagen: Medusa.
Østergård, Uffe
  1984 "Hvad er det 'danske' ved Danmark? Tanker om den 'danske vej' til kapitalismen, grundtvigianismen og 'dansk' mentalitet" (What is the "Danish" about Denmark? Thoughts on the Danish way to capitalism, Grundtvigianism and the "Danish" mentality). *Den Jysk Historiker*, Nr. 29–30.

Index

About the Author

Born in Philadelphia, Steven Borish took his B.A. in Sociology-Anthropology at Carleton College, Northfield, Minnesota. For two years he was a Peace Corps teacher in the Somali Republic, East Africa, and for one year taught fifth grade in an inner-city school in Philadelphia. He has also spent time studying how culture influences the educational process in Israeli kibbutzim. Although his primary professional interest is the cross-cultural study of education, he has a wide range of other interests as well.

After the successful completion of his doctorate in anthropology (Stanford University, 1982) and his initial fieldwork in Denmark (1983–84), he spent two years in postdoctoral research and study, including an M.S. degree in the Department of Biological Sciences, Stanford University. During his time at Stanford he studied genetics, plant physiology, biochemistry and paleoanthropology (with a special focus on the anatomy and evolutionary history of human walking).

His present fields of interest are anthropology and education (especially the human life cycle in cross-cultural perspective), human evolution, the ecological consequences of high technology, and the development of a critical perspective on Western science. He has taught courses in these areas at Stanford University, the University of Copenhagen, the University of Trondheim, and Swarthmore College where he was Visiting Assistant Professor of Anthropology from 1987–90. His main geographical area of interest is Scandinavia. He has been carrying out a study of education and socialization in Norway, with special focus on the Norwegian *barnehage*, or kindergarten, as a Fulbright Professor at the Norwegian Centre for Child Research (the University of Trondheim). His initial field research in Denmark was also supported by a Fulbright Grant.